BUREAU OF INTERNATIONAL RESEARCH
HARVARD UNIVERSITY AND RADCLIFFE COLLEGE

A TREATISE ON THE PERMANENT COURT OF INTERNATIONAL JUSTICE

THE MACMILLAN COMPANY
NEW YORK · BOSTON · CHICAGO · DALLAS
ATLANTA · SAN FRANCISCO

MACMILLAN & CO., Limited
LONDON · BOMBAY · CALCUTTA
MELBOURNE

THE MACMILLAN COMPANY
OF CANADA, Limited
TORONTO

THE PERMANENT COURT

OF

INTERNATIONAL JUSTICE

A TREATISE

BY

MANLEY O. HUDSON

MEMBER OF THE PERMANENT COURT OF ARBITRATION AND
BEMIS PROFESSOR OF INTERNATIONAL LAW
HARVARD LAW SCHOOL

NEW YORK

THE MACMILLAN COMPANY

1934

Set up and printed. Published August, 1934.

PRINTED IN THE UNITED STATES OF AMERICA

To

ELIHU ROOT

AND

JAMES BROWN SCOTT

who by a generation of effort
contributed to the establishment of the
Permanent Court of International Justice

To

BERNARD C. J. LODER

MAX HUBER

DIONISIO ANZILOTTI

AND

MINÉITCIRŎ ADATCI

who during its formative years
served as the Presidents of the
Permanent Court of International Justice

PREFACE

The Permanent Court of International Justice has now completed its twelfth year. In the course of this period, its constitutional law has been developed through the action of the Assembly and Council of the League of Nations and as a consequence of the action taken by various Governments, and the Court itself has laid the foundations of law and procedure upon which it will continue to build through the coming years. The time would seem to have arrived for comprehensive studies of the law of the Court for the assistance of lawyers who may appear before it and of others who must deal with its problems.

The present volume is designed to serve as such a study. The author has endeavored to follow the history of the Court since the creation of the Committee of Jurists which drafted its Statute in 1920. He has had exceptional opportunity for doing so, through connections from time to time with the Secretariat of the League of Nations and through the kindness of the Registrar of the Court. If the views here expressed should not commend themselves to the favor of the legal profession, they are based nevertheless upon a continuous study of the documents, upon numerous contacts with persons interested in the Court, and upon an unflagging interest in its activities.

The official publications of the Court are now very voluminous, as are also those of the League of Nations which relate to it. With respect to no other international institution and possibly with respect to no other public institution in the world is information available more adequately. Yet the very completeness of the documentation renders it sometimes difficult for one to answer a question which may arise, or to trace the development of a particular topic. It is not easy to thread one's way through the abundant literature concerning the Court; even with a large library at hand, a practitioner before the Court or a serious student of its problems may find difficulty in arriving at a conclusion concerning the precedents which have been established. So far as the author is aware, no book has heretofore

been published in any language which attempts a systematic and detailed study of the Court's entire procedure.

In its procedure and in its practice, the Court has shown throughout a willingness to make departures as the need for them has arisen, and the present procedure and practice are doubtless far from final. If the amendments to the Statute of the Court, annexed to the Protocol of September 14, 1929, should come into force, some changes must be made in the Rules. Account of the pending amendments has been taken in this volume, but its publication has not been withheld to await the uncertain event of their coming into force.

The author has been struck with the fact that the Permanent Court of International Justice has merely continued a process of international adjudication which began to be developed during the last century; at times, the Court has shown itself very aware of this continuity. This explains the inclusion here of Part I, which is devoted to "The Precursors of the Court," and it has been thought to justify the amount of space devoted to the history of the years before 1920. Nor has it seemed possible to omit the somewhat replete history of the establishment of the Court in 1920 and 1921, in Part II; much of the Court's activity is to be understood only in the light of this history. Part III on the organization of the Court is likewise essential to an appreciation of the Court's procedure. In Part IV on the jurisdiction of the Court, the writer has purposely refrained from the common classification of jurisdiction as *ratione personæ* and *ratione materiæ*, though the distinction has been embodied in the arrangement. Part V on procedure and practice and Part VI on the application of law, do not purport to be a connected account of the Court's dealing with the cases before it, though its entire jurisprudence has been analyzed under subject-headings. No attempt has been made to digest the Court's application of principles of substantive law.

Throughout this volume, citations have been made to the various series of the Court's publications which should enable a reader to pursue any point further. It is assumed that the reader will have at least Series A, Series B, and Series A/B available for this purpose. While the author has examined much of the unofficial literature, citations of it have been made only where notable contributions could be signalized. The bibliographies contained in Series E of the Court's publications facilitate a study of such literature; and they are so nearly complete that it has seemed unnecessary to include a bibliography here.

Several chapters of this book have been based upon studies previously published by the author; chapters 1 and 3 on articles published in the American Journal of International Law in 1932 and 1933; chapter 20 on a paper published in the Iowa Law Review (January, 1934); chapter 27 on a paper published in a volume dedicated to Professors Joseph H. Beale and Samuel Williston of the Harvard Law School; and chapter 28 on a paper published in a volume dedicated to Dean Orrin K. McMurray of the School of Jurisprudence of the University of California.

Acknowledgement is gratefully made of the aid given by the Bureau of International Research of Harvard University and Radcliffe College in supplying the assistance necessary for the completion of this work. The author desires to express his special indebtedness to Mr. Julius Stone, Solicitor of the Supreme Court in England, whose assistance in planning this volume has been most valuable; to Mr. A. H. Feller of the New York Bar, who has acted as a constant critic; and to Mr. Åke Hammarskjöld, Registrar of the Permanent Court of International Justice, who has been most generous in criticism and suggestion. Mr. Hugh McKinnon Wood of the Secretariat of the League of Nations and Professor George Grafton Wilson of Harvard University have also been very helpful in their suggestions. The author has been permitted to see advance proofs of a study entitled *Statut de la Cour permanente de Justice internationale, Eléments d'interprétation*, which has been prepared by Count Stauffenberg for the *Institut für ausländisches öffentliches Recht und Völkerrecht* under the direction of Professor Viktor Bruns; in a few instances, guidance has been taken from citations found in this study.

MANLEY O. HUDSON

Cambridge, Massachusetts,
June 1, 1934.

CONTENTS

PART I

PRECURSORS OF THE PERMANENT COURT OF INTERNATIONAL JUSTICE

CHAPTER 1. THE PERMANENT COURT OF ARBITRATION.

PART II

CREATION OF THE PERMANENT COURT OF INTERNATIONAL JUSTICE

CHAPTER 6. PROVISIONS FOR A COURT IN THE COVENANT.

Chapter 9. The Revision of the Statute.

PAGE

PART III

THE ORGANIZATION OF THE PERMANENT COURT OF INTERNATIONAL JUSTICE

CHAPTER 11. THE ELECTION OF MEMBERS OF THE COURT.

CHAPTER 12. THE RULES OF COURT.

PART IV

THE JURISDICTION OF THE PERMANENT COURT OF INTERNATIONAL JUSTICE

CONTENTS

PART V

PROCEDURE AND PRACTICE OF THE PERMANENT COURT OF INTERNATIONAL JUSTICE

CHAPTER 23. REPRESENTATIVES OF STATES BEFORE THE COURT.

PART VI

THE APPLICATION OF LAW BY THE PERMANENT COURT OF INTERNATIONAL JUSTICE

CHAPTER 27. THE LAW APPLICABLE BY THE COURT.

CHAPTER 28. INTERNATIONAL ENGAGEMENTS AND THEIR INTERPRETATION BY THE COURT.

APPENDICES

PART I

PRECURSORS OF THE PERMANENT COURT OF INTERNATIONAL JUSTICE

CHAPTER 1

THE PERMANENT COURT OF ARBITRATION

§1. **Arbitration in the Nineteenth Century.** Arbitration as a method of settlement of international disputes was greatly developed during the nineteenth century,[1] and it was employed more frequently in the later than in the earlier part of the century.[2] In most cases, resort to arbitration depended upon an *ad hoc* agreement between the States concerned; the tribunal to which a dispute was referred was created *ad hoc*, and it ceased to function when the particular dispute was disposed of. It was hardly before the middle of the century that States began to agree in advance to have resort to arbitration, and these agreements were usually very much restricted. General bipartite arbitration treaties were all but unknown prior to 1850;[3] and even when they became more numerous their provisions were seldom all-embracing. Increasingly, however, States began to agree in advance to arbitrate special questions.[4] In a few cases, provisions for the arbitration of certain disputes were included in multipartite instruments: the

[1] For lists of arbitrations during the nineteenth century, see 2 *Anales de la Corte de Justicia Centroamericana* (1912), p. 58; Darby, International Tribunals (4th ed., 1904), pp. 771–900; H. La Fontaine, "*Histoire sommaire et chronologique des arbitrages internationaux*," 4 *Revue de Droit International et de Législation Comparée* (1902), pp. 352, 558, 623; H. La Fontaine, *Pasicrisie Internationale* (1902), p. 651; Politis, *La Justice Internationale*, pp. 34–35; Ralston, International Arbitration from Athens to Locarno, pp. 345–355. See also, 5 Moore, International Arbitrations, pp. 4851ff.; Dreyfus, *L'Arbitrage International* (1892), pp. 154ff.

[2] De Lapradelle and Politis record 28 cases for the period from 1798 to 1855, and 42 cases for the period from 1856 to 1872. *Recueil des Arbitrages Internationaux*, I (1905), II (1924). La Fontaine lists 43 cases for the period from 1794 to 1860, and 134 cases for the period from 1861 to 1900. *Pasicrisie Internationale*, p. viii.

[3] For a list of arbitration treaties concluded between 1828 and 1914, see Denys P. Myers, "Arbitration Engagements," World Peace Foundation Pamphlet Series, Vol. V (1915), No. 5. Myers lists four treaties for the period from 1828 to 1850, and 38 for the period from 1851 to 1900. On a wider basis of inclusion, William R. Manning lists 228 arbitration agreements to which American states became parties between 1822 and 1910, only 19 of which were concluded before 1850. Manning, Arbitration Treaties among the American Nations (1924), p. ix.

[4] For lists of general and special compromissory clauses in treaties, see La Fontaine, *Pasicrisie Internationale*, p. x; Cory, Compulsory Arbitration of International Disputes (1932), p. 8.

Universal Postal Convention [5] of October 9, 1874 (Article 16), the General Act of Brussels [6] of July 2, 1890 (Article 55), and the Convention on Railway Freight Transportation [7] of October 14, 1890 (Article 57), are outstanding examples. A multipartite arbitration treaty, based upon a "plan" adopted by the Conference of American States held at Washington in 1889–90, was signed by the representatives of eleven American States on April 28, 1890, though it was never brought into force.[8] Progress both in the conduct of arbitrations and in the negotiation of agreements to arbitrate paved the way for a regularization of the process of arbitration; and at the end of the nineteenth century the time seemed to be ripe for the creation of a permanent agency for arbitration. Once that step had been taken the conclusion of arbitration agreements proceeded at an almost feverish pace.[9]

§2. **The Hague Convention of 1899.** The Convention for the Pacific Settlement of International Disputes of July 29, 1899, the greatest achievement of the first Peace Conference at The Hague in 1899, was in a sense a codification of the law of pacific settlement up to that time. It covered the subject of good offices and mediation; it provided for international commissions of inquiry; and it established a system of arbitration for which new agencies were created. The most significant part of the Convention relates to the organization of the Permanent Court of Arbitration, "competent for all arbitration cases unless the parties agree to institute a special tribunal." The Convention also outlines a scheme of arbitral procedure, which States desiring to do so may employ. The formal articles of the Convention have frequently been referred to as a model to be followed; but their provisions are inadequate, particularly as to the date of the Convention's coming into force and as to the effect of revision; nor was any provision made for later accession. On September 4, 1900, ratifications of the Convention were deposited at The Hague by seventeen of the signatory States, and the Convention may be said to have entered into force on that date; nine of the signatories deposited ratifications

[5] 65 British and Foreign State Papers, p. 13.
[6] 82 *id.*, p. 55.   [7] 82 *id.*, p. 771.
[8] Scott, International Conferences of American States (1931), p. 40.
[9] The collections of *Traités Généraux d'Arbitrage communiqués au Bureau International de la Cour Permanente d'Arbitrage,* 1st series (1911), 2d series (1914), 3d series (1921, 1928), 4th series (1929), 5th series (1932), contain the texts of 125 treaties concluded between 1899 and 1914. See also Chr. L. Lange, *L'Arbitrage Obligatoire en 1913* (Brussels, 1914).

thereafter.[10] On June 14, 1907, a protocol [11] was signed on behalf of the States which had ratified the Convention for the Pacific Settlement of International Disputes, for the purpose of enabling States not represented at the Conference of 1899 but invited to a second Conference of 1907 to adhere to the Convention. On June 15, 1907, a *procès-verbal* was opened to receive and record the adhesions; seventeen Latin-American States thus adhered to the Convention of July 29, 1899.[12]

§3. **The Hague Convention of 1907.** The Second Peace Conference at The Hague, in 1907, undertook a reëxamination of the Convention of 1899 with a view to its "improvement." The result was a new Convention for the Pacific Settlement of International Disputes of October 18, 1907. It contained 97 articles, instead of the original 61 in which many changes were made. The later convention was designed to "replace as between the contracting Powers" the earlier convention. It came into force on November 27, 1909, when eleven of the signatories deposited their ratifications.[13] Various States which ratified or adhered to the Convention of 1899 have not ratified the Convention of 1907, however; [14] for these States the Convention of 1899 remains in force, both *inter se* and *vis-à-vis* all other States which ratified or adhered to the Convention of 1899 and which may also have ratified or adhered to the Convention of 1907. Certain States have adhered to the later convention which were never bound by the earlier one.[15] In prac-

[10] The following signatories deposited ratifications: United States of America, Austria-Hungary, Belgium, Bulgaria, China, Denmark, France, Germany, Great Britain, Greece, Italy, Japan, Luxemburg, Mexico, Montenegro, Netherlands, Persia, Portugal, Rumania, Russia, Serbia, Siam, Spain, Sweden and Norway, Switzerland, and Turkey. Reservations were made by the United States of America, Rumania, Serbia and Turkey.

[11] For the text, see 100 British and Foreign State Papers, p. 276.

[12] These States were Argentina, Bolivia, Brazil, Chile, Colombia, Cuba, Dominican Republic, Ecuador, Guatemala, Haiti, Nicaragua, Panama, Paraguay, Peru, El Salvador, Uruguay, and Venezuela.

The opening of the 1899 Convention to adhesion by Latin-American States was due, at least in part, to the efforts of the United States of America and Mexico, whose Governments were authorized by the Second International Conference of American States, meeting at Mexico in 1902, to negotiate to this end. A protocol was signed at Mexico on January 15, 1902, by which fifteen American States recognized the principles set forth in the Hague Convention of 1899 to be "a part of Public International American Law." Scott, International Conferences of American States, p. 61.

[13] With reservations in some cases. For the texts of the reservations, see Scott, Hague Conventions and Declarations of 1899 and 1907, pp. 240–259.

[14] These include Argentina, Bulgaria, Chile, Colombia, Dominican Republic, Ecuador, Great Britain, Greece, Italy, Persia, Peru, Serbia (Yugoslavia), Turkey, Uruguay, and Venezuela. Paraguay's ratification of the 1907 Convention was not deposited until April 25, 1933.

[15] These are Czechoslovakia, Finland and Poland. Article 94 of the 1907 Convention seems to require an *entente ultérieure* as a condition precedent to such adhesion; on being notified of the desires of these States to adhere to the Convention, the Netherlands

tice, it seems to have been of little consequence whether a State which has ratified or adhered to the 1899 Convention has also ratified the 1907 Convention; in numerous instances States which have not ratified the latter convention have been parties to arbitrations under it.[16]

§4. **Legal Basis of the Permanent Court of Arbitration.** The Permanent Court of Arbitration now exists under the two conventions, that of 1899 and that of 1907.[17] By Article 20 of the former convention, the "signatory Powers" undertook to organize a Permanent Court of Arbitration; by Article 41 of the latter, the "contracting Powers" undertook to maintain the existing Permanent Court of Arbitration "as established by the first Peace Conference." The list of *Puissances contractantes* published annually by the *Conseil Administratif* therefore includes forty-five States [18] which are in some way active in their support of the Court and which have ratified or adhered to either or both of the two conventions; it does not include Austria,[19] Montenegro,[20] or the Union of Soviet Socialist Republics.[21] Both the Conventions of 1899 and 1907 provide (Articles 61: 96) for the possibility of denunciation, but neither has been denounced by any State.

§5. **Structure of the Court.** As an institution, the Permanent Court of Arbitration may be said to embrace three bodies: (1) a panel of members; (2) an International Bureau; and (3) an Administrative Council.

(1) The members of the Court, who are in no sense judges, are the persons nominated as such by the States parties to one or both of the Conventions of 1899 and 1907. Each State may name four

Government submitted them to the appreciation of the signatory States which gave their assent by failure to object. No formal agreement was entered into.

[16] For instance, Great Britain has not ratified the 1907 Convention, but has been a party to several arbitrations under it.

[17] As some of the "contracting Powers" are not parties to the Covenant of the League of Nations or the Protocol of Signature and Statute of the Permanent Court of International Justice, no question arises as to a possible modification of the Hague Conventions by these later instruments.

[18] Thirty-one of these States are parties to both Conventions.

[19] Austria does not consider itself a legal successor to Austria-Hungary, on behalf of which the two Conventions were ratified, and therefore does not participate *ipso facto* in conventions concluded by the Monarchy. Hungary, on the other hand, considers itself to be bound by the 1907 Convention, which had been made a part of Hungarian law. Neither Article 234 of the Treaty of St. Germain of September 10, 1919, nor Article 217 of the Treaty of Trianon of June 4, 1920, refers to the Conventions of 1899 and 1907.

[20] The territory of Montenegro now forms part of the territory of Yugoslavia.

[21] Though the Russian Emperor ratified both the 1899 and the 1907 Conventions, the Union of Soviet Socialist Republics has not in any way participated in maintaining the Court. In 1923, the payment of arrears in the Russian contributions from 1917 was undertaken by other States, as a result of a decision of the Administrative Council.

members, who should be "of known competence in questions of international law, of the highest moral reputation, and disposed to accept
the duties of arbitrator." In earlier years, the members usually numbered about 75; in later years they have numbered around 150.[22] It was
originally planned that the members of the Court should hold an inaugural meeting; but the plan was abandoned, and no attempt has
ever been made to assemble the members as such. Hence, the members
of the Court can hardly be said to form a *body* in a strict sense, and
they have never functioned as a body. Instead they form a *panel*
from which tribunals may be constituted, a tribunal to consist of one
or more members of the Court. The number of members of the Court
who have actually served as arbitrators is relatively small; in thirty-
three years, the total number of members has been about 450; but
only 29 members have served as members of tribunals.[23]

(2) The International Bureau, established at The Hague,[24] consists of the Secretary-General of the Permanent Court of Arbitration,
who has the rank of a Minister-Resident, and a small staff with usually
a first secretary; in 1933, the staff comprised a second secretary and
a subordinate personnel of three persons. The Secretary-General and
all of the personnel of the Bureau have always been of Dutch nationality,[25] though this is not required by the Conventions; in this sense,
therefore, the Bureau is not international. The Bureau acts as the
registry of the Permanent Court of Arbitration (Article 22 of the 1899
Convention, Article 43 of the 1907 Convention). It serves as the channel for communications relating to meetings of tribunals, and it has
charge of the archives and conducts the administration. It is author-

[22] Some of the parties to the conventions do not keep their national groups filled;
the *Rapport du Conseil Administratif* for 1933 lists 152 members on March 10, 1933.
[23] The United States of America, for instance, has had eleven members of the
Permanent Court of Arbitration, of whom only three have acted as members of tribunals.
[24] The Bureau has had its offices in the Peace Palace at The Hague since August 28,
1913, when the Peace Palace was inaugurated. Formerly, its offices were at 71 Prinse-
gracht, The Hague.
[25] The first Secretary-General, Baron Melvil de Lynden, served in that capacity
from October 1, 1900, to August 1, 1901. His successor, Mr. L. H. Ruyssenaers, served
from August 29, 1901, to October 1, 1905. Baron Michiels van Verduynen served as
Secretary-General from October 1, 1905, until his death on February 4, 1929. The present
Secretary-General, Dr. C. Crommelin, assumed office on April 18, 1929, having previously
acted as first secretary for twelve years.
Article 21 of the Statute of the Permanent Court of International Justice provides
that "the duties of Registrar of the Court shall not be deemed incompatible with those of
Secretary-General of the Permanent Court of Arbitration." When a vacancy in the
latter office was about to be filled in 1929, the Registrar drew this provision to the
attention of the President of the Administrative Council of the Permanent Court of
Arbitration. Publications of the Permanent Court of International Justice, Series E, No.
5, p. 246.

ized to place its premises and staff at the disposal of the contracting Powers for any special arbitration (Article 26, 1899; Article 47, 1907). It also acts as the registry for commissions of inquiry which meet at The Hague (Article 15, 1907). The Secretary-General of the Permanent Court of Arbitration usually acts as secretary-general of tribunals created within the framework of the Court, and frequently of special arbitral tribunals meeting at The Hague.

(3) The Administrative Council is composed of the Minister of Foreign Affairs of the Netherlands, as President, and of the diplomatic representatives at The Hague of States parties to the Conventions.[26] This Council, which has the direction and control of the International Bureau, meets with some frequency, and at least annually. Its first meeting was held on July 19, 1900, even before the first deposit of ratifications of the 1899 Convention. On September 19, 1900, the Council adopted a *règlement d'ordre*[27] and on December 8, 1900, a *règlement* for the Bureau;[28] these *règlements* are still in force. Its *procès-verbaux* are not published. A financial commission, on which the various States are represented in rotation, approves the annual budget of the International Bureau. The Council also nominates one member of the Council of Directors of the *Fondation Carnegie*, established by the Netherlands Government to administer the Peace Palace at The Hague. The Council publishes an annual report on the work of the Court, on the functioning of its administrative services, and on its expenditures.

§6. Finances of the Court. The Convention provides, Articles 29 (1899), 50 (1907), that the expenses of the International Bureau shall be borne by the Contracting States in the proportion established for the International Bureau of the Universal Postal Union; this proportion is changed from time to time by the revision of the Universal Postal Convention.[29] A State may choose that one of seven classes to which it wishes to belong, and the number of units which it is to pay will depend upon the class into which it places itself.[30] The payments

---

[26] In 1933, thirteen of the *Puissances contractantes* were not represented at The Hague and hence were not represented on the Administrative Council.

[27] For the text, see 94 British and Foreign State Papers, p. 722.

[28] For the text, see 94 *id.*, p. 724.

[29] It now depends on Article 24 of the Universal Postal Convention signed at London, June 28, 1929. 4 Hudson, International Legislation, p. 2880.

[30] In 1933, each unit was 165 florins; States in the first class contributed 25 units, and States in the seventh class, one unit. The United States of America, the Argentine Republic, China, France, Germany, Great Britain, Italy, Japan, and Turkey are in the first class.

are made to the Netherlands Government, which since 1900 has advanced the money necessary for meeting the budget of the Bureau. At times the arrears of payments have been considerable, some of the Contracting States having failed to make any payments for periods of as much as ten years. This system of meeting the expenses of the International Bureau works only because the expenses are not large,[31] and no State's contribution is very burdensome.

Under Articles 57 (1899), 85 (1907) of the Conventions, a party meets its own expenses in an arbitration, and the expenses of a tribunal are borne by the parties in equal parts. In addition to their expenses, members of the tribunals usually receive honoraria, the amounts of which are determined by the Governments concerned.[32]

§7. **Position of Members of the Court.** No imperative duties of any kind devolve on the members of the Permanent Court of Arbitration as such.[33] Possibly a member should hold himself in a position to accept an invitation to act as arbitrator, and yet such an invitation may be declined. Nor does one have any special privileges as a member of the Permanent Court of Arbitration. Under Article 24 of the 1899 Convention, a member of the Court is to enjoy diplomatic privileges and immunities while in the exercise of his duties and outside the territory of his own State; [34] Article 46 of the 1907 Convention confers this status only on a member of a tribunal. On the other hand, a member of the Court may be under a disability. In connection with the *Venezuelan Preferential Claims Arbitration* in 1903, strong objection was made to a member's acting as counsel before a tribunal,[35]

---

[31] In 1932, the expenses were 87,789.50 florins; in 1933, 87,784.23 florins. In the earlier years, the Bureau's expenses were less than half of this sum.

[32] The usual honorarium has been 25,000 gold francs. In the *North Atlantic Coast Fisheries Arbitration*, each member of the tribunal received £3,000; the members of the special tribunal in the *U. S.–Norwegian Arbitration* in 1922 each received $10,000.

[33] Apart from the Hague Conventions, however, the Statute of the Permanent Court of International Justice (Articles 4 and 5) provides for nominations of candidates in the elections of judges and deputy judges, by the national groups in the Permanent Court of Arbitration "belonging to the States mentioned in the Annex to the Covenant or to the States which join the League subsequently." In 1921, the national group "belonging to" the United States of America declined to admit that any duty or authority had been imposed on it by these articles of the Statute. League of Nations Document, A. 42. 1921. V. See § 246, *infra.*

[34] A French law of December 2, 1903, provided that alien members of a tribunal created under the Hague Convention of 1899 and sitting in France should enjoy diplomatic privileges and immunities. 68 *Bulletin des Lois* (12th ser.), p. 453; Dalloz, *Jurisprudence Générale* (1904), Part IV, p. 7; 98 British and Foreign State Papers, p. 848.

[35] The British Government protested against the appointment of M. Renault as counsel before the tribunal, because he was a member of the Permanent Court of Arbitration; counsel for Venezuela made a similar protest in general terms, on the ground that members acting as counsel would possess advantages over counsel who were not members.

but the objection did not prevail. The Convention of 1907 provides that a member of the Court may not act as agent, counsel or advocate before an arbitral tribunal except on behalf of the State which appointed him.[36] In the United States–Venezuelan arbitration in 1910, it was stipulated in the *compromis* that no member of the Court should appear as counsel.

§8. **Nature of the Court.** The name of the Permanent Court of Arbitration is really a misnomer,[37] and it was partly responsible for a deception of public opinion which led expectations to be entertained which could never be fulfilled. The Court is not in any accurate sense a tribunal, though it is quite commonly referred to as "the Hague tribunal." Instead, it is chiefly a device for facilitating the creation of tribunals and a machinery for aiding in the conduct of arbitral proceedings. Nor is the institution created in 1899 a *court;* and it is permanent only in the sense that a permanent International Bureau exists and that the Administrative Council is constituted as a continuing body. It is somewhat misleading therefore to speak of it as a *permanent court,* and the use of that name may have confused thinking about the Court of Arbitral Justice proposed in 1907 and about the Permanent Court of International Justice created in 1920. Having no existence as a *court,* the Permanent Court of Arbitration possesses no competence. Article 53 of the Convention of 1907 does appear to confer on the "Permanent Court" a limited competence to settle a *compromis* at the request of but one of the parties, in a dispute covered by a general treaty of arbitration made after the Convention came into force, on certain conditions, or in a dispute arising from contract debts claimed by one State as due to its nationals from another State provided an offer of arbitration has been accepted; but the article confers no competence in fact because of the way in which it must be carried out,[38] and no *compromis* has ever been drawn up under Article 53.

[36] Apparently, however, this disability does not prevent a member of the Court from giving legal advice. See the Rapporteur's statement in Scott, Reports to the Hague Conferences, p. 344. See, also, Scott, The Hague Peace Conferences, I, p. 294.

[37] See the Report of the 1920 Committee of Jurists, in *Procès-verbaux* of the Proceedings (The Hague, 1920), p. 698. Yet it may be noted that in the earlier years of the Permanent Court of Arbitration there was a tendency for States to choose members of tribunals who had frequently been chosen as such by other States; M. Renault, for example, was a member of seven tribunals constituted before 1914, and MM. Hammarskjöld, Fusinato and Savornin Lohman were members of five such tribunals.

[38] The explanation in Article 54 that the *compromis* is to be fixed by a commission of five members selected as provided in Article 45, robs Article 53 of its apparently compulsory feature.

§9. **Alternative Methods of Arbitration.** The Hague Conventions are in no sense agreements to arbitrate; the effort made at the Second Peace Conference to incorporate such an agreement into the 1907 Convention failed completely. Nor is a State which is a party to one or both of the Conventions under any duty to employ the agencies provided by the Conventions or to follow the procedure outlined in them, when it has agreed with another State which is also a party to arbitrate a question. Numerous arbitrations have been conducted since 1899 wholly outside the framework of the Conventions.[39] The statement in Article 21 (1899), Article 42 (1907), that the Permanent Court is "competent for all arbitration cases unless the parties agree to institute a special tribunal" means no more than that a tribunal may be recruited for any case out of the membership of the Court. Strictly, a provision for arbitration in accordance with or pursuant to the provisions of either Hague Convention is so indefinite as to have little meaning, though several agreements have contained such provisions. The Conventions envisage three different processes: (1) arbitration conducted by a tribunal of the Permanent Court of Arbitration; (2) arbitration conducted by a special arbitral tribunal; (3) arbitration conducted by summary procedure under Chapter IV of the Convention of 1907, by a tribunal which may or may not be composed of members of the Permanent Court of Arbitration. According to Article 24 (1899) and Article 45 (1907), all of the members of a tribunal must be chosen from the general list of the Court before the parties can be said to have had recourse to the Permanent Court of Arbitration. In its annual reports, the Administrative Council therefore lists as special arbitral tribunals those in which any one of the members was not a member of the Court;[40] even so, its list must be used with discrimination.

§10. **Cases before Tribunals of the Permanent Court of Arbitration.** The annual report of the Administrative Council for 1933 lists twenty-one *affaires d'arbitrage jugées,* of which six are said to have been before special arbitral tribunals.[41] The terms of submission in

---

[39] For a list of arbitrations since 1900, see Cory, Compulsory Arbitration of International Disputes (1932), pp. 235–238.

[40] It also lists the British-French tribunal in the case of the Chevreau Claim and the American-Swedish tribunal in the case of the *S.S. Kronprins Gustaf Adolf* and *S.S. Pacific,* as special tribunals, though the sole arbitrator in each of these cases was a member of the Permanent Court of Arbitration.

[41] *Rapport du Conseil Administratif de la Cour Permanente d'Arbitrage,* 1933, pp. 45–46.

these cases varied very much, and in some of them there was but a remote connection with the agencies of the Court.[42] To understand the precise rôle played by the Permanent Court of Arbitration, it is necessary to examine the facts in each of these twenty-one cases in some detail. On the other hand, certain arbitrations not listed in the reports of the Administrative Council, notably the American-British claims arbitration under the special agreement of August 18, 1910,[43] have as much relation to the Conventions for Pacific Settlement as some of those which are listed.

§11. **United States of America–Mexico:** *Pious Fund Case* (1902).[44] Under a "protocol of agreement" signed at Washington, May 22, 1902, this case was referred to a special tribunal consisting of four arbitrators and an umpire. Each party was to name two arbitrators, not nationals of either of the parties, and the umpire was "to be selected in accordance with the provisions of the Hague Convention" of 1899. All of the members of the tribunal were members of the Permanent Court of Arbitration, though this was not required by the protocol of agreement. It was provided in the agreement that the arbitrators should, unless otherwise stipulated, be controlled by the provisions of the Hague Convention of 1899. The tribunal was required to meet at The Hague in the quarters which might be provided by the International Bureau constituted under the Convention of 1899; later meetings were envisaged "at Brussels if the court should determine not to sit at The Hague." Prior to the signing of the protocol of agreement, the Mexican Government had first suggested the reference to "the Hague Tribunal," [45] and the two governments seem to have been agreed on this course. When the tribunal met at The Hague, it was taken to be a tribunal of the Permanent Court of Arbitration. The Secretary-General of the Permanent Court of Arbi-

---

[42] Two convenient collections of the awards of the tribunals have been published: James Brown Scott, Hague Court Reports (1916), and Hague Court Reports, second series (1932); and George Grafton Wilson, The Hague Arbitration Cases (1915). See also, James Brown Scott, *Les Travaux de la Cour Permanente d'Arbitrage de la Haye* (1921).

[43] Under this agreement certain claims were referred to arbitration under Chapter IV of the 1907 Convention, the tribunal to be constituted in accordance with Articles 87 and 59 of the Convention, and the procedure to be in accordance with certain of its provisions. Of the three original members of the tribunal, only one was a member of the Permanent Court of Arbitration at the time of his selection.

[44] *Recueil des Actes et Protocoles concernant le litige du "Fonds Pieux des Californies,"* published by the *Bureau International de la Cour Permanente d'Arbitrage*, The Hague, 1902; Scott, Hague Court Reports, p. 1. See also, Renault, *"Un premier litige devant la Cour d'Arbitrage de la Haye,"* 18 Annales des Sciences Politiques (1903), pp. 38–74.

[45] U. S. Foreign Relations, 1902, p. 778. The Government of the United States had first suggested arbitration, however.

tration was the secretary-general of the tribunal, which met from September 15 to October 14, 1902. The proceedings were conducted in public. The tribunal was asked to say whether a claim made by the United States was within the governing principle of *res judicata* by virtue of a previous arbitral award, and if not, to give such judgment as would seem to be just and equitable; by its award of October 14, 1902, the tribunal answered this general question in the affirmative. After the award was given, the members of the tribunal addressed a note to the president of the Administrative Council giving their suggestions on the procedure to be followed before the Permanent Court of Arbitration; these suggestions related to the functioning of the International Bureau as an intermediary for communications; the choice of presidents of the tribunals; the choice of languages and the appointment of agents and counsel with reference to such choice; the distinction between *l'instruction* and *les débats;* and the desirability of omitting in any future *compromis* provision relating to a revision of the award.[46]

§12. **Germany, Great Britain, and Italy–Venezuela:** *Preferential Claims* (1904).[47] This case was referred to "the tribunal at The Hague," under three protocols of May 7, 1903, entered into by Germany, Great Britain, and Italy, respectively, with Venezuela. The protocols, which were substantially identical, allowed "any nation having claims against Venezuela" to "join as a party in the arbitration." [48] The Emperor of Russia was invited to appoint three arbitrators "from the members of the Permanent Court at The Hague," none of whom should be a national of any of the signatory or creditor Powers. The Emperor of Russia first designated M. Mourawieff, M. Lardy, and Professor Matzen, all members of the

[46] For the text, see 5 American Journal of International Law (1911), Supp., p. 73. The note has not been published by the International Bureau.

[47] *Recueil des Actes et Protocoles concernant le litige entre l'Allemagne, l'Angleterre et l'Italie, d'une part, et le Vénézuela, d'autre part,* published by the International Bureau, The Hague, 1904; Scott, Hague Court Reports, p. 55. See also, Basdevant, *"L'Action coercitive anglo-germano-italienne contre le Vénézuela* (1902–1903)," 11 *Revue Générale de Droit International Public* (1904), pp. 362–458; Gaché, *Le Conflit vénézuélien et l'Arbitrage de la Haye* (1905); Hershey, "The Venezuelan Affair in the Light of International Law," 51 American Law Register (1903), pp. 249–267; Mallarmé, *"L'arbitrage vénézuélan devant la Cour de la Haye* (1903–1904)," 13 *Revue Générale de Droit International Public* (1906), pp. 423–500; Tello, *Venezuela ante el conflicto con las potencias aliadas, Alemania, Inglaterra e Italia en 1902 y 1903* (1905).

[48] The protocols of May 7, 1903, were adhered to by the United States, Belgium, France, Mexico, Netherlands, Spain, and Sweden and Norway, in the sense that these States formally joined with Venezuela as parties in the arbitration provided for. See Wilson, Hague Arbitration Cases, pp. 24, 27, 30; U. S. Foreign Relations, 1904, p. 511.

Permanent Court of Arbitration, but the two latter declined to serve because their States were interested as creditor Powers; later the Emperor appointed Professor Lammasch and M. de Martens, both members of the Permanent Court of Arbitration. M. Mourawieff was chosen by his colleagues as president. The protocols provided that, except as otherwise stipulated, the procedure should be regulated by the Convention of July 29, 1899. It was provided also that the tribunal should meet at The Hague on September 1, 1903; on that day, only one arbitrator was present, with agents of Germany, Spain, the United States, France, Great Britain, Italy, Netherlands, Sweden and Norway, and Venezuela. The members of the tribunal did not assemble until October 1, 1903; the Venezuelan representatives protested because of the delay, and their protest was followed by certain recriminations. The Secretary-General of the Permanent Court of Arbitration served as secretary-general of the tribunal. The question of languages gave considerable difficulty; the protocols provided for English as the official language, and after some objection by the French counsel, it was so recognized, with "the French language as subsidiary, since it is familiar to the members of the tribunal and to the majority of the representatives of the parties." Certain questions of procedure also gave difficulty. The principal question before the tribunal, whether Germany, Great Britain and Italy were entitled to preferential payment of their claims against Venezuela, was answered in the affirmative, in the award given on February 22, 1904. A concluding statement in the award invited the Government of the United States of America to see to the execution of that part of the award which dealt with an equal sharing of the expenses among the parties to the arbitration; this mandate having been declined by the United States,[49] it was assumed by the Secretary-General of the Permanent Court of Arbitration. At the closing session of the tribunal, the president made some remarks to which the Japanese Government later took formal exception. Following a precedent set by the tribunal in the *Pious Fund Case*, after the award was given the members of the tribunal addressed a note to the president of the Administrative Council giving their observations on certain questions of procedure;[50] account was taken of these observations by the Second Peace Con-

[49] U. S. Foreign Relations, 1904, p. 516.
[50] The text is to be found in the *Recueil des Actes et Protocoles*, not consecutively paged.

ference at The Hague, and they led to the introduction of certain amendments into the Convention.

§13. **France, Germany, and Great Britain–Japan:** *Japanese House Tax Case* (1905).[51] Under a protocol [52] of August 28, 1902, concluded by France, Germany and Great Britain, with Japan, this case was referred to a tribunal of three persons "who are members of the Permanent Court of Arbitration at The Hague." France, Germany and Great Britain were considered as a single party in the arbitration. Each party was to name one arbitrator, and the two arbitrators were to choose an umpire; failing any selection, the umpire was to be named by the King of Sweden and Norway, but the arbitrators were able to agree on the selection. Both arbitrators and the umpire were members of the Permanent Court of Arbitration. The Secretary-General of the Permanent Court of Arbitration was the secretary-general of the tribunal. Except as otherwise provided in the protocol, provisions of the Convention of July 29, 1899, were to apply. A problem of languages arose over a demand that German be one of the languages permitted, and the Japanese asked that the Japanese language also be permitted; it was decided that French should be the language of the tribunal, but that either French or English might be employed by the parties. The tribunal was asked to say whether, under treaties in force, buildings on lands held under perpetual lease were exempt from taxation other than that stipulated in the leases; this question was answered in the affirmative. The award was given on May 22, 1905; the Japanese member of the tribunal dissented both as to the conclusion and as to the reasons given for it.

§14. **France–Great Britain:** *Muscat Dhows Case* (1905).[53] Under an agreement of October 13, 1904, this case was referred to arbitration in accordance with the provisions of an arbitration treaty of October 14, 1903, the parties agreeing "that the decision of the

[51] *Recueil des Actes et Protocoles concernant le litige entre l'Allemagne, la France et la Grande-Bretagne, d'une part, et le Japon, d'autre part,* published by the Bureau International de la Cour Permanente d'Arbitrage, The Hague, 1905; Scott, Hague Court Reports, p. 77.

[52] The protocol was signed in French on behalf of France and Japan, in German on behalf of Germany and Japan, in English on behalf of Great Britain and Japan, and in Japanese on behalf of the four states; these may be considered as versions of a single instrument, though the form was unusual.

[53] *Recueil des Actes et Protocoles concernant le Différend entre la France et la Grande-Bretagne,* published by the Bureau International de la Cour Permanente d'Arbitrage, The Hague, 1905; Scott, Hague Court Reports, p. 93. See also, Bressonnet, *"L'Arbitrage franco-anglais dans l'affaire des boutres de Mascate,"* 13 *Revue Générale de Droit International Public* (1906), pp. 145–164.

Hague Tribunal shall be final." On all points not covered by the agreement, the provisions of the Hague Convention of 1899 were to apply. The agreement of October 13, 1904, provided that the arbitrators and umpire should be "chosen from among the members of the Hague Tribunal," not nationals of the parties. Each of the parties was to nominate one arbitrator and these arbitrators were to choose an umpire; failing their agreement, the umpire was to be chosen by the King of Italy. The arbitrators were unable to reach an agreement, and the King of Italy designated Dr. Lammasch as umpire. The International Bureau served as intermediary for communicating the cases and counter-cases, and the Secretary-General of the Permanent Court of Arbitration acted as secretary-general of the tribunal. The award was given on August 8, 1905, in French, with an official English translation; it dealt with the issue by France to certain subjects of Muscat, of papers authorizing them to fly the French flag, and with the nature of the privileges and immunities to be enjoyed in consequence of such issue. The proceedings were promptly published by the International Bureau.

§15. France–Germany: *Casablanca Case* (1909).[54] Under a protocol of November 10, 1908, and a *compromis* of November 24, 1908, this case was referred to an arbitral tribunal composed of five members, who were to be selected from the members of the Permanent Court of Arbitration. Each government was to choose two arbitrators, of whom one might be a national, and the four arbitrators were to choose an umpire. Such choices were duly made, M. Hammarskjöld being chosen as umpire. Communications were to be exchanged through the Bureau of the Permanent Court of Arbitration. The Secretary-General of the Permanent Court of Arbitration was secretary-general of the tribunal. Each of the parties agreed in advance to deposit with the International Bureau a sum of 3,000 florins to meet the expenses of the arbitration. The procedure was to be governed, on all points not covered by the *compromis,* by the provisions of the Hague Convention of 1907. Only the opening and closing sessions of the tribunal were public; the International Bureau was authorized, however, to make the *procès-verbaux* of the private sessions available to qualified persons.[55] The award, given on May 22, 1909, dealt with the settle-

---

[54] The award was published as an annex to the report of the Administrative Council for 1909. See also Scott, Hague Court Reports, p. 110; Gidel, *"L'Arbitrage de Casablanca,"* 17 *Revue Générale de Droit International Public* (1910), pp. 326–407.

[55] *Rapport du Conseil Administratif,* 1909, p. 15.

ment of the questions of fact and of law which had brought about certain incidents at Casablanca on September 25, 1908. Following the rendition of the award, a *procès-verbal* was signed by representatives of France and Germany, at Berlin, May 29, 1909, in which each government expressed its regret for the conduct of its officials which had been condemned by the tribunal.[56]

§16. **Norway–Sweden:** *Maritime Frontiers* (1909).[57] Under a convention of March 14, 1908, this case was referred to a special arbitral tribunal consisting of a president, not a national of either party, and two members, one Swedish and one Norwegian. The president was to have been chosen by the Queen of the Netherlands if the parties could not agree; but they succeeded in reaching agreement. The procedure was to be governed by Articles 62–85 of the Convention of 1907, as far as applicable. Only one of the members of the tribunal was a member of the Permanent Court of Arbitration. The Secretary-General of the Permanent Court of Arbitration was the secretary-general of the tribunal. After a preliminary meeting at The Hague, on April 28, 1909, the tribunal visited various places in the disputed territory, July 14–21, 1909; thereafter, August 28–October 23, 1909, its meetings were held at The Hague. Only the opening and closing sessions of the tribunal were public; but the *procès-verbaux* of the private sessions have been published.[58] The arbitral award, given on October 23, 1909, fixes the maritime boundary between Norway and Sweden in so far as it had not been fixed by the Royal Resolution of March 15, 1904.

§17. **United States of America–Great Britain:** *North Atlantic Fisheries* (1910).[59] Under a special agreement of January 27, 1909,

[56] Scott, Hague Court Reports, p. 120; 102 British and Foreign State Papers, p. 602.

[57] *Recueil des comptes rendus de la visite des lieux et des Protocoles des séances du Tribunal arbitral, constitué en vertu de la Convention du 14 mars 1908, pour juger la question de la délimitation d'une certaine partie de la frontière maritime entre la Norvège et la Suède,* published by the Bureau International de la Cour Permanente d'Arbitrage, The Hague, 1909; Scott, Hague Court Reports, p. 121. See also, Waultrin, *"Un conflit de limites maritimes entre la Norvège et la Suède: l'affaire des Grisbadarna,"* 17 *Revue Générale de Droit International Public* (1910), pp. 177–189.

The *Rapport du Conseil Administratif* for 1932 lists this case with an indication that it was before a special arbitral tribunal.

[58] See, however, the *Rapport du Conseil Administratif,* 1910, p. 15.

[59] The protocols are to be found in North Atlantic Coast Fisheries, Tribunal of Arbitration constituted under a Special Agreement signed at Washington, January 27, 1909, between the United States of America and Great Britain, published by the Permanent Court of Arbitration, The Hague, 1910. More complete proceedings, including documents presented to the tribunal, were published in 12 volumes, U. S. Sen. Doc. No. 870, 61st Cong., 3d sess. See also, Scott, Hague Court Reports, p. 141. For comment, see Anderson, "The Final Outcome of the Fisheries Arbitration," 7 American Journal of International

concluded in pursuance of an arbitration convention of April 4, 1908, this case was referred to a tribunal of arbitration "chosen from the general list of members of the Permanent Court at The Hague in accordance with the provisions of Article 45 of the Convention" of 1907.[60] The provisions of the latter convention, except Articles 53 and 54, were to apply to the proceedings. Cases and counter-cases were to be deposited with the International Bureau for transmission to the arbitrators. Difficulties arising in the future were to be "referred informally to the Permanent Court at The Hague for decision by the summary procedure provided in Chapter IV of the Hague Convention" of 1907. Three months were allowed for direct agreement on the composition of the tribunal, and agreement was reached upon the choice of five arbitrators, all of whom were members of the Permanent Court of Arbitration. The Secretary-General of the Permanent Court of Arbitration was the secretary-general of the tribunal, which held meetings from June 1 to September 7, 1910. The tribunal was called upon to answer seven elaborate questions relating to the execution of Article 1 of a convention of October 20, 1818, as to fishing rights, and to recommend rules for the determination of future questions on the subject. The award, given on September 7, 1910, was not on all points unanimous. Certain rules formulated by the tribunal for the future guidance of the parties were later elaborated and embodied in an agreement signed by representatives of the United States and Great Britain at Washington, July, 1912.[61] The tribunal thus acted in a legislative capacity.

§18.   United States of America–Venezuela: *Orinoco Steamship Company Case* (1910).[62] By an agreement of February 13, 1909; this

---

Law (1913), pp. 1–16; Balch, *"La Décision de la Cour Permanente d'Arbitrage au sujet des pêcheries de l'Atlantique dans le différend entre les États-Unis et l'Empire britannique,"* 13 *Revue de Droit International et de Législation Comparée* (1911), pp. 5–23; Basdevant, *"L'Affaire des pêcheries des côtes septentrionales de l'Atlantique entre les États-Unis d'Amérique et la Grand-Bretagne devant la cour de la Haye,"* 19 *Revue Générale de Droit International Public* (1912), pp. 421–582; Borchard, "The North Atlantic Coast Fisheries Arbitration," 11 Columbia Law Review (1911), pp. 1–23; Drago, *El arbitraje de las pesquerias del Atlántico norte entre la Gran Bretaña y los Estados Unidos de América* (1911); Lansing, "The North Atlantic Coast Fisheries Arbitration," 5 American Journal of International Law (1911), pp. 1–31; de Louter, *"L'Arbitrage dans le conflit anglo-américain concernant les pêcheries de l'Atlantique,"* 13 *Revue de Droit International et de Législation Comparée* (1911), pp. 131–157.

[60] Great Britain had not ratified the Hague Convention of 1907.

[61] Scott, Hague Court Reports, p. 221.

[62] *Protocoles des Séances du Tribunal d'Arbitrage constitué en exécution du compromis signé entre les États Unis d'Amérique et les États Unis du Vénézuela le 13 février 1909*, published by the Bureau International de la Cour Permanente d'Arbitrage, The Hague, 1910. Official English translations of the protocols and the award were published

case was submitted to a tribunal composed of three members, chosen "from the Permanent Court at The Hague." Each party was to select an arbitrator, and the two arbitrators were to choose a third arbitrator in accordance with Article 45 of the Convention of 1907. Nationals of the parties were excluded as arbitrators, and it was stipulated that no member of the Permanent Court of Arbitration could appear as counsel. The tribunal was to decide "in accordance with justice and equity." Each party was to deposit 15,000 francs with the International Bureau, for meeting the expenses of the tribunal. Except as otherwise provided, the procedure was to conform to the provisions of the Hague Convention of 1907,[63] particularly to the provisions of Chapter III. The Secretary-General of the Permanent Court of Arbitration was secretary-general of the tribunal. The tribunal was asked to decide whether a previous decision of the umpire of a mixed tribunal was void, and if so to decide the previously submitted claims on the merits. By its award of October 26, 1910, the tribunal declared the previous decision of the umpire void, in part, and to that extent it proceeded to give a fresh decision.

§19. **France–Great Britain:** *Savarkar Case* (1911).[64] Under an agreement of October 25, 1910, this case was referred to an arbitral tribunal "composed of five arbitrators chosen from the members of the Permanent Court of Arbitration." The exchange of cases, countercases and replies was to be effected through the "Bureau of the Permanent Court." By an exchange of notes on October 25, 1910, the parties agreed that any points arising in the arbitration not covered by the agreement were to be determined by the provisions of the Convention of 1907. The Secretary-General of the Permanent Court of Arbitration acted as secretary-general of the tribunal. At the re-

by the Bureau. See also Scott, Hague Court Reports, p. 226. For comment, see Dennis, "The Orinoco Steamship Company Case before the Hague Tribunal," 5 American Journal of International Law (1911), pp. 35–64; Nys, *"La revision de la sentence arbitrale,"* 12 *Revue de Droit International et de Législation Comparée* (1910), pp. 595–641; Scelle, *"Une instance en revision devant la Cour de la Haye, L'affaire de la* Orinoco Steamship Company," 18 *Revue Générale de Droit International Public* (1911), pp. 164–202.

[63] Venezuela had not ratified the Hague Convention of 1907.

[64] *Protocoles des Séances et Sentence du Tribunal d'Arbitrage entre la France et la Grande-Bretagne,* published by the Bureau International de la Cour Permanente d'Arbitrage, The Hague, 1911; Scott, Hague Court Reports, p. 275. See also, Anzilotti, *"Estradizione in transito e diritto d'asilo,"* 6 *Rivista di diritto internazionale* (1912), pp. 258–268; van Hamel, *"Les Principes du droit d'extradition et leur application dans l'affaire Savarkar,"* 13 *Revue de Droit International et de Législation Comparée* (1911), pp. 370–403; Kohler, *"Der Savarkarfall,"* 5 *Zeitschrift für Volkerrecht* (1911), pp. 202–21; Robin, *"Un différend franco-anglais devant la Cour d'arbitrage de la Haye (affaire de l'Hindou Savarkar),"* 18 *Revue générale de Droit International Public* (1911), pp. 303–352.

quest of the parties, only the opening and closing sessions of the tribunal were public, and the president left it to the parties to say whether the record of the proceedings would be made public; [65] the *procès-verbaux* were later published. The award, given on February 24, 1911, rejected a French claim that Savarkar should be restored to French custody by the British authorities.

§20. **Italy–Peru:** *Canevaro Case* (1912).[66] Under a *compromis* of April 20, 1910, concluded in execution of an arbitration treaty of April 18, 1905, this case was referred "to the Permanent Court of Arbitration at The Hague," to be decided "according to law." The two governments pledged themselves to designate the members of the arbitral tribunal within four months, but the *compromis* made no further provision for its creation. On April 27, 1910, an agreement was reached that the tribunal should be formed in accordance with Article 87 of the Hague Convention of 1907,[67] though it cannot be said to have been an "arbitration by summary procedure." The three members of the tribunal were all members of the Permanent Court of Arbitration. The Secretary-General of the Permanent Court of Arbitration filled the rôle of secretary-general of the tribunal. The award was given on May 3, 1912, to the effect that Peru should meet certain claims advanced by Italy on behalf of two Italian nationals; it has since been frequently cited on the law of dual nationality.

§21. **Russia–Turkey:** *Indemnity* (1912).[68] The *compromis* of July 22/August 4, 1910, recites that the parties, described as cosignatories of the Hague Convention of 1907, had resolved "in the conformity with the stipulations of the Hague Convention," to submit this case to arbitration. Each party was to select two arbitrators, and the four were to select an umpire; failing agreement on the selection of an umpire within two months, the selection was to be made by a third Power designated by the parties; if no third Power could be agreed

[65] *Rapport du Conseil Administratif*, 1911, p. 12.

[66] *Protocoles des Séances et Sentence du Tribunal d'Arbitrage constitué en exécution du compromis signé entre l'Italie et le Pérou le 20 avril 1910,* published by the Bureau International de la Cour Permanente d'Arbitrage, The Hague, 1912; Scott, Hague Court Reports, p. 284. See also, Boeck, *"La sentence arbitrale dans l'affaire Canevaro,"* 20 *Revue Générale de Droit International Public* (1913), pp. 317–371; Kohler, *"Die Lehren des Canevarofalles,"* 7 Zeitschrift für Volkerrecht (1913), pp. 1–10.

[67] Neither Italy nor Peru had ratified the Hague Convention of 1907.

[68] *Protocoles des Séances et Sentence du Tribunal d'Arbitrage constitué en vertu du compromis d'arbitrage signé à Constantinople entre la Russie et la Turquie le 22 juillet/4 août 1910,* published by the Bureau International de la Cour Permanente d'Arbitrage, The Hague, 1912; Scott, Hague Court Reports, p. 297. See also, Ruzé, *"Un arbitrage russo-turc,"* 15 *Revue de Droit International et de Législation Comparée* (1913), pp. 351–371.

upon, each party was to designate a Power, and the selection of the umpire was to be made by the two Powers designated; if the two Powers disagreed, provision was made for a designation by each of the parties of two members of the Permanent Court of Arbitration, so that the umpire might be selected by lot from the four designated, the drawing to be by the "International Bureau of the Permanent Court." Representation of the parties before the tribunal was to conform to Article 62 of the Hague Convention of 1907. Questions arising which had not been covered by the *compromis* were to be governed by the Hague Convention of 1907,[69] with the exception of those articles of which the Ottoman Empire had reserved acceptance. The umpire was eventually selected by the Swiss Government. Only two of the five members of the tribunal were members of the Permanent Court of Arbitration.[70] Meetings of the tribunal were held at The Hague, February 15, 1911 and October 28–November 11, 1912. The Secretary-General of the Permanent Court of Arbitration was secretary-general of the tribunal. The award was rendered on November 11, 1912, to the effect that the Imperial Ottoman Government was not obligated to pay interest damages demanded by the Imperial Russian Government on behalf of Russian claimants.

§22. **France–Italy:** *Carthage* and *Manouba Cases* (1913).[71] On January 26, 1912, the two governments agreed that the case of the *Carthage* should be referred for examination to the "Court of Arbitration at The Hague," under the Franco-Italian arbitration convention of December 23, 1903, renewed December 24, 1908; and that the case of the *Manouba* should "likewise be submitted for examination to the high international court established at The Hague." On March 6, 1912, two *compromis* were signed providing for an arbitral tribunal to be composed of five arbitrators, one of whom should be umpire, chosen by the two governments from among the members

---

[69] This convention had not been ratified by Turkey.

[70] For this reason, the tribunal is listed as a "special arbitral tribunal" in the annual reports of the Administrative Council.

[71] *Compromis, Protocoles des Séances et Sentences du Tribunal d'Arbitrage Franco-Italien,* published by the Bureau International de la Cour Permanente d'Arbitrage, The Hague, 1913; Scott, Hague Court Reports, pp. 329, 341. See also, Anzilotti, *"Le questioni di diritto sollevate dagli incidenti del 'Carthage' e del 'Manouba,'"* 7 Rivista di diritto internazionale (1913), pp. 200–236, 398–413, 502–523; Boeck, *"Les incidents franco-italiens des navires le 'Carthage,' le 'Manouba' et le 'Tavignano,'"* 39 Journal du Droit International Privé (1912), pp. 449–486; Ruzé, *"Un arbitrage franco-italien. L'affaire du 'Carthage' et l'affaire du 'Manouba,'"* 16 Revue de Droit International et de Législation Comparée (1914), pp. 101–136; Scelle, *"Die Fälle 'Carthage', 'Manouba,' 'Tavigliano,' in französischer Auffassung,"* 1 Jahrbuch des Völkerrechts (1913), pp. 544–567.

of the Permanent Court of Arbitration. Documents were to be filed with the Bureau of the Permanent Court of Arbitration, and each party was to deposit a sum for meeting expenses. On all points not covered by the *compromis*, the provisions of the Hague Convention of 1907 were to apply.[72] The two governments agreed on the selection of five arbitrators, and the tribunal met at The Hague, March 31– May 6, 1913. The Secretary-General of the Permanent Court of Arbitration was secretary-general of the tribunal. The awards were given on May 6, 1913, requiring the Italian Government to pay certain sums to the French Government as damages for the seizure of the two vessels.

§23. **France–Italy**: *Tavignano Case* (1912). On May 20, 1912, this case was referred to a commission of inquiry which rendered its report on July 23, 1912.[73] Under a *compromis* of November 8, 1912, it was referred to the tribunal to which the *Carthage* and *Manouba* cases had been referred.[74] On May 2, 1913, however, the parties reached an agreement which made it unnecessary to proceed with the arbitration,[75] and on May 3, 1913, the tribunal took note of the agreement and relinquished its jurisdiction.[76]

§24. **Netherlands–Portugal**: *Island of Timor* (1914).[77] Under a *compromis* of April 3, 1913, this case was submitted to a sole arbitrator to be chosen from the members of the Permanent Court of Arbitration. If the two governments could not agree on the choice, the choice was to have rested with the President of the Swiss Confederation; but M. Charles Edouard Lardy, a member of the Permanent Court of Arbitration, was chosen by the parties. The arbitrator was left free to choose the place where he would sit, but as all of the proceedings were in writing, this question was unimportant. The arbitrator was asked to decide upon part of a boundary between Dutch and Portuguese possessions in the Island of Timor, with reference to the execution of a convention of October 1, 1904. The *compromis* directed him to apply the treaties and the general principles of international law. The award of June 25, 1914, was communicated to the parties by the International Bureau, which had

---

[72] Italy had not ratified the Hague Convention of 1907.
[73] Scott, Hague Court Reports, pp. 413, 616. See § 36, *infra*.
[74] *Id.*, pp. 419, 621.   [75] *Id.*, pp. 421, 622.
[76] *Rapport du Conseil Administratif*, 1914, p. 13.
[77] *Sentence Arbitrale rendue en exécution du compromis signé à La Haye le 3 avril 1913 entre les Pays Bas et le Portugal*, published by the Bureau International de la Cour Permanente d'Arbitrage, Neuchâtel, 1914; Scott, Hague Court Reports, pp. 354, 574.

acted as intermediary in the exchange of documents. Apparently there was no secretary of the tribunal.

§25. **France, Great Britain, and Spain–Portugal:** *Religious Properties in Portugal* (1920).[78] By an agreement signed at Lisbon, July 31, 1913, in which the Parties were described as signatories of the Hague Convention of 1907,[79] claims relating to the expropriated properties of French, British, and Spanish nationals were referred to an arbitral tribunal constituted under the provisions for summary procedure set out in Chapter IV of the Convention. The tribunal was composed of three arbitrators, named in the agreement, all members of the Permanent Court of Arbitration. It was directed to decide in accordance with the conventional law applicable, and, that failing, with "the general provisions and principles of law and equity." Cases and counter-cases and replies and counter-replies were to be deposited with the International Bureau. Each of the parties was required to deposit 3,000 florins with the Bureau upon presenting its case. The procedure was governed by the provisions of the Convention of 1907, in so far as it was not covered by the agreement. Each of the claims presented was to be the subject of a separate award. The original periods set for the filing of documents were extended by the parties; and on August 13, 1920, an understanding was reached at Lisbon by which the French, British, and Portuguese Governments gave the tribunal "complete freedom in settling, according to equity and by a single judgment or several judgments," the claims submitted. The presentations were wholly in writing. In the case of the French claims, the tribunal gave a single award on September 2, 1920; the British claims were similarly disposed of by a single award on the same date.[80] On September 4, 1920, the tribunal rendered nineteen separate awards on the Spanish claims, seventeen of which were dismissed. The Secretary-General of the Permanent Court of Arbitration served as secretary-general of the tribunal.

[78] *Compromis, Protocoles des Séances et Sentences du Tribunal d'Arbitrage entre la Grande-Bretagne, l'Espagne et la France et le Portugal,* published by the Bureau International de la Cour Permanente d'Arbitrage, The Hague, 1920; Scott, Hague Court Reports (2 ser.), p. 1. See also, Ruzé, *"Portugal, Espagne, France et Grande-Bretagne— Cour permanente d'arbitrage de la Haye.—Sentences arbitrales au sujet des réclamations relatives aux biens des nationaux britanniques, espagnols et français,"* 29 *Revue Générale de Droit International Public* (1922), pp. 283–294.

[79] Great Britain and Spain had not ratified the Convention of 1907.

[80] "The Governments of France and Great Britain appear to have reached an agreement with Portugal upon the form and extent of the award to be entered in behalf of their subjects or citizens." James Brown Scott, in 15 American Journal of International Law (1921), p. 73.

§26. France–Peru: *Dreyfus Case* (1921).[81] Under a protocol of February 2, 1914, the two governments agreed to submit "to an arbitral tribunal sitting at The Hague" certain claims of French creditors and other claims. Each government was to appoint an arbitrator, and the two arbitrators were to choose an umpire in accordance with the provisions of Article 87 of the Hague Convention of 1907.[82] Documents were to be deposited with the International Bureau, which was charged with their transmission to the arbitrators and the parties. The procedure was to be governed, on points not covered by the protocol, by Chapter IV of the Convention of 1907. None of the members of the tribunal was a member of the Permanent Court of Arbitration, and the tribunal is listed as a special arbitral tribunal in the reports of the Administrative Council. The Secretary-General of the Permanent Court of Arbitration was secretary-general of the tribunal. An award was rendered on October 11, 1921, rejecting some of the French claims and upholding others.

§27. United States of America–Norway: *Seizure of Ships* (1922).[83] Under a special agreement of June 30, 1921, this case was referred to an arbitral tribunal constituted, except as otherwise provided, in accordance with Article 87 and Article 59 of the Convention of 1907. The agreement provided that certain Norwegian claims arising out of requisitions during the World War should be referred to arbitration conformably to the Hague Convention of 1907 and to an arbitration convention between the parties of April 4, 1908, renewed on June 16, 1913, and March 30, 1918. An arbitrator was to be appointed by each party and the two governments were to select a third arbitrator who was to be president; failing agreement, the third arbitrator was to be selected by the President of the Swiss Confederation, and such a selection was made. None of the arbitrators was a member of the Permanent Court of Arbitration. The Secretary-General of the Permanent Court of Arbitration was the secretary-general of the tribunal. The tribunal was to decide "in accordance with the principles of law and equity." When the award was ren-

---

[81] *Compromis, Protocoles des Séances et Sentence du Tribunal d'Arbitrage entre la France et le Pérou,* published by the International Bureau of the Permanent Court of Arbitration, The Hague, 1921; Scott, Hague Court Reports (2 ser.), p. 31. See also, Ruzé, *"France et Pérou [l'arbitrage franco-péruvien],"* 29 *Revue Générale de Droit International Public* (1922), pp. 256–283.

[82] Peru had not ratified the Convention of 1907.

[83] Proceedings of the Tribunal of Arbitration between the United States of America and Norway, published by the International Bureau, The Hague, 1922; Scott, Hague Court Reports, p. 39.

dered on October 13, 1922, the arbitrator appointed by the United States refused to attend the final session of the tribunal; his refusal, communicated to the Secretary-General of the Permanent Court of Arbitration and to the agents of the parties,[84] was grounded on the view that the other arbitrators had "disregarded the terms of submission and exceeded the authority" conferred on the tribunal.[85] This case is regarded as having been before a special arbitral tribunal, since the arbitrators were not members of the Permanent Court of Arbitration.[86] In paying the sum awarded, the Government of the United States denied that the award possessed "an authoritative character as a precedent." [87]

§28. United States of America–Netherlands: *Island of Palmas* (1928).[88] By an agreement of January 23, 1925, the two parties agreed to refer the decision of certain differences with respect to the sovereignty over the Island of Palmas (Miangas) "to the Permanent Court of Arbitration at The Hague." The tribunal was to consist of a sole arbitrator, designated by the two governments "from the members of the Permanent Court of Arbitration"; failing agreement he was to be designated by the President of the Swiss Confederation. The parties chose as arbitrator, M. Max Huber, a member of the Permanent Court of Arbitration, and at the time President of the Permanent Court of International Justice. Memoranda and counter-memoranda were to be exchanged by the two parties, and copies were thereafter to be transmitted to the "International Bureau of the Permanent Court of Arbitration for delivery to the Arbitrator." Requests by the arbitrator for further written explanations were to be addressed to the parties through the "International Bureau of the Permanent Court of Arbitration." Copies of the award were to be deposited with the "In-

[84] Annex to the Protocols of the United States-Norway Arbitration Tribunal, p. 161.

[85] A note in 17 American Journal of International Law (1923), p. 399, signed "C. P. A.," states that the letters from Mr. Anderson were "delivered when the award was announced," and that he was denied the privilege of filing a dissenting opinion.

[86] *Rapport du Conseil administratif*, 1922, p. 38.

[87] For the protest by the Secretary of State of the United States, addressed to the Norwegian Minister at Washington, February 6, 1923, see 17 American Journal of International Law (1923), pp. 287–289. *Cf.* Brooks-Scanlon Corporation *v.* U. S. (1924) 265 U. S. 106.

[88] Arbitral award rendered in conformity with the special agreement concluded on January 23, 1925, between the United States of America and the Netherlands, published by the International Bureau of the Permanent Court of Arbitration, 1928; Scott, Hague Court Reports (2 ser.), p. 83. See also, Jessup, "The Palmas Island Arbitration," 22 American Journal of International Law (1928), pp. 735–752; de Visscher, *"L'Arbitrage de l'Ile de Palmas* (Miangas)," 10 *Revue de Droit International et de Législation Comparée* (1929) pp. 735–762.

ternational Bureau at The Hague." The *compromis* required each of the parties to deposit £100 with the arbitrator "by way of advance of costs." The Secretary-General of the Permanent Court of Arbitration seems to have acted as secretary-general of the tribunal, though all of the proceedings were in writing. The award was given by the arbitrator on April 4, 1928, to the effect that the Island of Palmas (Miangas) forms in its entirety a part of Netherlands territory.

§29. **France–Great Britain**: *Chevreau Claim* (1931).[89] By a *compromis* of March 4, 1930, the French and British Governments agreed to submit to a sole arbitrator a claim by France on behalf of a French national arrested and detained during the World War. The two governments later selected as arbitrator M. Beichmann, who was a member of the Permanent Court of Arbitration though he was not named in that capacity. It was agreed also, that in all matters not covered by the *compromis,* the arbitrator should apply the procedure laid down in Chapter III of the Convention for the Pacific Settlement of International Disputes of July 29, 1899. The Secretary-General of the Permanent Court of Arbitration acted as secretary-general of the tribunal, which held meetings at the Peace Palace at The Hague, May 5–8, 1931. The tribunal was clearly a special arbitral tribunal, and it is so listed. By agreement of the parties, the award, given on June 9, 1931, was to remain secret for a period of three months, after which period it was to be "available to accredited inquirers and those who practise in the Peace Palace"; [90] it was not made available for publication until June, 1932.[91]

§30. **United States of America–Sweden**: *S.S. Kronprins Gustaf Adolf* and *S.S. Pacific* (1932).[92] Under an agreement of December 17, 1930, certain questions growing out of a demand for the indemnification of a Swedish corporation for the detention of its ships were "sub-

---

[89] *Compromis, Protocoles des Séances et Sentence du Tribunal d'Arbitrage constitué en vertu du compromis signé à Londres le 4 mars 1930 entre la France et le Royaume-Uni de Grande-Bretagne et d'Irlande du Nord,* distributed by the Bureau International de la Cour Permanente d'Arbitrage (not printed). A translation of the award is published in 27 American Journal of International Law (1933), p. 153.

[90] Letter of the Secretary-General of the Permanent Court of Arbitration, March 22, 1932.

[91] See Manley O. Hudson, "The Chevreau Claim between France and Great Britain," 26 American Journal of International Law (1932), p. 804.

[92] Arbitral Decision rendered in conformity with the special agreement concluded on December 17, 1930, between the Kingdom of Sweden and the United States of America (no place, no date). The record of proceedings and a photographic reprint of the arbitral decision have been published by the U. S. Department of State, Publication No. 402, in the Arbitration Series No. 5 (6). See also, Anna A. O'Neil, "United States-Sweden Arbitration," 26 American Journal of International Law (1932), pp. 720–734.

mitted to arbitration pursuant to the Convention for the Pacific Settlement of International Disputes, signed at The Hague, October 18, 1907, and the Arbitration Convention between the United States of America and Sweden, signed at Washington, October 27, 1928." In the event that the parties could not agree on the choice of a sole arbitrator, a tribunal of three members was to be constituted, one appointed by each party, and a third to be selected by the two parties. The parties agreed on the selection of M. Borel, who, though a member of the Permanent Court of Arbitration, was not described or nominated in that capacity. The special agreement of December 17, 1930, provided for the exchange of statements of facts and answers by the agents of the parties, which were later to be forwarded by the parties to the "International Bureau at The Hague" for transmission to the arbitrator. The tribunal met in Washington; its secretary, appointed by the arbitrator, was in no way connected with the International Bureau. The award given on July 18, 1932, in which Sweden's claim was disallowed, does not purport to have been given by a tribunal of the Permanent Court of Arbitration, nor was a copy of the award promptly communicated to the International Bureau; yet the case is listed among the *Affaires d'arbitrage jugées* in the report of the Administrative Council for 1932, with an indication that it was a special arbitral tribunal.

§31. **Awards of the Tribunals.** The provisions of the Conventions of 1899 and 1907 relating to the constitution of a tribunal envisage the selection of an umpire (Fr., *surarbitre*) who is to be the president of the tribunal. The normal function of an umpire is to decide in case of a difference between other members of the tribunal. "In legal terminology, an umpire is a person called in to decide between arbitrators who have failed to make an award." [93] This power is not conferred on the umpire by the Conventions, which on the contrary provide (Article 51, 1899; Article 78, 1907) that decisions are to be reached by majority vote; the term *umpire* is therefore "technically inaccurate." [94] Article 52 of the 1899 Convention provided that an award should be signed by each member of the tribunal; but Article 79 of the 1907 Convention provides for signature by the president and registrar or secretary. Though umpires have been selected in a number of cases, the awards represent the decisions not of umpires but of tribunals.

[93] 6 Moore, International Adjudications, p. ix.   [94] *Ibid.*

The awards of tribunals of the Permanent Court of Arbitration, and of the special arbitral tribunals served by the International Bureau, are usually published by the Bureau, though not in uniform style or in serial form. They lack the continuity and consistency which would constitute them a body of cumulating jurisprudence,[95] and in some of the cases they were not adequately grounded on citations of existing law.[96] Yet they accomplish with measurable satisfaction the object of international arbitration as stated in the Hague Conventions (Article 15, 1899; 37, 1907), namely "the settlement of disputes between States on the basis of respect for law." They have served and they will continue to serve as most important jural materials for the development of international law.[97]

§32. Appreciation of the Permanent Court of Arbitration. A review of the work of tribunals created with reference to the Hague Conventions for the pacific settlement of international disputes clearly points to the conclusion that over a period of thirty years the Conventions have served a very useful purpose. Unquestionably, States have been aided in the desire to resort to arbitration, both by the procedural provisions and by the existence of the agencies which constitute the Court. Of these agencies, the International Bureau is by no means the least important; it has served, even in arbitrations not conducted by members of the Permanent Court of Arbitration, as an impartial body through which negotiations and communications may be conducted; it has offered a *locus* in which tribunals may have their seats; and it has furnished a trained personnel upon which tribunals may rely. The existence of the panel of members of the Permanent Court of Arbitration, has frequently served to facilitate the selection of abritrators, though it has not offered escape from the difficulties of such a selection, and it has greatly encouraged the extension of agreements to arbitrate. Possibly it is not too early to say that the importance of the Court has diminished since the creation of the Permanent Court of International Justice; since the inauguration

---

[95] The following observation by Mr. Choate at the Second Peace Conference in 1907 still holds true: "The present Permanent Court has not gone far in the direction of establishing and developing international law. Each case is isolated, lacking both continuity and connection with the other." Scott, Proceedings of the Hague Peace Conferences, 1907, II, p. 596.

[96] For a severe criticism of the earlier awards, see Wehberg, The Problem of an International Court of Justice (translation by Charles G. Fenwick, 1918), pp. 29ff. On the other hand, some of the criticism of the awards has proceeded on misconceptions of the nature of the judicial process. See 1 Moore, International Adjudications, p. xc.

[97] See the excellent digest of the awards, in *Fontes Juris Gentium*, Series A, Sec. 1, Vol. 2.

of the latter, only one *compromis* has been concluded for creating a tribunal in the Permanent Court of Arbitration,[98] though in two additional cases special arbitral tribunals have been created with some reference to the Hague Conventions.[99] Yet situations may arise in which States will prefer tribunals composed of arbitrators of their own choice to the Permanent Court of International Justice with its fixed personnel, and the Permanent Court of Arbitration may still serve a useful purpose in the future. When its abolition was proposed to the First Assembly of the League of Nations in 1920, by the Argentine delegation, the proposal received no support, for "it was thought that this Court would still have a rôle to fill in certain international disputes which lend themselves more easily to arbitral decision than to an award based on strict rules of law."[100] Apart from this, however, the fact that the national groups in the Permanent Court of Arbitration now have the function of nominating candidates in the elections of members of the Permanent Court of International Justice, will doubtless tend to assure the continuance of the Permanent Court of Arbitration.

[98] In the Island of Palmas arbitration, between the United States of America and the Netherlands.
[99] The Chevreau Claim arbitration between France and Great Britain, and the Shipping Claims arbitration between the United States of America and Sweden. Four cases are listed among the *affaires d'arbitrage jugées* by the Administrative Council of the Permanent Court of Arbitration, in which the reference to arbitration has been made since 1920; in three of these cases, one party was the United States of America, which was not a party to the Protocol of Signature of December 16, 1920, setting up the Statute of the Permanent Court of International Justice.
[100] Records of First Assembly, Committees, I, pp. 514, 526.

CHAPTER 2

INTERNATIONAL COMMISSIONS OF INQUIRY

§33. The Hague Convention of 1899. The Convention for the Pacific Settlement of International Disputes, of July 29, 1899, contained (Article 9) a recommendation that for international differences involving neither honor nor vital interests and relating to points of fact, States should, so far as circumstances permit, institute international commissions of inquiry to elucidate the facts.[1] The Convention provided for the constitution of such commissions by the parties; the commissioners were to be appointed in accordance with the scheme laid down in Article 32 of the Convention for the appointment of members of arbitral tribunals. Agreements made *ad hoc* were to define the facts to be investigated and the powers of the commissioners. The parties were to supply commissions with all facilities necessary for understanding the facts in question, and both sides were to be heard. The report of a commission was to be limited to a statement of facts, and it was expressly stated not to have the character of an arbitral award. The parties to a difference were therefore left complete freedom in dealing with the report of a commission.

§34. The Hague Convention of 1907. Experience gained in connection with a single commission of inquiry set up in 1904 to deal with the North Sea Incident, was made the basis of proposals by the British, French and other delegations at the Second Peace Conference for extensive modifications of the provisions in the 1899 Convention relating to commissions of inquiry. Articles 9–14 of the 1899 Convention were expanded into Articles 9–35 of the 1907 Convention. New provisions were added for assessors, agents and counsel, and for the summoning of witnesses; the procedure was elaborately set

[1] See, generally, Albert Beaucourt, *Les Commissions internationales d'Enquête* (Arras, 1909); Maurice Bokanowski, *Les Commissions internationales d'Enquête* (Paris, 1908); Milosch Boghitchévitch, *Die Enquete-Kommissionen des Völkerrechtes* (Berlin, 1905); André le Ray, *Les Commissions internationales d'Enquête au XXme Siècle* (Saumur, 1910).

forth and assimilated in some measure to judicial procedure; and the International Bureau of the Permanent Court of Arbitration was given the function of acting as registry for commissions sitting at The Hague. The nature of the report by a commission of inquiry remained unaltered, however, though a provision was added that the report should be read at a public sitting of the commission.

§35. **The North Sea Incident (Dogger Bank Affair).**[2] In consequence of a suggestion made by the French Government, a declaration was signed by representatives of the British and Russian Governments on November 12/25, 1904, by which these Governments agreed to entrust to a commission of inquiry the "task of elucidating by means of an impartial and conscientious investigation the questions of fact connected with the incident which occurred during the night of October 8–9/21–22, 1904, in the North Sea (on which occasion the firing of the guns of the Russian fleet caused the loss of a boat and the death of two persons belonging to a British fishing fleet, as well as damages to other boats of that fleet and injuries to the crews of some of the boats)."[3] The commission was composed of five members; two were admirals in the British and Russian Navies, appointed by their Governments, respectively; one was an admiral of the United States Navy, named by the Government of the United States, and one an admiral of the French Navy, named by the Government of France; the fifth member was an admiral in the Austrian Navy, designated by the Austrian Government upon the invitation of the other four members.[4] The British and Russian Governments were represented in the commission by assessors, and an agent of each Government presented its views. The commission met at Paris, December 22, 1904, to February 26, 1905,[5] and it heard numerous witnesses in the course of its twenty-eight meetings. The International Bureau of the Permanent Court of Arbitration did not participate in the functioning of the commission. The report of February 26, 1905, was chiefly limited to a narration of events; the commissioners were not unanimous in placing the responsibility for the incident on

---

[2] Also known as the *Hull Affair.*

[3] For the text of the declaration, see *Archives Diplomatiques,* 1904, IV, p. 1323; Scott, Hague Court Reports, pp. 410, 614. For the correspondence relating to the North Sea Incident, see British Parliamentary Papers, Russia No. 2 (1905), Cd. 2350.

[4] In default of agreement, the designation was to have rested with the Austrian Government.

[5] The *procès-verbaux* are published in *Archives Diplomatiques,* 1905, II, pp. 450–491. For the *règlement* of the commission, see *id.,* I, p. 102.

the Russian admiral who ordered the firing.[6] Following the report, the Russian Government paid a sum of £65,000 to the British Government, and the incident was closed.[7]

§36. **The Tavignano, Camouna and Gaulois Inquiry.** Under an agreement signed at Rome, May 20, 1912, the French and Italian Governments undertook to establish a commission of inquiry "conformably to Part III of the Hague Convention of October 18, 1907" [8] to clear up the circumstances as to the capture and detention of the French mail steamer *Tavignano* by an Italian vessel on January 25, 1912, and as to the firing upon the *Camouna* and *Gaulois* by an Italian torpedo boat on the same day.[9] The commission was to be composed of three members, two naval officers appointed by the French and Italian Governments and a naval officer named by the British Government. It was entrusted with the task of investigating, marking and determining the exact geographic point where the *Tavignano* was captured and where the *Camouna* and the *Gaulois* were pursued and fired upon; of determining exactly the hydrography, configuration and nature of the coast and of the neighboring banks; and of making a written report on the results of its investigation. It was to meet at Malta, with power to meet elsewhere, and to make its report within fifteen days after its first meeting. On points not covered by the agreement, it was to be guided by the provisions of the Hague Convention of 1907. On July 23, 1912, the commission made a report, which, because of the uncertainty of the evidence and documents presented to it, was very inconclusive.[10] Following the rendering of this report, on November 8, 1912, the French and Italian Governments agreed to submit the *Tavignano Case* to an arbitral tribunal previously created to deal with the *Carthage* and *Manouba* cases.[11] This tribunal was to pronounce upon the facts, decide questions of law, and determine the amount of reparation which might be due. On May 2, 1913, before the tribunal had begun any deliberation, an agreement was reached by which the Italian Government undertook to pay to the French Government the sum of 5000 francs to

[6] *Archives Diplomatiques*, 1905, II, p. 491; Scott, Hague Court Reports (1916), pp. 404, 609.
[7] On the North Sea Incident, see the critical study of André Mandelstam, *"La Commission Internationale d'Enquête sur l'Incident de la Mer du Nord,"* 12 *Revue Générale de Droit International Public* (1905), pp. 161–190, 351–415.
[8] Italy had not ratified the Hague Convention of 1907.
[9] For the text of the agreement, see Scott, Hague Court Reports, pp. 417, 617.
[10] For the text of the report, see Scott, Hague Court Reports, pp. 413, 616.
[11] An agreement of April 15, 1912, had envisaged the possibility of this course.

indemnify the individuals who had suffered losses, and the French Government undertook to consider the affair as definitely settled.[12]

§37. The Tubantia Inquiry. On March 30, 1921, the Governments of Germany and the Netherlands entered into a convention by which they agreed to submit to a commission of inquiry the question of the cause of the sinking of the Netherlands steamship *Tubantia* on March 16, 1916.[13] Each party chose a member of the commission, the Danish and Swedish Governments were asked to choose one member each, and the Swiss Government was asked to choose a jurist as president of the commission. The procedure of the commission was to be in accordance with the applicable provisions of the Hague Convention of 1907; its meetings were not to be public and the protocols were not to be published; but the final report was to be read in public session and published. Memorials were deposited by the parties with the International Bureau of the Permanent Court of Arbitration. The commission began its meetings at The Hague on January 18, 1922; both witnesses and experts were heard. On February 27, 1922, a report was handed down,[14] in which the commission reached the conclusion that the *Tubantia* was sunk by the explosion of a torpedo launched by a German submarine. This report led to a settlement of the matter by the German and Netherlands Governments.

§38. Appreciation of the Commissions of Inquiry. In more than thirty years, only three commissions of inquiry have been created under the provisions of the Hague Conventions, and each of these commissions was charged with the investigation of a war-time incident between a belligerent and a neutral state. In one instance, that of the North Sea Incident, the situation may be said to have been quite serious; [15] this cannot be said of the other two instances, however. The commissions were too limited with respect to their reports for them to be more generally serviceable. Perhaps the provisions of the Hague Conventions may be thought to have influenced later

---

[12] Scott, Hague Court Reports, pp. 421, 612. See § 23, *supra*.

[13] For the text of the convention, see 20 Martens, N.R.G. (3 ser.), p. 613. An English translation is published in Scott, Hague Court Reports (2 ser.), p. 143.

[14] The report was published by the International Bureau of the Permanent Court of Arbitration. See also, Scott, Hague Court Reports (2 ser.), pp. 135, 211; 16 American Journal of International Law (1922), p. 485.

[15] See R. de la Penha, *La Commission d'Enquête sur l'incident Anglo-Russe de la Mer du Nord* (Paris, 1906), pp. 19ff. Various commentators have referred to the sinking of the *U.S.S. Maine* in 1898 as the kind of incident for which the commission of inquiry might have been particularly useful.

developments, though it is notable that they were not referred to by the Government of the United States in launching a plan for the promotion of peace through the establishment of permanent international commissions of investigation, on April 24, 1913.[16] Nor is it possible to trace to the Hague Conventions many of the characteristics of permanent commissions of investigation and conciliation established by numerous treaties since 1919.[17] In a sense, however, it may be said that the provisions in Article 15 of the Covenant have developed out of the provisions in the Hague Conventions; [18] the commissions of inquiry provided for by the Central American Convention signed at Washington, February 7, 1923,[19] and by the Inter-American Convention signed at Santiago, May 3, 1923,[20] also have many of the features of the Hague commissions. Certainly a significant departure was made by the Peace Conference in 1899 in providing this means of establishing the facts involved in a dispute, and efforts since that time have proceeded more smoothly because the initial step had been taken.

[16] U. S. Foreign Relations, 1913, p. 8.

[17] See Max Habicht, Post-War Treaties for the Pacific Settlement of International Disputes (1931), pp. 107off.

[18] See Hershey, Essentials of International Public Law and Organization (1927), p. 465. One may trace to the Hague Conventions, also, the Commission of Enquiry as to labor conventions, provided for in Articles 411–415 of the Treaty of Versailles and in the corresponding articles of other treaties of peace of that period.

[19] For the text, see 2 Hudson, International Legislation, p. 985.

[20] For the text, see id., p. 1006.

CHAPTER 3

THE CENTRAL AMERICAN COURT OF JUSTICE

§39. **Federation in Central America.** The organization of an international court in Central America was greatly facilitated by the fact that since their independence began the five Central American States have had a tradition of unity and solidarity. This tradition has persisted in spite of frequent dissensions, and it has found expression in numerous attempts at federation. Under the Spanish régime, the Vice-royalty of Guatemala included in its five provinces the territory now possessed by the five States. It was this dependency which declared its independence in 1821.[1] Two years later the Republic of the United States of Central America was formed, and it continued for some years. Later attempts at union were made in 1842, 1847, 1852, 1889, and 1895, all of which proved more or less abortive,[2] as was the latest attempt in 1921.[3] Unanimous agreement of the five States was not easy to achieve; distances were great and communications difficult; and no pressing need made union imperative. Yet the attempts at federation were renewed from time to time, over a period of a century. They had the effect of encouraging coöperation in many fields, and led to the efforts in 1902, 1907, 1921 and 1923 to create a judicial agency for the handling of disputes between the five States.

§40. **The Treaty of Corinto of 1902.** On January 20, 1902, four of the Central American States, Costa Rica, Honduras, Nicaragua and El Salvador, signed a treaty at Corinto, providing for compulsory arbitration and establishing a permanent tribunal of arbitration which

---

[1] On the history of these provinces, see the arbitral award of the King of Spain, of December 23, 1906. 35 Martens, N.R.G. (2 ser.), p. 563.

[2] A note on these attempts is published in U. S. Foreign Relations, 1917, p. 29. See also L. Moreno, *Historia de las Relaciones Interestatuales de Centroamérica* (Madrid, 1928); Dana G. Munro, The Five Republics of Central America (1918), c. 8; James Brown Scott, "The Central American Peace Conference of 1907," 2 American Journal of International Law (1908), p. 121; "The Central American League of Nations," World Peace Foundation, Pamphlet Series, Vol. VII (1917); 3 Miller, Treaties and other International Acts of the United States, p. 234.

[3] For the text of the Treaty of Union of January 19, 1921, see 5 League of Nations Treaty Series, p. 19; 1 Hudson, International Legislation, p. 600.

was to be instituted on September 5 of that year.[4] Each State was to nominate an arbitrator and an alternate to serve for terms of one year; the arbitrators named by parties to a dispute were not to sit; no seat of the tribunal was named, nor were any permanent officials provided for. Difficulties relating to boundaries, or with reference to boundary treaties, were to be submitted by the interested governments to a foreign arbitrator of American nationality. The treaty was ratified by Honduras on February 6, 1902, by El Salvador on March 24, 1902, and by Costa Rica on April 7, 1902.[5] The tribunal was installed at San José on October 2, 1902, and regulations were adopted on October 9, 1902.[6] A meeting of the tribunal to deal with Honduran-Nicaraguan relations was held early in 1907, without achieving any result.[7] On the whole, the system provided for by the Treaty of Corinto was highly artificial. The treaty was not referred to in the treaty of peace signed at San Salvador, November 9, 1903, by representatives of four republics, not including Costa Rica; [8] though it was "continued in force" by Article 4 of the treaty of peace signed by representatives of four republics at San José, September 25, 1906.[9] In February, 1907, the President of Honduras stated that the treaty of 1902 had been declared to be nonexistent.[10]

§41. **Influence of Peace Conferences at The Hague.** The Central American Peace Conference of 1907 assembled but a few weeks after the adjournment of the Second Peace Conference at The Hague, and its consideration of the problem of a permanent tribunal was influenced in some measure by the revision of the Convention for the Pacific Settlement of International Disputes and by the project formulated at The Hague for the creation of a Permanent Court of Arbitral Justice.[11] The influence seems to have been confined to a stimulus to action, however, for few ideas were borrowed from the work of the Second Peace Conference. During the year 1907, Guate-

---

[4] The text is published in 31 Martens, N.R.G. (2 ser.), p. 243; U. S. Foreign Relations, 1902, p. 881.

[5] Information as to Nicaragua is lacking; but an arbitrator was named by Nicaragua to sit in the tribunal.

[6] Minutes of Central American Peace Conference, 1907, Appendix 1, pp. 7–10. For the text of the *Acta de Instalación* and the *Reglamento*, see Descamps and Renault, *Recueil International des Traités du XX⁰ Siècle*, 1902, pp. 165, 166.

[7] U. S. Foreign Relations, 1907, II, p. 608; Moreno, *op. cit.*, p. 159.

[8] U. S. Foreign Relations, 1904, p. 351.

[9] 3 Tejada, *Tratados de Guatemala*, p. 391.

[10] U. S. Foreign Relations, 1907, II, p. 617.

[11] Luis Anderson, "Peace Conference of Central America," 2 American Journal of International Law (1908), p. 144.

mala, Nicaragua and El Salvador had adhered to the Convention of July 29, 1899, for the Pacific Settlement of International Disputes, and the same States later signed and ratified or adhered to the Convention of October 18, 1907; yet the scheme of tribunals which might be organized in the Permanent Court of Arbitration does not seem to have been taken into account by the Conference held at Washington in 1907.[12]

§42. **The Central American Peace Conference of 1907.** In 1906 difficulties between Guatemala and El Salvador, involving also Honduras, led to proposals of settlement by the United States and Mexico, which resulted in the preliminary convention of July 20, 1906, signed on board the *U.S.S. Marblehead*.[13] This was soon followed by the treaty of peace of September 25, 1906,[14] which, like the preliminary convention, envisaged arbitration by the Presidents of the United States and Mexico.[15] On September 25, 1906, also, a convention was signed setting up a Central American International Bureau.[16] Difficulties followed in 1907 between Honduras and Nicaragua, and led the United States and Mexico to propose a conference at Washington.[17] Preceding the conference, a peace protocol was signed by representatives of the five States at Washington, on September 17, 1907.[18] The five States accepted the invitation to a conference, which convened in Washington on November 14 and continued to December 20, 1907.[19] Delegates of the United States and Mexico attended the conference, but did not participate very actively in its deliberations. A proposal to revive the union of Central American States created a sharp division, being favored only by the delegations of Honduras and Nicaragua. A project for an Arbitral Court of Justice was presented by the delegation of El Salvador.[20]

---

[12] The conference was also influenced to some extent by the treaty concerning pecuniary claims of January 30, 1902, the text of which was published in the Minutes of the Central American Peace Conference, 1907, Appendix 1, p. 11.

[13] U. S. Foreign Relations, 1906, I, p. 851.

[14] 3 Tejada, *Tratados de Guatemala*, p. 391; U. S. Foreign Relations, 1906, I, p. 857.

[15] This seems to have been thought by Nicaragua to be inconsistent with the Treaty of Corinto. U. S. Foreign Relations, 1907, II, p. 608. In 1907, various proposals were made for arbitration between Honduras and Nicaragua, by the two heads of states.

[16] U. S. Foreign Relations, 1906, I, p. 863.

[17] U. S. Foreign Relations, 1907, II, p. 644.

[18] *Id.,* p. 644. Meetings of a preliminary conference were held in Washington, September 11, 16, 1917; the minutes are included in the Minutes of the Central American Peace Conference, 1907, pp. 5–11.

[19] Minutes of the Central American Peace Conference at Washington, 1907. Preparatory meetings were held on November 12 and 13.

[20] *Conferencia Centroamericana de Washington* (Managua, 1908), p. xii.

Nine instruments were signed on December 20, 1907: a general treaty of peace and amity with an additional convention, a convention establishing the Central American Court of Justice with an additional protocol, an extradition convention, two conventions establishing an International Central American Bureau and a pedagogical institute, a convention concerning future Central American Conferences, and a convention concerning railway communications.[21] Following the Conference of 1907, six Central American Conferences were held from 1909 to 1914, which dealt primarily with economic and fiscal matters.[22]

§43. **Instruments Relating to the Central American Court of Justice.** By Article 1 of the general treaty of peace and amity, the five States bound themselves always to "observe the most complete harmony, and decide every difference or difficulty that may arise amongst them, of whatsoever nature it may be, by means of the Central American Court of Justice, created by the Convention which they have concluded for that purpose on this date." The convention for the establishment of the court contained 28 articles, and a provisional article to which was annexed an article or "optional clause" relating to the court's jurisdiction, "in order that the legislatures may, if they see fit, include it in this Convention upon ratifying it."[23] The convention was supplemented by an additional protocol, correcting the text of Article 3. It was to remain in force during a period of ten years, counted from the date of the latest ratification. The ratifications were to be exchanged [deposited] by means of communications addressed to the Government of Costa Rica, which was to notify the other contracting States. The convention was ratified by El Salvador, January 20, 1908;[24] by Nicaragua, February 15, 1908;[25] by Costa Rica, February 28, 1908;[26] by Honduras, March 4, 1908;[27] and by Guatemala, March 12, 1908.[28] These ratifications were duly notified to Costa Rica in accordance with the provision in the convention.[29]

---

[21] The texts of these instruments are to be found in U. S. Foreign Relations, II, 1907, pp. 692–711, and in 2 American Journal of International Law (1908), Supp., pp. 219–265.

[22] See Moreno, *op cit.*, pp. 251–266; *República de Costa Rica, Memoria de la Secretaría de Relaciones Exteriores,* 1909, p. viii; 1910, p. ix; 1913, p. xv.

[23] The minutes of the conference state that the annexed article "was approved in the form of a recommendation" on December 13, 1907. Minutes, p. 70.

[24] Ramírez, *Pactos Internacionales de El Salvador* (1910), I, p. 84.

[25] *Convenciones Internacionales de Nicaragua* (1913), pp. 146, 182.

[26] *Colección de las leyes y decretos, República de Costa Rica,* 1908, *primer semestre,* p. 92.   [27] *La Gaceta de Honduras,* April 1, 1908, No. 3,016, p. 201.

[28] *Recopilación de las Leyes de la República de Guatemala,* 1908–1909, p. 349.

[29] Ramírez, *Pactos Internacionales de El Salvador* (1910), p. 116.

All the States except Costa Rica included the annexed article or "optional clause" in the convention as ratified.[30] On January 10, 1911, a convention was signed at Guatemala City by representatives of the five States, changing the seat of the court to San José.[31]

§44. **Constitution of the Court.** By Article 6 of the convention of December 20, 1907, the court was to consist of five justices, one of whom was to be appointed by the Legislative Power of each of the republics. Two substitute justices were to be appointed at the same time by the same authority in each republic. All appointments were to be for five years. Only jurists were to be appointed who possessed the qualifications which the laws of each country prescribed for the exercise of high judicial office, and who enjoyed the "highest consideration, both because of their moral character and their professional ability." Attendance of all five justices was required for a quorum of the court. The exercise of a profession, or the holding of a public office, was declared to be incompatible with the office of justice (Article 11). As the court represented "the national conscience of Central America," a justice might sit in a case in which the State appointing him was a party. A president and a vice-president were to be elected (Article 12) at the first annual session; in practice these officers were elected each year. The court was to organize the personnel of its office by designating a clerk, a treasurer, and the necessary subordinate employees; a single officer, called secretary-treasurer, served from May 25, 1908, to May, 1914, and his successor served from 1914 until the closing of the court. The minor officials consisted of a first and second clerk, a bookkeeper and an archivist.

During the first five-year period, the justices were as follows: *Costa Rica,* José Astúa Aguilar; *Guatemala,* Angel María Bocanegra; *Honduras,* Carlos Alberto Uclés; *Nicaragua,* José Madriz (succeeded in 1910 by Francisco Paniagua Prado, who was succeeded in 1911

---

[30] It is not clear whether five ratifications of the annexed article were required to give it force. Mr. Dana G. Munro says that the article was never ratified. The Five Republics of Central America, p. 215. The provisional article was expressly mentioned in the ratification of El Salvador. Ramírez, *op. cit.,* p. 92. Both the provisional and the annexed articles are included in the text of the convention published in *Convenciones Internacionales de Nicaragua,* Managua, 1913, p. 155, and in *La Gaceta de Honduras,* April 3, 1908, p. 202. The two articles are expressly included in Decree No. 749 of Guatemala, March 11, 1908. *Recopilación de Las Leyes de Guatemala,* 1910, p. 349. On the other hand, no reference to the two articles is made in the text or ratification appearing in *Colección de Leyes y Decretos de Costa Rica,* 1908, pp. 92–104.

[31] For the text, see *Tratados Vigentes de la República de Honduras* (Tegucigalpa, 1913), Part I, pp. 431–432. An English translation is published in U. S. Foreign Relations, 1911, p. 93.

by Daniel Gutiérrez Navas); *El Salvador,* Salvador Gallegos (succeeded in 1909 by Manuel I. Morales). During the second five-year period, the justices were: *Costa Rica,* Nicolas Oreamuno; [32] *Guatemala,* Angel María Bocanegra; *Honduras,* Saturnino Medal; *Nicaragua,* Daniel Gutiérrez Navas; *El Salvador,* Manuel Castro Ramírez. Of the eleven men who held the office of justice during the ten years, only one continued in office for the whole period. Unfortunately, the justices of the court seem never to have been looked upon as international officials of all five states; instead, they were usually regarded as officials of their respective States. This was an inevitable consequence of the provisions of the convention of 1907, which established no method for a coöperative election of the justices; their appointment by each State gave them a representative character. The justices were required by the convention (Article 9) to "take oath or affirmation prescribed by law before the authority that may have appointed them." A further circumstance giving the justices a national character was that some of them seem to have received their salaries directly from the States appointing them.

§45. **Salaries and Expenses.** The salaries of the justices appointed by States other than that in which the court had its seat, were fixed by the convention (Article 7) at $8,000 (*pesos en oro americano*), annually; the salary of the justice appointed by the State in which the court had its seat, was to be fixed by the government of that State. These salaries were to be paid through the treasury of the court; the provision (in Article 7) is not clear, but the inference is that each State was to bear the salary of the justice which it had appointed, though payment was to be effected through the treasurer of the court. In addition, each of the five States was to pay $2,000 (*pesos oro*) annually toward the ordinary and extraordinary expenses of the court. Each State bound itself to remit its contribution to the treasurer of the court, quarterly in advance. No provision seems to have been made for the payment of the justices' travelling expenses.[33] Though the published accounts are somewhat incomplete,[34] they indicate that some payments were made to justices directly by the

[32] Apparently, Marciano Acosta, substitute justice, was sitting at the time of the closing of the court. 46 Bulletin of the Pan American Union (1918), p. 540.

[33] Article 9 of the Rules of Court provided for the payment by the court of travelling expenses of substitutes.

[34] *Anales de la Corte de Justicia Centroamericana,* III, Nos. 1–8, p. 14; IV, Nos. 11–13, p. 43; V, Nos. 14–16, pp. 109–110; VII, Nos. 19–20, p. 16. See also Costa Rica, *Memoria de Relaciones Exteriores,* etc., 1917, pp. 83–86.

governments, and that considerable arrears in payments existed at various times.

§46. **Seat of the Court.** By Article 5 of the convention of 1907, it was provided that the court should sit in Cartago, Costa Rica, but that it might temporarily sit elsewhere. At the beginning, the Government of Costa Rica placed a building at the court's disposition; but at its inaugural session a gift by Mr. Andrew Carnegie of $100,000 was announced, to provide a permanent home for the court. This gift was partly used for a building which was not yet completed when it was destroyed by earthquake in 1910. The headquarters of the court were at once transferred to San José, where all later meetings were held. By a convention signed at Guatemala City, January 10, 1911, Article 5 of the convention of 1907 was amended to provide for the seat of the court at San José.[35] An unsuccessful effort was made by the municipality of Cartago to secure the return of the court to that city.[36] On May 22, 1911, Mr. Andrew Carnegie made a second gift of $100,000 for a building for the court at San José, to be erected under the supervision of the Government of Costa Rica. The construction of the second building was completed late in 1917.[37] When the court ceased to exist, in March, 1918, the possession of this building was handed over to the Costa Rican Government, and it now houses the Costa Rican Ministry of Foreign Affairs.

§47. **Sessions of the Court.** The inaugural session of the court was opened with great ceremony on May 25, 1908,[38] and this became the date for beginning the sessions of the succeeding years. The earthquake in Costa Rica on May 3, 1910, prevented a formal session of the court from that time until June, 1911. Except for that interim, the court seems to have remained in more or less continuous session, but the records available are so incomplete that information is lacking as to the number of meetings actually held. Article 49 of the rules adopted on December 2, 1911, provided that "the sessions of the Court shall be secret, except as otherwise decided;"[39] no complete

[35] For the text of the convention, see U. S. Foreign Relations, 1911, p. 93. It was ratified by Costa Rica, January 30, 1911; Guatemala, February 20, 1911; El Salvador, March 17, 1911; Nicaragua, December 30, 1911; Honduras, March 19, 1912.

[36] *República de Costa Rica, Memoria de la Secretaría de Relaciones Exteriores*, 1915, p. xvii.

[37] "The New Palace of the Central American Court of Justice," 44 Pan American Union Bulletin, 1917, pp. 734–739.

[38] Representatives of the United States and of Mexico participated in the inaugural ceremony.

[39] *Anales*, I, No. 4, p. 350; 8 American Journal of International Law (Supp., 1914), p. 190.

procès-verbaux were published in the *Anales*,[40] though Articles 43 and 44 of the rules required full records to be kept, and to be signed by all the justices.

§48. Status of the Justices. The convention of 1907 provided (Article 10) that "whilst they remain in the country of their appointment the regular and substitute justices shall enjoy the personal immunity which the respective laws grant to the magistrates of the Supreme Court of Justice, and in the other contracting Republics they shall have the privileges and immunities of diplomatic agents." This was slightly expanded, as to the use of shields and flags, by Article 33 of the rules. On September 21, 1908, El Salvador recognized the status of the justices and of the substitutes as that of ministers of the first class, assigning to the secretary of the court the status of a *chargé d'affaires;* [41] but the status of the justices was chiefly important in Costa Rica, where the seat of the court was located. In 1913, and again in 1916, Costa Rica proposed to the other States a permanent arrangement by which the justices would be given the status of diplomatic agents of the first class; [42] but this proposal was viewed by other States as tending to place the justices in the position of political representatives. In 1917, in proposing amendments to the convention of 1907, the permanent commission of the court suggested a clarification of Article 10 of the convention of 1907, "to avoid the difficulties which have arisen in practice." [43] At no time were the privileges and immunities of the justices made very definite.[44]

§49. Jurisdiction of the Court. By Article 1 of the convention of 1907, the five States bound themselves to submit to the court "all controversies or questions which may arise among them, of whatsoever nature and no matter what their origin may be, in case the respective Departments of Foreign Affairs should not have been able to reach an understanding." The court was also given jurisdiction over cases between a government and an individual who was a national of another state, either if they were cases of an international character, or if they concerned alleged violations of a treaty or convention; in such cases, it was not necessary that the individual's

---

[40] Though official, the *Anales* constitute a magazine of propagandist tendency, rather than a record of the court.   [41] *Anales,* III, Nos. 1–8, p. 10.
[42] *Idem,* p. 11; V, Nos. 14–16, p. 104.   [43] *Anales,* VII, Nos. 19–20, p. 37.
[44] *Cf.* S. Basdevant, *Les fonctionnaires internationaux* (1931); L. Preuss, "Diplomatic Privileges and Immunities of International Agents," 25 American Journal of International Law (1931) p. 699; J. Secretan, *Les immunités diplomatiques des représentants des États membres et des agents de la Société des Nations* (1928). *Cf.,* §366, *infra.*

claim be supported by his own government, but it was essential in a claim against a government that local remedies should have been exhausted or that a denial of justice should be shown. By common accord any case between a contracting government and an individual might be submitted to the court. The court might also take jurisdiction over international questions submitted to it by special agreement between one of the Central American States and a State outside of Central America, but no such question was ever submitted. The rules of court adopted on December 2, 1911, therefore, distinguished between the ordinary and the extraordinary or compromissory jurisdiction of the court. By Article 22 of the convention, the court was also given competence to determine its own jurisdiction, "interpreting the treaties and conventions germane to the matter in dispute, and applying the principles of international law." [45] By the "optional clause," included in the convention as ratified by all of the States except Costa Rica, the court was given jurisdiction over conflicts between the legislative, executive and judicial branches of a government "when as a matter of fact the judicial decisions and resolutions of the National Congress are not respected"; in such cases Article 4 of the rules required the court to be guided by "the public law of the respective State." Article 18 of the convention gave the court power to issue interim orders in any pending case "to the end that the difficulty shall not be aggravated and that things shall be conserved *in statu quo* pending a final decision"; this power was exercised on several occasions.

§50. **Rules of the Court.** Article 26 of the convention conferred on the court power to formulate rules of procedure and to determine the form and terms (*plazos*) not prescribed by the convention, its decisions being communicated to the States. Consideration of the court's *règlement* seems to have been begun on June 17, 1908,[46] but the rules were not adopted until December 2, 1911.[47] It is difficult to account for this delay in formulating the regulations.[48] The rules adopted go beyond the terms of the convention in many particulars; the most significant departure was made in Article 4 of the rules in the provision that "whenever for any reason the Court shall dis-

[45] This provision seems to have been taken from Article 48 of the Convention for the Pacific Settlement of International Disputes, of July 29, 1899. See Minutes of the Central American Peace Conference, 1907, p. 65.   [46] *Anales*, III, Nos. 1–8, p. 7.

[47] *Anales*, I, No. 4, pp. 339–353. An English translation of the rules is published in 8 American Journal of International Law (Supp., 1914), p. 179.

[48] See the note in *Anales*, I, No. 4, p. 382.

integrate," that is, lack the quorum of five judges required by Article 6 of the convention, "the judges present shall be constituted into a permanent commission" for the purpose of securing a quorum, attending to correspondence and directing the administration. The rules made liberal provision for challenging the judges (Article 26); laid down strict standards of incompatibility (Article 38); and outlined the general organization of the court.

§51. **Ordinance of Procedure.** The ordinance adopted on November 6, 1912,[49] in exercise of the power conferred on the court by Articles 13 and 26 of the convention, deals with numerous questions also covered by the rules of December 2, 1911. It gives detailed prescriptions for the procedure to be followed before and by the court. It provides (Article 35) for three kinds of judicial resolutions: decisions (*sentencias*), decrees (*autos*), and orders (*providencias*). Each action (*demanda*) had to be admitted before notification to the defendant, which was then to be given thirty or sixty days for filing its answer; this period might be prolonged by twenty days. In arriving at a decision, the justices were to vote on interrogatories framed by the President, and detailed requirements were laid down (Article 81) as to the record of the votes. Each judicial resolution required a majority of the votes; in case no majority was possible, Article 23 of the convention provided for calling in a substitute justice. The ordinance dealt at length with the challenge of judges, Article 15 envisaging a challenge of all members of the tribunal, for which a special deposit of $1,000 was required; and it prescribed in detail the manner in which evidence should be presented.

§52. **Decisions.** The court's decisions were required by the convention (Article 24) to be in writing, with a statement of reasons; this was supplemented by the requirement of a special *libro de fallos*, in Article 39 of the ordinance of procedure. Every final or interlocutory decision required the concurrence of at least three justices, though if such concurrence could not otherwise be attained, the substitute justices were to be called in. The convention required the decisions to be signed by all the justices of the court; but when the first decision was about to be given by the court, two of the justices refused to sign it. In most of the decisions, the *acts* of the court are set forth, showing the questions put and the votes of each of the justices

---

[49] *Anales*, II, Nos. 11–16, pp. 193–210. An English translation of the ordinance is published in 8 American Journal of International Law (Supp., 1914), pp. 194–213.

on each question. The decisions were not published in any uniform style; some of the later decisions appear in the *Anales*. Article 15 of the convention provided that the decisions of the court should be final. The Guatemalan delegation at the Central American Conference of 1907 was desirous of making it clear that this did not modify the previous agreement for reference to arbitration to be conducted by the Presidents of Mexico and the United States, in Article 5 of the convention of July 20, 1906; [50] and a declaration by the Guatemalan delegation was entered in the record of the session of December 14, 1907, by which Guatemala reserved "the right of resort to the good offices and friendly mediation of their Excellencies, the Presidents of the United States of America and Mexico, in the event of any difficulty in the execution of the findings" of the court.[51]

§53. **Law Applicable.** The convention provided that on points of fact the court was to be governed by its free judgment; on points of law, by the "principles of international law." The ordinance of procedure of November 6, 1912, provided (Article 72) that the court should consider the facts of a controversy "with absolute freedom of judgment," and the questions of law involved "according to the treaties and the principles of law." In the decisions of the court, there is little to indicate an attempt to formulate any special doctrines of Central American public law, though the views of the court, particularly in *El Salvador* v. *Nicaragua*, were influenced by the tradition of federation in Central America.

§54. **The Seating of Justice Navas.** On the elevation of Justice Madriz to the presidency of Nicaragua, Justice Paniagua Prado was elected to fill the vacancy and took his seat on the court on January 27, 1910.[52] It seems that in September, 1910, a new government in Nicaragua desired to relieve Justice Prado, and that a telegram signed by four of the justices was sent to the Nicaraguan Ministry of Foreign Affairs insisting upon a strict adherence to the treaty of 1907.[53] Arrears in the payment of his salary to the court by Nicaragua caused Justice Prado to return home. On January 13, 1911, the Provisional Assembly in Nicaragua elected Daniel Gutiérrez Navas as justice; its action was later confirmed by the Assembly, and Justice

---

[50] Minutes of the Central American Peace Conference, 1907, p. 61.
[51] *Idem*, p. 72. [52] *Anales*, I, No. 1, p. 67.
[53] These facts are recorded in *Protesta del Doctor Francisco Paniagua Prado, Magistrado de la Corte de Justicia Centroamericana* (Nicaragua, 1911), p. 5. This protest was addressed to the court, from León de Nicaragua, June 14, 1911.

Navas took the oath as a justice of the court. Upon his appearance at San José, the question arose whether the election of Justice Navas was valid. On June 22, 1911, three justices ruled that his credentials were in proper order, Justice Uclés dissenting.[54] A storm of public protest followed, as indicated by letters published at the time.[55] In the case of *Salvador Cerda* v. *Costa Rica,* the incumbency of Justice Navas was unsuccessfully challenged. He continued to serve until the end of the first five-year period, and was reëlected in 1913 for a second period of five years. He was at one time president, and on several occasions vice-president, of the court.

§55. **Cases before the Court.** Five cases [56] came before the court in each of its periods of five years. Of the ten cases, five were brought by individuals, and in each of them the plaintiff's case was declared to be inadmissible. In three cases the court itself took the initiative. In only two cases was an affirmative judgment rendered.

(1) *Honduras and Nicaragua* v. *Guatemala and El Salvador.* This case first came before the court as a result of its own initiative.[57] Having been advised, "through the instrumentality of the President of Costa Rica," of events indicating an invasion of Honduras and of a protest by Nicaragua to El Slavador which had invested these events "with an international character," the court felt itself "bound by its high mission to exhaust the recources of its friendly and well-intentioned intervention for the maintenance of peace and harmony." On July 8, 1908, telegrams were despatched to the Presidents of Guatemala, El Salvador, Honduras, and Nicaragua, urging a resort to the court; and in a telegram to the President of Costa Rica, the use of his offices was urged to the end that the conflict be brought before the court.[58] Formal complaints were subsequently lodged with the court by Honduras and Nicaragua against Guatemala and El Salvador, alleging that protection and encouragement had been given to a revolutionary movement in Honduras, claiming a violation of neutrality, and asking

[54] Article 12 of the rules adopted on December 2, 1911, provided that the appointment of justices was an "act of exclusive responsibility of the State" making the appointment.

[55] *Anales,* I, No. 1, pp. 12–99; II, Nos. 1–2, pp. 55–57; *id.,* Nos. 6–10, pp. 179–182.

[56] Strictly, not all of the matters considered by the court should be called cases.

[57] In a pamphlet of the World Peace Foundation, of February, 1917, entitled the "Central American League of Nations," it is said that States not parties to the difficulty haled the actual parties before the court. The telegrams published in *República de Costa Rica, Memoria de Relaciones Exteriores,* 1909, pp. vii–xi, seem to afford some basis for this statement; but the court was not originally seised of the case by Costa Rica, that State merely supplying the information on which it acted.

[58] 2 American Journal of International Law (1908), p. 836.

for interim protection. Two interlocutory decrees were issued by the court on July 13, 1908, calling upon Guatemala and El Salvador to refrain from military action and to take other measures, and calling upon Guatemala, El Salvador, and Nicaragua to maintain the *status quo* and to safeguard their neutrality with respect to the conflict in Honduras.[59] The final conclusions and decision (*sentencia*) of the court were handed down on December 19, 1908; [60] but as the decision was signed by only three of the justices, it would seem to have lacked validity as a decision under Article 24 of the 1907 convention. Guatemala had entered a plea of non-receivability on the ground that no negotiations between the parties had been conducted prior to Honduras' filing a complaint, and hence that the court lacked jurisdiction under Article 1 of the convention; [61] this plea was rejected. After an examination of the evidence submitted, the court held that El Salvador and Guatemala were "acquitted of the charges" and under no liability for damages. A dissenting opinion by Justice Madriz (Nicaragua), dated December 28, 1908, was later published privately.[62] One commentator on the case asserted soon afterward that "the Court performed its delicate mission under trying circumstances" and that its intervention had "prevented the outbreak of war in Central America." [63]

(2) *Diaz* v. *Guatemala*. On December 3, 1908, Dr. Diaz, a national of Nicaragua, filed a complaint against Guatemala alleging false arrest and imprisonment and asking for an indemnity. Deliberations of the court were held on January 13 and 16 and on February 3 and 10, 1909; on the last date Justices Aguilar, Bocanegra, and Suarez voted against admitting the claim, Justices Uclés and Madriz dissenting. Following these deliberations, the plaintiff unsuccessfully challenged one of the justices, alleging that he had furnished a copy of the plaintiff's complaint to a Guatemalan representative. Ap-

[59] *Id.* (1908), p. 838.
[60] Published by the court (183 pages), at San José in 1908; also in *Libro Rosado de El Salvador* (1908). For English translations, see 3 American Journal of International Law (1909), pp. 434–436, 729–736. See also Ramírez, *Cinco años en la Corte de Justicia Centroamericana* (1918), p. 31.
[61] *Defensa por el señor representante y abogado de Guatemala con motivo de la demanda del Gobierno de Honduras contra los de El Salvador y Guatemala* (Guatemala, 1908).
[62] *Voto del Magistrado por Nicaragua en la Corte de Justicia Centroamericana* (1908), San José: Maria v. de Lines. Justice Bocanegra (Guatemala) also gave a separate explanation of his vote.
[63] James Brown Scott, in 3 American Journal of International Law (1909), p. 436. See also, Joseph Wheless, "The Central American Court of Justice," 21 Case and Comment (1914), p. 551.

parently, no appearance was entered on behalf of Guatemala. In its resolution of March 6, 1909, the court held the complaint inadmissible because of lack of jurisdiction.[64] The personal security of the plaintiff while in Guatemala was "under the protection of the principles governing the Commonwealth of Nations, as international rights of man." Yet the plaintiff had not exhausted his local remedies, and this was a condition of the court's jurisdiction. The court refused to admit, by way of substitute, the allegation and proof that it was impossible and useless for the plaintiff to pursue local remedies, on the ground that this would constitute a defamation of Guatemala; *travaux préparatoires* were resorted to, indicating that such an exception had been rejected when the convention of 1907 was framed. Though two of the justices dissented in this case, all five of the justices signed the resolution.

(3) *The 1910 Revolution in Nicaragua.*[65] On April 11, 1910, Justice Paniagua Prado (Nicaragua) suggested that the court offer to mediate in the Estrada revolution which had been in progress in Nicaragua since the previous October. On April 27, 1910, telegrams were sent by the court to the leaders of the contending parties in Nicaragua, proposing an armistice for eight days to enable the court to mediate; and copies of these telegrams were sent to the other Central American States. This action of the court was warmly approved by the Secretary of State of the United States.[66] The suggestion of the court was declined by the Nicaraguan leaders. The earthquake of May 3, 1910, made it more difficult for the court to continue its activity, but after the removal to San José, a "permanent commission" was constituted to deal with the matter, consisting of three justices and the secretary. Offers of mediation were repeated and declined; on June 27, 1910, the President of the court communicated to the leaders a draft of bases for the settlement of the dispute; but the draft was not accepted.

(4) *Salvador Cerda v. Costa Rica.*[67] On September 27, 1911, the plaintiff, a national of Nicaragua living in Costa Rica, filed a complaint against Costa Rica, alleging a denial of the equal rights guaranteed to all Central Americans by the Treaty of Washington,

---

[64] *Resolución dictada en la demanda del Dr. don Pedro Andrés Fornos Díaz contra el Gobierno de la República de Guatemala* (San José, 1909). For an English translation, see 3 American Journal of International Law (1909), pp. 737–747. See also Ramírez, *op. cit.*, pp. 28–41.   [65] *Anales,* I, No. 2, pp. 146–164.

[66] U. S. Foreign Relations, 1910, p. 744.   [67] *Anales,* I, No. 3, pp. 199–214.

and of the rights given to him by the Constitution of Costa Rica. The plaintiff challenged the legality of Justice Navas' (Nicaragua) incumbency on the court. In its resolution of October 14, 1911, the court denied the capacity of the plaintiff to challenge a judge; "only the Governments signatories of the Convention establishing the Court have the right to raise questions as to the legality of its organization." The court also held that the plaintiff had not offered proofs of his Nicaraguan nationality, nor of the deprivation complained of, nor of his exhaustion of local remedies. For these reasons, the plaintiff's demand was rejected. Justice Uclés (Honduras) dissented and wrote a dissenting opinion, dealing chiefly with the challenge of Justice Navas. There is no indication that the Government of Costa Rica was represented.

(5) *The 1912 Revolution in Nicaragua.* On August 5, 1912, the court took cognizance of the existence of a new revolution in Nicaragua and decided to set up a commission to visit Nicaragua and to offer mediation if it seemed wise.[68] This commission, later called a Peace Commission, consisted of the Costa Rican, Salvadorean and Honduran justices and the secretary. On August 9, the commission started for Nicaragua, and it left that country with its mission unfulfilled, on September 3. Its report to the court, dated October 6, 1912, charged the Government of Nicaragua with disregard of the attempt of the commission to secure peace. Telegrams to the President remaining unanswered for several days, the commission decided to approach General Mena, one of the leaders of the rebelling forces. On August 21, a conference was held with this leader, who agreed to an armistice of not less than five days, and stated that he was willing for the members of the commission to represent him at Managua with a view to securing peace; he also offered to assist the commission in procuring transportation. The commission made special mention of the courteous reception accorded to it by the personnel of the rebel army. The same friendly treatment was received by the commission at the hands of General Zeledón, who also agreed to the arrangements for an armistice suggested by the commission, adding a statement to the effect that Nicaragua must govern herself, without foreign influence, and that all Nicaraguan citizens must be assured of their rights. At Managua, the commission received discouraging reports from "various persons in official circles," who

[68] *Anales*, II, Nos. 6–10, pp. 129–150.

declared that the President was determined to crush the revolution by force and would be strongly opposed to a move for peace. Nevertheless, on the following day, the commission presented a memorandum to the President proposing a five-day truce, during which time a conference should be held to determine the bases for peace. The commission was later received by President Diaz and his Foreign Minister "with irreproachable courtesy," but the proposals of the commission were rejected without discussion. Further efforts of the commission were unavailing, and it returned to San José. El Salvador, Honduras and the International Central American Bureau congratulated the court on the efforts of the commission.[69] The Government of El Salvador urged the court to take a firm stand in favor of peace, but did not institute a proceeding before the court; on October 27, 1912, the court replied that it considered further action useless, and the matter was closed.

(6) *Felipe Molina Larios* v. *Honduras.*[70] On November 28, 1913, the plaintiff, a national of Nicaragua, filed a claim for imprisonment, illegal search and expulsion against Honduras. It was alleged that on his arrival at Tela by boat from Costa Rica, the plaintiff had been arrested by order of the commandant of the port, held *incomunicado* for five days, and had later been expelled from Honduras by order of the President; also that his luggage and correspondence had been examined. The plaintiff excused his failure to exhaust the local remedies by alleging his inability to enter Honduras.[71] The court handed down its decision (*sentencia*) on December 10, 1913, declaring the case inadmissible because the claim failed to show that the plaintiff had exhausted local remedies. This decision, signed by the five justices, was concurred in by the justices of Nicaragua, Honduras and Guatemala; the justices of El Salvador and Costa Rica filed a joint dissenting opinion on December 17, 1913, declaring that Article 2 of the convention must be interpreted *con criterio humano,* in the sense that it must have been possible to invoke the local remedies against such deprivation as the plaintiff alleged. The plaintiff having shown that application to Honduras had not been open to him, the dissenting justices were of the opinion that the case was within the

---

[69] *Anales,* II, Nos. 6–10, pp. 185–192.   [70] *Anales,* III, Nos. 1–8, pp. 26–67.
[71] Article 2 of the convention of 1907 gives the court jurisdiction in cases brought by individuals, "provided that the remedies which the laws of the respective country provide against such violation shall have been exhausted or that denial of justice shall have been shown."

jurisdiction of the court.[72] Honduras does not seem to have been represented before the court.

(7) *Alejandro Bermúdez y Nuñez* v. *Costa Rica.*[73] On December 12, 1913, the plaintiff, a Nicaraguan national, filed a claim with the court based upon his expulsion from Costa Rica by the government of that country. The plaintiff had left Costa Rica by boat and had returned in the same way; on his return he was allowed to remain in Costa Rica only fifteen days. *Habeas corpus* having been denied, the plaintiff claimed that the decrees against refugees invoked against him applied only to foreigners, and not to Central Americans who were given equal rights with Costa Rican citizens by Article 6 of the General Treaty of Peace and Amity signed at Washington in 1907. The plaintiff asked to have his right to return to Costa Rica declared, but did not ask for damages. The representative of the Government of Costa Rica who appeared before the court renounced the exception of inadmissibility under Article 2 of the convention of 1907, concerning the exhaustion of local remedies. Costa Rica based its defence on the fundamental right of a State to deny asylum to aliens who constitute a prejudice or danger to society, and to prevent any conspiracy or expedition directed against the government of a neighboring State with which it is at peace. The decision (*sentencia*) of the court was handed down on April 7, 1914.[74] The court declared that the claim was without foundation, since residents in a country are under obligation to respect its neutrality, and that the Costa Rican decree of expulsion was legal in view of the fact that the claim itself manifested the part taken by the plaintiff in the revolution against the Government of Nicaragua. Dissenting opinions were filed by Justices Ramírez (El Salvador) and Medal (Honduras), to the effect that the plaintiff had been deprived of the rights given to Costa Rican citizens and also to other Central American citizens under the provisions of the Treaty of Peace and Amity of 1907.

(8) *Election of President González Flores of Costa Rica.*[75] On May 7, 1914, five individuals, nationals respectively of the five Central American States, by cablegram from Guatemala City, lodged with the court a protest against the election of Alfredo González Flores by the Costa Rican Congress as President of Costa Rica. The court

[72] See also Ramírez, *op. cit.,* p. 61.
[73] *Anales,* IV, Nos. 9–11, pp. 1–119; Ramírez, *op. cit.,* pp. 82–106.
[74] *Anales,* IV, Nos. 9–11, p. 84.
[75] *Anales,* IV, Nos. 11–13, pp. 1–12. See also Ramírez, *op. cit.,* pp. 107–110.

was asked to declare the election void as contrary to the Constitution of Costa Rica; to order a new election in conformity with the Constitution; and to declare that President Jiménez should continue until the election of his successor. The court did not recognize this request, since it was not presented in the proper form. On June 20, 1914, another request in the prescribed form was sent to the court from San José, signed by the Guatemalan and Salvadorean nationals in the name of the group. The court handed down a unanimous decision (*sentencia*) on July 3, 1914, declaring the protest to be inadmissible because it sought intervention in the internal affairs of Costa Rica and did not present a case of an international character. The action of nullifying an election was said to be a political one and, as such, not within the competence of the court; this was particularly true as to Costa Rica, since that State had decided in its legislative decree of February 25, 1908, not to accept the annexed article of the convention of 1907 which gave the court jurisdiction over conflicts between the different branches of a government.

(9) *Costa Rica* v. *Nicaragua.*[76] On March 24, 1916, the Costa Rican Government presented a demand to the court against the Government of Nicaragua, alleging that the conclusion of the convention of August 5, 1914,[77] between Nicaragua and the United States of America (called the Bryan-Chamorro Convention), with reference to an interoceanic canal, constituted a violation of the rights of Costa Rica under the Cañas-Jerez Treaty of April 15, 1858,[78] the Cleveland Award of March 22, 1888,[79] and the General Treaty of Peace and Amity signed at Washington, December 20, 1907. The complaint of Costa Rica[80] dealt at length with Costa Rican protests against the convention signed by representatives of the United States of America and Nicaragua at Managua, February 8, 1913, and against the secrecy with which it was negotiated and later superseded by the convention of August 5, 1914. Ratification of this latter convention had been

[76] *Anales*, V, Nos. 14–16, pp. 87–103, 122–129; U. S. Foreign Relations, 1916, pp. 841–842, 843–845; *República de Costa Rica, Memoria de la Secretaría de Relaciones Exteriores, 1916, Anexos*, pp. 63–137.
[77] 3 U. S. Treaties and Conventions, p. 2740. See §§ 56, 57, *infra.*
[78] *Colección de Tratados, República de Costa Rica* (1896), p. 149; 48 British and Foreign State Papers, p. 1049. This treaty provided that Nicaragua would consult Costa Rica before making any agreement relating to transit or a canal.
[79] U. S. Foreign Relations, 1888, I, p. 456.
[80] *Before the Central American Court of Justice, the Government of Costa Rica against the Government of Nicaragua* (Printed at National Printing Office, San José, Costa Rica). An English translation of Costa Rica's petition was published at Washington in 1916, by Gibson Brothers.

consented to by the United States Senate, with express reference to the protests of Costa Rica, Salvador and Honduras.[81] The court was asked to declare that the Bryan-Chamorro Convention violated the rights of Costa Rica in that Costa Rica was not consulted and in that its execution would jeopardize her rights of free navigation of the San Juan River and her rights in San Juan del Norte and Salinas Bay; Costa Rica also claimed that her rights in the ports and maritime waters of Nicaragua were jeopardized. The court was asked to say that these violations of Costa Rica's rights rendered the Bryan-Chamorro Convention void, because Nicaragua lacked the capacity to enter into it. Costa Rica also sought an interlocutory decree for the maintenance of the *status quo ante*, and requested that the Governments of the United States and Nicaragua be notified of the action.[82] On April 1, 1916, the Nicaraguan Minister of Foreign Affairs addressed a letter to the Secretary of the court, contending that the proceedings in the case were void and in violation of the Washington Convention of 1907, and asking the court to refuse to consider the complaint.[83] This letter was confirmed in a later communication of April 26, 1916. The absence of Justice Navas (Nicaragua) prevented the court from having a quorum for the consideration of the Costa Rican complaint until April 24, 1916. On May 1, 1916, the court adopted a resolution,[84] Justice Navas dissenting, reciting that it had jurisdiction of the complaint, and that the requirement of the exhaustion of diplomatic negotiations had been met; it was resolved that the complaint be received, that Nicaragua be notified and called upon to answer within sixty days, and that in the interim Costa Rica and Nicaragua should maintain the *status quo ante*. The court refused, however, to order a notification to the United States "because that government is not a party to this litigation." Each of the justices filed separate opinions.[85]

In spite of the resolution of the court, of which the two governments were informed, the Governments of the United States and Nicaragua proceeded to the exchange of the ratifications of the Bryan-Chamorro Convention on June 22, 1916.[86] On August 1, 1916, the

---

[81] On February 18, 1916. 3 U. S. Treaties and Conventions, p. 2742.
[82] On March 27, 1916, the Costa Rican Minister in Washington notified the Secretary of State of the United States that the proceeding had been instituted. U. S. Foreign Relations, 1916, p. 837.   [83] U. S. Foreign Relations, 1916, p. 843.
[84] *Anales*, V, Nos. 14–16, pp. 87–89; U. S. Foreign Relations, 1916, p. 841.
[85] *Anales*, V, Nos. 14–16, pp. 90, 95, 98, 100, 102.
[86] U. S. Foreign Relations, 1916, p. 849.

Nicaraguan Government addressed an answer to the secretary of the court,[87] again denying the competence of the court, and stating that if the court insisted upon taking an adverse decision Nicaragua would not abide by it. This communication seems to have reached the court on August 25. Meanwhile, on August 16, the court had granted an extension of twenty days for Nicaragua's reply. On August 31, 1916, the court declared that the cause was ready for hearing, and set September 11 as the date for a hearing. Representatives of Costa Rica appeared on that date, but no appearance was made in behalf of Nicaragua, whose protest against the court's assumption of juris- diction seems to have been repeated on September 7 and 9. On Sep- tember 22, fourteen interrogatories framed by the President were voted on by the five justices: on the jurisdiction of the court, the five justices voted affirmatively; on most of the queries, however, the Nicaraguan justice was a minority of one. The decision (*sentencia*) of the court was formulated on the basis of these votes, and was signed by the five justices and handed down on September 30, 1916.[88] Justice Navas (Nicaragua) delivered a dissenting opinion.[89] The decision affirmed the competence of the court, and declared that "the Government of Nicaragua has violated, to the detriment of Costa Rica, the rights granted to the latter by the Cañas-Jerez Boundary Treaty of April 15, 1858, the Cleveland Award of March 22, 1888, and the Central American Treaty of Peace and Amity of December 20, 1907." No declaration was made as to the validity of the Bryan-Chamorro Convention.

Following the announcement of the decision, a spirited exchange of communications took place between the Nicaraguan Government and the secretary of the court,[90] throughout which the former reiterated its refusal to abide by the decision. On November 9, 1916, the secretary of the court reviewed the whole matter in a communication sent to the Governments of Costa Rica, Guatemala, Honduras and El Sal- vador.[91] On November 24, 1917, Nicaragua addressed a statement

---

[87] *Anales*, V, Nos. 14–16, p. 122.
[88] *Anales*, V, Nos. 14–16, pp. 130–176. English translations are published in U. S. Foreign Relations, 1916, p. 862; 11 American Journal of International Law (1917), p. 181. The latter translation, reproducing a translation published by the Costa Rican Legation in Washington, seems to indicate erroneously that Justice Navas was not present when the decision was handed down.   [89] *Anales*, V, Nos. 14–16, p. 177.
[90] U. S. Foreign Relations, 1916, p. 888.
[91] U. S. Foreign Relations, 1916, p. 893; 11 American Journal of International Law (Supp. 1917), p. 3. For the replies to this communication, see *Anales*, VI, Nos. 16–18, pp. 1–6.

of its attitude to the governments of other Central American States,[92] contending that it was a case of *excès de pouvoir*.

(10) *El Salvador* v. *Nicaragua*. On August 28, 1916, the Government of El Salvador filed with the court a complaint against Nicaragua, asking that Nicaragua be enjoined from fulfilling the obligations undertaken in the convention signed with the United States of America on August 5, 1914, and asking for a preliminary injunction against any disturbance of the *status quo ante* by Nicaragua.[93] El Salvador contended that the convention would violate her rights of condominium in the Gulf of Fonseca,[94] which was said to belong to the category of "historic bays"; that the convention was contrary to Article 2 of the General Treaty of Peace and Amity of December 20, 1907, as well as to Article 2 of the Constitution of Nicaragua. Correspondence with the United States and Nicaragua was set out in the appendices. The original complaint relied upon the failure of Nicaragua to reply to a protest of May 4, 1916; an amendment to the complaint dealt with the Nicaraguan reply later received, and concluded that the diplomatic negotiations had been exhausted without a settlement. Additions to the complaint contended that the lease of the Great Corn and Little Corn Islands would violate Articles 2 and 9 of the general treaty of December 20, 1907. By a resolution of September 6, 1916,[95] from which Justice Navas (Nicaragua) dissented, the court admitted the complaint, and declared that negotiations had been exhausted; it ordered that Nicaragua be notified and allowed sixty days for reply, and directed the two parties to maintain the *status quo ante* until a final decision should be pronounced. By a resolution of October 2, 1916, the court admitted the additions to the Salvadorean complaint "in obedience to the universal rules of legal procedure." The period for the filing of a reply was later extended by twenty days, during which an appearance was entered on behalf of Nicaragua. The defense of Nicaragua was put in on February 6, 1917; it denied the jurisdiction of the court on the ground that a third State was involved, and asserted that diplomatic

[92] U. S. Foreign Relations, 1917, p. 1104.

[93] The text of the complaint, which bore the date of August 14, 1916, is not published in the *Anales*. It may be found in *Libro Rosado de El Salvador* (San Salvador, 1916). An English translation is published in U. S. Foreign Relations, 1916, p. 853.

[94] Salvador's claim of a condominium with Nicaragua and Honduras led to a protest by the latter, which refused to admit any condominium "in the waters of Fonseca Bay which correspond [belong] to Honduras." U. S. Foreign Relations, 1916, p. 890.

[95] *Anales*, V, Nos. 14–16, pp. 229–231; VI, Nos. 16–18, pp. 7–9.

negotiations had not been exhausted on the claim actually presented by El Salvador. Various documents were filed by Nicaragua as evidence. On February 9, 1917, the court declared that the time limits had expired, and fixed February 19 as the date for the hearing. On that day, representatives of both El Salvador and Nicaragua presented oral arguments to the court.[96] On March 2, the justices voted on 24 interrogatories framed by the President; Justice Navas (Nicaragua) voted with the other judges in favor of the court's jurisdiction, but on many of the questions he was in a minority of one. The decision (*sentencia*) of the court, signed by the five justices, was handed down on March 9, 1917,[97] and on March 12, 1917, Justice Navas (Nicaragua) filed a dissenting opinion.[98]

The court declared its competence to deal with the matter and overruled the exception taken by Nicaragua; it held that "by the concession of a naval base in the Gulf of Fonseca, the Bryan-Chamorro Convention of August 5, 1914, menaces the national security of El Salvador and violates her rights of condominium in the said Gulf," and that it violated Articles 2 and 9 of the General Treaty of Peace and Amity of December 20, 1907; it also held that "the Government of Nicaragua is under the obligation—availing itself of all possible means provided by international law—to reëstablish and maintain the legal status that existed prior to the Bryan-Chamorro Convention." On March 10, 1917, the representative of Nicaragua filed a protest, declaring that the decision was null and void and could not be respected by his government.[99] On April 16, 1917, the Nicaraguan Ministry of Foreign Affairs also addressed the court in this sense.[100] On July 14, 1917, the court replied to this latter communication, and on September 20, 1917, it requested the Governments of Costa Rica, Guatemala and Honduras to give their moral support to the end that the decision might be respected by Nicaragua. On November 24, 1917, Nicaragua addressed a note to each of the other States explaining and justifying its attitude.[1]

---

[96] *Anales*, VI, Nos. 16–18, pp. 21–95; *Alegato verbal de Señor Guerra, abogado del Gobierno de El Salvador en la vista del juicio promovido contra el Gobierno de Nicaragua* (San José, 1917).
[97] *Anales*, VI, Nos. 16–18, pp. 96–170. An English translation of the decision is published in 11 American Journal of International Law (1917), p. 674; and in U. S. Foreign Relations, 1916, p. 862.   [98] *Anales*, VI, Nos. 16–18, p. 171.
[99] *Idem*, p. 199.   [100] *Anales*, VIII, Nos. 19–20, p. 18.
[1] U. S. Foreign Relations, 1917, p. 1104. This note was in marked contrast to the attitude of the Nicaraguan delegation at the conference of 1907. *Conferencia Centroamericana de Wáshington* (Managua, 1908), pp. xii–xv.

§56. **The Bryan-Chamorro Convention.** Following the conclusion of the Hay-Pauncefote Treaty between the United States and
Great Britain on November 18, 1901, several attempts were made
by the United States and Nicaragua to conclude a treaty or convention which would provide for the United States some protection against
the building of a second interoceanic canal to compete with the
Panama Canal, and for Nicaragua funds with which to rehabilitate
its depleted treasury. A convention signed at Washington on June 6,
1911, was not ratified.[2] A second convention signed at Managua,
February 8, 1913, also failed of ratification.[3] A third convention was
signed at Washington, August 5, 1914, by Secretary of State Bryan
and the Minister of Nicaragua at Washington, Mr. Chamorro, and
ratifications were exchanged on June 22, 1916; [4] by this convention,
Nicaragua granted to the Government of the United States "in per-
petuity . . . the exclusive proprietary rights necessary and convenient
for the construction, operation and maintenance of an interoceanic
canal by way of San Juan River and the great Lake of Nicaragua
or by way of any route over Nicaraguan territory." For the protection of these rights, Nicaragua leased to the Government of the
United States for a period of 99 years Great Corn Island and Little
Corn Island, in the Caribbean Sea, and granted for a similar term
the right to establish, operate and maintain a naval base at any place
to be selected by the United States "on the territory of Nicaragua
bordering upon the Gulf of Fonseca." These leases and grants were
renewable at the option of the United States for a further period of
99 years. It was also provided that the territory leased and the
naval bases were to be subject exclusively to the laws and sovereign
authority of the United States during the period and its possible
extension. It was in consideration of these various stipulations that

[2] For the text, see 5 American Journal of International Law (1911), Supp., pp. 291–
293.
[3] The negotiation of this convention was conducted in considerable secrecy. A text
is published in Appendix L to the claim of Costa Rica against Nicaragua, before the
Central American Court of Justice. (An English translation of this claim was published
by Gibson Brothers, Washington, 1916.) A spirited defense of the convention, entitled
"American Policy in Nicaragua," by George T. Weitzel, one of the signers, is published
in Senate Document No. 334, 64th Congress, 1st session. See also George A. Finch, "The
Treaty with Nicaragua Granting Canal and Other Rights to the United States," 10
American Journal of International Law (1916), p. 344.
[4] For the English text, see 3 U. S. Treaties and Conventions, p. 2740. A Spanish text
may be found in *El Golfo de Fonseca y el Tratado Bryan-Chamorro, Documentos
Oficiales, Ministerio de las Relaciones Exteriores de El Salvador* (San Salvador, 1917),
p. 61. For comment, see Luis Anderson, "El Tratado Bryan-Chamorro," *Anales*, VII,
Nos. 19–20, p. 43.

the United States agreed to pay Nicaragua $3,000,000 on the date of the exchange of ratifications; this sum was later paid. When the Senate of the United States gave its advice and consent to ratification of the 1914 convention, on February 18, 1916, the resolution referred to the protests of Costa Rica, Honduras and El Salvador, and the action was taken with the understanding "that nothing in the said convention is intended to affect any existing right" of any of these States. A proclamation by the President of the United States, of June 24, 1916, recited that "the said understanding has been accepted by the Government of Nicaragua."

§57. **Protests against the Bryan-Chamorro Convention.**
Various States protested against the convention of 1914, or that of 1913, as affecting their interests.

(1) *By Colombia.* On August 9, 1913, Colombia made a formal protest to Nicaragua against the proposed lease of the Great Corn and Little Corn Islands, claiming that these islands were Colombian territory.[5] On February 6, 1916, Colombia protested to the United States that Great Corn Island and Little Corn Island were territory of Colombia and not of Nicaragua, relying upon the award rendered by the President of France on September 11, 1900.[6] In reply to this, the United States referred to a statement made by the French Minister of Foreign Affairs which seemed to limit the scope of the award of 1900.[7]

(2) *By Costa Rica.* The protests of Costa Rica to the United States were based on the incapacity of Nicaragua to enter into such a convention and the "contemptuous slight" of Costa Rica's rights.[8] The reply of the Secretary of State was that the United States was willing to enter into a similar treaty with Costa Rica. Later, the United States contended that the Washington treaties of 1907 had not affected the relations of the United States with Costa Rica under a protocol of December 1, 1900; Costa Rica seems to have denied

---

[5] U. S. Foreign Relations, 1913, p. 1032. By a treaty signed at Managua, March 24, 1928, of which ratifications were exchanged on May 5, 1930, Colombia renounced the sovereignty over the two islands, in Nicaragua's favor. 105 League of Nations Treaty Series, p. 337.

[6] U. S. Foreign Relations, 1916, p. 812. See also José Umaña Bernal, *El Tratado Chamorro-Bryan*, 8 Revista Jurídica (Colombia, 1917), p. 122; Antonio José Uribe, *Colombia y los Estados Unidos de America* (1931).

[7] U. S. Foreign Relations, 1916, p. 833.

[8] U. S. Foreign Relations, 1913, p. 1022; 1914, pp. 959, 962, 967; 1915, p. 1110; 1916, pp. 811, 814, 818. An account of Costa Rica's protests to the United States and to Nicaragua is also given in *República de Costa Rica, Memoria de la Secretaría de Relaciones Exteriores*, 1913, pp. vii-xv; 1915, p. xii; 1915, *Anexos*, pp. 58ff.

the validity of this protocol.[9] Costa Rica also protested to Nicaragua, especially with reference to the 1913 convention. The Costa Rican case against Nicaragua in the Central American Court of Justice, was based upon Article 6 of the Cañas-Jerez Treaty of April 15, 1858, providing for her enjoying perpetual rights of free navigation on certain parts of the San Juan River, and upon Article 8 of the same treaty providing for Nicaragua's consultation with Costa Rica with reference to any agreements for canalization or transit; the latter provided that "in the event the enterprise should cause no injury to the natural rights of Costa Rica, that [the] opinion shall be advisory." This article was interpreted in the Cleveland Award of March 22, 1888, somewhat broadly. In the court, four of the justices were of the opinion that "the Government of Nicaragua, by virtue of the eighth article of the Cañas-Jerez Treaty, [was] under the obligation to consult, in advance, the opinion of the Government of Costa Rica respecting injuries that might result to the latter in connection with the concessions contained in the Bryan-Chamorro Treaty." Costa Rica also relied, before the court, upon Article 9 of the Treaty of Peace and Amity of 1907, which provided that merchant ships of each State should be considered upon the sea, along the coasts and in the ports of all the States as national vessels, enjoying the same privileges as the latter; four of the justices of the court were of the opinion that the Bryan-Chamorro Convention violated Costa Rica's rights under this article.

(3) *By Honduras.* The resolution of the Senate of the United States of February 18, 1916, referred to a protest by Honduras. No other record of this protest is available to the writer.[10]

(4) *By El Salvador.*[11] On October 21, 1913, El Salvador protested to the United States against the proposed acquisition by the latter of a base in the Gulf of Fonseca.[12] This protest was renewed

---

[9] Identical protocols were signed by the United States with Costa Rica and Nicaragua, December 1, 1900. 1 U. S. Treaties and Conventions, p. 351; 2 *idem,* p. 1290. In a memorandum entitled "The Disturbing Influence in Central America of the Nicaraguan Canal Treaty with the United States of America" (Washington, 1917), Mr. Chandler P. Anderson argues that these protocols were never in force.

[10] The writer is informed that no record of a protest by Honduras exists in the archives of the Department of State in Washington.

[11] At an earlier period, El Salvador had urged the construction of a Nicaraguan Canal by the United States. U. S. Foreign Relations, 1883, p. 57.

[12] U. S. Foreign Relations, 1913, p. 1027. In 1917, the Ministry of Foreign Affairs of El Salvador published a collection of documents, entitled *El Golfo de Fonseca y el Tratado Bryan-Chamorro.* A "Manifesto from the Salvadorean People in Central America to the People of the United States," dated September 30, 1913, may be some indication of public opinion in El Salvador.

on February 9, 1916; [13] special reliance was placed on Article 3 of the general treaty of 1907, relating to the neutrality of Honduras.[14] In its protest to Nicaragua, of April 14, 1916, El Salvador contended that the Bryan-Chamorro Convention would seriously injure the "primordial" interests "not only of this Republic, but of all Central America." This contention was renewed before the Central American Court of Justice, the interest referred to as "primordial" being the interest of each Central American State in a federation which would embrace the whole territory of Central America, undismembered by any cession. El Salvador also contended before the court that the convention endangered her security, and cited the Magdalena Bay resolution adopted by the United States Senate in 1912; this contention was sustained by four justices of the court. The principal reliance, however, was on the condominium in the Gulf of Fonseca; on this point, four justices of the court admitted the existence of a condominium, El Salvador's rights in which were held to be violated by the Bryan-Chamorro Convention. In this connection the court cited the award in the *North Atlantic Coast Fisheries Arbitration.* El Salvador also relied on Article 2 of the Treaty of Peace and Amity of 1907, which declared that "every disposition or measure which may tend to alter the constitutional organization" of any State "is to be deemed a menace to the peace" of the five republics; on this point four justices agreed that "the concessions for a naval base in the Gulf of Fonseca and the lease of Great Corn Island and Little Corn Island" constituted a violation of Article 2, for "under the principles of public law there is an alteration of constitutional order—in perhaps its most serious and transcendental form—when a State supplants, in all or part of the national territory, its own sovereignty by that of a foreign country." El Salvador also contended before the court that the convention of 1914 violated Article 9 of the Treaty of Peace and Amity of 1907, as to the admission of merchant ships; this contention was likewise sustained by the votes of four justices of the court.

§58. **Effect of the Judgments on the Bryan-Chamorro Convention.** The Central American Court of Justice refused to pronounce the Bryan-Chamorro Convention to be void, though on El Salvador's complaint it declared that Nicaragua had an obligation to restore the

[13] U. S. Foreign Relations, 1916, p. 815.
[14] On the neutrality of Honduras, see Salvador Rodríguez González, "The Neutrality of Honduras and the Question of the Gulf of Fonseca," 10 American Journal of International Law (1916), p. 509.

status quo ante. Its judgments that treaty rights of Costa Rica and of El Salvador had been violated by Nicaragua might have had as consequence that these States were entitled to reparation from Nicaragua, and they may be of importance in a future determination of the extent of the rights acquired by the United States under Nicaragua's grants. Nicaragua's capacity to enter into the Bryan-Chamorro Convention can hardly be denied, however, even though that State may have lacked power to grant all that it purported to grant. Hence there can be little question of the validity of the Bryan-Chamarro Convention in international law, whatever question may arise as to its effect; the political desirability of the convention, from the viewpoint of Nicaragua or of the United States, is outside the scope of this inquiry.

An epilogue to this chapter of history was written on February 1, 1923, when a protocol was signed by representatives of the United States and Costa Rica, providing for consultation by the former with the latter as to the latter's interests involved in the possible construction of a Nicaraguan canal by the United States; [15] this protocol has not been ratified, however.

§59. **Closing of the Court.** The convention of 1907 which created the court provided (Article 17) that it should be considered to be "always in force during the term of ten years counted from the last ratification." The last ratification was effected by Guatemala, on March 12, 1908. The General Treaty of Peace and Amity of 1907 provided (Article 19) that it should remain in force for ten years, counted from the day of the exchange of ratifications, and that if one year before the expiration of this term, none of the parties had given special notice of intention to terminate the treaty, the period of ten years should be extended until one year after such notice; the convention of 1907 contained no corresponding article. On March 9, 1917, the Minister of Foreign Affairs of Nicaragua gave notice of an intention to terminate the convention of 1907 relating to the court, apparently in the apprehension that a year's notice was required.[16] Since the convention of 1907 and the general treaty of 1907 both related to the court, it was the view of the Salvadorean Government that the one could only be denounced with the other.[17] Article 27

---

[15] See Jesse S. Reeves, "Clearing the Way for the Nicaragua Canal," 17 American Journal of International Law (1923), p. 309.   [16] U. S. Foreign Relations, 1917, p. 30.

[17] *Idem,* p. 31. By Article 1 of the Tacoma Agreement of August 20, 1922, Honduras, El Salvador and Nicaragua declared that the Treaty of Peace and Amity of 1907 should be regarded as being in force beginning from that date, pending its revision. Conference on Central American Affairs, 1923, p. 6.

of the convention provided for a conference if any change of the political status of any of the States caused a suspension of the court; the desirability of such a conference was discussed during the summer of 1917, without any result. This left the provision limiting the duration of the convention to operate, and the convention therefore ceased to be in force on March 12, 1918. On that date, the court held its closing session and decided to hand over its archives and property to the Costa Rican Government.[18]

§60. **Effort to Revive the Court.** Throughout the later months of 1917 negotiations were under way with a view to a possible extension of the convention of 1907.[19] On July 17, 1917, the Government of Costa Rica addressed the governments of the other States, except Nicaragua, proposing that a conference be held at San José on September 15 to extend the life of the court and to revise generally the Washington conventions.[20] The Honduran reply accepted the idea of a conference and suggested a reconsideration of the proposal of union of the five States. El Salvador was likewise favorable to the holding of a conference, and suggested to the United States on August 23, 1917, that it send representatives to such a conference; a similar suggestion was also made to Mexico. The United States declined the suggestion because of its non-recognition of the Tinoco Government in Costa Rica. October 12 was later set as a date for the proposed conference; but it was never held. The justices of the court took cognizance of these negotiations, some of the communications exchanged by the governments having been placed before the court directly. On October 6, 1917, the secretary of the court, in a communication to the Minister of Foreign Affairs of El Salvador, set forth the reforms proposed by the permanent commission of the court composed of the justices of Guatemala, Honduras and El Salvador.[21] This proposals dealt with the following matters: clarification of the provision of Article 1 of the 1907 convention as to exhaustion of efforts at diplomatic settlement, and of the requirement for private persons to exhaust local remedies; provision for arbitrators to be appointed by States outside of Central America when parties before the court; provision for a permanent commission to take certain action without the concurrence of all of the justices; pro-

---

[18] U. S. Foreign Relations, 1918, p. 247.
[19] U. S. Foreign Relations, 1917, pp. 39–45.
[20] *Costa Rica, Memoria de relaciones exteriores,* etc., 1917, p. 6. For the later negotiations, see *id.,* pp. 8–64.   [21] *Anales,* VII, Nos. 19–20, pp. 32–42.

vision as to the diplomatic status of justices; provision for rotation
in the office of president; amendment of Articles 14 and 15 to provide
for filing of proofs after the filing of complaints; more flexible provisions for the calling of substitutes to constitute a quorum; relief from
the necessity of a signature of each decision by all the justices; provision for securing moral support for the court's decisions; amendment
of the General Treaty of Peace and Amity to provide for equality of
Central Americans in civil and political rights based on residence, and
to forbid any State to enter into treaties affecting other States without previous consent.

§61. Successor to the Court. Several years elapsed after the
closing of the Central American Court of Justice before any attempt
was made to establish a successor to it. In the Treaty of Union signed
at San José, January 19, 1921, on behalf of Costa Rica, Guatemala,
Honduras and El Salvador, provision was made (Article 5) for a
Supreme Court of the Federation, which was to have a competence
to deal with legal differences between two or more States.[22] This
treaty was ratified by three States, and therefore came into force
according to its terms on May 12, 1921. A "Political Constitution of
the Republic of Central America" was adopted at Tegucigalpa, September 9, 1921; [23] though a central government was actually set up
at Tegucigalpa, it endured for only a brief period, and plans for
the federation were soon abandoned.[24]

At a Conference on Central American Affairs, held in Washington
from December 4, 1922, to February 7, 1923, the 1907 treaties and
conventions were, to a large extent at least, superseded [25] by a series
of twelve new treaties and conventions, signed on February 7, 1923.
These included a treaty of peace and amity, a convention for the
establishment of an International Central American Tribunal, and a
convention for the establishment of international commissions of inquiry (to which the United States was also a party).[26] By the former
convention, the States bound themselves to submit to the tribunal envisaged "all controversies or questions which now exist between them

[22] For the text of the treaty, see 15 American Journal of International Law (Supp.,
1921), pp. 328–335; 5 League of Nations Treaty Series, p. 19; 1 Hudson, International
Legislation, p. 600.
[23] La Gaceta de Honduras, Sept. 29, 1921, pp. 873–883.
[24] See 11 League of Nations Treaty Series, p. 393.
[25] The general treaty of 1907 seems to have been denounced by Nicaragua in 1920.
[26] For the texts, see Supplement to 17 American Journal of International Law (1923),
pp. 70–132; Proceedings of the Central American Conference of 1923, pp. 287, 296, 392;
2 Hudson, International Legislation, pp. 901, 908, 985.

or which may hereafter arise, whatever their nature or origin," if they are not settled diplomatically or referred to other arbitration; but questions or controversies "which affect the sovereign and independent existence" of any State were excluded.

The new International Central American Tribunal was to be constituted from time to time as occasion might arise, and was to consist of persons to be selected from a permanent list of thirty jurists. Each of the five States was to name six persons for this list, four to be its nationals and two to be named from lists submitted by other Latin-American States and by the United States; the designations were to be communicated to the Ministry of Foreign Affairs of Honduras. Persons named on the permanent list were to serve for five years, and they were to enjoy the rank, privileges and immunities of ministers plenipotentiary while serving on the tribunal. In case a State should desire to submit a dispute to the tribunal, notice was to be given to the other State, and a protocol was to be signed, "in which the subject of the disputes or controversies shall be clearly set forth"; each State was to select an arbitrator from the permanent list, though it might not select one of its own appointees, and a third arbitrator was to be selected by the interested governments, or that failing by the other arbitrators, or that failing by lot. Two or more States having a common interest were to be considered as a single party for organizing a tribunal. If it should prove impossible for the States to agree, an alternative method of organizing the tribunal was provided. No permanent seat was fixed for the tribunal; and as no provision was made for a permanent budget, the expense of the tribunal in each case was to be borne by the parties. Decisions were to be taken by majority vote, and two annexes to the convention set forth elaborate rules of procedure, those in one annex being Articles 63–84 of the Convention on the Pacific Settlement of International Disputes, signed at The Hague, October 18, 1907. The convention was ratified by four States, and came into force on March 12, 1925, the date of the third ratification. El Salvador declined to ratify. The convention was to remain in force until January 1, 1934, "regardless of any prior denunciation, or any other cause"; and thereafter, it was to continue in force until one year following any State's notification of an intention to denounce it, though one or two denunciations were not to terminate the convention for other States so long as the latter remain three in number. The failure of El Salvador to ratify the convention may have crippled

the attempts to put its provisions into effect. The permanent list has never been completed,[27] and no tribunal has been organized under the convention to deal with any dispute.[28] The terms of the convention may have been affected by the general arbitration treaty of January 5, 1929, and the general conciliation convention of the same date, each of which has been ratified by three of the Central American States; but apparently the 1923 convention has not been denounced.

The convention of 1923 may be taken as an admission that the convention of 1907 was too ambitious. The latter followed the model of the project for a Permanent Court of Arbitral Justice which was promulgated at The Hague in 1907; while the former is modelled on the Permanent Court of Arbitration. The creation of the Permanent Court of International Justice seems to have had little influence on this effort in Central America; indeed the Protocol of Signature of December 16, 1920, has never been signed by Honduras, and though it was signed by the four other States, only El Salvador has ratified it and her ratification was not deposited at Geneva until August 29, 1930, on the eve of the general election of judges of the court.

The 1923 Treaty of Peace and Amity was denounced by Costa Rica and El Salvador, prior to January 1, 1934. On March 15, 1934, a new Central American Conference met at Guatemala City, and on April 12, 1934, a new Treaty of Confraternity was signed on behalf of the five

[27] Fifteen nominations were made by the Government of the United States in compliance with Article 3 of the convention. 20 American Journal of International Law (1926), p. 142. Costa Rica, Guatemala and Nicaragua each designated six persons. U. S. Treaty Information Bulletin No. 15, p. 1. Apparently no designations have been made by Honduras and El Salvador. In 1930, in connection with a dispute between Guatemala and Honduras, the government of the latter relied upon the non-existence of a complete list in refusing to submit the dispute to the International Central American Tribunal. It may also be noted that the 1923 convention does not appear to have been registered with the Secretariat of the League of Nations.

[28] In June, 1928, the Government of the United States suggested that a boundary dispute between Guatemala and Honduras be referred to a tribunal created under the convention. By a treaty signed at Washington on July 16, 1930, of which ratifications were exchanged October 15, 1931, the Governments of Guatemala and Honduras agreed to an arbitration of their boundary dispute by a special tribunal. The parties were unable to agree as to the capacity in which this tribunal should act, and a preliminary question was formulated to enable the tribunal to decide whether it should act as the International Central American Tribunal created by the convention of February 7, 1923, or as a special boundary tribunal. On January 8, 1932, the special tribunal, consisting of Chief Justice Charles Evans Hughes, Luis Castro-Ureña, and Emilio Bello-Codesido, decided this preliminary question, holding that it was bound to act as a special boundary tribunal and not as the International Central American Tribunal. Guatemala-Honduras Boundary Arbitration, Opinion and Judgment of the Special Tribunal on the Preliminary Question, Washington, 1932. The final opinion and award of the special tribunal was given on January 23, 1933. See F. C. Fisher, "The Arbitration of the Guatemalan-Honduras Boundary Dispute," 27 American Journal of International Law (1933), p. 403; 137 League of Nations Treaty Series, p. 231.

Central American States, containing a general provision for arbitration.[29]

§62. Appreciation of the Central American Court of Justice.
It would seem that the Central American Court of Justice was doomed
to failure from the outset. The provisions of the convention of 1907
gave it no chance to succeed, and opened to the justices temptations
which were bound to wreck their efforts. In the first place, the justices
were given no independent position; even if the five-year term was not
too short, the method of selection, the national oath, and the way
in which salaries were paid, prevented their enjoying sufficient independence of their governments. The deposing of Justice Paniagua
Prado in 1910 indicates that they had no security of tenure. In the
second place, the jurisdiction of the court was too large.[30] Even if it
was proper, in view of the widespread conception of Central America
as a unit, to allow individuals to bring suits against governments, it
was improper to give the justices the temptation to initiate proceedings
on the court's own responsibility, and the optional clause accepted
by four States was merely a courting of trouble. Contemporary opinion
in Central America seems to have regarded the court not simply as
a judicial institution, but also as a political agency for conciliation
and mediation and for the maintenance of peace. Was it not the
guardian of "the national conscience of Central America"? No court
could hold a judicial prestige which undertook the offices assumed by
this court in the revolutions in Nicaragua in 1910 and 1912. In 1917,
a Nicaraguan communication to the United States accused the court
of having "degenerated . . . into a center of lively intrigues." [31] In
the third place, the court never developed a satisfactory procedure.
The extent of its jurisdiction was such that its requirement of a
preliminary determination of admissibility may have been necessary,
but it was surely a mistake to make that determination without the
ordinary safeguards of judicial action.

Nor can it be said that the court exercised any great influence during
its short lease of life. None of the five cases in which individuals were
parties was a case of great practical importance, and the fact that all
of them were dismissed or declared to be inadmissible robs them of
any great significance in the development of the court's jurisprudence.
Of the five so-called cases in which only States were parties, three

[29] 10 Diario de Centro América, No. 31 (1934), p. 6.
[30] See Jean Eyma, *La Cour de Justice Centre-Américaine* (Paris, 1928), pp. 40–58.
[31] U. S. Foreign Relations, 1917, p. 35.

were undertaken on the court's own initiative and were of no juris-
prudential importance; two of these cases were very properly before
the court and presented problems of a legal nature which might have
given tests of its usefulness except for the fact that in both the am-
bitions of an overshadowing outside State deprived the action of the
court of reality.

Yet it is a matter for regret that this experiment in the administration of international justice was so short-lived, and that the convention
of 1907 was not revised and renewed in 1918. This was the first international court in modern history to be endowed with continuing functions. It had behind it a tradition of solidarity in Central America. Its
creation followed a period of frequent international dissension. It was
called upon to meet a real and pressing need. Its experience during ten
years ought to have been made the basis for changes in its constituent
law, and the suggestions made toward this end by the justices of the
court in 1917 pointed toward some of the reforms which might have
been effected. In a period of greater relative stability, a useful future
for the court might have been possible. It is unfortunate that the court's
lease on life expired during the World War, during a period of revolution in Mexico, and during a time of unusual unrest in Central
America itself.

CHAPTER 4

THE PROPOSED INTERNATIONAL PRIZE COURT

§63. Proposals for the Creation of an International Prize Court. During the eighteenth and nineteenth centuries, numerous proposals were advanced for the creation of an international prize court in which neutral States might be represented.[1] In 1875, the *Institut de Droit International* began a study of the question, and in 1887 it completed a *règlement international des prises maritimes*,[2] which envisaged (Section 100) the creation by each belligerent at the beginning of each war of an international tribunal for prize appeals, the belligerent to name the president and one member of the tribunal as well as three neutral States each of which should choose a member. The proposal of the Institute was never acted upon by any belligerent.[3] At the Second Peace Conference at The Hague, proposals for the creation of an international prize court were offered by both the British and the German delegations.[4] The German proposal envisaged the creation after the beginning of hostilities of an appellate tribunal composed of five members; each belligerent would choose an admiral as a member, and three members would be chosen by three neutral States of which one State should be named by each belligerent and a third by the two first named; appeals would be lodged with this tribunal

---

[1] See 2 Oppenheim, International Law (2 ed.), p. 559.

[2] *Annuaire de l'Institut de Droit International,* 1887–88, pp. 212, 239.

[3] In a few cases international tribunals have passed upon claims based upon the action taken by national prize courts. See, *e.g., The Circassian,* 3 Moore's Digest of International Arbitrations, p. 3152; 4 *id.,* p. 3911. In a circular note of November 3, 1909, the Secretary of State of the United States referred to the following additional cases as having been before an international tribunal after they had been decided by the Supreme Court of the United States: *The Hiawatha,* 2 Black 635, 4 Moore's Digest of International Arbitrations, 3902; *The Springbok,* 5 Wallace 154, 4 Moore, 3928; *The Sir William Peel,* 5 Wallace, 517, 4 Moore 3935; *The Volant,* 5 Wallace 179, 4 Moore 3950; *The Science,* 5 Wallace 178, 4 Moore 3950; *The Peterhoff,* 5 Wallace 28, 4 Moore 3838; *The Dashing Wave,* 5 Wallace 170, 4 Moore 3948; *The Georgia,* 7 Wallace 32, 4 Moore 3957; *The Isabella Thompson,* 3 Wallace 155, 3 Moore 3159; *The Pearl,* 5 Wallace 574, 3 Moore 3159; *The Adela,* 6 Wallace, 266, 3 Moore 3159. See U. S. Foreign Relations, 1910, p. 600.

[4] *Deuxième Conférence Internationale de la Paix, Actes et Documents,* II, pp. 1071, 1076. The subject was not on the agenda of the Conference of 1907.

either by a belligerent State or by an individual person; the International Bureau of the Permanent Court of Arbitration would serve as the registry of the court. According to the British proposal, each State with a merchant marine in excess of 800,000 tons would designate a judge and a deputy-judge of the proposed court; all the judges would sit in each case, except those appointed by the States parties to the litigation. The German and the British proposals were carefully studied by the Second Peace Conference, and the result was the adoption of the Prize Court Convention of 1907.

§64. The International Prize Court Convention of 1907. At the conclusion of the Second Peace Conference, on October 18, 1907, a convention providing for the creation of an international prize court was opened to signature,[5] and it was eventually signed on behalf of 33 States,[6] though in some cases with important reservations.[7] June 30, 1909, was set as the date for the deposit of ratifications, if the States then ready to ratify could furnish the proposed court with nine judges and nine deputy-judges; but no ratification was ever deposited. The Convention was to apply "as of right" only when all belligerents engaged in a war were parties to the Convention; conceivably, it might have been applied, i.e., the court might have functioned, with the consent of a single belligerent, though a State not a party was also engaged in the war. The limitation was a serious one, however, and if the Convention had come into force its application might have been very restricted. The Convention was to remain in force for twelve years, and to be "renewed tacitly from six years to six years unless denounced."

§65. Judges of the Proposed Court. The International Prize Court was designed to be composed of judges and deputy-judges appointed for six-year periods by the contracting States. Only "jurists of known proficiency in questions of international maritime law and of the highest moral reputation" were to be appointed. Fifteen judges were to constitute a full court, though nine would constitute a quorum. The task of apportioning the fifteen judicial seats was not really solved

---

[5] For the text of the convention, see *Deuxième Conférence Internationale de la Paix, Actes et Documents,* I, p. 668; Scott, Hague Conventions and Declarations of 1899 and 1907 (1915), p. 188.

[6] Eleven States represented at the Second Peace Conference failed to sign the convention. It was signed on behalf of Great Britain and Japan only after the conclusion of the London Naval Conference in 1909.

[7] Chile, Cuba, Ecuador, Guatemala, Haiti, Persia, El Salvador, Siam, Turkey and Uruguay signed with reservations as to Article 15 relating to the method of appointment of judges.

by the 1907 Conference. Article 15 of the Convention, to which various States made reservations, provided that the judges appointed by the United States of America, Austria-Hungary, France, Germany, Great Britain, Italy, Japan and Russia, should always be summoned to sit; while judges and deputy-judges appointed by other States were to sit by *rota* as provided for each of six years in a table annexed to the Convention. This arrangement was defended as being consistent with the principle of equality of States and as making allowance for differences in the size of the naval and merchant fleets of various States. Special provision (Article 16) was made, however, to allow a belligerent in a war to have the judge appointed by it take part in the settlement of all cases arising from the war; in this case, one of the judges entitled to sit by the *rota* was to be eliminated by lot. Various provisions in the Convention were designed to invest the judges with independence; they were to receive travelling expenses and *per diem* allowances, to enjoy diplomatic privileges and immunities when serving outside their own countries, and to take oaths of office before the Administrative Council of the Permanent Court of Arbitration. Regular meetings of the judges, apart from the cases arising in a particular war, were not envisaged, and the court was not therefore in any true sense *permanent*.

§66. **Administration of the Proposed Court.** The Convention provided that the Administrative Council of the Permanent Court of Arbitration should perform for the Prize Court the same functions as it performs for the Permanent Court of Arbitration, though when serving the former it was to be composed of representatives only of the contracting States. The International Bureau of the Permanent Court of Arbitration was to serve as the registry of the Prize Court, and the Secretary-General as its registrar. The Administrative Council was to apply to the States for funds for the Court; Article 47 of the Convention left in doubt the method of apportioning the general expenses, merely providing that they were to be borne by the contracting States "in proportion to their share in the composition of the Court as laid down in Article 15 and in the annexed table." The seat of the Prize Court was to be at The Hague, and, except in the case of *force majeure,* it could not sit elsewhere without the consent of the belligerents. A president and a vice-president were to be elected by the court itself, presumably when it was called together to deal with cases arising in a particular war.

§67. **Appeals to the Proposed Court.** Jurisdiction in matters of prize was recognized by the Convention to be vested, in the first instance, in the national prize courts of the belligerent captor. Appellate jurisdiction might also be exercised by national courts, as the Convention would have left it to the national law to say whether appeal to the international court should be immediate or after a national appeal; yet the national courts were to be limited to entertaining one appeal following the original suit. Provision was also made that if the national courts failed to give judgment within two years after the date of capture, the case could be taken directly to the International Prize Court. Appeal was to be allowed to the International Prize Court, on the ground that the national judgment was wrong in fact or in law, in two classes of cases: (1) when the judgment affected the property of a neutral State or individual; (2) when the judgment affected enemy property and related either to cargo on a neutral ship, or to an enemy ship captured in the territorial waters of a neutral State which has made no diplomatic claim, or to a seizure alleged to be in violation of an international convention or the laws of the captor. Appeals might be made in certain of these cases, either by a neutral State, or by a neutral individual, or by a national of an enemy State; but no appeal could be brought by a private person against his own State. A neutral individual might be forbidden by his own State to bring an appeal, or the State might undertake the proceedings in his place. The privilege of appealing to the court was restricted to contracting States and their nationals. The lodging of an appeal was to be effected by a written declaration in the national court which had given judgment or by a notice addressed to the International Bureau within 120 days after the rendering of the decision appealed against; this period was subject to extension. When a national court was given notice of an appeal, or informed by the International Bureau of an appeal, it was to be bound to transmit the record of the case to the International Bureau within seven days.

The provisions in the Convention for appeals from a national to an international court have had little influence on later developments, though they have led to suggestions that the Permanent Court of International Justice should be given appellate jurisdiction.[8] The opening of

---

[8] See particularly the proposals by Lord Robert Cecil in 1919. Miller, Drafting of the Covenant, I, p. 63. In 1929, the Government of Finland proposed to confer appellate jurisdiction on the Permanent Court of International Justice. See *infra*, § 412.

the proposed court to individuals has also had little influence on later developments, though it has exercised a certain spell over doctrinal writings.

§68. **Procedure in the Proposed Court.** The Convention provided for both written and oral procedure. The court was to have power to call for evidence, without resorting to compulsion or threats. The hearing of a case might proceed even though one party failed to appear, if it had been duly notified. The court's judgment, reached by majority vote, was to give the reasons on which it was based, and it had to be signed by the president and registrar. The judgment was to be pronounced in a public sitting, and thereafter the record was to be transmitted to the national prize court. The court was to have power to draw up its own rules of procedure, and to propose modifications in the procedural provisions of the Convention.

§69. **Effect of Judgments of the Proposed Court.** The provisions of the Convention with reference to the effect of the court's judgments were by no means complete. If the court pronounced a capture to be valid, the vessel or cargo in question was to be disposed of in accordance with the laws of the belligerent captor. If it pronounced void a capture which the national prize court had pronounced valid, the international court was to order a restitution of the vessel or cargo in question; but no machinery was created for the execution of such orders by the court. If the national prize court had pronounced a capture to be void, the international court might still allow damages. The contracting States were to undertake to submit in good faith to the decisions of the international court and to carry them out with the least possible delay.

§70. **Law Applicable in the Proposed Court.** When called upon to decide a question of law, the proposed court was to be governed first of all by the provisions of any treaty in force between the belligerent captor and the State which was the other party or a national of which was the other party. In the absence of applicable treaty provisions, the court was to apply (Article 7) the rules of international law, and where no generally recognized rules exist, it was to give judgment "in accordance with the general principles of justice and equity." In certain cases, also, the court was to apply the national law of the belligerent captor; though it was expressly recognized that the court might disregard a failure to comply with the procedure required by the laws of the captor, if it should be of

opinion that the consequences of complying therewith would be unjust and inequitable.

§71. **The London Naval Conference of 1908–1909.** After the Convention for the creation of an International Prize Court was opened to signature on October 18, 1907, it soon became apparent that its ratification was dependent upon the question of the law which the court would apply. No attempt was made at the Second Peace Conference to codify the existing law of maritime warfare. On February 27, 1908, the British Government proposed that a conference should be held "with the object of arriving at an agreement as to what are the generally recognized principles of international law within the meaning of paragraph 2 of Article 7 of the Convention, as to those matters wherein the practice of nations has varied, and of then formulating the rules which, in the absence of special treaty provisions applicable to a particular case, the court should observe in dealing with appeals brought before it for decision." [9] It was stated that the impression had been gained at the Second Peace Conference "that the establishment of the International Prize Court would not meet with general acceptance so long as vagueness and uncertainty exist as to the principles which the court, in dealing with appeals brought before it, would apply to questions of far-reaching importance affecting naval policy and practice." As "the rules by which appeals from national prize courts would be decided affect the rights of belligerents in a manner which is far more serious to the principal naval Powers than to others," the invitations were extended to the Governments of Austria-Hungary, France, Germany, Italy, Japan, Russia, Spain, and the United States of America, and later to the Netherlands. After a preliminary exchange of views on questions formulated by the British Government, representatives of all these States met at London, December 4, 1908–February 26, 1909, and drew up a *Déclaration relative au droit de guerre maritime,* commonly known as the Declaration of London.[10] Though it was agreed that the rules contained in the Declaration "correspond in substance with the generally recognized principles of international law," many of these rules were new and the Declaration had a clearly legislative intent. The Declaration was opened for signature on February 26, 1908, and it was signed on

[9] British Parliamentary Papers, Misc. No. 4, 1909, Cd. 4554. See also Gooch and Temperley, British Documents on the Origins of the War, 1898–1914, vol. 8, pp. 306ff.
[10] British Parliamentary Papers, Misc. No. 5, 1909, Cd. 4555. See Scott, The Declaration of London (1915).

behalf of all the States represented at the Conference. Some of these States proceeded to initiate the process of ratification,[11] but no ratification was ever deposited and the Declaration never came into force. Its fate was both mourned and acclaimed.[12]

§72. **Modification Proposed by the United States of America.** At the tenth plenary session of the London Naval Conference on February 22, 1909, the delegation of the United States of America pointed out that certain States might encounter constitutional difficulties in connection with the ratification of the convention for the creation of the International Prize Court,[13] and proposed that the Conference should draw up a protocol permitting any State to include in its ratification of the Convention a provision that instead of an appeal from its national courts to the International Prize Court, any prize case to which the State was a party might be submitted for inquiry *de novo* into the responsibility of the captor, with power in the International Prize Court to fix the damages to be paid by the captor for an illegal seizure.[14] The consideration of this proposal by the London Conference led to a *vœu* in the Final Protocol which suggested the conclusion of an arrangement to give effect to it.[15] Following the adjournment of the London Conference, the Government of the United States, on March 5, 1909, expressed its intention to push its proposal; on November 3, 1909, an identic circular note was sent by the Government of the United States to the Governments represented at the London Conference, making the proposal more definite. At a conference in Paris in March, 1910, representatives of the American, British, French, and German Governments drafted an additional protocol for giving effect to the proposal. On May 24, 1910, the Netherlands Government transmitted a draft protocol to

[11] The Declaration was submitted to the Senate of the United States, which on April 24, 1912, advised and consented to its ratification. A bill introduced into the British Parliament in 1910 to provide for appeals to the International Prize Court was later withdrawn; a second bill introduced in 1911 was passed in the House of Commons but failed of passage in the House of Lords.

[12] "The Declaration of London, even if it had been ratified by the belligerent Powers in the late war, was admittedly incomplete; and on the matters with which it did purport to deal would have proved both ineffective and unpractical." Sir H. Erle Richards, in British Year Book of International Law, 1921–22, p. 3.

[13] The difficulty felt by the United States' delegation related to allowing an appeal from a national judgment which might result in its reversal by an international tribunal. The question of constitutionality was much discussed in the United States. See 1 Scott, Hague Peace Conferences (1909), pp. 477ff.

[14] Proceedings of the International Naval Conference held in London, 1908–1909, British Parliamentary Papers, Misc. No. 5 (1909), Cd. 4555, p. 253.

[15] *Id.*, p. 379. See also, U. S. Foreign Relations, 1909, p. 317.

the signatories of the Convention, and on September 19, 1910, this protocol was opened to signature.[16]

§73. **The Additional Protocol of September 19, 1910.** In the additional protocol of September 19, 1910,[17] elaborate provision was made for actions for damages for injuries caused by captures. It was provided that States prevented by difficulties of a constitutional nature from accepting the Convention in its original form might declare in the instrument of ratification or adherence that recourse against them could only be exercised in the International Prize Court in the form of an action for damages. This necessitated a modification of various provisions of the Convention, in so far as they related to actions for damages; such actions were to be begun by means of written declarations or telegrams addressed to the International Bureau of the Permanent Court of Arbitration. The protocol was to form an integral part of the Convention, adherence to which was subordinated to adherence to the protocol. Though it was eventually signed by all the signatories of the original Convention, no ratifications were ever deposited [18] and the additional protocol failed to come into force.

§74. **Failure of the Prize Court Convention.** Despite the various efforts made to facilitate such a result, the prospect for the coming into force of the Convention creating the International Prize Court was never promising. First of all, complete agreement had not been reached in 1907 concerning the States whose appointees were to serve on the court as judges and deputy-judges. During the year 1908, interest centered on the work of the London Naval Conference, at the close of which the fate of the Prize Court Convention became bound up with the fate of the Declaration of London. During 1909 and 1910, the additional protocol was in process of being prepared for signature. By 1912, it was clear that the Declaration of London would not be ratified by certain States of greater naval strength, so

---

[16] For the history of these negotiations, see U. S. Foreign Relations, 1910, pp. 597–639; 1911, pp. 246–251.

[17] For the text, see 7 Martens, N.R.G. (3d ser.), p. 73. For an English translation, see Scott, Declaration of London (1915), p. 204; 5 American Journal of International Law, (1911), Supp., p. 95. For a discussion of the protocol, see George C. Butte, "The *Protocole additionnel* to the International Prize Court Convention," 6 American Journal of International Law (1912), p. 799.

[18] On February 15, 1911, the Senate of the United States gave its advice and consent to the ratification of the Convention of October 18, 1907, and the additional protocol of September 19, 1910. See 5 American Journal of International Law (1911), Supp., p. 99. In a message of December 7, 1911, President Taft stated that the two instruments had been ratified on behalf of the United States. U. S. Foreign Relations, 1911, p. xxii.

that even before the outbreak of war in 1914, the effort to create an international prize court had come to grief.

Looking back on this period, one may feel that the movement was never so important as it was then thought to be.[19] If the Prize Court was the "advance guard" of more extensive international judicial organization, as one observer stated,[20] it was so tied up with war that its successful functioning could never have produced an atmosphere favorable to judicial settlement. The conception, the plan, and some of the details have since been useful, but it is significant that with the large advance made in international organization since 1919 no suggestion has been made that such an institution is needed in the twentieth-century world.[21] International organization today is less tolerant of the fact of war; and present-day effort is facing a different goal.

[19] See Henry B. Brown, "The Proposed International Prize Court," 2 American Journal of International Law (1908), pp. 458–489.
[20] Mr. Elihu Root, in Proceedings of the American Society of International Law, 1912, p. 13.
[21] See, however, the suggestion of Professor E. M. Borchard, in 19 Iowa Law Review (1934), p. 175.

CHAPTER 5

THE PROPOSED COURT OF ARBITRAL JUSTICE[1]

§75. **Need for Such an Institution.** The agenda of the Second Peace Conference at The Hague in 1907 contained the following item: "Improvements to be made in the provisions of the Convention relative to the peaceful settlement of international disputes as regards the Court of Arbitration and the international commissions of inquiry." It soon became clear, however, that opinion was not to be satisfied with mere improvements in the 1899 Convention. Experience had been gained which seemed to the representatives of some States to justify the taking of a further step in international organization. The Permanent Court of Arbitration had existed since 1900, and four tribunals created within its framework had given awards; its inadequacy as a judicial institution was widely appreciated, and many of the delegations at the Second Peace Conference were convinced that it ought to be supplemented by the creation of a more permanent agency, with truly judicial characteristics. The chief criticisms of the process of arbitration set out in the 1899 Convention were that it was "difficult, time-consuming and expensive to set in motion,"[2] and that it afforded no basis for the cumulation of a body of jurisprudence. When the 1907 Conference assembled, it was seised with projects of the American and Russian delegations looking toward converting the Permanent Court of Arbitration into a truly

[1] See generally, Auguste Malauzat, *La Cour de Justice Arbitrale* (Paris, 1914); James Brown Scott, An International Court of Justice (New York, 1916); James Brown Scott, The Status of the International Court of Justice (New York, 1916); Hans Wehberg, *Das Problem eines internationalen Staatengerichtshofes* (English Translation by Fenwick, The Problem of an International Court of Justice, Oxford, 1918).

[2] The criticism of the expense was hardly justified by the facts with reference to the four tribunals which had been created out of the Permanent Court of Arbitration. The expense of the International Bureau was 42,499 florins in 1900, but less than 30,000 florins in all but one of the succeeding years to 1907. The extra expense of the Bureau for the *Pious Fund Case* was 208 florins; for the *Venezuelan Claims Case,* 1278 florins; for the *Japanese House Tax Case,* 433 florins; for the *Muscat Dhows Case,* 630 florins. Honoraria were also paid to the arbitrators by the parties and each party bore the expense of presenting its case. See Wehberg, The Problem of an International Court of Justice (Fenwick's translation), pp. 99ff; *supra,* § 6.

permanent body holding annual meetings. The American, British and German delegations later united in presenting a draft to the Conference; if the consideration of this draft did not convince the delegations of all the States represented that a new institution was needed, it enabled most of them to unite on this point and to join in the recommendation finally adopted by the Conference.

§76. **Action of the Hague Conference of 1907.** The Final Act of the Second Peace Conference, of October 18, 1907, signed on behalf of all States [3] represented with the exceptions of Paraguay and Turkey, contained the following *vœu:* "The Conference recommends to the signatory Powers the adoption of the annexed draft convention for the creation of a court of arbitral justice and the bringing it into force as soon as an agreement has been reached respecting the selection of the judges and the constitution of the Court." To this *vœu* was annexed a *projet d'une convention relative à l'établissement d'une cour de justice arbitrale* of 34 articles.[4]

§77. **The Draft Convention of 1907.** The draft convention annexed to the *vœu* contained in the Final Act of the Second Peace Conference called for the creation of a court "of free and easy access, composed of judges representing the various judicial systems of the world, and capable of ensuring continuity in arbitral jurisprudence." This was to be accomplished "without altering the status of the Permanent Court of Arbitration." The new court was to have its seat at The Hague, and to meet at least annually; and its needs were to be served by the Administrative Council and the International Bureau of the Permanent Court of Arbitration. It was to be competent to deal with all cases submitted to it, in virtue either of a general treaty or of a special agreement. A delegation of three judges, elected by the court, was to act in cases of arbitration by summary procedure as laid down in the Convention for the Pacific Settlement of International Disputes, and to conduct inquiries; it was also to be competent to settle the *compromis,* either if the parties agreed to leave this to the court, or upon the invitation of a single disputant in defined categories of cases. Only contracting States were to be allowed

---

[3] With a reservation by Switzerland as to the *vœu* concerning the creation of a Court of Arbitral Justice. *Deuxième Conférence Internationale de la Paix, Actes et Documents,* I, pp. 333, 580, 723. Numerous delegations made reservations when the *vœu* was adopted by the Plenary Conference, chiefly with reference to the principle of the equality of States. *Id.,* I, pp. 333–334. The delegations of Belgium, Denmark, Greece, Rumania, Switzerland and Uruguay abstained from voting on the adoption of the *vœu.*

[4] *Deuxième Conférence Internationale de la Paix, Actes et Documents,* I, p. 702.

access to the court. The procedure outlined was to be supplemented by rules drawn up by the court, and the court was to be given power to suggest to the States changes to be made in the procedure as established by the convention. The judgments were to contain statements of the reasons upon which they were based, but no direction was given as to the law which the court should apply. The convention was to be concluded for a limited period of twelve years, with a provision for automatic renewal subject to a possibility of denunciation.

§78. **The Question of Electing the Judges.** The draft convention of 1907 dealt mainly with the simpler problems involved in the creation of a court; the chief difficulty at the Second Peace Conference was to find some method by which the judges should be selected, and on this the draft was silent. One of the earliest proposals before the Conference, made by the Bulgarian delegation, called for the appointment of a competent person by each State and for the election of the judges by these persons from among themselves. The American, British and German delegations, proceeding upon the basis of population, and considering the criteria of industry and commerce, proposed that while each State should appoint one judge, certain States should have a permanent representation in the court, and that other States should have representation for varying periods of years according to a table of rotation. This seemed to involve a proposal also that parties to a case should be represented in the court. The Brazilian delegation envisaged the appointment of a judge by each State, and a division of the judges into three groups, each of which groups should sit in rotation for a period of years. Numerous other proposals were advanced.[5] Finally the American delegation proposed that a free election of fifteen judges should be held, a nomination to be made by each State and a vote to be taken through correspondence conducted by the International Bureau of the Permanent Court of Arbitration; this proposal received but scant support, and upon its defeat the effort to arrive at an agreement at the Second Peace Conference was abandoned.

§79. **Negotiations Following the Hague Conference of 1907.** Initiative toward further steps for putting into force the draft convention of 1907 was taken by the Government of the United States

[5] Mr. Denys P. Myers analyzed the various proposals, as follows: (1) rotation; (2) direct appointment; (3) indirect appointment; (4) direct election; (5) indirect election. Proceedings of the American Society for Judicial Settlement of International Disputes, 1913, p. 168.

of America. On February 22, 1909, the American delegation at the International Naval Conference in London proposed the adoption of a protocol providing that signatories of the convention creating the International Prize Court might stipulate in their ratifications of that convention that the prize court should be competent to deal with arbitral cases submitted to it by the signatories, and that it should accept this jurisdiction and follow in such cases the provisions of the 1907 draft convention for the establishment of a Court of Arbitral Justice.[6] The International Naval Conference pronounced itself incompetent to deal with the proposal.[7] On November 3, 1909, the Government of the United States, in a circular letter addressed to the British, Dutch, French, German, Italian, Japanese, Russian and Spanish Governments, repeated the proposal made at the London Conference, that the International Prize Court should be invested with the jurisdiction and functions of the proposed Court of Arbitral Justice.[8] The German Government suggested that the proper way of effecting this purpose would be by means of a supplementary convention, for drafting which a conference was suggested; the British and French Governments also suggested a conference. Informal negotiations were conducted at Paris in March, 1910, by "delegates" of the American, British, French and German Governments, and a draft convention was agreed to *ad referendum,* looking toward the creation of the Court of Arbitral Justice by a limited number of States.[9] A second meeting of these "delegates" was held in July 1910, at which the draft convention was revised.[10] These draft conventions were predicated upon the choice of a judge by each party to the convention, the judges to participate in the work of the court by the *rota* annexed to the convention for creating the International Prize Court. Further progress depended upon bringing into force the International Prize Court Convention, however, and failure of efforts in that direction made it impossible to go forward with the plan for creating a Court of Arbitral Justice.

[6] Proceedings of the International Naval Conference held in London, 1908–1909, British Parliamentary Papers, Misc. No. 5 (1909), Cd. 4555, p. 253.

[7] *Id.*, p. 223.

[8] U. S. Foreign Relations, 1910, p. 597. The date of the circular letter is given as October 18, 1909, in 4 American Journal of International Law, Supplement (1910), p. 114. The procedure suggested by the United States was clearly unsatisfactory, as various of the replies to the circular letter pointed out.

[9] U. S. Foreign Relations, 1910, p. 615.

[10] For an account of this whole effort, see the letter and memorandum addressed by Dr. James Brown Scott to the Minister for Foreign Affairs of the Netherlands, January 12, 1914. Scott, An International Court of Justice (1916). See also, Scott, The Status of the International Court of Justice (1916).

§80. **Results of the Effort.** Though the Court of Arbitral Justice planned in 1907 was never established, the promulgation of the project by the Second Peace Conference had a profound effect on world opinion in the succeeding years, and it later assisted in establishing a conviction, already quite general in 1914, that a new judicial institution was needed. Moreover, it supplied a set of definite ideas which could be used in fresh efforts in the future, and it was naturally taken as a point of departure when the Statute of the Permanent Court of International Justice was being drafted in 1920. Great credit is therefore due to the men who struggled so valiantly to establish the Court of Arbitral Justice, and it seems possible that without their effort the world would have been unprepared to take the step forward which was achieved in 1920.

PART II

CREATION OF THE PERMANENT COURT OF
INTERNATIONAL JUSTICE

PART II

CREATION OF THE PERMANENT COURT OF
INTERNATIONAL JUSTICE

CHAPTER 6

PROVISIONS FOR A COURT IN THE COVENANT

§81. The Situation in 1919. The progress of the World War from 1914 to 1918 had served to convince people in many countries that international organization was essential to maintaining peace in the future, and when hostilities were brought to a close in 1918, an unparalleled opportunity existed for launching a new effort in this direction. It had then become clear that no result was to be expected from the effort of the Second Peace Conference to create a Court of Arbitral Justice, and that a fresh attempt would have to be made which could not be limited by the discussions at The Hague in 1907. If an effective League of Nations was to be launched, the opinion of the time regarded it as essential that it should include a court to administer justice according to law, and the task of creating such a court became at once more simple because it could be undertaken in connection with plans for a larger organization. Inevitably, therefore, the revival of effort in this direction came to be associated with the League of Nations.

§82. Drafts Prior to the Peace Conference. The creation of an international court was foreseen in numerous unofficial drafts of the Covenant prior to the Peace Conference in 1919,[1] but preliminary consideration by governmental agencies of plans for the League of Nations seems to have put little stress on the importance of a court. The draft of a statute of the League of Nations prepared by a British

---

[1] See particularly Marburg, Development of the League of Nations Idea, II, pp. 721ff.; Kluyver, Documents on the League of Nations (1920), pp. 339ff.; Phillimore, Schemes for Maintaining General Peace, British Peace Handbooks, XXV, No. 160; Wehberg, *Die Pariser Volkerbundakte* (1919), pp. 58ff.; Wheeler-Bennett, Information on the World Court (1929), pp. 19–30; Lange, *"Préparation de la Société des Nations pendant la guerre,"* in *Les Origines et l'Œuvre de la Société des Nations,* I (1923), pp. 1–46; New York State Bar Association Proceedings, 1918, pp. 90ff.

An "American Society for the Judicial Settlement of International Disputes" had been organized in the United States in 1910, which published six volumes of proceedings. A magazine called "The World Court" was published in New York by a "World's Court League," from 1915 to 1919 (five volumes); this League advocated the establishment of an International Court of Justice.

committee in 1918 contained no reference to a court, though it envisaged the settlement of disputes by arbitration and as a result of reports on the facts by an international conference.[2] A French committee which elaborated a report in 1918 suggested the creation of an international tribunal and the assurance of the execution of its decisions by an international council.[3] A suggestion advanced by Colonel House (United States) in 1918 also provided for a court, with judges elected by the delegates of the members of a league;[4] it is significant that in presenting this draft to President Wilson, Colonel House stated that while he had been opposed to a court in the past, "in working the matter out it has seemed to me a necessary part of the machinery," and that "in time the court might well prove the strongest part" of that machinery.[5] President Wilson followed many of Colonel House's suggestions in his "first draft" for a league, but he made no reference to a court except in a general provision for the reference of disputes to arbitration and in a single reference to "judicial decision or arbitration" for disputes between members and non-members.[6] Nor did the proposals put forward by General Smuts at the end of 1918 envisage the creation of a court.[7] However, a draft for an international judicial organization, elaborated by committees of the Danish, Norwegian and Swedish Governments in 1918, contained detailed provisions for a court.[8]

§83. **Proposals at the Peace Conference.** In January 1919, Lord Robert Cecil (Great Britain) circulated at Paris a "draft sketch of a League of Nations" which referred to a "judicial body," explained as "the existing Hague organization, with any additions or modifications made by the League, or by the Peace Treaties."[9] In January 1919, also, President Wilson formulated two drafts[10] which like his earlier draft indicated that he did not think a court important; yet these drafts did provide for arbitration and for a possible appeal from an arbitral decision to a Body of Delegates,[11] and they continued to

---

[2] Miller, Drafting of the Covenant, II, p. 3.
[3] *Procès-verbaux de la Commission de la Société des Nations*, No. 1, p. 10; Miller, Drafting of the Covenant, II, p. 403.
[4] Miller, Drafting of the Covenant, II, p. 7. See also, Seymour, Intimate Papers of Colonel House, IV, pp. 30ff.   [5] Miller, Drafting of the Covenant, I, p. 13.
[6] *Id.*, II, p. 12.   [7] *Id.*, p. 23.
[8] *Betänkande rörande en Internationell Rättsordning . . . jämte förslag till Konvention* (Stockholm, 1919). A French translation of this draft convention and of the report concerning it, was published at Stockholm in 1919.
[9] Miller, Drafting of the Covenant, II, p. 63.   [10] *Id.*, II, pp. 65, 98.
[11] Such provisions were largely taken from Colonel House's draft of July 16, 1918. For a criticism of them, see Lansing, The Peace Negotiations (1921), pp. 126ff.

refer to the settlement of disputes by "judicial decision or arbitration." A "British Draft Convention" of January 20, 1919, provided for "the creation of a permanent Court of international justice," [12] though no definite plans were suggested and the provision was only incidental to the outline of a procedure for handling international disputes; it is interesting to note that this draft provided for a possible submission by a conference or council of disputes or questions to "a court of international law," and it was said that "in such case, the decision of the Court shall have no force or effect unless it is confirmed by the Report of the Conference or Council." When Lord Eustace Percy combined this British draft and a draft of President Wilson, he retained this provision, and added a new provision as follows: "Pending the creation of a permanent court of international justice, the court of international law referred to in this article shall be a tribunal of arbitration nominated by the Council from among the members of the Permanent Court created by the Convention for the Pacific Settlement of International Disputes." [13]

On January 25, 1919, at a plenary session of the Preliminary Peace Conference, a resolution approving the principle of the League of Nations and creating a committee "to work out the details" was adopted without reference to a court. Thereafter, Lord Robert Cecil seems to have insisted on some reference to a permanent court of international justice in lieu of certain provisions for arbitration,[14] though the Cecil-Miller draft [15] of January 27, 1919, barely mentioned it. Lord Cecil's suggestion at this time was the most complete outline of a court yet considered; [16] provisionally, five of nine judges were to be nominated by the Principal Allied and Associated Powers and were to select the other four judges from persons nominated by other members of the League. In his "notes on a Permanent Court," Lord Cecil conceived of it as both a court of appeal and a court of first instance; he foresaw difficulty in agreeing on a method of electing the judges "if the small states maintained the attitude they adopted in 1907," but replied that if these states entered the League at all "they must and will abandon the ideas of Barbosa." [17] On January 31, at a conference of American and British representatives, it was "agreed

---

[12] Miller, Drafting of the Covenant, II, p. 106.
[13] Miller, Drafting of the Covenant, II, p. 117.
[14] Id., I, p. 61.   [15] Id., II, p. 131.   [16] Id., I, p. 62.
[17] As a representative of Brazil, M. Ruy Barbosa had played a prominent rôle at the Second Peace Conference at The Hague in 1907. He was elected a judge of the Court in 1921.

that the provisions regarding the method of arbitration and particularly the appeal provisions" in President Wilson's drafts "were not essential, and that a general provision might be inserted for the creation of a Permanent Court."[18]   Shortly afterward, the Hurst-Miller draft was made, and it was this draft which was placed before the League of Nations Commission by President Wilson.

§84.   The Commission on the League of Nations. When the Commission set up under the resolution of January 25, 1919, began its work on February 3, 1919,[19] it had before it the Hurst-Miller draft presented by President Wilson, the text adopted by the French Ministerial Commission in 1918 submitted by M. Bourgeois, and an Italian draft scheme submitted by M. Orlando.[20]   The Italian draft definitely envisaged the creation of an international court of justice; it was to be composed of judges appointed by all the contracting States; the International Bureau of the Permanent Court of Arbitration was to serve as its registry; the court was to sit in sections, a section being composed of the President, one judge chosen by each litigant, and four judges elected by the court; the court was to have jurisdiction of cases submitted by *compromis* and of cases referred to it by the Council of the League of Nations on the demand of one party to a dispute. At its first meeting, the Commission decided to take the Hurst-Miller draft as the basis of its deliberations. Article 11 of this draft was as follows:

> The High Contracting Parties agree that whenever any dispute or difficulty shall arise between them which they recognise to be suitable for submission to arbitration, and which cannot be satisfactorily settled by diplomacy, they will submit the whole subject-matter to arbitration, and will carry out in full good faith any award or decision that may be rendered.

[18] Miller, Drafting of the Covenant, I, p. 67. Later explanations were given that there was not time at the Peace Conference to draft plans for the Court.

[19] The original members of the Commission were: *United States,* President Wilson and Colonel House; *British Empire,* Lord Robert Cecil and General Smuts; *France,* M. Léon Bourgeois and M. Larnaude; *Italy,* M. Orlando and M. Scialoja; *Japan,* Baron Makino and Viscount Chinda; *Brazil,* M. Pessôa; *Belgium,* M. Hymans; *China,* Dr. V. K. Wellington Koo; *Portugal,* M. Jayme Batalha Reis; *Serbia,* M. Vesnitch. Later the following were added: *Czechoslovakia,* M. Krámař; *Greece,* M. Venizelos; *Poland,* M. Dmowski; *Rumania,* M. Diamandy.

[20] The three drafts are reproduced in an annex to the minutes of the first session. Two sets of minutes exist, one in English and the other in French. Neither seems to have been approved by the Commission. Both texts are reproduced in Miller, Drafting of the Covenant, II, pp. 228–394, 395–538, and for convenience Miller's texts are referred to. The texts are also to be found in Miller's Diary at the Peace Conference, but it is less generally available.

When this Article 11 was considered on February 6, the Commission accepted the following addition proposed by Lord Robert Cecil:

> For this purpose the court of arbitration to which the case is referred shall be the court agreed on by the parties, or stipulated in any Convention existing between them.

Article 12 of the Hurst-Miller draft was as follows:

> The Executive Council will formulate plans for the establishment of a Permanent Court of International Justice, and this Court will be competent to hear and determine any matter which the parties recognise as suitable for submission to it for arbitration under the foregoing article.

When this Article 12 was considered on February 6, the text was changed at President Wilson's suggestion to read:

> The Executive Council shall formulate plans for the establishment of a Permanent Court of International Justice, and this Court shall when established be competent to hear and determine any matter which the parties recognise as suitable for submission to it for arbitration under the foregoing article.

M. Bourgeois drew attention to the fact that no mention had been made of the Permanent Court of Arbitration, which he thought had rendered notable services; but no change was made in consequence. On February 13, these articles were reported by the Drafting Committee as Articles 13 and 14, and as adopted by the Commission on that date they read as follows:

> *Article 13.* The High Contracting Parties agree that whenever any dispute or difficulty shall arise between them which they recognise to be suitable for submission to arbitration and which cannot be satisfactorily settled by diplomacy, they will submit the whole subject matter to arbitration. For this purpose the Court of arbitration to which the case is referred shall be the Court agreed on by the parties or stipulated in any Convention existing between them. The High Contracting Parties agree that they will carry out in full good faith any award that may be rendered. In the event of any failure to carry out the award, the Executive Council shall propose what steps can best be taken to give effect thereto.
> *Article 14.* The Executive Council shall formulate plans for the establishment of a Permanent Court of International Justice and this Court shall, when established, be competent to hear and determine any matter

which the parties recognise as suitable for submission to it for arbitration under the foregoing Article.

The articles appear in this form in the draft Covenant which was reported to the Preliminary Peace Conference on February 14, 1919, and published on that date. M. Bourgeois had repeated his desire to see the work of the Hague Conferences referred to, in vain; throughout this earlier period, an issue was drawn as to the connection between the system of Peace Conferences at The Hague and the new organization.[21]

§85. **Consultation with Neutral States.** On March 20 and 21, 1919, some of the members of the Commission on the League of Nations met with representatives of certain neutral States to consider the draft Covenant. The representatives of the Netherlands and Switzerland proposed amendments to Article 13; and those of Denmark, Norway, Sweden and Switzerland proposed amendments to Article 14.[22] A Spanish representative also insisted upon the principle of equality of States which was embodied in these proposals, and which he wished to see admitted. The proposals by neutral States did not lead to any modification of the draft, however.

§86. **Later Work of the Commission on the League of Nations.** On March 18, 1919, President Wilson and Lord Robert Cecil agreed upon an addition to Article 14 of the following words: "and also any issue referred to it by the Executive Council or Body of Delegates." [23] This embodied the conception of what was later called an advisory opinion; it had appeared in the draft of the French Ministerial Commission of 1918, in Colonel House's draft of July 16, 1918, in the British draft convention of January 20, 1919, and in the Italian draft submitted to the Commission at its first meeting, though for some time it had dropped out of the drafts under active consideration. At a meeting of the Commission on March 24, several amendments and additions were proposed to Article 14 as it appeared in the draft of February 13, 1919, notably by Lord Robert Cecil, M. Larnaude and M. Hymans. A significant addition suggested by

---

[21] The issue continued to give difficulty. See Miller, Diary at the Peace Conference, VII, p. 330. "The omission, which may be called systematic, in the acts of the Paris Conference, of any reference to the work of the first two Peace Conferences was a phenomenon of diplomatic history which was difficult to explain." Baron Descamps in Minutes of the 1920 Committee of Jurists, p. 155.

[22] Miller, Drafting of the Covenant, II, pp. 592ff. See also, Kluyver, Documents on the League of Nations (1920), pp. 168ff.

[23] Miller, Drafting of the Covenant, II, p. 585.

Lord Robert Cecil would have inserted after the word "determine" the words "any dispute or difference of an international character including." [24] Lord Robert Cecil also proposed the addition which he had agreed upon with President Wilson on March 18. M. Larnaude proposed that the court should be "competent to hear and determine: (*a*) any matter (Fr., *toute question*) which is submitted to it by the Body of Delegates or the Executive Council; (*b*) any matter arising out of the interpretation of the Covenant establishing the League; (*c*) any dispute" submitted by the parties with the consent of the Court and the Executive Council.[25] Several observations made on that occasion are of interest in view of later developments: M. Larnaude seems to have argued in favor of the selection of the judges by the Council rather than by the Assembly; Lord Robert Cecil thought that "in reality, the Assembly would establish the Court," but assumed that nominations of judges would be made to the members of the League by the Council; M. Krámař thought that the Court "would have to decide not only questions of law, but political questions as well." On March 26, a drafting committee was set up, and it made several important changes in the drafts of Articles 13 and 14. Provisions which finally became the second paragraph of Article 13 and the third sentence of Article 14 were adopted by the Commission on April 11, on the report of this committee. In the English version, Articles 13 and 14 assumed their final form, except for paragraphing, in a draft of April 5, approved on April 11, 1919. The French version assumed final form on April 21, 1919.[26] In the following form, the two articles were adopted by the Preliminary Peace Conference on April 28, 1919, and included in the conditions of peace communicated by the Allied and Associated Powers to the German delegation on May 7, 1919, and later embodied in the Treaty of Versailles:

Article 13

Les Membres de la Société conviennent que s'il s'élève entre eux un différend susceptible, à leur avis, d'une solution arbitrale et si ce

The Members of the League agree that whenever any dispute shall arise between them which they recognise to be suitable for

[24] The English minutes state that this proposal was adopted; the French minutes state that it was referred to the drafting committee.

[25] This proposal followed almost textually a recommendation by an unofficial Inter-Allied League of Nations Conference held in London, March 11–13, 1919. See Kluyver, Documents on the League of Nations, p. 309. M. Larnaude modified his proposals as a result of discussions in the Commission.

[26] Miller, Drafting of the Covenant, II, p. 791. See also *id.*, I, pp. 505ff.

différend ne peut se régler de façon satisfaisante par la voie diplomatique, la question sera soumise intégralement à l'arbitrage.

Parmi ceux qui sont généralement susceptibles de solution arbitrale, on déclare tels les différends relatifs à l'interprétation d'un traité, à tout point de droit international, à la réalité de tout fait qui, s'il était établi, constituerait la rupture d'un engagement international, ou à l'étendue ou à la nature de la réparation due pour une telle rupture.

La Cour d'arbitrage à laquelle la cause est soumise est la Cour désignée par les Parties ou prévue dans leurs conventions antérieures.

Les Membres de la Société s'engagent à exécuter de bonne foi les sentences rendues et à ne pas recourir à la guerre contre tout Membre de la Société qui s'y conformera. Faute d'exécution de la sentence, le Conseil propose les mesures qui doivent en assurer l'effet.

submission to arbitration and which cannot be satisfactorily settled by diplomacy, they will submit the whole subject-matter to arbitration.

Disputes as to the interpretation of a treaty, as to any question of international law, as to the existence of any fact which if established would constitute a breach of any international obligation, or as to the extent and nature of the reparation to be made for any such breach, are declared to be among those which are generally suitable for submission to arbitration.

For the consideration of any such dispute the court of arbitration to which the case is referred shall be the court agreed on by the parties to the dispute or stipulated in any convention existing between them.

The Members of the League agree that they will carry out in full good faith any award that may be rendered, and that they will not resort to war against a Member of the League which complies therewith. In the event of any failure to carry out such an award, the Council shall propose what steps should be taken to give effect thereto.

Article 14

Le Conseil est chargé de préparer un projet de Cour permanente de justice internationale de de le soumettre aux Membres de la Société. Cette Cour connaîtra de tous différends d'un caractère

The Council shall formulate and submit to the Members of the League for adoption plans for the establishment of a Permanent Court of International Justice. The Court shall be competent to

international que les Parties lui
soumettront. Elle donnera aussi
des avis consultatifs sur tout différend ou tout point, dont la
saisira le Conseil ou l'Assemblée.

hear and determine any dispute
of an international character which
the parties thereto submit to it.
The Court may also give an advisory opinion upon any dispute or
question referred to it by the
Council or by the Assembly.

§87. The German Counter-Proposals. On May 9, 1919, the
German delegation at the Peace Conference communicated to the President of the Conference a program containing suggestions on the
League of Nations,[27] and on the following day the President replied
that the German *projet* would be sent to the competent commission
formed by the Allied and Associated Powers.[28] No later meeting of
the Commission on the League of Nations was held, but a smaller
committee drafted a reply sent on May 22, which contained the
following paragraph: [29]

> The proposals of the German Government for the composition, juris-
> diction and procedure of a Permanent Court of International Justice
> (paragraphs 14–15, 29–36) have been carefully reviewed, and will be
> submitted for detailed consideration to the Council of the League of
> Nations, when it prepares a plan for the establishment of a Permanent
> Court in accordance with Article 14 of the Covenant.

As no change was made in the text of Articles 13 and 14 of the
Covenant in consequence of the German suggestions, it is unnecessary
to examine them in detail, though they contained several interesting
points; compulsory jurisdiction was to be conferred on a court, which
was also to have jurisdiction over complaints of private persons in
certain contingencies. The comment on the draft Covenant made by
the German delegation on May 29, 1919, did not deal in detail with
Articles 13 and 14, but insisted on a recognition of the principle
of state equality and on Germany's admission to the League of Nations. Nor did the Allied and Associated Powers refer to a court
in their final reply.

§88. The Austrian Counter-Proposals. The final conditions of
peace communicated to the Austrian delegation contained the text
of the Covenant in its final form, though the Austrian delegation had

---

[27] Miller, Drafting of the Covenant, II, p. 744. No specific suggestions seem to have
been made by the Bulgarian and Hungarian delegations.
[28] *Id.*, I, p. 539.   [29] *Id.*, I, p. 540.

previously indicated a desire that Austria should be admitted to membership in the League of Nations, and this desire had been favorably received by the Allied and Associated Powers. With its note of June 23, 1919, the Austrian delegation submitted suggestions for the text of Articles 12, 13 and 14 of the Covenant and an explanatory statement by Professor Lammasch; [30] these suggestions contained elaborate and somewhat definite provisions for creating a court. In his letter of July 9, 1919, the President of the Peace Conference stated that these proposals would be submitted to the Council of the League of Nations when it undertook the preparation of plans under Article 14 of the Covenant.

§89. The Covenant in the Treaties of Peace. The Covenant of the League of Nations became Part I of the treaties of peace between the Allied and Associated Powers and Germany, Austria, Bulgaria and Hungary, signed respectively at Versailles on June 28, 1919, at St. Germain-en-Laye on September 10, 1919, at Neuilly-sur-Seine on November 27, 1919, and at Trianon on June 4, 1920.[31] Each of these is a separate and distinct instrument, and the parties to the various instruments are not identical.[32] Some of the language of the Covenant is limited in its application to the treaty of which the Covenant forms a part, notably paragraph 1 of Article 5; [33] in a strict sense, therefore, one may say that there are four Covenants, though logic is not to be pressed so far as to say that they call for the creation of four Leagues of Nations. The Treaty of Versailles was the first of the four instruments to come into force, and the League of Nations

[30] For the text, see Kluyver, Documents on the League of Nations, pp. 142ff. For English and French translations, see Documents presented to the 1920 Committee of Jurists, pp. 130ff.

[31] The Treaty of Versailles came into force on January 10, 1920; the Treaty of St. Germain on July 16, 1920; the Treaty of Neuilly-sur-Seine on August 9, 1920, and the Treaty of Trianon on July 26, 1921. The Covenant was also embodied in the abortive Treaty of Sèvres, signed by representatives of the Allied Powers and Turkey on August 10, 1920.

[32] The signatories to the Treaty of Versailles were the United States of America, the British Empire, France, Italy, Japan, Belgium, Bolivia, Brazil, Cuba, Czechoslovakia, Ecuador, Germany, Greece, Guatemala, Haiti, Hedjaz, Honduras, Liberia, Nicaragua, Panama, Peru, Poland, Portugal, Rumania, Serb-Croat-Slovene State, Siam, Uruguay. Of these Bolivia, Brazil, Ecuador, Germany, Guatemala, Haiti, Hedjaz, Honduras, Liberia, Peru, and Uruguay were not signatories to the Treaty of St. Germain, or to the Treaty of Trianon. Bolivia, Brazil, Ecuador, Germany, Guatemala, Haiti, Honduras, Liberia, Nicaragua, Panama, Peru, and Uruguay were not signatories to the Treaty of Neuilly. China was a signatory of all these treaties except the Treaty of Versailles. Austria signed the Treaty of St. Germain only, Hungary the Treaty of Trianon only, and Bulgaria the Treaty of Neuilly only.

[33] This paragraph was added at a late stage of the drafting. See Miller, Drafting of the Covenant, I, p. 498.

was organized under the Covenant in that treaty; [34] yet it is not possible to say that the League of Nations exists solely under the Covenant as embodied in the Treaty of Versailles. The fact of the Covenant's inclusion in other treaties must be taken into account; [35] and this is done more easily since most of the obligations of the Covenant are imposed on Members of the League of Nations, and membership does not result in all cases from a State's signing and ratifying one of the treaties of peace. In spite of the reference to "the present Treaty" in Article 5, the Covenant has properly been regarded as a single instrument, forming a basic part of a general European settlement, and neither its setting nor its language is subject to a narrow or technical interpretation.[36] Articles 13 and 14 are identical in all four of the treaties, and they have been accepted by all Members of the League regardless of the method by which they became such.

§90. **The Name of the Court.** The name of the Court was fixed by the language of Article 14 of the Covenant, though conceivably it might have been open to the Members of the League of Nations to decide upon a different name when adopting the plans formulated by the Council. At the Second Peace Conference at The Hague in 1907 various names of a proposed court were discussed; "High International Court of Justice," and "International Court of Justice" were employed in drafts, but were finally discarded for "Court of Arbitral Justice." [37] This name had the disadvantage of raising questions as to possible differences between arbitration and adjudication, and it found little favor in subsequent usage. In numerous suggestions and drafts prior to the Peace Conference at Paris, various terms had been employed: "international court," "permanent international court," "international tribunal," "court of international law," "court of international justice," "international court of justice," and others. In the work of the Peace Conference itself various names were used, also: Colonel House proposed the creation of an "International

[34] Certain States became members of the League of Nations by acceding to the Covenant in the Treaty of Versailles. See Kluyver, Documents on the League of Nations, pp. 230–249. For the invitations to various States to accede, see 30 *La Paix par le Droit* (1920), p. 43.

[35] China is a member of the League of Nations by reason of ratification of the Treaty of St. Germain. League of Nations Official Journal, 1920, p. 300. See, also, Manley O. Hudson, "Membership in the League of Nations," 18 American Journal of International Law (1924), p. 436.

[36] See the memorandum signed by certain chiefs of Governments on May 6, 1919. Miller, Drafting of the Covenant, I, p. 489.

[37] See particularly, Scott, The Project Relative to a Court of Arbitral Justice (1920), pp. 18–19.

Court"; the French Committee spoke of an "International Tribunal" (*Tribunal international*); the Italian draft spoke of an "International Court of Justice" (*Corte internazionale di giustizia*); Lord Robert Cecil at first used the expression "an arbitral court." The expression "permanent court of international justice" first appears in the records of the Peace Conference in the British draft convention of January 20, 1919, though not as a name but as a descriptive phrase. It was retained in the later drafts of the Covenant, and capitalized as a name by the Drafting Committee in its report of April 5, 1919.[38]

The name has obvious advantages: it emphasizes the international character and the "permanence" of the new institution; the draftsmen of the Covenant desired to create something more than a system of *ad hoc* tribunals. One of the principal criticisms of the Permanent Court of Arbitration was that it was not what its name implied, not permanent. The name given in the Covenant also emphasizes the judicial nature of the new institution, which was to be a *court of justice;* in the minds of some persons the process of justice was to be distinguished from the process of arbitration. Yet the name has disadvantages, also: it is very similar to the name of the Permanent Court of Arbitration, so similar that public opinion does not easily distinguish between the two institutions. Nor is the order of words altogether happy; it was perhaps a permanent international court of justice rather than a permanent court of international justice which was intended.[39] Some attempts have been made to show that the name itself tended to prescribe certain characteristics of the court to be created; in its memorandum submitted to the Committee of Jurists in 1920, the Secretariat of the League of Nations stated that it is "a tenable position that the expression 'court of justice' in the first sentence [of Article 14] indicates that the Covenant has a tendency to make the Court competent to hear and determine disputes submitted to it by one party only." [40] It was also thought that "the expressions 'permanent' and 'of justice,' " in Article 14 were "to be taken as meaning 'accessible at all times' and 'applying the law.' " [41] Judge Loder seems to have found in the expression "court of justice" some suggestion of compulsory jurisdiction.[42] Such deductions are

[38] Miller, Drafting of the Covenant, II, p. 672.
[39] Sir Robert Borden (Canada) suggested "permanent international court of justice." Miller, Diary of the Peace Conference, VII, p. 234.
[40] Documents presented to the 1920 Committee of Jurists, p. 7.
[41] *Id.*, p. 113.   [42] British Yearbook of International Law, 1921–22, p. 12.

clearly negatived by the history of the drafting of the Covenant, though the records do not indicate that any very serious consideration was given to the name.

§91. **The Council's Mandate to Formulate Plans.** The first sentence of Article 14 confers a mandate on the Council to formulate plans (Fr., *un projet*) for the Court and to submit them to the Members of the League of Nations; only the English version adds "for adoption." No mention is made of the Assembly of the League of Nations in this connection, though it was clearly open to the Members of the League to employ that agency in connection with their consideration and adoption of the plans formulated. The report of the French Ministerial Commission had suggested that the Court be organized by an "international body," which was to consist of representatives of all members. The Hurst-Miller draft presented by President Wilson on February 3, 1919, referred only to the Council, and this was maintained in later drafts. The Danish and Swedish Governments proposed on March 21, 1919, that the task of creating the Court should be confided to the Assembly,[43] and on April 7, 1919, the Swedish delegation renewed this suggestion with a view to avoiding any "shadow of suspicion" that the creation of the Court was to be guided by political considerations.[44] When the matter was considered by the League of Nations Commission on April 11, 1919, Lord Robert Cecil stated that "in reality, the Assembly would establish the court." The action taken by the Council in submitting the plans to the Assembly in 1920 was generally regarded at the time as "an act of courtesy." [45]

The mandate of the Council was limited to formulating and submitting plans for the establishment of the Court. Once these plans had been formulated and submitted, it would seem that so far as Article 14 is concerned, the Council had no further duty with reference to such plans; and once the Court was established, it would seem that the first sentence of Article 14 confers on the Council no further competence with respect to it. In other words, the Council was thereafter *functus officio* in this respect; the force of the first sentence of Article 14 was spent when the plans were submitted and adopted, and an incorporation of Article 14 into the Statute by reference does not revive the provision. Therefore, the Council has no mandate

---

[43] Miller, Drafting of the Covenant, II, pp. 614–5.
[44] *Id.*, I, p. 451.   [45] Records of First Assembly, Committees, I, p. 299.

under Article 14 to propose amendments to the Statute adopted in 1920, though it may proceed to do so independently of the exhausted mandate conferred upon it. Yet it can hardly be said that this view has prevailed in practice.

§92. **Provisions in Article 14 on the Competence of the Court.** The purpose to be served by the second and third sentences of Article 14 was not clearly indicated by the records of the Peace Conference. Were they merely indications to the Council as to the nature of the plans to be formulated? Or were they agreements in advance by Members of the League of Nations as to the nature of the Court to be created? If the latter, how far did they restrict the Members of the League of Nations in their subsequent adoption of plans? Early drafts of Article 14 were based on the desire to postpone all questions as to the nature of the court to be established, though they connected Article 14 with the provisions for arbitration contained in the preceding article; the Hurst-Miller draft, placed before the League of Nations Commission on February 3, 1919, stated that the Court should "be competent to hear and determine any matter which the parties recognize as suitable for submission to it for arbitration under the foregoing article." On February 6, 1919, the Commission accepted a proposal of President Wilson to add the expression that the Court "when established" should be thus competent; this would clearly have meant that the Peace Conference was to determine the character of the Court to some extent. The words "when established" were dropped by the League of Nations Commission on the report of its drafting committee, on April 11, 1919, and at the same time the reference to Article 13 was eliminated. The final texts of the second and third sentences in Article 14 may be interpreted as agreements that the plans to be submitted to Members of the League should provide for the competence set forth. They were thus limitations on the mandate conferred on the Council,[46] though it must be noted that this interpretation does not seem to have been placed upon them by the Council. So interpreted, the two sentences would derive little significance from their later incorporation by reference into Article 1 of the Statute of 1920. Certainly these sentences did not preclude the Members

---

[46] M. Adatci (Japan) expressed this view before the Committee of Jurists in 1920, using it to show that the mandate of the Committee of Jurists was similarly limited. Minutes of the 1920 Committee of Jurists, p. 541. The question as to the limits of its competence gave great difficulty in the eleventh meeting of the Committee of Jurists. *Id.*, pp. 233-248.

of the League from later establishing a court of lesser or greater competence.[47]

§93. **Disputes of an International Character.** What is a "dispute of an international character"? It would seem that any dispute between States would have that character, and that a dispute between nationals of different States or between a State and a national of another State would lack it. The international character is not dependent on the subject matter of the dispute; this provision is not in juxtaposition to the provision in Article 15 as to disputes arising out of matters which by international law are solely within the domestic jurisdiction of one of the parties. The expression "dispute of an international character" was first used in Lord Robert Cecil's proposal at a meeting of the League of Nations Commission on March 24, 1919. Previous drafts had stated that the Court should be "competent to hear and determine any matter which the parties recognise as suitable for submission to it for arbitration under the foregoing article"; Lord Robert Cecil proposed to insert after the word "determine" the words "any dispute or difference of an international character including." The inclusion of these words pointed toward the Court's possessing obligatory jurisdiction, and for this reason the drafting committee modified the text,[48] dropping the words "including any matter." The expression "of an international character," originally a part of a proposal which was intended to confer on the Court obligatory jurisdiction, was thus retained as a proposed limitation on the Court's voluntary jurisdiction.

A construction seems to have been given to this expression in Article 14 by the British Government which would exclude from the Court's competence any dispute between two members of the British Commonwealth of Nations, though both are Members of the League of Nations;[49] as it was explained by Sir Cecil Hurst to the 1929 Committee of Jurists, "although the Dominions were

---

[47] The 1920 Committee of Jurists considered it obvious "that the constituent Statute of the Court can confer upon it the degree of competence which the States drawing up the Statute wish to give it." *Id.*, pp. 727–8.

[48] See Miller, Diary at the Peace Conference, VII, pp. 312, 468.

[49] In its protest against the registration of the Irish "treaty" of December 6, 1921, the British Government took the position that neither the Covenant of the League of Nations nor "any conventions concluded under the auspices of the League, are intended to govern the relations *inter se* of the various parts of the British Commonwealth." 27 League of Nations Treaty Series, p. 449. See also, 44 *id.*, p. 266. However, the 1931 British Commonwealth Merchant Shipping Agreement was registered at the request of the Union of South Africa, without protest. 129 *id.*, p. 177.

autonomous, a dispute between two of them or between a Dominion and Great Britain was not an international matter and could not technically be brought before the Court." [50] This view has not been taken by all members of the British Commonwealth of Nations, however.

§94. **Advisory Opinions.** The third sentence of Article 14 provides that "the Court may also give an advisory opinion upon any dispute or question referred to it by the Council or by the Assembly." The provision seems to have grown out of suggestions to be found in various early drafts of the Covenant. Colonel House's draft of July 16, 1918, proposed (Article 10) that "the Delegates may at their discretion submit to the Court such other questions as may seem to them advisable." [51] The report of the French Ministerial Commission of 1918 proposed that "the International Tribunal shall pronounce on all questions submitted to it either by the International Body or by a State having any dispute with another." [52] The British draft convention of January 20, 1919, included a provision for references to a court by the Conference or Council, and it was added that "in such case, the decision of the Court shall have no force or effect unless it is confirmed by the Report of the Conference or Council." [53] Similarly, the Italian draft presented to the League of Nations Commission in 1919 suggested that a court should have jurisdiction over "cases referred to it by the Council and brought forward by one of the parties only." [54] Yet this idea was not embodied in the earlier drafts actually discussed by the Commission. On March 24, 1919, Lord Robert Cecil proposed an additional text on which he and President Wilson had previously agreed, to the effect that the Court should be competent to hear and determine "any issue referred to it by the Executive Council or Body of Delegates." This addition was explained by the British delegation as follows: The power of the Council and Assembly to refer disputes to the Court for advice "will be indispensable for the settlement of some classes of disputes; but of course the opinion of the Court will have no force or effect unless confirmed by the Report of the Council or Assembly. It therefore in no

---

[50] Minutes of the 1929 Committee of Jurists, p. 72. Sir Cecil Hurst had previously expressed the view that "the common allegiance to the Crown prevents the relations between the different communities of the Empire from being international relations." Great Britain and the Dominions (Chicago, 1928), p. 55. See § 207, *infra.*

[51] Seymour, Intimate Papers of Colonel House, IV, p. 31; Miller, Drafting of the Covenant, II, p. 8.

[52] Miller, Drafting of the Covenant, II, p. 239.   [53] *Id.,* p. 111.   [54] *Id.,* p. 252.

way introduces the principle of obligatory arbitration." [55] The addition was later redrafted by the British delegation to read, "and also to advise upon any dispute or question referred to it by the Council or by the Body of Delegates." [56] The term "advisory opinion" was introduced by the drafting committee [57] on April 5, 1919, when Article 14 assumed its final form, but there was no extended consideration of its use, and the draftsmen do not seem to have been guided by any analogy to advisory opinions given by national courts.

§95. **Article 14 in relation to other Articles of the Covenant.** No specific reference to a court was made in any article of the original Covenant other than Article 14. By Article 13, the Members of the League agreed to submit certain disputes "either to arbitration or to enquiry by the Council." The process of arbitration was elaborated in Article 13, but the obligation of Members under Article 13 was limited to the arbitration of disputes "which they recognize to be suitable for submission to arbitration"; certain disputes were enumerated as "generally suitable"; and the parties to a dispute were to agree on the "court of arbitration" to be resorted to. In earlier drafts of the Covenant, Article 14 contained a reference to "the foregoing article," but it was dropped on March 31, 1919; though the word *arbitration* continued to be used in Article 15 to cover both arbitration and judicial settlement, this change in Article 14 had the effect of divorcing the conception of judicial settlement in Article 14 from the conception of arbitration in Articles 12 and 13.

By the fourth paragraph of Article 13, "the Members of the League agree that they will carry out in full good faith any award (Fr., *les sentences*) that may be rendered and that they will not resort to war against a Member of the League which complies therewith." Does this obligation apply to judgments of the Court created under Article 14? [58] If the reference to Article 13 had been retained in Article 14, there can be no doubt that the answer would have been in the affirmative; the suppression of that reference left the matter open

---

[55] Miller, Drafting of the Covenant, I, p. 416. On the other hand, Mr. Miller was of the opinion that the addition went "the whole length of permitting the Executive Council or Body of Delegates to compel arbitration." Miller, Diary at the Peace Conference, VI, p. 444. [56] Miller, Drafting of the Covenant, II, p. 670.

[57] *Id.*, p. 676. Mr. Miller has explained that the substitution of "give an advisory opinion" for "advise" indicated "that the function to be exercised is a judicial one." *Id.*, I, p. 406. See § 452, *infra*.

[58] At the first Assembly of the League of Nations, Lord Robert Cecil stated that "according to the Covenant, judgments were to be enforced." Records of First Assembly, Committees, I, p. 287. See § 449, *infra*.

to possible doubt, however, and the resolution of this doubt was one of the objects of amendments to the Covenant within a few years after it came into force.

§96. **Amendments to the Covenant.** Though no amendment has been made to Article 14 of the Covenant, on September 26, 1924, amendments came into force which added references to *judicial settlement* to the references to *arbitration* in Articles 12, 13 and 15.[59] In Article 12, an amendment inserted the words "or judicial settlement" after "arbitration," and the words "or the judicial decision," after "award of the arbitrators." Corresponding amendments were made in Articles 13 and 15, and the following new paragraph was inserted in Article 13: "For the consideration of any such dispute, the court to which the case is referred shall be the Permanent Court of International Justice, established in accordance with Article 14, or any tribunal agreed on by the parties to the dispute or stipulated in any convention existing between them." As submission to arbitration under Article 13 was optional, the insertion of this paragraph had little effect. These amendments had been proposed by the Second Assembly in 1921; the Committee of the Assembly stated in reporting them that "these proposals do not constitute changes in substance. They are merely drafting amendments. The procedure before the Permanent Court of International Justice has the same importance, under the existing text, as it would have under a text containing the modifications which are now proposed." [60] In spite of this statement it would seem possible to give greater effect to the amendment to the last paragraph of Article 13; the obligation to carry out "in full good faith any award *or decision* that may be rendered," and not to "resort to war against a Member of the League which complies therewith," would now seem to apply quite clearly to the judgments of the Permanent Court of International Justice. It is also provided that "in the event of any failure to carry out such an award *or decision,* the Council shall propose what steps should be taken to give effect thereto." Even a non-member of the League of Nations may have an obligation to carry out a judgment of the Court if it has accepted the invitation provided for in Article 17 of the Covenant.

§97. **Other Parts of the Peace Treaties.** The inclusion of the Covenant in Part I of each of the four treaties of peace necessitates

---

[59] For the texts of the protocols of amendment, see 1 Hudson, International Legislation, pp. 24, 26, 28.　　[60] Records of Second Assembly, Plenary Meetings, p. 698.

some consideration of other parts of those treaties which refer to the Court.[61] Part XIII of the Treaty of Versailles [62] bears a close connection with the Covenant, inasmuch as it provides for the International Labor Organization which is described as machinery "associated with that of the League of Nations," and of which all Members of the League of Nations are members. Articles 415–420, 423, and 426 of Part XIII refer to the Court; their substance was largely limited to a conferring of competence on the court to be created. Article 418 provided for the Court's indication of appropriate measures "of an economic character," which Governments "would be justified in adopting against a defaulting Government." It is doubtful whether these articles placed any limitation on the Members of the League in creating the Court; and in view of the provisions actually adopted in 1920, no difficulty has arisen from them.

The Treaty of Versailles did not contain the provisions on the protection of minorities to be found in the other treaties of peace. Article 69 of the Treaty of St. Germain, Article 57 of the Treaty of Neuilly, and Article 60 of the Treaty of Trianon confer a special jurisdiction on the Court with respect to such provisions, and provide that its decision "shall be final and shall have the same force and effect as an award under Article 13 of the Covenant."

§98. **The Court and the League of Nations.** The history of the drafting of the Covenant leaves no doubt that the Permanent Court of International Justice was envisaged at Paris as a part of the organization of the League of Nations. It was to be created by the Members of the League of Nations, after a consideration of plans formulated by the Council of the League of Nations; and it was to aid the Council and the Assembly in their dealing with international disputes. Most of the projects considered in drafting the Covenant proceeded on the assumption that the League to be organized should include a court as part of its machinery. While the possible participation of non-member States was not excluded, the conclusion is inescapable that the League was to include a court and that the court for which provision was made was not to be independent of the organs of the League which owe their existence to the Covenant itself.[63] It was for this reason that when the

---

[61] It is also to be noted that certain separate but contemporary treaties referred to the Court; for example, the treaties for the protection of minorities of 1919 and 1920.

[62] The same text constitutes Part XIII of the Treaty of St. Germain, Part XII of the Treaty of Neuilly, and Part XIII of the Treaty of Trianon.

[63] Article 415 of the Treaty of Versailles refers to "the Permanent Court of International Justice of the League of Nations."

Council of the League of Nations invited various jurists to serve on a committee to draft plans for the Court, on February 13, 1920, it stated in the invitation that "the Court is a most essential part of the organization of the League of Nations." [64] It was for this reason, also, that the Committee of Jurists reported in 1920: "The new Court, being the judicial organ of the League of Nations, can only be created within this League. As it is a component part of the League, it must originate from an organisation within the League, and not from a body outside it." [65] Though the Protocol of Signature which was drawn up in 1920 possesses an independent character,[66] the Statute annexed to it fulfills this conception of the Committee of Jurists in that the members of the Court are elected by the Assembly and the Council of the League of Nations, and the League of Nations as such is to bear the expenses of the Court. At the inaugural meeting of the Court, President Loder spoke of it as "one of the principal organs of the League," which "occupies within the League of Nations a place similar to that of the Judicature in many States." [67]

[64] League of Nations Official Journal, March 1920, p. 37.
[65] Minutes of the 1920 Committee of Jurists, p. 704.
[66] The French version of the first paragraph of the Protocol of Signature refers to the *Statut ci-joint de la Cour permanente de Justice internationale de la Société des Nations.*
[67] League of Nations Official Journal, 1922, p. 312.

CHAPTER 7

THE ADOPTION OF PLANS FOR THE COURT

§99. Preparation by Governments. Various neutral States in Europe, which had manifested an interest in the creation of a court by the Covenant itself, continued their consideration of plans for the court after the text of the Covenant had assumed final form. The Danish, Norwegian and Swedish Governments had committees at work, which had drawn up a draft of plans for a court early in 1919; [1] later these committees drew up separate drafts which were communicated to the Secretariat of the League of Nations.[2] The Netherlands Government also had a committee on the subject, and it took the initiative of inviting the three Scandinavian Governments and the Swiss Government to send representatives to a conference to combine their individual plans.[3] At this conference at The Hague, February 16–27, 1920,[4] a *projet* of 55 articles was adopted, though not with unanimity on all points, and its provisions were explained in an annexed *mémoire;* these were transmitted to the Secretary-General of the League of Nations by the Netherlands Government. The Committee of Jurists

[1] *Betänkande rörande en Internationell Rättsordning* (Stockholm, 1919). See also Kluyver, Documents of the League of Nations, p. 284 note.

[2] Following the Peace Conference at Paris, the Danish, Norwegian and Swedish committees held joint discussions, as a result of which the Danish and Norwegian committees elaborated new drafts, but the Swedish committee adhered to the earlier joint draft which had been submitted by the three Governments to the Peace Conference. A Danish *projet* of twenty articles, with an *exposé des motifs*, was communicated to the Secretary General of the League of Nations and to various Governments in November, 1919. The Swedish draft with the "considerations" explaining it was published in English and French at Stockholm in 1920. A report of the Norwegian committee, dated August 28, 1919, was published in English and Norwegian and possibly in other languages.

[3] In September, 1918, the Swedish Government had proposed to the Danish, Netherlands, Norwegian, Spanish and Swiss Governments that a conference should be held to discuss plans for a court.

[4] Denmark was represented by Otto Krag; the Netherlands by B. C. J. Loder, J. Limburg, and C. van Vollenhoven; Norway by Emil Huitfeldt and Mikael H. Lie; Sweden by Baron Marks von Wurtemburg and Baron W. Adelsward; and Switzerland by Gaston Carlin and Max Huber. The *protocole de clôture*, the *projet* and the *mémoire* were published in the *Conférence de la Haye pour l'élaboration d'un projet relatif à l'établissment de la Cour Permanente de Justice Internationale, prévu à l'article 14 du Pacte de la Société des Nations*, La Haye, Van Langenhuysen Frères, 1920. They are also published in *Grotius Annuaire Internationale*, 1919–1920, pp. 200 ff.

which made the original draft of the Statute of the Court later found "a very valuable source of information in the plan of the Five Powers." [5]

§100. **Establishment of the Committee of Jurists.** Even before the Covenant of the League of Nations came into force on January 10, 1920, it was contemplated that a committee of jurists should be set up to draft a plan for a court.[6] At its second meeting on June 10, 1919, the Organization Committee which was planning for the inauguration of the League of Nations requested the Acting Secretary-General to prepare, for consideration at a later meeting, a list of jurists who might be invited to form such a committee; [7] but no later meeting of the Organization Committee was held. At the second session of the Council of the League of Nations in February 1920, the Secretary-General submitted a memorandum containing such a list, and on February 12 and 13, 1920, the Council voted to invite the following "to form a committee to prepare plans for the Permanent Court of International Justice and to report to the Council": Satsuo Akidzuki (Japan), Rafael Altamira (Spain), Clovis Bevilaqua (Brazil), Baron Descamps (Belgium), Luis Maria Drago (Argentina), Professor Fadda (Italy), Henri Fromageot (France), G. W. W. Gram (Norway), B. C. J. Loder (Netherlands), Lord Phillimore (Great Britain), Elihu Root (United States),[8] and M. Vesnitch (Serb-Croat-Slovene Kingdom). Of these MM. Akidzuki, Drago, Gram, Fadda, Fromageot and Vesnitch either declined the invitation or resigned before the meeting of the Committee. On April 11, 1920, the Council invited M. Adatci (Japan) to serve on the Committee, and on May 14, 1920, MM. Hagerup (Norway), Ricci-Busatti (Italy) and de Lapradelle (France) were invited to serve. M. Clovis Bevilaqua did not attend the meetings of the Committee, though a draft was presented to it in his name; he was represented by M. Fernandes, whose appointment to succeed him was confirmed by the Council only after the adjournment of the Committee.[9] In the letter of invitation approved by the Council of the League of Nations on February 13, 1920, the Committee's attention was drawn to the plans which had been pre-

[5] Minutes of the 1920 Committee of Jurists, p. 697.

[6] This was contemplated as early as June, 1919. Seymour, Intimate Papers of Colonel House, IV, p. 480.

[7] Kluyver, Documents on the League of Nations, pp. 256, 283.

[8] On earlier overtures made to Mr. Root, see Miller, Diary at the Peace Conference, XX, pp. 346, 351.

[9] Minutes of the Council, Eighth Session, p. 32.

pared by States mentioned in the annex to the Covenant, and it was asked to invite other such States to "forward any proposals they may have prepared." [10] The Council also suggested that the Committee should not overlook assurances given to the Austrian and German Governments by the Allied and Associated Powers that their proposals would be examined.

§101. **Personnel of the Committee of Jurists.** As it was finally composed, the Committee of Jurists consisted of ten jurists, several of whom had been engaged in the work of the Hague Conferences, and some of whom later had a prominent part in the work of the Court itself.[11] M. Adatci, at the time the Minister of Japan at Brussels, was elected a judge of the Court in 1930, and became its president in 1931. M. Altamira, a professor at the University of Madrid, was elected a judge of the Court in 1921 and again in 1930. Baron Descamps, a senator and Minister of State in Belgium, had been a delegate to the Peace Conference at The Hague in 1899. M. Fernandes had been a delegate of Brazil at the Paris Peace Conference. Dr. Hagerup, a former prime minister of Norway, had been the first delegate of Norway at the Hague Conference of 1907. M. de Lapradelle, professor at the University of Paris, was a legal adviser to the French Foreign Office. M. Loder, a judge of the Netherlands Supreme Court, had been president of the conference at The Hague in 1920 which drafted a plan for the Court, and later became the Court's first president. Lord Phillimore, a member of the Privy Council in Great Britain, had been actively engaged in planning for the drafting of the Covenant. M. Ricci-Busatti, legal adviser to the Italian Ministry of Foreign Affairs, had been secretary to the Italian delegation at the Hague Conference of 1907. Mr. Elihu Root, as Secretary of State of the United States, had been responsible for the policy of the American delegation at the Hague Conference of 1907; his adviser, Dr. James Brown Scott, who played an important part in the work of the Committee, had been a technical adviser at the Second Peace Conference at The Hague, and had been actively engaged in the effort to establish the proposed Court of Arbitral Justice. With this composition, the Committee was thoroughly equipped for its work.

[10] No such invitation was extended.
[11] It was pointed out by the Secretary-General of the League of Nations that of the ten members of the Committee, five were "nationals of the five Great Powers and five nationals of smaller Powers." League of Nations Official Journal, June, 1920, p. 123. For biographical notes concerning the members of the Committee, see *id.*, pp. 71–72.

§102. **Work of the Committee of Jurists.**[12] By its resolution
of February 13, 1920, the Council authorized the payment of the
expenses of the Committee of Jurists out of the general funds of the
League, and the "formation of a small expert Secretariat to assist"
the Committee. The Secretary-General announced on May 14, 1920,
that the Secretariat would work under the direction of Commendatore
Anzilotti, Under Secretary-General of the League of Nations, and would
consist of the following members: M. Nippold, M. Winiarsky and
M. Åke Hammarskjöld, the last named a member of the Secretariat
of the League of Nations. As M. Nippold and M. Winiarsky did not
serve, M. Anzilotti acted as Secretary-General of the Committee of
Jurists, with M. Hammarskjöld as his deputy. In 1919, the provisional
Secretariat of the League of Nations had begun to prepare for this
work, by making a careful analysis of various proposals for the creation
of the Court; and this resulted in an elaborate memorandum to which
were annexed the texts of various documents: the Italian, German
and Austrian proposals at the Peace Conference, the convention for
the establishment of the Central American Court of Justice, the individual and joint drafts of the three Scandinavian committees, a
Swiss *avant-projet*, Draft Regulations drawn up by a Netherlands
Committee, and the plan of the five neutral states. This memorandum
was before the members of the Committee of Jurists before the Committee's meetings began.[13] The Netherlands Government invited the
Committee to hold its meetings at The Hague, and a majority of its
members expressed themselves as favoring the acceptance of this invitation.[14] At a private meeting on June 16, 1920, Baron Descamps
was elected President, and M. Loder Vice-President of the Committee.
M. Léon Bourgeois (France), who had played a prominent part in
the Hague Peace Conferences of 1899 and 1907, represented the
Council of the League of Nations at the first meeting of the Committee.

[12] In the publications of the League of Nations, the Committee was called "Advisory
Committee of Jurists."

[13] The memorandum and the annexes were published in Documents Presented to
the Committee of Jurists Relating to Existing Plans for the Establishment of a Permanent Court of International Justice, London (1920). The memorandum was largely
the work of Dr. John Pawley Bate, then a member of the Legal Section of the
Secretariat.

[14] M. Bourgeois later explained to the Council that "the choice of The Hague
had a real significance, and the reasons for the choice were understood by all. In these
surroundings, where for several centuries the traditions of International Law had been
alive, our representatives set to work." Minutes of the Council, Sixth Session, p. 167.
To the First Assembly, he stated that the meetings were held at The Hague "because
it seemed desirable to show that the conferences of 1899 and 1907 had not been for-
gotten." Records of First Assembly, Plenary, p. 436.

Altogether, the Committee held 35 meetings, from June 16 to July 24, 1920. An elaborate draft agenda,[15] prepared by the Secretariat, was not adopted; later, at the request of the Committee, the Secretariat framed a valuable synopsis [16] of various proposals, including those annexed to the Secretariat's memorandum, a draft of the International Parliamentary Union, and a draft of the Union Juridique Internationale, as well as the *projet* of the Hague Conference of 1907.

Differences which arose over the Committee's rules of procedure were soon smoothed out.[17] At its second meeting, Mr. Root proposed that the Committee adopt "as the basis for consideration of the subject referred to it the Acts and Resolutions of the Second Peace Conference at The Hague in the year 1907"; [18] but some members of the Committee favored proceeding more independently, and the resolution adopted merely stated that "the Committee starts its deliberations by paying homage to the work of the two Hague Conferences which have already prepared, with an outstanding authority, the solution of the problem of the organisation of the Court of International Justice." [19] In spite of this decision, the *projet* of 1907 was continually referred to during the deliberations of the Committee, and it was precisely the question left open by that *projet,* as to the method of electing judges, which caused the greatest difficulty and to which a large proportion of the Committee's time was given. The extent of the proposed Court's obligatory jurisdiction also gave difficulty, and some members of the Committee conceived its mandate to be limited by the limit on the mandate of the Council contained in the second sentence of Article 14 of the Covenant. However, the Committee was able to adopt unanimously a "draft-scheme" (Fr., *avant-projet*) of 62 articles, with only a mention of reservations by M. Adatci and M. Ricci-Busatti in its report.[20] Complete *procès-verbaux* of the meetings of the Committee were promptly published.[21]

---

[15] Minutes of the 1920 Committee of Jurists, p. 33.   [16] *Id.,* p. 51.
[17] Minutes of the 1920 Committee of Jurists, pp. 31, 113.
[18] *Id.,* p. 41.   [19] *Id.,* p. 43.
[20] These reservations related to the proposed obligatory jurisdiction.
[21] The Committee also adopted three resolutions (*vœux*) which went somewhat beyond its mandate. One of these resolutions recommended to the Council and Assembly the consideration of a proposal for the establishment of a High Court of International Justice "competent to try crimes constituting a breach of international public order or against the universal law of nations." Minutes, p. 748. The Third Committee of the First Assembly concluded that "there is no occasion for the Assembly of the League of Nations to adopt any resolution on this subject." Records of First Assembly, Committees, I, p. 589. The subject was later raised in the Assembly by Professor Pella (Rumania) in 1928. Records of Ninth Assembly, Committees, I, p. 35.

§103. **The Draft-Scheme before the Council.** When the draft-scheme of the Committee of Jurists came before the Council of the League of Nations at its eighth session at San Sebastian on August 3, 1920, explanations were offered by M. de Lapradelle who had been a member of the Committee. M. Léon Bourgeois made a report [22] which was adopted by the Council, in which he emphasized the solution of the difficulty as to election of judges which "the League of Nations, by its very existence, has made it possible to solve"; the seating of nationals of parties as judges; and the provisions for obligatory juris-diction. On the latter point, M. Tittoni (Italy) expressed a reservation, M. de Lapradelle explaining in reply that all Members of the League were "bound by a compulsory arbitration agreement" in the Covenant. On August 4, the Council requested M. Bourgeois to continue his study of the subject, and decided to communicate the draft-scheme to Members of the League of Nations, stating that "the Council would regard an irreconcilable difference of opinion on the merits of the scheme as an international misfortune of the gravest kind. . . . The failure would be great, and probably irreparable." [23] In the covering letter to Members of the League, it was made clear, however, that the Council would continue its examination of the draft-scheme. No consideration was given to the matter at the ninth session of the Council, but at the tenth session at Brussels extended consideration was given to it. The Council had before it observations submitted by the British and Italian, Norwegian [24] and Swedish [25] Governments.

On October 23, 1920, "the Council adopted the text of a number of articles [33, 34, 35, 57a] drafted on its instructions by Commendatore Anzilotti, Dr. van Hamel and Sir Cecil Hurst." [26] Mr. Balfour raised a question as to the languages of the Court, objecting to the proposal of the Committee of Jurists (Article 37) that the sole official language of the Court should be French. On October 26, 1920, M. Bourgeois made an elaborate report to the Council; [27] M. Caclamanos (Greece) also made a report on the question of languages, suggesting two official languages, "French and English." [28] The Coun-

---

[22] Minutes of the Council, Eighth Session, p. 164.
[23] *Id.*, p. 171.
[24] M. Hagerup later explained that the Norwegian observations "emanated from a Norwegian Commission of Investigation, and not from the Norwegian Government." Records of First Assembly, Committees, I, p. 279.
[25] These also emanated from a committee. *Id.*, p. 279.
[26] Minutes of the Council, Tenth Session, pp. 21, 160.
[27] *Id.*, p. 162.   [28] *Id.*, p. 176.

cil decided to communicate these reports to the Assembly.[29] A proposal to refer the draft-scheme back to the Committee of Jurists was not adopted. It seems also that the Secretariat was "instructed to bring the provisions of the scheme not amended by the Council into harmony with the amended parts";[30] it proceeded to draw up an amended text of the scheme, in which amendments were included to Articles 27, 29, 33, 34, 35, 36 *bis*, 37, 56, 57 *bis*; and this text, together with a complete documentation, was placed before the Assembly in November.[31] The most significant of the Secretariat's amendments was a proposed new text of Article 33, substituting for the obligatory jurisdiction of the Court, a statement that "the jurisdiction of the Court is defined by Articles 12, 13, and 14 of the Covenant." M. Bourgeois later explained that the Council "had restricted its examination to the question whether or not the draft-scheme was in conformity with the Covenant of the League, and to the possible political consequences of certain of its articles."[32]

Such, then, would seem to have been the "plans" formulated by the Council and submitted to the Members of the League, in discharge of its mandate under Article 14 of the Covenant.

§104. **The Draft-Scheme before the Assembly.** The "plans" transmitted by the Council were referred by the First Assembly of the League of Nations to its Third Committee. Under the chairmanship of M. Léon Bourgeois (France), the Third Committee held ten meetings between November 17 and December 16, 1919, and its personnel was such as to assure a sympathetic consideration of the "plans" before it. A sub-committee of the Third Committee, under the chairmanship of M. Hagerup (Norway), devoted eleven meetings to the subject, November 24 to December 10, 1920; five of the ten members of the sub-committee had previously served on the Committee of Jurists. Further amendments to the draft-scheme were formally submitted by the Argentine, Colombian and Panaman delegations; the Argentine delegation proposed the abolition of the Permanent Court of Arbitration, but the proposal seems to have received scant consideration.[33]

---

[29] *Id.*, p. 46.   [30] Records of First Assembly, Committees, I, p. 482.
[31] Records of First Assembly, Committees, I, pp. 411–495.
[32] *Id.*, p. 278.
[33] Records of First Assembly, Committees, I, p. 372. The report of the Third Committee to the Assembly states that it was thought that the Permanent Court of Arbitration "would still have a rôle to fill in certain international disputes which lend themselves more easily to arbitral decision than to an award [judgment] based on strict rules of law." Records of First Assembly, Plenary, p. 457.

The general discussion in the Third Committee related chiefly to the question of obligatory jurisdiction, and to the form to be given to the constitution of the court. The sub-committee examined the plan submitted by the Council in great detail, and in its unanimous report to the Third Committee,[34] it suggested numerous amendments. Consideration of this report was begun by the Third Committee on December 8, 1920; the draft was further amended by the Third Committee and in the amended form it was adopted unanimously and reported to the Plenary Assembly.

When the report of the Third Committee came before the Plenary Assembly on December 13, M. Bourgeois once more took a leading rôle. The Court's "relations with the League of Nations can be easily defined," he said; "it will be for the League to establish the Court and to draft its Statute. But from that moment, and so long as the League of Nations has not by its sovereign power altered those rules, the Court is independent." [35] Enthusiasm in the Assembly was dampened by the suppression of the provisions for obligatory jurisdiction proposed by the Committee of Jurists, a course which was attributed to the so-called "Great Powers." The opinion of many delegates seems to have been expressed by M. Fernandes (Brazil) when he said: "I was over-enthusiastic; to-day I am barely confident. I am waiting." [36] M. Loder exclaimed somewhat prophetically: "You are fighting against time; you will do so in vain." [37] Some further difficulty was also raised as to the manner proposed for the adoption of the draft. Only one slight amendment was made by the Plenary Assembly, however, and at a second meeting on December 13, the Assembly declared its unanimous approval of the draft Statute as amended.

§105. **Form of Adoption.** The question of the form in which plans should be adopted was not foreseen in the report of the Committee of Jurists,[38] but in the report adopted by the Council at Brussels it was stated: "It will be the duty of the General Assembly to draw up the terms of the future International Convention which is to be submitted for the signature of the Members of the League of Nations." [39] At a meeting of the Third Committee of the Assembly

---

[34] *Id.*, Committees, I, p. 526.   [35] Records of First Assembly, Plenary, p. 437.
[36] *Id.*, p. 449.   [37] *Id.*, p. 445.
[38] See, however, Lord Phillimore's statement, in Minutes of the 1920 Committee of Jurists, p. 236.
[39] Minutes of the Council, Tenth Session, p. 175.

on November 22, 1920, the question arose as to the form to be given
to the plans for the Court when adopted. M. Max Huber (Switzerland) stated that two alternatives were open, "a unanimous resolution
by the Assembly and an international convention ratified by different
States"; [40] for the first of these, he saw "difficulties of a constitutional
order." The matter was discussed in the sub-committee of the Third
Committee, where on December 10 it was suggested that there were
three possible solutions: (1) a unanimous vote of the Assembly,
(2) a diplomatic convention, and (3) a vote of the Assembly combined with a ratification. It was also suggested that the Court should
be established by a vote of the Assembly with a privilege for any
State to declare within a given time that it would not "adhere to the
Court." The sub-committee accepted a draft resolution proposed by
M. Fromageot (France),[41] calling for both the adoption of an Assembly resolution and the opening of a protocol to signature; it was
explained at the time that "the vote of the Assembly would result
in the establishment of the Court as an organisation under the League
of Nations, while the jurisdiction of the Court *ratione personæ* would
be determined by the ratification of States." [42] In the Third Committee, the suggestion that a resolution of the Assembly might be
ratified was opposed as a dangerous precedent which would weaken
the authority of the Assembly. When the sub-committee's proposal
had been adopted, the action was explained in the Third Committee's
report to the Assembly as having been taken "in view of the special
nature of the terms of Article 14 of the Covenant"; yet it would
seem that any of the proposals under consideration would have been
consistent with the terms of Article 14.

The question caused greater difficulty because it was never made
precisely clear what the rôle of the Assembly was, in connection with
the plans for the Court. M. Politis (Greece) stated to the Third
Committee that "the discussion in the Assembly was only a stage in
the preparation of the final plan to be submitted by the Council to
the Governments"; [43] later, however, he stated that the Assembly
"filled the rôle of a diplomatic conference." [44] It would seem that
the Council might be deemed to have submitted its plans to the Members of the League when on October 26, 1920, it resolved to com-

---

[40] Records of First Assembly, Committees, I, p. 281.
[41] Records of First Assembly, Committees, I, p. 617.
[42] *Id.*, p. 408.   [43] *Id.*, p. 299.   [44] *Id.*, p. 314.

municate the amended draft-scheme to the Assembly, and that the Members of the League might be taken to have used the Assembly as an agency through which they proceeded to the "adoption" of the plans.[45] The resolution adopted by the Assembly on December 13, 1920, however, left it to the Council to submit the Statute to the Members of the League.

§106. The Title of the Statute. Article 14 of the Covenant conferred on the Council a mandate for formulating "plans" (Fr., *un projet*) for the Court. In an address to the Committee of Jurists at The Hague on June 16, 1920, M. Bourgeois referred to *le statut* of the Court,[46] and the Committee of Jurists in its *vœux* referred to itself as constituted to prepare the "constituent statute" of the Court.[47] Yet the Committee of Jurists elaborated what it called a "draft-scheme" (Fr., *avant-projet*).[48] Frequent reference was made at the First Assembly to the "constitution" of the Court. M. Bourgeois seems to have used the word "statute" at a meeting of the Third Committee on December 8, 1920,[49] and M. Hagerup also used the term in a draft of a resolution on the same day.[50] The expression "organic statute" seems to have been used in the Third Committee on December 9, 1920.[51] No particular attention was given to the name, and the report of the Third Committee to the Assembly does not discuss it. The word "statute" seems to have expressed a certain consideration for the feelings of those delegates in the Assembly who insisted on the creation of the Court by the action of the Assembly itself; at the same time, it distinguished the action taken by the Assembly from the ordinary *resolutions* adopted by that body.[52] If the term was a novelty in in-

[45] It may even be contended that the Council was bound to submit the plans to the Members in the Assembly. See Schücking and Wehberg, *Die Satzung des Völkerbundes* (1921), p. 348.

[46] Minutes of the 1920 Committee of Jurists, p. 5.

[47] *Id.*, p. 747.

[48] At a meeting of the Committee of Jurists on June 29, 1920, Baron Descamps referred to the "organic statute" of the Court. *Id.*, p. 245.

[49] Records of First Assembly, Committees, I, p. 298.

[50] *Id.*, p. 552.

[51] Records of First Assembly, Committees, I, p. 302. As the published record is not a verbatim report of what was said, some doubt may be felt on this point.

[52] In the beginning various views were held as to the form to be given to the results of the Assembly's deliberations, and in some quarters it was urged that the term *acts* be employed for such results when unanimously adopted. At one time the view of the Swiss Government was that decisions adopted by the Assembly "constitute international acts, which in themselves impose international obligations." League of Nations Official Journal, 1922, p. 717. The distinction between resolutions and recommendations of the Assembly is of importance because of the nature of the vote required for each.

ternational legislation, it seems to serve a useful purpose, and it has been employed in subsequent instruments.[53]

§107. **The Assembly Resolution of December 13, 1920.** The action taken by the Assembly on December 13, 1920, was in the form of a resolution approving the Statute and providing for a separate instrument relating to its acceptance.[54] Though the Third Committee had presented this as two resolutions, it was adopted as a complete and single resolution.

Under the first paragraph of the resolution,

> The Assembly unanimously declares its approval of the draft Statute of the Permanent Court of International Justice—as amended by the Assembly—which was prepared by the Council under Article 14 of the Covenant and submitted to the Assembly for its approval.

This had the effect, at least, of giving final form to the Statute; if it was an approval of the Statute by all of the then Members of the League, it was not an agreement by them to be bound by it. Yet possibly no Member of the League could thereafter question the payment of the Court's expenses as decided upon by the Assembly, or the power of the Assembly and the Council to elect the judges.

A second paragraph of the resolution provided:

> In view of the special wording of Article 14, the Statute of the Court shall be submitted within the shortest possible time to the Members of the League of Nations for adoption in the form of a Protocol duly ratified and declaring their recognition of this Statute. It shall be the duty of the Council to submit the Statute to the Members.

The opening words of this paragraph were explained to have the purpose to "prevent this vote establishing a precedent for the future." The whole paragraph seems to be based on the theory that the Members of the League were acting on the "plans" submitted by the Council in accordance with the first sentence of Article 14. If the Assembly was merely assisting the Council in formulating plans to be submitted

---

[53] For example, the Statute on Freedom of Transit and the Statute on the Régime of Navigable Waterways of International Concern, annexed to the Barcelona Conventions of April 20, 1921. 1 Hudson, International Legislation, pp. 631, 645.

[54] The original draft of the Assembly resolution by M. Fromageot was adopted by the sub-committee of the Third Committee on December 10, 1920. Records of First Assembly, Committees, I, pp. 408, 617. Some modifications were made by the Third Committee. *Id.*, p. 317.

to the Members of the League, the question of a precedent could hardly have arisen. The concluding sentence of the paragraph had the effect of leaving to the Council the determination of the form of the protocol to be signed.

A third paragraph of the resolution provided:

> As soon as this Protocol has been ratified by the majority of the Members of the League, the Statute of the Court shall come into force and the Court shall be called upon to sit in conformity with the said Statute in all disputes between the Members or States which have ratified, as well as between the other States to which the Court is open under Article 35, paragraph 2, of the said Statute.

This was a departure in that the Statute was to be brought into force by a majority of the Members of the League of Nations. The Peace Conference at The Hague in 1907 had not dared to suggest the possibility of a similar course; nor does it seem to have occurred to the Committee of Jurists in 1920. In the First Assembly, itself, the provision received little consideration. The reference to the cases in which the Court is to be called upon to sit has no significance; it is an inaccurate description of the Court's jurisdiction.

A fourth paragraph of the resolution provided:

> The said Protocol shall likewise remain open for signature by the States mentioned in the Annex to the Covenant.

The object of this provision, as explained by M. Hagerup to the First Assembly, was to permit the United States of America to "adhere to the Statute." [55] It opens the Protocol to signature by Ecuador and the Hedjaz, as well as by the United States of America, all other States mentioned in the Annex to the Covenant being included under the second paragraph.

§108. **The Protocol of Signature.** The idea of a separate and complete diplomatic instrument giving force to a Statute adopted by the Assembly appeared late in the deliberations of the First Assembly; nor did the form of this instrument receive much attention. It was assumed that the instrument would deal with the acceptance of the jurisdiction of the Court under Article 36 of the Statute. It had first been proposed that the Members of the League should ratify the

---

[55] Records of First Assembly, Plenary, p. 441.

Assembly resolution.[56] M. Politis proposed a special convention.[57] M. Fromageot proposed a "protocol," [58] and when his proposal was adopted by the Third Committee on December 10, M. Loder "expressed the wish that the Protocol of Signature should be immediately prepared by the Secretariat, in order that it might be possible for the Government representatives to sign before leaving Geneva." [59] The Assembly's resolution of December 13, 1920, left the preparation of the "protocol" to the Council; and a draft prepared by the Secretariat was adopted by the Council without discussion on December 14, 1920,[60] and announced to the Assembly on December 17, 1920.[61] Though it bears the date of December 16, 1920, the instrument was available for signature at certain hours on December 17 and 18, and probably few if any of the signatures were affixed until after December 16. The title of the instrument is without legal significance.

§109. **Analysis of the Protocol.** By the first paragraph of the Protocol of Signature, "the Members of the League of Nations . . . declare their acceptance [Fr., *déclarent reconnaître*] of the adjoined Statute." As the Protocol itself provided that it might be signed by States mentioned in the Annex to the Covenant, it was clearly faulty drafting thus to limit the declarations of acceptance to Members of the League of Nations.[62] A second paragraph provides: "Consequently, they hereby declare that they accept the jurisdiction of the Court in accordance with the terms and subject to the conditions of the above-mentioned Statute." This provision is traceable to a confusion in the Assembly as to the effect of accepting the Statute; it can have no effect in conferring jurisdiction on the Court except on the terms of the "conditions" set forth in the Statute itself.[63] The Protocol is "subject to ratification." It was clearly faulty drafting that no provision was made for the coming into force of the Protocol itself upon the deposit of a certain number of ratifications; it was merely pro-

---

[56] Records of First Assembly, Committees, I, pp. 614–615.

[57] *Id.*, p. 616. M. Anzilotti had proposed a *"procès-verbal* of signature."

[58] *Id.*, pp. 611, 617.   [59] *Id.*, p. 315.

[60] Minutes of the Council, 11th Session, pp. 35, 137.

[61] Records of First Assembly, Plenary, p. 641.

[62] This drafting was responsible for a reservation proposed by the Government of the United States in 1926. See § 239, *infra*.

[63] It may be argued that a party to the Protocol of Signature has agreed to the Court's exercise of jurisdiction over disputes as to jurisdiction under paragraph 4 of Article 36, and in cases of applications for an indication of interim measures under Article 41, and in cases of applications to intervene. See § 404, *infra*. Judge Huber stated in 1922 that as a result of Article 53 of the Statute, "all States which had ratified the Statute had recognized the Court's right to decide, even in their absence, whether Articles 36 and 37 of the Statute were applicable in a given case." Series D, No. 2, p. 201.

vided that "the Statute of the Court shall come into force as provided in the above-mentioned decision," *i.e.*, the resolution of the Assembly of December 13, 1920, and that resolution provides that the Statute shall come into force "as soon as this Protocol has been ratified by the majority of the Members of the League." As the number of Members of the League has varied from time to time, did this mean a majority of the members on December 13, 1920, or a majority on the date of the deposit of some ratification? M. La Fontaine (Belgium) had stated to the Assembly on December 13, 1920, that "the signature of twenty-two States will suffice to enable the election of the judges of the Court to be made in the next session of the Assembly," [64] as the League of Nations then had forty-two members. Six States were admitted to membership in 1920, however, and in 1921 it was assumed that a deposit of the ratifications of twenty-five Members of the League was necessary to bring the Statute into force.[65]

The Protocol also provides that it "shall remain open for signature by the Members of the League of Nations and by the States mentioned in the Annex to the Covenant of the League." Numerous States have signed and ratified the Protocol since the Statute came into force in 1921. Though such action was too late to give these States a formal part in the creation of the Court, their action has had the effect of enlisting their support of the existing institution, and it may have the effect of enabling the Court to exercise, with reference to these States, certain kinds of incidental jurisdiction.

§110. **The Optional Clause.** The Italian Council for Diplomatic Litigation seems to have first suggested a "separate convention" for the acceptance of the Court's compulsory jurisdiction.[66] In the sub-committee of the Third Committee, an attempt was made to disassociate this proposal from the adoption of the Statute, and the sub-committee originally made no suggestion in line with the Italian proposal. Later, a proposal by M. Fernandes of an alternative text of Article 36 relating to the Court's obligatory jurisdiction, which

[64] Records of First Assembly, Plenary, p. 447. M. La Fontaine doubtless meant ratification instead of signature.

[65] It did not become necessary to decide the question in 1921. In February, 1921, a report of the Secretariat had stated that the deposit of ratifications by at least twenty-four members was needed to bring the Statute into force; counting the Argentine Republic, however, the League of Nations then had forty-eight members, so that a majority was not less than twenty-five.

[66] Records of First Assembly, Committees, I, p. 498. See also M. Ricci-Busatti's proposal to the Third Committee's sub-committee. *Id.*, p. 380.

States might accept if they chose,[67] was redrafted by the sub-committee [68] to avoid the alternative form, and it was approved with modifications by the Third Committee. No suggestion was made by the Third Committee of a text of an "optional clause" for declarations as to the Court's jurisdiction, nor was it mentioned in the Assembly on December 13, 1920. When a draft of the Protocol of Signature was submitted to the Council on December 14, however, a draft of an "optional clause" was included, and it seems to have been approved by the Council.[69] It constitutes merely one form for the declarations referred to in Article 36, paragraph 2. It is annexed to the Protocol of Signature,[70] and it has no independent status.

§111. **Coming into Force of the Statute.** On February 25, 1921, the Secretary-General of the League of Nations reported to the Council that the Protocol of Signature had been signed on behalf of twenty-seven Members of the League of Nations,[71] and the Council authorized the Secretary-General to proceed with steps for the nomination of candidates in the first election of judges. On February 21, 1921, the first ratification was deposited by Sweden. On March 3, 1921, a "pressing appeal" was made by the Council for the ratification of the Protocol.[72] On June 21, 1921, the Secretary-General of the League of Nations reported that the Protocol of Signature had been signed by representatives of thirty-nine Members of the League of Nations, and that ratifications had been deposited by Denmark, Italy and Sweden.[73] The task of securing the necessary number of ratifications was prosecuted with great vigor during the early months of 1921, and the Secretary-General reported that on September 1 twenty-two of the forty-one signatories had deposited ratifications, that six additional ratifications were in course of transmission for deposit, and that "the constitution of the Court is assured." [74] It seems unnecessary to fix the precise date on which the Statute came into force; the provision in the Assembly's resolution of December 13, 1920, to

[67] *Id.,* p. 553.
[68] *Id.,* p. 567. The Sub-committee seems to have conceived of its text as not "an amendment, but an addition to the Covenant." *Id.,* p. 408.
[69] Minutes of the Council, 11th Session, pp. 35, 137. The published records may not be complete on the history of the optional clause.
[70] The Council's resolution of May 17, 1922, refers to the "optional clause" as "the optional clause provided for by the additional protocol of December 16, 1920." League of Nations Official Journal, 1922, p. 545.
[71] Minutes of the Council, 12th Session, pp. 18, 115–116.
[72] League of Nations Official Journal, 1921, p. 213.   [73] *Id.,* p. 716.
[74] Minutes of the Council, 14th Session, pp. 11, 58; Records of Second Assembly, Plenary, p. 161.

which reference was made in the Protocol of Signature of December 16, 1920, was that the Statute should come into force "as soon as this Protocol has been ratified by a majority of the Members of the League." A deposit of the ratifications was not required for this purpose. It may be said, therefore, that the Statute came into force by September 1, 1921,[75] and this enabled the first election of judges to be held in that year. Since that date, various additional States have signed and ratified the Protocol of Signature; on September 14, 1933, it was reported that ratifications had been deposited by forty-nine Members of the League of Nations, and that signatures had been affixed on behalf of eight States which had not ratified.[76] The Protocol of Signature has now (January 1, 1934) been signed on behalf of all the present Members of the League of Nations except the Argentine Republic, Honduras, Iraq, Mexico and Turkey, and on behalf of Brazil, Costa Rica and the United States of America; it has been ratified by all the signatories except Bolivia, Costa Rica, Guatemala, Liberia, Nicaragua and the United States of America.

§112. **Possibility of Denunciation.** The Protocol of Signature of December 16, 1920, contains no provision for its denunciation, and the question has not arisen whether a party can escape from the obligations which it imposes. The extent of these obligations may be thought to render the question unimportant; perhaps it is less important for Members of the League of Nations than for States which are not members,[77] inasmuch as it seems unlikely that a State which remains a Member of the League of Nations will desire to have no part in maintaining the Court. A State withdrawing from membership in the League of Nations would have no duty to participate in the elections of members of the Court, nor to make any contribution to its expenses; but such withdrawal does not automatically effect a denunciation of the Protocol of Signature of 1920.[78] Conceivably, any State which is a party to the Protocol of Signature might wish to relieve itself of all responsibility for maintaining the Court, in addition to withdrawing from more active participation. In such a case, it may be

[75] Though the Protocol of Signature was not registered under Article 18 of the Covenant until October 8, 1921. 6 League of Nations Treaty Series, p. 379.

[76] For dates of the signatures and of the deposits of ratifications, see League of Nations Document, A.6(a). 1933. Annex, p. 9. See also the appendix, p. 579, *infra*.

[77] But see the statement by M. Pilotti (Italy) to the 1926 Conference of Signatories. Minutes of the 1926 Conference of Signatories, p. 16.

[78] Special provision is made in the Protocol of September 14, 1929, concerning the Accession of the United States, for withdrawal by the United States. See *infra*, §238 (8).

argued that in spite of the absence of a provision for denunciation the general principles of international law do not preclude a State's denunciation of an instrument entered into for the purpose of creating and maintaining an international institution; [79] but this argument loses some of its force because of the slight extent of the obligations resting on a party to the Protocol of Signature. Even if this argument were accepted, however, it might not apply to a denunciation of a declaration under Article 36, paragraph 2, of the Statute, accepting the Court's obligatory jurisdiction for an indefinite time. There may be good reason for saying that no obligation with reference to an international institution can be perpetual. It is to be noted that provisions for denunciation have been included in international instruments with reference to other institutions: for example, Article 61 (1899) and 96 (1907) of the Hague Conventions with reference to the Permanent Court of Arbitration. The Covenant provides (Article 1) that any Member of the League of Nations may "withdraw from the League" after two years' notice of its intention to do so, provided it has fulfilled "its international obligations" and "all its obligations under this Covenant"; and Article 11 of the Universal Postal Convention of June 28, 1929, provides for withdrawal from the Universal Postal Union.[80]

---

[79] M. Osusky (Czechoslovakia) made this argument to the 1926 Conference of Signatories. Minutes of the 1926 Conference of Signatories, p. 13. M. Dinichert (Switzerland) supported this position (*id.*, p. 15), but several other delegates opposed it. *Id.*, pp. 13–18.

[80] See 4 Hudson, International Legislation, p. 2875.

CHAPTER 8

THE DRAFTING OF THE STATUTE

§113. **Agencies Concerned in the Drafting.** Four agencies were principally concerned in the drafting of the Statute: the 1920 Committee of Jurists, the Council of the League of Nations, the sub-committee of the Third Committee of the First Assembly of the League of Nations, and the Third Committee of the First Assembly of the League of Nations. In its plenary sessions, the First Assembly of the League of Nations did little more than confirm the results of the work of its Third Committee and the latter's sub-committee.[1] To understand the genesis of any provision of the Statute, it is necessary to trace the drafts through the thirty-five meetings of the Committee of Jurists, June 16–July 24, 1920;[2] through the eighth and tenth sessions of the Council of the League of Nations, at San Sebastian July 30–August 5, and at Brussels October 20–28, 1920;[3] through the ten meetings of the sub-committee, November 24–December 7, 1920;[4] through the eight meetings of the Third Committee, November 17–December 11, 1920;[5]

[1] The First Assembly in plenary session made a single change in the draft before it, in Article 27.

[2] "*Procès-verbaux* of the Proceedings of the Committee of Jurists," The Hague (1920), pp. lv, 779 (herein referred to as Minutes of the 1920 Committee of Jurists). These minutes, in many cases only summarized, were revised from original minutes taken at the time which were not published. Some quotations from the original minutes were published in James Brown Scott, The Project of a Permanent Court of International Justice and Resolutions of the Advisory Committee of Jurists (1920). See also, Men and Policies, Addresses by Elihu Root (1924), pp. 321 ff.

It is a difficult task to trace the provisions of the Statute through the discussions of the Committee of Jurists. Until its 17th meeting, no definite text was taken as the basis of discussion. The Root-Phillimore plan, Minutes, pp. 298–301, 326–328, served as the basis from the 17th to the 24th meetings; a text prepared by a drafting committee, *id.*, pp. 561–571, served as the basis from the 25th to the 30th meetings. The 31st meeting was devoted to a second reading, and the final draft-scheme was signed at the 32nd meeting on July 23, 1920. *Id.*, p. 671.

[3] At this time the minutes of the Council were not included in the League of Nations Official Journal, but they were printed separately as Documents 20/29/14, 20/29/16 and were later published.

[4] Minutes of the sub-committee, in Records of First Assembly, Committees, I, pp. 331–408.

[5] Minutes of the Third Committee, in Records of First Assembly, Committees, I, pp. 273–330. The ninth and tenth meetings of the Third Committee were devoted to the resolutions of the Committee of Jurists and to the salaries of the members of the Court.

and through the twentieth and twenty-first plenary meetings of the
First Assembly, on December 13, 1920.[6] In addition to the drafts considered by these agencies, various official reports also deserve attention.
The report submitted by the Committee of Jurists to the Council [7] contains explanations of the Committee's draft-scheme, but parts of it can
hardly be taken to have represented the opinion of the Committee;
though the report was considered at three meetings of the Committee of
Jurists, it gives evidence of hasty preparation. Two reports made to
the Council by M. Bourgeois are also of interest.[8] The report submitted to the Third Committee by its sub-committee contains explanations of various suggested amendments,[9] as does also the report
submitted to the First Assembly by the Third Committee.[10] An *ensemble* of the relevant documents was published by the Secretariat of
of the League of Nations.[11]

§114. **Influence of Previous Drafts.** The work of the Committee
of Jurists was largely influenced by the deliberations of the Peace
Conferences at The Hague in 1899 and 1907, and by the "Five-Power
Plan" drawn up at the Conference held at The Hague in February
1920.[12] The Hague *projet* of 1907 for the creation of a Court of
Arbitral Justice furnished numerous ideas for the organization of the
Court, and many of the Committee's proposals with reference to the
procedure of the Court were borrowed from provisions in the "Five-
Power Plan," [13] which had in turn adapted them from the Hague
Conventions for Pacific Settlement. Indeed, a careful review of the

[6] Records of First Assembly, Plenary, pp. 436–501.
[7] The text of this report is published in Records of First Assembly, Committees,
I, pp. 422–464; Minutes of the 1920 Committee of Jurists, pp. 693–749.
[8] Minutes of the Council, 8th Session, pp. 164–169; 10th Session, pp. 162–175;
Records of First Assembly, Committees, I, pp. 464, 469.
[9] Records of First Assembly, Committees, I, pp. 526–548. See also *id.*, Plenary,
pp. 457–477.
[10] Records of First Assembly, Plenary, pp. 457–467; Committees, I, pp. 573–577.
[11] This *ensemble* includes: I, Documents Presented to the Committee of Jurists
relating to Existing Plans for the establishment of a Permanent Court of International
Justice, London (1920), pp. v, 373; II, *Procès-verbaux* of the Proceedings [Meetings]
of the Committee of Jurists, The Hague (1920), pp. lv, 779; III, Documents concerning the action taken by the Council of the League of Nations under Article 14 of the
Covenant and the adoption by the Assembly of the Statute of the Permanent Court,
Geneva (1921), pp. 284 (double).
    Where reference is made to this *ensemble* in this chapter, I is cited as "Preparatory
Documents," II as "Minutes of the 1920 Committee of Jurists," and III as "Documents."
As the "Documents" are not generally available, citations are given also to the Minutes
of the Council and to the Records of the First Assembly.
[12] Denmark, the Netherlands, Norway, Sweden and Switzerland were represented
at the February Conference at The Hague. See §99, *supra*. For a synopsis of various
preliminary drafts, see Minutes of the 1920 Committee of Jurists, pp. 53–99.
[13] For an analysis of the Articles of the Five-Power Plan relating to procedure, see
id., pp. 347–350.

history of the drafting of the Statute leaves the impression that it contains but few new ideas, and that many of its provisions are based upon drafts previously elaborated and upon previous experience.[14]

§115. **Article 1.**[15] *"A Permanent Court of International Justice is hereby established, in accordance with Article 14 of the Covenant of the League of Nations. This Court shall be in addition to the Court of Arbitration organized by the Conventions of The Hague of 1899 and 1907, and to the special Tribunals of Arbitration to which States are always at liberty to submit their disputes for settlement."*

This text was drafted by the Committee of Jurists, whose draft-scheme contained as an additional phrase in the first sentence, after the word "Justice," "to which parties [16] shall have direct access"; this phrase was deleted by the sub-committee of the Third Committee of the First Assembly, apparently because it was thought to be connected with the proposed system of obligatory jurisdiction which had been rejected.[17] The opening words, taken from Article 14 of the Covenant, give the Court its name, the indefinite article being replaced elsewhere in the Statute by the definite article. The reference to the Permanent Court of Arbitration was clearly inspired by a somewhat similar reference in Article 1 of the *projet* annexed to the first *vœu* of the Second Peace Conference at The Hague in 1907.[18] The reference to "special Tribunals of Arbitration" serves the purpose of maintaining a harmony with paragraph 3 of Article 13 of the Covenant,[19] and it emphasizes States' freedom to create tribunals *ad hoc.*

§116. **Article 2.** *"The Permanent Court of International Justice shall be composed of a body of independent judges elected regardless of their nationality from amongst persons of high moral character,*

[14] The elaborate memorandum prepared by the Secretariat of the League of Nations was seldom referred to in the work of the Committee of Jurists. For the text, see Preparatory Documents, pp. 1–119.

[15] This and the succeeding sections of this chapter reproduce and deal with the drafting of the text of the original Statute which was annexed to the Protocol of Signature of December 16, 1920. For some of the articles in the original Statute, provision is made for new texts by the Revision Protocol of September 14, 1929. See Chapter 9, *infra.* The complete text of the Statute is reprinted, p. 581, *infra.*

[16] The expression "contesting parties" is used in the report of the Committee of Jurists. Minutes of the 1920 Committee of Jurists, p. 699.

[17] Documents, p. 114; Records of First Assembly, Committees, I, p. 335.

[18] A draft considered by the Second Peace Conference in 1907 employed the expression "alongside of [Fr., *à côté de*] the Permanent Court of Arbitration." *Actes et Documents,* II, p. 657.

[19] Throughout the drafting of the Statute, a tendency was manifest to emphasize the questionable distinction between adjudication and arbitration. On this distinction, see 1 Moore, International Adjudications, pp. xxxviff.; Brierly, Law of Nations, pp. 176ff.

*who possess the qualifications required in their respective countries
for appointment to the highest judicial offices, or are jurisconsults of
recognized competence in international law."*

This text emanated from the Committee of Jurists, and no changes
were made at later stages except in punctuation. It is based in
part on the *projet* of 1907 with reference to a court of arbitral justice.
The expression "a body of independent judges" occasioned little debate in the Committee of Jurists, which desired to make the judges, so
far as possible, independent of the Governments of which they were
nationals.[20] The lack of such independence had been one of the
factors which wrecked the Central American Court of Justice. The
requirement that the judges be elected "regardless of their nationality"
seems to have been due to a desire of the Committee of Jurists to depart from the plan for choosing judges contained in the Prize Court
Convention of 1907,[21] and a desire to make it clear that the Great
Powers were not to be entitled to special representation in the Court.
Proposals to the Assembly by the Colombian [22] and Cuban [23] delegations
that judgeships should be allotted to various continents received but
scant consideration.[24] The text opens the door to the election of nationals
of States which do not participate in maintaining the Court, though M.
de Lapradelle expressed the opinion to the Committee of Jurists that
"for the time being a judge from the United States should be excluded." [25]

The qualification of "high moral character" derives from the
Hague Conventions for Pacific Settlement, Article 23 (1899), 44
(1907), whence it was copied without enthusiasm into the Hague
projet of 1907 (Article 2); it is impossible to conceive that the electors would vote for men who lacked this qualification, and its stipulation in the Statute seems to serve little purpose. The alternative requirement that judges must "possess the qualifications required in
their respective countries for appointment to the highest judicial offices," or be "jurisconsults of recognized competence in international
law," was the subject of some debate in the Committee of Jurists, and
a similar proposal had been debated at the Hague Conference of 1907.

[20] Minutes of the 1920 Committee of Jurists, p. 121.
[21] *Id.*, pp. 120ff.
[22] Documents, p. 72; Records of First Assembly, Committees, I, p. 525.
[23] Documents, pp. 72, 246; Records of First Assembly, Committees, I, p. 525;
Plenary, p. 487.
[24] Documents, p. 126; Records of First Assembly, Committees, I, p. 354.
[25] Minutes of the 1920 Committee of Jurists, p. 222.

The Hague Conventions for Pacific Settlement merely required the selection of persons "of known competence in questions of international law." In Article 2 of the Hague *projet* of 1907 the requirement was that judges *"devront remplir les conditions requises dans leur pays respectifs pour l'admission dans la haute magistrature, ou être des jurisconsultes d'une compétence notoire en matière de droit international."* In his report to the 1907 Conference, Dr. James Brown Scott explained the second part of this alternative as follows: *"Les auteurs du projet ne pouvaient méconnaître, d'ailleurs, que les autorités les plus compétentes en matière internationale se rencontrent souvent dans nos écoles et dans nos universités."* [26] On the suggestion of Lord Phillimore and Mr. Root, the Committee of Jurists in 1920 agreed to adopt the requirement as stated in the Hague *projet*.[27] The drafting committee later proposed to drop this wording and to require the choice of persons "of well-known experience . . . who possess a recognised competence in international law"; M. de Lapradelle explained that this attempted "to reconcile the Continental and Anglo-American points of view, the former of which preferred to have as international judges jurisconsults who were not judges by profession, whereas the latter preferred national magistrates. The committee had wished to exclude national judges who had not specialised in international law." [28] This led Mr. Root and Lord Phillimore to point out "the necessity of allowing certain countries to choose their international judges from among persons holding high judicial office." [29] M. Altamira pointed out, however, that some "national judges rarely have the opportunity of dealing with international questions." [30] In the end, the Committee of Jurists' draft-scheme reproduced almost textually the provision of the Hague *projet* on this point, and no change was made during the later consideration of the Statute.[31]

§117. Article 3. *"The Court shall consist of fifteen members: eleven judges and four deputy-judges. The number of judges and deputy-judges may hereafter be increased by the Assembly, upon the*

---

[26] *Actes et Documents*, I, p. 359.
[27] Minutes of the 1920 Committee of Jurists, p. 298.
[28] *Id.*, p. 553.   [29] *Id.*, p. 611.   [30] *Id.*, p. 612.
[31] The Director of the International Labor Office suggested an amendment to Article 2 which would have required for judges of a "special labor section" of the Court that they be "known for their impartiality with regard to the different economic tendencies." He also suggested an amendment to Article 3 that a special section of the Court should include "judges specially elected from amongst persons of recognized competence in labor legislation and social questions." Documents, p. 76; Records of First Assembly, Committees, I, p. 559.

proposal of the Council of the League of Nations, to a total of fifteen judges and six deputy-judges."

The determination that the Court should consist of a relatively small number of members depended on two considerations. First, it was important to overcome the contention that each State should be represented in the Court, and this was possible, as the experience at the Hague Conference in 1907 had shown, only if a satisfactory plan for the elections could be agreed upon. Second, it was necessary to consider the proper number of judges to compose a working tribunal. The 1907 *projet* had left both questions open; but the Prize Court Convention of 1907 (Articles 10, 14) envisaged the appointment of a judge and a deputy-judge by each State, only fifteen of whom were to function at any time. In some of the proposals made in connection with the work of the Paris Peace Conference, it was assumed that a scheme of election could be agreed upon and it was suggested that the Court should have fifteen members.[32] In various drafts before the Committee of Jurists in 1920, similar proposals were made. In the Committee of Jurists, itself, the opening discussion revealed a general desire to find a method of election, and the possibility of allowing each State to appoint a judge was never seriously considered.

As to the size of the Court, at different times members of the Committee of Jurists stressed the necessity of a court large enough to admit of challenges and inevitable absences and to represent various systems of legal thought, as well as the necessity of a court small enough to enable the judges to work together effectively and to include only persons of eminence.[33] It was also foreseen that the number should be susceptible of increase as more States were admitted to membership in the League of Nations and as the court's jurisdiction was extended.[34] The Root-Phillimore plan suggested eleven judges and four supplementary judges;[35] M. Loder wished to have but nine judges,[36] M. Adatci thirteen judges, Lord Phillimore fifteen judges and additional deputy-judges, M. de Lapradelle eleven judges.[37] The only proposal greatly out of line with the Root-Phillimore plan was that of M. Ricci-Busatti, who favored a panel of fifteen or twenty judges from which tribunals should be formed *ad hoc*.[38] When the draft-scheme was adopted, the question was raised whether action by

---

[32] Minutes of the 1920 Committee of Jurists, p. 55.
[33] Minutes of the 1920 Committee of Jurists, pp. 168ff.   [34] *Id.*, pp. 181, 441.
[35] *Id.*, p. 298. *Cf.*, the scheme of Baron Descamps, *id.*, p. 373.
[36] *Id.*, p. 169.   [37] *Id.*, pp. 168, 169, 171.   [38] *Id.*, pp. 177, 183.

the Council and Assembly to increase the number would require unanimity, but no attempt was made to dictate the answer.[39] No change was made in the text of the article in the Committee's draft-scheme, though Italian and British proposals were placed before both the Council and Assembly to suppress the post of deputy-judge,[40] and an Italian proposal would have eliminated the restriction on the increase which might later be made.[41] A British proposal that the number of judges be decreased to nine was opposed, because as "the Great Powers would always be represented on the Court," other States could not so easily agree on the distribution of fewer places.[42]

§118. **Article 4, paragraph 1.** *"The members of the Court shall be elected by the Assembly and by the Council from a list of persons nominated by the national groups in the Court of Arbitration, in accordance with the following provisions."*

This paragraph, which emanated from the Committee of Jurists, was the basis of the success which attended the effort to establish the Court. The problem of election had baffled and defeated the Hague Conference in 1907. The approach made in dealing with it in 1920 was largely due to the conception of the Court as an organ of the League of Nations. The existence of the Assembly and Council of the League of Nations afforded a possible escape from the deadlock of 1907. The Assembly was organized on the principle of state equality which had been so emphasized in 1907; on the other hand, the Council was organized to take account, in the allocation of permanent seats, of the wider interests in international affairs possessed by those States which had insisted on permanent representation on any court which might be created. Until this balance had been struck, proposals for the election of a small number of judges, though actually put forward,[43] had received but scant consideration; with the advance which the creation of the Assembly and Council represented, however, it became clear that the conception of the equality of States and that of the hegemony of "Great Powers," were no longer irreconcilable. Yet the proposal made by the Committee of Jurists was evolved only through protracted discussion.

[39] Minutes of the 1920 Committee of Jurists, p. 554.
[40] Documents, pp. 28, 70; Records of First Assembly, Committees, I, pp. 496, 591.
[41] Documents, p. 28; Records of First Assembly, Committees, I, p. 497. Various other amendments were proposed. See Documents, pp. 43, 72, 76, 117.
[42] Documents, p. 117; Records of First Assembly, Committees, I, p. 340.
[43] See Mr. Choate's proposal at the Second Peace Conference at The Hague in 1907. *Actes et Documents*, II, p. 698.

The election of judges by votes of the States from a list of nominees of the several States was suggested by Switzerland early in 1919,[44] and a somewhat similar suggestion for election by a "Congress of States" was made by the German delegation at the Peace Conference.[45] The creation of a special electoral college composed of members of the Permanent Court of Arbitration to elect the judges from among persons nominated by the States was proposed in the Scandinavian project of 1919; [46] the Swedish committee continued to insist on this proposal after the Covenant of the League of Nations was established,[47] but the Danish and Norwegian Committees then proposed that the judges should be elected by the Assembly from among candidates nominated by the States,[48] a suggestion which had previously been made by the Austrian delegation at the Peace Conference.[49] Early in 1919, also, the Netherlands committee proposed elections by a permanent Administrative Council modelled on that of the Permanent Court of Arbitration,[50] the candidates being nominated partly by the bodies exercising the highest legal functions in each State and the law faculties of the universities, and partly by the governments. The Netherlands proposal is interesting in that it allowed for a greater voting power of certain States in the electoral body. The Secretariat of the League of Nations seems to have suggested that one body should nominate and another body should elect the judges.[51] The "Five-Power Plan" suggested that the judges should be elected by the Assembly from among candidates nominated by the States Members of the League of Nations.[52]

When the discussion was opened in the Committee of Jurists, the principle of equality of States was greatly emphasized on the one hand, and on the other hand Lord Phillimore urged that "the Court must have behind it material force," which would be possible "only if it includes representatives of the Great Powers." [53] A more useful approach was made by Mr. Root who drew upon an analogy in the history of the United States to suggest that it might be "possible that the solution of the problem would be found by articulating the new organization with the political organization of the League." "Would it be possible," he asked, "to vest the power of elec-

[44] Preparatory Documents, p. 257.   [45] Id., p. 125.   [46] Id., pp. 173–5.
[47] Id., pp. 237–9.   [48] Id., pp. 203, 229–231, respectively.
[49] Id., p. 131. See also the proposal of the Inter-Parliamentary Union in 1919, id., p. 335, and of the Union Juridique Internationale, id., p. 345.
[50] Id., pp. 279–81.   [51] Preparatory Documents, p. 89.   [52] Id., p. 303.
[53] Minutes of the 1920 Committee of Jurists, p. 106.

tion of judges both in the Assembly and in the Council?" [54]
Later, Mr. Root proposed "concurrent votes of the Assembly and the
Council." [55] To some members of the Committee who sought a
recognition of State equality, these suggestions seemed "premature." [56]
Baron Descamps proposed election by members of the Permanent
Court of Arbitration, a proposal which M. de Lapradelle observed
"tended to renew the historical connection which was broken by the
Covenant." [57] Lord Phillimore preferred direct action by Governments.
Gradually, support developed for the suggestions made by Mr. Root
in a memorandum providing for election by the Council and Assembly
from a list of names furnished by the members of the Permanent Court
of Arbitration, each national group proposing not less than two nor
more than four names.[58] M. de Lapradelle came to the conclusion
that since it was a question of creating "a new organism forming part
of the League of Nations, it is only right that the election should be
entrusted to the two chief organs of this League." [59] It was assumed
by certain members of the Committee that their own States would
never be willing to submit a case to a court on which they were not
represented; this raised the question of participation by judges who
were nationals of parties before the Court, as well as the question of
the size of the Court. These and other matters had to be discussed
generally before any conclusion on the method of election could be
reached, and as this discussion progressed it became apparent that
the new Court would be related in many ways to the Council and
Assembly of the League of Nations. Issue was not joined until the
sixteenth meeting of the Committee of Jurists, by which time the
question was whether the election should be by the Assembly and the
Council, or by the Assembly alone. Mr. Root insisted that the former
plan had the advantage of "removing any possibility of unfairness by
giving the small nations the veto on everything which took place in
the Council, and by giving the large nations a veto on all the decisions taken by the Assembly." [60] Baron Descamps could see this
only as an "organized antagonism," but the Committee as a whole
found it a possible solution. In the report of the Committee, it was said

[54] Minutes of the 1920 Committee of Jurists, p. 109. See also Scott, Project of a
Permanent Court, pp. 32ff.   [55] Minutes of the 1920 Committee of Jurists, p. 121.
[56] Id., pp. 123-4.   [57] Minutes of the 1920 Committee of Jurists, p. 148.
[58] Id., p. 166. An excellent account of the debate on this point is given in Scott,
Project for a Permanent Court, pp. 29-48.
[59] Minutes of the 1920 Committee of Jurists, p. 150.
[60] Id., p. 389.

that the "only possible system for the formation of the Court was that of equal and simultaneous election by the Council and the Assembly." [61] Yet this conclusion had been reached by the Committee of Jurists only after a protracted discussion.

The device of having nominations made by members of the Permanent Court of Arbitration was simultaneously suggested by M. Loder [62] and by Mr. Root.[63] It was offered by M. Loder as a means of preventing political intrigues in the elections, because of the "moral weakness of all political bodies." More important, however, was the fact that the suggestion offered a link with the Permanent Court of Arbitration at a time when it was being stoutly insisted that the elections should be conducted by the members of that institution. Other reasons which have been assigned seem to be apocryphal rationalizations.[64]

When the plan proposed by the Committee of Jurists came before the Council, M. Bourgeois said that it gave satisfaction to the cherished principle of equality, "to exactly the same degree as in the Covenant, and he thought that "by its very existence," the League had made it possible to solve the difficulty.[65] Later, he insisted that "the system presented by the Committee of Jurists" be "maintained in its entirety." [66] Certain proposals were made, however, to amend the provision for nomination of candidates by the "national groups of the Permanent Court of Arbitration"; a Norwegian committee attacked these provisions on the ground that the candidates of various countries might be members of the Permanent Court of Arbitration, and that the national groups of such members had been "organised for another object"; it therefore suggested direct nominations by Governments.[67] No change of substance was made by the First Assembly.

The expression "national groups in the Permanent Court of Arbitration" is not to be found in the Hague Conventions setting up the Permanent Court of Arbitration.

§119. Article 4, paragraph 2. *"In the case of Members of the League of Nations not represented in the Permanent Court of Arbitration, the lists of candidates shall be drawn up by national groups appointed for this purpose by their Governments under the same con-*

---

[61] *Id.*, p. 700.   [62] *Id.*, pp. 147, 160.   [63] *Id.*, pp. 150, 166.
[64] Such reasons are stated in Scott, Project for a Permanent Court, p. 55.
[65] Documents, p. 24; Records of First Assembly, Committees, I, p. 466.
[66] Documents, p. 49; Records of First Assembly, Committees, I, p. 477.
[67] Documents, p. 31; Records of First Assembly, Committees, I, p. 501.

ditions as those prescribed for members of the Permanent Court of Arbitration by Article 44 of the Convention of The Hague of 1907 for the pacific settlement of international disputes."

The draft-scheme of the Committee of Jurists took no account of the fact that some of the Members of the League of Nations, entitled to vote in the Assembly in the election of judges, would be debarred from participation in the nomination of candidates if such nomination was entrusted only to members of the Permanent Court of Arbitration; this would be true, particularly, of the British Dominions and of certain States to which accession to the Hague Conventions was not open as of right.[68] It was to take account of this fact that the British delegation in the First Assembly proposed an addition to allow Governments of Members of the League having no "national groups" in the Court of Arbitration to make nominations.[69] The sub-committee of the Third Committee adopted the more ingenious solution embodied in the text of this paragraph.[70]

§120. **Article 5, paragraph 1.** *"At least three months before the date of the election, the Secretary-General of the League of Nations shall address a written request to the members of the Court of Arbitration belonging to the States mentioned in the Annex to the Covenant or to the States which join the League subsequently, and to the persons appointed under paragraph 2 of Article 4, inviting them to undertake, within a given time, by national groups, the nomination of persons in a position to accept the duties of a member of the Court."*

This text was largely drafted by the Committee of Jurists. As it was first proposed in the Root-Phillimore plan,[71] the request was to be made to all members of the Permanent Court of Arbitration, and only to them. The Committee finally adopted a limitation which confined nominations to those members appointed by States mentioned in the Annex to the Covenant or by States which subsequently joined the League of Nations.[72] The sub-committee of the Third Committee of the Assembly added the provision for requests to be made to persons appointed under the amended text of Article 4, paragraph 2.[73]

[68] Under Article 60 (1899), 94 (1907) of the Hague Conventions for pacific settlement, adhesion is subject to the agreement of the Contracting Powers. See §3, *supra.*
[69] Documents, p. 70; Records of First Assembly, Committees, I, p. 591.
[70] Documents, p. 117; Records of First Assembly, Committees, I, pp. 338–339.
[71] Minutes of the 1920 Committee of Jurists, p. 299.
[72] *Id.,* p. 674.
[73] Documents, p. 120; Records of First Assembly, Committees, I, p. 343.

At the suggestion of M. Negulesco (Rumania), the words "within a given time" were added by the Third Committee.[74]

§121. **Article 5, paragraph 2.** *"No group may nominate more than four persons, not more than two of whom shall be of their own nationality. In no case must the number of candidates nominated be more than double the number of seats to be filled."*

The draft-scheme of the Committee of Jurists proposed the following text: "No group may nominate more than two persons; the nominees may be of any nationality." At one time, however, the Committee had decided that a maximum of six nominations might be made by any group. Mr. Root expressed the hope that "so many concordant expressions of opinion would be obtained from the various countries that the election would be thereby virtually decided." [75] Some of the members of the Committee of Jurists had thought it desirable that members of the Permanent Court of Arbitration should meet for a common consideration of their nominations. Numerous other questions were raised in the Committee of Jurists; *e.g.*, whether members of the Permanent Court of Arbitration could nominate themselves, and whether governments should have any control of their nominations. The Third Committee of the Assembly adopted a proposal of M. La Fontaine (Belgium) to increase the number of possible nominees to four,[76] and to divide the number between nationals and non-nationals,[77] thus returning to a suggestion previously made to the Committee of Jurists by Mr. Root.[78] The increase in the number of nominees was made "to give the different groups a larger opportunity to propose candidates of universally known competence but of a nationality other than that of the nominating group." [79] The second sentence of the paragraph was also added by the Third Committee, with little discussion, to take care of the special situation which may exist in by-elections.[80]

§122. **Article 6.** *"Before making these nominations, each national group is recommended to consult its Highest Court of Justice, its Legal Faculties and Schools of Law, and its National Academies and*

[74] Documents, p. 100; Records of First Assembly, Committees, I, p. 303.
[75] Minutes of the 1920 Committee of Jurists, p. 409.
[76] Norwegian and Swedish proposals to increase the number to six were not adopted. Documents, pp. 31, 36; Records of First Assembly, Committees, I, pp. 503, 508.
[77] Documents, p. 101; Records of First Assembly, Committees, I, p. 304.
[78] Minutes of the 1920 Committee of Jurists, pp. 166, 408. This suggestion seems to have originated in the Five-Power Plan, Article 6.
[79] Documents, p. 172; Records of First Assembly, Committees, I, p. 568.
[80] Documents, p. 107; Records of First Assembly, Committees, I, p. 405.

national sections of International Academies devoted to the study of Law."

This text came from the draft-scheme of the Committee of Jurists. It was based on suggestions found in the "Five-Power Plan" and presented by M. Altamira; [81] they were opposed by M. Ricci-Busatti, who preferred to leave the nominating groups "free to consult whomsoever they might wish." [82] In its report, the Committee of Jurists stated that "only a moral obligation to take this advice exists, there is no legal obligation; the nomination is not rendered void if one of these bodies is not consulted; and even if they are all consulted there is no definite obligation to choose the name of the person who has received most support from them." [83] In the sub-committee of the Third Committee of the Assembly, the British and Italian representatives proposed to suppress this provision, but an even vote on the proposal resulted in the maintenance of the text.[84]

§123. **Article 7.** *"The Secretary-General of the League of Nations shall prepare a list in alphabetical order of all the persons thus nominated. Save as provided in Article 12, paragraph 2, these shall be the only persons eligible for appointment.*

"The Secretary-General shall submit this list to the Assembly and to the Council."

This text emanated from the Committee of Jurists, except that the arrangement was changed by the Third Committee of the Assembly. The "Five-Power Plan" had suggested that the list should indicate the number of nominations of each candidate, without disclosing who had made the nominations; but this idea was not approved by the Committee of Jurists which desired to leave the point to the determination of the Secretary-General himself.[85] The necessity of a choice from the list, from which only the joint conference may depart under Article 12, was designed to avoid any possibility that the majority of judges might be elected from outside the list of candidates submitted to the Council and the Assembly. The adoption of the text occasioned no debate in the Council or in the Assembly.

§124. **Article 8.** *"The Assembly and the Council shall proceed independently of one another to elect, firstly the judges, then the deputy-judges."*

[81] Minutes of the 1920 Committee of Jurists, pp. 158, 436.
[82] *Id.*, p. 436.   [83] *Id.*, p. 707.
[84] Documents, p. 118; Records of First Assembly, Committees, I, p. 341.
[85] Minutes of the 1920 Committee of Jurists, p. 432.

The Committee of Jurists had proposed the following text for this article: "The Assembly and the Council shall proceed to elect by independent voting first the judges and then the deputy-judges." It was first suggested to the Committee that the Assembly and Council should act "separately"; [86] but "independent" voting was accepted as the equivalent of "separate" voting.[87] Questions were raised as to the simultaneous or successive action by the Assembly and by the Council, but no proposal was made by the Committee of Jurists in either sense. In the sub-committee of the Third Committee, the Italian representative proposed the addition of the word "simultaneously," to insure that one electoral body "should not influence the other's decision," but little support was given to the proposal.[88] The successive voting on judges and deputy-judges was accepted without much debate in the Committee of Jurists.[89]

§125. **Article 9.** *"At every election, the electors shall bear in mind that not only should all the persons appointed as members of the Court possess the qualifications required, but the whole body also should represent the main forms of civilization and the principal legal systems of the world."*

This text was drafted by the Committee of Jurists, and no change was made by the Assembly except for a slight redrafting of the French version. M. Adatci suggested to the Committee of Jurists that "all different kinds of civilisation must be taken into account, among them the civilisation of the Far East, of which Japan was perhaps the principal representative." [90] Baron Descamps suggested a reference to "principal legal systems," [91] in line with the provision in Article 1 of the Hague *projet* of 1907,[92] and he supported the suggestion as an assurance to the "Great Powers" of their having nationals in the Court.[93] Some opposition was manifested on the ground that as the Court was to apply international law, "there was no need to have national systems of law represented." [94] In its report,[95] the Committee of Jurists

---

[86] In the Root-Phillimore plan, *id.,* p. 298.

[87] *Id.,* p. 396.

[88] Documents, p. 118; Records of First Assembly, Committees, I, p. 341.

[89] Minutes of the 1920 Committee of Jurists, p. 401.

[90] Minutes of the 1920 Committee of Jurists, p. 136.

[91] *Id.,* pp. 111, 356.

[92] In his instructions to the American delegates to the 1907 Hague Conference, Secretary of State Root said that the "judges should be so selected from the different countries that the different systems of law and the principal languages shall be fairly represented." Quoted in *Id.,* p. 403.

[93] *Id.,* pp. 362, 371.   [94] *Id.,* pp. 363, 365.   [95] *Id.,* p. 710.

stated that it did not intend to refer "to the various systems of international law"; the intention was to ensure that "no matter what points of national law may be involved in an international suit, all shall be equally comprehended." The reference to "main forms of civilization" was said to be an essential condition "if the Permanent Court of International Justice is to be a real World Court for the Society of all Nations." In the Third Committee of the Assembly, the Colombian delegation desired to provide also for "the geographical representation of the different Continents," but a proposal in this sense was rejected.[96] In the general election of judges in 1921, seven of the eleven successful candidates were Europeans; in 1930, only nine of the fifteen successful candidates were Europeans.

§126. **Article 10, paragraph 1.** *"Those candidates who obtain an absolute majority of votes in the Assembly and in the Council shall be considered as elected."*

This paragraph was drafted by the Committee of Jurists. Before it was finally determined that the election should be by the Assembly and the Council, some difficulties were encountered as to possible procedure by the two bodies. It was pointed out, for instance, that representatives of some States might vote in both bodies, and to meet this inequality, it was suggested that "delegates of those States whose representatives had already voted on the Council" might be excluded from voting in the Assembly.[97] At various times, also, the suggestion was made that a particular majority vote, *e.g.*, three-fourths, should be required in the Assembly; at no time does it seem to have been proposed that a simple majority should be sufficient. The Root-Phillimore plan suggested requiring "the votes of a majority of those present and voting in each body." [98] In accepting this principle, the members of the Committee do not seem to have thought of the possible out-voting of the "Great Powers" in the Council as a result of the enlargement of the Council.[99] When the matter arose in the sub-committee of the Third Committee of the Assembly, M. Adatci (Japan) asked whether

---

[96] Documents, pp. 72, 101; Records of First Assembly, Committees, I, pp. 304, 525.
[97] Minutes of the 1920 Committee of Jurists, p. 387.
[98] *Id.*, p. 298.
[99] In 1920 the Council of the League of Nations consisted of the representatives of eight States, four of which were so-called Great Powers entitled to permanent representation; in 1922, the number of States non-permanently represented was increased to six, in 1926 to nine, and in 1933 to ten. The Council may now consist of fifteen members, five of whom would represent States entitled to permanent representation; Japan and Germany have not been represented, however, since the announcements of their intentions to withdraw from the League of Nations.

a "majority of the members present" was provided for, and "it was pointed out that this question had already been decided in the affirmative by the Covenant of the League."[100]

§127. Article 10, paragraph 2. *"In the event of more than one national of the same Member of the League being elected by the votes of both the Assembly and the Council, the eldest of these only shall be considered as elected."*

The text proposed by the Committee of Jurists was somewhat different: "in the event of more than one candidate of the same nationality being elected." The Committee of Jurists stated in its report that "the Court can never include more than one judge of the same nationality," this rule being thought necessary "to ensure the representation of the main forms of civilization and the principal legal systems" and "to enable as many States as possible to have a share in the composition of the Court."[1] In the sub-committee of the Third Committee of the Assembly, the Canadian delegation raised the question of the meaning of "nationality," and desired to amend the provision as the proposed text "might give rise to the false interpretation that a Canadian could not sit in the Court at the same time as a judge of the United Kingdom."[2] The sub-committee therefore formulated the text which was adopted.[3] A suggestion to insert in the paragraph a general definition of nationality for the purposes of the Statute was not approved.[4] No reason was advanced for preferring the eldest of the persons voted for, and this seems to have been adopted as "an artificial means for attaining a result."[5] The French and English versions of this Article have quite different meanings; the English term "national" is not the exact equivalent of the French term *ressortissant.*

§128. Article 11. *"If, after the first meeting held for the purpose of the election, one or more seats remain to be filled, a second and, if necessary, a third meeting shall take place."*

This text was drafted by the Committee of Jurists. It served prin-

---

[100] Documents, p. 119; Records of First Assembly, Committees, I, p. 342.

[1] Minutes of the 1920 Committee of Jurists, p. 713. No such rule is to be found in the Statute, however. See §257, *infra.*

[2] Documents, pp. 118, 120; Records of First Assembly, Committees, I, pp. 342, 344. For a discussion of a related problem, see Minutes of the 1929 Committee of Jurists, pp. 70–71, 84–87; §257, *infra.*

[3] The text has the curious result of making it possible for "more than one national" of a State which is not a Member of the League of Nations to be elected.

[4] Documents, p. 121; Records of First Assembly, Committees, I, p. 344.

[5] Minutes of the 1920 Committee of Jurists, p. 557.

cipally to lay a basis for the application of Article 12, and it was not debated in the Third Committee of the Assembly. It does not exclude the possibility of further meetings before a joint conference is set up.

§129. **Article 12, paragraph 1.** *"If, after the third meeting, one or more seats still remain unfilled, a joint conference consisting of six members, three appointed by the Assembly and three by the Council, may be formed, at any time, at the request of either the Assembly or the Council, for the purpose of choosing one name for each seat still vacant, to submit to the Assembly and the Council for their respective acceptance."*

Except for a slight change, this text emanated from the Committee of Jurists. The idea of a "joint conference" to reconcile divergent views of the Assembly and the Council first appeared in the discussions of the Committee of Jurists as a proposal for a "conciliation committee," [6] later called a "committee of mediation." [7] The suggestion seems to have been made by Mr. Root, on analogy to the conference committees set up from time to time to reconcile the divergent views of the two Houses of the Congress of the United States.[8] It was proposed to the Committee of Jurists that the joint conference should have final power of selection,[9] but Lord Phillimore insisted that "the formal appointment should always be left to the two bodies," and this view prevailed.[10] The duty of choosing "one name for each seat still vacant" was laid down, to prevent the joint conference from listing a number of persons and thus requiring a later choice by the Assembly and the Council.[11] M. Adatci, a member of the Committee of Jurists, stated to the Second Assembly of the League of Nations in 1921 that "when we drew up the Statute" of the Court, "we were all of opinion that necessity would never arise to have recourse to Article 12." [12]

§130. **Article 12, paragraph 2.** *"If the Conference is unanimously agreed upon any person who fulfils the required conditions, he may be included in its list, even though he was not included in the list of nominations referred to in Articles 4 and 5."*

This paragraph embodies in substance a proposal made by the Committee of Jurists, which adopted it only after prolonged debate. It was thought that unless the joint conference was given complete freedom, it might fail to achieve results. On the other hand, it was

---

[6] Minutes of the 1920 Committee of Jurists, p. 127. [7] *Id.*, p. 399.
[8] *Id.*, p. 433. See also Scott, Project of a Permanent Court, p. 67.
[9] Minutes of the 1920 Committee of Jurists, p. 381. [10] *Id.*, p. 399.
[11] *Id.*, p. 557. [12] Records of Second Assembly, Plenary, p. 256.

feared that too many of the judges might be chosen in this way, without regard to the limitations set for ordinary nominations; Mr. Root replied: "Such a high standard of competence and moral authority would be established by laying down that the lists should be drawn up by the members of the Permanent Court of Arbitration, that it would be inconceivable that the person selected from outside this list, would not conform to the standard." [13] The report of the Committee of Jurists indicates various situations in which a departure from the list of nominees might be desirable; and the requirement of unanimity in the joint conference is explained as a "guarantee . . . to prevent an arbitrary choice made under the political influences of two such essentially political bodies as the Assembly and the Council." [14]

§131. Article 12, paragraphs 3 and 4. *"If the joint conference is satisfied that it will not be successful in procuring an election, those members of the Court who have already been appointed shall, within a period to be fixed by the Council, proceed to fill the vacant seats by selection from amongst those candidates who have obtained votes either in the Assembly or in the Council.*

"In the event of an equality of votes amongst the judges, the eldest judge shall have a casting vote."

These paragraphs with slight modifications were drafted by the Committee of Jurists. The Root-Phillimore plan proposed that if differences should prove to be "ultimately irreconcilable," the choice should "devolve upon the judges who have already been agreed upon." [15] At one time it was proposed that the joint conference should have three days for reaching agreement.[16] In the sub-committee of the Third Committee of the Assembly, the words "if the joint conference is not successful in procuring an election" were replaced by the words "if the joint conference is satisfied that it will not be successful in procuring an election"; the object of this amendment, which originated in a proposal of the British delegation, was to enable the joint conference to make several attempts to reach an agreement.[17] The text seems to indicate that after a failure of a joint conference (Fr., *commission médiatrice*) the voting is not to be resumed in the Assembly and the Council.

---

[13] Minutes of the 1920 Committee of Jurists, p. 433.   [14] *Id.*, pp. 712–3.
[15] Minutes of the 1920 Committee of Jurists, p. 298.   [16] *Id.*, p. 563.
[17] Documents, p. 122; Records of First Assembly, Committees, I, pp. 345–346.

§132. **Article 13, paragraphs 1 and 2.** *"The members of the Court shall be elected for nine years.*

"They may be re-elected."

This text emanated from the Committee of Jurists. Several of the preliminary plans submitted to the Committee had suggested a term of nine years, though others suggested six years, twelve years and life tenure; [18] ten years was also proposed by members of the Committee. The nine-year term was selected as a convenient compromise.[19] The Committee pointed out in its report that this term assured a "continuity of jurisprudence," and made possible an elimination of judges who had forfeited confidence.[20] Apparently little consideration was given by the Committee of Jurists to the simultaneous expiration of the terms of all of the judges. A system which would call for the election of a certain number of judges at intervals of several years might have prevented the possibility of a court composed wholly of new judges; but it was doubtless thought to be undesirable because judges may be reëlected, because the number eleven finally decided upon does not evenly divide, and because an election of the larger number of judges presents fewer difficulties than an election of a smaller number. As the Committee of Jurists pointed out in its report, "the free play offered to States at the time of election, by a general redistribution of seats every nine years, is very desirable."

§133. **Article 13, paragraph 3.** *"They shall continue to discharge their duties until their places have been filled. Though replaced, they shall finish any cases which they may have begun."*

This text emanated from the Committee of Jurists. The limit placed on the continuance of the term of office is somewhat indefinite, and no precise date was fixed on which newly elected judges should assume office; this *lacuna* in the Statute had to be filled by the rules of court. The first sentence in this paragraph was partly due to uncertainty as to the meetings of the Assembly and the Council of the League of Nations; the Covenant does not prescribe annual meetings of the Assembly, and it was thought that the two electoral bodies might be unable to hold an election of judges' successors in time to prevent a hiatus. The second sentence in the paragraph seems to have been borrowed from Article 9 of the "Five-Power Plan" drawn up at The Hague in 1920. M. de Lapradelle objected to it on the ground

---

[18] Minutes of the 1920 Committee of Jurists, p. 57.
[19] For the discussions, see *id.*, pp. 194–6, 441–2. Members of the Permanent Court of Arbitration are appointed for six years; but the Hague *projet* of 1907 suggested a twelve-year term for judges in a court of arbitral justice.   [20] *Id.*, p. 714.

that if a judge failed of reëlection, it would be harmful to the Court to allow him to continue in function after he had "lost the confidence of the League of Nations," but the objection was overruled by the Committee.[21] No change was made in this paragraph either in the Council or the Assembly.

§134. **Article 14.** *"Vacancies which may occur shall be filled by the same method as that laid down for the first election. A member of the Court elected to replace a member whose period of appointment had not expired will hold the appointment for the remainder of his predecessor's term."*

This text emanated from the Committee of Jurists. The Root-Phillimore plan proposed that judges elected to fill vacancies should serve for nine years,[22] following in this respect the provision in Article 3 of the Hague *projet* of 1907. Baron Descamps thought "it would undermine the whole system of election if each judge elected at a by-election was to be appointed for nine years," and he expressed the opinion that by-elections would not always be necessary because a senior deputy-judge would fill a vacancy;[23] his views met determined opposition, mainly on the ground that they would tend to destroy the representative character of the Court.[24] Their rejection did not make agreement possible, however, and for some time the members of the Committee were not agreed as to the term for which vacancies should be filled.[25] In the sub-committee of the Third Committee of the Assembly, the British representative proposed to omit the second sentence of this article, and to avoid a break in the continuity of the Court by allowing by-elections for the period of nine years;[26] this was supported on the ground that a judge elected for a short unexpired term would be in a "precarious position." As the votes in the sub-committee were even, the amendment was rejected. In the Third Committee, itself, the proposal to suppress the second sentence was renewed and defeated.[27]

§135. **Article 15.** *"Deputy-judges shall be called upon to sit in the order laid down in a list.*

"This list shall be prepared by the Court and shall have regard firstly to priority of election and secondly to age."

In substance this article originated with the Committee of Jurists,

[21] Minutes of the 1920 Committee of Jurists, pp. 451–2.
[22] Minutes of the 1920 Committee of Jurists, p. 300.
[23] *Id.*, p. 465.   [24] *Id.*, pp. 467ff.   [25] *Id.*, p. 575.
[26] Documents, p. 122; Records of First Assembly, Committees, I, p. 348.
[27] Documents, p. 101; Records of First Assembly, Committees, I, p. 305.

though the Hague *projet* of 1907 had also envisaged the appointment of deputy-judges. Baron Descamps first proposed six *suppléants,* in addition to nine judges,[28] following a suggestion in several of the preliminary drafts; [29] and he seems to have conceived of them as necessary for filling vacancies among the judges.[30] While the plan met with some opposition, it was useful in fixing a relatively small number of judges and in making certain at the same time that the Court would not be crippled from a lack of personnel. M. de Lapradelle explained the purposes of deputy-judges to be: (1) the practical purpose of filling vacancies, and (2) the political purpose of satisfying countries who had no nationals among the judges; [31] it is not clear that this statement was approved by the Committee, however. M. de Lapradelle also insisted upon having deputy-judges "in order to imbue future judges with the spirit which must pervade the Court," and to provide "young judges who can from time to time do duty on the Court and keep in constant touch with it." [32] At one time it was proposed that the order in the list should also depend on the number of votes received in the election.[33] In the Assembly the substance of the Committee's text was approved without debate.

§136. **Article 16.** *"The ordinary members* [Fr., *les membres] of the Court may not exercise any political or administrative function. This provision does not apply to the deputy-judges except when performing their duties on the Court.*

"Any doubt on this point is settled by the decision of the Court."

The Committee of Jurists had proposed a somewhat different text of the first paragraph: "The exercise of any function which belongs to the political direction, national or international, of States, by members of the Court during their terms of office, is declared incompatible with their judicial duties." Preliminary plans before the Committee contained various proposals on this subject.[34] Baron Descamps insisted upon a statement as to incompatibilities in lieu of a provision for challenges.[35] Lord Phillimore saw it as an "advantage for an international judge to belong at the same time to the Bench of his own country," and he did not consider participation in the judicial work of the House of Lords in Great Britain as a political function.[36] M. Adatci thought that judges should "resign their national occupa-

---

[28] Minutes of the 1920 Committee of Jurists, p. 143.
[29] *Id.,* pp. 54–56.
[30] *Id.,* p. 195.
[31] *Id.,* p. 457.
[32] *Id.,* p. 400.
[33] *Id.,* pp. 561, 565.
[34] Minutes of the 1920 Committee of Jurists, p. 67.
[35] *Id.,* p. 173.
[36] *Id.,* p. 191.

tions in order to internationalize themselves," or as he preferred to put it "to deify themselves." [37] Mr. Root desired to prevent a judgeship "from being considered as an incident in a political career." [38] It was early agreed in the Committee that the duties of a professor or a magistrate were not incompatible with those of a judge.[39] Some difference of opinion arose as to the extent to which the system of incompatibilities should apply to deputy-judges, and as to the consequence of a judge's engaging in an incompatible activity; [40] on this latter point, it was proposed to the Committee that such engaging should be considered a resignation.[41] The report of the Committee recognized that men of the caliber desired would be needed in their own countries for positions which they could not readily leave, and it stated that "a great judge or a great professor . . . must be allowed to continue" his functions as such even after his election, and that "an eminent member of Parliament may retain his legislative function." [42] It was made clear that the incompatibility proposed applied to "international political duties" in connection with the work of the League of Nations, but not to membership in the Permanent Court of Arbitration.

In the sub-committee of the Third Committee of the Assembly,[43] dissatisfaction with the Committee's text was expressed. M. Huber (Switzerland) anticipating that the Court would have "little to do," did not wish to be too strict; M. Fromageot (France) did not share this premise, and desired to "disengage the judge from his previous occupations." The sub-committee redrafted the article, and stated in its report that in England the exercise of the functions of judge in the House of Lords was not to be considered an incompatibility.[44] The article assumed its final form in the Third Committee, which added the second sentence to avoid an "excessive measure" as to the deputy-judges.[45]

§137. **Article 17, paragraph 1.** *"No member of the Court can act as agent, counsel or advocate in any case of an international nature. This provision only applies to the deputy-judges as regards cases in which they are called upon to exercise their functions on the Court."*

This paragraph states a disability, as distinguished from an incom-

---

[37] *Id.*, p. 187.   [38] *Id.*, p. 462.   [39] *Id.*, p. 192.
[40] Minutes of the 1920 Committee of Jurists, p. 573.   [41] *Id.*, p. 462.
[42] *Id.*, pp. 715-6.
[43] Documents, pp. 123-5; Records of First Assembly, Committees, I, pp. 349-352.
[44] Documents, pp. 208, 528.
[45] Documents, pp. 102, 172; Records of First Assembly, Committees, I, pp. 305, 573.

patibility or a disqualification. The first sentence was drafted by the Committee of Jurists, and the second sentence was added by the Third Committee of the Assembly. Experience in the early years of the Permanent Court of Arbitration [46] had led to the inclusion in Article 62 of the 1907 Convention for Pacific Settlement of the following:

> The members of the Permanent Court may not act as agents, counsel or advocates except on behalf of the Power which appointed them members of the Court.

Article 7 of the Hague *projet* of 1907 provided (paragraph 2):

> A judge cannot act as agent or advocate before the Court of Arbitral Justice or the Permanent Court of Arbitration, before a special tribunal of arbitration or a commission of inquiry, nor act for one of the parties in any capacity whatsoever so long as his appointment lasts.

These texts were taken as the basis of its draft by the Committee of Jurists,[47] which desired to make no distinction in this respect between judges and deputy-judges. No extended consideration was given to the point in the Third Committee of the Assembly, beyond the addition of the second sentence.[48]

§138.   Article 17, paragraphs 2 and 3. *"No member may participate in the decision of any case in which he has previously taken an active part, as agent, counsel or advocate for one of the contesting parties, or as a member of a national or international Court, or of a commission of enquiry, or in any other capacity.*

"Any doubt on this point is settled by the decision of the Court."

These texts emanated from the Committee of Jurists. Paragraph 2 is based [49] on the first paragraph of Article 7 of the Hague *projet* which was as follows:

> A judge may not exercise his judicial functions in any case in which he has, in any way whatever, taken part in the decision of a national tribunal, of a tribunal of arbitration, or of a commission of inquiry, or has appeared in the suit as counsel or advocate for one of the parties.

Baron Descamps would have gone further to say that a judge may not participate in a case in which he, or a member of his family or a connection up to and including the third degree has a "direct personal in-

---

[46] See §7, *supra*.   [47] Minutes of the 1920 Committee of Jurists, pp. 461, 494.
[48] Documents, pp. 102, 107; Records of First Assembly, Committees, I, pp. 305, 312.
[49] Minutes of the 1920 Committee of Jurists, p. 461.

terest." [50] There was little discussion of the two paragraphs, either in the Committee of Jurists or in the Third Committee of the Assembly.

§139. **Article 18.** *"A member of the Court cannot be dismissed unless, in the unanimous opinion of the other members, he has ceased to fulfil the required conditions.*

"Formal notification thereof shall be made to the Secretary-General of the League of Nations, by the Registrar.

"This notification makes the place vacant."

Except for a rephrasing of the second paragraph, this text emanated from the Committee of Jurists. The Root-Phillimore draft stated the matter positively, and made dismissal depend upon a determination of incapacity or unfitness for the performance of judicial functions.[51] M. de Lapradelle wished to suppress any such article, as the colleagues of an incompetent judge would never have the moral courage to vote for his exclusion, and the danger in his retention would not be great.[52] Lord Phillimore wished to retain such a provision to operate *in terrorem*, though he thought it probable that no action would ever be taken under it.[53] In a proposal submitted to the Council at Brussels, the Italian Council deemed the requirement of unanimity to be too strict, and suggested a four-fifths vote instead.[54] The sub-committee of the Third Committee of the Assembly introduced into the article only the requirement that the notification to the Secretary-General of the League of Nations should be by the Registrar.[55]

Various preliminary drafts had suggested an age limit for the judges, but the suggestion was not seriously considered by the agencies engaged in the drafting of the Statute.

§140. **Article 19.** *"The members of the Court, when engaged on the business of the Court, shall enjoy diplomatic privileges and immunities."*

The Committee of Jurists had proposed for this article:

The members of the Court when outside their own country, shall enjoy the privileges and immunities of diplomatic representatives.

Somewhat similar provisions had been included in Articles 24 (1899), 46 (1907) of the Hague Conventions for Pacific Settlement, in the Hague *projet* of 1907 (Article 5), and in the Convention of 1907 on

[50] Minutes of the 1920 Committee of Jurists, p. 376.   [51] *Id.*, pp. 299–300.
[52] *Id.*, p. 453.   [53] *Id.*, p. 453.
[54] Documents, p. 28; Records of First Assembly, Committees, I, p. 497.
[55] Documents, pp. 70, 127; Records of First Assembly, Committees, I, pp. 356, 591.

the Central American Court of Justice (Article 10). It seems to have been agreed in the Committee of Jurists that "judges should enjoy diplomatic privileges under the same conditions as diplomats," *i.e.*, "not only during their residence in Holland, but also in countries through which they would have to travel on their way to and from their duties." [56] In the sub-committee of the Third Committee of the Assembly, reference was made to Article 7 of the Covenant of the League of Nations, on the basis of which the British representative proposed to drop the restriction contained in the words "outside their own country." The revision of the text was voted by the sub-committee to bring it into accord with Article 7 of the Covenant, but it was agreed that "the question of the situation of judges in their own countries should not be prejudiced by the solution adopted." [57]

§141. Article 20. *"Every member of the Court shall, before taking up his duties, make a solemn declaration in open Court that he will exercise his powers impartially and conscientiously."*

This article was drafted by the Committee of Jurists. The Hague *projet* of 1907 provided (Article 5):

> Before taking their seat, the judges and deputy-judges must, before the Administrative Council, swear or make a solemn affirmation to exercise their functions impartially and conscientiously.

The Root-Phillimore plan had suggested: [58]

> Every judge or supplementary judge shall, at the first sitting at which he is to be present, solemnly declare that he will exercise his functions in accordance with international law.

The Committee of Jurists took Article 5 of the Hague *projet* as the basis of its proposal.[59] M. de Lapradelle referred to the oath as not denationalizing but super-nationalizing the judges.[60] This article was not discussed in the Council or in the Assembly.

§142. Article 21. *"The Court shall elect its President and Vice-President for three years; they may be re-elected.*

"It shall appoint its Registrar.

"The duties of Registrar of the Court shall not be deemed incom-

---

[56] Minutes of the 1920 Committee of Jurists, p. 479.
[57] Documents, pp. 128, 208; Records of First Assembly, Committees, I, pp. 356, 529.
[58] Minutes of the 1920 Committee of Jurists, p. 326.
[59] *Id.*, p. 478.   [60] *Id.*, p. 534.

patible with those of Secretary-General of the Permanent Court of Arbitration."

This text was drafted by the Committee of Jurists, though it has some points in common with the Hague *projet* of 1907. Lord Phillimore thought that "it would be dangerous to make the Presidency of the Court too important a post," and that the President should rather be *primus inter pares*. He proposed a term of office of three years; and he said that "if the president were made eligible for reëlection, it was almost certain that a good president would keep his appointment for 9 years." [61] An issue was raised in the Committee as to the participation of deputy-judges in the elections by the Court; and a proposal to allow their participation was rejected. [62] The provisions concerning the Registrar occasioned little debate in the Committee, and considering what the Registry of the Court has now become, the importance of the post was unduly minimized. M. Hagerup desired that the Registrar should be called Secretary-General. Several members of the Committee thought that one person should serve both the new Court and the Permanent Court of Arbitration, [63] to avoid useless expenditure and to establish a close connection between the two institutions. [64] No changes in the Committee's draft were proposed, either in the Council or in the Assembly, and the article was not debated further.

§143. **Article 22.** *"The seat of the Court shall be established at The Hague.*

"The President and Registrar shall reside at the seat of the Court."

This text was drafted by the Committee of Jurists. Baron Descamps proposed that The Hague should be chosen as the seat of the Court, not only as "an act of courtesy," but also because The Hague was already the seat of the Permanent Court of Arbitration, and because it was desirable "to separate the political functions of the League of Nations from its judicial functions by assigning different seats to the two groups of institutions. [65] M. Adatci said that "in Japan, when The Hague is mentioned, it means Peace and Justice." [66] The Hague was chosen by the unanimous vote of the Committee, because "a high tradition of pacific hopes and legal progress" surrounds it. [67]

Many of the preliminary drafts, including the "Five-Power Plan"

[61] Minutes of the 1920 Committee of Jurists, p. 456.   [62] *Id.,* p. 459.
[63] Compare Article 12 of the Hague *projet* of 1907.
[64] Minutes of the 1920 Committee of Jurists, p. 455.
[65] Minutes of the 1920 Committee of Jurists, p. 203.   [66] *Ibid.*
[67] *Id.,* p. 718. M. de Lapradelle had objected to any statement of the reasons for choosing The Hague. *Id.,* p. 204.

(Article 13), provided that all judges should reside at the seat of the Court, and this was also urged by some members of the Committee. Lord Phillimore foresaw "unfortunate consequences" if the judges were in "daily contact without occupation," [68] though he admitted that distant countries would be at some disadvantage if judges were not required to be domiciled at The Hague.[69] The decision of the question of residence seems to have turned upon an expectation that "at the outset" the Court would have little to do.[70] The requirement in the second paragraph of the Article was finally adopted as an element of the Court's "permanence." [71] The text adopted by the Committee of Jurists was not modified by the First Assembly.

§144. **Article 23.** *"A session of the Court shall be held every year.*

"Unless otherwise provided by Rules of Court, this session shall begin on the 15th of June, and shall continue for so long as may be deemed necessary to finish the cases on the list.

"The President may summon an extraordinary session of the Court whenever necessary."

This text with a slight change was that of the Committee of Jurists. Fortunately a proposal made to the Committee, similar to Article 14 of the Hague *projet* of 1907, that the Court should not have to meet if there was no business to come before it, was rejected; the Committee of Jurists decided expressly that the Court should meet annually "even though there might be no cases to deal with." [72] The date fixed for the annual session was not much debated; in the First Assembly it was explained to the sub-committee of the Third Committee that "June had seemed to be the most favorable month, since at that time the judges would probably be less burdened by their ordinary occupations." [73]

§145. **Article 24.** *"If, for some special reason, a member of the Court considers that he should not take part in the decision of a particular case, he shall so inform the President.*

"If the President considers that for some special reason one of the members of the Court should not sit on a particular case, he shall give him notice accordingly.

"If in any such case the member of the Court and the President disagree, the matter shall be settled by the decision of the Court."

The substance of this text was proposed by the Committee of

---

[68] Minutes of the 1920 Committee of Jurists, p. 186.   [69] *Id.*, p. 189.
[70] *Id.*, p. 718.   [71] *Id.*, p. 188.   [72] *Id.*, pp. 516, 574.
[73] Documents, p. 128; Records of First Assembly, Committees, I, p. 358.

Jurists as a substitute for a proposed right of challenging judges.[74] It clearly belongs with that part of Article 17 which deals with disqualifications; it was originally only part of a proposal which in a sense got lost in the draft-scheme of the Committee of Jurists.[75] Its purpose was not explained in the report of the Committee, and the debate in the Assembly does not throw much light on the need for it. A slight amendment was made in paragraph 1, where "should not" (Fr., *devoir ne pas*) was substituted for "cannot" (Fr., *ne pouvoir*);[76] this amendment was explained in the report of the Third Committee as intended to make it clear that it is not an impossibility, but the moral duty of abstention, which the paragraph is aimed to cover.[77]

§146. **Article 25.** *"The full Court shall sit except when it is expressly provided otherwise.*

"If eleven judges cannot be present, the number shall be made up by calling on deputy-judges to sit.

"If, however, eleven judges are not available, a quorum of nine judges shall suffice to constitute the Court."

The substance of this text emanated from the Committee of Jurists, though it is modelled on Article 14 of the Hague *projet* of 1907. The provision that "the full Court shall sit" was the subject of a protracted debate. Baron Descamps proposed that the Court should sit in sections or in chambers;[78] this was in line with a desire to make the court small, manifested by most of the preliminary drafts.[79] Lord Phillimore said that the Court must always sit *in pleno* so that "it should make use of all its resources."[80] On the other hand, no basis was found for the exclusion of certain members of the Court from sitting. M. Ricci-Busatti desired a large number of judges from which tribunals would be constituted as in the Permanent Court of Arbitration. It was only as the debate progressed that the members of the Committee came to the view that the Court must always sit *in pleno*.[81] Lord Phillimore explained that "the number eleven would be merely nominal; cases of illness and absence would always reduce the num-

---

[74] Minutes of the 1920 Committee of Jurists, p. 298. The subject of challenges had figured very prominently in the Five-Power Plan. Lord Phillimore thought that the right of challenge was a "Continental institution" which was unnecessary. *Id.*, p. 472.

[75] *Id.*, pp. 472–5, 574, 613.

[76] Documents, p. 129; Records of First Assembly, Committees, I, p. 359.

[77] Documents, p. 208; Records of First Assembly, Plenary, p. 460.

[78] Minutes of the 1920 Committee of Jurists, pp. 49, 111, 143.

[79] *Id.*, p. 71.   [80] *Id.*, p. 169.   [81] *Id.*, pp. 517, 526.

ber to nine." [82] In the sub-committee of the Third Committee, the British representative proposed that the number of judges be reduced to nine, with seven to constitute a quorum; [83] and an Italian amendment would have provided that each party should have the right to demand that a decision be postponed if less than eleven judges were sitting.[84] Neither of these amendments was adopted. It seems that the article might have been drafted to contain special provision for the enlargement of the Court; as such provision is lacking, however, nine judges or deputy-judges continue to constitute a quorum, though the total number of judges and deputy-judges was increased in 1930 to nineteen. The use of the term "judges" in the third paragraph seems to take insufficient account of the provision in the second paragraph, but it clearly includes deputy-judges.

§147. Article 26. *"Labour cases, particularly cases referred to in Part XIII (Labour) of the Treaty of Versailles and the corresponding portions of the other Treaties of Peace, shall be heard and determined by the Court under the following conditions:*

"The Court will appoint every three years a special chamber of five judges, selected so far as possible with due regard to the provisions of Article 9. In addition, two judges shall be selected for the purpose of replacing a judge who finds it impossible to sit. If the parties so demand, cases will be heard and determined by this Chamber. In the absence of any such demand, the Court will sit with the number of judges provided for in Article 25. On all occasions the judges will be assisted by four technical assessors sitting with them, but without the right to vote, and chosen with a view to ensuring a just representation of the competing interests.

"If there is a national of one only of the parties sitting as a judge in the Chamber referred to in the preceding paragraph, the President will invite one of the other judges to retire in favour of a judge chosen by the other party in accordance with Article 31.

"The technical assessors shall be chosen for each particular case in accordance with rules of procedure under Article 30 from a list of "Assessors for Labour cases" composed of two persons nominated by each Member of the League of Nations and an equivalent number nominated by the Governing Body of the Labour Office. The Govern-

---

[82] Minutes of the 1920 Committee of Jurists, p. 526.
[83] Documents, p. 117; Records of First Assembly, Committees, I, p. 340.
[84] Documents, p. 29; Records of First Assembly, Committees, I, p. 497.

ing Body will nominate, as to one-half, representatives of the workers, and as to one-half, representatives of employers from the list referred to in Article 412 of the Treaty of Versailles and the corresponding articles of the other Treaties of Peace.

"In Labour cases the International Labour Office shall be at liberty to furnish the Court with all relevant information, and for this purpose the Director of that Office shall receive copies of all the written proceedings."

This text originated in the First Assembly. Articles 415–17 and 423 of the Treaty of Versailles provide for the jurisdiction of the Court with respect to labor cases. The Director of the International Labor Office drew these provisions to the attention of the Council at an early date, and his communication was placed before the Committee of Jurists.[85] The draft-scheme of the Committee of Jurists made no special provision for labor cases, however, though it proposed a special chamber of three judges for cases by summary procedure. The Director of the International Labor Office later formulated numerous amendments to the draft approved by the Council at Brussels, and these were placed before the Assembly;[86] he proposed the election of certain judges who were experts in labor legislation and social questions, and the representation of workmen and employers on the Court when labor cases were heard. In the sub-committee of the Third Committee, the French representative supported the latter suggestion.[87] The British delegation proposed a plan for a special chamber of five judges for labor cases,[88] to be assisted by four assessors who should act in an advisory capacity;[89] Sir Cecil Hurst explained that a special chamber was necessary to prevent the Court's being too large after assessors had been added, and to create a small body of judges who might specialize on labor questions. Some members of the sub-committee favored the hearing of labor cases by the full court, in order to maintain the representative character of the Court,[90] but a small chamber was decided upon with a view to developing specialists.[91] In reporting to the Third Committee, the sub-committee suggested that labor disputes might present features "not of an exclusively legal char-

[85] Minutes of the 1920 Committee of Jurists, pp. 248, 257.
[86] Documents pp. 74–80; Records of First Assembly, Committees, I, pp. 557–565.
[87] Documents, pp. 129, 151; Records of First Assembly, Committees, I, pp. 361, 394.
[88] Documents, p. 70; Records of First Assembly, Committees, I, p. 592.
[89] Documents, p. 146; Records of First Assembly, Committees, I, p. 388.
[90] Documents, pp. 149ff.; Records of First Assembly, Committees, I, pp. 391ff.
[91] Documents, p. 153; Records of First Assembly, Committees, I, pp. 396–397.

acter." [92] The Director of the International Labor Office, appearing before the Third Committee, was somewhat critical of the draft offered by the sub-committee, insisting that assessors be given the character of real judges.[93] As a result of his insistence, the Third Committee added the last paragraph of Article 26, which clearly applies only to contentious cases.[94] The desire to have among the judges specialists on labor legislation and labor problems can hardly be said to have been realized in practice.

§148. Article 27. *"Cases relating to transit and communications, particularly cases referred to in Part XII (Ports, Waterways and Railways) of the Treaty of Versailles and the corresponding portions of the other Treaties of Peace shall be heard and determined by the Court under the following conditions:*

"The Court will appoint every three years a special chamber of five judges, selected so far as possible with due regard to the provisions of Article 9. In addition, two judges shall be selected for the purpose of replacing a judge who finds it impossible to sit. If the parties so demand, cases will be heard and determined by this chamber. In the absence of any such demand, the Court will sit with the number of judges provided for in Article 25. When desired by the parties or decided by the Court, the judges will be assisted by four technical assessors sitting with them, but without the right to vote.

"If there is a national of one only of the parties sitting as a judge in the chamber referred to in the preceding paragraph, the President will invite one of the other judges to retire in favour of a judge chosen by the other party in accordance with Article 31.

"The technical assessors shall be chosen for each particular case in accordance with rules of procedure under Article 30 from a list of "Assessors for Transit and Communications cases" composed of two persons nominated by each Member of the League of Nations."

This text originated in the First Assembly. A draft proposed by the British delegation [95] was modified in the sub-committee of the Third Committee to conform in general to the article on labor cases. At the same time the Second Committee of the First Assembly was engaged in creating the Communications and Transit Organization of the League

[92] Documents, p. 209; Records of First Assembly, Plenary, p. 460.
[93] Documents, p. 105; Records of First Assembly, Committees, I, p. 309. M. Thomas stated that conflicts between capital and labor "were far from involving mere points of law." Documents, p. 106; Records of First Assembly, Committees, I, p. 310.
[94] Series D, No. 2, p. 98.
[95] Documents, p. 71; Records of First Assembly, Committees, I, p. 592.

of Nations with a competence to act as an agency of conciliation in international disputes, and some fears were expressed that a conflict might arise between that organization and the Court. The technical character of transit and communications questions, such as those which might arise under Part XII of the Treaty of Versailles, was emphasized, as well as the optional character of the jurisdiction of the chamber. In the Third Committee,[96] some opposition to the draft was expressed, on the ground that the technical questions involved in transit and communications cases would already have been dealt with by experts. A slight amendment in the second paragraph, substituting "when desired by the Parties or decided by the Court" for the words "on all occasions" was voted in the plenary session of the First Assembly on December 13, 1920.[97]

§149. Article 28. *"The special chambers provided for in Articles 26 and 27 may, with the consent of the parties to the dispute, sit elsewhere than at The Hague."*

This text originated in the First Assembly, as it relates only to articles which were not discussed in the Committee of Jurists. A British draft [98] included it as a part of the proposal for special chambers, and as such it was adopted with little discussion.[99] No suggestion was ever made for requiring the consent of the States in whose territory the chambers were to sit, in line with Article 60 of the Hague Convention for Pacific Settlement of 1907. The view was taken in the sub-committee of the Third Committee of the First Assembly that the extra expense of a meeting elsewhere than at The Hague would be borne by the parties.[100]

§150. Article 29. *"With a view to the speedy despatch of business, the Court shall form annually a chamber composed of three judges who, at the request of the contesting parties, may hear and determine cases by summary procedure."*

This text emanated from the Committee of Jurists, which clearly borrowed the conception from Chapter IV of the Hague Convention for Pacific Settlement of 1907. The earlier Hague Convention of 1899 contained no provisions on summary procedure, and in 1907 the French delegation suggested the addition of a provision for compulsory sum-

[96] Documents, p. 105; Records of First Assembly, Committees, I, p. 310.
[97] Documents, p. 254; Records of First Assembly, Plenary, p. 499.
[98] Documents, p. 71; Records of First Assembly, Committees, I, p. 592.
[99] Documents, pp. 107, 155; Records of First Assembly, Committees, I, pp. 312, 400.
[100] Documents, p. 155; Records of First Assembly, Committees, I, p. 400.

mary arbitration procedure where a convention to which more than two States were parties was the subject of the dispute.[1] The Hague *projet* of 1907 (Articles 6, 18) also envisaged a dealing with cases by summary procedure, and this was proposed in various drafts submitted to the Committee of Jurists in 1920.[2] Such a general opinion existed that the proposal was not debated at length in the Committee of Jurists,[3] and the draft was easily arrived at after the determination that the Court should normally sit *in pleno*. No changes were made by the First Assembly.

§151. **Article 30.** *"The Court shall frame rules for regulating its procedure. In particular, it shall lay down rules for summary procedure."*

This text emanated from the Committee of Jurists, which from the beginning showed a desire to leave the Court to a large extent free in the control of its procedure.[4] A proposal of Baron Descamps requiring approval of the rules of procedure by the Council and the Assembly [5] was not taken up by the Committee. The Council suggested the addition of a reference to rules "governing the conditions under which the Vice-President shall take up his duties," [6] but this reference was abandoned by the sub-committee of the Third Committee.[7] A question was raised in the Committee of Jurists as to the power of the Court to supply by its rules omissions in its Statute, and it was answered affirmatively.[8]

§152. **Article 31.** *"Judges of the nationality of each contesting party shall retain their right to sit in the case before the Court.*

"If the Court includes upon the Bench a judge of the nationality of one of the parties only, the other party may select from among the deputy-judges a judge of its nationality, if there be one. If there should not be one, the party may choose a judge, preferably from among those persons who have been nominated as candidates as provided in Articles 4 and 5.

"If the Court includes upon the Bench no judge of the nationality

---

[1] *Actes et Documents*, II, pp. 764, 874–5; Scott, Reports to the Hague Peace Conferences, pp. 467–8.

[2] Minutes of the 1920 Committee of Jurists, p. 89. The drafts of Norway, Sweden, Denmark, Netherlands, and the Five Powers all contained such provisions.

[3] *Id.*, pp. 619–20, 647.

[4] Minutes of the 1920 Committee of Jurists, p. 248. Article 30 follows the provision in Article 32 of the Hague *projet* of 1907.   [5] *Id.*, p. 50.

[6] Documents, pp. 56–57; Records of First Assembly, Committees, I, p. 487.

[7] Documents, p. 129; Records of First Assembly, Committees, I, p. 360.

[8] Minutes of the 1920 Committee of Jurists, p. 647.

of the contesting parties, each of these may proceed to select or choose a judge as provided in the preceding paragraph.

"Should there be several parties in the same interest, they shall, for the purpose of the preceding provisions, be reckoned as one party only. Any doubt upon this point is settled by the decision of the Court.

"Judges selected or chosen as laid down in paragraphs 2 and 3 of this article shall fulfil the conditions required by Articles 2, 16, 17, 20, 24 of this Statute. They shall take part in the decision on an equal footing with their colleagues."

This text, the substance of which was drafted by the Committee of Jurists, represents one of its principal achievements, for the scheme for electing the judges would probably never have been adopted without it.[9] The article at once distinguishes the Court from national courts, the considerations governing the creation of the latter being quite different. M. Adatci supported the participation of national judges as essential to the completeness of the Court's examination of a case,[10] and he proposed the appointment of judges *ad hoc* wherever a litigant state did not have a representative among the judges sitting in the Court.[11] Lord Phillimore proposed the appointment of judges *ad hoc,* to sit as "assessors with voting powers," [12] but this qualification was dropped in the Root-Phillimore plan.[13] M. de Lapradelle suggested that if both parties had nationals among the judges, they should be allowed to participate; that if only one party had a national among the judges he should give up his seat, and both parties should then be represented by assessors; and that if neither party had a national among the judges then the appointment of assessors "would be avoided." [14] He assumed that "a national judge would always record his disapproval of a sentence unfavorable to his country"; [15] Lord Phillimore dissented from this, citing the *Alaska Boundary Arbitration.*[16] M. Loder opposed the participation of national judges as "a characteristic essentially belonging to arbitration," [17] and desired to limit them to acting in an advisory capacity; he was also troubled about the possibility of an even number of judges.[18] M. Ricci-Busatti thought

---

[9] Cf., Article 16 of the 1907 Prize Court Convention.
[10] Minutes of the 1920 Committee of Jurists, pp. 168, 529.
[11] Minutes of the 1920 Committee of Jurists, p. 165.
[12] *Id.,* p. 169.   [13] *Id.,* p. 327.   [14] *Id.,* pp. 172, 198, 535.   [15] *Id.,* p. 531.
[16] *Id.,* p. 533. In the award of the Alaska Boundary Tribunal of October 20, 1903, Baron Alverstone, who had been appointed by Great Britain, joined with the members appointed by the United States in upholding the United States' contentions on certain points. See U. S. Foreign Relations, 1903, p. 543; 98 British and Foreign State Papers, p. 152.   [17] Minutes of the 1920 Committee of Jurists, p. 531.   [18] *Id.,* p. 534.

it a difficulty that judges should derive their authority from different sources, ordinary judges from their international election and judges *ad hoc* from appointment by their own Governments.[19] Mr. Root insisted that "nations should be able to go before the Court with the certainty that their case would be fully understood"; [20] he urged the participation of national judges chiefly, however, as a practical way for getting States to consent.[21] It was the practical appeal of the provision which led to its adoption, relatively late in the deliberations of the Committee.[22] In its report the Committee admitted that it would be "logical" that national judges should abstain from sitting, and that its proposal made the Court resemble a court of arbitration more nearly than a court of justice; but it replied that "States attach much importance to having one of their subjects on the Bench when they appear before a Court of Justice." [23]

In his report to the Council at Brussels, M. Bourgeois (France) stated that the essential condition in this respect was "complete equality." [24] The Norwegian and Swedish committees proposed to amend the draft by excluding national judges in every case.[25] The sub-committee of the Third Committee gave little consideration to the article; it accepted an Italian amendment adding the second sentence in the fourth paragraph; but it refused to accept a second Italian proposal to add to the last paragraph a provision that judges *ad hoc* should not "be included in the quorum of nine or of eleven judges stipulated in Article 25," since in the opinion of the sub-committee that went without saying.[26] The Third Committee adopted the amended draft without discussion.

§153. Article 32. *"The judges shall receive an annual indemnity to be determined by the Assembly of the League of Nations upon the proposal of the Council. This indemnity must not be decreased during the period of a judge's appointment.*

"The President shall receive a special grant for his period of office, to be fixed in the same way.

"The Vice-President, judges and deputy-judges, shall receive a grant for the actual performance of their duties, to be fixed in the same way.

---

[19] Minutes of the 1920 Committee of Jurists, p. 532. [20] *Id.*, p. 532.
[21] *Id.*, p. 538. [22] *Id.*, p. 561. [23] *Id.*, p. 722.
[24] Documents, p. 48; Records of First Assembly, Committees, I, p. 475.
[25] Documents, pp. 34, 36; Records of First Assembly, Committees, I, pp. 505, 509.
[26] Documents, p. 210; Records of First Assembly, Committees, I, p. 532.

"*Travelling expenses incurred in the performance of their duties shall be refunded to judges and deputy-judges who do not reside at the seat of the Court.*

"*Grants due to judges selected or chosen as provided in Article 31 shall be determined in the same way.*

"*The salary of the Registrar shall be decided by the Council upon the proposal of the Court.*

"*The Assembly of the League of Nations shall lay down, on the proposal of the Council, a special regulation fixing the conditions under which retiring pensions may be given to the personnel of the Court.*"

The substance of this text was proposed by the Committee of Jurists. A number of the preliminary drafts contained provisions as to salaries and pensions.[27] The problem of remuneration was connected with various other problems, chiefly those of residence and incompatibility, and the Committee's judgment was influenced by the prevailing anticipation that the judges would not have much to do. At various times, the amount of a judge's salary was discussed in the Committee. Lord Phillimore suggested "the same sum as that paid to the highest English judges, that is to say, £5,000"; [28] Mr. Root thought that the sum of 6,000 florins, which was provided for the judges of the proposed court of arbitral justice in the Hague *projet* of 1907, was "quite out of the question"; [29] M. de Lapradelle wished deputy-judges to be paid the salary of ordinary judges,[30] and his proposal led to an extended debate; it was at one time suggested that a deputy-judge should receive one-third of the salary of a judge.[31] It was concluded that the Committee did not have the necessary information for proposing a definite amount, and it was desired to leave the Council and the Assembly free in the matter; [32] the report of the Committee did not deal with the subject. M. Bourgeois, as *rapporteur* of the Council, intimated that judges' salaries should be divided into small fixed salaries, and liberal daily allowances for the actual performance of their duties.[33] The sub-committee of the Third Committee redrafted the provision on pensions and made it applicable to all of the Court's personnel,[34] and not merely to members.

---

[27] Minutes of the 1920 Committee of Jurists, p. 67.
[28] Minutes of the 1920 Committee of Jurists, pp. 480, 483.
[29] *Id.*, p. 486.   [30] *Id.*, p. 487.   [31] *Id.*, pp. 485, 492.   [32] *Id.*, p. 577.
[33] Documents, p. 49; Records of First Assembly, Committees, I, p. 476.
[34] Documents, p. 130; Records of First Assembly, Committees, I, p. 361. See, however, the amended text of Article 32 annexed to the Revision Protocol of September 14, 1929. See also §362, *infra*.

§154. **Article 33.** *"The expenses of the Court shall be borne by the League of Nations, in such a manner as shall be decided by the Assembly upon the proposal of the Council."*

This text was drafted by the Committee of Jurists. The Root-Phillimore draft proposed that "the expenses of the Court shall be borne by the League of Nations"; [35] it was also proposed to the Committee that States Members of the League of Nations should contribute to the expenses in equal shares.[36] The text adopted left it to the Assembly to decide such questions as contributions by States not Members of the League of Nations,[37] though the Assembly probably has no other power than that of reaching an agreement with such States as to the contributions which they will pay. In the sub-committee of the Third Committee of the Assembly, an Italian proposal was made that since the expenses of the Court should be borne as were other expenses of the League itself the article should be deleted; this proposal was withdrawn on its being pointed out that the article was indispensable for the purpose of having the Members of the League not parties to the Protocol of Signature support a part of the cost.[38] During the discussion of Articles 31 and 32 it was stated that the distinction between States to which the Court is open by right and those which merely have access to it, lay chiefly in the distribution of the expenses.[39]

§155. **Article 34.** *"Only States or Members of the League of Nations can be parties in cases before the Court."*

This text grew out of a proposal by the Committee of Jurists that "the Court shall have jurisdiction to hear and determine suits between States." In the Committee of Jurists, the Prize Court Convention of 1907 was referred to as conferring a wider competence; [40] access to the court of arbitral justice proposed in 1907 would have been limited, under Article 21 of the Hague *projet*, to the contracting States. M. Loder was opposed to the exclusion of individuals as parties,[41] and his views received some support from M. de Lapradelle.[42] Lord Phillimore thought that "a State would never permit itself to be sued before a court by a private individual." Mr. Root and Baron Descamps thought that the Court should be able to deal with private interests only when a Government "made them international by adopt-

[35] Minutes of the 1920 Committee of Jurists, p. 326.
[36] *Id.*, p. 495.   [37] *Id.*, pp. 577–8.
[38] Documents, p. 131; Records of First Assembly, Committees, I, p. 362.
[39] Documents, p. 140; Records of First Assembly, Committees, I, p. 378.
[40] Minutes of the 1920 Committee of Jurists, p. 205. See §67, *supra*.
[41] Minutes of the 1920 Committee of Jurists, p. 206.   [42] *Id.*, p. 210.

ing them as its own." [43] M. Ricci-Busatti stated that "private individuals are not subjects of international law and it is entirely within the realm of that law that the Court is called upon to act." [44] The protection of minorities was referred to in the discussion,[45] and a proposal dealing with claims submitted by States on behalf of individuals and national minorities [46] was considered but rejected.[47] A question was raised as to a special *locus standi* for the League of Nations,[48] but it was not discussed. The decision on the exclusion of individuals [49] was said in the Committee's report to have been taken "without prejudice to any subsequent development" of the Court.[50]

In the sub-committee of the Third Committee, where the article was redrafted, it was agreed that the Council of the League of Nations could not be a party before the Court.[51] The sub-committee stated that all Members of the League of Nations were to be assimilated to States, under this article, and modified the text accordingly; and it recognized that States might "present themselves as joint parties before the Court." [52]

§156. **Article 35.** *"The Court shall be open to the Members of the League and also to States mentioned in the Annex to the Covenant.*

"The conditions under which the Court shall be open to other States shall, subject to the special provisions contained in treaties in force, be laid down by the Council, but in no case shall such provisions place the parties in a position of inequality before the Court.

When a State which is not a Member of the League of Nations is a party to a dispute, the Court will fix the amount which that party is to contribute towards the expenses of the Court."

[43] *Id.,* pp. 207, 216.   [44] *Id.,* p. 208.   [45] *Id.,* pp. 204, 216.   [46] *Id.,* p. 566.
[47] *Id.,* p. 580. It may be of interest to note that during the drafting of the Polish Minorities Treaty at the Paris Peace Conference, Lord Cecil made a proposal to the Committee on New States providing that "as soon as the Permanent Court of International Justice shall have been established and shall have settled the necessary procedure, any Polish citizen or group of citizens" aggrieved by a violation of the stipulations for protection of minorities "may appeal to that Court, and the Court may give such decision and make such order as it shall think right." The Committee on New States submitted alternative texts to the Supreme Council, which on June 17, 1919, "decided that States only, and not individuals, should have the right of appeal to the Permanent Court of International Justice." Minutes of the Committee on New States, pp. 45, 77; Miller, Diary at the Peace Conference, XIII, pp. 103, 170.
[48] Minutes of the 1920 Committee of Jurists, p. 579.
[49] *Id.,* p. 580.   [50] *Id.,* p. 723.
[51] Documents, p. 140; Records of First Assembly, Committees, I, p. 378. In its session at Brussels, the Council had reached this conclusion also. Minutes of the Council, 10th session, pp. 170–171.
[52] Documents, p. 210; Records of First Assembly, Committees, I, p. 532.

This text was drafted in the First Assembly. The Committee of Jurists had proposed the following (Article 32):

> The Court shall be open of right to the States mentioned in the Annex to the Covenant, and to such others as shall subsequently enter the League of Nations. Other States may have access to it. The conditions under which the Court shall be open of right or accessible to States which are not Members of the League of Nations shall be determined by the Council, in accordance with Article 17 of the Covenant.

In opening the discussion on this point, Baron Descamps referred to the Hague *projet* of 1907 which, in Article 21, limited access to the proposed court to "contracting States"; in reply M. de Lapradelle drew attention to the changes wrought since 1907.[53] The problem was closely connected with that of obligatory jurisdiction, as to which it was thought that no obligation could be imposed on States not members of the League of Nations, or on Members of the League in respect of suits by non-members.[54] Article 17 of the Covenant seemed to afford a basis for a wider competence,[55] and the reference to Article 17 of the Covenant was stoutly insisted upon in the Committee.[56] It was easy to agree that the Court should be open to States named in the Annex to the Covenant. The reference to conditions to be set by the Council seems to have been chiefly to a condition as to payment of a share of the expenses of the Court.[57] It is not clear, however, that this was the view of the sub-committee of the Third Committee of the Assembly, where it was desired to take account of provisions in the Treaties of Peace under which the Central Powers would be parties before the Court; the words "subject to the special provisions contained in treaties in force" were inserted in the second paragraph with this object.[58] The sub-committee was particularly desirous that the rights of parties before the Court should be equal, and to this end it inserted the last clause of paragraph 2.[59] It also adopted a proposal of the Canadian delegation, for meeting the situation of the British Dominions, to add the words "to the Members of the League of Nations" in paragraph 1.[60] In the report of the Third Committee to the As-

---

[53] Minutes of the 1920 Committee of Jurists, p. 224. *Cf.*, Article 47 of the Hague Convention for Pacific Settlement of 1907.

[54] Minutes of the 1920 Committee of Jurists, pp. 270, 648.

[55] *Id.*, p. 223.   [56] *Id.*, p. 581.   [57] *Id.*, pp. 220, 580-1.

[58] Documents, pp. 141-4; Records of First Assembly, Committees, I, pp. 378-382.

[59] Documents, p. 141, 144; Records of First Assembly, Committees, I, pp. 379, 384.

[60] Documents, p. 145; Records of First Assembly, Committees, I, p. 385.

sembly, it was made clear that the phrase "Members of the League" referred to future as well as present members; and it was recognized that the conditions of access to be laid down by the Council should be "in conformity with Article 17 of the Covenant," though the reason for this is not clear.[61]

§157. Article 36. *"The jurisdiction of the Court comprises all cases which the parties refer to it and all matters specially provided for in Treaties and Conventions in force.*

"The Members of the League of Nations and the States mentioned in the Annex to the Covenant may, either when signing or ratifying the protocol to which the present Statute is adjoined, or at a later moment, declare that they recognize as compulsory ipso facto *and without special agreement, in relation to any other Member or State accepting the same obligation, the jurisdiction of the Court in all or any of the classes of legal disputes concerning:*

   (a) *the interpretation of a treaty;*

   (b) *any question of international law;*

   (c) *the existence of any fact which, if established, would constitute a breach of an international obligation;*

   (d) *the nature or extent of the reparation to be made for the breach of an international obligation.*

"The declaration referred to above may be made unconditionally or on condition of reciprocity on the part of several or certain Members or States, or for a certain time.

"In the event of a dispute as to whether the Court has jurisdiction, the matter shall be settled by the decision of the Court."

This article represents the result of the greatest contest waged in the creation of the Court. In the Committee of Jurists, the desire prevailed to confer on the Court a broad compulsory jurisdiction, as had been suggested in various preliminary plans,[62] though the experience of the Hague Peace Conferences in 1899 and 1907 had not been such as to justify large hopes of success in this direction.[63] The actual wording of Article 14 of the Covenant seemed to some members of the Committee to exclude a possibility of compulsory jurisdiction,[64] though Articles 12 and 13 of the Covenant supplied a coun-

---

[61] Documents, p. 210; Records of First Assembly, Plenary, p. 462.

[62] Minutes of the 1920 Committee of Jurists, p. 81.

[63] This experience was frequently referred to in the Committee of Jurists, and not too accurately.   [64] See especially *id.*, pp. 228, 231, 233ff.

terbalancing factor. Mr. Root looked upon the provisions of the Covenant as expressing only a "general intention," [65] and he thought that the Committee should make any recommendations which it deemed useful. At one time, the Committee considered a possible recommendation that Article 14 should be modified.[66] It was taken for granted that only Members of the League of Nations could be asked to confer such jurisdiction on the Court. Compulsory jurisdiction was strongly insisted upon by M. Loder.[67] Lord Phillimore proposed that "in the absence of any convention to the contrary," the Court should "be deemed to be the Court of Arbitration mentioned in Article 13 of the Covenant." [68] Several members of the Committee desired to confine the compulsory jurisdiction to defined categories of disputes, as had been suggested in the "Five-Power Plan," and Baron Descamps proposed a transaction limiting it to "cases of a legal nature" which he proceeded to define.[69] In supporting this proposal, Mr. Root thought that the limits of compulsory jurisdiction should be clearly laid down, since "States would not accept a court which had the right to settle disputes in accordance with rules established" by itself; and he recalled the failure of the International Prize Court Convention.[70] For the definition of "cases of a legal nature," the enumerations in paragraph 2 of Article 13 of the Covenant were later adopted.[71] The draft finally adopted by the Committee [72] contained three articles relating to obligatory jurisdiction, which was limited, however, to disputes which could not be settled by diplomatic means, following in this respect Articles 20 (1899), 41 (1907) of the Hague Conventions for Pacific Settlement. The report of the Committee stated its desire to "take an important step in the direction" indicated by the Hague Conference of 1907; great reliance was placed on Article 13 of the Covenant, somewhat in neglect of its limited text. Reservations made by M. Adatci and M. Ricci-Busatti were mentioned in the report.[73]

This proposal by the Committee of Jurists was the outstanding feature of the draft-scheme to occupy the attention of the Council and the Assembly. When the Council met at San Sebastian, M. Tittoni (Italy) at once stated that "it was unprecedented for one State to bring

---

[65] Minutes of the 1920 Committee of Jurists, p. 240.   [66] Id., pp. 231–2, 241–2.
[67] Id., p. 249.   [68] Id., p. 253.   [69] Id., p. 272.
[70] Id., pp. 286, 309.
[71] M. de Lapradelle proposed that the English text of the Covenant be taken as the basis of the Committee's work. Id., p. 287.
[72] Id., pp. 583, 615–19.   [73] Id., p. 727.

another State before a tribunal without its assent and to condemn it by default; and such a procedure would in practice only be tolerated by the smaller countries." [74] When the Council met at Brussels, it had before it the report of the Italian Council for Diplomatic Litigation which suggested that provisions for obligatory jurisdiction should be left to a "separate convention," [75] and a note by Mr. Balfour (Great Britain) observing that the draft-scheme went "considerably beyond the Covenant." [76] The Council proceeded to approve a series of amendments eliminating obligatory jurisdiction; [77] and a suggestion was made that this feature of the draft should be referred to "authorities on international law" for further study. [78] M. Bourgeois, as *rapporteur*, stated that "in reality a modification in Articles 12 and 13 of the Covenant is here involved," and since it would give the Court jurisdiction conferred on the Council, he thought the Council should take no initiative to such an end. [79] He pointed out that the Council was not opposed to compulsory jurisdiction, however, and that the matter might be considered at a future date.

In the First Assembly, the debate was very heated. The Argentine delegation urged obligatory jurisdiction, to avoid making the Court "merely an arbitration tribunal," and this received the support of the Brazilian, Panama, and Portuguese representatives, some of whom insisted squarely that if certain articles of the Covenant conflicted with the idea of obligatory jurisdiction they would have to be amended. [80] Lord Robert Cecil (South Africa) thought that jurisdiction could not be given to the Court relating to matters involving "vital interests," and he wished to leave the Court to "develop organically." [81] M. Hagerup (Norway) preferred the solution of the Committee of Jurists, [82] but fell back on the Italian suggestion of a special treaty to provide for it. Even M. Loder (Netherlands) abandoned his stand in face of the danger of an irreconcilable disagreement. [83] M. La Fontaine (Belgium) attributed the opposition to "the two fetiches of unanimity and sovereignty," and he urged that the jurisdiction of the United

[74] Documents, p. 20; Minutes of the Council, 8th session, p. 33.
[75] Documents, p. 29; Records of First Assembly, Committees, I, p. 498.
[76] Documents, p. 38; Records of First Assembly, Committees, I, p. 511.
[77] Documents, p. 44; Minutes of the Council, 10th session, p. 161.
[78] Documents, p. 43; Minutes of the Council, 10th session, p. 45.
[79] Documents, p. 47; Minutes of the Council, 10th session, pp. 167ff.
[80] Documents, p. 91; Records of First Assembly, Committees, I, p. 287.
[81] Documents, p. 91; Records of First Assembly, Committees, I, p. 287.
[82] Documents, p. 92; Records of First Assembly, Committees, I, p. 289.
[83] Documents, p. 91; Records of First Assembly, Committees, I, p. 288.

States Supreme Court be taken as a model.[84] Sir Cecil Hurst (Great Britain) saw the "true solution in mutual bipartite treaties."[85] In the sub-committee, this idea was supported by M. Politis (Greece), who foresaw "a network of separate conventions extending the jurisdiction of the Court."[86]

The sub-committee adopted the amendments approved by the Council because it did "not seem possible to arrive at unanimity except on the basis of the principles laid down in the Council's draft."[87] In the Third Committee, the struggle was renewed, however. M. Fernandes (Brazil) proposed that alternative texts be adopted, to either of which a Member of the League of Nations might adhere.[88] This idea was adopted by the sub-committee, on special reference, in the form of an optional provision for obligatory jurisdiction.[89] M. Huber (Switzerland) welcomed this by saying that "to make possible a universal agreement on compulsory jurisdiction" would constitute "almost as great a step in advance as the establishment" of the Court.[90] The provision for an optional declaration accepting obligatory jurisdiction was thus adopted by the Third Committee,[91] though the "optional clause" was not drafted until later.[92] In the plenary meeting of the First Assembly on December 13, 1920, the effort to retain obligatory jurisdiction was renewed, particularly by M. Loder (Netherlands), M. La Fontaine (Belgium), and M. Blanco (Uruguay), but the draft was adopted unanimously without any amendment dealing with the Court's jurisdiction.

The enumerations in Article 36 follow almost textually those in paragraph 2 of Article 13 of the Covenant, which were expanded from Article 16 (1899), 38 (1907) of the Hague Conventions for Pacific Settlement, and from a *vœu* of the Hague Peace Conference of 1907.[93] The last paragraph of Article 36 was proposed by the Committee of Jurists in a different form, as a part of its suggestion of obligatory

[84] Documents, p. 94; Records of First Assembly, Committees, I, p. 292.
[85] Documents, p. 94; Records of First Assembly, Committees, I, p. 294.
[86] Documents, p. 142; Records of First Assembly, Committees, I, p. 380.
[87] Documents, p. 211; Records of First Assembly, Committees, I, p. 533.
[88] Documents, p. 168; Records of First Assembly, Committees, I, p. 553. This proposal was very similar to a proposal made by the Swiss delegation at the Second Peace Conference at The Hague in 1907. *Actes et Documents,* II, p. 888.
[89] Documents, p. 170; Records of First Assembly, Committees, I, p. 566.
[90] Documents, p. 107; Records of First Assembly, Committees, I, p. 313.
[91] Documents, pp. 108, 110; Records of First Assembly, Committees, I, pp. 314, 317.
[92] The optional clause attached to the Protocol of Signature first appears in the draft approved by the Council on December 14, 1920. See §110, *supra.*
[93] The enumerations were included in Article 13 of the Covenant from the "Phillimore Plan" of March 20, 1918. See Miller, Drafting of the Covenant, II, p. 4.

jurisdiction; it was to apply only to "a dispute as to whether a certain case comes within any of the categories above mentioned." As it was retained by the Third Committee of the Assembly, there is nothing to indicate that disputes as to whether the Court has jurisdiction must arise out of other provisions in Article 36.

§158. **Article 37.** *"When a treaty or convention in force provides for the reference of a matter to a tribunal to be instituted by the League of Nations, the Court will be such tribunal."*

This text originated in a suggestion by the Council [94] which was redrafted by the sub-committee of the Third Committee of the Assembly; [95] having proposed a general obligatory jurisdiction, the Committee of Jurists had not found it necessary to deal with this special point.[96] When the Council rejected obligatory jurisdiction, the point became important because of certain articles in the Treaties of Peace, particularly Articles 336 and 376 of the Treaty of Versailles and corresponding articles of other Peace Treaties of 1919 and 1920.[97]

§159. **Article 38.** *"The Court shall apply:*

"1. International conventions, whether general or particular, establishing rules expressly recognized by the contesting States;

"2. International custom, as evidence of a general practice accepted as law;

"3. The general principles of law recognized by civilized nations;

"4. Subject to the provisions of Article 59, judicial decisions and the teachings of the most highly qualified publicists of the various nations, as subsidiary means for the determination of rules of law.

"This provision shall not prejudice the power of the Court to decide a case ex æquo et bono, *if the parties agree thereto."*

The enumerations in the first paragraph were drafted by the Committee of Jurists, which, however, proposed to make the order enumerated an order of successive application. Baron Descamps' original proposal of such enumerations met with some opposition; [98] his references to the "legal conscience of civilized nations," based on the preamble of the Hague Convention concerning the laws and customs of war on land, recall the conception on which the Central American Court of Justice was established.[99] M. de Lapradelle preferred to say

---

[94] Documents, p. 44; Minutes of Council, 10th session, p. 161.
[95] Documents, p. 143; Records of First Assembly, Committees, I, p. 382.
[96] See the Minutes of the 1920 Committee of Jurists, p. 724.
[97] On the effect of this provision, see §406, *infra.*
[98] Minutes of the 1920 Committee of Jurists, pp. 294ff., 306, 322.
[99] See §44, *supra.*

that the Court should "judge in accordance with law, justice and equity," to which M. Hagerup replied that "equity was a very vague conception . . . not always in harmony with justice." [100] Frequent reference was made to Article 7 of the Prize Court Convention of 1907. The question was discussed whether the Court could ever refuse to decide because there was no law on the question before it, because of a *non liquet*.[1] Mr. Root urged a limited statement as a condition of the acceptance of obligatory jurisdiction, mentioning the fate of the Prize Court Convention;[2] but he later submitted a redraft of Baron Descamps' ideas which met with general approval and was adopted.[3] Lord Phillimore explained the expression "general principles of law" to mean "maxims of law."[4] The proposed requirement of a "successive order" gave some difficulty.[5]

The Council of the League of Nations approved the addition in (4) of the introductory phrase, "subject to the provisions of Article 59."[6] In the sub-committee of the Third Committee of the Assembly, the Argentine delegation wished to add a reference to "the rules drawn up by the Assembly of the League of Nations in the performance of its duty of codifying international law";[7] but this was rejected. The sub-committee adopted the concluding paragraph of Article 38, which had been mentioned[8] but not proposed by the Committee of Jurists, with little discussion;[9] it was merely explained as giving "a more flexible character" to the provision.[10] The sub-committee also dropped the introductory phrase as to successive order which had been opposed by the Italian Council for Diplomatic Litigation.[11] The report of the sub-committee lists it as one of the Court's important tasks "to contribute, through its jurisprudence, to the development of international law."[12]

§160. Article 39. *"The official languages of the Court shall be French and English. If the parties agree that the case shall be con-*

---

[100] Minutes of the 1920 Committee of Jurists, pp. 295, 296.
[1] Minutes of the 1920 Committee of Jurists, pp. 296, 307ff., 317, 332, 338. See §516, *infra.*
[2] *Id.*, pp. 308ff. [3] *Id.*, pp. 584, 649. [4] *Id.*, p. 335. [5] *Id.*, pp. 337-8.
[6] Documents, p. 44; Minutes of the Council, 10th session, p. 161. It is to be noted that the French version of sub-paragraph 4 contains no equivalent for the English "of the various nations"; but the Revision Protocol of September 14, 1929, provides for adding an equivalent in the French version.
[7] Documents, pp. 68, 145; Records of First Assembly, Committees, I, pp. 386, 519.
[8] Minutes of the 1920 Committee of Jurists, p. 296.
[9] Documents, p. 157; Records of First Assembly, Committees, I, p. 403.
[10] Documents, p. 211; Records of First Assembly, Committees, I, p. 534.
[11] Documents, p. 28; Records of First Assembly, Committees, I, p. 499.
[12] Documents, p. 211; Records of First Assembly, Committees, I, p. 534.

ducted in French, the judgment will be delivered in French. If the parties agree that the case shall be conducted in English, the judgment will be delivered in English.

"In the absence of an agreement as to which language shall be employed, each party may, in the pleadings, use the language which it prefers; the decision of the Court will be given in French and English. In this case the Court will at the same time determine which of the two texts shall be considered as authoritative.

"The Court may, at the request of the parties, authorize a language other than French or English to be used."

The Committee of Jurists, following a number of the preliminary drafts including the "Five-Power Plan," [13] had proposed that the Court's official language should be French, and that on request the use of another language might be authorized by the Court.[14] When the draft-scheme came before the Council at Brussels, Mr. Balfour (Great Britain) observed that "the Treaty of Versailles puts the two languages on an equality," and that "the League of Nations itself carries on its business in French and English"; and he thought it would be "unfortunate to make an exception in respect of the Permanent Court." [15] Viscount Ishii (Japan) supported this view.[16] On October 27, 1920, M. Caclamanos (Greece) presented a report to the Council,[17] suggesting a redraft of the Article in substantially its final form; when this redraft was adopted by the Council, M. Bourgeois (France) abstained from voting. Both in the Third Committee of the Assembly and in its sub-committee, the Spanish delegation offered an amendment to add as a final paragraph, "this authorization cannot be refused when it is requested by all the parties to a dispute"; this was rejected,[18] and no substantial change was made in the article as drafted by the Council.

[13] Minutes of the 1920 Committee of Jurists, p. 99. The Hague Conventions for Pacific Settlement of 1899 and 1907 and the *projet* of 1907 left the matter of languages to the tribunal.

[14] It seems to have been agreed that the draft-scheme and report of the Committee of Jurists would be drawn up in French only, and translated into English. *Id.*, p. 552. Dr. Scott states that the Committee "simply registered the fact that French is today the language of the polite world, of the diplomatic world, of international conferences, and therefore" of the proposed Court. Scott, Project of a Permanent Court, p. 114.

[15] Documents, p. 39; Records of First Assembly, Committees, I, p. 513. Mr. Balfour also insisted that the United States of America should have an opportunity to express an opinion on this question.

[16] Documents, p. 42; Minutes of the Council, 10th session, p. 20.

[17] Documents, p. 51; Minutes of the Council, 10th session, pp. 44, 176.

[18] Documents, pp. 73, 102, 134; Records of First Assembly, Committees, I, pp. 306, 367, 598.

§161. **Article 40.** *"Cases are brought before the Court, as the case may be, either by the notification of the special agreement, or by a written application addressed to the Registrar. In either case the subject of the dispute and the contesting parties must be indicated.*

"The Registrar shall forthwith communicate the application to all concerned.

"He shall also notify the Members of the League of Nations through the Secretary-General."

To this, as to most of the articles relating to procedure, the Committee of Jurists seems to have given only scant attention. Article 38 of its draft-scheme provided, in place of paragraph 1:

> A State desiring to have recourse to the Court shall lodge a written application addressed to the Registrar. The application shall indicate the subject of the dispute, and name the contesting parties.

This was based on Article 30 of the "Five-Power Plan." The text was redrafted and given its final form by the sub-committee of the Third Committee of the Assembly,[19] in order to distinguish between cases submitted by the unilateral action of a State and cases submitted by the agreement of two or more States. The Committee of Jurists explained "all concerned" in the second paragraph to mean "the contesting parties and also any others who might conceivably feel called upon to intervene in the case."[20] The purpose of the third paragraph seems to have been "to take the place of a provision regulating publicity," though it is also related to intervention.[21]

§162. **Article 41.** *"The Court shall have the power to indicate, if it considers that circumstances so require, any provisional measures which ought to be taken to reserve the respective rights of either party.*

"Pending the final decision, notice of the measures suggested shall forthwith be given to the parties and the Council."

The Committee of Jurists drafted the second paragraph of this Article in its final form; for the first paragraph, it suggested:

> If the dispute arises out of an act which has already taken place or which is imminent, the Court shall have the power to suggest if it considers that circumstances so require, the provisional measures that should be taken to preserve the respective rights of either party.

---

[19] Documents, p. 134; Records of First Assembly, Committees, I, p. 368.
[20] Minutes of the 1920 Committee of Jurists, p. 734.   [21] *Id.*, pp. 587, 734.

As stated in the report of the Committee of Jurists,[22] the idea of interim protection was taken from various treaties between the United States and other States, the so-called "Bryan Treaties"; but a somewhat similar provision had been included in Article 18 of the Convention creating the Central American Court of Justice. M. Fernandes' suggestion that the provisional measures should be supported by effective penalties was rejected by the Committee of Jurists, which took the view that "there is no question here of a definite order, even of a temporary nature, which must be carried out at once."[23] The sub-committee of the Third Committee of the Assembly substituted "indicate" for "suggest" in the text proposed by the Committee of Jurists; the introductory phrase was dropped by the Third Committee, so that "all possible cases might be covered,"[24] and the remainder of the paragraph was slightly redrafted. In a report of the Third Committee, it was stated that the article as amended covered "omissions which infringe a right as well as positive acts."[25] The word "reserve" in the English version seems to have crept in as a printer's error for "preserve."[26]

§163. Article 42. *"The parties shall be represented by agents.*
"They may have the assistance of counsel or advocates before the Court."

This text was drafted by the Committee of Jurists in substantially its final form. The Hague Conventions for Pacific Settlement, Articles 37 (1899), 62 (1907), provided for agents and counsel or advocates, as did also the Netherlands' draft of 1919 and the "Five-Power Plan";[27] and the provision seems to have been borrowed by the Committee of Jurists with little discussion.[28] The sub-committee of the Third Committee of the Assembly declined to accept an amendment proposed by the Argentine delegation that the second paragraph should read, "they may have counsel or advocates to represent them or to plead before the Court."[29] An amendment proposed by the Director of the International Labor Office was rejected, also.[30]

[22] Minutes of the 1920 Committee of Jurists, p. 735.   [23] *Id.,* pp. 588, 735.
[24] Documents, p. 103; Records of First Assembly, Committees, I, p. 307.
[25] Documents, p. 172; Records of First Assembly, Plenary, p. 467. See also, the German request of October 14, 1927, in Series A, No. 12, pp. 6–7.
[26] Though the word "preserve" was included in all previous drafts, it was rendered as "reserve" in the text approved by the First Assembly on December 13, 1920. Records of First Assembly, Plenary, p. 475.
[27] *Cf.,* Articles 25 and 26 of the Prize Court Convention of 1907.
[28] Minutes of the 1920 Committee of Jurists, pp. 588, 650.
[29] Documents, pp. 68, 135; Records of First Assembly, Committees, I, pp. 370, 520.
[30] Documents, p. 80; Records of First Assembly, Committees, I, p. 564.

§164. **Article 43.** *"The procedure shall consist of two parts: written and oral.*

"The written proceedings shall consist of the communication to the judges and to the parties of Cases, Counter-Cases and, if necessary, Replies; also all papers and documents in support.

"These communications shall be made through the Registrar, in the order and within the time fixed by the Court.

"A certified copy of every document produced by one party shall be communicated to the other party.

"The oral proceedings shall consist of the hearing by the Court of witnesses, experts, agents, counsel and advocates."

This text was in substance drafted by the Committee of Jurists in three separate articles, which were based on provisions in the "Five-Power Plan," [31] and on Articles 39, 40, 45 (1899) and Articles 63, 64, 70 (1907) of the Hague Conventions for Pacific Settlement. The Committee of Jurists stated in its report: [32]

> Whereas in the case of the Permanent Court of Arbitration of The Hague the former [written procedure] only need be used, as it alone is essential, both phases, written and oral, are equally necessary in the case of the Permanent Court.

Its proposals were rearranged by the sub-committee of the Third Committee, on the suggestion of the Italian delegation.[33]

§165. **Article 44.** *"For the service of all notices upon persons other than the agents, counsel and advocates, the Court shall apply direct to the government of the State upon whose territory the notice has to be served.*

"The same provision shall apply whenever steps are to be taken to procure evidence on the spot."

No change was made in this text as submitted by the Committee of Jurists (Article 43). The bases of its proposal seem to have been Articles 25 and 76 of the 1907 Hague Convention for Pacific Settlement,[34] which had been rephrased in various preliminary drafts, particularly in Article 49 of the "Five-Power Plan." It is to be noted that action by a State may have to be authorized by its local law, as was recognized in Article 76 of the Hague Convention for Pacific

---

[31] Minutes of the 1920 Committee of Jurists, p. 737.
[32] *Ibid.*
[33] Documents, pp. 30, 135; Records of First Assembly, Committees, I, pp. 370, 499.
[34] Minutes of the 1920 Committee of Jurists, p. 589.

Settlement of 1907; and on occasion the article may be of little use in the absence of such authorization.[35]

§166. Article 45. *"The hearing shall be under the control of the President or, in his absence, of the Vice-President; if both are absent, the senior judge shall preside."*

This text emanated from the Committee of Jurists (Article 44), whose draft dealt with "the proceedings" instead of "the hearing," and the "direction" instead of the "control" of the President. It followed Article 34 of the "Five-Power Plan," which was based on the provision in Articles 41 (1899), 66 (1907) of the Hague Conventions for Pacific Settlement. The changes were made by the sub-committee of the Third Committee of the Assembly, without explanation. The English version does not completely correspond with the French version.

§167. Article 46. *"The hearing in Court shall be public, unless the Court shall decide otherwise, or unless the parties demand that the public be not admitted."*

The Committee of Jurists proposed on this subject (Article 45): "The hearing in Court shall be public, unless the Court, at the written request of one of the parties, accompanied by a statement of his reasons, shall otherwise decide." The "Five-Power Plan" (Article 34) had proposed simply that the debates should take place in public session. This represented a decided departure from the provision in Articles 41 (1899), 66 (1907) of the Hague Conventions for Pacific Settlement that the discussions "are public only if it be so decided by the tribunal, with the assent of the parties." [36] In its report, the Committee of Jurists stated that it wished to reverse "the diplomatic custom of secrecy inherent in the jurisdiction of the Court of Arbitration," and it emphasized the "exceptional" character of a decision to sit in secret which the Court might or might not take at the request of both parties.[37] In the sub-committee of the Third Committee of the Assembly, M. Fromageot (France) proposed "to return to the principle of 1907 which made non-publicity the rule and publicity the exception"; "States must not be assimilated to individuals," he said, and hence "it must not be necessary to conduct suits between States

---

[35] On this point, attention should be drawn to a statute of the United States of July 3, 1930, as amended June 7, 1933, concerning the subpœna of witnesses. 46 U. S. Statutes 1005; Session Laws, 73d Congress, 1st session, p. 117.

[36] But see Article 39 of the 1907 Prize Court Convention.

[37] Minutes of the 1920 Committee of Jurists, p. 738.

in such a way as to embitter their mutual relations." [38] M. Hagerup (Norway) feared that publicity "would open the way for influences which would interfere with the course of justice," and he declared that "the question had not been sufficiently examined at The Hague." [39] M. Ricci-Busatti (Italy) thought that "publicity would prevail in practice, if not openly, then by indirect means." [40] The final text of the article was adopted by the sub-committee by a close vote. [41] In practice, hearings before the Court are invariably public. [42]

§168. Articles 47 and 48. (47) *"Minutes shall be made at each hearing, and signed by the Registrar and the President.*

"These minutes shall be the only authentic record."

(48) *"The Court shall make orders for the conduct of the case, shall decide the form and time in which each party must conclude its arguments, and make all arrangements connected with the taking of evidence."*

These texts were proposed by the Committee of Jurists (Articles 46 and 47); they were not the subject of extended discussion, either in the Committee of Jurists [43] or in the Assembly. Articles 35 and 41 of the "Five-Power Plan," following Articles 41 and 49 (1899), 66 and 74 (1907) of the Hague Conventions for Pacific Settlement, clearly served as their bases.

§169. Articles 49 and 50. (49) *"The Court may, even before the hearing begins, call upon the agents to produce any document, or to supply any explanations. Formal note shall be taken of any refusal."*

(50) *"The Court may, at any time, entrust any individual, body, bureau, commission or other organization that it may select, with the task of carrying out an enquiry or giving an expert opinion."*

The draft-scheme of the Committee of Jurists contained the substance of these texts (Articles 48 and 49), and they were never a subject of extended discussion. A proposal by M. Adatci to add a provision permitting consultation of "the technical bodies instituted by the League of Nations" was considered and rejected. [44] Article 49 is clearly based on Article 44 (1899), 69 (1907) of the Hague Conventions for Pacific Settlement.

---

[38] Documents, pp. 135, 137; Records of First Assembly, Committees, I, pp. 370, 372.
[39] Documents, p. 137; Records of First Assembly, Committees, I, p. 373.
[40] *Ibid.*   [41] Records of First Assembly, Committees, I, p. 373.
[42] The records are published in Series C of the Court's publications.
[43] Minutes of the 1920 Committee of Jurists, pp. 589, 590, 650.
[44] Minutes of the 1920 Committee of Jurists, p. 589.

§170. **Article 51.** *"During the hearing, any relevant questions are to be put to the witnesses and experts under the conditions laid down by the Court in the rules of procedure referred to in Article 30."*

The draft-scheme of the Committee of Jurists had proposed the following text (Article 50):

> During the hearing in Court, the judges may put any questions considered by them to be necessary, to the witnesses, agents, experts, advocates, or counsel. The agents, advocates and counsel shall have the right to ask, through the President, any questions that the Court considers useful.

The first sentence of the Committee's draft was based on Articles 47 (1899), 72 (1907) of the Hague Conventions for Pacific Settlement, substantially reproduced in Article 40 of the "Five-Power Plan" with the *caveat* that questions put were not to be taken as expressions of opinion by the tribunal or its members. The matter was not discussed at length by the Committee of Jurists.[45] In the sub-committee of the Third Committee of the Assembly, the British delegation proposed to delete the second sentence of the draft; Sir Cecil Hurst explained that the draft was "based on the Continental system of procedure," and that "the British Government, in accordance with the Anglo-American system, would prefer to give more liberty to the judges." [46] The sub-committee adopted the final text by a narrow vote.[47]

§171. **Article 52.** *"After the Court has received the proofs and evidence within the time specified for the purpose, it may refuse to accept any further oral or written evidence that one party may desire to present unless the other side consents."*

This text was drafted by the Committee of Jurists (Article 51), and it was never discussed at any length.[48] A substantially similar provision is to be found in Articles 42 (1899), 67 (1907) of the Hague Conventions for Pacific Settlement.

§172. **Article 53.** *"Whenever one of the parties shall not appear before the Court, or shall fail to defend his case, the other party may call upon the Court to decide in favour of his claim.*

"The Court must, before doing so, satisfy itself, not only that it has jurisdiction in accordance with Articles 36 and 37, but also that the claim is well founded in fact and law."

---

[45] Minutes of the 1920 Committee of Jurists, p. 590.
[46] Documents, p. 135; Records of First Assembly, Committees, I, p. 369.
[47] *Ibid.*   [48] Minutes of the 1920 Committee of Jurists, pp. 590, 650.

The substance of this article was contained in the draft-scheme of the Committee of Jurists (Article 52). A somewhat similar provision appeared in Article 15 of the Convention creating the Central American Court of Justice, in Article 40 of the Prize Court Convention of 1907, and in a number of the post-war drafts including the "Five-Power Plan." In view of the Committee of Jurists' proposal for obligatory jurisdiction, it seemed necessary to include this provision for judgments by default, though this was the subject of some opposition.[49] In the report of the Committee of Jurists, special justification is given of the requirement that a State should support its claim before it may be entitled to a default judgment; and it is stated that in formulating this article the Committee "drew its inspiration from the example set by English national legal practice, and the legal practice of the American Supreme Court in interstate litigation."[50] At the suggestion of the Italian delegation, the sub-committee of the Third Committee dropped a proposed requirement that the judgment be "supported by substantial evidence."[51]

§173. **Article 54.** *"When, subject to the control of the Court, the agents, advocates and counsel have completed their presentation of the case, the President shall declare the hearing closed.*

"The Court shall withdraw to consider the judgment.

"The deliberations of the Court shall take place in private and remain secret."

The substance of this article appeared in the draft-scheme of the Committee of Jurists (Article 53). It was never the subject of extended consideration. The ideas were taken from provisions in Articles 50 and 51 (1899), 77 and 78 (1907) of the Hague Conventions for Pacific Settlement, whence they had been embodied in Article 45 of the "Five-Power Plan."

§174. **Article 55.** *"All questions shall be decided by a majority of the judges present at the hearing.*

"In the event of an equality of votes, the President or his deputy shall have a casting vote."

This text was drafted by the Committee of Jurists (Article 54). It was the subject of little discussion, either in the Committee of Jurists,[52] or in the Assembly. It restates Article 27 of the Hague *projet*

---

[49] Minutes of the 1920 Committee of Jurists, p. 590.   [50] *Id.*, p. 740.
[51] Documents, pp. 30, 136; Records of First Assembly, Committees, I, pp. 370, 499. The Italian Council for Diplomatic Litigation considered these words "useless and dangerous."   [52] Minutes of the 1920 Committee of Jurists, pp. 591, 650.

of 1907, omitting a provision for not counting the vote of a junior judge when the votes are equal [53] and substituting the casting vote of the President. Various preliminary drafts included similar provisions, particularly Article 45 of the "Five-Power Plan."

§175. Article 56. *"The judgment shall state the reasons on which it is based.*

"It shall contain the names of the judges who have taken part in the decision."

This article was drafted by the Committee of Jurists (Article 55). It was never a subject of lengthy discussion,[54] being based almost textually on Article 28 of the Hague *projet* of 1907, and Article 79 of the 1907 Hague Convention for Pacific Settlement. The "Five-Power Plan" contained a substantially similar provision.

§176. Article 57. *"If the judgment does not represent in whole or in part the unanimous opinion of the judges, dissenting judges are entitled to deliver a separate opinion."*

The Committee of Jurists had proposed (Article 56) that dissenting judges should "be entitled to have the fact of their dissent or reservations mentioned" in the judgment, but that the "reasons for their dissent or reservations" should not be expressed. Article 52 of the 1899 Hague Convention for Pacific Settlement provided for a record of dissent, but this provision was omitted in Article 79 of the 1907 Hague Convention, and no provision for dissenting opinions was included in the Hague *projet* of 1907. A provision for inclusion in the judgment of "the purport of the dissenting findings" appeared in Article 46 of the "Five-Power Plan," however. The Committee of Jurists refused to accept a suggestion that reasons for dissent might be stated,[55] this being thought particularly undesirable in the case of national judges.[56] When the draft-scheme of the Committee of Jurists came before the Council, M. Bourgeois suggested an amendment,[57] and the Council approved the following text: [58] "If the judgment does not express wholly or partially the unanimous opinion of the judges, those dissenting have the right to add to it a statement of their individual opinion." In the sub-committee of the Third Committee,

---

[53] Such a provision was contained in earlier drafts of the Committee of Jurists. *Id.*, p. 570.　　　　[54] Minutes of the 1920 Committee of Jurists, pp. 591, 650.
[55] Minutes of the 1920 Committee of Jurists, p. 591.　　　[56] *Id.*, p. 742.
[57] Documents, p. 50; Records of First Assembly, Committees, I, p. 478. Its object was stated to be to assure that "the play of the different judicial lines of thought would appear clearly." *Ibid.*
[58] Documents, p. 44; Minutes of the Council, 10th session, p. 161.

M. Loder found this idea "foreign to Continental procedure" and fraught with "danger to the authority of the Court," chiefly because of the national judges.[59] The Italian delegation proposed the suppression of the article, but it was retained by the sub-committee in spite of the opposition.[60]

§177. Article 58. *"The judgment shall be signed by the President and by the Registrar. It shall be read in open Court, due notice having been given to the agents."*

This article was drafted by the Committee of Jurists (Article 57), but it was never discussed at length.[61] It is based on Articles 79 and 80 of the 1907 Hague Convention for Pacific Settlement, and on Article 28 of the Hague *projet* of 1907; and possibly those articles may be taken into account in its interpretation.[62] A proposal of the Argentine delegation to require signature also by the participating judges was not taken up in the Assembly.[63]

§178. Article 59. *"The decision of the Court has no binding force except between the parties and in respect of that particular case."*

This text found no place in the draft-scheme of the Committee of Jurists, though it is clearly in line with Article 84 of the 1907 Hague Convention on Pacific Settlement. In substance it was proposed by the Council in its meeting at Brussels.[64] Mr. Balfour foresaw that the decisions of the Court would "have the effect of gradually moulding and modifying international law," and he wished to leave it open to a State to protest "not against a particular decision," but "against any ulterior conclusions to which that decision may seem to point."[65] M. Bourgeois therefore proposed what became the final text, and it was said to be a statement of what Article 61 of the Committee of Jurists' draft "indirectly admits."[66] Little consideration was given to this article in the First Assembly.[67]

---

[59] Documents, p. 136; Records of First Assembly, Committees, I, p. 371.

[60] Documents, p. 138; Records of First Assembly, Committees, I, p. 375.

[61] Minutes of the 1920 Committee of Jurists, pp. 591, 650.

[62] Thus, as it was explained to the Hague Conference of 1907, the signature by the President does not indicate that the judgment expresses his views. See Scott, Proceedings of the 1907 Conference, I, p. 385.

[63] Documents, p. 69; Records of First Assembly, Committees, I, p. 520.

[64] Documents, p. 44; Minutes of the Council, 10th session, p. 161. A very similar provision was contained in Article 46 of the Swiss *avant-projet* of 1919.

[65] Documents, p. 38; Records of First Assembly, Committees, I, p. 512.

[66] Documents, p. 50; Records of First Assembly, Committees, I, p. 478.

[67] An amendment proposed by the Argentine delegation to the Committee of Jurists' Article 35 was in an opposite sense to the latter part of Article 59. Documents, p. 68; Records of First Assembly, Committees, I, p. 519. Similarly Lord Cecil's "Suggestions" in 1919 had provided for the Court's decisions to be "binding precedents for itself." Miller, Drafting of the Covenant, I, p. 62.

§179. Article 60. *"The judgment is final and without appeal. In the event of dispute as to the meaning or scope of the judgment, the Court shall construe it upon the request of any party."*

This text was proposed by the Committee of Jurists (Article 58), with the phrase "in the event of uncertainty" in the English version instead of "in the event of dispute." It was based on Articles 54 (1899), 81 and 82 (1907) of the Hague Conventions for Pacific Settlement, and provisions in Articles 57 and 58 of the Netherlands draft of 1919. The proposal was not discussed at length, either in the Committee of Jurists,[68] or in the First Assembly. An Argentine proposal to include sanctions in the Article was not approved.[69]

§180. Article 61. *"An application for revision of a judgment can be made only when it is based upon the discovery of some fact of such a nature as to be a decisive factor, which fact was, when the judgment was given, unknown to the Court and also to the party claiming revision, always provided that such ignorance was not due to negligence.*

"The proceedings for revision will be opened by a judgment of the Court expressly recording the existence of the new fact, recognizing that it has such a character as to lay the case open to revision, and declaring the application admissible on this ground.

"The Court may require previous compliance with the terms of the judgment before it admits proceedings in revision.

"The application for revision must be made at latest within six months of the discovery of the new fact.

"No application for revision may be made after the lapse of ten years from the date of the sentence."

This article with exception of the fourth paragraph follows a draft by the Committee of Jurists. It is based upon Articles 55 (1899), 83 (1907) of the Hague Conventions for Pacific Settlement, and the ideas appear in some form in most of the post-war drafts.[70] A time limit was added by the Committee of Jurists; and because of its fear "that a party might delay compliance with a sentence until the expiration of this period" in the hope of discovering some new fact, the third paragraph was added.[71] In the first paragraph, the sub-committee of the Third Committee dropped the qualification "new" in respect

---

[68] Minutes of the 1920 Committee of Jurists, pp. 591, 650.
[69] Documents, p. 64; Records of First Assembly, Committees, I, p. 520.
[70] Minutes of the 1920 Committee of Jurists, pp. 91–3.   [71] *Id.*, p. 745.

of the fact which might base an application for revision; and in the fifth paragraph, on an Italian proposal, it substituted "ten years" for the "five years" proposed by the Committee of Jurists.[72] On a proposal by the Canadian delegation, the fourth paragraph was added by a narrow vote, though M. Ricci-Busatti (Italy) pointed out that "the discovery of the new fact was a very indefinite point of departure."

§181. **Article 62.** *"Should a State consider that it has an interest of a legal nature which may be affected by the decision in the case, it may submit a request to the Court to be permitted to intervene as a third party.*

"It will be for the Court to decide upon this request."

This text was drafted by the Committee of Jurists (Article 60),[73] which gave the explanation in its report that a State may intervene as a plaintiff, or as a defendant, or to claim "exclusive rights," or to ask the withdrawal of a party.[74] The Committee wished to exclude "political intervention." It agreed to leave open the question whether there would have to be a judge of the nationality of the intervening State on the bench.[75] The text was not extensively discussed in the First Assembly. The sub-committee of the Third Committee refused to add a provision allowing intervention by the International Labor Office and other similar international institutions.[76] Article 62 may come to have importance in connection with attempts to secure a uniform application of international legislation.

§182. **Article 63.** *"Whenever the construction of a convention to which States other than those concerned in the case are parties is in question, the Registrar shall notify all such States forthwith.*

"Every State so notified has the right to intervene in the proceedings: but if it uses this right, the construction given by the judgment will be equally binding upon it."

This text is substantially that proposed by the Committee of Jurists (Article 61); it is based on Articles 56 (1899), 84 (1907) of the Hague Conventions for Pacific Settlement. It provides for intervention in certain cases, which the Court cannot deny.[77] In preliminary drafts, the concluding provision gave the judgment the effect of

---

[72] Documents, p. 139; Records of First Assembly, Committees, I, p. 375.
[73] Minutes of the 1920 Committee of Jurists, pp. 592–4.
[74] *Id.*, p. 746.   [75] *Id.*, p. 593. See §385, *infra.*
[76] Documents, pp. 155, 213; Records of First Assembly, Committees, I, pp. 400, 537.
[77] Minutes of the 1920 Committee of Jurists, pp. 594, 746.

res judicata as to the intervening party.[78] The article was the subject of little discussion in the Assembly.

§183. **Article 64.** *"Unless otherwise decided by the Court, each party shall bear its own costs."*

This text was drafted by the Committee of Jurists (Article 62). It was adopted with little discussion, either in the Committee of Jurists,[79] or in the Assembly. Article 29 of the Hague *projet* of 1907 provided that "each party pays its own costs and an equal share of the costs of the trial," and Articles 57 (1899), 85 (1907) of the Hague Conventions for Pacific Settlement are similar in effect. In the sub-committee of the Third Committee, the British delegation suggested an addition which would enable a departure from the rule to be made "by the agreement of the parties"; the British view was stated to be that "the costs of the suit should be borne by the losing party, except in the case of agreement between the parties." [80] In its report, "the sub-committee unanimously recognise that the terms of this article do not prevent division of the costs between the parties in accordance with an agreement between them." [81]

§184. **Advisory Opinions.** The following text was proposed by the Committee of Jurists (Article 36):

> The Court shall give an advisory opinion upon any question or dispute of an international nature referred to it by the Council or Assembly.
>
> When the Court shall give an opinion on a question of an international nature which does not refer to any dispute that may have arisen, it shall appoint a special Commission of from three to five members.
>
> When it shall give an opinion upon a question which forms the subject of an existing dispute, it shall do so under the same conditions as if the case had been actually submitted to it for decision.

The Root-Phillimore proposal would have restricted the giving of advisory opinions to "any subject or question" submitted by the Council or Assembly. [82] Mr. Root later explained that he was opposed to the Court's giving an advisory opinion "with reference to an existing dispute," [83] though he seems to have abandoned this position.[84] M. de Lapradelle envisaged a smaller number of judges to deal with a request

---

[78] *Id.*, pp. 571, 594, 650.
[79] Minutes of the 1920 Committee of Jurists, pp. 594, 651.
[80] Documents, pp. 71, 139; Records of First Assembly, Committees, I, pp. 376, 593.
[81] Documents, p. 213; Records of First Assembly, Committees, I, p. 537.
[82] Minutes of the 1920 Committee of Jurists, p. 548.
[83] *Id.*, p. 584.   [84] *Id.*, p. 585.

for an opinion on a "theoretical question." [85] The text received but scant consideration. [86] The report of the Committee of Jurists refers to the Court's advisory jurisdiction as being "apart from its judicial competence"; [87] if an opinion is given "in the abstract," it is "simply advisory, so that the Court must not be bound by this opinion should the question come before it as a concrete case." Even when a dispute is involved, the advisory opinion "would not have the force of a sentence binding upon the two parties"; [88] the Committee suggested that national judges should sit in this latter case, however.

In the First Assembly, the Italian delegation wished to redraft the article and to delete the last paragraph, [89] and the Argentine delegation wished to allow the Government of any Member of the League of Nations to request an advisory opinion. [90] The Director of the International Labor Office proposed that the Governing Body of the International Labor Office be permitted to make requests for advisory opinions. [91] When the sub-committee of the Third Committee began its consideration of the proposed article, it was recognized that "the report explaining the difference in procedure between the two cases had not been sufficiently discussed by the Committee of Jurists." [92] M. Hagerup mentioned the Aaland Islands dispute as one in which an advisory opinion might have been requested. [93] M. Ricci-Busatti thought that "in practice it would be impossible for the Court to draw a distinction between the cases contemplated for the second and third paragraphs of Article 36." [94] M. Fromageot thought that "it was to be regretted that the Covenant gave to the Court advisory capacities." The sub-committee first decided to delete the last paragraph of the article; [95] but when a redraft was undertaken, the drafting committee reported unanimously that the article should be suppressed as unnecessary, inasmuch as "the Court could

---

[85] Minutes of the 1920 Committee of Jurists, p. 584.
[86] *Id.*, p. 649.   [87] *Id.*, p. 730.   [88] *Id.*, p. 731.
[89] Documents, p. 30; Records of First Assembly, Committees, I, p. 499.
[90] Documents, p. 68; Records of First Assembly, Committees, I, p. 519.
[91] Documents, p. 79; Records of First Assembly, Committees, I, p. 563.
[92] Documents, p. 146; Records of First Assembly, Committees, I, p. 386.
[93] *Ibid.* In a report to the Council on July 11, 1920, proposing that a preliminary question in the Aaland Islands dispute be referred to a committee of jurists, Mr. Balfour (Great Britain) declared that this question would have been referred for advisory opinion to the Court, "had that body already been established." Minutes of the Council, 7th session, p. 61.
[94] Documents, p. 146; Records of First Assembly, Committees, I, p. 387. Yet it is to be noted that this distinction is made in the amendment to Article 71 of the Rules, adopted by the Court in 1927. See §337, *infra.*
[95] Documents, p. 146; Records of First Assembly, Committees, I, p. 388.

not refuse to give advisory opinions" under Article 14 of the Covenant.[96] By unanimous vote the sub-committee made a recommendation
in this sense; in its report, it stated that advisory opinions "should, in
every case, be given with the same quorum of judges as that required
for the decision of disputes"; and that the draft of the Committee of
Jurists "here entered into details which concerned rather the rules
of procedure of the Court." [97] The suppression of the article does not
appear to have been discussed by the Third Committee. Thus the
Statute of the Court came to be adopted with no express reference to
advisory opinions.[98]

[96] Documents, p. 156; Records of First Assembly, Committees, I, p. 401.
[97] Documents, p. 211; Records of First Assembly, Committees, I, p. 534.
[98] On the incorporation of the provision for advisory opinions in Article 14 of the
Covenant by the reference in Article 1 of the Statute, see §450, *infra*.

CHAPTER 9

THE REVISION OF THE STATUTE

§185. **Lack of Provision for Amendment.** It is an unfortunate *lacuna* in the Statute of the Court annexed to the Protocol of Signature of December 16, 1920, that it makes no provision for the adoption of future amendments. The possibility of including such a provision was not discussed by the Committee of Jurists at The Hague in 1920, nor does it seem to have been referred to when the draft-scheme was being prepared for the approval of the First Assembly. Yet it must have been obvious that no text could be framed which would be completely satisfactory for all time to come. The omission was the more singular because of the provision which had been made for the amendment of the Covenant of the League of Nations. Article 26 of the Covenant permits amendments to the Covenant to "take effect when ratified by the Members of the League whose representatives compose the Council and by a majority of the Members of the League whose representatives compose the Assembly"; and it takes into account the general principle that a State cannot be bound by legislation to which it has not assented by providing that "no such amendment shall bind any Member of the League which signifies its dissent therefrom, but in that case it shall cease to be a Member of the League." [1] The Covenant had not been in force for two years when various amendments were projected, including amendments to Article 26 itself, and some of these amendments have been brought into force.[2] Moreover, provision had been made for the amendment of the constitution of the International Labor Organization as contained in Part XIII of the Treaty of Versailles of June 28, 1919, and in the corresponding parts of other treaties of peace; Article 422 of the Treaty of Versailles provides that amendments to Part XIII "which are adopted

---

[1] For a commentary on Article 26 of the Covenant, see Manley O. Hudson, "Amendment of the Covenant of the League of Nations," 38 Harvard Law Review (1925), pp. 903–942.
[2] See 1 Hudson, International Legislation, pp. 18–42.

by the [International Labor] Conference by a majority of two-thirds of the votes cast by the Delegates present shall take effect when ratified by the States whose representatives compose the Council of the League of Nations and by three-fourths of the Members." [3] In view of the situation as it existed in 1920, therefore, it was an amazing lack of foresight which caused the draftsmen of the Statute of the Court to fail to include a provision for the amendment of the Statute.

§186. **Method of Amendment.** Though the Statute fails to envisage any process of amendment, its provisions cannot be immutable. The general rule of international law is that a modification in an international instrument may be effected by all the parties. Yet the question arises whether all the parties to the Protocol of Signature can amend the Statute without the coöperation of the Assembly and perhaps of the Council of the League of Nations. The Statute was approved by the First Assembly in 1920 before the Protocol of Signature was opened to signature, yet the resolution of the Assembly did not purport to give force to the Statute. In view of the close relation of the Court to the League of Nations, and particularly of the provision in Article 33 of the Statute that "the expenses of the Court shall be borne by the League of Nations," the Assembly's approval at some time was essential, as a practical matter; and since there has never been a time when all the Members of the League of Nations were parties to the Protocol of Signature, such approval may have been legally necessary. [4] If all the Members of the League of Nations should become parties to the Protocol of Signature, perhaps the Statute might be amended without any action taken in the Council or Assembly; or if all the parties to the Protocol of Signature desired to divorce the Court from the League of Nations completely, the Statute might be amended by their action alone. Otherwise, however, it would seem to be necessary that any amendment of the Statute must be accepted in some way by all the Members of the League.

§187. **Necessity of Unanimous Consent.** Action by the parties to the Protocol of Signature with a view to the amendment of the Statute is governed by a general principle of international law that in the absence of specific provisions to the contrary the stipulations of an international instrument can be modified only with the consent

---

[3] One amendment, to Article 393, was projected in 1922, but it did not come into force until June 4, 1934. See 1 Hudson, International Legislation, pp. 248–253.

[4] See the remarks of M. Rolin (Belgium), Records of Ninth Assembly, First Committee, pp. 39–40.

of all parties.[5] If this principle has not been universally observed in connection with the maintenance of international institutions,[6] it is nevertheless generally accepted as one of the basic principles of international legislation. Applied to the Statute, it involves the necessity of consent by each State or Member of the League of Nations which may have signed and ratified, or which may have adhered to, the Protocol of Signature of December 16, 1920, before any amendment to the Statute can be put into effect. It is to be noted, however, that the general principle of international law does not require that such consent be manifested in any particular way; it may even be informal.

§188. French Proposal of 1928. For six years after the inauguration of the Court in 1922, no proposals were advanced for the amendment of the Statute. This was not wholly due to satisfaction with the work of the Court; it was due, rather, to a feeling that further experimentation was not wise until the Court had been placed on firm foundations. With the approach of a general election of judges in 1930, however, the occasion seemed to be presented for some changes to be made. Though there was no widespread dissatisfaction, some events in the history of the Court itself may have encouraged such an effort; the decision of the *Lotus Case* by an evenly divided Court in 1927, the difficulty in securing a full attendance of judges at other than the summer sessions, the frequent summoning of deputy-judges, and delays in the disposition of cases, possibly contributed to produce a willingness to consider changes which might be made. The French delegation in the Ninth Assembly of the League of Nations took the initiative in this direction, and having secured the support of other delegations, on September 7, 1928, it submitted a draft resolution to the Assembly on behalf of twenty delegations.[7] A statement accompanying the draft mentioned "the ever-growing number of matters referred" to the Court and "certain defects revealed by eight years of work." No explanation was offered to the Assembly as to what these defects were, however. M. Fromageot (France) explained to the First Committee that the draft resolution was "quite innocuous," that it contained not "so much as the

---

[5] The London Protocol of January 17, 1871, contains a formal statement of this principle. 61 British and Foreign State Papers, p. 1198; Hudson, Cases on International Law, p. 998.

[6] By a protocol of April 21, 1926, the Convention of June 7, 1905, creating the International Institute of Agriculture, seems to have been modified without the consent of all parties. See 3 Hudson, International Legislation, p. 1857.

[7] Records of Ninth Assembly, Plenary, p. 55.

shadow of a criticism against the Court," and that "there must be no risk of upsetting an organism which was working extremely well"; [8] but he failed to say why the proposed examination of the Statute was thought to be desirable. As *rapporteur* for the First Committee, M. Cassin (France) later explained that it was intended not to revise but to reëxamine the Statute, "with a view to remedying such defects as experience may have brought to light." [9]

§189. **Assembly Resolution of September 20, 1928.** When the French proposal came before the First Committee of the Assembly, some apprehension was expressed that the process of amendment with the assent of all parties to the Protocol of Signature could not be completed before 1930. The First Committee approved a draft resolution on September 15, 1928,[10] omitting a proposed statement, "in view of Article 14 of the Covenant of the League of Nations, under which the Council is responsible for preparing the Statute of the Court with a view to its submission to the Assembly for approval." On September 20, 1928, the Assembly adopted the resolution in the following form: [11]

> The Assembly:
> Considering the ever-increasing number of matters referred to the Permanent Court of International Justice;
> Deeming it advisable that, before the renewal of the term of office of the members of the Court in 1930, the present provisions of the Statute of the Court should be examined with a view to the introduction of any amendments which experience may show to be necessary;
> Draws the Council's attention to the advisability of proceeding, before the renewal of the term of office of the members of the Permanent Court of International Justice, to the examination of the Statute of the Court with a view to the introduction of such amendments as may be judged desirable, and to submitting the necessary proposals to the next ordinary session of the Assembly.

§190. **The 1929 Committee of Jurists.** Having before it the Assembly's resolution, on December 14, 1928, the Council of the League of Nations decided to entrust the study of the Statute to a Committee of Jurists with "wide terms of reference"; [12] and it named the following to constitute the Committee: M. Fromageot (France), M. Gaus

---

[8] Records of Ninth Assembly, First Committee, pp. 33–35. [9] *Id.*, Plenary, p. 110.
[10] Records of Ninth Assembly, First Committee, p. 40. [11] *Id.*, Plenary, p. 112.
[12] League of Nations Official Journal, 1929, pp. 35, 56.

(Germany), Sir Cecil Hurst (Great Britain), M. Ito (Japan), M. Politis (Greece), M. Raestad (Norway), M. Rundstein (Poland), M. Scialoja (Italy), M. Urrutia (Colombia), M. van Eysinga (Netherlands), and Mr. Elihu Root (United States.) [13] The Council also invited the President and the Vice-President of the Court "to participate in the work of the Committee." The chairman of the Supervisory Commission, M. Osusky (Czechoslovakia), was later asked to assist the Committee; and on March 9, 1929, M. Pilotti (Italy) was invited to become a member of the Committee.[14] On March 9, 1929, the Council decided to refer to the Committee the question of the accession of the United States of America, that question being related to the problem of revision.

The Committee of Jurists held fifteen meetings at Geneva, March 11–19, 1929.[15] The President and Vice-President of the Court accepted the invitation to be present at the meetings of the Committee, with the reservation that their presence was not to be taken to indicate an opinion that any revision was necessary; they did not vote, however.[16] The Committee drafted amendments to eighteen articles of the Statute, and proposed the addition of four new articles on advisory opinions. On June 12, 1929, the Council of the League of Nations decided to communicate the Committee's report [17] to the Members of the League of Nations and to the States mentioned in the Annex of the Covenant, and to convoke a "conference of States parties to the Statute" for the purpose of "examining the amendments." [18] In this latter action, the Council followed the precedent which it had set in 1926 in convoking a conference of signatories to deal with the proposed accession by the United States to the Protocol of Signature of December 16, 1920.[19]

[13] Mr. Root was later named by the President of the Council; he was the only member of the committee who had served as a member of the Committee of Jurists in 1920.   [14] League of Nations Official Journal, 1929, p. 566.
[15] The Committee's minutes are published in League of Nations Document, C. 166. M. 66. 1929. V. In the publications of the League of Nations, the Committee is referred to as the "Committee of Jurists on the Statute of the Permanent Court of International Justice."
[16] Minutes of the 1929 Committee of Jurists, p. 25. The Registrar of the Court also assisted the Committee in the drafting.
[17] League of Nations Official Journal, 1929, p. 1113. A separate report was made on the accession of the United States. See §234, infra.   [18] Id., p. 997.
[19] It seems very doubtful whether the expedient of a more or less independent conference of signatories would ever have been resorted to, if both the Conferences of 1926 and 1929 had not been concerned with the proposed accession by the United States of America, which was not a member of the League of Nations. It is to be noted, however, that Brazil was represented at the Conference of Signatories in 1929, after its withdrawal from membership in the League of Nations.

§191. **The Conference of Signatories of 1929.** At the Conference of Signatories, which held five meetings in Geneva, September 4–12, 1929,[20] forty-eight States or Members of the League of Nations were represented,[21] including several States which had signed but had not ratified the Protocol of Signature of December 16, 1920. The work of the Conference was mainly devoted to a study of the amendments to the Statute proposed by the Committee of Jurists and to the drafting of a protocol for putting these amendments as revised and amplified into force. The Conference stopped short, however, of attempting to promulgate in any form the draft protocol and amendments which it "adopted"; nor did it open the draft protocol to signature. Instead, it appointed *rapporteurs* to present the results of its work to the Tenth Assembly of the League of Nations, then in session.[22] On September 12, 1929, the President of the Conference, M. van Eysinga, addressed a letter [23] to the President of the Tenth Assembly of the League of Nations and to the chairman of the First Committee of the Tenth Assembly, communicating to them the texts of the draft protocol and amendments as adopted by the Conference, as well as a draft of a resolution which the Assembly might adopt. It was suggested that the Assembly should "by a suitable resolution, adopt for its part the amendments to the Statute of the Court and the draft protocol relating thereto," and that in this event there would be no obstacle to opening the draft protocol to signature.

§192. **Assembly Resolution of September 14, 1929.** The First Committee of the Tenth Assembly comprised among its members a large number of the men who had represented their Governments at the 1929 Conference of Signatories, as well as a number of those who had served on the 1929 Committee of Jurists. The First Committee had before it the report which had been submitted to the Council by the 1929 Committee of Jurists; consideration of this report was postponed pending the discussion of the report in the 1929 Conference of Signatories, though the chairman of the First Committee was careful to point out that the Assembly's position in the matter was safeguarded.[24] On September 13, 1929, after a brief discussion, the First Committee

---

[20] The minutes of the Conference are published in League of Nations Document, C. 514. M. 173. 1929. V.
[21] *Id.*, p. 5. The *rapporteur* of the First Committee of the Tenth Assembly stated that fifty-four States or Members of the League of Nations were represented. Records of Tenth Assembly, Plenary, p. 115.   [22] Minutes of the 1929 Conference, p. 53.
[23] *Id.*, p. 78.   [24] Records of Tenth Assembly, First Committee, p. 57.

adopted the draft resolution relating to the amendments and the draft protocol placed before it by President van Eysinga's communication,[25] and its *rapporteur* informed the plenary Assembly that the First Committee was "in entire agreement with the views expressed by the Conference [of Signatories] as regards the revision of the Court's Statute." [26] With little discussion the Assembly adopted the following resolution proposed by the First Committee, on September 14, 1929: [27]

> The Assembly adopts the amendments to the Statute of the Permanent Court of International Justice and the draft Protocol which the Conference convened by the Council of the League of Nations has drawn up after consideration of the report of the Committee of Jurists, which met in March 1929 at Geneva and which included among its members a jurist of the United States of America. The Assembly expresses the hope that the draft Protocol drawn up by the Conference may receive as many signatures as possible before the close of the present session of the Assembly and that all the Governments concerned will use their utmost efforts to secure the entry into force of the amendments to the Statute of the Court before the opening of the next session of the Assembly, in the course of which the Assembly and the Council will be called upon to proceed to a new election of the members of the Court.

§193. **The Revision Protocol of September 14, 1929.** In pursuance of the decision taken by the Conference of Signatories on September 12, 1929, and of the Assembly resolution of September 14, 1929, the Protocol drafted by the Conference of Signatories was opened to signature on September 14, 1929.[28] This Protocol provided that it should "be presented for signature to all the signatories of the Protocol of December 16, 1920," and to the United States of America. Though reference is made in the Protocol to "the amendments which are set out in the Annex," the provisions in the Annex were drafted on a different basis, for it is there provided that certain articles of the Statute are to be replaced by a "new text" (Fr., *nouvelle rédaction*) in each case. It was provided that after the Protocol had entered into force, the new provisions should form part of the Statute and that the provisions of the original articles which had been made the subject of amendment should be abrogated; and that thereafter "any acceptance of the Statute" should "constitute an acceptance of the Statute as

---

[25] *Id.,* pp. 9, 70.   [26] *Id.,* Plenary, p. 436.   [27] *Id.,* p. 121.
[28] For the text, see League of Nations Document, C. 492. M. 156. 1929. V; 1 Hudson, International Legislation, p. 582; *infra,* p. 631. In the publications of the League of Nations, the Protocol is referred to as a Protocol on the "revision of the Statute."

amended." The new texts of the articles to which amendments were proposed must be dealt with *seriatim* and in detail.

§194. **New Article 3.** This text provides for fifteen judges, and omits the provisions for four deputy-judges and for the Assembly's increasing the number of judges upon the proposal of the Council. The amendment was proposed by the Committee of Jurists, which in its report stated that "practical experience suggested the desirability of abolishing the post of deputy-judge"; [29] though deputy-judges had frequently been called upon to sit, they were not subject to the same disabilities as judges. M. Fromageot observed that judges might be tempted to be absent because deputy-judges were at hand to take their places.[30] The change was also connected with various proposals that judges should be required to reside at The Hague. The report of the Committee of Jurists explained that the omission of the provision for power of the Assembly to increase the number of judges was "to avoid the risk of an exaggeration which might cause misconception." [31] In the Conference of Signatories, there was no disposition to retain the deputy-judges, though the Cuban representative was opposed to any change in Article 3, and voted against the amendment in the Conference.[32] M. Rundstein (Poland) sought to maintain the provision as to a possible increase in the number of judges, but this was rejected.[33]

§195. **New Article 4.** A new third paragraph is to be added to the original article, as follows:

> The conditions under which a State which has accepted the Statute of the Court but is not a Member of the League of Nations, may participate in electing the members of the Court shall, in the absence of a special agreement, be laid down by the Assembly on the proposal of the Council.

This addition was not considered by the Committee of Jurists. At the Conference of Signatories, the representative of Brazil asked that Brazil's situation in regard to the Court since its withdrawal from membership in the League of Nations, should be "regularized in a clear and precise manner." [34] Brazil desired to continue its contribu-

---

[29] Minutes of the 1929 Committee of Jurists, p. 119.   [30] *Id.*, p. 28.
[31] *Id.*, p. 119.   [32] Minutes of the 1929 Conference, p. 30.   [33] *Id.*, pp. 28–30.
[34] Minutes of the 1929 Conference, p. 75. Brazil ceased to be a Member of the League of Nations in 1928. On March 27, 1933, Japan gave notice of an intention to withdraw from membership in the League of Nations, and on October 21, 1933, similar notice was given by Germany; if this intention is carried out, Japan and Germany will be in the same position as Brazil.

tion to the expenses of the Court, and at the same time to participate "on a footing of equality" in the elections of judges. To meet this situation, the drafting committee of the Conference proposed an addition to Article 4, as well as an addition to Article 35.[35] The addition to Article 4 was adopted by the Conference with a slight modification of the original proposal.[36]

§196. New Article 8. The amended text drops the words "firstly the judges, then the deputy-judges," and substitutes "the members of the Court." This amendment was a consequence of the suppression of the post of deputy-judge in Article 3, and as such it called for no extended consideration.

§197. New Article 13. The amendment consists in the addition of two paragraphs, as follows:

> In the case of the resignation of a member of the Court, the resignation will be addressed to the President of the Court for transmission to the Secretary-General of the League of Nations.
> This last notification makes the place vacant.

The original Statute contains no provision concerning resignations. In the 1920 Committee of Jurists, M. Altamira had proposed a recognition of the right of a judge to resign, but the Committee thought such a provision unnecessary.[37] Only two judges have resigned from membership in the Court: Judge Moore resigned by addressing a letter to the Secretary-General of the League of Nations on April 11, 1928; [38] Judge Hughes resigned by addressing telegrams to the Secretary-General of the League of Nations and to the President of the Court, on February 14, 1930.[39] In each of these cases, the resignation was later accepted by the Council of the League of Nations provisionally, subject to the concurrence of the Assembly.[40]

The text of the new paragraphs was drafted by the Committee of Jurists, which stated that "doubts have been felt as to the procedure to be adopted in such cases," and that while the view should be adopted that the resignation becomes final on its transmission to the League of Nations, this transmission should be effected by the Presi-

---

[35] Minutes of the 1929 Conference, p. 76.   [36] Id., p. 50.

[37] Minutes of the 1920 Committee of Jurists, p. 554. Lord Phillimore said there was a "natural right" to resign. Id., p. 612.

[38] Series E, No. 4, p. 26.   [39] Series E, No. 6, p. 17.

[40] This was explained by the Secretary-General of the League of Nations to be necessary because both the Council and the Assembly had participated in the election. Minutes of the 1929 Committee of Jurists, p. 38.

dent of the Court "in order that he may, if desirable, be able to satisfy himself that the decision of the judge concerned is irrevocable." [41] It was pointed out in the discussions of the Committee of Jurists that this "implied that a judge could resign of his own right," *i.e.*, that no acceptance of the resignation was required.[42] In the Conference of Signatories, only the word "last" was inserted in the second new paragraph.[43]

§198. **New Article 14.** The second sentence of the original Article 14 was transferred to the new Article 15, and after the first sentence the following was added: "subject to the following provision: the Secretary-General of the League of Nations shall, within one month of the occurrence of the vacancy, proceed to issue the invitations provided for in Article 5, and the date of the election shall be fixed by the Council at its next session." In proposing to the Committee of Jurists that Article 14 should be amended, M. Fromageot drew attention to the possibility of "prolonged vacancies" under the existing Statute, contending that a seat might remain vacant for fifteen months if the vacancy occurred just three months prior to a regular session of the Assembly.[44] It was the desire of the Committee of Jurists "to establish a somewhat elastic system" which would allow a prompt filling of vacancies. This might in some cases, as the Council shall decide, involve the holding of extraordinary sessions of the Assembly.[45] The amendment gave rise to no discussion in the Conference of Signatories.

§199. **New Article 15.** This article in the original Statute, providing for lists of deputy-judges, was suppressed in consequence of the abolition of the post of deputy-judge. The new text is identical with the second sentence of Article 14 in the original Statute.

§200. **New Article 16.** The new text suppresses the distinction between ordinary judges and deputy-judges, and adds a new disability for all members of the Court that they may not "engage in any other occupation of a professional nature." M. Fromageot, in proposing to the Committee of Jurists that this article should be amended, suggested that members of the Court should "devote themselves exclusively to this high function" and should not "exercise any other functions." [46] Some members of the Committee desired to leave this question to "the conscience of the individual judges." [47] The dis-

---

[41] Minutes of the 1929 Committee of Jurists, p. 119.   [42] *Id.*, pp. 46–7.
[43] Minutes of the 1929 Conference, p. 31.
[44] Minutes of the 1929 Committee of Jurists, pp. 37–8.   [45] *Id.*, pp. 111–112.
[46] Minutes of the 1929 Committee of Jurists, p. 42.   [47] *Id.*, p. 44.

cussion followed the consideration of an amendment to Article 23, and the drafting was influenced accordingly. The Committee of Jurists adopted the addition in its final form,[48] but explained in its report that judges might be members of the Permanent Court of Arbitration, and might act as arbitrators or as conciliators when their duties on the Court permitted.[49] The proposal was the subject of some discussion in the Conference of Signatories; a Cuban proposal to restrict the disability to the exercise of "political functions" was rejected, and the Conference adopted the draft of the Committee of Jurists with the understanding that "occupation of a professional nature" was to be interpreted "in the widest sense," and to cover the activity of a director of a company.[50] It seems to have been agreed in the Conference, also, that a judge should not hold a post as a professor.

§201. **New Article 17.** The first paragraph of Article 17 in the original Statute provides:

> No member of the Court can act as agent, counsel or advocate in any case of an international nature. This provision only applies to the deputy-judges as regards cases in which they are called upon to exercise their functions on the Court.

The Committee of Jurists proposed that the first sentence of this paragraph should be retained, stating in its report that in view of the new Article 16, it would not "be possible to infer *a contrario*" that a member is "free to exercise the said functions in a case which is national in character." [51] In the Conference of Signatories, Sir Harrison Moore (Australia) proposed the deletion of the paragraph, but accepted the deletion of the words "of an international nature." [52] The new text therefore reads: "No member of the Court may act as agent, counsel or advocate in any case." The suppression of the second sentence in the first paragraph was a consequence of the amendment to Article 3. No amendment was made in the second and third paragraphs of Article 17.

§202. **New Article 23.** In the original Statute, Article 23 reads as follows:

> A session of the Court shall be held every year.

---

[48] Minutes of the 1929 Committee of Jurists, p. 45.   [49] *Id.*, p. 120.
[50] Minutes of the 1929 Conference, p. 33.
[51] Minutes of the 1929 Committee of Jurists, p. 120.
[52] Minutes of the 1929 Conference, p. 34.

Unless otherwise provided by Rules of Court, this session shall begin on the 15th of June, and shall continue for so long as may be deemed necessary to finish the cases on the list.

The President may summon an extraordinary session of the Court whenever necessary.

The new text provides:

The Court shall remain permanently in session except during the judicial vacations, the dates and duration of which shall be fixed by the Court.

Members of the Court whose homes are situated at more than five days' normal journey from The Hague shall be entitled, apart from the judicial vacations, to six months' leave every three years, not including the time spent in travelling.

Members of the Court shall be bound, unless they are on regular leave or prevented from attending by illness or other serious reason duly explained to the President, to hold themselves permanently at the disposal of the Court.

Dissatisfaction with the delays incident to convoking the Court had been one of the reasons for undertaking a study of the Statute. The judges' record of attendance had also been far from satisfactory, and in proposing an amendment to this article, the Committee of Jurists may have been influenced by the abortive session of the Court, November 12–21, 1928, when adjournment was necessitated by the illness of a single deputy-judge whose presence was necessary to a quorum. The increase of the number of judges to fifteen, the permanence of sessions, the duty to attend, long leave for judges who live in places distant from The Hague, and increase of salaries, were all related questions.

The Committee of Jurists desired to "bring the written rules into harmony with the facts" as to the frequency with which extraordinary sessions of the Court had been held.[53] It emphasized the importance of judges' attendance by stating an imperative duty, and it attempted to equalize the burden which performance of this duty would entail by providing for long leave to certain of the judges. For the first paragraph, the Committee of Jurists proposed: "The Court shall remain permanently in session except during the judicial vacations, the dates and duration of which shall be fixed by the Court at the end of each year for the following year." The Conference of Signatories

[53] Minutes of the 1929 Committee of Jurists, p. 121.

dropped this concluding phrase, to leave greater latitude to the Court.[54] Slight amendments were also made in the second paragraph as proposed by the Committee of Jurists.[55] The third paragraph was adopted by the Conference without change.[56] On the effect of the changes, an observation made to the Committee of Jurists by M. Politis is of interest: "Under the new organization which the Committee had adopted, it was anticipated that the Court would have seven months' work a year and three months' vacation; there remained two other months, which would be covered by various public holidays, travelling and so forth." [57]

§203. **New Article 25.** The second and third paragraphs of Article 25 in the original Statute were amended to read as follows:

Subject to the condition that the number of judges available to constitute the Court is not thereby reduced below eleven, the Rules of Court may provide for allowing one or more judges, according to circumstances and in rotation, to be dispensed from sitting.

Provided always that a quorum of nine judges shall suffice to constitute the Court.

The new second paragraph was originally proposed to the Committee of Jurists as an amendment to Article 23. The proposal was warmly supported by Mr. Root, who drew an analogy to the practice of the Supreme Court of the State of New York; he desired to enable the Court to make adjustments so that some of its members might be engaged on one case while others were engaged on another.[58] The Committee entered a *caveat* in its report, however, to the effect that no ground should be given for a suspicion "that the Court has in a given case been specially composed for the purpose of affecting the decision of the case." [59] The new third paragraph was partly due to the amendments introduced into Article 23. The Conference of Signatories accepted the amendments with little discussion.[60]

§204. **New Article 26.** The modifications of the original article are as follows: (1) In the fourth and fifth sentences of the second paragraph, merely drafting changes were made, in correspondence with the new Article 25. (2) The third paragraph was deleted to allow the participation of national judges in all cases and because of the text of the new Article 31. (3) A new fourth paragraph was inserted

---

[54] Minutes of the 1929 Conference, p. 38.   [55] *Ibid.*   [56] *Id.,* p. 39.
[57] Minutes of the 1929 Committee of Jurists, p. 56.
[58] Minutes of the 1929 Committee of Jurists, p. 74.   [59] *Id.,* p. 121.
[60] Minutes of the 1929 Conference, p. 39.

to allow the parties to resort to summary procedure as provided in the new Article 29. The changes provided chiefly for a possible recourse to summary procedure for labor cases, and for the participation of national judges *ad hoc*.[61] The Committee of Jurists consulted the Director of the International Labor Office with reference to these amendments, and he offered no objection.[62] The text proposed by the Committee was accepted by the Conference of Signatories.[63]

§205. **New Article 27.** The modifications introduced into the original article correspond to those introduced into Article 26. When the Committee of Jurists consulted the League of Nations Advisory and Technical Committee on Communications and Transit with reference to these alterations, the latter pointed out that no resort had been had to the special chamber provided for by Article 27; it expressed the opinion that the Court *in pleno* should deal with cases relating to disputes as to transit and communications questions, and that on the technical aspects of such questions the assessors were not likely "to afford the Court any real assistance"; [64] and it suggested as an alternative to the suppression of the article, that resort to summary procedure should be permitted. This reply was not debated at length,[65] but the Committee of Jurists decided to retain the article as modified.[66] In the Conference of Signatories, the Danish representative stated that his Government preferred to abolish this special chamber for transit and communications cases, and to constitute a special chamber for international commercial disputes.[67] The Conference adopted the text of the Committee of Jurists, however.

§206. **New Article 29.** The changes in Article 29 provide for enlarging the chamber for summary procedure from three to five judges, and for the Court's selecting two judges as substitutes. In the Committee of Jurists, it was thought that the Court's exclusion of national judges from the chamber for summary procedure may have been a reason for the fact that but little use had been made of this

---

[61] Minutes of the 1929 Committee of Jurists, pp. 47–48, 50, 52–53, 121–122.

[62] *Id.*, pp. 53, 69.   [63] Minutes of the 1929 Conference, pp. 38–40.

[64] Minutes of the 1929 Committee of Jurists, p. 69.

[65] *Id.*, p. 74.   [66] *Id.*, p. 122.

[67] Minutes of the 1929 Conference, p. 40. In 1930, a proposal was submitted to the Preliminary Conference with a view to Concerted Economic Action, at Geneva, for "the establishment of a permanent body for arbitration and conciliation." This proposal resulted in the creation of a group of experts for dealing with economic disputes, by the Council of the League of Nations on January 28, 1932. League of Nations Official Journal, 1932, pp. 463, 596. See also, 26 American Journal of International Law (1932), p. 353.

procedure; [68] the increase of the number of judges in the chamber would allow two national judges to be included on each occasion. The second change makes Article 29 correspond with Articles 26 and 27 with respect to substitutes. The amendments were adopted by the Conference of Signatories without discussion.[69]

§207. **New Article 31.** The alterations made in the original text of Article 31 are the following: (1) in the first paragraph, "each of the contesting parties" is substituted for "each contesting party"; (2) in the second paragraph, the word "only" is dropped and the reference to deputy-judges is omitted with some consequent redrafting; (3) in the third paragraph, the changes are merely verbal; (4) a new paragraph is added providing for the participation of national judges in the chambers, to replace other members of the chamber; (5) in the final paragraph, the drafting is modified, the reference to Article 16 is suppressed, and in the concluding phrase the words "on an equal footing" are replaced by the words "on terms of complete equality." The discussion in the Committee of Jurists brought forth an interesting suggestion by M. Politis that judges *ad hoc* should be chosen from a list of assessor judges, two of whom would be named by each Member of the League of Nations, on analogy to the lists of assessors provided for in Articles 26 and 27; [70] but this suggestion was not adopted. The discussion also led Sir Cecil Hurst to raise the question as to the meaning of "nationality" with reference to the British Empire; he desired "to coördinate the practice of the Court and that of the Council of the League" in this respect.[71] He contended that an English judge would not be qualified to represent the local law of a Dominion in the same manner as would a national judge,[72] yet at the same time he denied the possibility of the Court's dealing with a dispute between Great Britain and a Dominion, as "the relations between them were not international." [73] Sir Cecil Hurst refrained from proposing an amendment because a "close study" of the Statute had convinced him that it was unnecessary,[74] but he asked that his interpretation be embodied in the Committee's report; in the face of considerable opposition, voiced particularly by M. Politis, this request was withdrawn.[75]

---

[68] Minutes of the 1929 Committee of Jurists, pp. 49–50.
[69] Minutes of the 1929 Conference, p. 40.
[70] Minutes of the 1929 Committee of Jurists, p. 54.   [71] *Id.*, p. 70.
[72] *Id.*, p. 71.   [73] *Id.*, p. 72.   [74] *Id.*, p. 84.
[75] *Id.*, pp. 85–87. For a discussion of the question raised by Sir Cecil Hurst, see Walter Pollak, "The Eligibility of British Subjects as Judges of the Permanent Court of International Justice," 20 American Journal of International Law (1926), p. 714. See also, §257, *infra*.

The precise texts of the amendments proposed in Article 31 were only hurriedly considered by the Committee of Jurists.[76] No change was made in them by the Conference of Signatories, though M. Cohn (Denmark) took occasion to observe that equality would be better attained if each party could appoint a judge *ad hoc* where only one of the parties had a national among the judges, such national being required to retire from the bench for that particular case.[77]

§208. **New Article 32.** The text of Article 32 was almost completely redrafted by the Committee of Jurists. M. Politis explained that the original text was based on "the assumption that there would only be occasional meetings of the Court," and that the requirement of permanent sessions necessitated a reconsideration of the "system of remuneration." [78] The principal changes proposed by the Committee were the following: (1) that the annual indemnity and the *per diem* grants to judges be consolidated into an annual salary; (2) that the salary of the Registrar should be fixed by the Assembly instead of by the Council, on the proposal of the Court; (3) that the payment of travelling expenses and pensions should be governed by regulations made by the Assembly; and (4) that salaries, indemnities and allowances should be free of all taxation.[79] The Committee's proposals were adopted by the Conference of Signatories without discussion.[80]

§209. **Discussion of Article 33.** This article was sharply criticized by M. Urrutia (Colombia) and M. Scialoja (Italy) before the Committee of Jurists,[81] but no amendment was adopted by the Committee. M. Osusky thought that to touch this article "would be to upset the entire financial system of the League." [82]

§210. **Discussion of Article 34.** An interesting discussion of this article in the Committee of Jurists turned on the possibility of the League of Nations' being a party before the court.[83] No amendment was recommended, though a harmonization of the French and English versions was seriously considered.

§211. **New Article 35.** The amendment to Article 35 consists in the addition of the following at the end of the third paragraph: "This provision shall not apply if such State is bearing a share of the expenses of the Court." This is intended to avoid a double assessment

[76] Minutes of the 1929 Committee of Jurists, p. 92.
[77] Minutes of the 1929 Conference, p. 41.
[78] Minutes of the 1929 Committee of Jurists, p. 55.
[79] The third and fourth of these proposals are in accordance with the practice under the original Statute. See §359, *infra.*   [80] Minutes of the 1929 Conference, p. 41.
[81] Minutes of the 1929 Committee of Jurists, p. 57.   [82] *Id.,* p. 73.   [83] *Id.,* pp. 57–61.

for the expenses of the Court against States which may be parties to the Protocol of Signature and not Members of the League of Nations. The matter was discussed briefly in the Committee of Jurists,[84] but the amendment was formulated by the Conference of Signatories [85] as a result of a Brazilian proposal.

§212. **New Article 38.** The amendment to Article 38 consists in the addition of the words *"des différents nations"* in the French version to "bring it into literal conformity with the English text." [86]

§213. **New Article 39.** The amendment to Article 39 consists of substituting the words "at the request of any party" for the words "at the request of the parties," in the third paragraph. This makes it clear that the Court may authorize the use of a language other than French or English in cases where this is requested by only one party. As explained to the Committee of Jurists, the Court had thus interpreted the original text.[87]

§214. **New Article 40.** The amendment to Article 40 consists in adding at the end of the last paragraph the words, "and also any States entitled to appear before the Court." [88] This is explained in the report of the Committee of Jurists [89] as designed "to bring the text of the Statute into line with Article 73 of the present Rules of Court," and it was desired to do this because it was proposed to embody the latter in the new Article 66 of the Statute. It was adopted by the Conference of Signatories without discussion.[90]

§215. **New Article 45.** The amendment to Article 45 changes only the English version of the original article, which did not correspond with the French version. The control of hearings is made to depend not on the "absence" of the President, but on his being "unable to preside"; and the same applies to the Vice-President. It was pointed out to the Committee of Jurists that under the Rules the President could not preside if he were a national of a party to the case before the Court.[91]

§216. **Discussion of Article 55.** An interesting question was raised in the consideration of this article by the Committee of Jurists,

[84] Minutes of the 1929 Committee of Jurists, pp. 62, 73–74, 124.
[85] Minutes of the 1929 Conference, pp. 42, 49–51.
[86] Minutes of the 1929 Committee of Jurists, p. 62.
[87] Minutes of the 1929 Committee of Jurists, p. 62. See Series C, No. 3, Vol. I, p. 18.
[88] On the meaning of this phrase, see §398, *infra.*
[89] Minutes of the 1929 Committee of Jurists, p. 124.
[90] Minutes of the 1929 Conference, p. 42. *Cf.*, §398, *infra.*
[91] Minutes of the 1929 Committee of Jurists, p. 65.

whether a judge might abstain from voting on a question before the Court. It seems to have been agreed that abstention was not "compatible with the duties of a judge," [92] and this view has since been taken by the Court.[93]

§217. **Discussion of Article 57.** The consideration of this article by the Committee of Jurists led M. Fromageot to propose that the judgments of the Court should be given in the name of the Court alone, with no indication of divisions among the judges and no dissenting opinions; [94] he wished to make it impossible for Governments to know how their nationals on the Court had voted, and he deemed it unwise to put the independence of the judges to the test of openly opposing their own Governments. Sir Cecil Hurst thought that this proposal would "destroy the Court." Mr. Root thought that "no member of the Court would consent to rest under an imputation of acquiescing in views which he did not hold, and the judges would naturally defend themselves in private." [95] M. Politis stated that even if the representatives of Anglo-Saxon countries were to ask for the suppression of dissenting opinions, he would feel himself obliged to oppose the request, because he felt these opinions to be of such "immense advantage to international law." [96] The Vice-President of the Court, M. Huber, stated that the possibility of the publishing of dissenting opinions "made it necessary for the Court to examine very carefully the different points of view brought forward by the judges, and to state clearly the reasons for its awards." [97] At a later date, Sir Cecil Hurst proposed an amendment to Article 57 which would recognize, in addition to dissenting opinions, separate opinions by judges who found themselves in the majority of the Court but did not agree with the statement of reasons given for the majority's conclusions; [98] he argued in favor of this amendment that the judgments of the Court were unnecessarily long, and that the existing system of the Court weakened the judgments by making it necessary for them "to embody several views." President Anzilotti stated that this was already the procedure followed by the Court in practice, and the Committee of Jurists decided that Article 57 should not be amended. Several members of the Committee thought that the Court's judgments were too long, however.

---

[92] Minutes of the 1929 Committee of Jurists, p. 65.
[93] Series E, No. 9, p. 174. See also §506, *infra.*
[94] Minutes of the 1929 Committee of Jurists, p. 50.
[95] *Id.,* p. 51. [96] *Ibid.* [97] *Id.,* p. 52.
[98] Minutes of the 1929 Committee of Jurists, pp. 65–66.

§218. **New Articles on Advisory Opinions.** The original Statute contains no express provision concerning advisory opinions, and the Court's procedure with reference to them has depended solely upon the Rules of Court. In connection with the consideration of the proposed accession to the Protocol of Signature by the United States of America, a Conference of Signatories in 1926 had agreed that certain provisions concerning advisory opinions contained in the Rules of Court might be given the same force which they would have had if they had been embodied in the Statute. M. van Eysinga proposed to the 1929 Committee of Jurists that the rules be studied with a view to the incorporation of certain of their provisions into the Statute.[99] He attributed the action of the Third Committee of the First Assembly in omitting any mention of advisory opinions in the original Statute to a desire to leave the Court entirely free in this respect; but the need of this safeguard had ceased to exist when after several years' experience "it was possible to form an accurate idea of the working of the procedure in respect of advisory opinions." This view was accepted by the Committee of Jurists; the Vice-President of the Court, M. Huber, supported it as tending to a "codification" of the experience to date. The Director of the International Labor Office submitted a memorandum to the Committee of Jurists, emphasizing the need for a coördination of Article 14 of the Covenant and Article 423 of the Treaty of Versailles, and stating that the Court itself should "formulate an authoritative interpretation, bringing these two clauses into line." [100] This memorandum provoked some discussion in the Committee of Jurists as to the nature of the function of the Council and Assembly in requesting advisory opinions desired by the International Labor Organization, but the Committee contented itself with submitting the memorandum to the Council.[1] In proposing that the substantive provisions of the Rules with reference to advisory opinions be "transferred" to the Statute "in order to give them a permanent character," the Committee of Jurists pointed out that this was "particularly desirable today in view of the special circumstances attending the possible accession of the United States" of America.[2]

§219. **New Article 65.** This text reproduces *verbatim* Article 72 of the Rules of Court adopted on March 24, 1922, in which no change has been made by the Court in the revisions down to that of Febru-

---

[99] Minutes of the 1929 Committee of Jurists, pp. 66–68.   [100] *Id.,* pp. 102–104.
[1] Minutes of the 1929 Committee of Jurists, pp. 75–76.   [2] *Id.,* p. 125.

ary 21, 1931. The effect of writing this provision into the Statute would be to deprive the Court of power to change it.

§220. **New Article 66.** The first paragraph reproduces *verbatim* the first paragraph of Article 73 of the Rules of Court, as adopted on March 24, 1922, and amended on July 31, 1926, with the omission of a requirement of notice to the Members of the Court. The second and third paragraphs reproduce *verbatim* the second and third paragraphs of Article 73 of the Rules of Court as amended on July 31, 1926, except that the French version of the second paragraph was slightly amended to conform to the English version. The fourth paragraph (numbered "2") reproduces *verbatim* the fourth paragraph (numbered "2") in Article 73 of the Rules of Court as amended on July 31, 1926, with a change of the order of the words "States, Members" to "Members, States."[3] As proposed by the Committee of Jurists, the text would have omitted the reference to international organizations; this led to a protest by the Director of the International Labor Office,[4] and after a lengthy discussion the Conference of Signatories restored such a reference as it exists in Article 73 of the Rules of Court.[5]

§221. **New Article 67.** This text is based upon the first sentence of Article 74 of the Rules of Court as amended on July 31, 1926, the only changes being that the provision that "the Court shall deliver its advisory opinions in open Court," is substituted for the provision in the Rules that "advisory opinions shall be read in open Court," and the mention of "States" is placed after that of "Members of the League." As proposed by the Committee of Jurists, the text would have omitted reference to international organizations. This led to a protest by the Director of the International Labor Office,[6] and after a lengthy discussion the Conference of Signatories restored such a reference as it exists in Article 74 of the Rules of Court.[7]

§222. **New Article 68.** The Committee of Jurists proposed the following text for this article: "In the exercise of its advisory functions, the Court shall apply Articles 65, 66, and 67. It shall further be guided by the provisions of the preceding chapters of this Statute to the extent to which it recognizes them to be applicable to the case." This was explained in the Committee's report to take "account of the fact that the Court may be called upon to give advisory opinions both

---

[3] Minutes of the 1929 Conference, p. 49.   [4] *Id.*, p. 74.   [5] *Id.*, pp. 43–46, 75.
[6] Minutes of the 1929 Conference, p. 74.   [7] *Id.*, pp. 43–46, 75.

in contentious and in non-contentious matters," and it was said that certain provisions of the Statute applicable in the former would not be applicable in the latter cases, *e.g.*, Article 31.[8] When the proposal came before the Conference of Signatories, the first sentence was suppressed as serving no useful purpose.[9] After a discussion "with an enthusiastic gentleman from across the Atlantic,"[10] Sir Cecil Hurst (Great Britain) proposed a redrafting of the second sentence, in the interest of clarity.[11] In supporting this proposal, M. Fromageot (France) thought it essential that when asked for an advisory opinion relating to a dispute, the Court should hear the parties to the dispute; "it was therefore quite natural to lay down in the Statute of the Court that, in regard to advisory opinions, the Court should proceed in all respects in the same way as in contentious cases."[12] In line with these views,[13] the text of the new article was made to read as follows: "In the exercise of its advisory functions, the Court shall further be guided by the provisions of the Statute which apply in contentious cases to the extent to which it recognizes them to be applicable." Though this text may lend itself to misconstruction,[14] it still leaves the control of advisory procedure in the hands of the Court.

§223. **Appreciation of the Amendments.** It is to be noted, first of all, that the amendments fail to deal with the most important *lacuna* in the Statute of December 16, 1920, *viz.*, the absence of any provision for a process of amendment. Experience in the endeavor to bring about the ratifications of the Revision Protocol of September 14, 1929, has demonstrated the seriousness of this defect in the Statute. The failure of the 1929 Committee of Jurists and the 1929 Conference of Signatories to deal with the matter can only be explained by the fact that one of the reservations offered by the United States of America in connection with its proposed accession to the

---

[8] Minutes of the 1929 Committee of Jurists, p. 125.
[9] Minutes of the 1929 Conference, p. 48. [10] Mr. S. O. Levinson, of Chicago.
[11] Minutes of the 1929 Conference, pp. 46–47, 75.
[12] *Id.*, p. 48. It is to be noted that the Court had previously on September 7, 1927, amended Article 71 of its Rules by inserting as paragraph 2: "On a question relating to an existing dispute between two or more States or Members of the League of Nations, Article 31 of the Statute shall apply. In case of doubt the Court shall decide."
[13] M. Fromageot's statement is reproduced in the letter of President van Eysinga to the President of the Assembly and the Chairman of the First Committee. *Id.*, p. 78.
[14] In a report by Senators Fess and Walsh to the United States Senate, on June 1, 1932, the new Article 68 was construed to make applicable the rule that "if the question in reference to which the advisory opinion of the Court is requested is involved in a dispute between two nations, the request will not be entertained or the opinion given, except the parties to the controversy join in the request or assent to the action solicited." 72d Congress, 1st session, Senate Report No. 758, p. 9.

Protocol of Signature, states that the Statute "shall not be amended without the consent of the United States." This led to the inclusion in the United States Accession Protocol of September 14, 1929, of the provision (Article 3) that "no amendment of the Statute of the Court may be made without the consent of all the Contracting States." Only political considerations could have dictated this result.

In the second place, it is to be noted that the amendments are of widely varying importance, and few of them effect significant changes. Sir Cecil Hurst insisted in vain that the Committee of Jurists should confine itself to proposing "changes which were of urgent and real importance" and which would justify "the exercise of pressure by the Council on States in order to obtain their ratifications before September 1930." [15] M. Politis (Greece), acting as *rapporteur* of the First Committee in the Tenth Assembly, characterized most of the amendments as of "secondary importance." [16] The work of the Committee of Jurists was in some measure stultified by the pressing need for bringing the amendments into force by September 1930, and by the oft-repeated declaration that it was not intended to "recast" the Statute.

It is also to be noted that some of the reforms which the amendments were designed to effect were possible without any amendment of the Statute. It was within the power of the Assembly to increase the number of the judges of the Court and to provide for them adequate salaries, and such action was taken in 1930. It was also within the power of the Court to modify its rules as to sessions and other matters, though the pending amendments to the Statute may have operated to influence the revision of the Rules effected on February 21, 1931.

These considerations may have contributed to the delay in bringing the amendments into force. The Assembly of the League of Nations has not faltered, however, in its insistence on the desirability of that end. In 1930, it expressed the hope that States would proceed to ratify the Revision Protocol "as soon as possible"; [17] in 1931, it reaffirmed this expression; [18] and in 1932, it addressed an "urgent appeal" to States to take such action.[19]

[15] Minutes of the 1929 Committee of Jurists, p. 40.
[16] Records of Tenth Assembly, Plenary, pp. 117–118.
[17] Records of Eleventh Assembly, Plenary, p. 132.
[18] Records of Twelfth Assembly, Plenary, p. 139.
[19] Records of Thirteenth Assembly, Plenary, p. 91.

§224. **Failure of the Protocol to Enter into Force in 1930.** The decision taken in 1928, calling for a study of possible amendments to the Statute, was largely due to the thought that any desirable amendments should be brought into force before the second general election of judges in 1930, and for this reason the work of revision had been hurried. Recent experience had shown, however, that it was extremely difficult to obtain a large number of ratifications in so short a period as one year. The drafting committee of the Conference of Signatories gave its attention to this question and prepared the following text, which was adopted by the Conference without discussion and incorporated in the Protocol of September 14, 1929, as paragraph 4: [20]

> The present Protocol shall enter into force on September 1, 1930, provided that the Council of the League of Nations has satisfied itself that those Members of the League of Nations and States mentioned in the Annex to the Covenant which have ratified the Protocol of December 16, 1920, and whose ratification of the present Protocol has not been received by that date, have no objection to the coming into force of the amendments to the Statute of the Court which are annexed to the present Protocol.

This text clearly met the requirement that each of the signatories of the Protocol of December 16, 1920, which had ratified it, should consent to the amendments to the Statute; it was novel in providing that the consent should be required only in such form that the Council might be satisfied that it existed, *i.e.*, that there was no objection.[21] If it had been necessary to raise the question, the point might have been made that this provision for bringing the amendments into force would have required that each State or Member of the League of Nations which had ratified the Protocol of December 16, 1920, should be a signatory of the Revision Protocol of September 14, 1929.

On May 12, 1930, the Council of the League of Nations took cognizance of the fact that few signatures had been affixed to the Revision Protocol of September 14, 1929, and directed the Secretary-General to ask States and Members of the League to express their opinions as to the entry into force of the Protocol. The Secretary-General's communication of June 4, 1930, was followed by a telegraphic communication on August 20, 1930. When the Council met to con-

---

[20] Minutes of the 1929 Conference, p. 51.
[21] Mr. A. P. Fachiri has described this provision as "a revolution in the history of international agreements." 11 British Year Book of International Law (1930), p. 98.

sider the matter on September 9, 1930, the situation was as follows:
of the forty-five signatories which had then ratified the Protocol of
December 16, 1920, only thirty-two had ratified the Revision Protocol
of September 14, 1929; eight had stated that they would raise no objection to the coming into force of the amendments (as had also the
United States of America); Brazil and Uruguay had stated that constitutional provisions prevented their agreeing without parliamentary
authorization; Cuba had expressed definite opposition; and Abyssinia
and France had expressed no attitude.[22] The Council was therefore
unable to satisfy itself that there was no objection, and the amendments to the Statute failed to come into force as contemplated in
the Revision Protocol of September 14, 1929. The second general
election of judges was later held under the original provisions of the
Statute, though the nominations had to be made before the fate of
the amendments was known.

§225. **Later History of the Revision Protocol.** The new situation with reference to the Revision Protocol of 1929 was considered
by the Eleventh Assembly in 1930. Several courses were then open:
(1) to declare the Revision Protocol to be dead, on the ground that
the provision in paragraph 4 of the Protocol contained the only reference to its coming into force and the conditions set had failed to be
realized; (2) to keep the Protocol alive in the hope of its later coming
into force; or (3) to prepare a new protocol for putting the amendments into force. The second course was adopted by the Eleventh Assembly. It involved the determination of the conditions under which
the amendments might still become effective, and attention had to be
given to the consequences of the amendments' coming into force
during the term of the newly-elected members of the Court. After a
prolonged discussion in the First Committee of the Assembly,[23]
M. Pilotti (Italy) reported its conclusion to the Assembly, that "the
Protocol of September 14, 1929, could not now come into force until
it has been ratified by all the States which ratified the former Protocol
of December 16, 1920." [24] The resolution adopted by the Eleventh
Assembly therefore invited further ratifications, and the invitation
was repeated by the Assembly in 1931 and 1932.

On January 1, 1934, the Revision Protocol had been signed on

[22] League of Nations Official Journal, 1930, p. 1313.
[23] Records of Eleventh Assembly, First Committee, pp. 8–27, 41–42.
[24] *Id.*, Plenary, p. 131.

behalf of all the signatories of the Protocol of Signature of December 16, 1920; and it had been ratified on behalf of all the States or Members of the League of Nations which had ratified the 1920 Protocol, except Abyssinia, Brazil, Panama and Peru.

§226. The Cuban Reservations.[25] When the Tenth Assembly adopted its resolution of September 14, 1929, no opposition was voiced by the Cuban delegation; nor was any objection made by that delegation when, after the Council had noted that the Revision Protocol could not come into force in September 1930, the Eleventh Assembly proceeded to increase the number of judges and to increase the salaries of judges. Yet after the Revision Protocol had been signed on behalf of Cuba on January 5, 1931, on the same date a ratification was offered for deposit, containing reservations as to paragraph 4 of the Protocol and as to the amendment to Article 23 of the Statute; moreover, in a covering letter written by the Cuban Secretary of State, the Secretary-General of the League of Nations was asked to take note of the view of the Cuban Government that "the Protocol will not affect the position of judges already elected." [26] When these reservations and statement were communicated to the various Governments, the replies indicated that while no objection was raised to the reservation to paragraph 4 of the Protocol (which had become *functus officio*), many Governments were unable to accept the reservation to the new text of Article 23 of the Statute, and the statement in the covering letter was regarded as relating to a matter within the competence of the Court itself.[27] On March 14, 1932, after protracted negotiations, an instrument was deposited at Geneva by which the Cuban reservations were withdrawn.[28]

§227. The United States and the Revision Protocol. When the amendments to the Statute were being drafted in 1929, proposals were under consideration for the adhesion of the United States of America to the Protocol of Signature of December 16, 1920, and some of the amendments proposed were designed to facilitate that adhesion. The Protocol for putting into effect the amendments and a protocol on the adhesion of the United States were opened to signature on the same day. The latter envisaged an adhesion to the "Protocol of Signature

---

[25] For a fuller treatment of this subject, see Manley O. Hudson, "The Cuban Reservations and the Revision of the Statute of the Permanent Court of International Justice," 26 American Journal of International Law (1932), p. 590.
[26] League of Nations Document, C. L. 4. 1931. V.
[27] *Id.*, A. 81. 1931. V.   [28] *Id.*, C. L. 50. 1932. V.

of the Statute of the Permanent Court of International Justice" without any reference to the pending amendments.[29] It was possible, however, that the amendments would be brought into force before the
adhesion of the United States became effective, and it was desired
that in this event the United States' adhesion should involve an acceptance of the amended instead of the original Statute; otherwise, the
United States would be adhering to a text which no longer existed. The
simple way of providing for this event would have been a provision in
the protocol relating to the adhesion by the United States; though the
question was raised in the Committee of Jurists when this protocol
was being drafted,[30] it had been ignored in the text proposed, and for
delicate political reasons the draft of the Committee of Jurists was
adopted without any substantial modifications by the Conference
of Signatories.[31] In this situation, it seemed necessary to the Conference of Signatories that a suggestion should be made that the
United States should act simultaneously on the Protocol of Signature
of December 16, 1920, the Revision Protocol of September 14, 1929,
and the Protocol relating to United States' Accession of September 14,
1929; [32] and "to safeguard entirely the situation of the United States
with regard to the amendments," it was provided in the protocol relating to the amendments (paragraph 7) that "for the purposes of the
present Protocol, the United States of America shall be in the same
position as a State which has ratified the Protocol of December 16,
1920." This had the effect of making it necessary for the Council to
satisfy itself that the United States had no objection to the coming
into force of the amendments, before it might proceed in September
1930 to declare that the Revision Protocol had come into force. On
December 9, 1929, the three Court protocols were signed on behalf
of the United States, and on June 25, 1930, the Secretary of State
of the United States informed the Secretary-General of the League
of Nations that he perceived "no reason to object to the coming into
force, between such nations as may have become parties thereto, of
the amendments to the ~tatute . . . which have not been ratified by
the United States

---

[29] League of Natio   ᴎ3. M. 157. 1929. V; 1 Hudson, International
Legislation, p. 591. See s.
    [30] Minutes of the 1929   ᴉsts, p. 80.
    [31] Minutes of the 1929
    [32] *Id.*, p. 80. See also M   ᴑ the Tenth Assembly. Records of Tenth
Assembly, Plenary, p. 118.   [33] Series E, No. 8., p. 59.

When the Revision Protocol failed to come into force in 1930, the question arose as to the necessity of a formal ratification of that protocol by the United States, as a condition precedent to its coming into force. If ratification is required by each of the States or Members of the League of Nations which has ratified the Protocol of Signature of December 16, 1920, and if the United States is in the same position with reference to the Revision Protocol as a State which has ratified the Protocol of December 16, 1920, then it would seem that a ratification by the United States is essential to the coming into force of the Revision Protocol. On the other hand, it is hardly a situation where the States and Members of the League of Nations which have ratified the Protocol of December 16, 1920, can be prevented from proceeding to put the amendments into force without formal action by the United States; and until the United States has effectively adhered to the Protocol of December 16, 1920, the agreement of these States and Members among themselves would seem to make it possible for them to waive any effect of paragraph 7 of the Revision Protocol as a condition to the amendments' coming into force. The position taken by the Secretary of State of the United States on June 25, 1930, might be relied upon in connection with such a waiver.

CHAPTER 10

PARTICIPATION OF STATES NOT MEMBERS OF THE LEAGUE OF NATIONS

§228. **Possibility of Such Participation.** From the beginning it has been anticipated that States not members of the League of Nations might participate in the maintenance of the Court. Certain States may become parties to the Protocol of Signature of December 16, 1920, which have never been members of the League; or States which are parties may withdraw from membership in the League. The resolution adopted by the First Assembly of the League of Nations on December 13, 1920, provided (paragraph 4) that the protocol to which the Statute was to be annexed should "remain open for signature by the States mentioned in the Annex to the Covenant." This provision had been adopted by the sub-committee of the Third Committee,[1] whose *rapporteur*, M. Hagerup (Norway), explained to the Assembly: "This means that the United States of America can adhere to the Statute. You know that a representative of the United States of America, a man of the highest authority and the greatest competence, Mr. Elihu Root, took part in the preparation of the Hague Scheme. The party to which he belongs will soon come into power, and, though they have not yet decided to enter the League of Nations, they have proclaimed in a resolution that they are quite prepared to accept the Court." [2] From this statement it is quite clear that the object of the provision was to enable the United States to become a party to the Protocol; however, the language was also applicable to two other States, Ecuador and the Hedjaz, which were mentioned in the Annex to the Covenant and which were not members of the League of Nations. The provision in the Assembly resolution was also embodied in the fourth paragraph of the Protocol of Sig-

[1] Records of First Assembly, Committees, I, pp. 408, 617.
[2] Records of First Assembly, Plenary, p. 441. It is not clear to the writer what the resolution was to which M. Hagerup referred.

nature of December 16, 1920, where it was stated that the Protocol of Signature should "remain open for signature by the Members of the League of Nations and by the States mentioned in the Annex to the Covenant of the League." [3]

The United States of America is the only State which has expressed a desire to sign or adhere to the Protocol of Signature and which was not at the time a member of the League of Nations. The problem of the participation of States not members of the League of Nations in the maintenance of the Court is therefore, in part, a problem as to the adhesion by the United States; but it is also a problem of the continued participation of States which have ceased to be members of the League of Nations and which while they were members had become parties to the Protocol of Signature of December 16, 1920.

§229. Effect of Withdrawal from the League of Nations. Under Article 1 of the Covenant, a Member of the League of Nations may "withdraw from the League"; two years' notice of its intention to withdraw must have been given, and the withdrawal is conditioned upon the fulfilment of "all its international obligations and all its obligations" under the Covenant. Costa Rica withdrew from the League in 1927, and Brazil in 1928; Spain's notice of intention to withdraw was cancelled before the expiration of the two-year period. On March 27, 1933, Japan gave notice of an intention to withdraw from membership in the League of Nations; and on October 21, 1933, Germany gave a similar notice.[4] Clearly during the two-year period, a State remains a member of the League of Nations, and its position as a party to the Protocol of December 16, 1920, is in no way affected by the notice. Nor is that position changed by an effective withdrawal.[5] A State may contribute to the expenses of the Court without membership in the League, and the amendment to Article 4 of the Statute, annexed to the Revision Protocol of September 14, 1929, would

---

[3] The French version, which is clearly defective, provided that the Protocol should remain open "à la signature des États visés à l'annexe du Pacte de la Société." Series D, No. 1 (2d ed.), p. 7.

[4] On October 27, 1933, the German Government notified the Court that it did not intend to proceed with two suits pending before the Court, in which it was the applicant. Series A/B, No. 59, p. 195; No. 60, p. 202.

[5] But see the statement made to the 1926 Conference of Signatories by M. Pilotti (Italy). Minutes of the 1926 Conference of Signatories, p. 16. A protocol of signature annexed to a treaty of April 19, 1933, between Japan and the Netherlands, envisaged the possibility that Japan's legal position vis-à-vis the Court might be changed in consequence of Japan's withdrawal from membership in the League of Nations.

envisage the possibility of participation in the election of the members of the Court by "a State which has accepted the Statute of the Court, but is not a Member of the League of Nations." As the Protocol of Signature of December 16, 1920, was never ratified by Costa Rica, Brazil is the only State which is now in that position. In 1929, the Brazilian Government expressed a desire to contribute to the expenses of the Court in a proportion to be agreed,[6] but no agreement has been made; [7] the amount of any such contribution is to be determined with reference to what a State might have been called upon to pay as a Member of the League of Nations.

§230. The United States' Proposal of 1926.[8] The texts of the Protocol of Signature and the Statute of the Court were communicated to the Government of the United States on February 4, 1921, and their receipt was acknowledged on August 15, 1921. On February 24, 1923, the President of the United States transmitted a message to the Senate, asking for its advice and consent to the adhesion by the United States to the Protocol of Signature of December 16, 1920, upon certain "conditions and understandings" set out in an accompanying letter of February 17, 1923,[9] by the Secretary of State. On January 27, 1926, the Senate of the United States adopted a resolution giving its "advice and consent" to the proposed adhesion by the United States "subject to the following reservations and understandings," to be accepted "through an exchange of notes" by "the Powers signatory to such Protocol": [10]

[6] Records of Tenth Assembly, Plenary, p. 435.

[7] Up to 1933, Brazil had made no contribution to the expenses of the Court since her withdrawal from the League in 1928; contributions have been made by Brazil for the expenses of the International Labor Office, however. See League of Nations Document, A. 3. 1933. X, p. 54.

[8] The texts of documents relating to the United States' proposal are collected in Hudson, The World Court, 1921–1934 (World Peace Foundation, Boston, 1934), pp. 218–289.

[9] These "conditions and understandings" were as follows:

"1. That such adhesion shall not be taken to involve any legal relation on the part of the United States to the League of Nations or the assumption of any obligations by the United States under the Covenant of the League of Nations constituting Part I of the Treaty of Versailles.

"2. That the United States shall be permitted to participate through representatives designated for the purpose and upon an equality with the other States members, respectively, of the Council and Assembly of the League of Nations, in any and all proceedings of either the Council or the Assembly for the election of judges or deputy judges of the Permanent Court of International Justice, or for the filling of vacancies.

"3. That the United States will pay a fair share of the expenses of the Court as determined and appropriated from time to time by the Congress of the United States.

"4. That the Statute for the Permanent Court of International Justice adjoined to the Protocol shall not be amended without the consent of the United States." U. S. Senate Document No. 309, 67th Congress, 4th Session, p. 7.

[10] U. S. Senate Document No. 45, 69th Congress, 1st Session. For detailed studies

1. That such adherence shall not be taken to involve any legal relation on the part of the United States to the League of Nations or the assumption of any obligations by the United States under the Treaty of Versailles.

2. That the United States shall be permitted to participate through representatives designated for the purpose and upon an equality with the other States, members, respectively, of the Council and Assembly of the League of Nations, in any and all proceedings of either the Council or the Assembly for the election of judges or deputy-judges of the Permanent Court of International Justice or for the filling of vacancies.

3. That the United States will pay a fair share of the expenses of the Court as determined and appropriated from time to time by the Congress of the United States.

4. That the United States may at any time withdraw its adherence to the said Protocol and that the Statute for the Permanent Court of International Justice adjoined to the Protocol shall not be amended without the consent of the United States.

5. That the Court shall not render any advisory opinion except publicly after due notice to all States adhering to the Court and to all interested States and after public hearing or opportunity for hearing given to any State concerned; nor shall it, without the consent of the United States, entertain any request for an advisory opinion touching any dispute or question in which the United States has or claims an interest.[11]

of the reservations, see Manley O. Hudson, "The American Reservations and the Permanent Court of International Justice," 22 American Journal of International Law (1928), pp. 776–796; Herbert Kraus, "La Cour . . . et les États-Unis d'Amerique," 7 Revue de Droit International et de Législation Comparée (1926), p. 281.

An earlier draft of the second part of the fifth reservation, which had not been proposed by the Secretary of State, provided: "That the United States shall be in no manner bound by any advisory opinion of the Permanent Court of International Justice not rendered pursuant to a request in which it, the United States, shall expressly join in accordance with the statute for the said court adjoined to the protocol of signature of the same to which the United States shall become signatory." The final form of the reservation, introduced in the Senate on January 23, 1926, seems to have been due to a memorandum by a "well-known international jurist . . . in official life," presented to the Senate on January 18, 1926. 67 Congressional Record, p. 2293. It was later reported that Judge John Bassett Moore, at that time a judge of the Court, had assisted in drafting the resolution. New York Times, January 28, 1926, p. 1. It may be noted in this connection that when the Court's rules were being framed, Judge Moore had expressed doubts about the Court's giving advisory opinions. Series D, No. 2, pp. 383–398. He had opposed the admission of any possibility of the Court's giving secret opinions, and had supported the general assimilation of advisory to contentious procedure. Id., p. 160. When in 1923 Judge Altamira proposed to provide for secret procedure with reference to advisory opinions, Judge Moore presented an able and effective comment in which he opposed "any abatement whatever from the judicial character of the Court's proceedings." Series D, No. 2 (add.), pp. 293–296.

[11] A further "understanding," set out in the Senate resolution but of which acceptance by other States was not stipulated for, would require that recourse to the Court for the settlement of a difference between the United States and any other State could be "had only by agreement thereto through general or special treaties" between the parties. This follows a stock form which had been employed by the United States in a reservation to

On February 12, 1926, the Government of the United States communicated the text of this resolution to the various signatories of the Protocol of December 16, 1920, asking to be informed whether the reservations and understandings were acceptable. On March 2, 1926, the Secretary of State of the United States addressed a communication to the Secretary-General of the League of Nations, informing him of the adoption of the Senate's resolution, and stating that the signature of the United States would not be affixed to the said Protocol until the Governments of the States signatory thereto should have signified in writing their acceptance of these "conditions, reservations, and understandings." [12] When this communication came before the Council of the League of Nations on March 18, 1926,[13] the Council expressed the opinion that as the Protocol of Signature of 1920 is a "multilateral instrument," "the special conditions on which the United States desire to accede to it should also be embodied in a multilateral instrument," and could not "appropriately be embodied in a series of separate exchanges of notes." It proposed to all the Governments which had received from the United States a copy of the Senate resolution that their replies should indicate "the need of a general agreement," and it invited these Governments and that of the United States to be represented at a conference with the object of framing such a general agreement.

§231. The Conference of Signatories of 1926. Forty signatories of the Protocol of Signature were represented at the Conference of Signatories held at Geneva, September 1–23, 1926.[14] With somewhat questionable courtesy the Government of the United States declined the invitation to be represented, on the ground that no "useful purpose could be served by the designation of a delegate"; the Secretary of State stated that the reservations were "plain and unequivocal," and that no "new agreement" was necessary to give effect to them beyond

the 1907 Hague Convention for the Pacific Settlement of International Disputes; it was intended to limit the power of the Executive by requiring the advice and consent of the Senate to any *compromis*.

A second statement was made in the Senate resolution to the effect that adherence by the United States should not be construed to require a departure from the "traditional policy" of non-entanglement in the political affairs of other States, or an abandonment of the "traditional attitude toward purely American questions." This, too, is a stock form which had been employed by the United States in reservations to the 1899 and 1907 Hague Conventions for the Pacific Settlement of International Disputes. Its significance is not juridical.

[12] League of Nations Official Journal, 1926, p. 628.   [13] *Id.*, pp. 535–536.

[14] The minutes of the Conference were published by the Secretariat of the League of Nations. Document V. Legal. 1926. V. 26. Not all of the States represented at the Conference had ratified the Protocol of Signature of December 16, 1920.

the "assent of each signatory by direct exchange of notes," a mode of procedure which he had "no authority to vary." [15] This left the Conference "incomplete," as its President, M. van Eysinga (Netherlands), pointed out at the beginning of its deliberations, in that it had to proceed without any clarification of the views of the Government of the United States.[16] Emphasis was laid on the fact that the signatories were represented solely in their capacity as signatories, and not as members of the League of Nations; and to avoid any impression that the reservations of the United States were being considered by an organ of the League of Nations, the Conference met, not at the Secretariat, but at the International Labor Office.[17] The reservations of the United States were studied "with a strong desire to satisfy them in the largest possible measure," and the opinion was expressed in the Final Act of the Conference that the proposed adhesion by the United States "necessitates an agreement between the United States and the signatories of the Protocol." [18] Conclusions were formulated in the Final Act to serve "as the basis of the replies" to be sent by the signatories to the Government of the United States, and a preliminary draft of a "protocol of execution" was elaborated and annexed to the Final Act, which was recommended for signature by the signatories and by the United States. The President of the Conference was directed to transmit to the Government of each of the signatories a model of a letter of reply to the United States.

§232. **Proposed Acceptance of United States' Reservations.** The 1926 Conference of Signatories found no difficulty in accepting the first three reservations proposed by the United States. Nor did it raise any objection to the fourth reservation, though it proposed that "in order to assure equality of treatment . . . the signatory States, acting together and by not less than a majority of two-thirds, should possess the corresponding right to withdraw their acceptance of the special conditions attached by the United States . . . in the second part of the fourth reservation and in the fifth reservation." [19] With reference to the first part of the fifth reservation, the Conference drew attention to Articles 71–74 of the Rules of Court, and particularly

[15] Minutes of the 1926 Conference, p. 71.

[16] This had the result of leading delegates to the Conference to scan the records of the debates in the United States Senate, as published in the Congressional Record, in their effort to understand the United States' position. See the excellent study by Quincy Wright, in 21 American Journal of International Law (1927), p. 1.

[17] Minutes of the 1926 Conference, pp. 10–11.

[18] Minutes of the 1926 Conference, p. 75.   [19] Minutes of the 1926 Conference, p. 77.

to the amendments to Articles 73 and 74 effected by the Court on July 31, 1926, after the United States had offered its reservations; [20] and it expressed a willingness to study "the possible incorporation of certain stipulations of principle" in the proposed protocol of execution. The second part of the fifth reservation gave considerable concern, however, because of the "great importance" attached by the Members of the League of Nations to the value of advisory opinions, and because it was feared that the fifth reservation might have the effect of diminishing the value of advisory opinions. A distinction was drawn between an advisory opinion relating to a dispute to which the United States might be a party, and an advisory opinion relating to a dispute or question with regard to which the United States should claim an interest though not a party. With reference to the former case, the Conference merely referred to the Court's "advisory opinion No. 5 (Eastern Carelia)" which seemed to the Conference "to meet the views of the United States." [21] With reference to the latter case, the Conference was prepared to assure to the United States a "position of equality with States represented either on the Council or in the Assembly of the League of Nations"; but as no decision had yet been taken on the question whether unanimity was required in the Council or the Assembly for the adoption of a request for an advisory opinion, the Conference found it "impossible to say with certainty whether in some cases, or possibly in all cases, a decision by a majority is not sufficient." It therefore envisaged a "supplementary agreement" to deal with "the manner in which the consent provided for in the second part of the fifth reservation will be given," but no attempt was made at the time to draft such a "supplementary agreement."

§233. **Results of the 1926 Conference.** The Conference of Signatories achieved its purpose to a very limited extent. Its suggestions led to a large measure of uniformity in the replies made by certain signatories to the Government of the United States, though some sig-

---

[20] It cannot be said that the Court had been led by the proposals of the United States to make the amendments in its rules adopted in 1926, for the revision had been on its agenda since June 17, 1925. When the resolution adopted by the United States Senate on January 27, 1926, was mentioned at a meeting of the Court on July 26, 1926, Judge Moore stated that he "thought that the Court should discuss and decide any question without reference to the situation in the United States." Series D, No. 2 (add.), p. 198. "On July 30, 1926, the Court decided to abstain from any decision or discussion on the question of the American reservations; and the President construed the Court's vote as implying that the Court wished to assume a purely passive attitude and not to lend itself even to indirect coöperation in the work of the Conference called to consider the American reservations." Series E, No. 3, p. 195.

[21] Minutes of the 1926 Conference, p. 79. See §464 (4), *infra*.

natories did not reply in the sense recommended.[22] On the other hand, the recommendations of the Conference were not received with favor by the Government of the United States, and for more than two years the negotiations were not pursued. The signing of a treaty for the renunciation of war as an instrument of national policy, on August 27, 1928, may have produced some willingness on the part of the Government of the United States to give more hospitable consideration to the recommendations of the Conference, and on the eve of the assembling of the Committee of Jurists charged with the study of the Court's Statute with a view to its amendment, the United States reopened the negotiations. In a letter addressed to each of the signatories on February 19, 1929,[23] the Secretary of State of the United States referred to "some elements of uncertainty in the bases" suggested by the Conference of Signatories, "which seem to require further discussion." Inasmuch as the powers and procedure of the Council might be changed by an amendment of the Covenant, and "the ruling of the Court in the Eastern Carelia case and the rules of the Court are also subject to change at any time," the view was expressed that the draft protocol of 1926 "would not furnish adequate protection to the United States." It was said that "there seems to be but little difference" of opinion regarding the substance of the "rights and interests" of the United States "as an adherent to the Court Statute," and "an informal exchange of views" was suggested. On February 19, 1929, also, the Secretary of State informed the Secretary-General of the League of Nations of the letters addressed to the signatories. On March 9, 1929, the Council of the League of Nations requested the Committee of Jurists created under its resolution of December 14, 1928, "to consider the present situation as regards accession of the United States of America" and "to make any suggestions which it feels able to offer with a view to facilitating such accession on conditions satisfactory to all the interests concerned." [24] The membership of Mr. Elihu Root in the 1929 Committee of Jurists seemed to offer a happy augury for this course, and the general situation gave promise of better results than in 1926.

---

[22] Twenty-four Governments followed the recommendations of the Conference of Signatories in their replies to the United States; fifteen sent mere acknowledgments; five unconditionally accepted the reservations; and three indicated that they would accept. The Greek Government's acceptance of the reservations was sent on March 12, 1926, before the Council had decided to convoke a conference. See Series E, No. 4, p. 126.

[23] United States Department of State, Publication No. 44, p. 33.

[24] League of Nations Official Journal, 1929, p. 564.

§234. **The 1929 Committee of Jurists.** The Committee of Jurists created to study the Court's Statute with a view to its amendment, began its consideration of the question of the accession of the United States at its first meeting on March 11, 1929. Mr. Root offered a "suggested redraft of Article 4 of the [draft] protocol of 1926," [25] dealing chiefly with "the manner in which shall be made known whether the United States claims an interest and gives or withholds its consent" to the Court's giving an advisory opinion. He emphasized that "his proposals were intended to cover exceptional and extremely improbable cases." [26] Though the members of the Committee were at first disposed to deal with the precise points made in the letter addressed to the various signatories by the Secretary of State on February 19, 1929, various redrafts of Mr. Root's suggestions were offered and referred to a sub-committee, which reported a draft [27] based upon a proposal submitted by Sir Cecil Hurst.[28] This draft was adopted by the Committee in amended form on March 18, 1929,[29] with an explanatory report,[30] and communicated to the Council of the League of Nations. On June 12, 1929, the Council "adopted" the report and draft protocol, and directed that the texts be communicated to the Government of the United States and to the signatories to the Protocol of December 16, 1920; it also decided to place the question on the agenda of the Tenth Assembly and to transmit the texts to the Assembly, in view of its "being, like the Council, a body whose procedure in regard to the method of seeking advisory opinions from the Court would be affected by the adoption of the protocol proposed." [31] On August 31, 1929, the Council referred the report and the draft protocol to the Conference of Signatories which was to convene a few days later; and similar action was later taken by the Tenth Assembly.

§235. **The Conference of Signatories of 1929.** At the opening session of the second Conference of Signatories on September 4, 1929, the Secretary-General of the League of Nations stated that he was informed [32] that the Secretary of State of the United States was of the

---

[25] For the text, see Minutes of the 1929 Committee of Jurists, p. 9. These minutes were published by the Secretariat of the League of Nations, as Document C. 166. M. 66. 1929. V.   [26] *Id.*, p. 15.

[27] *Id.*, p. 106. The sub-committee consisted of Mr. Root and Sir Cecil Hurst; its draft was not limited to a redraft of Article 4 of the 1926 draft protocol.

[28] *Id.*, p. 16.   [29] *Id.*, pp. 82, 132.   [30] *Id.*, p. 130.

[31] League of Nations Official Journal, 1929, p. 998.

[32] The Secretary-General did not at the time divulge that the source of his information was an *aide-mémoire* from the Minister of the United States at Berne. This was later published by the United States Department of State. Publication No. 44, p. 41.

opinion that the draft protocol drawn up by the Committee of Jurists would effectively meet the reservations of the United States and would constitute a satisfactory basis for the adhesion of the United States.[33] No change was proposed in this text by the Conference of Signatories, and on September 5, 1929, the President of the Conference addressed a letter to the President of the Tenth Assembly and to the chairman of its First Committee,[34] stating that the Conference had accepted the draft protocol "unanimously and without alteration," and had decided to refer it to the First Committee of the Tenth Assembly.

§236. **Action of the Tenth Assembly.** The draft protocol prepared by the Committee of Jurists was unanimously approved by the First Committee of the Tenth Assembly, without discussion.[35] On September 14, 1929, it was adopted without discussion by the Tenth Assembly,[36] and it was opened to signature on the same day.

§237. **The Protocol of September 14, 1929.** The Protocol of September 14, 1929,[37] can come into force, according to its terms (Article 7), only when ratifications have been deposited with the Secretariat of the League of Nations by "all States which have ratified the Protocol of December 16, 1920, and also the United States." It seems clear that the first of these expressions does not apply merely to the States and Members of the League of Nations which had ratified the Protocol of Signature on September 14, 1929; various States have ratified the Protocol of Signature since that date, and the requirement must be that ratifications be deposited by all States which shall have ratified the Protocol of Signature as of the time when it is possible for the Protocol of September 14, 1929, to come into force.[38] On January 1, 1934, the Protocol of Signature of December 16, 1920, had been ratified by 49 States or Members of the League of Nations; of these, all except Abyssinia, Brazil, Chile, Haiti, Panama, Paraguay, Peru, and El Salvador, had on that date deposited ratifications of the Protocol of September 14, 1929. Both Protocols were signed on behalf of the United States on December 9, 1929, but on January 1, 1934, they had not been ratified by the United States.

---

[33] Minutes of the 1929 Conference, p. 9.   [34] *Id.*, p. 74.
[35] Records of Tenth Assembly, First Committee, p. 8.   [36] *Id.*, Plenary, p. 122.
[37] For the text, see League of Nations Document, C. 493. M. 157. 1929. V; 1 Hudson, International Legislation, p. 591; *infra*, p. 646.

[38] The attention of the Committee of Jurists was called to the references in the draft protocol to "States signatories," "Contracting States," and "States which have ratified," and these references were all made advisedly. 1929 Committee Minutes, pp. 77, 78. It is to be noted that the text refers to signatories as "States," and not as "Members of the League of Nations or States," which is the usual form.

§238. Analysis of the Protocol for the Accession of the United States.[39] The preamble to the Protocol of September 14, 1929, sets forth an agreement "upon the following provisions" regarding the adherence [40] of the United States "subject (Fr., *sous condition*) to the five reservations formulated by the United States in the resolution adopted by the Senate on January 27, 1926." This statement seems to indicate that the five reservations offered by the United States are being consented to, *in toto,* and that in connection with the giving of this consent certain stipulations are to be laid down in the following provisions; it is the "adherence," and not the "following provisions," which is subject to the reservations. The text of the Senate resolution was not annexed to the Protocol, though M. Politis had suggested that course to the Committee of Jurists; [41] but it may possibly be taken to have been incorporated into the Protocol by the reference in the preamble.

(1) *Article 1. "The States signatories of the said Protocol accept the special conditions attached by the United States in the five reservations mentioned above to its adherence to the said Protocol upon the terms and conditions set out in the following Articles."*

This provision constitutes an acceptance by the Signatories of "the special conditions attached by the United States," though the acceptance seems to be limited by the concluding phrase. The French version, *"acceptent, aux termes des conditions spécifiées dans les articles ci-après,"* makes it clear that the acceptance is subject to the provisions in the following articles; yet the acceptance of the reservations would seem to be complete, to the extent that their substance is not covered or diminished by a later article of the Protocol.

(2) *Article 2. "The United States shall be admitted to participate, through representatives designated for the purpose and upon an equality with the signatory States Members of the League of Nations represented in the Council or in the Assembly, in any and all proceedings of either the Council or the Assembly for the election of judges or deputy-judges of the Permanent Court of International Justice, provided for in the Statute of the Court. The vote of the*

---

[39] See, also, Philip C. Jessup, The United States and the World Court (1929), pp. 14–58.

[40] The text of the Protocol uses the word "adherence" (in French *adhésion*). In the publications of the League of Nations, the word "accession" is used in the title given to the Protocol. Adherence, adhesion and accession have the same significance in this connection.

[41] Minutes of the 1929 Committee of Jurists, pp. 78–80.

United States shall be counted in determining the absolute majority of votes required by the Statute."

The first sentence of this article follows quite closely the second reservation offered by the United States, though it omits a specific reference to the filling of vacancies; the second sentence was not included in the reservations. The text was drafted at the 1926 Conference of Signatories, and no change was later made. It would have the effect of amending Articles 4, 8, 10, and 12 of the Statute, by creating electoral bodies consisting of the Assembly and the Council of the League of Nations plus representatives of the United States of America; a further amendment to Article 4 of the Statute, in line with this provision, is contained in the new text of Article 4 annexed to the Revision Protocol of September 14, 1929.

(3) *Article 3. "No amendment of the Statute of the Court may be made without the consent of all the Contracting States."*

This text, which originated in the 1926 Conference of Signatories, generalizes a provision in the fourth reservation proposed by the United States. It adds nothing to the situation which would exist if it were omitted. Unfortunately, it tends to perpetuate the *lacuna* in the Statute due to its failure to provide an easier method of amendment in line with the provision in Article 26 of the Covenant of the League of Nations. Fortunately, however, it does not specify any form for the giving of consent, and it leaves open the possibility of a future resort to the method of amendment adopted in paragraph 4 of the Revision Protocol of September 14, 1929.

(4) *Article 4. "The Court shall render advisory opinions in public session after notice and opportunity for hearing substantially as, provided in the now existing Articles 73 and 74 of the Rules of Court."*

The first part of the fifth reservation offered by the United States was "that the Court shall not render any advisory opinion except publicly after due notice to all States adhering to the Court and to all interested States and after public hearing or opportunity for hearing given to any State concerned." The 1926 Conference had proposed as a provision of its draft protocol that "the Court shall render advisory opinions in public session." The amplification contained in the 1929 text would constitute an addition to the Statute which would make it impossible for the Court to effect any substantial change in Articles 73 and 74 of the Rules of Court as they were adopted on March 24, 1922, and amended on July 31, 1926. If the Revision

Protocol of September 14, 1929, should come into force, however, most of the substantial provisions of Articles 73 and 74 of the Rules would be incorporated into the Statute, as Articles 66 and 67 thereof, and Article 4 of the Protocol for the adhesion of the United States would then have lost much of its force.

(5) *Article 5, paragraph 1. "With a view to ensuring that the Court shall not, without the consent of the United States, entertain any request for an advisory opinion touching any dispute or question in which the United States has or claims an interest, the Secretary-General of the League of Nations shall, through any channel designated for that purpose by the United States, inform the United States of any proposal before the Council or the Assembly of the League for obtaining an advisory opinion from the Court, and thereupon, if desired, an exchange of views as to whether an interest of the United States is affected shall proceed with all convenient speed between the Council or Assembly of the League and the United States."*

Article 5 represents the chief contribution made by the 1929 Committee of Jurists. The second part of the fifth reservation offered by the United States was that the Court should not "without the consent of the United States, entertain any request for an advisory opinion touching any dispute or question in which the United States has or claims an interest." The 1926 Conference of Signatories had feared that this provision might lend itself to a possible interpretation which would diminish the value of advisory opinions "in connection with the functioning of the League of Nations." [42] The proposal made by Mr. Root to the 1929 Committee of Jurists was designed to lay down "the manner in which shall be made known whether the United States claims an interest and gives or withholds its consent"; [43] and it was explained as "intended to provide against a very rare and improbable contingency." [44] Mr. Root's original draft expressly envisaged a possibility that the United States might be unable "to find the submission of the question so important for the general good as to call upon the United States to forego its objection in that particular instance, leaving the request to be acted upon by the Court without in any way binding the United States"; and a provision followed for the exercise of the power of withdrawal. [45] M. Raestad (Norway) took this to mean that "in case of disagreement, if the

[42] Minutes of the 1926 Conference, p. 79.
[43] Minutes of the 1929 Committee of Jurists, p. 9.
[44] *Id.*, p. 13.
[45] *Id.*, p. 9.

Council or the Assembly maintained its request for an advisory opinion, contrary to the wishes of the United States, the United States would not insist on exercising its right of veto and would withdraw from the Permanent Court." [46]

The introduction in the text finally adopted seems to assume the unqualified acceptance of the second part of the fifth reservation of the United States, by which the power of the Court to "entertain any request" would be limited; and it is to be noted that the remaining part of the paragraph relates not to the Court's power but to the procedure before the Council or Assembly. Yet interpretations given to the text by some members of the Committee of Jurists gave another emphasis. M. van Eysinga stated: "There might be a section of public opinion in America which desired to claim the right of veto in cases where a request for an advisory opinion had not been unanimous. The Committee now learned that the United States would be content if it were allowed to withdraw in such circumstances." [47] Sir Cecil Hurst explained to the 1929 Conference of Signatories that the text was "in reality a method of saying: 'For the purpose of giving satisfaction to the fifth condition embodied in the Senate resolution, the Secretary-General shall, through any channel designated for that purpose, inform the United States, etc.'" He added that if the result of the discussion did not give satisfaction to the United States, "it would be remembered that the United States had the power to withdraw if necessary." [48] If this interpretation were accepted, it would seem that no absolute bar would be created to the Court's entertaining a request touching a dispute or question in which the United States has or claims an interest, without the consent of the United States; perhaps the interpretation finds some support in the reference to a stay of proceedings (Fr., *la procédure sera suspendue*) in the second sentence of the second paragraph of this Article. In the report adopted by the Committee of Jurists, it was emphasized that "the provisions of the Article have purposely been framed so as to afford a measure of elasticity in its application"; and that if the provisions of the article failed to give it satisfaction, the United States "would be fully justified in withdrawing from the arrangement." [49] It seems clear that the Committee of Jurists was careful to avoid anticipation of possible but improbable consequences of its drafting, and for this reason it

[46] Minutes of the 1929 Committee of Jurists, p. 17. [47] *Id.*, p. 20.
[48] Minutes of the 1929 Conference, p. 18.
[49] Minutes of the 1929 Committee of Jurists, p. 131.

refrained from any complete exposition of the meaning of the text adopted. It was engaged in an effort to reconcile differing views, a process in which it is sometimes less profitable to seek clarity than to arrive at acceptable ambiguity.[50]

It may also be noted that some confusion has existed in the United States as to the proper interpretation of the effect of Article 5. The Secretary of State of the United States said in a letter to the President on November 18, 1929:[51] "Whenever a dispute to which we are a party is involved, no opinion on that dispute can be rendered unless we consent. When we claim an interest, although no dispute exists, we can, if we so desire, bring our great influence to bear against the rendering of such an opinion with the same legal standing as if we were a member of the Council or the Assembly of the League of Nations; and, in the extremely unlikely event of our being unable to persuade the majority of the Council or the Assembly that our interest is real and that the request for the opinion should not proceed, we may withdraw from membership in the Court without any imputation of unfriendliness." A different emphasis was given by Mr. Elihu Root, when on January 21, 1931, he told a committee of the United States Senate that "so long as we remain in that court, so long the court is barred from passing upon any question as to which we interpose an objection or claim an interest and refuse to consent."[52] Mr. Root's view was later adopted by the Secretary of State of the United States.[53]

The first paragraph of Article 5 provides that an exchange of views between the United States and the Council or Assembly before which a proposal for requesting an advisory opinion may be pending, shall

---

[50] Of the numerous discussions of this problem, see "Innoxius," *"L'Adhésion des États-Unis au Protocole de Signature du Statut de la Cour,"* 10 *Revue de Droit Internationale et de Législation Comparée* (1929), p. 784.

[51] Department of State Publication, No. 44, p. 12.

[52] United States Senate Executive Document No. 1, 72d Congress, 1st session, p. 64. Mr. Root was later asked whether "the United States would have an absolute veto power which would take away the jurisdiction of the Court from rendering an advisory opinion"; and he replied, "Absolutely." *Id.,* p. 73. On the weight to be attached to a draftsman's subsequent interpretation of an instrument, see Lord Halsbury's statement in *Hilder* v. *Dexter,* [1902] A.C. 474, 477.

For a somewhat elaborate discussion of the point made by Mr. Root, see Proceedings of the American Society of International Law, 1931, pp. 61–91.

[53] In a letter addressed to Senator Borah by Secretary Stimson, on March 22, 1932. See U. S. Senate Report No. 758, 72d Congress, 1st session, p. 59. In a report made on June 1, 1932, by Senators Walsh and Fess, the view was taken that "the difference as a practical matter between the original reservation V and the protocol of accession" was "so slight, even though the Root construction be rejected, as to approach the vanishing point." *Id.,* p. 14.

be held, if desired, with a view to their reaching an agreement as to whether any interest of the United States is involved in the dispute or question to which the advisory opinion would relate. When a question was raised in the Committee of Jurists as to the extent of this provision, Sir Cecil Hurst explained that the words "before the Council or the Assembly of the League" had been inserted to make it "clear that the provisions of the Article would not apply when the request for an advisory opinion came from an outside body and when it was not likely to be seriously entertained by the Council or the Assembly"; he urged "that the question of informing the United States should be left to the good sense and discretion of the Secretary-General and the Council," and he therefore opposed a suggestion that the word "serious" be inserted before the word "proposal." [54] The exchange of views provided for is limited to the question whether an interest of the United States is involved; it can hardly be assumed that if an interest of the United States is found to exist other States would necessarily find the United States' withholding of consent justified, and no doubt the exchange of views would be directed toward persuading the United States to give its consent.

(6) *Article 5, paragraph 2. "Whenever a request for an advisory opinion comes to the Court, the Registrar shall notify the United States thereof, among other States mentioned in the now existing Article 73 of the Rules of Court, stating a reasonable time-limit fixed by the President within which a written statement by the United States concerning the request will be received. If for any reason no sufficient opportunity for an exchange of views upon such request should have been afforded and the United States advises the Court that the question upon which the opinion of the Court is asked is one that affects the interests of the United States, proceedings shall be stayed for a period sufficient to enable such an exchange of views between the Council or the Assembly and the United States to take place."*

This paragraph is clearly directed to the Court. The first sentence would require the Court to adopt a special procedure as to the United States, with respect to each request for an advisory opinion; with reference to other States, the Court does not fix "a reasonable time limit" for the filing of written statements unless it considers them "likely to be able to furnish information." The second

[54] Minutes of the 1929 Committee of Jurists, pp. 77-78.

sentence of this paragraph provides merely for a stay of proceedings in certain cases; it was explained in the report of the Committee of Jurists that "the desirability of obtaining an advisory opinion may only become apparent as the session of the Council is drawing to a close and when it may not be possible to complete the exchange of view [sic] before the members of that body separate." [55] The stay of proceedings may possibly be regarded as preliminary to the Court's declaration that it cannot entertain the request; consent by the United States or a withdrawal of the request by the Council, as a result of the exchange of views, would obviate the necessity for such a declaration.

(7) *Article 5, paragraph 3. "With regard to requesting an advisory opinion of the Court in any case covered by the preceding paragraphs, there shall be attributed to an objection of the United States the same force and effect as attaches to a vote against asking for the opinion given by a Member of the League of Nations in the Council or in the Assembly."*

This paragraph is based upon a provision in Article 4 of the draft protocol of 1926, which was retained in the proposal made by Mr. Root in 1929. It relates not to the Court's entertainment of a request for an advisory opinion, but to the power of the United States to prevent the Council from making a request. The provision represents a return to the idea of equality between the United States and the States represented in the Assembly or the Council, with respect to any objection to a request's being made to the Court. It, therefore, raises the question whether a unanimous vote in the Council or the Assembly is needed for a request, which so preoccupied the 1926 Conference of Signatories. The "objection of the United States" to which force is to be given does not seem to be limited to an objection based on a claim of interest, and in this respect, the United States would enjoy equality; yet the introductory words seem to assume that the objection would have been advanced in the course of the "exchange of views" mentioned in the two preceding paragraphs. If the Court had been seised of a request before the exchange of views had taken place, and if the Council or Assembly did not thereafter withdraw the request because of the objection of the United States, it would seem to be for the Court itself to

[55] Minutes of the 1929 Committee of Jurists, p. 131. See also the observations of M. van Eysinga, *id.*, pp. 20–21.

attribute force and effect to the objection. In this event, if the Court should decide that unanimity is required, it might hold itself to be no longer seised of the request.

(8) *Article 5, paragraph 4. "If, after the exchange of views provided for in paragraphs 1 and 2 of this Article, it shall appear that no agreement can be reached and the United States is not prepared to forego its objection, the exercise of the powers of withdrawal provided for in Article 8 hereof will follow naturally without any imputation of unfriendliness or unwillingness to co-operate generally for peace and goodwill."*

This paragraph originated in the proposal by Mr. Root. It seems to afford to the United States an option between foregoing its objection and withdrawing, if no agreement can be reached. It applies only "after the exchange of views" has taken place, and the exchange referred to is only as to the question "whether an interest of the United States is affected." The text seems to be unduly restricted, for the statement as to "the exercise of the powers of withdrawal" ought to apply even though an agreement has been reached on the United States' having an interest. This suggests that the "agreement" referred to should not be limited to the subject matter of the exchange of views provided for, but might relate to the desirability of the request for the opinion. The reservation offered by the United States envisaged a withholding of consent rather than the offering of an objection (Fr., *opposition*); but a withholding of consent by the United States would clearly be an "objection" within the meaning of this paragraph. The whole paragraph is of little substance.

(9) *Article 6. "Subject to the provisions of Article 8 below, the provisions of the present Protocol shall have the same force and effect as the provisions of the Statute of the Court and any future signature of the Protocol of December 16, 1920, shall be deemed to be an acceptance of the provisions of the present Protocol."*

The first part of this article would incorporate the provisions of the Protocol into the Statute of the Court, and would give effect to some of them, particularly to Articles 2 and 4, as amendments to the Statute; [56] yet, as they remain subject to the provisions of Article 8 of the Protocol, these amendments might later be cancelled by a

---

[56] Of course it is not accurate to say that the provisions of the Protocol are to "have the same force and effect" as the provisions of the Statute; what is meant is that they shall have the force and effect of amendments to the provisions of the Statute.

special procedure. The Committee of Jurists thought it necessary to assure that later signatories of the Protocol of Signature of December 16, 1920, *i.e.*, States which sign that Protocol subsequently to the coming into force of the Protocol of September 14, 1929, would also accept the special terms of the American adherence. It would seem that this would have been true if nothing had been said on the point; for an effective modification of the Statute would have to be accepted by any later signatory of the Protocol of Signature of December 16, 1920. The Committee of Jurists seems to have contemplated ratification subsequent to the new Protocol's coming into effect by States on whose behalf the Protocol of 1920 had been signed previously; but a proposal to substitute "ratification" for "signature" was not accepted.[57]

(10) *Article 7. "The present Protocol shall be ratified. Each State shall forward the instrument of ratification to the Secretary-General of the League of Nations, who shall inform all the other signatory States. The instruments of ratification shall be deposited in the archives of the Secretariat of the League of Nations.*

"The present Protocol shall come into force as soon as all States which have ratified the Protocol of December 16, 1920, and also the United States, have deposited their ratifications."

The first paragraph of this article follows a standard form in multipartite instruments opened to signature at Geneva. The second paragraph requires that the unanimous consent necessary be expressed by formal ratifications; the 1929 Conference of Signatories did not here adopt the innovation as to consent which was included in paragraph 4 of the Revision Protocol of September 14, 1929.

(11) *Article 8. "The United States may at any time notify the Secretary-General of the League of Nations that it withdraws its adherence to the Protocol of December 16, 1920. The Secretary-General shall immediately communicate this notification to all the other States signatories of the Protocol.*

"In such case, the present Protocol shall cease to be in force as from the receipt by the Secretary-General of the notification by the United States.

"On their part, each of the other Contracting States may at any time notify the Secretary-General of the League of Nations that it desires to withdraw its acceptance of the special conditions attached by

[57] Minutes of the 1929 Committee of Jurists, p. 81.

the United States to its adherence to the Protocol of December 16, 1920. The Secretary-General shall immediately give communication of this notification to each of the States signatories of the present Protocol. The present Protocol shall be considered as ceasing to be in force if and when, within one year from the date of receipt of the said notification, not less than two-thirds of the Contracting States other than the United States shall have notified the Secretary-General of the League of Nations that they desire to withdraw the above-mentioned acceptance."

The fourth reservation offered by the United States stipulated "that the United States may at any time withdraw its adherence to the said Protocol" of December 16, 1920. The 1926 Conference of Signatories proposed that the signatory States should possess a "corresponding right" to withdraw their acceptance of the American reservation, in order that "the *status quo ante* could be reëstablished if it were found that the arrangement agreed upon was not yielding satisfactory results."[58] It decided, however, "to invest the exercise of such a right with the character of a collective decision taken by a sufficiently large majority to ensure that it is inspired exclusively by objective considerations arising from the discovery of some serious practical difficulty."[59] The text of the 1926 Conference, in Article 7 of the draft protocol, was more limited than that adopted in 1929. Under the latter, however, the privilege of withdrawal is not really reciprocal. The United States alone may withdraw its adherence to the Protocol of 1920; but any withdrawal by another of the Contracting States will apply only to its acceptance of the United States adherence, and it will have to be supported by two-thirds of the Contracting States before it becomes effective. The period of one year within which such support must be rallied is so short for action by thirty-three or more States that withdrawal by other Contracting States would be impossible except in case of very serious dissatisfaction. This arraying of the United States on one side and of "the other Contracting States" on the other, lends color to a suggestion that the Protocol is in reality a bilateral arrangement.[60]

§239. **Reservations Accepted without Reference.** Two of the reservations offered by the United States were accepted without any special reference to them in the Protocol of September 14, 1929,

[58] Minutes of the 1926 Conference, p. 77.   [59] *Id.*, pp. 53–56.
[60] See Proceedings of the American Society of International Law, 1931, p. 77.

though the general reference to the five reservations, contained in Article 1 of the Protocol, may be taken to have covered them.

The first reservation offered was a *caveat* "that such adherence shall not be taken to involve any legal relation on the part of the United States to the League of Nations or the assumption of any obligations by the United States under the Treaty of Versailles." The first part of this reservation was expressly agreed to in the Final Act of the 1926 Conference of Signatories,[61] and it was not later dealt with; yet it contains a flat contradiction of the basic provisions contained in the Protocol of September 14, 1929. Indeed, it contradicts the statement in the second reservation offered by the United States, for participation in the elections of judges by the Assembly and the Council would seem to involve a legal relation to the League of Nations. The reservation was justified by the faulty drafting of the Protocol of Signature of December 16, 1920, which begins with the words "the Members of the League of Nations." The second part of the reservation was merely superfluous, for by no stretch of imagination could the United States be thought to be assuming any obligation under the Treaty of Versailles as a result of its adherence.

The third reservation offered by the United States was "that the United States will pay a fair share of the expenses of the Court as determined and appropriated from time to time by the Congress of the United States." This also was agreed to in the Final Act of the 1926 Conference of Signatories, and it was not later discussed. The President of the 1926 Conference thought that it "could hardly be called a reservation"; [62] yet it is to be noted that it assures to the United States a privilege which is not possessed by States which are Members of the League of Nations, the privilege of determining the amount of its own contribution.[63]

---

[61] Minutes of the 1926 Conference, p. 77.

[62] Minutes of the 1926 Conference, p. 12.

[63] Article 33 of the Statute makes no provision for contributions to the Court's expenses by the States not members of the League of Nations to which the Protocol of Signature was opened for signature. Article 22 of the League of Nations Financial Regulations provides: "States not Members of the League which have been admitted members of any organization of the League shall, in the absence of any contrary provision, contribute towards the expenses of the organization concerned as nearly as possible in the proportion in which they would contribute to such expenses if they were members of the League." League of Nations Document, C. 3(1). M. 3(1). 1931. X. See §352, *infra*.

In other connections in which the United States has met a part of special expenses incurred by the League of Nations, the amount of its contribution has been computed with reference to the amount paid by the largest contributor to the League's budget, *i.e.*, by Great Britain. In 1933, Great Britain's share of the League's budget amounted to 105 units, each unit being 33,016.43 Swiss francs, and 7.95 per cent of each contribu-

§240. **Defective Drafting of the 1929 Protocol.** The Protocol for the Accession of the United States contemplates an accession to the Protocol of Signature of December 16, 1920, to which the Statute was annexed, and it completely fails to take account of the Revision Protocol of September 14, 1929, to which various amendments to the Statute were annexed. If the Protocol for the Accession of the United States should come into force after the Revision Protocol has come into force, the former would according to its terms have the effect of making the United States a party to the Protocol of Signature of December 16, 1920, with the original Statute annexed, whereas that Statute would already have been amended. This defect in the Protocol for United States' accession will be cured, for all practical purposes, however, if the United States also ratifies the Revision Protocol; by its simultaneous ratification of the Protocol of December 16, 1920, the Revision Protocol, and the Protocol for the United States' Accession, the United States would become, in effect, a party to the amended Statute if the Revision Protocol has previously been brought into force; and to the unamended Statute if the Revision Protocol has not previously been brought into force. It was for the purpose of taking care of the position of the United States in this regard, that provision was made in paragraph 7 of the Revision Protocol that "for the purposes of the present Protocol, the United States of America shall be in the same position as a State which has ratified the Protocol of December 16, 1920"; this afforded the United States an opportunity to object to the coming into force of the amendments to the Statute, but no such objection was made.

§241. **Importance of American Participation.** The long and difficult road which has been travelled to effectuate the participation of the United States in the maintenance of the Court may be said to have been due to exaggerations, both on the part of the signatory States and on the part of the United States. The importance of American participation was exaggerated in the First Assembly in 1920, in the two Conferences of Signatories, and in the elections of judges. For twelve years, the Court has been maintained without aid from the United States, and it would be difficult to say that the value of its functioning was in any important respect diminished by American

tion was to be paid over to the Court. On this basis the share of the Court's expenses payable by the United States for 1933 would have been 7.95 per cent of 105 × 33,016.43 Swiss francs, or 275,604.65 Swiss francs (about $53,205 gold).

abstention. At no time did the United States propose to make any large contribution; at no time has it proposed to become a party to the "Optional Clause." For a period, agreements were made in various exchanges of notes between the United States and other States [64] looking toward a possible insertion of provisions relating to the Court into arbitration treaties; but the requirement in the Senate Resolution of January 27, 1926, that recourse to the Court should be had by the United States "only by agreement thereto through general or special treaties" would have made it impossible for such provisions to go far toward increasing the Court's jurisdiction. If in a few cases during the decade following 1922 the United States might have gone before the Court as a party, this would not have added greatly to the Court's prestige. The desire of the signatory States for American participation was probably based in part upon the hope that it would lead the United States to play a larger rôle in international coöperation.[65]

It is equally true, on the other hand, that the course followed by the United States has been largely dictated by exaggerations. In American opinion, mere participation in maintaining the Court has been viewed as the assumption of an important rôle in coöperation to maintain the world's peace. A very different estimate would doubtless have prevailed if the United States had been a member of the League of Nations. "Membership in the Court" appeared as a substitute for membership in the League, or as leading necessarily toward the latter; in spite of the American Government's past record in urging the establishment of a court, the step was looked upon in some quarters as one of involvement. This caused the fears expressed in the Senate resolution of January 27, 1926, and the seeking of a very special position for the United States. The spirit of nationalism prevailing led not only to unfounded criticism of the structure and work of the Court, but also to a distrust of the purposes which it might be made to serve.

[64] With Great Britain, June 23, 1923; with France, July 19, 1923; with Japan, August 23, 1923; with Portugal, September 5, 1923; with Norway, November 26, 1923; with the Netherlands, February 13, 1924; with Sweden, June 24, 1924; with Liberia, February 10, 1926. See U. S. Treaty Series, Nos. 674, 679, 683, 735, 680, 682, 708, 747. An exchange of notes between the United States and the Netherlands on August 21, 1924, also envisaged a possible agreement for referring to the Court claims arising under a convention concerning the prevention of smuggling of intoxicating liquors. *Id.*, No. 712. A similar exchange of notes was made by the United States and Cuba, March 4, 1926. *Id.*, No. 738.

[65] See Records of First Assembly, Plenary, p. 441.

PART III

THE ORGANIZATION OF THE PERMANENT
COURT OF INTERNATIONAL JUSTICE

CHAPTER 11

THE ELECTION OF MEMBERS OF THE COURT

§242. **The System of Elections.** The provisions of the Statute which deal with the election of members of the Court represent the greatest triumph achieved in creating the Court. The problem of election had baffled the 1907 Hague Conference in its effort to create a Court of Arbitral Justice, and a very unsatisfactory solution had been given to the problem when that Conference sought to create an International Prize Court. The difficulty had been in reconciling the demands of the more powerful States for certain representation and the insistence of other States on the principle of equality. By 1920, however, a similar difficulty had been surmounted in the creation of the League of Nations; full recognition was given to the claims of the larger States in the provisions for permanent representation on the Council, while all Members of the League were entitled to equal representation in the Assembly. The 1920 Committee of Jurists took advantage of this fact to propose that the election of judges of the Court should be entrusted to the Assembly and the Council, and the proposal was greeted with general satisfaction. It is the existence of these two bodies which makes possible the maintenance of the Court under the present Statute.

Article 13 of the Statute provides that "the members of the Court shall be elected for nine years," [1] and under Article 14 a member elected to fill a vacancy serves only "for the remainder of his predecessor's term." This means that the membership is completely reconstituted at the end of each nine-year period. Given the difficulties to be overcome when the method of election had to be agreed upon in 1920, perhaps no other plan could have been adopted at

---

[1] M. Politis (Greece) proposed to the 1929 Committee of Jurists that the term "should be increased from nine to twelve years, with the hope that, in future, it would be found possible to go even further and to appoint the international judges for life." Minutes of the 1929 Committee of Jurists, p. 44.

that time; yet this feature of the system has been the subject of some criticism on the ground that the continuity of the Court's work would be better safeguarded if the terms of members of the Court did not expire simultaneously.[2] Assuming a Court of fifteen members, the terms might have been so arranged that five members would have been elected every three years; such a system might have produced more continuity, and at the same time it might have reduced the possibility of bargaining in the elections.[3] The provision in Article 13 of the Statute that members may be reëlected has in practice worked to produce the first of these advantages, however.

§243. **The Nomination of Candidates.** Only those persons who have been nominated by a national group in the Permanent Court of Arbitration or by a national group set up under the second paragraph of Article 4 of the Statute, may be said to be candidates in an election. Article 4 refers to "national groups in the Court of Arbitration" generally; but Article 5 restricts the invitations to be issued by the Secretary-General to "members of the Court of Arbitration belonging to the States mentioned in the Annex to the Covenant or to the States which join the League subsequently."[4] As these two categories of States may not include all the States represented in, or entitled to representation in the Permanent Court of Arbitration, the privilege of making nominations may not extend to all the members of the latter.[5] Governments of various "Members of the League of Nations not represented in the Permanent Court of Arbitration" have appointed national groups for the purpose of making nominations; they include the Governments of Albania, Austria, Czechoslovakia, Estonia, Finland, Latvia, Lithuania and Poland, as well as various members of the British Commonwealth of Nations.[6] In practice, the

---

[2] The question arose before the 1920 Committee of Jurists in a proposal that elections to fill vacancies should be for a full period of nine years. See Minutes of the 1920 Committee of Jurists, pp. 194, 465.

[3] It is to be noted that the terms of Members of the League of Nations nonpermanently represented on the Council do not now expire simultaneously.

[4] In the meaning of this phrase in Article 5, members of the Permanent Court of Arbitration "belong to" the States which appointed them, though they may be nationals of other States. Siam has recently appointed non-nationals.

[5] In 1933, however, every State actually represented in the Permanent Court of Arbitration was a member of the League of Nations or mentioned in the Annex to the Covenant. Though Russia was a party to the 1899 and 1907 Conventions, no members of the Permanent Court of Arbitration have been appointed by the Union of Soviet Socialist Republics; and Montenegro is no longer to be regarded as a "Contracting Power." See *supra*, §4.

[6] Czechoslovakia, Finland and Poland are now "represented in the Permanent Court of Arbitration." Several States entitled to representation in the Permanent Court of Arbitration have failed to designate members of that body; under Article 4 of the

Secretary-General of the League of Nations requests that appointments of such groups under the second paragraph of Article 4 of the Statute be notified to him, in advance of the despatch of the invitations provided for in Article 5.

The Secretary-General's invitation to the national groups to undertake the nomination of candidates must be sent out "at least three months before the date of the election"; it is usually sent at a date even longer in advance. It is not necessary for the Secretary-General to obtain the authority of the Council for issuing these invitations if the date of the election is known; such authority is obtained in practice, however. The invitations are addressed to the members of the national groups individually, but they are sent to the ministry of foreign affairs of each country for transmission to the addressees. The invitation is accompanied by reproductions of the relevant texts, and in 1930 the Secretary-General drew attention to the recommendation adopted by the Assembly on September 14, 1929. The national groups are invited to make the nominations "within a given time," the period being determined by the Secretary-General; in practice the nominations are not required to be in the hands of the Secretary-General by the date set, and later nominations are always received. Though the invitations are addressed to individuals, the nominations must be made by the national groups; several individual members of a group cannot make nominations, each independently of the others.

In 1929, the Committee of Jurists which was considering amendments to the Statute suggested that the Assembly adopt a "recommendation" that the Secretary-General in issuing invitations to national groups should request that they satisfy themselves that their nominees "possess recognised practical experience in international law" and "are at least able to read both the official languages of the Court and to speak one of them," and should recommend that the groups "attach to each nomination a statement of the career of the person nominated showing that he possesses the required qualifications." [7] In the 1929 Conference of Signatories, some opposition was manifested to the qualification of "recognised practical experience in international law," as an addition to Article 2 of the Statute,[8] and

Statute, such States may create special national groups to make nominations, if they are members of the League of Nations.

[7] Minutes of the 1929 Committee of Jurists, p. 129.

[8] Minutes of the 1929 Conference, pp. 25–28, 52–53. The opposition led by the representative of Norway was motivated by a desire to prevent the election of legal advisers to Foreign Offices, as a regular practice.

the opposition was renewed when the Tenth Assembly voted on September 14, 1929, to associate itself with the following recommendation by the Conference: [9]

> The Conference recommends that, in accordance with the spirit of Articles 2 and 39 of the Statute of the Court, the candidates nominated by the national groups should possess recognised practical experience in international law and that they should be at least able to read both the official languages of the Court and to speak one of them; it also considers it desirable that to the nominations there should be attached a statement of the careers of the candidates justifying their candidature.

Article 7 of the Statute requires the Secretary-General to submit to the Assembly and the Council a list of the persons nominated, "in alphabetical order." This list gives an indication of the source of the nominations in each case.[10] Only candidates whose names appear on the Secretary-General's list may be elected, in the first instance; if the Assembly and the Council are unable to agree, a joint conference of six members may by unanimous vote select a person for its report to the electoral bodies, even though his name is not included on the Secretary-General's list.

§244. **Voting in the Assembly and in the Council.** Though this is not required by the Statute, the meetings of the Assembly and of the Council for the purposes of elections are held simultaneously.[11] Care is taken to prevent either body from knowing in advance the results of the balloting in the other,[12] and in practice the requirement in Article 8 of the Statute that the two bodies "proceed independently" is applied quite strictly. Article 21 of the Assembly's rules of procedure [13] requires that "all decisions relating to individuals shall be taken by a secret ballot," and this is applied in the elections. The voting is conducted in public sessions of the Assembly; on the other hand, the Council's voting is conducted at a private meeting. Article 10 of the Council's rules of procedure, as codified in the Rules adopted on May 26, 1933, is applied, providing: "All decisions con-

[9] Records of Tenth Assembly, Plenary, pp. 119–121; *id.*, Committees, I, pp. 10–11. This recommendation was brought to the attention of the national groups in 1930.

[10] See, *e.g.*, League of Nations Official Journal, 1920, p. 811; League of Nations Document, A. 31. 1930. V.

[11] The 1920 Committee of Jurists declined to recommend a text which would have fixed different days for the voting in the Council and the Assembly. Minutes of the 1920 Committee of Jurists, pp. 396–397.

[12] In the beginning, this practice was due to the Assembly's jealousy of the Council.

[13] See Document C. 220. M. 92. 1932. V; 1 Hudson, International Legislation, p. 132.

cerning persons shall be taken at a private meeting. On the demand of any member of the Council, the voting shall be by secret ballot." [14] A majority of the members of the Council must be present. In both the Assembly and the Council, "an absolute majority of the votes" is required for an election, by Article 10 of the Statute; in practice, this seems to mean an absolute majority of the votes cast. It is the President of the Assembly who makes public declaration of the result of the voting by both the Assembly and the Council.

§245. **Preparations for the First Election in 1921.**[15] The hope had been expressed in the First Assembly that it would be possible for the first election of members of the Court to be held in 1921.[16] In some quarters, it was thought that no election could be held until the Statute had come into force, however, and the ratifications of twenty-five States or Members of the League of Nations were required to bring the Protocol of December 16, 1920, and the annexed Statute, into force. Only the Swedish Government's ratification had been deposited when on February 29, 1921, the Council of the League of Nations authorized the Secretary-General to take steps for the conditional nomination of candidates.[17] Strenuous efforts were made by the Secretariat of the League of Nations to expedite the ratifications of the Protocol of Signature, and a sufficient number of ratifications was effected to bring the Statute into force on or before September 1, 1921.[18] On April 1, 1921, the Secretary-General asked the Members of the League of Nations and the States mentioned in the Annex to the Covenant to inform him of the composition of their national groups in the Permanent Court of Arbitration or of their national groups created under Article 4 of the Statute for the purpose of making nominations; [19] and on June 2, 1921, a formal invitation was addressed to members of the national groups to make nominations of candidates by August 15, 1921, conditioned on the elections taking place at the forthcoming Assembly.[20] Though the composition of some of the national groups under Article 4 was not notified to the

---

[14] League of Nations Official Journal, 1933, p. 900.

[15] For a study of the various elections, see Manley O. Hudson, "The Election of Members of the Permanent Court of International Justice," 24 American Journal of International Law (1930), p. 718.   [16] Records of First Assembly, Plenary, p. 467.

[17] Council Minutes, 12th Session, pp. 18, 115–6.   [18] See *supra*, §111.

[19] League of Nation Official Journal, 1921, pp. 246–7, 314. The letter also suggested the appointment of members of the Permanent Court of Arbitration by signatories of the Hague Conventions which were not represented in that body. On April 25, 1921, 38 States were represented in the Permanent Court of Arbitration by 122 members.

[20] *Id.*, pp. 426–7.

Secretary-General within the time limit set, they were invited to make nominations.[21]

§246. Nominations in 1921. Thirty-four national groups sent in nominations of eighty-nine candidates for the first election.[22] The Secretary-General did not refuse to list nominations received after the date set, August 15, 1921, for on that date nominations had been received from only twenty-four groups; to allow for delays in transmission, the list was not closed until September 5, 1921. In some cases, the nominations were communicated to the Secretary-General of the League through the group's Ministry of Foreign Affairs; this practice is not foreseen in the Statute, and it might tend to deprive the national group of some of its independence. The members of the Permanent Court of Arbitration appointed by the United States of America declined to make any nomination on the ground of lack of competence under the 1907 Hague Convention for Pacific Settlement.[23] In spite of the requirement in Article 5 of the Statute that persons nominated should be "in a position to accept the duties of a member of the Court," some of the nominating groups seem to have acted without having ascertained this, and nine of the nominees withdrew their names from consideration. In the list of nominees submitted to the Assembly and Council by the Secretary-General, under Article 7 of the Statute, indication was given of the nationality of each candidate, and of the groups by which he had been nominated; [24] the actual ballot placed before the Assembly [25] gave only the names of the candidates in alphabetical order with an indication of their

---

[21] League of Nations Official Journal, 1921, p. 428.

[22] League of Nations Document, A. 30. 1921. V. To aid in the appointment of judges *ad hoc* under Article 31 of the Statute, the list is published in the Annual Report of the Court. Series E, No. 1, pp. 28–45.

[23] The invitations to members of the United States group were not promptly transmitted to them after they had been received by the Secretary of State; the delay led the Secretary-General to send the invitations a second time, and the repeated invitations did not pass through the hands of the Secretary of State. On September 15, 1921, the American group replied to the Secretary-General's invitation as follows: "Considering that our appointment by the President as members of the Permanent Court of Arbitration was, under the Hague Convention of 1907, to perform the functions contemplated in that Convention and that your invitation to nominate candidates for judges of the new Permanent Court of International Justice is under another treaty, to which the United States is not a party, and in respect of which no authority has been conferred upon us, we reluctantly reached the conclusion that we were not entitled to make official nominations for the new Court." League of Nations Document, A. 92. 1921. V. In 1923, however, the American group composed of the same members made nominations, and nominations have since been made by it. In 1930, the Ecuadorean group also expressed doubt as to its competence to make nominations.

[24] League of Nations Official Journal, 1921, p. 811.

[25] League of Nations Document, A. 65. 1921.

nationality. Only one candidate received as many as seven nominations in 1921.

§247. **The General Election of 1921.** Some nervousness was felt in the Second Assembly as to the procedure to be followed in the election, and on September 13, 1921, the day before the election was to begin, the President of the Assembly gave an elaborate explanation of the proposed procedure.[26] While the Council was to meet in private,[27] it had been decided that the Assembly should meet in public. The voting was to be by secret ballot, the results of each poll being announced to the Assembly. Rule 21 of the Assembly was to be applied to restrict the voting on each later ballot to the unsuccessful candidates who obtained the greatest number of votes on the previous ballots, the number of such candidates to be not more than twice the number of places remaining to be filled. The election was begun in both the Assembly and the Council on September 14, 1921.[28] The two bodies acted simultaneously, care being taken that neither should know the list of the other until the lists were ready for comparison. On the first ballot in the Assembly, nine candidates received an absolute majority of the votes cast: M. Altamira (Spain), M. Alvarez (Chile), M. Anzilotti (Italy), M. Barbosa (Brazil), M. de Bustamante (Cuba), Viscount Finlay (Great Britain), M. Loder (Netherlands), M. Oda (Japan), and M. Weiss (France). Thereafter, the Assembly decided that its Rule 21 should not be applied to exclude any candidate in later ballots.[29] On the second ballot, one candidate, Mr. Moore (U.S.A.), received a majority, but on the third and fourth ballots no candidate had a majority. On the fifth ballot, held after an interval, the Assembly's list of eleven candidates was completed, M. Huber (Switzerland) having received a majority. On comparison with the Council's list, nine candidates whose names appeared on both lists were declared to be elected; M. Alvarez and M. Huber, whose names appeared on the Assembly's list, were not on the Council's list. At a later meeting of the Assembly on the same day, a sixth ballot yielded two names which were also on the Council's second list, of M. Huber and M. Nyholm (Denmark), and this completed the

[26] Records of Second Assembly, Plenary, pp. 222–3.

[27] No provision of the Statute requires the Council to act in private, but this is in line with the usual practice of the Council when it chooses individuals for posts, and the practice has persisted in all the elections of judges. No account of the election appears in the published minutes of the Council.

[28] Records of Second Assembly, Plenary, pp. 235–8.

[29] This precedent has been followed at the subsequent elections.

election of eleven judges. Four ballots were then taken in the Assembly for the election of the deputy-judges; three of the names on the Assembly's list, M. Negulesco (Rumania), M. Wang (China), and M. Yovanovitch (Serb-Croat-Slovene State), were also on the Council's third list. An eleventh ballot was then taken in which the Assembly again chose M. Alvarez (Chile); but the Council chose M. Descamps (Belgium). After a twelfth ballot in the Assembly and a new ballot in the Council, these respective choices were adhered to. The President of the Assembly then raised the question of applying Article 12 of the Statute to set up a joint conference, and the Assembly decided that a joint conference should be set up. On September 15, the Assembly and Council elected their respective members of the conference.[30] On September 16, the joint conference recommended the election of M. Beichmann (Norway),[31] and soon afterward he was elected by both the Assembly and the Council as the fourth deputy-judge.[32]

Thus, the election was accomplished in three days, after thirteen ballots in the Assembly, its successful termination being made possible by the device of the joint conference. All of the successful candidates accepted their election.[33] One or more votes were cast for only fifty-five of the eighty candidates whose names were on the Assembly ballot, indicating that some of the nominations were hardly more than a compliment paid to the nominees.

§248. The Election of 1923. The death of Judge Barbosa on March 1, 1923, created a vacancy, for which an election was authorized by the Council on April 17, 1923. The invitations issued by the Secretary-General requested nominations to be made by August 1, 1923, but the list was not closed until September 3. Thirty-one candidates were nominated by forty national groups; [34] twenty-two of these groups nominated M. Pessôa (Brazil). The voting took place on September 10, 1923, and M. Pessôa received a majority of the votes cast on the first ballot both in the Assembly and in the Council.

---

[30] Records of Second Assembly, Plenary, pp. 273, 279. When in 1921 the Assembly was considering the nomination of its representatives in the joint conference, Mr. H. A. L. Fisher (British Empire) laid down three general principles in which the Assembly seems to have acquiesced: (1) the Assembly's representatives should be delegates of States not represented on the Council; (2) the Assembly's representatives should represent different systems of law; and (3) the Assembly's representatives should not be immediately concerned in the issue between the two prominent candidates. Records of Second Assembly, Plenary, p. 258. These principles are not to be found in the Statute, however.

[31] Id., p. 281.　　　　　[32] Id., p. 291.　　　　　[33] Id., p. 293.

[34] League of Nations Document A. 37. 1923. V.

§249. **The Election of 1928.** On April 11, 1928, Judge Moore addressed a letter to the Secretary-General of the League of Nations, presenting his resignation and expressing a desire that it should take effect "as soon as the presence of the statutory full court, without my attendance, at the opening of the regular session, on June 15th next, is reasonably assured." [35] On being informed of the letter, the Court asked Judge Moore to reconsider, but he replied that he was unable to alter his decision. As resignation is not provided for, either in the Statute or in the Rules, the resignation was accepted by the Council provisionally, subject to the concurrence of the Assembly; the resignation was not finally accepted until September 4, 1928, when the Assembly concurred in the action of the Council. Meanwhile, however, the Secretary-General had taken the necessary steps to secure the nomination of candidates for an election to fill the vacancy. Twenty-six candidates were nominated by thirty-nine national groups,[36] of which thirty nominated Mr. Charles Evans Hughes (U.S.A.). The election took place on September 8, 1928, and Mr. Hughes received a majority of the votes cast on the first ballot both in the Assembly and in the Council.

§250. **The Election of 1929.** The death of Judge Weiss on August 31, 1928, and that of Lord Finlay on March 9, 1929, created two vacancies in the Court. Since the vacancies occurred at separate times, the Secretary-General addressed to the national groups separate invitations in respect of each vacancy, and two lists of candidates were communicated to the Assembly.[37] Twenty-five candidates were nominated by thirty-seven national groups for the vacancy created by the death of Judge Weiss; M. Fromageot (France) was nominated by twenty-five of these groups. Twenty-four candidates were nominated by thirty-five national groups for the vacancy created by the death of Lord Finlay; Sir Cecil Hurst (Great Britain) was nominated by twenty-nine of these groups.[38] In the Tenth Assembly of the League of Nations, the general committee made a special report on the procedure to be followed, recommending that the two vacancies be filled simultaneously and that all candidates nominated for either

---

[35] Series E, No. 4, p. 26.   [36] League of Nations Document A. 32. 1928. V.

[37] League of Nations Document, A. 26. 1929. V.

[38] An unusual feature of these nominations was that the British national group consisted of one man who nominated himself. In the House of Commons of the British Parliament, the Secretary of State for Foreign Affairs seems to have accepted responsibility for this nomination, which he attributed to a "previous government." 230 British Parliamentary Debates, p. 399.

vacancy should be eligible for both vacancies; [39] the constitutionality of such a procedure is difficult to justify. These recommendations were accepted by the Assembly and followed by the Council, both of which bodies proceeded to hold the election on September 19, 1929. Fifty-two delegations voted in the Assembly, and on the first ballot Sir Cecil Hurst and M. Fromageot received a majority of the votes cast; as their names were also on the Council's list they were declared elected. Both accepted and assumed office immediately.[40]

§251. The Election of a Successor to Judge Hughes in 1930. On February 14, 1930, by telegrams addressed to the Secretary-General of the League of Nations and the President of the Court, Judge Hughes resigned and requested that his resignation take effect immediately. On May 12, 1930, the resignation was accepted by the Council "subject to the concurrence of the Assembly," and the Secretary-General was requested to take steps for the eventual selection of a successor.[41] The list of nominations circulated to the Assembly contained the names of sixteen candidates, of whom eleven were nationals of the United States; these candidates were nominated by thirty-two national groups, of which eight nominated Mr. Frank B. Kellogg and seven nominated Dr. James Brown Scott, both nationals of the United States.[42] The Assembly did not take any action toward expressly concurring in the Council's acceptance of Judge Hughes' resignation, but on September 17, 1930, both the Assembly and the Council proceeded to the election. Mr. Kellogg received thirty of forty-seven valid votes cast in the Assembly on the first ballot, and as his name was on the Council's list he was declared to be elected. He accepted and assumed office immediately.

§252. Nominations for the General Election in 1930. Invitations were despatched by the Secretary-General to national groups to make nominations for the second general election, on March 21, 1930. In a memorandum accompanying the invitation, the national groups were asked to "observe that the candidates whom they nominate on the present occasion may, if elected members of the Court, be called upon to occupy their office either under the conditions laid down by

[39] Records of Tenth Assembly, Plenary, p. 450.
[40] Records of Tenth Assembly, Plenary, pp. 126, 153. The terms of the successful candidates began on October 1, 1929.
[41] Judge Hughes was requested to take part in the session of the Court in June, 1930, but found himself unable to do so. Series C, No. 18—I, p. 9. Even if he was not still a member of the Court, he was eligible to sit under Article 13 of the Statute.
[42] League of Nations Documents A. 33. 1930. V; A. 33 (a). 1930. V.

the existing Statute of the Court or under those which would result from the entry into force of the amendments to the Statute" annexed to the Revision Protocol of September 14, 1929.[43] The memorandum also drew attention to the nature of the proposed amendments, and to the salaries and pensions to which judges were entitled. In response to the invitation, fifty national groups nominated sixty candidates.[44] Though the Secretary-General had asked that nominations be sent to him by August 1, 1930, nominations were accepted which were received after the opening of the Assembly in September. The list presented to the Assembly indicated the nominations received by each candidate, and contained a statement of his career based on information received from the national groups. One candidate received as many as twenty-two nominations, and eight candidates were nominated by six or more groups. Several nominees withdrew from candidacy, among them Judge Huber and Judge Pessôa, both of whom declined to stand for reëlection.[45]

§253. **Demand of the Latin–American States.** On July 19, 1930, the representatives of twelve Latin-American States addressed a letter to the Secretary-General of the League of Nations, stating that the Governments of these States considered that Latin-American States "should be represented in the Court in the same proportion as on the Council" of the League of Nations, and that "of the fifteen members of the Court, three should be nationals of Latin-American States." It was stated that "the maintenance of this proportion is particularly necessary in view of the probability of an increase in the near future in the number of American countries which are Members of the League."[46] Of the twelve Governments on behalf of which this demand was made, seven—Colombia, Guatemala, Honduras, Nicaragua, Paraguay, Peru and El Salvador—had not at the time ratified the Protocol of Signature of December 16, 1920, and only two of the twelve had become bound by the "optional clause"; nor had any of the twelve States ever been represented in a case before the Court. The Secretary-General of the League of Nations communicated the letter

---

[43] League of Nations Document, Annex to M.L.3 and 3 (a). 1930. V.

[44] League of Nations Documents A. 31. 1930. V.; A. 31 (a), 1930. V.; A. 31 (c), 1930. V.

[45] Judge Loder also declined to stand for reëlection.

[46] League of Nations Official Journal, 1930, p. 1321. It may be recalled that at the First Assembly of the League of Nations in 1920 Colombian and Cuban proposals to allot the judgeships to various continents had been rejected. Records of First Assembly, Committees, I, p. 354. See § 125, *supra*.

to the Assembly,[47] and it was also brought to the attention of the Council.

§254. The General Election in 1930. In advance of the session of the Eleventh Assembly, the Secretary-General circulated a note concerning the election which drew attention to the proposed amendments to the Statute, to the financial regulations applicable to members of the Court, and to the procedure to be followed. On September 12, 1930, the Council formulated a proposal that in view of the fact that the Revision Protocol of September 14, 1929, had not been brought into force, the number of judges should be increased from eleven to fifteen; this increase was effected by the Assembly on September 25, 1930, and the action greatly facilitated the general election which followed. The First Committee of the Assembly reported its view that if the Revision Protocol of September 14, 1929, should enter into force at some future date, "it would have no effect upon the term of office of judges elected at the present Assembly,"[48] and that thereafter the deputy-judges to be elected would "no longer be called upon to exercise their functions"; the election seems to have been conducted with this understanding.

The Assembly and Council proceeded to the election on September 25, 1930.[49] On the first ballot fourteen candidates received an absolute majority of the 52 votes cast in the Assembly: M. Adatci (49 votes), M. Anzilotti (40), M. Fromageot (40), Sir Cecil Hurst (40), M. Altamira (38), Jonkheer van Eysinga (38), M. Guerrero (38), Baron Rolin-Jaequemyns (38), Mr. Kellogg (35), Count Rostworowski (34), M. Schücking (34), M. Wang (32), M. de Bustamante (31), and M. Negulesco (30). On the second, third and fourth ballots, no candidate received a majority; the Cuban delegate then proposed a recess, but the Assembly proceeded to a fifth ballot on which M. Urrutia received 23 of 45 valid votes.[50] On comparison with the Council's list, the latter was found to contain the names of the candidates who had been successful in the first ballot in the Assembly, and these fourteen candidates were declared elected. At a later meeting on the same day, the balloting in the Assembly was resumed. On the sixth to ninth ballots, no candidate received a majority in the Assembly. On the tenth ballot M. A. Hammarskjöld

[47] League of Nations Document A. 31. 1930. V, p. 23.
[48] Records of Eleventh Assembly, Plenary, p. 131.
[49] *Id.*, pp. 134–140. The published minutes of the Sixtieth Session of the Council contain no account of the election.   [50] A blank vote was not counted. *Sed quære.*

received a majority, but the Council's second list contained the name of M. Urrutia. An eleventh ballot was then taken in the Assembly, in which M. Urrutia obtained a majority, and as his name appeared on the Council's third list he was declared to be elected. The election of the deputy-judges then followed. On the first ballot in the Assembly, M. Redlich received a majority of the votes; on the second ballot, M. Novacovitch and M. Erich received a majority, and on the fourth ballot M. Rodrigo Octavio de Langgaard Menezes received a majority. The Council's list contained the names of M. Erich, M. Novacovitch and M. Redlich and they were declared to be elected deputy-judges; the Council's list also contained the name of M. da Matta. A fifth ballot in the Assembly gave M. da Matta a majority, but the Council had meanwhile shifted to M. Rodrigo Octavio de Langgaard Menezes. A sixth ballot in the Assembly gave a majority to M. da Matta, who also received a majority in the Council, and he was declared elected.

The election was thus completed in a single day, without setting up a joint conference, with a total of seventeen ballots in the Assembly and with a comparison of six lists drawn up by each of the electoral bodies. None of those elected declined to accept. A notable feature of this election was that Jonkheer van Eysinga (Netherlands) was elected a judge although he had not been nominated by the national group of the Netherlands.

§255. **Members of the Court, 1922–1930.** From many points of view, the five elections held from 1921 to 1930 resulted in giving to the Court during its first period a very satisfactory composition. Though it was the subject of some criticism, in geographical representation, in range of experience, and in commanding eminence, the roster of the Court was probably as strong as that which any possible system of elections might have produced. Most of the judges elected in 1921 and since were members of the Permanent Court of Arbitration. A brief biographical note concerning each of the members may convey some impression of the strength of the Court.[51]

Judge B. C. J. Loder (Netherlands), born in 1849, had long been a judge of the Netherlands Supreme Court. He was a founder of the International Maritime Committee, and had taken part in various

---

[51] These biographical notes are based upon the material appearing in the annual reports. Series E, No. 1, pp. 14–27; No. 5, pp. 25–26, 33; No. 6, pp. 20–21; No. 7, pp. 21–41.

conferences on maritime law. From 1917, he had been active in the planning for the creation of a court; he had served as vice-president of the 1920 Committee of Jurists and as president of the Conference held at The Hague in February 1920.

Judge André Weiss (France), born in 1858, was an eminent professor of international law, with a wide experience as legal adviser to the French Ministry of Foreign Affairs and in international arbitrations. He had been a delegate to the Paris Peace Conference in 1919. He was the author of a celebrated treatise, *Traité de droit international privé* (6 vols.). He died on August 31, 1928, and was succeeded by Judge Fromageot.

Lord Finlay (Great Britain), born in 1842, was for many years a member of the British Parliament, and he had served as Solicitor-General, Attorney-General, and Lord Chancellor in Great Britain. He died on March 9, 1929, and was succeeded by Sir Cecil Hurst.

Judge D. G. Nyholm (Denmark), born in 1858, had a previous judicial career extending over twenty-eight years, as a member of the Court of Appeal at Copenhagen and as a judge of the Mixed Court at Cairo.

Judge John Bassett Moore (United States of America), born in 1860, had been for thirty years a professor of international law at Columbia University, and had had a wide experience in the Department of State at Washington, in international conferences and in international arbitrations. His *History and Digest of International Arbitrations* (6 vols.) and his *Digest of International Law* (8 vols.) are in use throughout the world. He resigned on April 11, 1928, and was succeeded by Judge Hughes.

Judge Antonio S. de Bustamante (Cuba), born in 1865, for thirty years a professor of international law at Havana, had long been in public life in Cuba. He was a delegate to the Peace Conference at The Hague in 1907, and to the Paris Peace Conference in 1919. His publications on international law were widely known; he drafted the Bustamante Code of Private International Law of 1928.

Judge Rafael Altamira (Spain), born in 1866, had been a professor at the University of Oviedo and the University of Madrid, actively interested in comparative law, and had had some experience in international arbitrations. As a member of the 1920 Committee of Jurists, he had participated in drafting the Statute of the Court.

Judge Yorozu Oda (Japan), born in 1868, had been a professor at

Kyoto University, interested chiefly in Japanese and Chinese administrative law.

Judge Dionisio Anzilotti (Italy), born in 1869, had long been a professor of international law at Florence, Palermo, Bologna and Rome, and a legal adviser to the Italian Ministry of Foreign Affairs. In 1919, he became Under-Secretary-General of the League of Nations, and in that capacity he had played an important rôle in the launching of plans for the Court. He was the founder of the *Rivista di Diritto internazionale*.

Judge Max Huber (Switzerland), born in 1874, had been for twenty years a professor at Zurich. He had served as a delegate to the Peace Conference at The Hague in 1907, and as legal adviser to the Political Department of the Swiss Federal Council, and had been active in the early work of the League of Nations.

Judge Ruy Barbosa (Brazil), born in 1849, had been in public life in Brazil, and had served as a delegate to the Peace Conference at The Hague in 1907. He died on March 1, 1923, without having attended any session of the Court, and was succeeded by Judge Pessôa.

Judge Epitacio da Silva Pessôa (Brazil), born in 1865, elected to succeed Judge Barbosa in 1923, had been President of Brazil, and had served as Minister of Justice and as *Procureur-Général*. He was a delegate to the Paris Peace Conference in 1919, and had been active in the codification of Brazilian and international law.

Judge Charles Evans Hughes (United States of America), born in 1862, elected to succeed Judge Moore in 1928, had been Governor of the State of New York, Justice of the Supreme Court of the United States, and Secretary of State of the United States, and had participated in numerous international conferences. He resigned on February 15, 1930, upon his appointment as Chief Justice of the Supreme Court of the United States, and was succeeded by Judge Kellogg.

Judge Henri Fromageot (France), born in 1864, elected to succeed Judge Weiss in 1929, had long been legal adviser to the French Ministry for Foreign Affairs. He had had a wide experience in international conferences and in international arbitrations; from 1913 to 1922, he was president of the Anglo-American Pecuniary Claims Tribunal; from 1920 to 1929 he was closely identified with the work of the League of Nations, and he was a member of the 1929 Committee of Jurists. Prior to his election as judge, he had served on the Court as judge *ad hoc* on two occasions.

Sir Cecil Hurst (Great Britain), born in 1870, elected to succeed Lord Finlay in 1929, had been for many years legal adviser to the British Foreign Office, and he had had a prominent part in many international conferences, particularly in the Peace Conference at Paris in 1919 and in the work of the Council and Assembly of the League of Nations from 1920 to 1929. He was a member of the 1929 Committee of Jurists. In several cases, he had been counsel before the Court.

Judge Frank B. Kellogg (United States of America), born in 1856, elected to succeed Judge Hughes in 1930, had been a member of the Senate, Ambassador to Great Britain, and Secretary of State of the United States, and he was widely known as co-author of the Treaty for the Renunciation of War signed at Paris, August 27, 1928.

Deputy-Judge M. Yovanovitch (Yugoslavia), born in 1855, had been Minister of Justice, and President of the Court of Appeal and of the Court of Cassation at Belgrade.

Deputy-Judge F. V. N. Beichmann (Norway), born in 1859, had been a judge and president of the Court of Appeal at Trondhjem. He had played a prominent rôle in international conferences on the unification of law, and in various international arbitrations.

Deputy-Judge Demètre Negulesco (Rumania), born in 1875, had been a judge and a professor at Bucharest, and had served as a delegate to the first and second Assemblies of the League of Nations.

Deputy-Judge Wang (China), born in 1881, had been Minister of Justice and Minister of Foreign Affairs, judge of the Supreme Court and president of the Codification Commission in China. His English translation of the German Civil Code was a notable achievement.

§256. Members of the Court since 1930.[52] At the general election in 1930, Judges Kellogg, Fromageot, de Bustamante, Altamira, Anzilotti and Hurst were reëlected, and Deputy-Judges Negulesco and Wang were elected judges. The increase in the number of judges made place for the election of seven new judges, and produced a wider geographical distribution; it is to be noted, however, that no national of a Scandinavian State was included in the new roster of the Court, a fact which did not escape comment at the time.

Judge Minéitcirô Adatci (Japan), born in 1870, had been a professor of diplomatic history and international law in Japan, and had

---

[52] These biographical notes are based upon the material appearing in Series E, No. 7, pp. 21–41.

had a long career in the diplomatic service. In 1904–1905, he acted as judge of various prize courts during the Russo-Japanese War. He had served as Minister to Mexico and as Ambassador at Brussels and at Paris. As a member of the 1920 Committee of Jurists and a delegate to the First Assembly of the League of Nations, he had been prominently identified with the drafting of the Statute of the Court. He was for a number of years a delegate to the Assembly and the representative of Japan on the Council and on the Governing Body of the International Labor Organization. In 1923 he was president of the International Labor Conference.

Judge J. Gustavo Guerrero (El Salvador), born in 1876, had been Minister of Foreign Affairs, and had served as Minister to Italy, to Spain, to France and to the Vatican. He had played a prominent rôle in the Council and Assembly of the League of Nations, and in numerous international conferences, particularly conferences devoted to the codification of international law. In 1929 he served as president of the Tenth Assembly.

Baron Rolin-Jaequemyns (Belgium), born in 1863, had served as a judge in the Congo. He had had a large experience in international conferences, having been a delegate to the Peace Conference at The Hague in 1899; he had served as Belgian High Commissioner in the Rhineland, and had been identified with the work of the League of Nations from 1928 to 1930. For some years he was editor of the *Revue de Droit International et de Législation Comparée*.

Count Michel Jean César Rostworowski (Poland), born in 1865, had been a professor of international and constitutional law at Cracow, and had been prominently identified with the codification of Polish law and also of international law. During several years he was a member of the Polish delegation at the Assembly of the League of Nations. Prior to his election as judge, he had served on the Court as judge *ad hoc* on four occasions.

Judge Francisco José Urrutia (Colombia), born in 1870, had been Minister of Foreign Affairs and President of the Senate in Colombia, as well as Minister to Brazil, Spain and Switzerland. From 1920 to 1930, he was active in the work of the League of Nations and of numerous international conferences, acting as delegate to all sessions of the Assembly prior to his election, as a representative on the Council, and as a member of the 1929 Committee of Jurists.

Judge Walther Schücking (Germany), born in 1875, had been

professor of international law at Göttingen, Breslau, Marburg, Berlin and Kiel, and director of the Institute of International Law at Kiel. He was for some years a member of the Reichstag, and prior to his election as judge he had served on the Court as judge *ad hoc* on two occasions. His publications on international organization are notable.

Jonkheer W. J. M. van Eysinga (Netherlands), born in 1878, had been professor of public and international law at Gröningen and at Leyden. He had served for some years in the Ministry of Foreign Affairs and on the International Rhine Commission, and had been a member of the Netherlands delegation to each of the Assemblies of the League of Nations from 1920 to 1930. He had taken a prominent part in the work of the League of Nations Organization for Communications and Transit, and had served as a member of the 1929 Committee of Jurists and as president of the two conferences of Signatories of the Court Protocol in 1926 and 1929.

Deputy-Judge Joseph Redlich (Austria), born in 1869, had been a professor at Vienna and at Harvard University. He had been for some years a member of the Austrian Parliament, and had served as Minister of Finance.

Deputy-Judge José Caeiro da Matta (Portugal), born in 1877, had been professor of international law at Lisbon and a Member of Parliament. He had represented Portugal at numerous international conferences and in several international arbitrations.

Deputy-Judge Mileta Novacovitch (Yugoslavia), born in 1878, had been professor of international law at Belgrade, and had been a delegate to the second and fifth Assemblies of the League of Nations.

Deputy-Judge Rafael Waldemar Erich (Finland), born in 1879, had been a Member of Parliament and Prime Minister in Finland, and a professor of international law at Helsingfors. He had served as Minister to Switzerland and to Sweden, and had represented Finland at numerous international conferences. He was a delegate to the Assembly of the League of Nations from 1921 to 1930.

§257. **Nationality of Successful Candidates.** The second paragraph of Article 10 of the Statute provides that "in the event of more than one national of the same Member of the League being elected by the votes of both the Assembly and the Council, the eldest of these only shall be considered as elected." The French version is more accurately phrased, in that it does not assume to nullify an election already accomplished; it has a very different meaning, also, in that

it refers to *ressortissant* instead of *national*.[53] The Statute does not expressly confer on any body the power to determine who has been elected, and it would doubtless be for the Assembly and the Council to make the determination, at least in the first instance, if any question arose as to the application of this paragraph of Article 10. Several nationals of the same Member of the League may be nominated as candidates in an election, and if each of two nationals (*ressortissants*) of the same Member should receive a majority of votes in the Assembly and the Council at the same election, those bodies should declare only the elder of the two to be elected. Such a declaration would be necessary in order that further balloting might be conducted. In most cases, this would probably produce no difficulty; cases might arise, however, in which vexing questions of multiple nationality would be involved.

The question has been discussed, for instance, whether under Article 10 a British national of the United Kingdom of Great Britain and Northern Ireland and a British national of a Dominion which is a Member of the League of Nations would both be eligible to election.[54] This question was not resolved when an interpretation of the word "nationality" in Article 31 was being discussed by the 1929 Committee of Jurists.[55] The French version of Article 10 of the Statute would clearly allow a *ressortissant* of the United Kingdom and a *ressortissant* of a Dominion to be elected at the same election; the same person would hardly be a *ressortissant* of two Members of the League of Nations, but under the nationality laws prevailing in the British Commonwealth of Nations [56] many persons have the nationality of two Members of the League of Nations. The meaning of the term "nationality" as it is used in the English version of Article 10 may be determined to be in some measure independent of national laws by which nationality is conferred.[57]

The Statute does not lay it down as a principle that two persons

---

[53] The French version reads: *"Au cas où le double scrutin de l'Assemblée et du Conseil se porterait sur plus d'un ressortissant du même Membre de la Société des Nations, le plus âgé est seul élu."*

[54] See Walter Pollak, "The Eligibility of British Subjects as Judges of the Permanent Court of International Justice," 20 American Journal of International Law (1926), p. 714.

[55] Minutes of the 1929 Committee of Jurists, pp. 70–71, 84–87. See §207, *supra*.

[56] See Flournoy and Hudson, Nationality Laws, pp. 59–150.

[57] The term "national" (Fr., *ressortissant*) is used in Articles 10 and 27 of the Statute, and the term "nationality" (Fr., *nationalité*) is used in Articles 2, 5 and 31. As a general rule, the term "national" has no significance in international law other than that of describing a person upon whom a State or a Member of the League of Nations has conferred its nationality.

possessing the same nationality may not be judges of the Court at the same time.[58] The second paragraph of Article 10 seems to apply only to successful candidates at the same election; strictly, it does not prevent the election at a by-election of a national of a Member of the League, one of whose nationals has previously been elected at a general election, nor does it in terms prevent the election on the same occasion of two or more nationals (*ressortissants*) of a State which is not a member of the League of Nations. It should also be noted that under Article 31 a State may choose as judge *ad hoc* a national of another State, one of whose nationals is already among the judges on the bench.[59]

§258. **Appreciation of the System of Nominations.** The six elections which have been held to date enable certain observations to be made, both on the system of nominations and on the system of elections provided for in the Statute. The system of nominations by national groups instead of by Governments or other agencies served a convenient purpose at the time of its adoption in 1920, in that it provided a useful link between the Permanent Court of International Justice and the Permanent Court of Arbitration. It was also thought to have the advantages (1) of securing the independent selection of competent candidates by men who are not necessarily under government influence, and (2) of leaving the representatives of Members of the League of Nations freer in their voting in the elections by the Assembly and the Council. The first of these advantages has been realized to some extent, although some national groups have clearly conceived it to be their function to express the Government's will.[60] The second advantage foreseen has probably materialized, also. On the other hand the system has some disadvantages: it is not clearly understood,[61] and the small national groups may not always select the strongest nominees. Various Governments have not kept full their

---

[58] The history of the drafting of Article 10 leaves no doubt that this was intended, however. See *infra*, §127.

[59] This was the situation, for instance, when the Court gave its opinion in 1931 on *Polish War Vessels in Danzig*. Series A/B, No. 43, p. 128.

[60] In most cases the nomination by the national group is transmitted to the Secretary-General through the Ministry of Foreign Affairs; in some cases, it is the Minister of Foreign Affairs who makes the communication. A few of the national groups draw up formal *procès-verbaux* which are transmitted to the Secretary-General.

[61] In 1921, nominations were offered by the Government of Paraguay in its own name; owing to the lateness of the communication, the question of listing them did not arise. In 1928, the Canadian representative in the Assembly attempted to withdraw the candidacy of nominees of the Canadian national group. Some Governments have considered their Assembly delegations competent to make nominations.

quotas in the Permanent Court of Arbitration, and have thus deprived the electors of the judgment of four members of a national group.[62] Some groups are composed of men who may have been appointed for a purpose wholly unrelated to the system of elections,[63] and who may have little first-hand knowledge either of the temper of the electoral bodies or of the needs of the Court itself. Some groups are not careful to consult their nominees in advance, and frequently make nominations of persons not "in a position to accept the duties of a member of the Court." One cannot escape the conclusion that some of the nominations are made simply for the purpose of paying compliments. Only a few of the groups seem to have complied with the recommendation contained in Article 6 of the Statute that they should consult the highest Court of Justice, the faculties of law, and academies devoted to the study of law, though observance of this recommendation might help to build a professional support for the Court.[64] In spite of these facts, it must be said that on the whole the system of nominations has worked with quite satisfactory results.

Though consultation by a national group with other national groups is not provided for in the Statute, the number of groups which nominated the same candidates in the earlier elections indicates that informal consultation takes place on a very wide scale. The facts that a single candidate received the nominations of thirty national groups in the 1928 election, and that one candidate in the second general election received the nominations of twenty-two national groups, show conclusively that the groups coöperate among themselves. This may have the result of limiting the choice of the electoral bodies in practice, but the limitation is due to a unity of judgment which is clearly desirable; [65] it also tends to simplify the elections by the Assembly and by the Council.

[62] On several occasions, a nomination has been made by a "group" having but one member.

[63] This may not be true as to members of the Permanent Court of Arbitration appointed since 1921.

[64] Some of the groups are careful to state that this recommendation has been followed, when making their nominations.

Article 6 of the Statute refers to "national sections of International Academies devoted to the study of Law." The 1920 Committee of Jurists listed the Institute of International Law, the American Institute of International Law, the *Union Juridique Internationale,* the International Law Association, and the Iberian Institute of Comparative Law; most of these organizations have no organized national sections, however.

[65] To some extent, the record to date fulfils the hope expressed by Mr. Root to the 1920 Committee of Jurists that "so many concordant expressions of opinion would be obtained from the various countries that the election would be thereby virtually decided." Minutes of the 1920 Committee of Jurists, p. 409.

§259. **Appreciation of the System of Elections.** In view of the long struggle as to the method of election which preceded 1920, it must be said that the system laid down in the Statute of the Court has worked with surprising ease and with remarkable success. Yet perhaps the chief reason for the system actually devised has disappeared. In 1920, the so-called "Great Powers" held four permanent seats in a Council composed of representatives of eight States, with a possibility that a fifth "Great Power" would also accept a permanent seat. This fact was chiefly responsible for the willingness of the "Great Powers" to create a court in which no States were to be entitled to representation. At the present time, however, the Council has been enlarged in such a way that so-called "Great Powers" hold but five permanent seats in a body which may be composed of representatives of fifteen States. Yet this change has led to no suggestion of a modification in the method of election.

The Statute clearly excludes the idea of State *representation* on the Court; in each of the general elections to date, however, each of the States permanently represented on the Council has seen one of its nationals chosen. It is an idle expression in the Statute that the judges will be elected "regardless of their nationality"; the demand made by certain Latin-American States in 1930, even though it was based on the representation of "the main forms of civilisation and the principal legal systems of the world" as provided for in Article 9 of the Statute, indicated how remotely that expression corresponds with the facts. The practice which has prevailed on four occasions of filling a vacancy by electing a person of the same nationality as the previous incumbent, might well become a dangerous precedent.

Resort to the ultimate method for breaking a deadlock in the elections which is provided for in Article 12 of the Statute, has not yet been necessary, but at some future time it may serve a useful purpose; on the other hand, the provision for a joint conference in Article 12 of the Statute is a happy one, and it certainly facilitated the first election in 1920 even if the choice might have been completed without it. Recently, as shown by the later voting in the 1930 election, the Council and Assembly have shown a decided disposition to respect each other's preferences.

The chief criticism to be made of the system of elections is that as no age limit is fixed for the candidates, the electoral bodies have shown too little disposition to give to the factor of age the importance

which it deserves. In 1921, three judges were elected who had already passed the age of seventy, and two of them failed to survive the expiration of their terms. In 1930, one judge was elected who had already attained the age of seventy-four. On the other hand, too little attention has been paid to the importance of active-mindedness in the candidates, of which age affords a partial test. The average age of the judges elected in 1921 was over sixty, and of the judges elected in 1930 it was almost sixty.[66]

On the whole, however, the system of elections must be pronounced a success which augurs well for the future maintenance of the Court.

[66] The possibility of an age limit was discussed at the 1929 Conference of Signatories. Minutes of the 1929 Conference, p. 33. An age for the compulsory retirement of judges, which would serve much the same purpose as an age limit at the time of election, was proposed by Colonel House in an early draft of the Covenant of the League of Nations; the retiring age proposed was seventy-two. Seymour, Intimate Papers of Colonel House, IV, p. 31.

CHAPTER 12

THE RULES OF COURT

§260. **Rôle of the Court in Determining Its Procedure.**
Throughout the discussions of the Committee of Jurists in 1920, the desire prevailed to leave the Court free to frame rules governing its own procedure. Article 30 of the Statute puts no qualification on the Court's power to "frame rules for regulating its procedure"; the French version is perhaps broader than the English, empowering the Court to determine *"par un règlement le mode suivant lequel elle exerce ses attributions."* The article seems to have been given the wider meaning of the French version by the Court. It is to be noted, however, that the Statute itself lays down certain rules of procedure,[1] and to this extent the power of the Court is limited. The rules are therefore to be considered as supplementing the provisions contained in the Statute.[2] The rules adopted bear the designation of "Rules" (Fr., *règlement*), though they appear under the rubric "Rules of Court" (Fr., *Réglement de la Cour*) in the official publications. In framing its original rules, the Court was called upon to break new ground; there were few precedents to guide it. It was early suggested that two sets of rules should be adopted by the Court, one to be its Rules of Court, and the other to be its Rules of Procedure;[3] though the suggestion met with no favor at the time, in 1931 the Court formulated tentative rules of practice as distinguished from the Rules of Court.[4]

§261. **Composition of the Court in Framing Rules.** At the beginning of the preliminary session of the Court, the question arose whether deputy-judges should be asked to participate in framing the

---

[1] M. Hammarskjöld has suggested that the assumption that the Court was to have compulsory jurisdiction dominated the drafting of these rules in the Statute. 3 *Revue de Droit International et de Législation Comparée* (1922), p. 136. In some cases different rules might have been laid down in the Statute if the rejection of that assumption had been foreseen by the Committee of Jurists.

[2] Series D, No. 2, p. 106.

[3] Series D, No. 2, pp. 103, 106. Article 23 of the Statute refers to "Rules of Court"; Articles 26, 27 and 51 mention "the rules of procedure" under Article 30.

[4] Series D, No. 2 (2d add.), pp. 268, 300.

Court's rules. The first meeting, at which Judges Barbosa and de Bustamante were absent, was attended by Deputy-Judges Beichmann and Yovanovitch; by vote of the judges, five to four, it was decided that the other two deputy-judges should be invited to take part in the preliminary session.[5] M. Negulesco accepted this invitation, and hence three deputy-judges took part in the framing of the original Rules. When in 1925 a question arose as to the revision of Article 3 of the Rules, on June 17, 1925, it was "recognized that it would be preferable to deal with this matter at a session at which all the deputy-judges were present." [6] On June 19, 1926, however, the Court decided that "the Statute did not permit the convocation of the deputy-judges for the purpose of the revision of the Rules." [7] The deputy-judges therefore took no part in framing the revision of 1926, though it is to be noted that all the judges were present at the eleventh session which effected this revision; certain suggestions made by absent deputy-judges were, however, placed before the Court by the President as his own suggestions.[8] The deputy-judges were not invited to take part in the twentieth session, though three judges were absent, and they therefore took no part in framing the Rules of 1931.[9] Nor are they to participate in the general revision contemplated by the Court by its decision of May 12, 1931.[10]

§262. **The Rules of March 24, 1922.** The greater part of the Court's preliminary session, January 30 to March 24, 1922, was devoted to the preparation of the original Rules. When the session began, the Court had before it drafts by M. Loder, M. Altamira, and the Secretariat of the League of Nations.[11] At the fourth meeting, a committee on procedure was appointed to draw up a "questionnaire embodying the main points to be settled in the Rules"; yet some of the questions to be regulated were necessarily determined in the course of the process of organizing the Court.[12] A discussion of the questionnaire continued from the sixth to the eighteenth meetings of the Court, when the committee on procedure was reconstituted as a drafting committee. Its draft,[13] based on the Secretariat's draft, was considered by the Court in first reading from the twentieth to the twenty-eighth meetings; its re-draft [14] was considered in second reading from the thirtieth

---

[5] Series D, No. 2, p. 2. *Cf., id.*, p. 239. The presence of two deputy-judges was required to complete the number of eleven fixed by paragraph 2 of Article 25 of the Statute. *Id.*, p. 111.   [6] Series D, No. 2 (add.), pp. 7, 242.   [7] *Id.*, p. 5.
[8] *E.g., id.*, p. 19.   [11] Series D, No. 2, pp. 249, 253, 274.   [13] *Id.*, p. 424.
[9] Series E, No. 7, p. 291.   [12] *Id.*, p. 415.   [14] *Id.*, p. 481.
[10] *Id.*, p. 290.

to the thirty-eighth meetings. A special committee was created to harmonize the English and French versions, and this Committee proposed various amendments to the French version which were approved on the second reading.[15] The final English and French versions were adopted unanimously at the fortieth meeting on March 24, 1922.[16] The Rules were signed by the President and Registrar, "in the same manner as a judgment of the Court." [17] The minutes of the Court in its preliminary session, but not the verbatim record,[18] were promptly published,[19] containing the rules as finally adopted; but no separate edition of the Statute and Rules was published at the time.[20]

§263. **The Revision of July 31, 1926.** The power of the Court to revise its rules derives from Article 30 of the Statute. Though a reservation of this power had been proposed in 1922,[21] the Rules as adopted did not reserve it. Soon after the original Rules came into force, suggestions began to be made that they should be revised; particularly that the rules dealing with advisory procedure were insufficient. On September 4, 1923, Judge Altamira made a formal suggestion,[22] and in 1923–24 a draft was presented by the President and Vice-President.[23] A slight addition to Article 2 of the Rules was adopted on January 15, 1925.[24] On June 17, 1925, the Court decided to undertake a revision in 1926; [25] the purposes of the revision were later stated by the President to be to supplement the Rules on matters as to which no decision had been reached, and to incorporate interpretations placed on the existing Rules by the Court's jurisprudence.[26] Numerous suggestions were made to this end,[27] and a draft intended to codify existing practice and to fill gaps was prepared by the Registrar.[28] The revision was undertaken at the eleventh session, and occupied the attention of the Court during twenty-seven meetings be-

---

[15] Series D, No. 2, p. 556. The deliberations of the Court had been based upon a French version.

[16] *Id.,* p. 232. For an excellent commentary on the 1922 rules, see Å. Hammarskjöld, *"Le Règlement de la Cour Permanente de Justice Internationale,"* 3 *Revue de Droit International et de Législation Comparée* (1922), pp. 125–148.

[17] Series D, No. 2, p. 106.   [18] *Id.,* p. 234.   [19] Series D, No. 2.

[20] Series D, No. 1, of the Court's Publications first appeared in 1926. It contains both the 1926 and the 1922 Rules. Apparently a publication by the *Institut Intermédiaire International,* entitled *The Permanent Court of International Justice, Statute and Rules,* which appeared in 1922, served in lieu of an official edition of the Statute and the original Rules prior to 1926. Series E, No. 1, p. 125 note.

[21] Series D, No. 2, p. 424.

[22] Series D, No. 2 (add.), p. 293. For observations by Judge Moore, see *id.,* p. 294.

[23] *Id.,* p. 281. See the observations of Judge Huber, *id.,* p. 254.

[24] Series E, No. 1, pp. 13, 127.   [27] *Id.,* pp. 246–277.

[25] Series D, No. 2 (add.), p. 5.   [28] *Id.,* p. 304.

[26] *Id.,* pp. 242–3.

tween June 22 and July 31, 1926. Revised Rules were adopted on the latter date, embodying amendments to 32 of the 75 articles, and against some opposition they were put into effect immediately.[29]

§264. **The Amendment of September 7, 1927.** On September 1, 1927, Judge Anzilotti proposed the addition of a paragraph after paragraph 1 of Article 71 of the Rules. The proposal was considered at two meetings of the twelfth session, September 2 and 7, 1927, and after a report by a committee it was adopted and put into force on the latter date.[30] Judge Anzilotti had thought it desirable to raise the question "at a time when no affair for advisory opinion was actually pending"; [31] his proposal related to the participation of the judges *ad hoc* provided for in Article 31 of the Statute, in connection with the giving of advisory opinions relating to disputes. This had been proposed by the 1920 Committee of Jurists in Article 36 of its draft-scheme; it had also been proposed to and rejected by the Court in 1926.[32] Though some doubts were expressed by members of the Court, the committee appointed gave strong support to the proposal,[33] and it was adopted by nine votes to two.

§265. **The Revision of February 21, 1931.** While the revision of 1926 was the result of criticism within the Court itself, the revision of 1931 was clearly the result of outside pressure. When the Revision Protocol of September 14, 1929, failed to come into force as contemplated in September 1930, a committee of jurists reported to the Council of the League of Nations that it would be desirable to call to the Court's attention the possibility of its effecting certain changes in line with the proposed amendments to the Statute through the exercise of its power to regulate its procedure; the committee mentioned particularly the "nature of the leave granted" to members of the Court, and "the system of permanent sessions." [34] This report led the Eleventh Assembly of the League of Nations, on September 25, 1930, to adopt the following resolution: [35]

[29] Series D, No. 1. The minutes of the Court dealing with the revision are published in Series D, Addendum to No. 2. For an excellent commentary on the 1926 rules, see Å. Hammarskjöld, *"Le Règlement Revisé de la Cour Permanente de Justice Internationale,"* 8 *Revue de Droit International et de Législation Comparée* (1927), pp. 322–359.

[30] Series E, No. 4, pp. 72–78.

[31] A request was actually pending, but owing to the seating of a deputy-judge the question raised by Judge Anzilotti did not arise. *Id.*, p. 77.

[32] Series D, No. 2 (add.), pp. 185–193.

[33] Series E, No. 4, pp. 75–77.

[34] League of Nations Official Journal, 1930, p. 1466.

[35] Records of Eleventh Assembly, Plenary, p. 132.

The Assembly requests the Permanent Court of International Justice to examine the suggestions contained in Part II, paragraphs 1 and 2, of the report of the Committee of Jurists which was submitted to and approved by the Council of the League of Nations on September 12, 1930, and expresses the hope that the Court will give consideration to the possibility of regulating, pending the coming into force of the Protocol of September 14, 1929, concerning the revision of the Statute of the Court, the questions of the sessions of the Court and the attendance of the judges, on the basis of Article 30 of the Statute as annexed to the Protocol of December 16, 1920.

When the newly-elected judges met for the reorganization of the Court on January 15, 1931, they included several of the men who had been prominently identified with the attempt to revise the Court's Statute. The new Court was therefore not reluctant to proceed in accordance with the suggestions in the Assembly's resolution, and from January 21 to February 21, it devoted some thirty meetings to a consideration of modifications of the Rules. While the conclusion was reached that it was inexpedient "at the beginning of the period of office of the judges recently elected, to undertake a fresh general revision," certain questions of an urgent nature were considered in addition to those suggested by the Assembly. The revised Rules put into effect on February 21, 1931, embodied amendments in eighteen of the revised Rules adopted in 1926.[36] On May 12, 1931, the Court decided to undertake a "methodical examination" of the Rules with a view to a later general revision, and certain subjects were selected for this purpose, to be studied by four committees.[37] The coming into force of the Revision Protocol of September 14, 1929, would clearly involve further amendments of the Rules.

§266. **Arrangement of the Rules.** The Rules are divided into a preamble and two chapters; Chapter I relates to "the Court" and Chapter II to its "Procedure." The chapters are divided into "Headings," which are divided into Sections, in which subtitles are given. This arrangement has undergone no change during the various revisions, except that the subtitle "Revision" adopted in 1922 was changed in 1926 to read "Revision and Interpretation." The arrangement has little significance, and is designed merely to aid a reading of the

---

[36] Series D, No. 1 (2d ed.). The minutes of the Court are published in Series D, second Addendum to No. 2.
[37] Series E, No. 7, pp. 108, 290; Series E, No. 9, pp. 62–63.

Rules.[38] The articles are numbered, and great care has been exercised to avoid any new numbering in the course of the successive revisions. The paragraphs in the articles bore no numbers in 1922; numbers were introduced in 1926 for certain paragraphs in Articles 35, 66 and 73, and in 1931 in Article 27, to enable "new provisions to be inserted without altering the numbering of the articles themselves." [39] In 1931, the Registrar raised the question of numbering the paragraphs of all articles, but no decision has been taken to that effect.[40]

§267. 1931 Rules, Article 1.[41] This article has undergone no change since it was adopted in 1922. It is designed to fill a *lacuna* in Article 13 of the Statute. A question might have been raised as to whether the Court was acting *intra vires* in dealing with the terms of office of its members; but as some rule was necessary, it seems desirable that the Court should have dealt with it, subject to action by the Assembly and the Council of the League of Nations. The term of office of the judges elected in 1921 was taken to have commenced on January 1, 1922, "owing to an interpretation given to the Statute by the Secretary-General of the League of Nations." [42] Judge Anzilotti foresaw a possibility that the elections might be postponed, and "if the new elections took place only after the expiration of a period of nine years, the judges replaced would have to give up their seats immediately, and could not continue in office until January 1st of the year following the election"; [43] but this view was not shared by a majority of the judges.

§268. 1931 Rules, Article 2. This text was adopted in 1922, with the exception of a slight verbal modification in the English version of the last paragraph made in 1931.[44] Priority of election at the same session of the electoral bodies was early rejected as a basis of precedence.[45] In 1925, a fifth paragraph was added to the article providing

[38] Series D, No. 2, p. 224.   [39] Series D, No. 2 (2d add.), p. 103.

[40] *Id.*, pp. 103–4. A proposal had previously been made in the Assembly of the League of Nations that paragraphs in the Statute and Rules should be numbered.

[41] The texts of this and other articles are omitted here because a more or less complete revision of the Rules is anticipated as a consequence of the coming into force of the Revision Protocol of September 14, 1929. The texts of all the rules adopted to date are reproduced in the appendix, *infra*, p. 653.

[42] Series D, No. 2, pp. 107, 168. Salaries of the judges were paid from January 1, 1922. The terms of office of judges elected to fill vacancies are taken to begin on the first day of the month following their election, though both the Statute and the Rules are silent on this point.

[43] Series D, No. 2, pp. 107, 168.   [44] Series D, No. 2 (2d add.), p. 131.

[45] Series D, No. 2, pp. 110, 588. In 1922, birth certificates seem to have been required for determining seniority. Series D, No. 2 (add.), p. 44.

that a retiring president should sit on the right of the President; [46] it seems to have been intended to apply to a retiring president only during the term of his immediate successor. Though the addition was retained after some debate in 1926,[47] it was omitted in 1931 when the retiring president, Judge Anzilotti, renounced the privilege.[48] A seniority attained does not survive a general election of members of the Court.[49]

§269. **1931 Rules, Article 3.** The greater part of this article was adopted in 1922. A paragraph adopted at that time, relating to deputy-judges' finishing cases in which they have sat, was dropped in 1926 for reasons which are not clear.[50] The concluding paragraph of the article was amended in 1931 by the insertion of the reference to Article 71 of the Rules.[51] The drafting of the article in 1922 gave rise to numerous questions concerning the extent of the participation of deputy-judges in the work of the Court.[52]

§270. **1931 Rules, Article 4.** The first paragraph of this article as adopted in 1922 closed with the words "exceeding eleven"; the concluding words, "exceeding the number of regular judges fixed by the Statute," were adopted in 1926, to foresee a possible increase in the number of judges.[53] No changes have been made in the second and third paragraphs as adopted in 1922. In connection with the second paragraph, it was at one time proposed that the selection of a judge might be made by a majority of parties "taking joint action in a case"; [54] the question was also raised whether intervening parties might appoint judges *ad hoc*.[55] In 1926, Judge Pessôa's proposal that in some cases judges of the nationality of some of several parties in the same interest should be excluded from sitting, was the subject of extended discussion.[56] A proposal by President Huber that the President should be empowered to invite provisionally several parties in the same interest to appoint a judge *ad hoc* was not accepted.[57] The third paragraph of this article is a definite addition to Article 31 of the Statute.

---

[46] Series E, No. 1, pp. 13, 127.
[47] Series D, No. 2 (add.), pp. 14–17. While this addition was in force, the retiring president, with the Vice-President, was frequently consulted by the President on doubtful questions as to the powers of the President.
[48] Series D, No. 2 (2d add.), p. 131.   [49] Series E, No. 7, p. 276.
[50] Series D, No. 2 (add.), pp. 19–22. But see Å. Hammarskjöld, in 8 *Revue de Droit International et de Législation Comparée* (1927), p. 328.
[51] Series D, No. 2 (2d add.), p. 131.   [55] *Id.*, pp. 177, 215.
[52] Series D, No. 2, pp. 169–176.   [56] Series D, No. 2 (add.), pp. 25, 29, 269.
[53] Series D, No. 2 (add.), pp. 23–4.   [57] *Id.*, pp. 29–32, 247.
[54] Series D, No. 2, p. 118.

The reference in the first paragraph of this article to a choice by one or more of the parties of "a judge *ad hoc* of their nationality", is clearly erroneous, as a judge *ad hoc* need not possess the nationality of the State which chooses him.

§271. **1931 Rules, Article 5.** No change has been made in this article since its adoption in 1922. Article 20 of the Statute requires that "each member of the Court" shall "make a solemn declaration" that "he will exercise his powers impartially and conscientiously." A draft of the declaration proposed by the Secretariat in 1922 sought "to emphasize the fact that the Court was an organ of the League of Nations." [58] Judge Huber suggested that the members might make the declaration collectively, but the Court decided otherwise.[59] The third paragraph of the article indicates that "after a new election of the whole Court," the President and Vice-President may be elected by members of the Court who have not yet made the declaration. Judges who are reëlected in a general election must thereafter make a new declaration.

§272. **1931 Rules, Article 6.** No change has been made in this text as it was adopted in 1922. The text of Article 18 of the Statute has been interpreted to require the collaboration of deputy-judges in this case,[60] though clearly deputy-judges might not be in a position to know all the facts. Some doubt was felt by members of the Court as to the desirability of a rule on the point,[61] but it was adopted with little discussion.[62]

§273. **1931 Rules, Article 7.** This text was framed in 1922, and no change has since been made. Various questions were raised, as to the nomination of assessors by the parties, as to the Court's consultation of "some competent body," as to the nationality of the assessors to be chosen, and as to the freedom of the Court to decide that assessors should be chosen.[63] The reference to the Governing Body of the International Labor Office is badly drafted.

§274. **1931 Rules, Article 8.** This text was adopted in 1922. The question arose in connection with the Court's consideration of the presence of assessors at its private deliberations and with the drafting of Article 31 of the Rules.[64] As no use has been made of assessors, a practice with reference to them has not been established.

[58] Series D, No. 2, p. 13. [61] *Id.*, p. 51. [63] *Id.*, pp. 34–8, 40–42, 112–14.
[59] *Ibid.* [62] *Id.*, pp. 122, 177. [64] *Id.*, pp. 195, 204.
[60] Series D, No. 2, pp. 174–5, 514–16.

§275. **1931 Rules, Article 9.** In 1931, two changes were made in this article as it had been adopted in 1922. In paragraph 1, it was originally provided that the election should take place "at the end of the ordinary session immediately before the normal termination of the period of office" of the incumbents; [65] in paragraph 3, the original text made reference to a possible extraordinary session of the Court to fill vacancies. Article 21 of the Statute fixes the duration of the term for which the President and Vice-President are to serve, but fails to fix the time of commencement or of termination. When the first President of the Court was elected on February 3, 1922, both preliminary and final votes were taken; [66] but this procedure was not stereotyped in the Rules. The Court rejected a proposal that deputy-judges should be allowed to take part in the elections.[67]

§276. **1931 Rules, Article 10.** No change has been made in this article as it was adopted in 1922. In 1931, the President asked for an interpretation of "work and administration" (*les travaux et les services*) as used in this article; his request gave rise to a lengthy discussion, but various amendments proposed were not adopted.[68]

§277. **1931 Rules, Article 11.** This text, as adopted in 1922, was modified in 1931 to provide for the Vice-President's taking the place of the President, should the latter be "unable to fulfil his duties," instead of "unable to be present." This brought the English version into conformity with the original French version, which was not changed.[69]

§278. **1931 Rules, Article 12.** As it was adopted in 1922, this article required the President to "reside within a radius of ten kilometers from the Peace Palace at The Hague," [70] and limited his "main annual vacation" to three months. Article 22 of the Statute merely requires the President to reside "at the seat of the Court"; this was interpreted to mean "within a distance of ten kilometers of the Peace Palace." [71] In 1931, it was thought that no rule on the subject was necessary; [72] the reference to the President's vacation was suppressed; and a new text based on the original text of Article 13 as modified in 1926, was drafted to assure that in no case should the Court lack a person authorized to act as President. No method is prescribed for

---

[65] See Series D, No. 2 (2d add.), pp. 135–6.
[66] Series D, No. 2, p. 4.   [68] Series D, No. 2 (2d add.), pp. 139–144.
[67] *Id.*, pp. 173–4.   [69] Series D, No. 2 (2d add.), p. 181.
[70] Prior to 1926, the French version of the Rules required the President to be domiciled within ten kilometers of the Peace Palace.
[71] Series D, No. 2, p. 14.
[72] Series D, No. 2 (2d add.), pp. 137–9.

determining who is the oldest judge to discharge the duties of President, after a new election of the whole court and before a President is elected; and the third paragraph of this article may result in giving the duties of President to a judge who has had no previous experience in the Court.

§279. **1931 Rules, Article 13.** The 1922 Rules contained no disqualification of the President from acting as such in a case in which he is a national of a party. In 1926, President Huber proposed a rule on the subject, to avoid a possibility that a case might be decided by the casting vote of a President who was a national of one of the parties; [73] this proposal was adopted by the Court as an addition to Article 13.[74] In 1931, the provision was redrafted, to replace the reference to seniority with a reference to length of service and age; this did not change the meaning of the text.

§280. **1931 Rules, Article 14.** This text was adopted in 1922,[75] except for an amendment in 1931 to paragraph 3 which placed the election of members of the Chambers in the "last quarter of the year." It was originally proposed that the President should be a member of the chamber for summary procedure *ex officio*,[76] and that a definite order should be fixed for the summoning of substitutes; neither of these proposals was adopted. The Court was agreed that a judge appointed a member of a special chamber was bound to discharge his duties as such.[77]

§281. **1931 Rules, Article 15.** No change has been made in this article as it was framed in 1922. It is difficult to discover any purpose served by the first paragraph, in view of the provisions in Articles 26 and 27 of the Statute which quite clearly limit the special chambers to five judges. The question was raised, however, as to the application of paragraph 3 of Article 31 of the Statute, where neither party has a judge of its nationality sitting in the Chamber, and the Court was opposed to such application; [78] it is to be noted, however, that if the Revision Protocol of September 14, 1929, comes into force, the new text of Article 31 of the Statute will require a different course in the composition of the special chambers. The second paragraph of the article was designed to prevent any modification in the composition of a chamber without a corresponding change in the number,[79] either

---

[73] Series D, No. 2 (add.), p. 248.   [74] *Id.*, p. 33.
[75] A slight change was made in the French version in 1926.
[76] Series D, No. 2, p. 112.   [78] Series D, No. 2, pp. 192–3.
[77] *Id.*, pp. 30–1.   [79] *Id.*, p. 184.

by the Court itself or on the initiative of the parties.[80] A suggestion of a definite order for summoning judges to complete the chambers when necessary, was not adopted.

§282. **1931 Rules, Article 16.** This text was framed in 1922. The admission of deputy-judges to the special chambers was proposed as a measure for assuring the representation of various legal systems; but the proposal was not adopted.[81] The text was criticized in 1931 as being out of harmony with the Statute, but no change was made.[82]

§283. **1931 Rules, Article 17.** A simpler text of this article was adopted in 1922.[83] The first Registrar had previously been elected at the second meeting of the preliminary session in 1922.[84] In 1926, two changes were made on the proposal of the Registrar. A provision was added that each election should be for a full period of seven years, though Judge Anzilotti questioned whether one group of judges could bind a succeeding group in this way.[85] The Registrar pointed out that "the period of seven years corresponded to the period of office of directors of the Secretariat of the League of Nations to whom the Registrar was assimilated," and he stated that the 1920 Committee of Jurists had intended that "this period should overlap two of the nine years' periods of the judges' tenure of office." [86] A second change in 1926 was the addition of the provision for a deputy-registrar, that post having previously been created in 1925. In the revision of 1931, a second sentence was added in the first paragraph, and a new second paragraph was added; [87] and a provision for a casting vote by the President was dropped, "on the ground that such a provision was inconsistent with the system of a secret ballot." [88]

§284. **1931 Rules, Article 18.** The first paragraph of this article was adopted in 1922. The second paragraph originally provided that "the other members of the Registry shall make a similar declaration before the President, the Registrar being present"; this was dropped in 1926, and the present second paragraph was substituted.

§285. **1931 Rules, Article 19.** As adopted in 1922, this article required the Registrar to reside within ten kilometers of the Peace Palace; the Statute required him to reside at the seat of the Court.

---

[80] Series D, No. 2, p. 427.
[81] *Id.*, p. 31. See also pp. 193–4.
[82] Series D, No. 2 (2d add.), pp. 145–8.
[83] Series D, No. 2, pp. 122–3, 242.
[84] Series D, No. 2, p. 7.
[85] Series D, No. 2 (add.), p. 40.
[86] *Ibid.* See Series E, No. 5, p. 247.
[87] Series D, No. 2 (2d add.), pp. 150–1, 207. It was said in 1931 that "documents submitted in previous elections had been defective in various respects."
[88] *Id.*, p. 210.

In 1926, this provision was extended to the deputy-registrar. These requirements were dropped in 1931, when also the provision for the Registrar's "main annual vacation" was changed to a provision for a "holiday."

§286. **1931 Rules, Article 20.** The first paragraph of this article originally applied to the "staff of the Registry." This was changed in 1926 to "the officials of the Registry, other than the Deputy-Registrar," and a second paragraph was added based upon the provision dropped from the original Article 18.

§287. **1931 Rules, Article 21.** As adopted in 1922, Article 21 provided: "The regulations for the staff of the Registry shall be adopted by the President on the proposal of the Registrar, subject to subsequent approval by the Court." The Registrar explained that the approval of the Court was required because the regulations "contained certain financial provisions which could not become operative without the express consent of the Court." [89] When the first staff regulations were approved by the Court on March 22, 1922, the President explained that they "constituted a contract with the members of the staff." [90] In 1931, the opening sentence of this article was taken from Article 22 of the original Rules; and the first sentence was added in the second paragraph, after the Registrar had explained that "the contents of the Regulations" were determined "by the Regulations made for the Geneva staff" of the League of Nations. [91] The general concordance of the two sets of regulations, he explained, was "necessary to enable officials of the Registry to be promoted into the Secretariat and *vice versa*." [92] The new text was drafted by the Registrar. [93]

§288. **1931 Rules, Article 22.** In the text of this article as adopted in 1922, the appointment of a substitute for the Registrar was entrusted to the President. By a modification in 1926 it was entrusted in the first instance to the Court, and account was taken of the new post of Deputy-Registrar. Slight changes were made in 1931, in addition to the transfer of the first sentence of the original text to Article 21.

§289. **1931 Rules, Article 23.** No change has been made in this text since its adoption without discussion in 1922. [94] The separate classification of decisions and advisory opinions was not changed in 1931,

---

[89] Series D, No. 2, p. 190.
[90] *Id.*, p. 225.
[91] Series D, No. 2 (2d add.), p. 142.

[92] *Id.*, p. 153.
[93] *Id.*, pp. 208, 295.
[94] Series D, No. 2, p. 124.

though Article 28 of the 1931 Rules looks toward minimizing that distinction.

§290. **1931 Rules, Article 24.** The first paragraph of this article was transferred from Article 25 in 1926; it does not deal with the problem of the channel through which the Registrar acting on behalf of the Court will communicate with Governments.[95] The second paragraph was framed in 1926, based on part of the original text of this article as adopted in 1922. Originally, there was also a provision that "during hours to be fixed by the President, the Registrar shall receive any documents." No change was made in the text in 1931, though several proposals of amendment were discussed.[96]

§291. **1931 Rules, Article 25.** This text was adopted in 1922 as the second paragraph of the article;[97] the first paragraph of the original article was transferred to Article 24 in 1926.

§292. **1931 Rules, Article 26.** This text was adopted in 1922, with changes in 1926 referring to the Deputy-Registrar.

§293. **1931 Rules, Article 27.** As it was drafted in 1922, this article included paragraph "6" as a second paragraph, and in the first paragraph it provided merely that "in the year following a new election of the whole Court the ordinary annual session shall commence on the fifteenth of January." This date was fixed to avoid compelling "many of the members of the Court to travel during the Christmas and New Year holidays."[98] Certain members of the Court made an effort in 1926 to delete the first paragraph,[99] in curious disregard of the necessity of the Court's always being organized. Article 23 of the Statute fixed the annual sessions to begin on June 15, "unless otherwise provided by Rules of Court"; some disposition to change this date was manifested in 1922.[100] In 1926, the question was discussed at some length;[1] Judge de Bustamante thought that the Court should "not be at the mercy of States or other Parties," and that the judges' "personal work would not allow them to be surprised by convocations summoning them for a date which was not known in advance."[2] In 1931 a general desire had come to exist that some change be made.

The new text of Article 23 of the Statute, annexed to the Revision

---

[95] *Id.*, pp. 124, 196, 451. A drafting committee expressed the view in 1922, that "the Court will have to conform to the varying wishes and usages of the several Governments." See also Series D, No. 2 (2d add.), p. 154; § 401, *infra*.

[96] Series D, No. 2 (2d add.), pp. 155–6, 209.

[97] Series D, No. 2, p. 123.

[98] Series D, No. 2, p. 186.

[99] Series D, No. 2 (add.), pp. 42–45.

[100] Series D, No. 2, p. 99.

[1] Series D, No. 2 (add.), pp. 46–51.

[2] *Id.*, p. 50.

Protocol of September 14, 1929, would require the Court to "remain permanently in session," and the prolonged discussions in the Court in 1931 were influenced accordingly. Many proposals were made; [3] Judge van Eysinga wished the Court to meet "at the beginning of the year, when the whole world was returning to work after the Christmas holidays"; [4] February 1 was proposed "to enable judges from distant countries to pass Christmas and the New Year at home," [5] and this date was finally chosen in preference to the third Tuesday after Easter. [6] The matter was complicated because it was connected with such matters as extraordinary sessions, duration of sessions, long leave, and obligatory attendance. Nor was it simplified by the disagreement as to the extent of the Court's competence under Article 23 of the Statute. [7]

Paragraph 2 as to the duration of the sessions gave considerable difficulty, for the conception of a continuous session had to be reconciled with the text of the existing Statute. The session list is more explicitly defined than formerly, in the new Article 28; the agenda may also include "administrative matters." [8] It was finally decided that the President, and not the Court, should declare the session closed. [9]

Paragraph 3 was intended as an indication to the President of circumstances in which he is to act under Article 23 of the Statute to convoke extraordinary sessions. [10] The Court felt itself compelled by the existing Statute to retain extraordinary sessions.

The new paragraph 4 was due to the proposed amendment to Article 23 of the Statute. Judge Fromageot wished to introduce the text with a provision that the members of the Court should "at all times be exclusively at the disposal of the Court." [11] The text adopted [12] draws a distinction between judges and deputy-judges. Sir Cecil Hurst wished it to be plain that judges "could not discharge their obligations by merely attending an opening meeting" of a session; and it was agreed that "to be present at" meant "to attend throughout the session."

Paragraph 5 embodies a suggestion which was due to the proposed amendment to Article 23 of the Statute. The problem was connected with the more general one of judicial vacations, and there was some

---

[3] Series D, No. 2 (2d add.), pp. 20–88.
[4] Id., p. 32.
[5] Id., p. 57.
[6] Series D, No. 2 (2d add.), p. 57.
[7] Id., p. 60.
[8] Id., p. 72.
[9] Id., pp. 74–5.
[10] Id., pp. 75, 206–7.
[11] Series D, No. 2 (2d add.), p. 17.
[12] Id., pp. 78, 98–101.

disposition to say that such vacations should be rigidly fixed in the Rules.[13]

§294. **1931 Rules, Article 28.** As adopted in 1922, this article provided for a "list of cases" and a "list for each session," and it was possible for the Court to add to the latter after the beginning of a session; "extracts from the above list" and "a list of cases for revision" were also provided for. The session list was to include questions submitted for advisory opinion and cases in which written proceedings were concluded; this distinction was made "because, originally, no written proceedings had been contemplated in the case of advisory opinions." [14] No change was made in 1926, except for the correction of a slight error in the French version, but in 1931 the article was entirely recast. In proposing a new draft of the first paragraph, Judge Fromageot desired "to prevent unjustified preference being given to one case over another." [15] The Court drew a sharp distinction between the "general list" and the "session list," and it sought in vain to avoid the use of the word "list" with reference to both.[16] It was agreed that the general list would include cases for revision, and should be drawn up retrospectively to begin with the first case dealt with by the Court in 1922.[17] The possibility of varying the order of cases in the session list was considered at length.[18] Care was taken to avoid special lists for the chambers.[19] The provision for adjournments was made elastic, partly with a view to taking care of requests for advisory opinions; [20] and adjournment was distinguished from extension of time. A proposal of a special paragraph relating to measures of interim protection was not adopted.[21]

§295. **1931 Rules, Article 29.** This article has not been changed since it was adopted in 1922. A proposal to amend it was not adopted in 1931.[22]

§296. **1931 Rules, Article 30.** When the first sentence of this article was adopted in 1922, opinion was divided as to whether adjournment was possible in other circumstances.[23] The second sentence

---

[13] *Id.*, p. 76. On January 30, 1931, the Court adopted a resolution declaring that "the Court considers it desirable that it should not be convened between July 1 and October 1, except for urgent cases." *Id.*, p. 80.

[14] Series E, No. 5, p. 248.

[15] Series D, No. 2 (2d add.), p. 92.   [16] *Id.*, pp. 104–6.

[17] *Id.*, p. 164. The retrospective list was published in a note by the Registrar, with Series A/B, No. 40.

[18] Series D, No. 2 (2d add.), pp. 117–121.   [21] *Id.*, pp. 92–5, 104.

[19] *Id.*, pp. 126, 130, 159–164.   [22] *Id.*, pp. 201–4, 297.

[20] *Id.*, pp. 107–112.   [23] Series D, No. 2, pp. 187–8.

was added in 1926,[24] excluding judges *ad hoc* from being counted in determining a quorum; this fills a *lacuna* in Article 25 of the Statute. No amendment was made in 1931.[25]

§297. **1931 Rules, Article 31.** The first paragraph of this article was adopted in substance in 1922, the provision for administrative matters being added in 1926. The second paragraph was adopted in 1922, except for the reference to the Deputy-Registrar adopted in 1926; it covers the possibility of having assessors present at the Court's deliberations. The third paragraph has not been changed since 1922; in 1926 it was made clear that the Court wished to preserve the possibility of an exchange of written notes as part of the deliberations.[26] The first part of the fourth paragraph was adopted in 1922; in 1926, the provision was added that voting should be in an order inverse to that of precedence,[27] in line with a decision which the Court had taken on July 19, 1922.[28] The fifth paragraph was adopted in 1922. The sixth[29] and seventh paragraphs were adopted in 1926, on the proposal of the Registrar, as embodying a decision previously taken by the Court.[30] The eighth paragraph was adopted in 1926; it does not clearly add to the provisions of Article 57 of the Statute.

§298. **1931 Rules, Article 32.** This text dates from 1922. Only the Rules relating to contentious procedure, Articles 33–70, may be varied by the Court on the proposals of the parties concerned. The matter was discussed at length by the Court;[31] as originally proposed by Judge Moore, the article would have permitted a varying of the Rules contained in the Statute. A proposal by Judge Anzilotti would have enabled the Court to vary the Rules *proprio motu*.[32] In 1926, the article was explained as affording "the Court the possibility of exercising control over proposals of the parties whilst indicating a desire to take such proposals into account."[33]

§299. **1931 Rules, Article 33.** No change has been made in this text since 1922.[34] The questions raised related chiefly to the extent to which the parties should be allowed to fix time-limits. As to the moment when a time-limit should begin to run, it was assumed that this would be fixed by the Court. In 1926, Judge Pessôa proposed an addition

---

[24] Series D, No. 2 (add.), pp. 53–4.
[25] But see Series D, No. 2 (2d add.), pp. 201–4.
[26] Series D, No. 2 (add.), p. 59.
[27] *Id.*, p. 60.
[28] Series E, No. 1, p. 255.
[29] On the application of this paragraph, see Series E, No. 8, pp. 269–70.
[30] Series D, No. 2 (add.), pp. 63–5, 232, 308. See Series E, No. 1, p. 270.
[31] Series D, No. 2, pp. 52–4, 57–61.
[32] *Id.*, p. 129.
[33] Series D, No. 2 (add.), p. 68.
[34] Series D, No. 2, pp. 54–67, 129–132.

that parties could not appeal from an order by the President; this proposal was not accepted, but it seems to be recognized that no right of appeal exists.[35] In two cases in which special agreements defined time-limits in terms of "months," the Court has taken a month to consist of twenty-eight days.[36]

§300. 1931 Rules, Article 34. As adopted in 1922, this article provided: "All documents of the written proceedings submitted to the Court shall be accompanied by not less than thirty printed copies certified correct. The President may order additional copies to be supplied." The amended text was adopted in 1926, proposed by the Registrar on the basis of his experience.[37] In practice, an application or a special agreement does not fall within the operation of this rule.

§301. 1931 Rules, Article 35. Paragraph "(1)" of this article was drafted in 1926, in elaboration of the provisions adopted in 1922.[38] It had been pointed out in 1922 that the provisions were not complete as to "addresses." In 1926, the Registrar proposed various changes, relating in part to the names and selection of agents,[39] to meet "difficulties which had arisen in the relations with certain agents." [40] A failure to state names of agents is not necessarily fatal to an application.[41]

Paragraph "(2)" had no counterpart in the earlier Rules, and its adoption in 1926 gave rise to an extended debate.[42] The question of the conditions under which the Court was to be open to States not Members of the League of Nations and not mentioned in the Annex to the Covenant was discussed by the Court at length in 1922, and it was decided to address a letter to the Council of the League of Nations asking to be informed of the use which the Council intended to make of the powers conferred upon it by the second paragraph of Article 35 of the Statute, particularly whether it was intended to issue "a general regulation covering all possible cases, instead of dealing with each separate case as it arose." [43] The letter also contained various suggestions as to the general rules which the Council might lay down; it was stated that "the suggestion was made during the discussion in the Court that the Council might find it preferable to waive the powers, which it derived from Article 35, to fix conditions of admission." On May 17, 1922, the Council adopted its resolution on the

---

[35] Series D, No. 2 (add.), pp. 68-9.
[36] Series E, No. 4, p. 284.
[37] Series D, No. 2 (add.), pp. 70, 308.
[38] Series D, No. 2, pp. 133-5, 198-200.
[39] Series D, No. 2 (add.), pp. 308-9.
[40] *Id.*, pp. 72-5, 233.
[41] Series E, No. 8, p. 256.
[42] Series D, No. 2 (add.), pp. 75-7, 104-7.
[43] Series D, No. 2, pp. 69-72, 76-7, 34, 343-7. This initiative may have been due to a suggestion by the Council itself.

subject,[44] and the text was annexed to the article adopted by the Court in 1926; in general, it may be said that the resolution corresponds with the suggestions made by the Court. It is to be noted that paragraph "(2)" contains no indication of the way in which the Court proposes to exercise its power under the third paragraph of Article 35 of the Statute, as to fixing contributions by parties not members of the League of Nations.

Paragraph "(3)" is substantially the text adopted in 1922.[45] It was emphasized in the discussion that the parties should be agreed on resort to a special chamber under Articles 26 and 27 of the Statute.

§302. **1931 Rules, Article 36.** The first paragraph of this article was adopted in 1922;[46] the second paragraph was added in 1926 on the proposal of the Registrar,[47] as a codification of the Court's practice up to that time.

§303. **1931 Rules, Article 37.** No change has been made in this article since it was adopted in 1922.[48] It was thought desirable that the Registrar should be "able to quote a definite authority when refusing to undertake translations for the parties." [49]

§304. **1931 Rules, Article 38.** The text of Article 38 as adopted in 1922 was transferred to Article 42, and the present text was substituted in 1926. Though the question was discussed in 1922,[50] no provision was then made concerning preliminary objections; but the Court's experience in the *Mavrommatis Case* and in the case on *German Interests in Polish Upper Silesia* led to several proposals along this line in 1926.[51] Two conceptions were held of the preliminary objection or plea to the jurisdiction: on the one hand, that it was to be dealt with as a part of the proceedings on the merits; on the other hand, that it was to be dealt with as a more or less independent proceeding; it was feared that the former procedure might compel States to plead to the merits where the Court lacked jurisdiction. Some members of the Court were opposed to any general rule requiring the separation of the question of jurisdiction from that of the merits; emphasis was placed on the fact that the Court was not in the position of a national court in this respect. It was suggested that decisions as to jurisdiction might be provisional. It was agreed that the Court could decide in each case

---

[44] League of Nations Official Journal, 1922, pp. 526, 545. See §397, *infra*.
[45] Series D, No. 2, pp. 134–5, 199–200.
[46] Series D, No. 2, p. 135.
[47] Series D, No. 2 (add.), pp. 77–8.
[48] Series D, No. 2, pp. 69, 135–6.
[49] *Id.*, p. 205.
[50] *Id.*, pp. 77–8.
[51] Series D, No. 2 (add.), pp. 78–94.

whether objections to jurisdiction and the merits would be dealt with at the same session.[52] The discussion failed to indicate any clear distinction between pleas to the jurisdiction and other possible preliminary objections.

§305. **1931 Rules, Article 39.** No change has been made in this text since 1922. At that time the Court considered whether documents should be presented simultaneously or successively, and whether one order could be adopted for cases submitted by special agreement and another for cases submitted by application. M. Beichmann pointed out the difficulty in many cases of saying which party was plaintiff; and Judge Moore "thought that, in the case of a special agreement, the question of plaintiff and defendant did not logically arise." [53] It was agreed that in cases submitted by special agreement, simultaneous presentation should be the general rule, and that such presentation might be agreed upon by the parties in cases submitted by application. After some discussion of the submission of replies, it was agreed that in the case of simultaneous presentation there should be a "right of reply," and that in other cases "both parties should have a right to present an equal number of documents of procedure." [54] It was assumed that in cases submitted by application, the application and the applicant's case would form a single document.[55] The phraseology seems to have been carefully considered.[56]

§306. **1931 Rules, Article 40.** This text was adopted in 1922, with little discussion,[57] and no change has since been made.

§307. **1931 Rules, Article 41.** This article, as adopted in 1922, conferred on the President the power to fix the date for the commencement of the oral proceedings. In 1931, this power was conferred on the Court, or the President if the Court is not sitting, in consequence of the new provisions as to sessions.[58] In 1922, Judge Anzilotti wished the article to foresee the possibility that parties might waive oral proceedings; M. Beichmann wished to provide for an intermediate stage between written and oral proceedings which might be used for such purposes as the taking of evidence on commission.[59] In practice, the rule is taken to mean that the date for the commencement of the oral proceedings shall not be fixed before the termination of the written proceedings, if the former are to be held.

[52] Series D, No. 2 (add.), p. 94.
[53] Series D, No. 2, p. 72.
[54] Series D, No. 2, p. 75.
[55] *Id.*, pp. 137–8.
[56] *Id.*, pp. 137, 207.
[57] *Id.*, p. 208.
[58] Series D, No. 2 (2d add.), p. 173.
[59] Series D, No. 2, p. 140.

§308. **1931 Rules, Article 42.** The first paragraph of this article was adopted in 1922, without the provision for forwarding copies of documents to parties, which was added in 1926 to bring the Rules into harmony with Article 43 of the Statute.[60] The complete *dossier* under this rule includes the documents of procedure and some of the correspondence; it does not include applications or special agreements.

The second paragraph, adopted in 1922 as Article 38, was transferred to this article in 1926; it was designed to enable Governments to decide as to the desirability of intervention.[61] Judge Anzilotti thought that Article 46 of the Statute gave parties "the right to institute secret proceedings." [62] In 1931, the Registrar explained that cases and counter-cases are communicated to all Governments only when they appear in Series C of the Court's publications.[63] The "hearing" of the parties under this rule is conducted in writing.

The third paragraph was added in 1931 on the proposal of the Registrar; [64] while the publication of documents was viewed as "giving food for polemics," it was preferred to the encouragement of "unfounded rumours."

The second and third paragraphs of this article have been applied by analogy in advisory procedure.[65]

§309. **1931 Rules, Article 43.** This text dates from 1922, when it was adopted with little discussion.[66]

§310. **1931 Rules, Article 44.** This text dates from 1922. Article 39 of the Statute empowers the Court, at the request of the parties, to authorize a language other than French or English to be used; in this case, the party concerned must arrange for the translation into English or French.[67] If a witness uses another language, it is the translation of his testimony which is taken to be authoritative.[68]

§311. **1931 Rules, Article 45.** This text has not been changed since its adoption in 1922.[69] Lord Finlay proposed that the order in which counsel and witnesses should be heard should be decided by the Court in each case; the text does not deal with the order in which counsel should be heard. Some members of the Court had interpreted

---

[60] Series D, No. 2 (add.), p. 103.

[61] Series D, No. 2, pp. 152, 205–6. Governments not infrequently request that they receive the documents in cases to which they are not parties. The German and Italian Governments made such requests in the *Serbian Loans Case*. Series C, No. 16–III, p. 798.

[62] Series D, No. 2, p. 153.

[63] Series D, No. 2 (2d add.), p. 173.

[64] *Id.*, pp. 173–4.

[65] Series E, No. 8, p. 262.

[66] Series D, No. 2, pp. 140, 208. *Communiqués* issued by the Registrar are marked non-official. Series E, No. 1, p. 270.

[67] Series D, No. 2, pp. 141, 208.

[68] Series E, No. 3, p. 201.

[69] Series D, No. 2, pp. 81, 142, 208–9.

Articles 43 and 54 of the Statute to indicate that counsel should be heard after oral evidence had been taken. The concluding clause was designed to assure that, even though counsel had been heard before witnesses were examined, they should be permitted to comment on the testimony.

§312. **1931 Rules, Article 46.** This text was adopted in 1922; [70] in employing the terms "agents, advocates or counsel," it follows the usage in Articles 42 and 54 of the Statute.

§313. **1931 Rules, Article 47.** This text dates from 1922. It was designed to give the Court control of the introduction of evidence, following the English system.[71] The text seems to envisage a direct communication between the parties which is not elsewhere provided for in the Statute or in the Rules.

§314. **1931 Rules, Article 48.** This text dates from 1922.[72] Some question was raised whether under Article 54 of the Statute the Court could take the initiative in calling witnesses, but this power was rested on Article 50 of the Statute. It was agreed that the Court had no power to compel the attendance of witnesses, and its action is therefore subject to Article 44 of the Statute. A party may request the Court to act under this Rule.

§315. **1931 Rules, Article 49.** This text dates from 1922.[73] A proposal that a provision should be added that the Court could not order an enquiry on the territory of any State a party to a dispute, without its consent, was not accepted.

§316. **1931 Rules, Article 50.** This text was adopted in 1922. A suggestion that the Court should administer oaths to witnesses was opposed "in the interests of freedom of conscience," and on the ground that the Court had no power to punish for perjury.[74] The language in which the witness should make the declaration is not covered.[75] It was agreed, however, that a witness should not be compelled "to violate professional secrecy," [76] though in 1926 it was not clear how this would be determined.[77]

§317. **1931 Rules, Article 51.** This text was adopted in 1922. It was Lord Finlay's insistence that witnesses should be examined in the first instance "by those who had summoned them," [78] though a pro-

---

[70] Series D, No. 2, pp. 142, 209.
[71] Series D, No. 2, pp. 142–3.
[72] *Id.*, pp. 145–6, 209–11, 232.
[73] *Id.*, pp. 209–11.
[74] Series D, No. 2, pp. 82–3.

[75] *Id.*, p. 146.
[76] *Id.*, p. 211.
[77] Series D, No. 2 (add.), p. 132.
[78] Series D, No. 2, p. 83.

posal had been made that the President should have this function.[79] It was agreed that the President could not prevent a judge from asking a witness a question.[80]

§318. **1931 Rules, Article 52.** This text was adopted in 1922. It was first agreed that witnesses should be paid by the Court, the expense being charged to the losing party.[81] Judge Huber criticized the expression "losing party" as not well chosen, and proposed the deletion of the phrase as to charging expenses, because "it was undesirable to introduce the principle of the payment of the expenses of the Court by the parties; these expenses should, according to the Statute, be borne by the League of Nations." [82] This proposal was agreed to, and the article was redrafted.[83] It does not apply to a witness who appears at the instance of a party.

§319. **1931 Rules, Article 53.** This text dates from 1922, when it was adopted with some opposition.[84] "Enquiry" seems to be used here in a wider sense than the taking of oral testimony.

§320. **1931 Rules, Article 54.** A less definite text was adopted in 1922,[85] and the present text was substituted in 1926. The earlier text required the approval by a witness of the record of his testimony; defects in this rule seem to have been exposed in the case relating to *German Interests in Polish Upper Silesia.* Various questions arose in 1926, whether a witness' approval was essential to the validity of his testimony, whether he could approve by proxy, whether signature was required, whether approval should take place at the hearing at which the testimony was given. The matter was complicated by the possibility that various languages might be used by witnesses. After a lengthy discussion,[86] a text was adopted which did not meet some of the questions debated. As to the report of statements by agents, advocates or counsel, a decision had been taken on January 24, 1925, restricting corrections of formal changes.[87]

§321. **1931 Rules, Article 55.** The first paragraph of this text was adopted in 1922.[88] The second paragraph was added in 1926.[89]

§322. **1931 Rules, Article 56.** As adopted in 1922, this article provided: "Before the oral proceedings are concluded, each party

[79] Series D, No. 2, p. 303.
[80] *Id.,* pp. 146, 211. See §493, *infra.*
[81] *Id.,* p. 82.
[82] *Id.,* p. 146.
[83] Series D, No. 2, p. 232.
[84] *Id.,* pp. 147, 212.
[85] *Id.,* pp. 148, 212, 232.
[86] Series D, No. 2 (add.), pp. 132–46, 148–51.
[87] *Id.,* p. 143. See, however, Series E, No. 1, pp. 268–9, 271; No. 7, p. 295.
[88] Series D, No. 2, pp. 148, 212.
[89] Series D, No. 2 (add.), p. 146.

may present his bill of costs." This was an optional provision. The present text was substituted in 1926.[90] It fails to indicate how the Court will proceed in allowing a bill of costs, and as no order for the payment of costs has been made, there has been no application of this rule.

§323. **1931 Rules, Article 57.** The text of this article as adopted in 1922, in which no change was made until 1931, provided in two paragraphs: "When the Court is not sitting, any measures for the preservation in the meantime of the respective rights of the parties shall be indicated by the President. Any refusal by the parties to conform to the suggestions of the Court or of the President, with regard to such measures, shall be placed on record." Much more elaborate provisions had been proposed by Judge Nyholm,[91] and Lord Finlay suggested that in case of a refusal of a party to comply with measures indicated damages should be stipulated in the judgment.[92] The text was adopted in 1922 with little discussion,[93] and it was not discussed in 1926; but in 1931 the revised text was the subject of an extended consideration.[94] Judge Anzilotti explained that the 1922 text was based on the assumption that the Court would meet but rarely, and in view of the change in Article 27 he thought a new text was necessary. Judge Fromageot raised the questions of the Court's deliberation on requests for interim measures, and of the necessity of a request; he preferred the word "order" to "indicate," but this suggestion was withdrawn when it was explained that the term "indicate" as used in Article 41 of the Statute had been borrowed from the Bryan treaties, advisedly. Several members of the Court expressed regret that the Statute left so little latitude to the Court on this point. Judge Negulesco raised the question of a possible agreement of the parties relating to interim measures. The 1931 text establishes priority and urgency for requests for interim measures, confines the exercise of the power of indication to the Court, establishes the Court's competence *proprio motu,* and requires that the parties be given opportunity to be heard. It omits, however, the reference to a party's refusal to conform to the Court's suggestions as contained in the 1922 text, to which Judge Fromageot had proposed an addition of notice to the Council of the League of Nations.[95]

---

[90] Series D, No. 2 (add.), pp. 146–8.
[91] Series D, No. 2, pp. 376–7.
[92] *Id.,* p. 77.
[93] *Id.,* pp. 77, 148, 212.
[94] Series D, No. 2 (2d add.), pp. 181–200.
[95] Series D, No. 2 (2d add.), p. 297.

§324. **1931 Rules, Article 58.** This text has not been changed since its adoption in 1922, when the subject of intervention was considered at great length.[96] The provisions of Articles 62 and 63 of the Statute called for interpretation. Some members of the Court desired to restrict intervention under Article 62 to cases in which the Court derived jurisdiction under paragraph 2 of Article 36 of the Statute; Judge Anzilotti pointed out that "States would hesitate to have recourse to the Court if they had reason to fear that third parties would intervene in their cases." [97] Other members considered this view as contrary to the Statute.[98] Nor were the members of the Court agreed as to the extent of the "interest of a legal nature" which would serve as a basis for intervention; Lord Finlay thought that it would be sufficient if the interests of the intervening State "might be affected by the attitude adopted by the Court" in the case, while Judge Anzilotti thought "an actual legal interest in the dispute" essential.[99] The Court rejected a proposal to provide for the appointment of judges *ad hoc* by intervening States.[100] The text adopted fails to resolve the principal questions raised in the debate, and it is limited to intervention under Article 62 of the Statue. In 1926, a proposal to delete the second paragraph of Article 58 was rejected by 7 votes to 4,[1] and other amendments proposed were not accepted.[2] Intervention, strictly speaking, is not allowed in connection with requests for advisory opinions.[3]

§325. **1931 Rules, Article 59.** The first and second paragraphs of this article were adopted with little discussion in 1922; the third and fourth paragraphs were added in 1926, the latter for the purpose of avoiding "any delay as a result of intervention at a late stage." [4]

§326. **1931 Rules, Article 60.** As adopted in 1922, this article was more restrictive. The first paragraph of the 1922 text provided: "Any State desiring to intervene, under the terms of Article 63 of the Statute, shall inform the Registrar in writing at latest before the commencement of the oral proceedings." Article 63 of the Statute was taken to confer a right to intervene,[5] and the phrase "declaration of

---

[96] Series D, No. 2, pp. 86–97, 151, 176–7, 214–17, 349–52.
[97] *Id.*, p. 87.
[98] Judge Altamira pointed out that Article 62 of the Statute was drafted on the assumption that the Court was to have compulsory jurisdiction, and that it was not modified when compulsory jurisdiction was rejected. *Id.*, p. 89.
[99] Series D, No. 2, pp. 89, 90.
[100] *Id.*, pp. 177, 215.
[1] Series D, No. 2 (add.), p. 152.
[2] *Id.*, pp. 152–7, 163–7.
[3] Series E, No. 1, p. 258. See §410, *infra.*
[4] Series D, No. 2 (add.), pp. 152–7, 234–5.
[5] Series D, No. 2, p. 87.

intervention" was proposed to cover it by M. Beichmann.[6] It was pointed out that Articles 62 and 63 of the Statute might be applicable simultaneously. The opinion was expressed that "the right to inspect documents was a necessary corollary of the right to intervene."[7] In 1926, Judge de Bustamante pointed out that the 1922 article did not apply to Members of the League of Nations not States.[8] Some difficulty was anticipated if all parties to an international convention should ask to be permitted to intervene in a case, and Judge Anzilotti said that Article 63 of the Statute did not provide for "true intervention," since a State might merely submit observations. President Huber proposed that it should be made clear that only conventions were in question on which the application was based,[9] and for the interpretation of which the Court possessed jurisdiction. The text adopted in 1926 [10] retained in the third paragraph a provision based on the second paragraph of the 1922 text. No provision analogous to that in Article 59 was added, however. No change was made in this article in 1931. As only one case of intervention has occurred, the rules have not been tested in practice.

§327. **1931 Rules, Article 61.** This text dates from 1922. It provides for both a settlement by agreement and an agreed discontinuance of proceedings.[11] There was some disposition to say that the Court might give judgment in accordance with the agreement of the parties,[12] and Judge Huber found this authorized by Article 38 of the Statute; it was thought, however, that such judgments "might have a detrimental effect upon the development of case-law." Nor was such a suggestion adopted when it was renewed in 1926.[13]

§328. **1931 Rules, Article 62.** The first paragraph of this text was adopted in 1922, with the exception of "(10) the number of the judges constituting the majority contemplated in Article 55 of the Statute," which was added in 1926. The second paragraph as adopted in 1922 read: "The opinions of judges who dissent from the judgment, shall be attached thereto should they express a desire to that effect." A new text of the second paragraph was substituted in 1926. No part of the text was discussed at length in 1922.[14] By 1926 the practice had become established to permit judges to have their dissents merely

---

[6] Series D, No. 2, pp. 151, 349.
[7] *Id.*, p. 216.
[10] Series D, No. 2 (add.), pp. 161, 167, 235.
[11] The latter is due to the *Tavignano Case* in a tribunal of the Permanent Court of Arbitration. See §23, *supra.*
[12] Series D, No. 2, pp. 154, 217.
[8] Series D, No. 2 (add.), p. 158.
[9] *Id.*, pp. 160, 161.
[13] Series D, No. 2 (add.), pp. 167–71.
[14] Series D, No. 2, pp. 78, 155, 217.

mentioned,[15] on the ground that the greater right included the lesser.[16] Four problems were raised in 1926:[17] (1) compulsory recording of names of dissenting judges; (2) record of dissents; (3) annexing of reasoned opinions, not published, to minutes of a private sitting; and (4) mention of votes on judgments and the naming of the majority. The result was a new text of the second paragraph,[18] which was adopted in connection with the new text of the third paragraph of Article 71. On February 17, 1928, the Court adopted a resolution requiring dissenting opinions to be submitted normally after the first reading of the draft judgment or opinion,[19] but no provision to this effect has been incorporated in the Rules. An amendment to Article 62 was proposed in 1931, but it was not discussed.[20]

§329. **1931 Rules, Article 63.** As adopted with little discussion in 1922,[21] this article provided: "After having been read in open Court the text of the judgment shall forthwith be communicated to all parties concerned and to the Secretary-General of the League of Nations." A new text was substituted in 1926, to distinguish between copies sent to parties and those sent to others, and omitting the provision for communicating the text to the Secretary-General of the League of Nations.[22]

§330. **1931 Rules, Article 64.** This text was adopted in 1922 with little discussion, and it has not since been changed.[23]

§331. **1931 Rules, Article 65.** As adopted in 1922, this article related to a collection of judgments only, and it led to Series A of the Court's publications. Though the collection was to be published "under the responsibility of the Registrar," it had been agreed in 1922 that it "should be published under the authority of the Court."[24] In 1931, at the suggestion of the Registrar,[25] the two collections of judgments and advisory opinions were combined into a single collection; this has called for the amalgamation of Series A and Series B of the Court's publications into Series A/B.

§332. **1931 Rules, Article 66.** As adopted in 1922,[26] this article related only to revision. In 1926, the Court adopted a proposal that

---

[15] Series D, No. 2 (add.), p. 313.
[16] *Id.*, p. 215.
[17] *Id.*, p. 219.
[18] *Id.*, pp. 171–3, 200–23.
[22] Series D, No. 2 (add.), pp. 173–4. It is the Court's practice to supply parties with not more than 25 copies of judgments and orders. Series E, No. 7, p. 298.
[23] Series D, No. 2, p. 218.
[24] Series D, No. 2, p. 155.

[19] Series E, No. 4, p. 291.
[20] Series D, No. 2 (2d add.), p. 294.
[21] Series D, No. 2, pp. 155, 217.
[25] Series D, No. 2 (2d add.), pp. 209, 296.
[26] Series D, No. 2, pp. 155–6, 218.

interpretation should be covered,[27] to take account of precedents established by the Court;[28] it was pointed out that Article 60 of the Statute provided for "construing" a judgment. The view was expressed that an application for an interpretation was a "new proceeding"; and it seems to have been agreed that jurisdiction of such a proceeding was compulsory, though a door was opened for preliminary objections on this account.[29] Article 13 of the Statute does not require the composition of the Court for construing a judgment to be the same as that when the judgment was given.[30] No change in the text was made in 1931.

§333. **1931 Rules, Article 67.** This text was adopted in 1922, with little discussion,[31] and it has not since been amended.

§334. **1931 Rules, Article 68.** This article as adopted in 1922 provided merely that on receipt of the application the President should convene the Chamber for Summary Procedure. In 1926, this was thought to be too rigid,[32] and the new text was designed to leave greater latitude to the President. No change was made in 1931.

§335. **1931 Rules, Article 69.** This text, except for slight modifications introduced in 1926, was adopted in 1922. Lord Finlay was of the opinion that summary procedure should be limited to oral proceedings, while M. Beichmann, basing his argument on Article 90 of the 1907 Hague Convention for Pacific Settlement, wished it to be conducted exclusively in writing.[33] The text was based on neither of these views.[34] Judge Oda proposed that a case begun in the Chamber for Summary Procedure might be transferred to the full court, but the proposal was defeated by 7 votes to 5.[35] The changes made in 1926 take account of different ways in which cases may be submitted to summary procedure, and of both simultaneous and successive presentation of documents;[36] in other words, the article takes account of the possibility of an application as the document instituting a summary proceeding.

§336. **1931 Rules, Article 70.** No change has been made in this text since its adoption in 1922.[37] It was desired to make it clear that a judgment given by the Chamber for Summary Procedure is a judgment of the Court itself.

---

[27] Series D, No. 2 (add.), pp. 313–4.
[28] *Id.*, p. 174.
[29] Series D, No. 2 (add.), pp. 176–9.
[30] Series E, No. 4, p. 295.
[31] Series D, No. 2, pp. 159, 218.
[32] Series D, No. 2 (add.), pp. 180–1, 236.
[33] Series D, No. 2, p. 158.
[34] *Id.*, pp. 158, 218.
[35] *Id.*, pp. 100–2, 159.
[36] Series D, No. 2 (add.), pp. 182–3.
[37] Series D, No. 2, pp. 158, 218–9.

§337. **1931 Rules, Article 71.** The first sentence of the first paragraph of this article was adopted in 1922; a second paragraph adopted at that time provided that "the opinions of dissenting judges may, at their request, be attached to the opinion of the Court." In a memorandum of February 18, 1922,[38] Judge Moore stated that the question of advisory opinions had caused "much confusion"; after reviewing the history of the texts, he submitted various propositions for discussion, among others that the Court was not obliged to render such opinions "unconditionally and on request," that the giving of advisory opinions was "not an appropriate function of a Court of Justice" and would tend to obscure and change the character of the Court, that the Court should not seem to invite requests for such opinions, and that the Court should deal with each application on its merits without formulating a general rule. Early in its session, the Court decided that advisory opinions should be given by the full Court, that Article 26 of the Statute did not refer to them, and that the same procedure would be adopted for them as for judgments.[39] M. Beichmann stated that "as regards advisory opinions, there was [to be] no written procedure properly so called."[40] The subject was not fully discussed, and the text was adopted with no clashes of opinion.[41]

By 1926, a new appreciation of the importance of advisory opinions was evident. On September 4, 1923, a proposal had been made by Judge Altamira envisaging the possibility of a secret procedure as to advisory opinions,[42] upon which Judge Moore had commented at length;[43] Judge Altamira's proposal was later withdrawn. Various other proposals were before the Court in 1926: that oral proceedings be dispensed with as to advisory opinions, that judges *ad hoc* be allowed to participate, that dissenting opinions be suppressed, and that the votes be recorded. These proposals were debated at length.[44] Various judges were opposed to the introduction of judges *ad hoc,* as being contrary to the Statute, and this proposal was rejected by 7 votes to 3. The proposal that dissenting opinions be suppressed was rejected by 8 votes to 3. By a vote of 6 to 5, the article was amended by adding the second sentence in the first paragraph: "They shall mention the number of the judges constituting the majority." The second paragraph was also redrafted to allow dissenting judges to attach "either an

---

[38] Series D, No. 2, pp. 383–98.
[39] *Id.*, pp. 98–9.
[40] *Id.*, p. 194.
[41] *Id.*, p. 219.

[42] Series D, No. 2 (add.), pp. 293.
[43] *Id.*, pp. 294–6.
[44] *Id.*, pp. 184–223.

exposition of their individual opinion or the statement of their dissent."
This was in accord with previous practice.[45]

In 1927, Judge Anzilotti renewed a proposal defeated in 1926,
that judges *ad hoc* should be allowed to participate in giving advisory
opinions.[46] A committee reported at this time that "where there are
in fact contending parties, the difference between contentious cases
and advisory cases is only nominal"; and it recommended the adoption
of the proposal, the significance of which had been illustrated by the
case relating to the *Jurisdiction of the European Commission of the
Danube* then pending. Whereas the proposal was defeated in 1926
by 7 votes to 3, it was adopted in 1927 by 9 votes to 2. A new second
paragraph was therefore added to the article, effective from September 7, 1927.[47] In the application of this paragraph, a criterion has been
applied that States which have been invited to be represented in the
Council of the League of Nations when the request was voted, may
appoint judges *ad hoc*.[48] No change was made in this article in 1931.

§338. **1931 Rules, Article 72.** This text was adopted in 1922,[49]
and no change was later made.

§339. **1931 Rules, Article 73.** The first paragraph of this article
as adopted in 1922 provided for notice to Members of the League of
Nations and "to the States mentioned in the Annex to the Covenant"; [50]
this latter was changed in 1926 to read, "to any States entitled to appear
before the Court." The 1922 text contained as a second paragraph:
"Notice of such request shall also be given to any international organizations which are likely to be able to furnish information on the
question." This was suppressed in 1926, when the present text of the
second, third and fourth paragraphs was adopted. When the text of
1922 was under discussion, Judge Anzilotti expressed the view "that
the Council should, in the interests of the peace of the world, have
the right to ask the Court for secret advice." [51] Lord Finlay and
Judge Moore thought that "the practice of giving opinions which were

---

[45] Series E, No. 1, pp. 256–7.
[46] Series E, No. 4, pp. 75–78. See Å Hammarskjöld, in 8 *Revue de Droit International et de Législation Comparée* (1927), pp. 354–355. But see Series E, No. 1, p. 252.
[47] The amended article was published at the time in Series D, addendum to No. 1.
The English and French versions of the added paragraph are not in accord; the former
says that "in case of doubt the Court shall decide," while the latter provides only for
the case of *contestation*.
[48] Series E, No. 7, p. 303.
[49] Series D, No. 2, pp. 159–160, 219.
[50] In practice it was held that the enumeration in the 1922 text was not exhaustive.
Series E, No. 1, pp. 250, 263.
[51] Series D, No. 2, p. 160.

not made public would be a deathblow to the Court as a judicial body," and this view was adopted by 11 votes to 1. Some difference of opinion was expressed, also, as to the time when notice should be given, and as to the States to which it should be given.[52] Various amendments were proposed by the Registrar in 1926.[53] There was some discussion as to the nature of the "international organizations" which might be consulted, but as the Court itself had the initiative no necessity appeared to define them.[54] No change in the text was made in 1931.

The coming into force of the Protocol of September 14, 1929, relating to the accession of the United States, would render it impossible for the Court to change the substance of this article; and the coming into force of the Revision Protocol of September 14, 1929, would incorporate the article with only slight changes into a new Article 66 of the Statute.

§340. 1931 Rules, Article 74. As adopted in 1922, this article read as follows: "Any advisory opinion which may be given by the Court and the request in response to which it was given, shall be printed and published in a special collection for which the Registrar shall be responsible." When this text was adopted, several members of the Court expressed the view that an opinion should not be published until it had been communicated to the body which had requested it.[55] In pursuance of the provision, Series B of the Court's publications was established. In 1926, the 1922 text was maintained, but two new paragraphs were added to precede it, on the proposal of the Registrar, who explained the new paragraphs as a "codification of the Court's practice." [56] In 1931, the 1922 text was dropped, in view of the decision embodied in Article 65 to issue a single collection of the judgments, orders and advisory opinions.[57]

The coming into force of the Protocol of September 14, 1929, relating to the adhesion of the United States, would make it impossible for the Court to change the substance of the provisions of this article; and the coming into force of the Revision Protocol of September 14, 1929, would incorporate the substance of the first sentence into a new Article 67 of the Statute.

§341. 1931 Rules, Article 75. This text dates from 1922. When it was adopted, "it was understood that before correcting clerical

---

[52] Series D, No. 2, pp. 219–20.   [53] Series D, No. 2 (add.), p. 315.
[54] *Id.*, pp. 224–5, 237. See, however, Series E, No. 8, pp. 273–4.
[55] Series D, No. 2, pp. 160.   [57] Series D, No. 2 (2d add.), p. 209.
[56] Series D, No. 2 (add.), pp. 228, 316.

errors, the Court or the President should ascertain that the parties gave their consent." [58] In 1931, the Registrar proposed to delete this text, but the proposal was not adopted.[59] The article has never been applied, in practice.

[58] Series D, No. 2, pp. 161, 221.　　　[59] Series D, No. 2 (2d add.), pp. 209, 296.

CHAPTER 13

THE REGISTRY

§342. The Office of Registrar. Article 21 of the Statute provides for the appointment of a Registrar by the Court, and it adds that the Registrar's duties "shall not be deemed incompatible with those of the Secretary-General of the Permanent Court of Arbitration." At no time have the duties of the two offices been conferred upon a single person,[1] though a combination would possess obvious advantages and it would not in any way militate against the interests of either the Permanent Court of International Justice or the Permanent Court of Arbitration. The provision in the Statute was partly due to a desire to connect the two institutions.[2] When the Statute was being drafted there was little appreciation of the importance of the post of Registrar, and the developments which have made the office so vital to the functioning of the Court were in no way foreseen. The Registrar is today much more than a clerk of court. He is the "head" of an institution called the Registry, nowhere mentioned in the Statute;[3] as an administrative official he has manifold duties, which include the handling of the Court's finances; he has custody of the seals of the Court; he is the chief representative of the Court *vis-à-vis* Governments, the organs of the League of Nations, and the general public; he conducts important negotiations on behalf of the Court; and he plays a responsible rôle in the actual functioning of the Court as a judicial body.

§343. Dignity of the Office. The Court has very wisely invested the office of Registrar with a becoming dignity. Article 18 of the Rules

---

[1] In 1929, when a vacancy in the post of Secretary-General of the Permanent Court of Arbitration was about to be filled, the Registrar addressed a letter to the President of the Administrative Council of the Permanent Court of Arbitration relative to the provision in Article 21 of the Statute. Series E, No. 5, p. 246.

[2] Partly also to a desire for economy. Minutes of the 1920 Committee of Jurists, p. 455; Series D, No. 2, p. 242.

[3] Yet ten articles of the Rules are devoted to the Registry.

Other names have been suggested for the Registry, particularly "The Office of the Registrar."

requires of him a solemn declaration, to be made at a meeting of the full Court. The Registrar sits with the judges at a public meeting of the Court, wearing a robe. He is present at all sessions of the Court,[4] and he assists the drafting committees appointed by the Court to prepare the texts of its judgments and opinions. He has large powers which in addition to his administrative responsibilities give him an actual share in the work of the Court.[5] He is protected from embarrassment by the resolution forbidding the acceptance of decorations without the consent of the Court.[6] He enjoys the diplomatic privileges and immunities and special facilities conferred on the members of the Court.[7] At Geneva, also, the post has been dignified. Though the Registrar has not formally been assimilated to the higher officials of the Secretariat of the League of Nations,[8] as the Court's "competent official" he is given large responsibilities in connection with the application of the League's Financial Regulations.

§344. Appointment of the Registrar. The appointment, "election," of the Registrar is governed by Article 17 of the Rules, which has tended to become more detailed through the various revisions. Only members of the Court may propose candidates, though in 1922 the Court received applications.[9] Since 1931, it is recognized that "experience in connection with the work of the League of Nations" should be considered as a qualification of a candidate; but the Rules place no restriction on the possible choice by the Court, other than nomination by a member of the Court. The election is by a secret ballot, an absolute majority being required; and the casting vote given to the President by the earlier Rules was abolished in 1931, as being inconsistent with the secrecy of the ballot. While deputy-judges may participate in the nomination of candidates, their participation in the election is not provided for in Article 17; in 1922 the deputy-judges present

---

[4] A meeting of the judges without the Registrar or his deputy would not be a legal meeting of the Court.

[5] This is shown by the rôle played by the Registrar in connection with the revisions of the Court's Rules.

[6] Series E, No. 3, p. 178.

[7] Series E, No. 4, p. 58. In relation to the Netherlands authorities the Registrar ranks with the Secretary-General of the Permanent Court of Arbitration, considered as an international official. See §370, *infra*.

[8] In 1922, the Court seems to have envisaged assimilation to the post of Director of the Secretariat of the League of Nations. Series D, No. 2, pp. 6–7. In 1930, a League of Nations Committee of Thirteen proposed assimilation to the post of Under-Secretary-General. In function, the office of Registrar is more nearly comparable with that of the Secretary-General of the League of Nations.

[9] Series D, No. 2, p. 242. In 1930, it was recognized that members of the "old" Court might put forward candidates for consideration by the "new" Court. Series E, No. 7, p. 280.

participated in the choice of the first Registrar, and two deputy-judges were present when he was reëlected in 1929. Every election, even an election to fill a vacancy, is for a term of seven years, which begins to run on January 1 following the election.[10] The Registrar may be re-elected, however, and the Court has declared that the only object of the seven-year limit is to enable the Court, if necessary, to terminate the incumbency; the "principle of stability" has been adopted, instead of the system of rotation which prevails for the higher posts in the Secretariat of the League of Nations.[11] The wisdom of this provision is clear; it assures to the Court the immense advantage of its being able to capitalize experience gained.

§345. **The Office of Deputy-Registrar.** The Statute includes no provision for the post of Deputy-Registrar and the original Rules made no provision for it, though the possibility of creating such a post was mentioned in 1922.[12] The Court created the post in 1925, and the 1926 Rules make provision for it. In general, the Deputy-Registrar is selected in the same way as the Registrar; he shares the functions of the Registrar and acts as a substitute for him; when so acting his powers and duties are assimilated to those of the Registrar.

§346. **The Staff Regulations.** The organization of the Registry is determined by the Court upon proposals submitted by the Registrar.[13] The 1922 Rules provided (Article 21) for Regulations for the Staff of the Registry, to be adopted by the President on the proposal of the Registrar, subject to subsequent approval by the Court;[14] in 1931, it was added that the regulations should be drawn up with regard to the organization decided upon by the Court and should conform as far as possible to the Staff Regulations of the Secretariat of the League of Nations. On March 22, 1922, the original Regulations were approved by the Court.[15] They applied to the officials of the Registry exclusive of the subordinate personnel, but not to the Registrar himself;[16] and the President explained that they "constituted a contract

---

[10] The term of seven years was chosen because Directors in the Secretariat of the League of Nations were appointed for this term, and to assure a continuity over the nine-year periods for which judges are elected. Series D, No. 2, p. 7.

[11] Series E, No. 5, p. 247.

[12] Judge Altamira proposed a candidate for the post in 1922. Series D, No. 2, p. 271.

[13] For the original plan proposed by the Registrar, see Series D, No. 2, p. 310.

[14] It seems that the President merely satisfies himself that the regulations are in general accordance with the Staff Regulations of the Secretariat of the League of Nations. Series D, No. 2 (2d add.), p. 153.

[15] Series D, No. 2, p. 225. For the text, see *id.*, pp. 530–532.

[16] The term "officials of the Registry" is generally used to exclude the Registrar.

with the members of the Staff." [17] Several revisions of the Regulations have been made,[18] the latest text being that adopted by the President on February 6, 1931, and approved by the Court on February 20, 1931.[19] Since the revision of January 1, 1926, they have provided that on questions relating to rights and duties of officials of the Registry they are to be supplemented by the Registrar, having regard to the provisions of the Staff Regulations of the Secretariat of the League of Nations and the International Labor Office. Since the beginning, they have been subject to modification by the Registrar with the approval of the President, and have provided that the Registrar shall take into consideration any proposal of modification made by as many as three members of the Staff. The 1931 Regulations now in force (14 articles) deal with appointments, categories, salaries and allowances, hours of work, holidays and leave, pensions and discipline.

§347. **Instructions for the Registry.** The duties of the Registrar and of officials of the Registry are set out in the Instructions, which under the third paragraph of Article 26 of the Rules are approved by the President on the submission of the Registrar. The original Instructions [20] have been amended,[21] and those now in force were approved on December 20, 1928. The Instructions (77 articles) deal in detail with the position and duties of both the Registrar and the officials of the Registry.

§348. **The Personnel of the Registry.** On February 3, 1922, M. Åke Hammarskjöld (Sweden) who had previously acted for a short time as Secretary of the Court was elected Registrar for a period of seven years,[22] and on August 16, 1929, he was reëlected for a like term.[23] Owing partly to his previous experience in connection

---

[17] On the contractual nature of the engagement of officials, see the report of a committee of jurists to the First Committee of the Thirteenth Assembly in 1932. Records of Thirteenth Assembly, Fourth Committee, p. 206; Series E, No. 9, p. 194.

[18] Series E, No. 1, p. 81; No. 2, p. 36; No. 5, p. 54; No. 7, pp. 75–6.

[19] The 1931 revision took effect as from Jan. 1, 1931. Series E, No. 7, p. 75. The text is reprinted in the appendix, *infra*, p. 681.

[20] Series E, No. 1, p. 86.

[21] *Id.*, No. 2, p. 40; No. 5, p. 58. The text is reprinted in the appendix, *infra*, p. 685.

[22] M. Hammarskjöld had been the chief member of the Secretariat placed at the Court's disposal by the Secretary-General of the League of Nations. His candidacy for the post of Registrar was suggested by the President of the Court. Series D, No. 2, p. 7. He is now an Envoy Extraordinary and Minister Plenipotentiary of H. M. the King of Sweden.

[23] Series E, No. 6, p. 41. The Registrar's first term began on February 1, 1922. Series D, No. 2, p. 579. However, under the third paragraph of Article 17 of the 1922 Rules, the seven-year period has been taken to have begun on January 1, 1923, so as to expire at the end of 1929. His second term began on January 1, 1930.

with the drafting of the Court's Statute and owing to the continuity of his service, his work has been of inestimable value to the Court.

Three persons have held the post of Deputy-Registrar: M. Paul Ruegger (Swiss) from 1926 to 1928, M. Julio López Oliván (Spanish) from 1929 to 1931; and M. L. J. H. Jorstad (Norwegian) since February 1, 1931.

The Staff of the Registry comprises established, temporary, and auxiliary officials. The appointment of established officials is regulated by the Staff Regulations; such officials are appointed for seven years, but the appointments are automatically renewable until the age limit is reached. The appointments may be terminated under certain conditions by the Court or by the official concerned. Temporary officials are appointed for periods of more than six months but less than seven years, while auxiliary officials are appointed for special occasions. Under Article 20 of the Rules all appointments except that of the Deputy-Registrar are made by the Court on the proposal of the Registrar. No attempt is made to follow a strict principle of national distribution of the posts in the Registry, though the Court has envisaged the appointment of persons who had knowledge of the Spanish and of the Slav languages; [24] knowledge of the official languages of the Court would necessarily restrict any selections on the basis of nationality. The Staff Regulations (Article 6) fix ten categories for officials, based on the minimum salaries paid. In 1930, the Registrar described the framework (*cadre*) of organization, then incomplete, as follows: [25]

  (A) The editing secretaries;
  (B) The technical departments:
     (1) Establishment and Accounts Department (including messengers);
     (2) Printing Department;
     (3) Archives and Library;
     (4) Department for distribution of documents;
     (5) Shorthand, Typewriting, and Roneographing Department.
  (C) The lady secretaries.

A list of the established and temporary officials is published each year.[26]

---

[24] Series E, No. 3, p. 181; No. 4, p. 271.
[25] Series E, No. 7, p. 67. In 1931, a Documents Department was added under (B).
[26] In Series E, Chapter 1. See Series E, No. 9, p. 32 for a list of 27 officials, which does not include the Registrar.

As the possibilities of promotion within the Staff of the Registry are limited, the Registrar has urged "that it should be possible for officials of the Court to be transferred . . . to posts at Geneva, the only means open to them of obtaining promotion within the framework of the League." [27] The 1933 Staff Regulations of the Secretariat of the League of Nations give a preference to officials of the Court when appointments are to be made from outside the Secretariat.[28]

§349. **The Work of the Registry.** The work of the Registry has been described by the Registrar [29] under four headings: (1) judicial; (2) diplomatic; (3) administrative; and (4) linguistic.

(1) The Instructions for the Registry (Article 3) make the Registrar "responsible for the preparation of cases for consideration by the Court," and direct him to assist the Court's drafting committees in the preparation of the texts of judgments and opinions. They make the Registrar responsible also (Article 16) for seeing that the prescribed forms are followed in documents submitted to the Court, and he is empowered (Article 17) to ask for additional information with regard to requests for advisory opinions. These duties are carried out with a view to saving the Court's time; and to the same end "in all cases of some complexity, the Registry provisionally assembles beforehand—subject to the personal researches which it is the duty of each judge to undertake—judicial and historical precedents, the text of treaty or legislative provisions and the opinions of publicists bearing upon the matter" involved.[30]

(2) The diplomatic work of the Registry consists of conducting the necessary correspondence with reference to cases before the Court; [31] conducting negotiations and correspondence with Governments as to general questions, particularly with the Netherlands Government and with the organs of the League of Nations; handling relations with the press, including the preparation of *communiqués;* and the preparation of the publications of the Court with reference to its jurisdiction, including its annual reports.

(3) The administrative work of the Registry is very heavy. In

---

[27] Series E, No. 6, p. 45.

[28] This principle is applied more easily in view of the fact that the Court's personnel is sometimes lent to the Secretariat. See Series E, No. 9, p. 196, note.

[29] Series E, No. 7, pp. 64ff.

[30] *Id.*, pp. 64–5. For an example, see Series C, No. 16—I, pp. 240ff.

[31] As between the President and the Registrar, correspondence is divided in accordance with the provisions of Article 24 of the Rules and Article 3 of the Instructions for the Registry. See also Series D, No. 2 (2d add.), pp. 153–156.

part it is set forth in the Instructions for the Registry. It comprises the internal administration proper, *e.g.*, questions relating to staff, premises, equipment, purchases and accounts; financial administration, including preparation of the budget and seeing it through the Assembly; the routine of preparing and distributing documents, of keeping archives and of maintaining a library; [32] and the preparation and printing of the Court's publications.

(4) The linguistic work of the Court occupies the time of a large part of the Staff. Interpretations at meetings of the Court, translations, and the maintenance of- a two-language system involve work which is both "administrative and substantial." [33]

§350. **Division of Work.** All of the duties of the Registry are performed under the immediate direction of the Registrar. To some extent, however, a division of labor is provided for in the Instructions for the Registry; specific duties are there set out for the editing secretaries, the archivist, the accountant-establishment officer, and the printing department.

§351. **The Publications of the Court.** No small part of the work of the Registry is connected with the publications of the Court, which appear in both French and English, and which have been organized on a most satisfactory basis. Indeed, it may be said that no public institution in the world is better documented; certainly it is doubtful whether any other judicial institution publishes such a complete record of its activities.[34] The six series of the Court's publications [35] have now been reduced to five, with the combination of Series A

[32] In addition to its use of the Peace Palace Library, the Court built up a small private library during its earlier years. In 1929, the Court requested additional funds for purchases for this library, in order that a library of private law might be available to it. Series E, No. 6, p. 52. In 1930, the Assembly voted to increase the budget item for this library from 500 to 10,000 florins. A working arrangement was then made by the Secretary-General of the League of Nations with the President of the Committee of Directors of the Carnegie Foundation. Series E, No. 7, p. 85; No. 8, p. 52. The Court's library, which is the property of the League of Nations, is housed in the premises of the Peace Palace Library.

[33] The expenditure for the linguistic work of the Court was partly accounted for in 1932 by the fact that "not all the present judges are sufficiently acquainted with the two official languages of the Court even to understand them." Series E, No. 8, p. 329.

[34] Nine volumes of a German edition of some of the Court's publications have been published by the *Institut für Internationales Recht* at Kiel, "with the authorization of the Registrar and subject to his control." Series E, No. 5, p. 291; No. 8, p. 321. Translations of the judgments and opinions into other languages, such as those into Spanish by the *Instituto Ibero-Americano de Derecho Comparado,* possess no official character.

[35] Catalogues of the Court's publications are issued by the Registry from time to time. A periodical "confidential bulletin" is prepared by the Registry for the use of members of the Court, but it is not given outside distribution. See Series E, No. 6, p. 294; Å. Hammarskjöld, in 25 Michigan Law Review (1927), p. 343. For a list of the Court's publications, see the appendix, *infra,* pp. 702, 708.

and Series B into Series A/B in 1931. Series A was a collection of the judgments of the Court, including some of the orders, and Series B was a collection of advisory opinions. Under Article 65 of the 1931 Rules, Series A/B was established, to include judgments, orders and advisory opinions; it is arranged, paged and indexed so as to form annual volumes. Series C, in which a new consecutive numbering was adopted in 1931, contains acts and documents relating to the judgments and opinions of the Court; these include, in addition to the documents of the written proceedings, the correspondence relating to cases before the Court, *procès-verbaux* of the Court's public sittings, records of the oral proceedings, and the texts of relevant treaties or other documents. Series D contains acts and documents concerning the organization of the Court.

Series E of the publications, containing the annual reports, was inaugurated in 1925. These reports were begun [36] in response to suggestions made in the Fifth Assembly of the League of Nations and to a Council resolution of December 8, 1924.[37] Though they are called reports, they are not addressed to any body; yet they are designed to inform the Assembly and a wider public of the Court's activities, and the date of publication is slightly in advance of the meeting of each Assembly. They constitute an invaluable source of information. The arrangement is kept more or less uniform from year to year; the contents deal with the structure of the Court and the Registry, the governing instruments, the jurisdiction, the judgments, orders and opinions, digests of decisions taken, publications, finances, and bibliographical lists. Series F of the Court's publications contains general indexes.

The distribution of the Court's publications is governed by Article 25 of the Instructions, and by the contracts for publishing made by the Registrar.[38]

---

[36] Series E, No. 1, pp. 7–9.

[37] League of Nations Official Journal, 1925, p. 124.

[38] On the publishing contracts concluded by the Registrar with A. W. Sijthoff's Publishing Co. of Leyden, see Series E, No. 1, p. 273. The system of publication was investigated and approved by the League of Nations Supervisory Commission in 1928. Series E, No. 4, p. 315. The publisher has agents for the sale of the Court's publications in some thirty-two countries.

CHAPTER 14

THE FINANCES OF THE COURT

§352. **Method of Meeting the Court's Expenses.** There is abundant evidence that when the plans for its establishment were being perfected in 1920, the Court was regarded as an organ of the League of Nations.[1] This partly explains the failure of its founders to envisage any independent method for meeting the Court's expenses. The expenses of the International Bureau of the Permanent Court of Arbitration are borne by the "Contracting States" in the proportion fixed for the International Bureau of the Universal Postal Union; as they are not large, no great difficulties have arisen in that system.[2] Article 31 of the 1907 Hague *projet* for a Court of Arbitral Justice was more general, providing that the expenses should be borne by the "Contracting States", to which the Administrative Council was to apply for funds. The original Covenant of the League of Nations also provided that the expenses of the Secretariat should be "borne by the Members of the League in accordance with the apportionment of the expenses of the International Bureau of the Universal Postal Union"; when the First Assembly considered the problems of the budget in 1920, it had already begun to appear that difficult questions were involved in the allocation of the expenses, to which the solution given by the Covenant was not satisfactory.[3]

Since agencies had been created for collecting and disbursing the funds of the League of Nations, it would have meant both duplication and difficulty in 1920 to have created an independent method of financing the Court; and the view that the Court was to be an organ of the League of Nations led quite naturally to the provision in Article 33 of the Statute that "the expenses of the Court shall be

---

[1] See §98, *supra.*

[2] See *supra*, §6. For a comparison between the expenses of the Court and those of the Permanent Court of Arbitration, see Series E, No. 8, pp. 329–330.

[3] These problems led to the amendment to Article 6 of the Covenant, which was proposed in 1921 and came into effect on August 13, 1924. See 1 Hudson, International Legislation, p. 20.

borne by the League of Nations, in such a manner as shall be decided by the Assembly upon the proposal of the Council." This gives the Assembly complete power over the finances of the Court, though Article 35 of the Statute confers on the Court itself the power to fix the contribution to be paid by a State which is a party to a dispute before the Court but which is not a member of the League of Nations.[4] The provisions of the Statute do not place on a party to the Protocol of December 16, 1920, any obligation to contribute to the budget of the Court, and it is only under the decisions of the Assembly that States which are Members of the League of Nations are obligated to contribute. Up to this time, the obligation to contribute has rested on all Members of the League of Nations, even though they are not parties to that Protocol. No mention is made in the Statute of States which may be parties to the Protocol of December 16, 1920, but which are not members of the League of Nations.[5] Contributions by such States are referred to in the League of Nations Financial Regulations; [6] but it would seem that the Assembly is without power to

---

[4] The new Article 35 of the Statute, annexed to the Revision Protocol of September 14, 1929, if it comes into force, will confine the Court's power to those cases in which the State is not already bearing a share of the Court's expenses.

In the case of the *S.S. Wimbledon,* no contribution was demanded from Germany, on the ground that "generally speaking, it was not the intention of the Statute that it should be possible to require a contribution from States summoned to appear before the Court under articles of the Peace Treaties giving the Court compulsory jurisdiction." Series E, No. 3, p. 197. In the case of the *German Interests in Polish Upper Silesia* in 1926, Germany was asked to pay the Court 35,000 florins. Series C, No. 11—III, p. 1293. In the *Lotus Case* in 1927, Turkey was asked to pay the Court 5,000 florins. Series C, No. 13—II, p. 459. In the *Brazilian Loans Case* in 1929, no contribution was asked from Brazil, which had been a Member of the League of Nations when the case was submitted. Series E, No. 6, p. 287.

[5] Under the new Article 4 of the Statute, annexed to the Revision Protocol of September 14, 1929, such States might participate in the elections of members of the Court on conditions to be laid down, in the absence of a special agreement, by the Assembly on the proposal of the Council; these conditions might require contributions by such States.

The Protocol of September 14, 1929, concerning the accession of the United States of America, does not expressly refer to a contribution to be made by the United States, but it provides for the acceptance of the five reservations offered by the United States, one of which stated "that the United States will pay a fair share of the expenses of the Court as determined and appropriated from time to time by the Congress of the United States." While it is not to be anticipated that this would cause any difficulty, it would place the United States in the special position of determining by itself the amount of its contribution.

[6] Article 22 of the Financial Regulations in force on January 1, 1931, provides that "States not Members of the League which have been admitted members of any organisation of the League shall, in the absence of a contrary provision, contribute towards the expenses of the organisation concerned as nearly as possible in the proportion in which they would contribute to such expenses if they were Members of the League." This may apply only where the condition was included in the invitation to participate, however. The Supervisory Commission has established the principle that funds paid to the Court by States not Members of the League of Nations "will be exclusively devoted to the expenditure of the Court." See the Supervisory Commission's report for 1933, in League of Nations Document, A. 5. 1933. X, p. 9; Series E, No. 9, p. 205.

place on them an obligation to contribute. It is to be noted, also, that States appearing before the Court, if they contribute to the Court's expenses as Members of the League of Nations or otherwise, pay no fees of any kind to the Court. An early suggestion by the Council of the League of Nations that the expenses of the Court might partly be met by fees was disapproved by the Court; [7] in 1933, however, the Court authorized the Registrar to inform the parties in future cases that a future decision might be taken by which the expenses of printing the parties' written and oral statements in Series C of the Court's publications would be charged to the parties themselves; such a decision would be regrettable.[8]

§353. **The League of Nations Budget for the Court.** The annual budget of the League of Nations is divided into parts, one of which is the budget for the Court. This is voted by the Assembly each year, for the following calendar year. Each Member of the League of Nations is obligated to contribute to this budget, whether or not it is a party to the Protocol of Signature of December 16, 1920. It has been a difficult task to allocate the number of units of the whole budget which each State is to pay, and for various reasons this number varies from year to year. In the 1933 allocation,[9] the total was 1012½ units, 105 of which were allocated to the United Kingdom of Great Britain and Northern Ireland, 79 to France and to Germany, 60 to Italy and to Japan, and only ½ of one unit was allocated to Nicaragua. Each unit for 1933 was 33,016.43 Swiss francs.

In practice, a fixed per cent (in 1933, 7.95 per cent) of each payment made by a Member of the League of Nations to the Treasurer at Geneva is deposited to the credit of the Court in a bank at The Hague. Under this system, and with the possibility of drawing on the working-capital fund,[10] the Court has never been without the funds necessary for meeting its expenses.

§354. **Provisions for Expenditures.** The only provisions in the Statute relating to expenditures to be made by or on behalf of the Court are to be found in Article 32, and they are quite incomplete. The fixing of all salaries and allowances is left to the Assembly, acting on the proposal of the Council, except that the salary of the Registrar

[7] Series E, No. 3, p. 196.   [8] Series E, No. 9, p. 168.
[9] League of Nations Official Journal, 1932, p. 1675.
[10] On several occasions, the Court has drawn on the working-capital fund, the object of which is "to meet temporarily normal requirements of regular organizations of the League which cannot be paid out of income at the time when they are due to be met." Article 33 of the Financial Regulations of the League of Nations.

is to be fixed by the Council on the proposal of the Court. Each judge is to receive an "annual indemnity," and the amount may not be reduced during a judge's term of office; a "special grant" to the President is provided for, and "a grant for the actual performance of their duties" is to be paid to the Vice-President, the judges and the deputy-judges; "grants" to *ad hoc* judges are envisaged; and travelling expenses of judges and deputy-judges are to be refunded. Pensions to all "the personnel of the Court" are to be paid in accordance with a "special regulation" to be adopted by the Assembly on the proposal of the Council.[11] Nothing is said about general administrative expenses, however; nor about the salaries of officials of the Registry. Nor is any power specifically conferred on the Court to determine what its expenses shall be. Yet the provisions and *lacunæ* in the Statute cannot be said to impair the judicial independence of the Court, which is in this respect in a position very similar to that of a national court.

§355. **Preliminary Budget Arrangements.** The first and second budgets of the League of Nations contained items to cover the expense necessary for the establishment of the Court,[12] and the third budget for 1921, adopted in 1920, included an item of 650,000 francs (later reduced to 500,000 francs) for the Court's expenses.[13] In the fourth budget for 1922, the item was for 1,500,000 francs. As from February 21, 1922, the Court's services took over from the Secretariat of the League of Nations the accounts and the administration of funds placed to its credit at The Hague.[14] In February 1922, also, by arrangement between the President of the Court and the Secretary-General of the League of Nations,[15] a "permanent imprest" system was established as a temporary expedient, under which at the end of each month the Registrar reported the expenditure of that month and the estimated expenditure for the following month; the Secretariat kept the Court in funds, with the balance not falling below 100,000 florins; and the account was operated by the joint signatures of the President and the Registrar of the Court. During the negotiations

---

[11] Under the new Article 32, annexed to the Revision Protocol of September 14, 1929, these provisions are entirely recast. One of the principal changes is that the Registrar's salary is to be fixed by the Assembly on the proposal of the Court.

[12] Records of First Assembly, Committees, II, pp. 106, 107, 118.

[13] Records of First Assembly, Plenary, p. 707. The Council had previously approved a memorandum by the Secretary-General which proposed an item of 1,500,000 francs for the Court. *Id.*, Committees, II, p. 122.

[14] Series E, No. 1, p. 279.

[15] For the exchange of letters, see League of Nations Official Journal, 1922, p. 565.

in 1922, the President of the Court proposed that the "permanent imprest" system should be replaced by a permanent arrangement, under which the Court itself should propose its budget for adoption by the Assembly, and on March 24, 1922, the Court proceeded to authorize budget estimates for 1923 to be submitted to the "authorities of the League of Nations." [16] The President's proposal was referred by the Council to the Supervisory Commission, which recommended that "the Court should, like the International Labor Office, have its own independent budget," that it should share proportionately in each contribution received by the League of Nations, and that it might be granted advances from the working capital fund of the League of Nations. These recommendations were approved by the Third Assembly, and their substance was embodied in the Financial Regulations of the League of Nations.

§356. **Financial Regulations of the League of Nations.** The financial status of the Court was placed on a definite basis by the Financial Regulations first adopted by the Assembly on September 29, 1922, and put into force on January 1, 1923.[17] While some amendments have been made to the original Regulations, the provisions relating to the Court have undergone little modification. As revised and in force on January 1, 1931,[18] the Regulations deal with the Court as one of several "autonomous organisations," the word *autonomous* signifying a separate financial administration without implying "any wider consequences." Under Article 7 of the Regulations, the financial administration of an autonomous organization is independent of that of the Secretariat, subject to the provisions of the Regulations. A "competent authority" and a "competent official" are designated for the purpose of the Regulations with respect to each autonomous organization; for the Court, the "competent authority" is the Court itself, or by delegation from the Court its President, and the "competent official" is the Registrar or his duly authorized deputy.[19] Competent officials of autonomous organizations supply data to the Secretary-General, though he seems to have no responsibility for framing the

---

[16] Series D, No. 2, pp. 233, 581.

[17] For the text of the Financial Regulations of 1922, see Records of Third Assembly, Plenary, II, p. 207. For an analysis of the Regulations as they affect the Court, see Series E, No. 1, pp. 281ff.

[18] For the text, see League of Nations Document, C. 3 (1). M. 3 (1). 1931. X (Edition brought up to date on January 1, 1933); 1 Hudson, International Legislation, p. 149.

[19] On the Registrar's activities as "competent official," see Series E, No. 8, pp. 331–336.

Court's budget; [20] provision is made in the Regulations for the submission of supplementary estimates also. A Supervisory Commission of five members appointed by the Assembly reports on the budget, which can be adopted by the Assembly only after a report by its Fourth Committee. The contributions due from Members of the League of Nations are determined, since 1924, by the Assembly. As each contribution is received, the Regulations provide (Article 26) that a share is to be distributed to the competent officials of the autonomous organizations, in the proportion of the estimates, and such organizations also share in the working-capital fund,[21] out of which advances may be made to cover current requirements. The accounts of each organization must be audited, three times annually, by an auditor who reports to the Supervisory Commission.[22] Representatives of the Court are entitled to appear before the Supervisory Commission, the Fourth Committee of the Assembly, and even the Assembly itself.[23]

§357. **Internal Financial Administration.** The Financial Regulations (Articles 39, 40) require the competent official of each organization to make rules concerning the control of liabilities and payments and to ensure economy, and these rules must be communicated to the Supervisory Commission. For the Court, these rules are embodied in the Instructions for the Registry, Articles 28–41 of which deal with financial questions. Under these rules, the Registrar frames the budget estimates and after their approval by the Court or the President, communicates them to the Secretary-General for transmission to the Supervisory Commission. The Registrar represents the Court before the Supervisory Commission when the estimates are under consideration,[24] and later before the Fourth Committee of the Assembly. Few changes have been made in the estimates submitted. Once the budget is voted by the Assembly, transfers from one

[20] In practice the Court's budget estimates are submitted to the Supervisory Commission without modification by the Secretary-General, and it seems that the Secretary-General is not thought to have power to modify them.

[21] The nature and purpose of this fund are explained in Articles 31–33 of the Financial Regulations.

[22] The Registrar's office is visited four times each year by the Deputy-Auditor of the League of Nations, and generally once each year by the Auditor. Monthly statements are also made to the Auditor by the Registrar. Series E, No. 8, p. 336.

[23] In 1922, Judge Moore represented the Court in dealing with certain questions at the Third Assembly. Beginning in 1922, the Court has been represented at Geneva each year by the Registrar or his deputy. In 1927, certain members of the Court met with certain members of the Supervisory Commission at The Hague, when the latter was considering the emoluments of deputy-judges. Series E, No. 3, p. 195.

[24] He may also represent the Court before the Supervisory Commission with respect to other matters. Series E, No. 8, p. 334 note.

item to another may be effected by the Court,[25] subject to limitations set out in Article 29 of the Regulations and Article 36 of the Instructions.[26] Only the Registrar may incur liabilities in the name of the Court; when he deems it necessary, he obtains the previous authorization of the Court or the President. Statements of account are prepared by the Registrar, annually, and after submission to the Court (or the President if the Court is not sitting), they are forwarded to the Supervisory Commission. Records are kept of all appropriations, liabilities, and capital requisitions. Though the accounts are kept in Dutch florins, the Court's budget is voted in gold francs.

§358. **The Budgets of the Court.** The annual budgets of the Court vary with the activities of the Court, and with the decisions by the Council and Assembly as to the remuneration of its members and its personnel. The budget estimates of the Court prepared by the Registrar are submitted to the Court if it is in session, otherwise to the President, during the latter part of March.[27] The following table shows the financial provision for the Court year by year (in florins unless otherwise noted): [28]

	Appropriated	*Expended*
1920		124,499.84 (francs)
1921	500,000.00 (francs)	339,603.43 (francs)
1922	1,500,000.00 (francs)	1,276,228.75 (francs)
1923	935,625.70	745,990.54 [a]
1924	921,739.83	580,127.35
1925	915,796.76	847,950.48
1926	915,838.32	791,789.44
1927	1,029,177.83	859,083.55
1928	1,042,296.56	960,812.76
1929	1,082,839.37	819,457.14
1930	1,088,804.81	799,820.69
1931	1,302,288.50 [b]	1,159,769.86
1932	1,278,781.00	1,214,854.32
1933	1,277,076.25	2,332,568.00 (francs)
1934	2,538,827.00 (francs)	

[a] In 1923, actual receipts were below expenditures, necessitating advances by the Secretariat of the League of Nations from the working-capital fund.

[b] The original estimates submitted on behalf of the Court for 1931, were increased, owing to the decisions taken by the Assembly.

[25] Limited transfers of sub-items of the same item may be made by the Registrar.

[26] In 1932, certain transfers by the Registrar were authorized by the Assembly, if the Revision Protocol of September 14, 1929, should come into force. Records of Thirteenth Assembly, Fourth Committee, p. 246.

[27] On the preparation of the Court's budget estimates, see Series E, No. 8, pp. 332ff.

[28] These figures are taken from Series E and from the records of the Assembly of the League of Nations. The budgets are now published in the League of Nations Official Journal, where the amounts of Court appropriations are also given in francs. A rough calculation makes the florin equivalent to two gold francs; in 1924, the equivalent was fixed at 2.083 gold francs.

The current budget consists of two sections, one of which deals with ordinary expenditures, the other of which deals with capital account.[29]

§359. Salaries of Members of the Court. The subject of the salaries of members of the Court was first considered by the Council in the report of M. Léon Bourgeois of October 27, 1920, when certain principles were laid down.[30] On December 10, 1920, the Council requested the Third Committee of the First Assembly to make proposals to the Assembly on behalf of the Council, as it was felt to be necessary that some decision should be arrived at before an election of the judges.[31] The first schedule proposed was that contained in a memorandum of the Secretariat in December, 1920; [32] suggestions made by the British delegation and by M. Hagerup on behalf of certain members of the Third Committee varied widely.[33] The ninth and tenth meetings of the Third Committee were devoted to considering the subject,[34] and the following scale was reported to and adopted by the First Assembly on December 18, 1920: [35]

		Dutch florins	
President:			
Annual salary		15,000	
Special allowance		45,000	
Total			60,000
Vice-President:			
Annual salary		15,000	
Duty-allowance (200 × 150) (maximum)		30,000	
Total			45,000
Ordinary Judges:			
Annual salary		15,000	
Duty-allowance (200 × 100) (maximum)		20,000	
Total			35,000
Deputy-Judges: [36]			
Duty-allowance (200 × 150) (maximum)		30,000	

Duty allowances are payable from the day of departure until the return of the beneficiary.

[29] For the 1934 budget in detail, see League of Nations Official Journal, 1933, pp. 1250ff.   [30] Minutes of the Council, 10th session, pp. 171–173.
[31] Id., 11th session, pp. 27, 136.
[32] Records of First Assembly, Committees, I, p. 580.
[33] Id., pp. 583–584.   [34] Id., pp. 319–326.
[35] Records of First Assembly, Plenary, p. 766.
[36] In the earlier years of the Court, the deputy-judges were called upon so frequently that "they received total emoluments amounting to a sum hardly less than that received by regular judges." Series E, No. 3, p. 194.

An additional allowance of 50 florins per day is assigned for each day of actual presence at The Hague to the Vice-President and to the ordinary and deputy-judges.

Allowances and salaries are free of all tax.

No changes were made in this scale during the first nine-year period. In 1929, however, the Committee of Jurists charged with the study of amendments to the Statute was of the opinion that a revision of the scale would be in line with the proposals for a more permanent functioning of the Court and with the new requirements as to judges' engaging in no other occupations; it proposed a revised text of Article 32 of the Statute, under which judges would receive an annual salary supplemented by a *per diem* indemnity, and a draft resolution fixing the following scale for the emoluments of members of the Court:

	Dutch florins
President:	
Annual salary	45,000
Special indemnity	15,000
Vice-President:	
Annual salary	45,000
Allowance for each day on duty (100 × 100)	10,000 (maximum)
Members:	
Annual salary	45,000
Judges referred to in Article 31 of the Statute:	
Indemnity for each day on duty	100
Allowance for each day of attendance	50

This resolution was adopted by the Tenth Assembly, on September 14, 1929, "subject to the entry into force of the amendments proposed in the Court's Statute," the new scale to become effective on January 1, 1931. At the same time and subject to the same condition, the Assembly adopted a resolution concerning the repayment of judges' travelling expenses.[37]

When the amendments to the Statute failed to enter into force in 1930, the Council and Assembly were confronted with a situation which seemed to call for some intermediate solution. On September 25, 1930, on the proposal of the Council, the Assembly adopted a new scale of salaries and allowances as from January 1, 1931, to prevail

[37] Records of Tenth Assembly, Plenary, pp. 114, 432.

in the interim until the Assembly's resolution of September 14, 1929 should become applicable, as follows:

	Dutch florins
President:	
Annual salary	35,000
Special allowance	25,000
Vice-President:	
Annual salary	35,000
Allowance of 50 florins for each day of duty as a judge up to a maximum of	10,000
Allowance of 50 florins for each day on which he acts as President up to a maximum of	10,000
Judges:	
Annual salary	35,000
Allowance of 50 florins for each day of duty up to a maximum of	10,000
Deputy and National Judges: [38]	
Allowance of 150 florins for each day of duty up to a maximum of	30,000

Rules regarding the payment of allowances and indemnities to members of the Court, drawn up by the Registry on the instructions of the President, were published in 1930.[39] These rules deal with subsistence allowances, duty allowances, travelling expenses, and missions away from the seat of the Court; they codify the provisions in force and the decisions and practice of the competent financial authorities.

The Assembly resolutions of December 18, 1920, and September 25, 1930, provide that salaries and allowances paid to members of the Court shall be free of all taxes; it was recognized, however, that "the decisions of the Assembly may be inoperative as against the fiscal laws applied in the different countries," and members of the Court are to be reimbursed by the League of Nations for any taxes which they are obliged to pay on their salaries.[40] The new text of Article 32 of the Statute, annexed to the Revision Protocol of September 14, 1929, would make the salaries, indemnities and allowances of judges and the Registrar free of all taxes, *vis-à-vis* States which have accepted the Statute.

[38] Judges who continue to act in a case already begun, even after the expiration of their terms of office, under Article 13 of the Statute, are assimilated for purposes of remuneration to deputy and *ad hoc* judges. Series E, No. 8, p. 247.

[39] Series E, No. 6, p. 343. The rules were approved in 1928.

[40] Records of First Assembly, Plenary, pp. 748, 766; Records of Eleventh Assembly, Plenary, p. 132. Reimbursement does not apply to taxes on pensions.

§360. **Remuneration of Judges ad hoc and Assessors.** By a resolution of September 23, 1922, the Assembly of the League of Nations [41] established the allowances to be paid to judges *ad hoc* selected under Article 31 of the Statute, as follows:

Daily duty allowance	Florins	150
Daily subsistence allowance	"	50

The same resolution of the Assembly fixed a daily subsistence allowance to be paid to assessors serving under Articles 26 and 27 of the Statute, as follows:

Daily subsistence allowance:

1. Persons habitually residing at The Hague	Florins	25
2. Other persons	"	50

Travelling expenses are refunded both to judges *ad hoc* and to assessors. However, if assessors sit at the request of the parties, the Assembly's resolutions provide that their allowances and travelling expenses must be paid by the parties in accordance with rules to be made by the Court; and such rules were adopted by the Court on January 20, 1923.[42]

§361. **Expenses of Witnesses and Experts.** The Court's budget carries an item each year for the expenses of witnesses and experts. Under Article 52 of the Rules, witnesses who appear at the instance of the Court are to receive indemnities out of the funds of the Court; the expenses of other witnesses are met by the parties which produce them. When a committee of experts was created in the *Chorzów Factory Case* in 1928, the President fixed the fees to be paid to the experts in accordance with their own proposal; 20,000 florins were to be paid to each expert, and an additional 2,000 florins were to be paid to the chairman of the Committee,[43] in addition to travelling expenses; but in view of the termination of the inquiry these sums were reduced.[44] To meet these expenses, the parties made deposits in advance.[45]

§362. **Pensions of Members of the Court.** Article 32 of the Statute provides for a special regulation as to retiring pensions for "the personnel of the Court," to be adopted by the Assembly on the proposal of the Council. The question was raised in the Council

[41] For the proposal of the Council, see League of Nations Official Journal, 1922, p. 786.   [42] Series E, No. 1, p. 291.
[43] Series C, No. 16—II, pp. 23, 40.   [44] *Id.*, p. 57.
[45] See the Court's order of September 13, 1928. Series A, No. 17, p. 99.

in 1923, and in 1924 it decided to submit to the Assembly proposals made by the Supervisory Commission.[46] On September 30, 1924, the Assembly adopted regulations [47] under which the judges were normally entitled to pensions upon retirement after five years of service, at the age of 65 years; power was given to the Court to waive these two conditions in exceptional cases, however. The maximum retiring pension was fixed at 15,000 florins, the amount being equivalent to one-thirtieth of the "salary in respect of each period of twelve months passed in the service of the Court." The pension is payable monthly during the lifetime of the beneficiary. Limited power was reserved by the Assembly to amend the regulations, and on September 25, 1930, on the proposal of the Council, the Assembly adopted revised regulations to apply to personnel of the Court holding office on January 1, 1931, or thereafter.[48] In the revised regulations, a provision was added as to judges who resign.[49] The regulations do not provide for pensions to widows and children, though that subject was considered in the Tenth Assembly.[50] Nor is it provided that pensions paid shall be free from taxation.[51]

§363. Salary of the Registrar. The power to determine the salary of the Registrar rests with the Council, acting on the proposal of the Court; the provision in Article 32 of the Statute is in this respect out of line with the general policy which leaves to the Assembly the fixing of the salaries to be paid out of funds of the League of Nations.[52] On February 3, 1922, the Court proposed a salary of 12,000 florins a year, and an allowance of 15,000 florins a year.[53] On July 17, 1922, the Council, after a report by the Supervisory Commission, fixed the Registrar's salary at 22,000 florins a year for a period of five years, at the end of which period the amount was to be reconsidered.[54] On

---

[46] League of Nations Official Journal, 1924, pp. 1284, 1383ff.

[47] Series D, No. 1, p. 30; Records of Fifth Assembly, Plenary, pp. 190–1.

[48] Records of Eleventh Assembly, Plenary, p. 133. See also the regulations of September 14, 1929, in Records of Tenth Assembly, Plenary, p. 431.

[49] When he resigned in 1928, Judge Moore waived his right to a pension. Series E, No. 4, p. 26.

[50] In 1932, the Assembly authorized a payment of the equivalent of three months' salary to the widow or children (under 18 years of age) of a deceased judge. League of Nations Official Journal, 1932, p. 1596.

[51] Series E, No. 7, p. 103.

[52] This provision has been criticised in the Assembly, where the view seems to have been taken that "it does not invalidate the sovereign right of the Assembly on budgetary measures." Series E, No. 8, p. 44. The new text of Article 32 of the Statute, annexed to the Revision Protocol of September 14, 1929, would confer this power on the Assembly, which would act only on the proposal of the Court.

[53] Series D, No. 2, p. 6.

[54] League of Nations Official Journal, 1922, p. 787.

August 31, 1922, at the insistence of the Court, the Council decided that the salary should rise by successive annual increments of 1250 florins to the sum of 27,000 florins.[55] In 1927, when a general reduction in salaries of permanent officials was under consideration owing to an ascertained decrease in the cost of living, the Registrar offered to accept a reduction of his salary.[56] In 1929, the Court made a proposal with reference to the Registrar's salary for the seven-year period beginning in 1930, viz., that it be increased by four annual increments to 32,000 florins.[57] In 1930, the whole subject of salaries payable by the League of Nations was re-examined by a committee of thirteen set up by the Assembly, and this committee recommended that the salary of the Registrar should be assimilated to the salary of an under-Secretary-General, i.e., that it be from 55,000 to 75,000 francs, with a possible entertainment allowance, if requested by the Court, of 12,500 francs.[58] In 1931, a new committee of thirteen recommended the adoption of the Court's proposal of 1929. On May 21, 1931, the Council fixed the Registrar's salary on the scale of 27,000 florins, with four increments to 32,000 florins, and recommended to the Assembly that this new scale be operative as from January 1, 1930.[59]

The Registrar benefits as one of the "personnel of the Court" from the regulations as to pensions adopted by the Assembly on September 30, 1924, and September 25, 1930. Subject to certain conditions, his pension is payable only on retirement after seven years' service and it begins at the age of 65; it is equivalent to one-fortieth of the salary received for each twelve months of service, with a maximum of 10,000 florins.[60]

§364. **Salaries of Officials of the Registry.** The salary of the Deputy-Registrar was originally fixed by the Court at 14,000–17,000 florins. Provisions for the salaries and allowances of the officials of the Registry are included in the Court's Staff Regulations.[61] The higher salaries are subject to increases to certain maximums, and were formerly subject to divisions into a fixed part and a part which

---

[55] League of Nations Official Journal, 1922, p. 1162. In Series E, No. 1, p. 292, it is stated that the allowance of the Registrar was 10,000 florins, and the salary 12,000 increasing to 17,000 florins.   [56] Series E, No. 4, p. 329.

[57] Series E, No. 7, p. 73.   [58] Id., p. 72; Series E, No. 9, p. 199 note.

[59] The Registrar renounced certain benefits of the increase for 1932. Series E, No. 8, p. 45.

[60] Records of Eleventh Assembly, Plenary, p. 133.

[61] Series E, No. 1, p. 294; No. 4, p. 228; No. 5, p. 76. See infra, p. 681.

varies with the cost of living.[62] The salaries paid range from 12,000–15,000 to 2,000–3,500 florins. In recent contracts, a provision is included that the salary of an official may be modified by a decision of the Assembly.[63]

Provision is made for the payment by the Court of one-half the premium on sickness insurance policies. Officials of the Registry (not including the Registrar) were required to participate in the Provident Fund established by the League of Nations in 1923; and the contribution of each official, deducted from his salary, was matched by a contribution paid by the Court. In 1930, the committee of thirteen proposed a pension scheme for officials of the Registry, to replace the compulsory Provident Fund,[64] providing for old age pensions, invalidity pensions, and pensions for the surviving consort and orphans; on October 3, 1930, the Assembly adopted this proposal as embodied in a series of Staff Pensions Regulations which came into force on January 1, 1931. A representative of the Registrar may sit with the administrative board which administers the pension fund. The Staff Pensions Regulations were modified in 1931.

In 1927, the Assembly of the League of Nations established an Administrative Tribunal for dealing with complaints by officials who had no other means of resorting to judicial procedure for enforcing their contracts. At the desire of the Court, this Tribunal might be opened to officials of the Registry; [65] under the Staff Pensions Regulations of 1931 the Tribunal has jurisdiction to deal with disputes concerning pensions to which officials of the Registry are parties.[66]

§365. **Premises Occupied by the Court.** Each year the budget of the Court includes an item for meeting the expenses of the premises occupied by the Court, and the topic therefore calls for consideration in connection with the Court's finances. The existence of the Peace Palace at The Hague was one of the factors which led to the selection of The Hague as the seat of the Court.[67] That Palace

---

[62] The variable part of these salaries was 20 per cent; it could be modified on a 10 per cent variation in cost of living, by a salaries adjustment committee. A reduction was made in 1928. The salaries were stabilized as from January 1, 1929.

[63] Series E, No. 8, p. 45. In the absence of such a clause, the Assembly does not have power to reduce the salaries of officials of the Registry. See the report of a committee of jurists, in Records of Thirteenth Assembly, Fourth Committee, p. 206.

[64] Series E, No. 6, p. 46.

[65] Series E, No. 4, p. 53; No. 8, p. 47. The Statute of the Tribunal gives it no jurisdiction with respect to officials of the Registry, but the Court's annual reports refer to this possibility. For the text of the Statute and rules of the Tribunal, see 1 Hudson, International Legislation, pp. 212, 217.   [66] Series E, No. 9, p. 34.

[67] It is referred to in the report of the 1920 Committee of Jurists, Minutes, p. 718.

was a gift by Mr. Andrew Carnegie to the Carnegie Foundation, a corporation organized under the laws of the Netherlands. Negotiations were begun in 1921, between the Secretary-General of the League of Nations and the President of the Board of Directors of the Carnegie Foundation, with a view to reaching an arrangement concerning the Court's occupancy of the Peace Palace. Declarations and letters were exchanged by the two officials, November 15 and November 29, 1921,[68] fixing the details of the arrangement for 1922. They provided for the Court's exclusive use of certain parts of the Peace Palace and the non-exclusive use of other parts, for which the League of Nations was to pay an annual sum of 50,000 florins. The arrangement was later extended for 1923. A permanent arrangement, negotiated by the Registrar who acted on behalf of the Secretary-General, and a representative of the Foundation, was approved by the Secretary-General and the President of the Board of Directors and became effective from March 8, 1924.[69] Like the earlier arrangement, it envisaged a possibility that the Court might be dissolved or transferred from the Peace Palace. The annual contribution by the League of Nations was reduced to 40,000 florins. The space available to the Court under this arrangement was grossly inadequate, as it did not even admit of a separate office for each of the judges; and in 1927 a supplementary arrangement was negotiated to meet the needs of the Court more adequately.[70] Additional space was to be made available by a remodelling of parts of the Peace Palace, for the purpose of which the Netherlands' Government advanced to the Foundation 240,000 florins as a loan without interest. To enable the Foundation to repay this loan, it was agreed that the League of Nations should pay the Foundation the additional sum of 10,000 florins, each year from 1929 to 1952. This remodelling was completed in 1929.[71] The available space again proved to be inadequate when in 1930 the number of the judges was increased from eleven to fifteen, and in 1929 negotiations were opened by the Secretary-General with a view to meeting the Court's new needs. A plan submitted by the Foundation in 1931 was not approved by the Supervisory Commission; [72] after prolonged negotiations a modified plan was approved by the Supervisory Commission, the Fourth Committee of the Assembly and

---

[68] Series E, No. 1, pp. 109, 110. Some differences arose in the interpretation of this arrangement. *Id.*, p. 112.
[69] Series E, No. 1, pp. 112–119.   [70] Series E, No. 4, pp. 63–67.
[71] Series E, No. 5, pp. 78–80.   [72] Series E, No. 7, p. 83.

the Assembly, and put into effect on December 1, 1932, by a rider to the arrangement of 1924.[73] Under this plan, the Court is to have new space available, necessitating the removal of the Academy of International Law to a building to be constructed in the grounds of the Peace Palace. For this purpose, the Netherlands Government advanced 273,400 florins as a loan without interest, and this sum is to be repaid by the League of Nations to the Carnegie Foundation, in annual instalments of 10,000 florins payable until 1960. The budget of the Court for 1933 includes an item of 60,000 florins for payment by the League of Nations to the Carnegie Foundation.[74] The cost of the premises occupied by the Court is an item in the independent budget of the Court, but the responsibility for the arrangements with the Carnegie Foundation rests with the Secretary-General of the League of Nations. In this respect, the Court has not assumed the independence which it enjoys in connection with other parts of its budget; [75] however, the negotiations on behalf of the Secretary-General are frequently conducted by the Registrar of the Court.

[73] Series E, No. 9, pp. 48ff.   [74] League of Nations Official Journal, 1932, p. 1669.
[75] Chattels used by the Court, such as furniture and office equipment, seem to be the property of the League of Nations. The question has been mooted whether the Court has a juridical personality, enabling it to hold, lease and transfer property; but it seems quite unimportant for all practical purposes.

CHAPTER 15

DIPLOMATIC PRIVILEGES AND IMMUNITIES

§366. **Provisions of the Statute.** Article 19 of the Statute of the Court follows Articles 24 (1889), 46 (1907) of the Hague Conventions for Pacific Settlement in providing that "the members of the Court, when engaged on the business of the Court, shall enjoy diplomatic privileges and immunities." The scope of this text is somewhat broader than that in the Hague Conventions, however, for it is not restricted in its application to the period of absence of the members from their own countries. While it is possible to find that limitation in the construction given to the text when it was adopted,[1] it is essential to the independence of the Court that its members should enjoy some privileges and immunities even within the territory of the State of which they are nationals. It is to be noted that paragraph 4 of Article 7 of the Covenant is similarly broad in scope; it provides that "representatives of the Members of the League and officials of the League when engaged on the business of the League shall enjoy diplomatic privileges and immunities."

The question arises as to the extent to which this paragraph of Article 7 of the Covenant may be applicable to the personnel of the Court. Members of the Court are clearly not "representatives of the Members of the League," but conceivably they might be included under "officials of the League" as that term is used in the Covenant; in view of the provisions of Article 19 of the Statute, this question could not arise for a Member of the League which is a party to the Protocol of Signature of December 16, 1920, but it may arise for Members of the League which are not parties to that protocol.

The text of Article 19 does not apply to the Registrar nor to officials of the Registry; in practice the tendency is to apply Article 19 to the Registrar and to leave the officials of the Registry to benefit by

---

[1] The subcommittee of the Third Committee of the First Assembly decided that "the question of the situation of the judges in their own country should not be prejudiced" by the text adopted. Records of First Assembly, Committees, I, p. 358.

the provision in Article 7 of the Covenant.[2] Nor does Article 19 apply to agents and counsel representing States before the Court,[3] or to witnesses and experts who may be called to appear.

§367. **Rank of Members of the Court.** In 1922, the Court decided to send to the Council of the League of Nations a memorandum on the rank and title of the judges,[4] in which the question of rank was said to be "closely bound up with the question of the dignity of the Court"; the Court itself preferred "to avoid fixing any rank rather than to fix a rank which might not be consonant" with its dignity. Two alternative solutions were suggested to the Council: (1) that the judges of the Court should have the rank of national judges in the various countries; (2) that their rank should be determined on analogy to that of officials of the diplomatic service. The second solution was preferred, and it was suggested to the Council that the judges might rank after ambassadors and might take precedence over ministers plenipotentiary. It was recognized, however, that a national as opposed to an international rank might be given, and that each country might give to its nationals among the members of the Court a fixed national rank, such as that of minister plenipotentiary or ambassador. The Council was not disposed to view the matter very seriously; in its reply to the President of the Court,[5] it pointed out that no general solution of such questions had been attempted for officials of the League, but that questions of precedence had been settled only "in so far as was necessary in each particular case." The Council therefore suggested that the Court follow a similar course; and that as the matter had arisen only at The Hague, questions of protocol should be settled with the Netherlands Government.

§368. **Negotiations with the Netherlands Government.** With the seat of the Court established at The Hague, numerous questions have arisen as to the manner in which Article 19 of the Statute as to the members of the Court, and Article 7 of the Covenant as to the officials of the Registry, should be applied by the Netherlands

---

[2] Series E, No. 1, p. 103; No. 3, p. 178; No. 4, p. 58.

[3] It would seem to follow from the Netherlands Government's consent to the establishment of the seat of the Court at The Hague that the Netherlands is bound to permit agents and counsel to have access to the Court, even though they represent a Government which the Netherlands may not have recognized or with which it might be at war.

[4] Series D, No. 2, pp. 48–49, 332–33.

[5] League of Nations Official Journal, 1922, pp. 521, 568.

Government. Some concessions were made by the Netherlands Government in the course of the earlier years, relating chiefly to tax exemptions,[6] but the negotiation of a formal agreement was postponed until 1927. In the interim, the situation at The Hague seems to have caused some embarrassment to members of the Court, as well as to others concerned. On April 6, 1927, a memorandum was addressed to the Netherlands Minister of Foreign Affairs by the President of the Court, emphasizing the necessity of a definite *protocole*, particularly as to the status of the members of the Court.[7] The reply of the Minister of Foreign Affairs, of November 25, 1927,[8] was deemed by the Court to be unsatisfactory, as it tended "to treat the Court as if it were a Netherlands institution." On December 5, 1927, the Court resolved to request the League of Nations "to regulate the matter from an international point of view," the members of the Court maintaining meanwhile "an absolute reserve with regard to any invitations addressed to them which might in any way influence the ultimate solution of the question."[9] On December 13, 1927, the Registrar addressed a letter to the Secretary-General of the League of Nations, requesting that "the question of the external status of members of the Court" be placed before the Council, and the letter was accompanied by an elaborate memorandum on the subject.[10] On March 9, 1928, a consideration of the matter was postponed by the Council, its *rapporteur* having arranged for a resumption of negotiations by the President of the Court and the Netherlands Minister of Foreign Affairs.[11] The renewed negotiations, begun on March 28, 1928, resulted in a formal exchange of notes on May 22, 1928, recording an agreement "on some of the points at issue" in the form of four "general principles", supplemented by "rules of application."[12] This agreement was at once communicated to the Secretary-General of the League of Nations, and on June 5, 1928, the Council took formal note of it.[13]

§369. The "General Principles" of May 22, 1928. While the general principles agreed upon by the President of the Court and the Netherlands Minister of Foreign Affairs are more liberal than

---

[6] Series E, No. 4, p. 59 note. Salaries of members of the Court are exempt from taxation under the Assembly resolution of December 18, 1920, and under the later resolutions.   [7] League of Nations Official Journal, 1928, p. 981.
[8] *Id.*, p. 982.   [9] League of Nations Official Journal, 1928, p. 980.
[10] *Id.*, pp. 980, 982.   [11] *Id.*, p. 431.
[12] *Id.*, pp. 985–987. See also Series E, No. 4, pp. 57–61.
[13] League of Nations Official Journal, 1928, p. 886.

the "established custom" set out in the latter's letter of November 25, 1927, they can hardly be said to be altogether satisfactory from the point of view of the Court as an international institution. The diplomatic privileges and immunities of members of the Court and of the Registrar are assimilated to those of heads of missions accredited to the Queen of the Netherlands; the Court is given a position analogous to that of the Diplomatic Corps, but the latter takes precedence at official ceremonies to which both are invited; a member of the Court who is not of Netherlands nationality enjoys precedence in relation to the Netherlands authorities as if he were a minister plenipotentiary accredited to the Queen, the Registrar's position in this respect being the same as that of the Secretary-General of the Permanent Court of Arbitration.[14] In view of the provision in Article 7 of the Covenant, also, higher officials of the Court are to enjoy "the same position as regards diplomatic privileges and immunities as diplomatic officials attached to legations at The Hague."

§370. **Rules of Application.** The rules or regulations agreed upon for the application of the four general principles do not supersede the concessions which had been granted by the Netherlands Government prior to 1927.[15] They deal separately with the members of the Court and the Registrar, and with the Deputy-Registrar and the officials of the Court. Members and the Registrar, not of Netherlands nationality, are to enjoy in Netherlands territory the privileges and immunities granted in general to heads of diplomatic missions; a wife and unmarried children share the position of the head of the family if they reside with him and have no profession; the "private establishment," which includes teachers, private secretaries and servants, shares the position of that of a head of a diplomatic mission. A member of the Court or a Registrar of Netherlands nationality enjoys immunity from the jurisdiction of local courts with respect to official acts, and his salary is exempt from direct taxation. As to the Deputy-Registrar and other officials of the Court, a distinction is drawn between "higher officials" and others, and for this purpose the higher officials comprise "at the present time" the Deputy-Registrar and the editing secretaries. The higher officials, not of Netherlands

---

[14] The latter's position is described in the exchange of notes as "that of an international official." Series E, No. 4, pp. 62–3. The Secretary-General of the Permanent Court of Arbitration has the rank of a Minister Resident of the Netherlands Government. See § 5, *supra*.

[15] These concessions are contained in thirteen letters, dated from 1922 to 1927, listed in Series E, No. 4, p. 59 note.

nationality, are accorded the privileges and immunities generally granted to diplomatic officials attached to legations; in determining precedence, the Deputy-Registrar ranks as a counsellor of legation and an editing secretary as a secretary of legation. Higher officials of Netherlands nationality enjoy immunity from jurisdiction of local courts with respect to official acts, and their salaries are exempt from direct taxation. With the approval of the President, the Registrar may waive the jurisdictional immunity of an official accused of a violation of law. The Netherlands authorities are to make no objection to the issuance by the competent authorities of the Court of identity cards to officials of the Court.[16] Where any question as to external status of Court officials is in doubt, it is to be decided with regard to the provisions made for corresponding officials of the League of Nations at Geneva.[17]

§371. **Provisions by Other Governments.** The agreement of May 22, 1928, between the President of the Court and the Netherlands Minister of Foreign Affairs, constitutes a *modus vivendi* for the application of Article 19 of the Statute and Article 7 of the Covenant (in part) by the Netherlands Government. It does not purport to lay down any general interpretation of Article 19, nor does the action taken by the Council of the League of Nations on June 5, 1928, constitute a basis for a more general application of the agreement. Most of the questions arising in connection with the application of Article 19 will probably concern action of the Netherlands Government; yet questions may arise with reference to action taken by other Governments. Though the seat of the Court is fixed at The Hague, it might become necessary for the Court to meet at some other place, and this is not precluded by the Statute. Under Article 28 of the Statute, special chambers of the Court may sit elsewhere than at The Hague; under Article 50, the Court may direct an enquiry to be undertaken elsewhere, and members of the Court may be charged with conducting it; under Article 44, the Court may un-

---

[16] This question had been the subject of some prior negotiations. League of Nations Official Journal, 1928, p. 984.

[17] In 1926, a *modus vivendi* was concluded by the Secretary-General of the League of Nations and the Swiss Federal Council. League of Nations Official Journal, 1926, pp. 1407, 1422.

On the general subject, see S. Basdevant, *Les Fonctionnaires Internationaux* (1931); S. Kauffmann, *Die Immunität der Nicht-Diplomaten* (1932); L. Preuss, "Diplomatic Privileges and Immunities of Agents Invested with Functions of an International Interest," 25 American Journal of International Law (1931), p. 694; J. Secretan, *Les Immunités Diplomatiques* (1928); C. van Vollenhoven, "Diplomatic Prerogatives of Non-Diplomats," 19 American Journal of International Law (1925), p. 469.

dertake "to procure evidence on the spot." Moreover, members of the Court may encounter difficulties with their own Governments, or with Governments whose territories they must traverse to reach The Hague. In any of these cases, the scope of application of Article 19 by States other than the Netherlands may become important to the functioning of the Court. Yet no attempt has been made to make precise the obligations of a State under Article 19 of the Statute or to secure a uniform application of its provisions, and the Council of the League of Nations has not seemed to be disposed to act except as problems have actually arisen. This seems to leave to each State the interpretation to be given to Article 19.[18] As few questions have arisen, there has been no general tendency for States to formalize their attitudes,[19] and the practice is not yet sufficient for a final solution of the problem to be foreseen.

§372. **Attitude of Rumania.** On August 28, 1929, the Rumanian Minister of Foreign Affairs addressed a letter to the President of the Court, stating that Rumania accepted the interpretation of Article 19 as embodied in the agreement concluded between the Court and the Netherlands Government in 1928, relating to the privileges and immunities of the members of the Court and the Registrar.[20] It was further stated that members of the Court not of Rumanian nationality, "whether in Rumania or abroad," will rank for purposes of precedence in relation to Rumanian authorities as ministers plenipotentiary accredited to the King of Rumania; that members of the Court of Rumanian nationality will rank as Rumanian ministers plenipotentiary; and that under Article 19 of the Statute the members of the Court would enjoy the diplomatic privileges and immunities generally accorded to heads of missions accredited to the King of Rumania. The text of the letter was also communicated to the Secretary-General of the League of Nations;

---

[18] Some States make provisions in their laws for certain privileges and immunities to be given to international officials. Hungary accords certain privileges, for example, to members of international courts. See Feller and Hudson, *Diplomatic and Consular Laws and Regulations* (1933), I, p. 677. Poland accords customs exemptions to representatives of international institutions, among which the Court is mentioned explicitly. *Id.*, II, p. 1018.

[19] A questionnaire circulated by the Committee of Experts for the Progressive Codification of International Law in 1926 dealt with the privileges and immunities of the "judges and staff" of the Court. In reply, the German Government expressed the opinion that the subject should be covered in a separate agreement; the Swiss Government stated that the problem as to the Court was the same as that as to the League of Nations. See League of Nations Document, C. 196. M. 70. 1927, pp. 77, 85, 135, 249.   [20] Series E, No. 6, p. 50.

and it was stated in a covering letter that without desiring to pre-judge the question so far as other Governments were concerned, the Rumanian Government was of the opinion that "the members of the Court should have the same status as diplomatic representatives of the highest category received or accredited." [21] This action of the Rumanian Government may have been intended to raise the question of a uniform application of Article 19, but the communication was not considered by the Council of the League of Nations, and it has led to no formulation of a common attitude by the parties to the Protocol of Signature of December 16, 1920.

§373. **Obligations of States under Article 19.** In providing that members of the Court shall enjoy diplomatic privileges and immunities, Article 19 of the Statute imposes on each party to the Protocol of Signature of December 16, 1920, certain obligations which are clear in purpose though indefinite in content. Whether or not the privileges and immunities to be accorded are identical with those given to diplo-mats, each party to the Protocol of Signature may be taken to have agreed that it will accord to any member of the Court, whether or not its national, such privileges and immunities as will enable him to per-form his duties on the Court effectively. These privileges and im-munities must include, at the least, a freedom to travel to and from the seat of the Court, and a freedom to communicate with the Court or its members. If the analogy to diplomats is not to be the guide, then the general principle must be that no State should deny to mem-bers of the Court those facilities which are essential to the Court's performance of its functions.[22] In this respect Article 19 is re-enforced by the principle of good faith which must underlie any appli-cation of the provisions of the Statute, and which is essential to the Court's **functioning**.

Quite apart from the obligations existing, however, it is desirable that privileges and immunities be accorded to members of the Court which will support the Court's dignity and prestige as an international institution. On the whole, it seems that the Court has not been sufficiently exigent in this matter. The judges as a body

---

[21] League of Nations Official Journal, 1929, p. 1863.

[22] An Italian law of June 16, 1927, requires Italian nationals who enter the service of another Government or of a public international institution to obtain the authoriza-tion of the Ministry of Foreign Affairs or of a competent diplomatic authority, and to abandon such service upon the order of the Government. *Raccolta delle Leggi d'Italia*, 1927, Vol. VI, p. 5932. The possible application of such a law to judges of the Court might raise serious difficulties. See also Article 274 of the Italian Penal Code, 1930.

ought not to be assimilated to a diplomatic corps, and a proper respect for the Court as an institution demands that its members be given precedence as high international officials over the representatives of any single State.[23] New standards are needed for determining the status of high international officials, and they should be developed without a slavish regard for the past.

[23] On this point, the suggestion has been made by M. Raoul Genet that Article 19 of the Statute should be revised. Genet, *"Un Problème de Préséances,"* 14 *Revue de Droit International et de Législation Comparée* (1933), p. 254.

CHAPTER 16

PROBLEMS OF THE COURT'S ORGANIZATION

§374. **Sessions of the Court.** After the election of the members of the Court in September 1921, initiative was taken by the Secretary-General of the League of Nations to inform them that their salaries would be paid as from January 1, 1922,[1] and to summon them to meet at The Hague on January 30, 1922. Nine of the eleven judges and two of the four deputy-judges responded to the summons.[2] A representative of the Secretary-General of the League of Nations was also present at the earlier meetings of the session; and a member of the Secretariat of the League of Nations, M. Å. Hammarskjöld, served as Acting Secretary of the Court on the designation of the Secretary-General. Judge Loder was asked to take the chair, pending the election of a President. Adopting a suggestion of the Secretary-General of the League of Nations, the Court held a public inaugural meeting on February 15, 1922. The preliminary session, which continued until March 24, 1922, was entirely devoted to administrative questions and to the preparation of the Rules. It was only when the Rules were adopted on March 24, 1922, that the Court may be said to have been prepared to exercise its jurisdiction.

Article 23 of the Statute requires a session of the Court to be held every year; the date of June 15, which is prescribed "unless otherwise provided by Rules of Court," was changed in the 1931 Rules to February 1. The annual session has been held each year, whether or not any case was ready for hearing;[3] and the Court has shown it-

---

[1] Series E, No. 1, p. 12. Article 1 of the Rules of Court provides that the term of office of judges and deputy-judges shall commence on January 1 of the year following their election; the Statute is strangely silent on this point. When a person is elected to fill a vacancy, his term is taken to begin on the first day of the month following his election.

[2] Only two deputy-judges were summoned by the Secretary-General, to fill the places of judges who were unable to be present. The Court later invited the other two deputy-judges to attend, and one of them accepted.

[3] The eighth session, which began on June 15, 1925, was adjourned from June 19 to July 15, because a case was not ready for hearing. Series E, No. 3, p. 183.

self reluctant to postpone the date for the opening of this session.[4] Article 23 also empowers the President to summon an extraordinary session whenever necessary.[5] The distinction between ordinary and extraordinary sessions has no substantial significance [6] and it ought to be abolished.[7] During its first twelve years, in addition to the preliminary session of 1922, the Court held thirty sessions, of which twelve were ordinary sessions and eighteen were extraordinary.[8] In no year during the first nine-year period was the Court in session for 200 days, the basis upon which the budget was framed; in 1925 and 1927, the busiest years of this period, the sessions lasted for only 185 days.[9] The dates of some of the sessions overlap the dates of others; though the twenty-sixth session continued from October 14, 1932 until April 15, 1933, the twenty-seventh session was opened on February 1, 1933, and was closed on April 19, 1933.[10] No cases were heard in the twenty-seventh session. On January 30, 1931, the Court adopted a resolution expressing the opinion that it was "desirable that it should not be convened between July 1 and October 1 except for urgent cases." [11]

The question has arisen whether a session of the Court can be held to which all of the judges have not been summoned. Under Article 23 of the Statute and Article 27 of the 1931 Rules, no special convocation would seem to be needed for the Court's annual ordinary session; the assembling of the judges for the annual session is in a sense automatic. Extraordinary sessions must be summoned by the President, however, and it would seem that all of the judges should be summoned before an extraordinary session may be held.[12] In practice, however, all the judges are not summoned for each extraordinary session; notice only is sent to those judges who are ap-

---

[4] Series E, No. 3, pp. 183, 185.
[5] Under Article 27 of the 1931 Rules, an extraordinary session may be convoked for dealing with an administrative question.
[6] However, the Court has refused to revise at an extraordinary session an administrative decision taken at an ordinary session. Series E, No. 2, p. 193; No. 3, p. 183.
[7] The new text of Article 23, annexed to the Revision Protocol of September 14, 1929, would abolish this distinction.
[8] For the dates of the sessions, see Series E, No. 9, p. 90; *infra*, p. 701. The serial numbering of the sessions begins with the session after the preliminary session of 1922.
[9] In 1922, the Court was in session for 113 days; in 1923, 149 days; in 1924, 81 days; in 1925, 185 days; in 1926, 160 days; in 1927, 185 days; in 1928, 182 days; in 1929, 121 days; in 1930, 117 days; in 1931, 197 days; in 1932, 207 days; and in 1933, 164 days.
[10] The seventeenth session also overlapped the sixteenth session in 1929.
[11] Series E, No. 7, p. 285.
[12] Paragraph 4 of Article 27 of the Rules seems to envisage a summons even to a judge on leave.

parently unable to be present on the date fixed. The presence of the Registrar or his deputy would appear to be essential for a session of the Court.

The cloture of a session is declared by the President; this may be done by order, at any rate when it is inconvenient or impossible for the full Court to take a decision.[13]

§375. **Quorum.** Article 25 of the Statute provides that "the full Court shall sit except when it is expressly provided otherwise," and it envisages a "full court" of eleven judges. The question has arisen whether, since the increase of the number of judges from eleven to fifteen, eleven judges continue to constitute a "full court." The question was answered affirmatively in the Eleventh Assembly of the League of Nations,[14] and later by the Court itself.[15] Article 25 also provides that if "eleven judges are not available, a quorum of nine judges shall suffice to constitute the Court"; this provision was not affected by the increase in the number of judges in 1930. A judge *ad hoc* is not to be counted among the nine judges necessary for a quorum, nor a deputy-judge sitting as a national judge.[16] With the larger number of judges elected in 1930, it has not been difficult for the Court to have a quorum; previously, however, even though the deputy-judges were frequently called upon, difficulty was experienced on this score, and on several occasions it seriously interfered with the work of the Court. At the fifteenth session of the Court, a bare quorum of judges and deputy-judges was present, in addition to a judge *ad hoc,* and when one deputy-judge fell ill, the session had to be closed,[17] with the result that a delay of six months occurred in disposing of the *Serbian Loans Case* which was then before the Court.[18] On the date set for the opening of the seventeenth session a quorum was lacking; [19] and a session of the Court arranged for October 14, 1931, when a case was ready for hearing, had to be postponed until April 18, 1932, because of the unavailability of certain judges.[20]   In

---

[13] Series E, No. 5, p. 252; No. 9, p. 160.
[14] Records of the Eleventh Assembly, Plenary, p. 131.
[15] Series E, No. 7, p. 289.
[16] Series D, No. 2 (add.), pp. 53–54; Series E, No. 3, p. 188. See §146, *supra*.
[17] The cloture was effected by order of the President.
[18] Series E, No. 5, pp. 249, 251. In this case, the agents seem to have discussed the possibility of an agreement that the case should be disposed of by the eight available judges. Series C, No. 16—III, p. 805, 808. Clearly, the Court cannot act as such with only eight judges present.   [19] Series E, No. 6, p. 284.
[20] In this instance, however, the terms of some of the judges whose presence was necessary had expired.

1926, the Court took the view that a judge's abstention from voting does not affect the existence of a quorum;[21] but at the twenty-sixth session, 1932–1933, when the abstention of several judges reduced the number of votes recorded to less than nine, the voting was held to have had no effect.[22] This rule is to be applied, doubtless, only when the vote has to do with the disposition of a case. Minutes of a meeting at which a quorum is lacking are not treated as official without later adoption by the Court.[23]

§376. **Attendance of the Judges.** One of the recurring problems of the Court has been to assure the attendance of the judges at its sessions. One of the judges elected in 1921 failed to attend any of the three sessions held before his death in 1923. In the first nine-year period, other judges were absent at most of the sessions held during the winter months,[24] and several of the judges were absent at about half the sessions, as the following table indicates:

SESSIONS 1922–1930—Attendance of the Judges

Judges	Pre.	1	2	3	4	5	6	7	8	9	10	11	12	13	14	15	16	17	18	19
Altamira	P	P	PA	P	A	P	P	P	P	P	P	P	P	P	P	P	P	P	P	P
Anzilotti	P	P	P	P	P	P	P	P	P	P	P	P	P	P	P	P	P	P	P	P
Barbosa	A	A	A	..	..	..	..	..	..	..	..	..	..	..	..	..	..	..	..	..
Bustamante	A	P	A	P	A	P	A	A	P	A	A	P	PA	A	P	A	P	P	P	A
Finlay	P	P	P	P	P	P	P	P	P	P	P	P	P	P	A	P	P	..	..	..
Fromageot	..	..	..	..	..	..	..	..	..	..	..	..	..	..	..	..	..	..	P	A
Huber	P	A	P	P	P	P	P	P	P	P	P	P	P	P	P	P	P	P	P	P
Hughes	..	..	..	..	..	..	..	..	..	..	..	..	..	..	..	P	P	..	..	..
Hurst	..	..	..	..	..	..	..	..	..	..	..	..	..	..	..	..	..	..	P	P
Kellogg	..	..	..	..	..	..	..	..	..	..	..	..	..	..	..	..	..	..	..	P
Loder	P	P	P	P	P	P	P	P	P	P	P	P	P	P	P	P	P	P	P	P
Moore	P	P	P	P	A	P	A	A	A	A	A	P	P	A	..	..	..	..	..	..
Nyholm	P	P	P	P	P	P	P	P	A	P	P	P	P	P	P	P	PA	PA	P	P
Oda	P	P	A	P	P	P	P	P	P	P	A	A	P	P	PA	P	A	P	P	P
Pessôa	..	..	..	..	A	P	A	A	P	A	A	P	PA	A	P	A	P	P	PA	A
Weiss	P	P	P	P	P	P	P	P	P	P	PA	P	PA	P	PA	..	..	..	..	..

P—present; A—absent; PA—present at part of the session only; dots indicate that a person was not a member of the Court at the time.

[21] Series E, No. 3, p. 188. See also, Series D, No. 2 (add.), p. 62.
[22] Series E, No. 9, p. 161.
[23] Series E, No. 5, p. 252. Such minutes of the fifteenth session were approved by the Court at its sixteenth session.
[24] M. Fromageot stated to the 1929 Conference of Signatories that "the result was that, in the summer, cases would be heard by a normally constituted Court, whereas in the winter they would be heard by an almost exclusively European Court." Minutes of the 1929 Conference of Signatories, p. 22.

On the other hand, some of the deputy-judges were present during the first nine-year period as often as were some of the judges, as the following table indicates:

SESSIONS 1922–1930—Attendance of the Deputy-Judges

Deputy-Judges	Pre.	1	2	3	4	5	6	7	8	9	10	11	12	13	14	15	16	17	18	19
Beichmann......	P	P	P	A	P	A	P	P	A	P	P	A	PA	P	P	P	PA	PA	A	P
Negulesco.......	P	P	P	A	A	A	P	P	A	P	P	A	PA	P	A	P	P	P	A	P
Wang..........	A	A	A	P	P	A	A	P	P	A	A	A	A	P	A	A	PA	PA	A	A
Yovanovitch....	P	A	A	A	P	A	P	P	A	P	P	A	PA	P	A	P	A	A	P	P

This was one of the problems which led to the proposal made in 1928 to consider the revision of the Statute, and the new text of Article 23 of the Statute annexed to the Revision Protocol of September 14, 1929, would place on members of the Court the imperative duty "to hold themselves permanently at the disposal of the Court" unless "they are on regular leave or prevented from attending by illness or other serious reason duly explained to the President." The substance of this provision was incorporated in Article 27 of the 1931 Rules; yet since that time the record of attendance has not been wholly satisfactory, as the following table indicates:

SESSIONS 1931–1933—Attendance of the Judges

Judges	20	21	22 [25]	23	24	25 [26]	26	27	28	29	30
Adatci......................	P	P	PA	P	P	PA	P	P	P	P	P
Altamira....................	PA	P	P	P	P	P	A	A	A	A	A
Anzilotti...................	P	P	P	P	P	P	P	P	P	P	P
Bustamante.................	A	A	P	A	A	PA	A	A	A	A	PA
van Eysinga................	P	P	PA	P	P	PA	P	P	P	P	P
Fromageot..................	P	P	P	P	P	PA	P	P	P	P	P
Guerrero...................	P	P	PA	P	P	PA	P	P	P	P	P
Hurst......................	P	P	P	P	P	PA	P	PA	P	P	P
Kellogg....................	A	P	PA	A	A	PA	A	A	A	A	PA
Negulesco..................	P	P	P	P	A	P	P	P	P	P	P
Rolin-Jaequemyns..........	P	P	P	P	P	PA	P	P	P	P	P
Rostworowski..............	P	P	P	P	P	PA	P	P	P	P	P
Schücking..................	P	P	P	P	P	PA	P	P	P	P	P
Urrutia....................	P	PA	P	P	P	PA	P	P	P	P	A [27]
Wang.....................	A	A	P	P	P	PA	P	P	P	P	P

P—present; A—absent; PA—present at part of the session only; dots indicate that a person was not a member of the Court at the time.

[25] The absence of Judge van Eysinga and Judge Guerrero at a part of this session was due to an application of Article 24 of the Statute.

[26] The absence of several judges at a part of this session was due to an application of Article 13 of the Statute.   [27] On leave.

The real difficulty with reference to the attendance of the judges arises from the advanced age of some of them,[28] and from the fact that, particularly during the earlier period, some of them have had other interests.[29]

The 1931 Rules inaugurated a system by which judges whose homes are situated at more than five days' normal journey from The Hague, and who by reason of the fulfillment of their duties in the Court are obliged to live away from their country, are entitled to a long leave of six months in each period of three years. Not more than two judges may be on such leave at one time, and the order of leaves was to be laid down in a list. A roster drawn up in 1931 was announced in order that Governments might know the composition of the Court during each year; it was modified in 1932, however, and the system was not brought into operation until 1933.[30]

§377. **The Presidency.** Under Article 21 of the Statute, the President's term is fixed at three years. Judge Loder, who was elected President on February 3, 1922, served until the end of 1924. On September 4, 1924, Judge Huber was elected President for the years 1925–1927. On December 6, 1927, Judge Anzilotti was elected President for the years 1928–1930. On January 16, 1931,[31] Judge Adatci was elected President for the years 1931–1933, though he had not previously been a member of the Court. On December 2, 1933, Sir Cecil Hurst was elected President for the years 1934–1936. Deputy-judges took part in the first election, but in none of the later elections.

In 1930, the Court decided that in any third phase of the *Free Zones Case* between France and Switzerland, the Court should be presided over by the judge who had held the office of President during the previous phases of the case; [32] Judge Anzilotti therefore presided over the Court in 1932 during the third phase of that case, "in so far as concerned deliberations and proceedings connected with the decision," though this did not wholly relieve President Adatci of his duties as President.[33] Under Article 13 of the Rules, as amended in 1926, the President may not act as such in a case in which the State

[28] This affords an argument for fixing a maximum age limit for members of the Court at the time of their election.
[29] See Series E, No. 7, p. 285.   [30] See Series E, No. 9, p. 161.
[31] Article 12 of the Rules provides that "after a new election of the whole Court, and until the election of the President and Vice-President, the duties of President are discharged by the oldest judge."
[32] Series E, No. 7, p. 275. *Quære,* whether this decision was binding on the Court in 1932.   [33] Series E, No. 8, p. 247.

of which he is a national is a party; [34] this does not necessarily apply to an order fixing the time-limits in such a case, however.[35]

Article 55 of the Statute provides that "in the event of an equality of votes, the President or his deputy shall have a casting vote" (Fr., *voix prépondérante*). The English and French versions seem to carry different meanings: a "casting vote" would seem to be a second vote to be cast by the President when an equality prevails, and the casting vote of the President might differ from his original vote; a "preponderant vote" would seem to mean that where equality prevails preponderance is to be assigned to the vote which has been cast by the President, with the result that this vote would be taken as decisive. In practice, the sense of the English version has prevailed, and on numerous occasions the President has given a casting vote which was not in accord with his previous vote.[36] The judgment of the Court in the *Lotus Case* was adopted by the casting vote of the President.[37] The President does not have a casting vote in elections by the Court.

A judge of the Court has no powers and no special rank as a consequence of his former service as President. In 1925, the retiring President was given a seat at the right of the President, and provision for this was inserted in Article 2 of the 1926 Rules; this provision was omitted in the 1931 Rules, however, and the practice was discontinued.

Since the revision of the Rules in 1931, certain powers previously exercised by the President must be exercised by the Court itself. Yet the Presidency of the Court has become a more important office than was envisaged by the draftsmen of the Statute. The expectation of the 1920 Committee of Jurists that the President would be *primus inter pares* has hardly been fulfilled; nor has the Court reëlected its President as had been anticipated.

§378. The Vice-Presidency. Judge Weiss was elected Vice-President of the Court on February 7, 1922, and he was reëlected on September 4, 1924, and on December 6, 1927; he therefore served as Vice-President from 1922 until his death in 1928. He was succeeded by Judge Huber, who had formerly served as President. On Janu-

[34] The possibility of the President's giving a casting vote seems to make this rule essential.
[35] See the President's note in the case relating to the *Statute of Memel*, in which the Vice-President acted as President. Series C, No. 59, p. 606.
[36] Series E, No. 3, p. 216; No. 4, p. 291; No. 6, p. 299; No. 7, p. 298; No. 9, p. 174. See also Fischer Williams, Chapters on Current International Law and the League of Nations (1929), p. 228.
[37] Series A, No. 10, p. 32. Six of twelve judges also dissented from certain recitals in the order given in the second phase of the *Free Zones Case*. Series A, No. 24, p. 20.

ary 17, 1931, Judge Guerrero was elected Vice-President for the years 1931–1933, and on December 2, 1933 he was reëlected for the years 1934–1936.

The Vice-President has rarely acted as President,[38] and he has presided over the Court during the conduct of only one proceeding; in 1932, in view of the fact that President Adatci was a national of one of the parties, Vice-President Guerrero replaced him under Article 13 of the Rules, while the Court was dealing with the case relating to the *Statute of Memel*.[39]

§379. **Special Chambers.** The Court has regularly constituted the chambers for labor cases and for cases relating to transit and communications, as provided in Articles 26 and 27 of the Statute, for each three-year period. In addition, assessors have been named for each of these chambers, and a list of them is published in the annual reports; it is to be noted, however, that all Members of the League of Nations have not availed themselves of the privilege of appointing assessors. No case has come before either of these chambers, and neither has ever met. As the President of each chamber is designated by the Court itself, the organization of the chambers is complete without any meeting. The two special chambers differ in that technical assessors must always sit with the judges in the chamber for labor cases,[40] while their sitting in the chamber for cases relating to transit and communications depends on the desire of the parties or the decision of the Court. Either of the special chambers may sit elsewhere than at The Hague. Under the new text of Article 31 of the Statute, annexed to the Revision Protocol of September 14, 1929, national judges would sit in the special chambers in each case, and judges who are regular members of a chamber may be called upon to give up their places as such for a particular case.[41]

§380. **Chamber for Summary Procedure.**[42] The Chamber for Summary Procedure, provided for in Article 29 of the Statute, has

---

[38] On July 4, 1933, Vice-President Guerrero acted as President and issued orders fixing time-limits in two cases.   [39] Series A/B, Nos. 47, 49.

[40] The selection of the assessors to act in a case may raise very difficult problems, to which Article 7 of the Rules does not give any definite solution. Only Members of the League of Nations may appoint assessors.

[41] The Danish Government desired to abolish the special chamber for transit and communications cases in 1929, and to substitute a chamber for international commercial disputes. Minutes of the 1929 Conference of Signatories, p. 40. See §205, *supra*.

[42] The Court's deliberations are held in *Chambre du Conseil*, for which no English equivalent seems to have been found. The *Chambre du Conseil* is to be sharply distinguished from the Chamber for Summary Procedure and the special chambers.

been regularly constituted each year, but little use has been made of it. In 1924, this procedure was employed for the case relating to the *Interpretation of the Treaty of Neuilly,* and a judgment was given by the Court sitting as a Chamber for Summary Procedure on September 12, 1924; and on an application for an interpretation of this judgment, a second judgment was given by the Court in this chamber on March 26, 1925. The same judges composed the chamber on both occasions,[43] and oral proceedings were not called for in either case. The fact that so little use has been made of this chamber [44] has been attributed to the failure of the Statute to provide for the participation in the chamber of judges *ad hoc;* [45] the new text of Article 31 of the Statute, annexed to the Revision Protocol of September 14, 1929, would fill this *lacuna.* It seems doubtful, however, whether this change will produce more frequent appeals to the chamber. Proceedings in the Chamber for Summary Procedure are deemed to be urgent.

The new texts of Articles 26 and 27 of the Statute, annexed to the Revision Protocol of September 14, 1929, provide for recourse to the Chamber for Summary Procedure in labor cases and in cases relating to transit and communications, if the parties so request; and the new text of Article 29 provides for five instead of three members of the Chamber for Summary Procedure, with two substitutes.

§381. **Precedence among the Members of the Court.** The three categories of judges, deputy-judges and judges *ad hoc* are ranged in that order for purposes of seniority. Under Article 2 of the Rules and Article 15 of the Statute, precedence within each of the categories of judges and deputy-judges is determined first by the date of election and second by age. All the judges elected at the same general election are taken to have been elected simultaneously, and among them precedence is determined by age. After a general election, judges who have been reëlected do not necessarily take precedence over other judges. Precedence in the seating of the retiring president was established in 1924 and provided for in the 1926 Rules; but the provision was omitted from the 1931 Rules.

§382. **Composition of the Court under Article 13 of the Statute.** While the composition of the Court may be varied during a ses-

---

[43] Series E, No. 1, p. 57.
[44] A suggestion by the Registrar that summary procedure might be resorted to in the *Serbian Loans Case* was not accepted by the parties. Series C, No. 16—III, pp. 792, 796.
[45] Records of Thirteenth Assembly, First Committee, p. 8.

sion, no change may be made, except of necessity, while the Court is dealing with a particular case.[46] It is provided in Article 13 of the Statute that members of the Court "shall finish any cases which they may have begun" (Fr., *continuent de connaître des affaires dont ils sont déjà saisis*), even though they have been replaced.[47] The view has been taken by the Court that this refers only to judges who have ceased to belong to the Court or to one of the chambers.[48] The principle underlying Article 13 seems to have been more extensively applied in 1922, for the 1922 Rules (Article 3) provided that "a deputy-judge who has begun a case shall be summoned again, if necessary out of his turn, in order to continue to sit in the case until it is finished"; this provision was dropped in 1926, however. In the application of the principle, a determination must be made as to when a case is finished.

In practice, Article 13 is not taken to require that the Court should have the same composition when it deals with the merits of a case as it may have had in dealing with a request for interim protection; *e.g.*, a judge *ad hoc* may not have been present when the latter action was taken, or a judge who participated in the consideration of the request may not take part in the hearing on the merits.[49] The composition of the Court for the merits of the *Mavrommatis Case* was not the same as its composition for dealing with the question of jurisdiction; this was true also of the case relating to *German Interests in Polish Upper Silesia*. Under Article 66 of the Rules, Article 13 of the Statute is made to apply to proceedings for revision or interpretation of a judgment; but as these proceedings are quite independent of the original proceeding in which the judgment was given, there seems to be no necessity for this extension. The Court which dealt with the request for an interpretation of Judgments Nos. 7 and 8 was not of the same composition as the Court which gave those judgments.[50]

The application of Article 13 may create serious difficulties, as the Court's experience in the *Free Zones Case* between France and Switzerland has shown. After the Court had disposed of the first phase of that

---

[46] See Series E, No. 9, p. 160.

[47] In the 1929 Committee of Jurists, the interpretation of this article was the subject of some confusion. Minutes of the 1929 Committee of Jurists, p. 42.

[48] Series E, No. 4, p. 295.   [49] Series E, No. 9, p. 164.

[50] In the case on the interpretation of Judgment No. 3, it was decided that the Chamber for Summary Procedure should be presided over by the judge who had been its president when the judgment was given. Series E, No. 3, p. 191.

case in 1929, its composition was changed by the resignation of Judge Hughes, and by the election of Judges Fromageot, Hurst, and Kellogg. At the extraordinary session, convoked for October 22, 1930, to hear the case in its second phase, three members of the Court who had sat in the first phase were unable to attend; hence, the Court was reconstituted by the summoning of the regular judges available and of the number of deputy-judges necessary to complete a quorum, and the Court decided that it could not continue to deal with the case if the agents of the parties objected.[51] The agents made their declarations of assent in open court,[52] and these declarations were reproduced in the order of December 6, 1930.[53] For the third phase of the case in 1932, the Court had the same composition as for the second phase, except for the absence of Judge Nyholm, deceased; it thus included four judges who after January 1, 1931, were no longer members of the Court.[54]

§383. **Temporary Absence of Participating Judges.** It has frequently happened that a judge who was participating in the hearing of a case was compelled to be absent during a part of the hearings, or during a part of the Court's deliberations. Such absence will not ordinarily necessitate a reconstitution of the Court. On some occasions, the hearings have been continued in the temporary absence of a judge, without objection by the parties, and this judge has been permitted to continue to sit in the case.[55] On other occasions, the absent judge has been dropped from the further hearings in the case.[56] The Court's deliberations and preliminary discussions have sometimes been continued in the absence of a sitting judge, a quorum being present; on some occasions they have been postponed. If a judge does not participate in the final deliberation on a judgment or opinion, his name is not included among the names of judges composing the Court for that case. In the first *Mavrommatis Case,* a judge who participated in the proceedings left The Hague before the final draft of the judgment

---

[51] The Court later recognized that the parties may have a "right, in view of the reconstitution of the Court, to demand to reargue the whole case." Series A/B, No. 46, p. 107.

[52] Series E, No. 7, p. 275.

[53] Series A, No. 24, p. 8. It is to be noted that the parties did not express the same reasons for giving their assent, however.

[54] These judges were assimilated, for purposes of remuneration, to deputy-judges and judges *ad hoc.* Series E, No. 8, p. 247. For a sharp criticism of the course adopted in the *Free Zones Case,* see Series A/B, No. 46, pp. 201–202.

[55] Series C, No. 16—III, p. 817; Series C, No. 18—II, p. 272; Series E, No. 2, p. 157; No. 3, p. 187; No. 7, p. 288; No. 9, p. 161.

[56] Series E, No. 3, p. 187.

was adopted, but a statement was appended to the judgment that "he declared he was unable to agree to the conclusions of the judgment"; [57] this procedure seems to be wholly unjustifiable. A judge who is absent when a judgment is adopted, perhaps when a judgment is delivered, ought not to assume and ought not to be permitted to assume a position as to the conclusions reached. The Court has not been sufficiently exigent in this matter.

§384. **The Deputy-Judges.** During the first period of nine years, the deputy-judges were frequently called upon to sit upon the bench; one or more of them was present at the preliminary session and at all but one of the nineteen sessions held thereafter; all four of the deputy-judges sat in the seventh and thirteenth sessions.[58] The 1929 Committee of Jurists reported, therefore, that "the deputy-judges have in fact been placed on a footing of equality with the ordinary judges in regard to the work performed"; it accordingly proposed the abolition of the post of deputy-judge and an increase in the number of the judges,[59] and amendments to the Statute to this end were annexed to the Revision Protocol of September 14, 1929. When that protocol failed to enter into force in 1930, the Assembly's action did not go beyond the step of increasing the number of judges, though the Assembly's *rapporteur* recognized that "the practical effect of the increase would be to render superfluous, save in quite exceptional cases, recourse to the deputy-judges." [60] Since the beginning of the twentieth session of the Court in 1931, no deputy-judges have been summoned; the post has therefore lost much of its importance, and on the coming into force of the Revision Protocol it will disappear altogether. Yet the possibility that under Article 31 of the Statute a deputy-judge may be designated by his State to act as judge *ad hoc* in a case in which it is a party, gives some importance to the post so long as it is not abolished. Moreover, under the Court's interpretation of Article 18 of the Statute as embodied in Article 6 of the Rules, the deputy-judges must be summoned for any application of the provisions relating to the dismissal of a member of the Court.

---

[57] Series A, No. 11, p. 24. See also, Series B, No. 7, p. 21, for a similar case. In the case of the *Peter Pázmány University*, Judge Kellogg left The Hague "before the terms of this judgment were finally settled," but it was stated that "he concurred in the conclusions reached by the Court"; Judge de Bustamante left The Hague before the judgment was delivered, but it was stated that he concurred also. Series A/B, No. 61, p. 250.

[58] Series E, No. 5, p. 251; No. 7, p. 288. See §376, *supra*.

[59] Minutes of 1929 Conference of Signatories, p. 57.

[60] Records of Eleventh Assembly, Plenary, p. 131.

§385. **Judges ad hoc.** Though the term "judge *ad hoc*" is not employed in the Statute, Article 31 provides for the appointment of judges *ad hoc* in two situations. (1) Where only one party has a national among the judges upon the bench (*i.e.*, sitting or prepared to sit in the case),[61] the other party may appoint a judge *ad hoc* if it has no national among the deputy-judges, or if it has among the deputy-judges a national who is not able to sit.[62] (2) Where neither party has a national among the judges on the bench, each may select a judge *ad hoc*. Article 31 applies in terms only to the Court's exercise of contentious jurisdiction;[63] since 1927, however, it has been extended to the exercise of advisory jurisdiction, and this extension will be required by the Statute if the Revision Protocol of September 14, 1929, comes into force. Under Article 71 of the Rules, as amended in 1927, Article 31 of the Statute is to be applied in advisory proceedings where the question relates "to an existing dispute."[64]

The choice of a judge *ad hoc* is to be made "preferably" from among the persons nominated by national groups for the elections of judges, and for this purpose a cumulative list of nominees is included in the Court's annual reports.[65] In practice, however, Governments pay little attention to this list; eleven of the fourteen persons who acted as judges *ad hoc* from 1922 to 1933 had not been nominated by national groups. Nor is any good reason to be seen for this "preference"; State A should not be in any way bound to designate as judge *ad hoc* one of its nationals who has been nominated by a national group of either State A or State B. Moreover, as no limit is set by the text of Article 31, it may apply to "persons who have been nominated as candidates" many years before a judge *ad hoc* is to be selected, and such persons may at the time be of very advanced age. The provision of the Statute confers on the nominations by national groups

---

[61] In the *Lotus Case*, the French Government was allowed to name a judge *ad hoc* because of the illness of Judge Weiss. Series E, No. 4, p. 274.

[62] In the *Serbian Loans Case*, the Yugoslav deputy-judge being unable to respond to a summons, his Government was allowed to appoint a judge *ad hoc*. Series E, No. 5, p. 252.

[63] Doubt has been expressed as to the right of a State which intervenes in a proceeding to appoint a judge *ad hoc*. Series D, No. 2, pp. 177, 215. In the *Wimbledon Case*, Poland waived this right. Series C, No. 3, Vol. 1, p. 117.

[64] *Cf.*, the distinction drawn in Article 36 of the draft scheme of the 1920 Committee of Jurists. Minutes of the 1920 Committee of Jurists, p. 680. One criterion employed by the Court for determining whether a question relates to an existing dispute is the opening of formal proceedings before the Council of the League of Nations.

[65] See Series E, No. 9, pp. 18–21. The various suggestions for amendments to paragraph 2 of Article 31, made to the 1929 Committee of Jurists, seem quite impractical. See Minutes of the 1929 Committee of Jurists, pp. 54–55.

an importance which they may not merit; in practice it is questionable whether the mere fact of such nomination offers much guarantee that the nominees possess the necessary qualifications.

A person designated as a judge *ad hoc* must fulfill the conditions required by Articles 2, 16,[66] 17, 20, 24, of the Statute; the most important of these conditions is that he should not previously have taken an active part as agent, counsel, or advocate in the particular case. On several occasions the Court seems to have satisfied itself as to the fulfilment of this condition.[67] The caliber of the judges *ad hoc* who have been appointed has been such as to inspire confidence in their usefulness. Some of the men who have served in this capacity have afterward been elected members of the Court: thus, Judge Schücking, Count Rostworowski, Judge Fromageot, and Deputy-Judge Novacovitch. In a few cases, however, the appointments made have been questionable. In the *Serbian Loans Case,* a reservation was made by the President of the Court when he was notified of the designation by the Serb-Croat-Slovene State of a diplomat in active service as judge *ad hoc,* and a different person was then designated; [68] in the *Eastern Greenland Case,* however, diplomats in active service sat as judges *ad hoc.*[69]

A State has chosen the same person to act as judge *ad hoc* on several occasions.[70] Though such judges are frequently classed as "national judges," the Statute does not require them to be nationals of the States which choose them; [71] Danzig, for instance, has chosen Professor Viktor Bruns, a German national, in three cases.[72] "Several parties in the same interest" (Fr., *cause commune*) are to be reckoned as one party, for this purpose; [73] the application of this provision in connection with the request for an advisory opinion on

[66] The reference to Article 16 has been dropped in the new Article 31, annexed to the Revision Protocol of September 14, 1929.

[67] For example, in the *Lotus Case.* Series C, No. 13—II, p. 433.

[68] Series C, No. 16—III, p. 811.

[69] Apparently, such a judge *ad hoc* must obtain release from his diplomatic function as from the day he enters upon his duties as a judge. Series E, No. 9, p. 162.

[70] The same judge *ad hoc* must renew his solemn declaration for each case in which he acts.

[71] Article 4 of the Rules, however, deals with cases in which parties "are entitled to choose a judge *ad hoc* of their nationality." This limitation is not justified by the text of the Statute.

[72] This may result in the Court's including on the bench more than one national of the same State.

[73] The English and French versions of Article 31 of the Statute may be given different meanings. Parties in the same interest may not make common cause in the protection of that interest.

the *Austro-German Customs Régime* gave some difficulty.[74] Under Article 4 of the Rules, the "several parties in the same interest" must agree upon the choice of a judge *ad hoc,* or they will be taken to have renounced the right of designation. In the case relating to the *Jurisdiction of the Oder Commission,* the fact that one of several parties in the same interest had a national on the bench, *viz.,* Denmark, precluded the others of the several parties in the same interest, *viz.,* Czechoslovakia, Great Britain, Germany, France and Sweden, from having any right to designate a judge *ad hoc.*[75]

By the former practice, the Court drew the attention of the Government concerned to its right to appoint a judge *ad hoc* wherever the existence of this right appeared evident; since 1931, however, the practice has been changed. It is no longer necessary for a Government to await an invitation from the Court; if it considers itself entitled to do so under Article 31 of the Statute, it may proceed to make an appointment.[76] In one instance, States interested in an advisory opinion agreed to waive their rights to appoint judges *ad hoc.*[77] An appointment is notified to the Court, which may decide as to admitting the person appointed to sit.[78] No person may sit as judge *ad hoc* until he has made the declaration provided for in Article 20 of the Statute.

The presence of a judge *ad hoc* is not counted in determining whether a quorum exists,[79] but Article 31 of the Statute provides that a judge *ad hoc* shall take part in the decision on an equal footing with the members of the Court. Thus, it has been recognized that judges *ad hoc* should participate in decisions relating to a preliminary objection, and a judge *ad hoc* appointed by an original party has participated in a judgment on an application to intervene; on the other hand, it has been held that the presence of judges *ad hoc* is not necessary for decisions relating to fixing the dates for proceedings, or to a request

---

[74] In this case, the Court gave an order refusing to permit the appointment of a judge *ad hoc* by Austria or Czechoslovakia, with five judges dissenting. Series A/B, No. 41, p. 88. See Mandelsloh, *"Der Antrag Österreichs auf Zulassung eines Richters ad hoc im Zollunionsverfahren,"* 3 *Zeitschrift für ausländisches öffentliches Recht und Völkerrecht* (1932), p. 523.   [75] Series C, No. 17—II, pp. 8–9.

[76] Series C, No. 59, p. 605; No. 68, p. 244; Series E, No. 8, p. 252. The change in the practice seems to have little justification.

[77] Series C, No. 15—I, p. 245; Series E, No. 5, p. 262. See also Series C, No. 68, p. 246.

[78] In the case of the *Austro-German Customs Régime,* the Court decided to await a request before determining whether a judge *ad hoc* could be appointed to sit.

[79] The subcommittee of the Third Committee of the First Assembly, rejecting an amendment to the proposed text of the Statute offered by the Italian delegation, in this sense, interpreted the text of the Statute to require that judges *ad hoc* should not be counted for purposes of a quorum. Records of First Assembly, Committees, I, p. 532.

for indication of interim measures,[80] or to the appointment of a judge *ad hoc* by another party,[81] or to the presidency of the Court in a later stage of the proceedings,[82] or to the termination of a proceeding.[83] It has been said to be "desirable that judges *ad hoc* should be appointed sufficiently early to be able, like their regular colleagues, to follow step by step the proceedings in the case"; and that this would mean that "they should be appointed before the expiration of the time-limit fixed for the filing of the first document of the written proceedings." [84]

A question was raised in the 1929 Committee of Jurists as to the interpretation of the word "nationality" in Article 31, in its application to members of the British Commonwealth of Nations. Sir Cecil Hurst proposed that Article 31 "should be interpreted to mean that it did not exclude the right of a Dominion to appoint to the Court a judge *ad hoc* even though an English judge should also be a member." [85] This proposal was not adopted by the Committee, and the discussion brought out opposition to such an interpretation. The application of Article 31 in this respect may depend to some extent upon the meaning given to the second paragraph of Article 10 of the Statute, the English and French versions of which are at variance. If two British subjects, one from the United Kingdom and another from a Dominion, or from two Dominions, may be elected judges of the Court under Article 10, it would seem to be easier to arrive at the interpretation of Article 31 proposed by Sir Cecil Hurst. Apart from such a determination, however, if a British judge did not possess the nationality of a Dominion, it would seem to be possible for that Dominion to appoint a judge *ad hoc* for a case in which it is a party, even though a British judge is sitting on the bench.

The theory on which judges *ad hoc* are appointed is not clearly brought out by the provisions in the Statute. Two theories have been advanced. (1) That a party before the Court should have on the bench a judge who is acquainted with its own system of law and its local conditions. On this theory, perhaps a judge *ad hoc* should be of

---

[80] Series A, No. 12, p. 10. Judges *ad hoc* did participate, however, when the Court decided on the Norwegian request for the indication of interim measures, in the *Southeastern Greenland Case*, in 1932, and it was held in this case that Article 31 of the Statute was applicable. The participation of judges *ad hoc* in such cases may be made to depend on the amount of delay involved. Series E, No. 9, p. 162.

[81] Series E, No. 5, p. 252.   [82] Series E, No. 7, p. 291.

[83] See the orders of May 11 and May 12, 1933. Series A/B, Nos. 55 and 56. See also Series E, No. 9, p. 162.

[84] Series E, No. 9, p. 161. See also Series C, No. 57, p. 426.

[85] Minutes of the 1929 Committee of Jurists, pp. 70-71, 84-87. See §§207, 257, *supra*.

the nationality of the party appointing him, and each of "several parties in the same interest" should be entitled to have a judge *ad hoc;* yet neither of these points is met by the provisions in the Statute. (2) That parties before the Court should be on a basis of equality in this respect, a national judge being present to explain the views of each party; on this theory, it would not have been necessary to provide for the appointment of judges *ad hoc* when none of the parties has a national among the members of the Court.[86] The two theories were confused in the report of the 1920 Committee of Jurists.[87] On any theory, the provision for judges *ad hoc* lends color to the idea of representation of States in the Court. The best argument for this provision is the practical one that it facilitated the acceptance of the Statute.

§386. **Participation of National Judges.** A national judge may be either a judge or a deputy-judge who possesses the nationality of a party, or a judge *ad hoc* designated by a party. Prior to 1920, the problem had been much discussed whether nationals of the parties should be permitted to participate in a case. At the Second Peace Conference at The Hague there was some insistence on their exclusion,[88] and it is notable that this view was adopted in the draft elaborated by the conference at The Hague in February, 1920. The provisions in Article 31 of the Statute were stated by the 1920 Committee of Jurists to have the effect that "our Court more nearly resembles a court of arbitration than a national court of justice." [89] Yet the experience of the Court since 1922 cannot be said to have confirmed the doubts entertained as to the provisions allowing the participation of national judges.

Since 1922, national judges have participated in numerous judgments and opinions of the Court.[90] Though they have frequently supported the contentions of their own Governments by dissenting from the position taken by the majority of the Court, on several occasions they have refused to support their Governments' contentions. In the *Wimbledon Case,* Judge Anzilotti (Italy) dissented from the judgment

---

[86] The principle of equality is not applied, also, in a case in which some but not all of several parties in the same interest have nationals among the judges on the bench.

[87] Minutes of the 1920 Committee of Jurists, pp. 721-722. *Cf. id.,* pp. 528ff. See also, Records of First Assembly, Committees, I, p. 475.

[88] See Wehberg, The Problem of an International Court of Justice (1918), pp. 55-59.   [89] Minutes of 1920 Committee of Jurists, p. 722.

[90] See Norman L. Hill, "National Judges in the Permanent Court of International Justice," 25 American Journal of International Law (1931), p. 670.

given by the Court, in opposition to the position taken by the Italian Government.[91] In the *Mavrommatis Jerusalem Concessions Case*, Lord Finlay (Great Britain) and M. Caloyanni (Greece), judge *ad hoc*, concurred with the majority in a judgment which did not sustain certain contentions of Great Britain and of Greece.[92] In the *Tunis-Morocco Case*, Judge Weiss (France) joined in the unanimous opinion of the Court which opposed the contention made by the French Government.[93] The advisory opinion concerning *Jurisdiction of the Danzig Courts* was given by a unanimous Court, with Danzig and Polish judges *ad hoc* participating; [94] similarly the advisory opinion concerning *Greco-Bulgarian Communities*, with the participation of Greek and Bulgarian judges *ad hoc*.[95] In the advisory opinion on *Railway Traffic between Lithuania and Poland*, Count Rostworowski (Poland) concurred in the unanimous opinion which was unfavorable to the Polish Government's contentions.[96] In the *Southeastern Greenland Case*, the Norwegian judge *ad hoc*, M. Vogt, did not dissent from the order of August 3, 1922, dismissing the Norwegian request for interim protection.[97] Though the judgment of the Court in the case concerning the interpretation of the *Statute of Memel* was largely unfavorable to contentions advanced by the British, French, and Japanese Governments, the judges possessing these nationalities did not dissent.[98] This record seems to indicate that national judges have shown a certain amount of independence, and that judges *ad hoc* do not always consider themselves as representatives of the State which appointed them.[99] As a rule, however, judges *ad hoc* have not failed to support the position of their Governments, even when this placed them in a minority of one. The publication of dissenting opinions has a value in this connection, in that it discourages a national judge from taking a merely partisan attitude.

Moreover, the tendency has been to increase, rather than to diminish, the participation of national judges. In 1927, the amendment of Article 71 of the 1926 Rules provided for the application of Article 31 of the Statute in advisory procedure where the question relates to an existing dispute; and the new text of Article 31 of the Statute, annexed to the Revision Protocol of September 14, 1929, pro-

---

[91] Series A, No. 1, p. 35.   [92] Series A, No. 5.   [93] Series B, No. 4.
[94] Series B, No. 15.   [95] Series B, No. 17.   [96] Series A/B, No. 42.
[97] Series A/B, No. 48, p. 277.   [98] Series A/B, No. 49.
[99] It seems difficult to share on this point the views of Mr. Lauterpacht, in his *Function of Law in the International Community* (1933), pp. 230–231.

vides for the participation of national judges in the special chambers and in the Chamber for Summary Procedure.

§387. **Disqualifications of Judges.** The second paragraph of Article 17 of the Statute disqualifies a member of the Court in a case in which he has previously taken an active part as agent, counsel, or advocate, or as a member of national or international court or of a commission of inquiry, or in any other capacity. On several occasions, members of the Court have submitted their doubts on this point to the Court itself. In 1928, the Court decided that Judge Huber was not disqualified in the *Free Zones Case* by reason of the fact that he had been legal adviser to the Swiss Federal Council during a certain period before the dispute had arisen; [100] this was formally confirmed in 1929.[1] In 1931, the Court held that a judge was not disqualified in a particular case because he had participated in the drafting of a convention the interpretation of which was in issue.[2] In several cases of requests for advisory opinions, members have informed the Court of their previous activities in connection with a consideration of the same or similar questions by the Council of the League of Nations, and the attitude of the Court has been dictated by its appreciation of the facts in each case.[3] The Rules make no provision for a party's suggestion that a judge is disqualified,[4] and no such suggestion has been advanced; yet the provision in Article 17 of the Statute is so peremptory in character that it must be open to a party to take advantage of it by raising a question for the Court's decision.

Article 24 of the Statute creates both a privilege and a possible disqualification for the judges. It is clearly necessary that a judge be given the privilege of withdrawing from the Court while it is dealing with a case in which for some special reason he feels that he should not take part. In this event, the judges must inform the President; the decision must be taken by the Court if the President and the judge disagree.[5] Perhaps the "special reason" should be one which can be explained to the President or to the Court, though in the earlier

---

[100] Series E, No. 4, p. 270. Judge Huber raised the question on this occasion.
[1] Series E, No. 6, p. 282.   [2] Series E, No. 8, p. 251.
[3] See Series E, No. 7, pp. 277, 287.   [4] See Series E, No. 1, p. 247.
[5] It may well be argued that the third paragraph of Article 24 ought not to be applied to a case under the first paragraph of the article. This view does not seem to have been taken by the Court, however, and the history of the drafting of the text does not sustain the argument. See Minutes of the 1920 Committee of Jurists, pp. 300, 472.

years the view was taken that Article 24 is designed to apply to "personal reasons."[6] A withdrawal should take place before and not during the hearings,[7] though this might not always be possible. In reliance on Article 24, Judge Urrutia withdrew from the Court in 1931, because of his previous activities in the Council of the League of Nations in connection with the question on *German Minority Schools in Polish Upper Silesia;* the President's examination of the documents led him to share Judge Urrutia's opinion in this instance.[8] The same procedure was followed in 1931 when Vice-President Guerrero and Judge van Eysinga withdrew from the Court when it dealt with the case concerning *Railway Traffic between Lithuania and Poland.*[9]

The second paragraph of Article 24 creates a possible disqualification when the President considers that for some special reason a judge should not sit in a particular case; if the President and the judge disagree, the matter is to be settled by the decision of the Court. No case has occurred in which the President on his own initiative has stated that a judge ought not to sit. It would seem to be clear that a party cannot raise before the Court any question of applying Article 24.

§388. **Incompatibilities.** Article 16 of the Statute provides that "the ordinary members [Fr., *les membres*] of the Court may not exercise any political or administrative function." The extent of this disability of a judge was discussed at the preliminary session of the Court in 1922, and opinions were expressed as follows: [10]

(*a*) that there was incompatibility between the functions of judge of the Court and the functions of a member of an institution such as the *Conseil du contentieux* of the Italian Foreign Office;

(*b*) That there was no incompatibility between the functions of a judge and the functions of a member of a Government commission for preparing copyright legislation;

(*c*) that there was no incompatibility between the functions of a judge and the functions of a member of a Government commission for testing candidates for the diplomatic service;

(*d*) that the judges, or in case of doubt the Court, should decide in

---

[6] Series E, No. 3, p. 186; No. 7, p. 288.   [7] Series E, No. 7, p. 287.
[8] Series C, No. 52, p. 106.   [9] Series C, No. 54, p. 304.
[10] Series E, No. 1, p. 247. Article 16 of the Statute is referred to in Article 31 as applying to judges *ad hoc;* the view has been taken that it begins to apply to judges *ad hoc* when they enter upon their duties as such. Series E, No. 9, pp. 161–162.

each instance whether there is incompatibility between their functions as judges and participation in cases of private international law;

(e) that, except in special cases upon which the Court might be called upon to decide, participation in negotiations even of a non-political character was inadmissible;

(f) that the judges might take part in international conferences which were connected with the development of law.

The question of incompatibility has frequently arisen, and on occasion the Court has approved the exercise of various international and national functions by its members. It has decided, for instance, that Judge Altamira might properly continue in his position as Spanish Senator. In 1925, a question arose in connection with the appointment of a judge as president of a conciliation commission under one of the Locarno agreements, and the President formulated the principle that where a conciliation commission is set up by an agreement which confers jurisdiction on the Court if the conciliation commission fails to reach a settlement, an "effective incompatibility" exists; [11] this view was confirmed by the Court in 1930.[12] A year later, however, the view was adopted that "there was no sufficient justification for this distinction," and it was recognized that members of the Court might properly be members of commissions of conciliation or inquiry.[13] In 1931, the members of the Court seem to have been of the opinion that "any function which compelled a person to follow the instructions of his government, regardless of his personal views, was 'political.'" This would quite clearly preclude a member of the Court from representing his Government at an international conference, even at a conference for the development of international law; it was thought at the time to preclude a judge from representing his Government at a session of the International Labor Conference, or from making "an official pronouncement at a banquet regarding his government's international policy in a certain limited respect." [14] The Court has shown increasing solicitude on this point.

The new text of Article 16, annexed to the Revision Protocol of September 14, 1929, provides that "the members of the Court may not exercise any political or administrative function, nor engage in any other occupation of a professional nature." This amendment was due to an impression that members of the Court had allowed other in-

[11] Series E, No. 1, p. 178.
[12] Series E, No. 7, p. 276.
[13] Series E, No. 7, p. 277.
[14] Series E, No. 7, p. 278.

terests to interfere with the Court's work during its earlier years; [15] and the contemplated increase in the salaries would remove any excuse for judges' having other occupations. The 1929 Conference of Signatories intended that the addition to Article 16 should be "interpreted in the widest sense." [16]

§389. **Discipline.** No power to discipline its members is expressly conferred on the Court, apart from the power of dismissal set out in Article 18 of the Statute. The latter power has not been exercised by the Court,[17] and only one case of what might be called discipline has arisen. In 1929, a deputy-judge who was a national of a party before the Court failed to respond to a summons to attend a session under circumstances which seemed to indicate an intention thereby to modify the composition of the Court in the case before it; the failure seems to have been explained, but the Court addressed a letter to the deputy-judge which drew his attention to the "danger" to the "Court's authority" involved in any purpose to change the Court's composition in a particular case.[18] A power to discipline one of its members must reside in the Court, even apart from the power of dismissal; and if a flagrant case should arise, it would doubtless be exercised. If, for instance, a member of the Court should act as agent in a case of an international nature, in violation of Article 17 of the Statute, the case would clearly call for action by the Court, and such action might fall short of dismissal.

§390. **Acceptance of Decorations.** On July 30, 1926, the Court adopted a resolution forbidding the acceptance of decorations by members of the Court, by the Registrar, or by officials of the Registry, "without the consent of the Court," [19] and as a general rule the vote of the Court must be by secret ballot. Such consent has on some occasions been denied, and on others it has been granted.[20] Doubtless cases may arise in which the acceptance of a decoration would excite no unfavorable comment; yet it seems to be a point on which the Court should not take any risks, and a definite rule should forbid

---

[15] However, President Anzilotti explained to the 1929 Committee of Jurists that "the case had never yet occurred where a judge had refused to discharge his duties on the ground of other professional occupations." Minutes of the 1929 Committee of Jurists, p. 45.   [16] Minutes of the 1929 Conference, pp. 33, 78. See §200, *supra*.

[17] The 1920 Committee of Jurists seems to have contemplated an application of Article 18 only in cases of physical incapacity. Minutes of the 1920 Committee of Jurists, pp. 452–453, 717. Article 6 of the Rules carries no suggestion of this limitation.

[18] Series E, No. 6, p. 283.   [19] Series E, No. 3, p. 178.
[20] Series E, No. 4, p. 270; No. 5, p. 246; No. 7, p. 276.

the acceptance of decorations from any source by any member of the Court, the Registrar or an official of the Registry, during his term of office. In this respect, the Court is in a different position from the Secretariat of the League of Nations, because of the absolute necessity of its avoiding any appearance of a basis for favoritism; the Staff Regulations of the Secretariat ought not therefore to serve as the model on this point.[21]

§391. Vacancies. Article 14 of the Statute provides for the filling of vacancies, but except for Article 18 the Statute lays down no procedure for determining that a vacancy exists. A vacancy may be created by the death of a member of the Court, or by the resignation of a member of the Court, or by the dismissal of a member of the Court under Article 18 of the Statute. The "normal procedure" in case of the death of a member of the Court is for the Court to notify the Secretary-General of the League of Nations in order that steps may be taken to fill the vacancy.[22] In the event of a resignation, it seems from the procedure followed in two instances [23] that the resignation must be accepted by the Council and the Assembly. No case has arisen where the application of Article 18 has created a vacancy. The new text of Article 14 of the Statute, annexed to the Revision Protocol of September 14, 1929, is designed to expedite the filling of vacancies, though it is left to the Council to fix the date of each election; and the new text of Article 13, annexed to the Revision Protocol of September 14, 1929, requires a resignation to be addressed to the President of the Court, whose notification of it to the Secretary-General "makes the place vacant."

§392. Employment of Experts. The Court is empowered by Article 50 of the Statute to entrust any individual, body, bureau, commission or other organization with the task of carrying out an enquiry or of giving an expert opinion. This contemplates either the use of an existing organization, or the creation of an organization *ad hoc*. The permanent committees of the League of Nations are thus available for use by the Court. The final paragraph of Article 26 of

[21] The Staff Regulations of the Secretariat of the League of Nations, edition of March, 1933, provide (Article 1) that "no official of the Secretariat may, during the term of his appointment, accept from any Government any honor or decoration except for services rendered before appointment."

[22] Series E, No. 5, p. 245. The death of Judge Barbosa in 1923 was notified to the Court by the Secretary-General, however.

[23] In connection with the resignation of Judge Moore in 1928 and that of Judge Hughes in 1930. Series E, No. 4, p. 27; No. 6, p. 17.

the Statute may be taken to recognize the propriety of resort to the International Labor Office; and in connection with a request for an advisory opinion, the Council has suggested that the Advisory and Technical Committee for Communications and Transit should be available for assistance to the Court.[24] In only one case, however, has the Court acted under Article 50 of the Statute. In 1928, a committee of three experts was established by order of the Court, to conduct an enquiry which would enable the Court to fix the amount of the indemnity to be paid by the Polish Government to the German Government in the case of the *Factory at Chorzów;* [25] before its work was completed, however, the committee was dissolved by the President because of the termination of the case before the Court as a result of an agreement between the parties.[26]

§393. **The Court's Public Relations.** Aside from its very useful documentation, the Court makes little effort to cultivate relations with the public; it seems to be content that the public's estimate of its work should depend on the results achieved, without any special organization for making the results known. Under Article 24 of the Rules,[27] the Registrar replies to inquiries from the press, and Article 43 requires him to publish in the press all necessary information as to the date and hour fixed for public sittings; *communiqués* marked unofficial are issued both before and after such sittings are held.[28] A post of press official has not been filled, however,[29] and the present policy of the Court is that it will not avail itself of the assistance of the Secretariat of the League of Nations for *liaison* with the press.[30]

[24] Series E, No. 8, p. 273.
[25] Series A, No. 17, p. 99; Series C, No. 16—II, pp. 17–24.
[26] Series A, Nos. 18/19, p. 14. See §497, *infra.*
[27] See also Article 24 of the Instructions for the Registry, Series E, No. 5, p. 62.
[28] Series E, No. 3, p. 182. On a few occasions, public sittings have been held at which no cases were argued. See Series E, No. 4, p. 286.
[29] Series E, No. 7, p. 282.   [30] Series E, No. 8, p. 248.

PART IV

THE JURISDICTION OF THE PERMANENT COURT
OF INTERNATIONAL JUSTICE

CHAPTER 17

ACCESS TO THE COURT

§394. Limitations in the Statute. Article 34 of the Statute provides that "only States or Members of the League of Nations can be
parties in cases before the Court." [1] Two categories of parties, "States
or Members of the League of Nations," are mentioned because it is
possible that some Members of the League of Nations, original members or members admitted under Article 1 of the Covenant, may not
be States; for example, certain members of the British Commonwealth of Nations which are Members of the League of Nations are
not generally referred to as States. [2] The possibility of an individual's
being a party before the Court is clearly excluded by Article 34. Nor
can a society, an association or a corporation be a party, even though
it is public in character; the League of Nations, for example, cannot
be a party in a case before the Court. In proceedings relating to requests for advisory opinions, "international organisations" may be
admitted to furnish information to the Court under Article 73 of the
Rules, and they may be represented before the Court in oral hearings;
but as there are no *parties* in such proceedings, this involves no
derogation from Article 34 of the Statute. [3]

§395. Categories of Possible Parties. Article 35 of the Statute
opens the Court to all Members of the League of Nations "and also to
States mentioned in the Annex to the Covenant." So far as the Mem-

---

[1] In the *Serbian Loans Case*, the Court stated that "this principle has its origin
in Article 14 of the Covenant." Series A, No. 20/21, p. 17.

[2] It seems to be the contention of certain members of the British Commonwealth
of Nations that a dispute between two or more of them does not constitute an international dispute and cannot be brought before the Court, however. See Minutes of the
1929 Committee of Jurists, p. 72. Such a limitation was embodied in the declarations
accepting the Court's compulsory jurisdiction under Article 36 of the Statute, by all
of the members of the British Commonwealth of Nations except the Irish Free State.

[3] The provision in Article 7 of the Rules that "with regard to the questions referred
to in Article 26 of the Statute," the President shall consult the Governing Body of the
International Labor Office, has to do only with the selection of assessors. Series D,
No. 2, pp. 40–42, 112–113.

bers of the League of Nations are concerned, the Court is open to them without regard to whether they are parties to the Protocol of Signature of December 16, 1920. Under Article 33 of the Statute, the expenses of the Court are to "be borne by the League of Nations, in such a manner as shall be decided by the Assembly upon the proposal of the Council." Though it might be open to the Assembly to decide that Members of the League of Nations which are not parties to the Protocol of December 16, 1920, need not contribute to the funds of the League of Nations available for meeting the expenses of the Court, no such decision has been taken; and it is therefore logical that all the Members of the League of Nations which contribute to the Court's expenses should have access to it. This is not true, however, of the States which are mentioned in the Annex to the Covenant, but are not Members of the League of Nations—at the present time the United States of America, Ecuador and the Hedjaz.[4] It was the desire to secure the coöperation of the United States of America which led the First Assembly of the League of Nations to open the Protocol of December 16, 1920, to signature by such States; [5] and this may also explain the opening of the Court to them without condition.

No special provision is made for States which may have withdrawn from membership in the League of Nations. Such States may, like Brazil, be parties to the Protocol of Signature of December 16, 1920, but this is not a category to which the Court is open; they may, like Brazil, be mentioned in the Annex to the Covenant, and if so the Court is open to them; or they may, like Costa Rica,[6] be in neither of these categories, and in this case the Court is open to them only under paragraph 2 of Article 35.[7]

The second paragraph of Article 35 provides that the Court shall be open to States not Members of the League of Nations and not mentioned in the Annex to the Covenant, on conditions to be laid down by the Council of the League of Nations. The creation of this special category seems to have been due to the position in 1920 of Germany and other States opposed to the Allied Powers during the War, and to a desire to safeguard the provisions of the peace treaties relating to

---

[4] The Hedjaz has been combined with the Nejd, and both are now parts of the Kingdom of Saudi Arabia. There can be little doubt that the Kingdom of Saudi Arabia has replaced the Hedjaz as a State to which the Court is open under paragraph 1 of Article 35 of the Statute.

[5] Records of First Assembly, Plenary, p. 441.

[6] The Protocol of Signature of December 16, 1920, has been signed but not ratified on behalf of Costa Rica.   [7] See Series E, No. 6, p. 287.

the jurisdiction of the Court; it was not due to a desire to exclude any State from appearing before the Court.

§396. **"Treaties in Force."** Article 35 of the Statute provides, however, that the conditions shall be laid down by the Council "subject to the special provisions contained in treaties in force" (Fr., *sous réserve dispositions particulières des traités en vigueur*). The object of this provision, which was added by the subcommittee of the Third Committee of the First Assembly, was to safeguard the provisions in the peace treaties under which States not members of the League of Nations and not named in the Annex to the Covenant had agreed that certain cases might be taken before the Court, *e.g.*, Article 386 of the Treaty of Versailles.[8] In such cases, it is clear that any conditions set by the Council are not to conflict with the provisions of such treaties in force; it may be argued, also, that they are not to be applicable in a case covered by "special provisions contained in treaties in force." Some difficulty may arise in determining the time as of which the treaty is to be in force; is it the time when the Council acted, on May 17, 1922, or is it the time when a case arises? Is the expression "treaties in force" in Article 35 equivalent to the expression "treaties and conventions in force" in Article 36? There can no doubt that the latter expression refers to the future. Is the expression in Article 35 analogous to "a treaty or convention in force" referred to in Article 37? It seems doubtful whether the latter is to be applied in the future indefinitely. Article 35 may have been intended to safeguard provisions in the peace treaty made with Turkey;[9] yet the Treaty of Lausanne was not signed until July 24, 1923, and did not come into force until August 6, 1924.

In the revision of the Rules in 1926, the Court seems to have preferred to leave open the question as to the meaning of "treaties in force."[10] In the *Wimbledon Case* in 1923, in which the Court's jurisdiction was based on Article 386 of the Treaty of Versailles, no declaration was required of Germany. In connection with its sixth judgment, on the question of jurisdiction in the case of *German Interests in Polish Upper Silesia,* the Court decided not to require Germany to

---

[8] Records of First Assembly, Committees, I, pp. 378–382. In the report of the Third Committee to the First Assembly, it is said: "The access of other States to the Court will depend either on the special provisions of the treaties in force (for example, the provisions of the Treaties of Peace concerning the right of minorities, labor, etc.), or else on a resolution of the Council." Records of First Assembly, Plenary, p. 462.

[9] The treaty of Sèvres of August 10, 1920, was never brought into force.

[10] Series D, No. 2 (add.), pp. 76, 104ff.; Series E, No. 3, p. 198.

make the declaration referred to in the Council's resolution of May 17, 1922; [11] this would seem to indicate that the conditions laid down by the Council may not apply where a special provision in a treaty in force is applicable. In the same case, it was agreed by the parties that Article 23 of the Geneva Convention of May 15, 1922, fell within the category of "matters specially provided for in treaties and conventions in force," mentioned in Article 36 of the Statute, and the Polish Government did not dispute that the suit was duly submitted "in accordance with Articles 35 and 40 of the Statute"; [12] yet the Geneva Convention did not come into force until June 3, 1922. Here, then, the Council's resolution was not applied to a case which was covered by special provisions in a treaty in force, but the treaty was not concluded until 1922. If the implications of this decision were carried out, it would be possible for two States to escape the Council's conditions by entering into a treaty; indeed, if special agreements were included among treaties in force, the Council's resolution might never be applicable. It is clearly necessary for some restrictive meaning to be given to this provision in Article 35; it ought to be confined to treaties relating to the liquidation of the war, and the action taken in the case of *German Interests in Polish Upper Silesia* ought not to serve as a general precedent.

§397. The Council's Resolution of May 17, 1922. At its preliminary session in 1922, the Court decided to address a letter to the Council of the League of Nations concerning action to be taken by the Council under the second paragraph of Article 35 of the Statute.[13] The President's letter of February 21, 1922, suggested that the powers of the Council should be considered as subordinate to the main principles that (*a*) any State should have a right of recourse to the Court, and (*b*) all parties admitted before the Court should have a right "to be placed in a position of absolute legal equality." [14] It was concluded, therefore, that the conditions fixed by the Council could "hardly involve more" than a duty to carry out the Court's decisions in good faith in accordance with the last paragraph of Article 13 of the Covenant and a duty to contribute to the Court's expenses.[15] This

[11] Series E, No. 1, p. 261.
[12] Series A, No. 6, p. 11.
[13] This decision was due to a suggestion made by the Secretary-General of the League of Nations. Series D, No. 2, p. 63. See §301, *supra*.
[14] Series D, No. 2, p. 345.
[15] Contribution to the expenses of the Court was not made a condition to the Court's being open to a State. The report of the Third Committee to the First

letter was considered by the Council on May 12, 1922,[16] and its decision was taken by a resolution adopted on May 17, 1922.[17]

(1) The first paragraph of the Council's resolution sets a single condition for access to the Court by a State not a member of the League of Nations and not mentioned in the Annex to the Covenant: *viz.*, that it shall previously have deposited with the Registrar a declaration "by which it accepts the jurisdiction of the Court, in accordance with the Covenant of the League of Nations and with the terms and subject to the conditions of the Statute and Rules of the Court, and undertakes to carry out in full good faith the decision or decisions of the Court and not to resort to war against a State complying therewith." This reference to the Covenant was doubtless due to the mention of Article 13 of the Covenant in the President's letter of February 21, 1922; the phrasing of the concluding part of the condition is based on the first sentence of paragraph 4 of Article 13. The reference to the Covenant is more general, however. It seems extremely doubtful whether any jurisdiction is conferred on the Court by the Covenant; nor do the Statute and Rules confer more than incidental jurisdiction. An acceptance referring to the Covenant, the Statute and the Rules, can therefore involve nothing in the way of an obligation to submit to the Court's jurisdiction. The undertaking required to be contained in the declaration does not tend to produce "inequality before the Court," but it may produce inequality in the position of parties after the Court has rendered a judgment; for even if Members of the League of Nations have this obligation under paragraph 4 of Article 13 of the Covenant with reference to the judgments of the Court, no such obligation rests on States not members but mentioned in the Annex to the Covenant.

(2) The second paragraph of the Council's resolution provides for either particular or general declarations; the latter may be equivalent to a declaration recognizing the Court's compulsory jurisdiction under Article 36, paragraph 2, of the Statute, but it will not necessarily involve an obligation for Members of the League or States mentioned in the Annex to the Covenant which have made or may make declarations under Article 36. This provision is indeed

Assembly had suggested that the Council's resolution might "lay down conditions of access in conformity with Article 17 of the Covenant." Records of First Assembly, Plenary, p. 462. This suggestion had been made by the 1920 Committee of Jurists. Minutes of the 1920 Committee of Jurists, p. 725.

[16] League of Nations Official Journal, 1922, pp. 526, 609.

[17] *Id.*, p. 545. For the text of the Council's resolution, see appendix, *infra*, p. 667 n.

curious, and it is not surprising that no such general declaration has been made.

(3) The third paragraph of the Council's resolution merely provides for the custody of the declarations and their communication to Members of the League of Nations, to States mentioned in the annex to the Covenant, "to such other States as the Court may determine," and to the Secretary-General of the League of Nations.

(4) The fourth paragraph of the Council's resolution reserves the power of the Council to modify the resolution, even so as to affect "existing declarations." No modification has yet been considered, however.

(5) The fifth paragraph of the Council's resolution provides that "all questions as to the validity or the effect" of a declaration shall be decided by the Court. This would seem to open a door to the Court's determination of the effect of an undertaking analogous to that in Article 13 of the Covenant, a duty which the Court would probably be reluctant to assume.

§398. Action on the Council's Resolution by the Court. The Council's *rapporteur* suggested that the Council's resolution should be communicated to the Court and that the Court should be requested "to give effect to the resolution." [18] On June 28, 1922, the Court decided to communicate the resolution to States not members of the League of Nations but mentioned in the Annex to the Covenant,[19] and to the following additional States not at the time members of the League of Nations and not mentioned in the Annex to the Covenant: Dominican Republic, Georgia, Germany, Hungary, Iceland, Liechtenstein, San Marino, Mexico, Monaco, Danzig (through Poland), and Turkey. These States seem to have been selected in consequence of a decision by the Court on June 23, 1922, to communicate the resolution "to all States recognized *de jure*." [20] On June 16, 1925, the Court decided to communicate the resolution to Afghanistan, Egypt and "Russia." [21]

[18] League of Nations Official Journal, 1922, p. 609. The Secretariat of the League of Nations seems to have suggested that the Court should, if it saw fit, communicate the resolution to States not members of the League of Nations. Series E, No. 1, p. 144.

[19] The Court later "ceased to communicate with the Hedjaz, as all communications have been returned." Series E, No. 1, p. 261. It has also discontinued sending communications to Georgia.

[20] *Id.,* p. 260. If the decision of June 23, 1922, refers to recognition by other States, interesting questions may arise as to the number of States which must have accorded recognition, and as to the account to be taken by the Court of a recommendation by the Council or Assembly that recognition should be withheld.

[21] Series E, No. 1, p. 144.

The effect of this communication by the Court is not clear; it seems to have been interpreted to mean that these States are "entitled to appear before the Court," as that expression is used in the Rules,[22] though this was not expressly stated in the communication.[23] It would doubtless be within the power of the Council, under Article 35 of the Statute, to exclude any State not a member of the League of Nations and not mentioned in the Annex to the Covenant from appearing before the Court; but the Council does not seem expressly to have authorized the exercise of any power of selection or exclusion by the Court.[24] While it may be for the Court to say whether a particular community is a State, some danger might be involved in conferring upon it the political function of selecting the States to which it should be open. The Court's Rules, as revised in 1926, provide particularly in Articles 36, 42, 63 and 73 for communications to be made to "States entitled to appear before the Court," [25] and for this purpose it must have a list.[26] Various of the States to which the Council's resolution has been communicated have subsequently changed their positions: the Dominican Republic, Germany, Hungary, Mexico and Turkey have become Members of the League of Nations; and Georgia has become a part of the Union of Soviet Socialist Republics.

In 1926, the text of the Council's resolution was annexed to Article 35 (2) of the revised Rules, though apparently only for information in connection with the application of the rule; such reproduction of the text has not changed its legal effect, though it clearly facilitates the framing of declarations under the resolution.

§399. **Declarations under the Council's Resolution.** Only two declarations have been made in accordance with the Council's reso-

---

[22] Series E, No. 2, p. 87; No. 3, p. 98; No. 4, p. 128; No. 5, p. 150; No. 6, p. 172; No. 7, p. 180; No. 8, p. 143.
[23] According to information supplied by the Registrar.
[24] The reference in paragraph 3 of the resolution "to such other States as the Court may determine" applies only to the communication of declarations by the Court.
[25] The new Articles 40 and 66 of the Statute, annexed to the Revision Protocol of September 14, 1929, also employ the expression "States entitled to appear before the Court."
[26] At the present time (June 1, 1934) such a list would include the 57 Members of the League of Nations; the United States of America, Brazil, Ecuador and Saudi Arabia (Hedjaz), as States mentioned in the Annex to the Covenant; and Afghanistan, Danzig, Egypt, Iceland, Liechtenstein, San Marino, Monaco, and "Russia," as States to which the Council's Resolution of May 17, 1922, has been communicated. It should also include Costa Rica, which is not named in the Annex to the Covenant, which is no longer a member of the League of Nations, and which is not a party to the Protocol of Signature of December 16, 1920, but which may take advantage of the Council's Resolution of May 17, 1922. The total number of States or Members of the League of Nations to which the Court is open is therefore 70.

lution. On two occasions before its admission to the League of Nations, Germany was a party in cases before the Court, but no declaration was made on either occasion.[27] When oral proceedings were begun in the *Lotus Case,* on August 2, 1927, the following declaration signed by the Turkish *chargé d'affaires* at The Hague was stated to have been filed with the Registry and was read in Court: [28]

> The undersigned, being duly empowered by the Government of the Turkish Republic, hereby declares, in accordance with the terms of paragraph 2 of Article 35 of the Rules of the Permanent Court of International Justice, that he accepts, on behalf of that Government, the aforesaid Court's jurisdiction for the dispute which has arisen between the Government of the Turkish Republic and the Government of the French Republic as a result of the collision which occurred on August 2nd, 1926, between the steamships *Boz-Kourt* and *Lotus,* which dispute has formed the subject of the Special Agreement signed by the delegates of the two Governments on October 12th, 1926, and filed on behalf of those Governments with the Registry of the Court on January 4th, 1927.

It might have been questioned whether this declaration was a compliance with the requirement set by the Council in the first paragraph of the resolution of May 17, 1922. On November 18, 1931, a similar declaration was given on behalf of the Turkish Government, in reference to the case concerning the *Delimitation of Territorial Waters* between the island of Castellorizo and the coasts of Anatolia.[29]

§400. **Access Possible to All States.** Under the Council resolution of May 17, 1922, it would seem to be possible for any *State* to have access to the Court, even though the resolution has not been formally communicated to it. If Andorra or Nepal or one of various other communities should seek to come before the Court, a question might arise, which it would be for the Court to decide under Article 34, whether the political organization offering itself as a party is indeed a State. No indication has been given by the Court as to the criteria which it may apply in determining statehood for this pur-

---

[27] In the *Wimbledon Case,* in which Germany was respondent, jurisdiction was based on Article 386 of the Treaty of Versailles. In the case concerning *German Interests in Polish Upper Silesia,* in which Germany was applicant, it was agreed by the parties that Article 23 of the Geneva Convention of May 15, 1922, was a matter provided for in a treaty in force within Article 36 of the Statute. See Series E, No. 1, p. 261.

[28] Series C, No. 13—II, pp. 9, 28.

[29] Series C. No. 61, p. 9; Series E, No. 8, p. 255. This case was later withdrawn Series A/B, No. 51.

pose.[30] When the Court was approached as to the conditions on which the "Confederacy of Six Nations of the Grand River" might submit to the Court "certain differences with the United States of America and Great Britain," the Registrar's reply merely referred to Articles 34 and 35 of the Statute, and this was later approved by the Court.[31]

§401. **Channels for Communication with Governments.** It seems to have been recognized at the Court's preliminary session that in determining the channels through which it would communicate with Governments, "the Court will have to conform to the varying wishes and usages of the several Governments"; and that the Governments should be approached to ascertain these "wishes and usages." [32] On March 27, 1922, the Registrar requested the Secretary-General of the League of Nations to ask Members of the League of Nations to state their desires in this respect; and the Governments of certain States not members of the League of Nations were approached directly by the Registrar. The Governments of all the States to which the Court is open did not reply promptly, and a reminder was sent to them in 1928. The annual reports of the Court list the results of the inquiries; fifty-seven states have indicated channels to be used for direct communications emanating from the Court.[33] In most cases, the Court is asked to address the Ministry of Foreign Affairs or a corresponding department of the Government, though in some instances this is to be done through the legation at The Hague; in a relatively few cases, the Government is to be addressed through its legation at The Hague. Where no desire has been expressed, the Court communicates either with the legation at The Hague or with the Ministry of Foreign Affairs. Article 35 of the Rules of Court requires that applications and special agreements, or notifications of the latter, shall indicate the permanent addresses at the seat of the Court to

[30] In 1922, the Court decided to communicate the Council's resolution "to all States recognized *de jure*" or "to all recognized States." Series E, No. 1, p. 260; No. 3, p. 197. Danzig has been recognized as a "juridical personality" for the purpose of appointing a judge *ad hoc* in a proceeding relating to a request for an advisory opinion. Series E, No. 4, p. 296. And the Court has looked upon Danzig as a State. Series A/B, No. 44, pp. 23–25. On the other hand, it has said that the European Commission of the Danube is not a State. Series B, No. 14, p. 64.

[31] Series E, No. 8, p. 158.

[32] Series D, No. 2, pp. 197, 451. Article 44 of the Statute seems to have furnished the *point de départ* for this action.

[33] Series E, No. 8, pp. 144–147. On the channel for the Court's communication with Danzig, see Series E, No. 6, p. 302. Communications emanating from the Court may be in English or in French; English is commonly employed in communications addressed to English-speaking countries.

which notices and communications are to be sent; [34] while a case is pending before the Court, the parties are addressed through their agents.

No limitation exists on the agency through which a Government may address a communication to the Court, but the Court may require a communication to be confirmed by the Minister of Foreign Affairs or by the diplomatic representative at The Hague.[35] Communications by Governments are normally addressed to the Registrar, though in some cases they are addressed to the President and sent to the Registrar.

§402. **Requests by Individuals.** On numerous occasions individuals have sought to approach the Court with claims against Governments; [36] such requests have frequently been made by stateless persons. In response, it is the practice of the Registrar to state that under Article 34 of the Statute the Court has no jurisdiction to deal with such requests.[37] In one case in 1922, the Court decided that an application by an individual relating to minority protection should be transmitted to the Secretary-General of the League of Nations with a request that it should be circulated to members of the Council; [38] it is difficult to justify this procedure, however.

Although it is not open to individuals, of course the claims of individuals may be advanced by their Governments before the Court. "International law does not prevent one State from granting to another the right to have recourse to international arbitral tribunals in order to obtain the direct award to nationals of the latter State of compensation for damage suffered by them as a result of infractions of international law by the first State." [39] In the *Mavrommatis Case*, the Court declared that "once a State has taken up a case on behalf of one of its subjects before an international tribunal, in the eyes of the latter the State is sole claimant," and it will appear "asserting its

---

[34] For an explanation of the purpose of this rule, see Series C, No. 18—I, p. 1041.

[35] In 1932, when applications were addressed to the Court by the Czechoslovak Government's agent-general before the Mixed Arbitral Tribunals, the Court directed the Registrar to obtain the confirmation by the Czechoslovak Government of the appointment of its agent before the Court. Series E, No. 9, p. 164.

[36] Series E, No. 1, pp. 155–8; No. 2, p. 96; No. 3, pp. 109–12; No. 4, p. 138; No. 5, pp. 162–165; No. 6, pp. 181–2; No. 7, pp. 191–5; No. 8, pp. 157–8; No. 9, pp. 86–88.

[37] Series E, No. 1, p. 159. [38] *Id.*, p. 254.

[39] *Chorzów Factory Case*, Series A, No. 17, p. 28. See Travers, "La Cour permanente de justice internationale et les interêts privés," 52 *Journal de Droit International* (1925), p. 29; Sobolewski, "La Cour permanente de Justice internationale et les droits et interêts des particuliers," 38 *Revue Générale de Droit International Public* (1931), p. 420.

own rights." [40] In the *Serbian Loans Case,* the special agreement made the controversy submitted to the Court appear to be a dispute between the Serb-Croat-Slovene Government and the French bond-holders; but the French Government having intervened on behalf of the bondholders, the Court found itself seised by the special agreement of a difference of opinion between the two Governments, which though "fundamentally identical with the controversy" between the Serb-Croat-Slovene Government and the bondholders, was nevertheless "distinct therefrom." [41] In such cases, the reparation due may correspond to the damage suffered by individuals, but as the rights and interests of individuals are "always in a different plane to rights belonging to a State," the injury to the individual and the injury to the State are not identical; and as the Court declared in the case of the *Chorzów Factory,* "the reparation due by one State to another does not change its character by reason of the fact that it takes the form of an indemnity for the calculation of which the damage suffered by a private person is taken as the measure." [42]

If a State asserts before the Court a claim of one of its nationals, the conduct of the case, so far as the Court is concerned, is entirely in the hands of the State itself. Hence no question can arise as to the representation of the national before the Court. [43]

[40] Series A, No. 2, pp. 12, 13. See also the *Chorzów Case,* Series A, No. 17, pp. 27–28. In the *Wimbledon Case,* the company which had suffered injury was referred to as if it had been the applicant. Series A, No. 1, p. 32.

[41] Series A, Nos. 20/21, pp. 17–18. In this case, Judge Pessôa, dissenting, stressed the fact that the French Government was proceeding on behalf of unidentified French nationals. *Id.,* pp. 64–65.

[42] Series A, No. 17, pp. 27–28. Judge Nyholm, dissenting in this case, insisted on regarding the State as the "mandatory" for its nationals. *Id.,* p. 96.

[43] Thus it was agreed by the 1920 Committee of Jurists that "the right of a private individual, associated with his Government in a suit, to have an agent of his own, is a domestic question concerning the individual and his Government." Minutes of the 1920 Committee of the Jurists, p. 340.

CHAPTER 18

THE JURISDICTION OF THE COURT

§403. **Provisions of the Covenant.** Article 1 of the Statute may be taken to have incorporated by reference certain provisions in Article 14 of the Covenant of the League of Nations, and Article 14 provides for two sources of jurisdiction: (1) a submission by the parties of a dispute of an international character; (2) a reference by the Council or by the Assembly of a dispute or question for advisory opinion. The first of these is covered by the broader provision for reference by the parties in Article 36 of the Statute; Article 14 therefore adds to the Statute only the provision for advisory jurisdiction.

Other articles in the Covenant may be examined for their effect on the Court's jurisdiction, either as having been somehow incorporated in the Statute, or as falling into the category of "treaties and conventions in force" mentioned in Article 36 of the Statute. It would seem, however, that the provisions in other articles of the Covenant cannot be said to have been incorporated by reference into the Statute, for the reference to Article 14 does not comprise them. Nor does the relation between the Court and the League of Nations make the Covenant applicable generally. Even if other articles in the Covenant are to be regarded as applicable to the Court, it seems clear that their provisions do not furnish a source of jurisdiction for the Court. Article 12 of the Covenant, before it was amended, obligated a Member of the League of Nations to submit "any dispute likely to lead to a rupture" either to arbitration or to inquiry by the Council; as amended in 1924, it leaves to Members of the League of Nations the choice of judicial settlement as a third course. Article 13 of the Covenant, before it was amended, left the Members of the League of Nations free to determine what disputes should be recognized by them as suitable for submission to arbitration and free to choose an agency for that purpose; as it was amended in 1924, this freedom has not been curtailed. Article 15 of the Covenant, in

its original form and as amended in 1924, expressly recognizes that Members of the League of Nations need not submit to arbitration or judicial settlement even disputes "likely to lead to a rupture." The expression "judicial settlement" as used in the amended text of the Covenant does not necessarily refer to the Court,[1] as some other tribunal might be chosen. The Court would not be justified, therefore, in taking either Article 12, or Article 13, or Article 15 as a source of jurisdiction. In fulfillment of obligations undertaken therein, Members of the League of Nations may proceed to confer jurisdiction on the Court; but the articles do not operate automatically to give the Court any jurisdiction.

§404. The Protocol of Signature. The protocol opened to signature at Geneva on December 16, 1920, contains a reference to the jurisdiction of the Court which seems to require explanation. Signatories of the Protocol first declare their acceptance of the "adjoined Statute"; then "consequently," they declare their acceptance of "the jurisdiction of the Court in accordance with the terms and subject to the conditions of the above-mentioned Statute." This language creates an impression that a party to the Protocol necessarily accepts, i.e., confers on the Court, some measure of jurisdiction; but an examination of the Statute tends to dissipate the impression. If a State does not agree to a reference of a case to the Court, and if it is not a party to a "treaty or convention in force" providing a "matter" as to which the Court is to have jurisdiction, and if it does not make a declaration under paragraph 2 of Article 36, its "acceptance" of the Court's jurisdiction in accordance with the Statute means little more than its consent that an institution which it helps to maintain may exercise the contentious jurisdiction conferred by other States and the advisory jurisdiction conferred by Article 14 of the Covenant. A party to the Protocol of Signature is not bound by its acceptance of the Statute to make any use of the Court; it does not thereby subject itself in any way to the Court's exercise of contentious jurisdiction. In this respect the Court is like the Permanent Court of Arbitration; a State may join in the maintenance of either institution without conferring any jurisdiction. By becoming a party to the Protocol of Signature, a State merely consents to the operation of the Statute as a whole.

[1] This was the object of the amendments proposed in 1921, however, though it was explained at the time that they were only modifications of form. Records of Second Assembly, Plenary, pp. 698, 827.

The language of the Protocol may have a meaning, however, in connection with action which may be taken by the Court incidentally to its exercise of jurisdiction otherwise conferred. Thus, two States which are before the Court under a special agreement may have to submit to intervention by a third State; the Court's allowing such intervention would be incidental to its exercise of jurisdiction under the special agreement, "in accordance with the terms" of the Statute. Moreover, the Court may indicate measures of interim protection, even in advance of its determination whether jurisdiction has been conferred upon it to deal with the merits of a case; under Article 36 of the Statute, it may deal with a dispute as to its jurisdiction upon the application of one State; and under Article 60 of the Statute, the Court has obligatory jurisdiction for construing a judgment previously given.[2] In this limited sense, then, a party to the Protocol of Signature may be said to have conferred a jurisdiction on the Court.

§405. **Provisions of the Statute.** Article 36 of the Statute provides four sources of the Court's jurisdiction: (1) references by the parties; (2) special provisions in "treaties and conventions in force"; (3) declarations recognizing jurisdiction "as compulsory *ipso facto* and without special agreement"; and (4) paragraph 4, under which the Court has competence to decide disputes as to its own jurisdiction. Article 37 is in a sense an amplification of the second of these sources. Several additional articles of the Statute relate to the exercise of jurisdiction incidental to that conferred: thus, Article 41 as to the indication of provisional measures of interim protection; Article 48, as to making orders for the conduct of a case; Article 49, as to calling upon agents to produce documents; Article 53, as to the Court's proceeding in the absence of a party; Articles 60 and 61, as to the construction and revision of judgments.[3] Intervention as provided for in Articles 62 and 63 of the Statute may be said to constitute an independent source of the Court's jurisdiction. Under Article 63, a State has a right to intervene, and thus to procure an adjudication of its relations with the preëxisting parties before the Court, if it is a party to a convention which the Court is called upon to construe in the pending case; under Article 62, it rests with the Court to say whether intervention will be permitted, and the Court should

---

[2] This is stated by Judge Anzilotti, in Series A, No. 13, p. 23.

[3] It may be noted, also, that under Article 40 of the Rules conclusions stated in a counter-case "may include counter-claims, in so far as the latter come within the jurisdiction of the Court." See, also, Articles 26 and 27 of the Statute.

only admit such intervention if, in its opinion, the existence of an "interest of a legal nature which may be affected by the decision" in the pending case, is sufficiently demonstrated.[4]

The exercise of the Court's jurisdiction does not depend upon the appearance of all the parties; under Article 53 of the Statute, the Court may decide in favor of a party's claim in the absence of the other party, if it is satisfied that it has jurisdiction under Article 36 or Article 37 of the Statute and that the claim is well founded in fact and in law.

§406. **Article 37 of the Statute.** Article 37 of the Statute provides that "when a treaty or convention in force provides for the reference of a matter to a tribunal to be instituted by the League of Nations, the Court will be such tribunal." The article raises some difficult questions, both in its application to treaties and conventions in force in 1921 when the Statute became operative, and in its application to treaties and conventions coming into force after that date. It was intended by the subcommittee of the Third Committee of the First Assembly[5] to take account of provisions in the peace treaties of 1919 and 1920 for referring certain questions to the "jurisdiction instituted for the purpose by the League of Nations."[6] With respect to such provisions, it is not clear that the parties to the Protocol of Signature, which may not include all Members of the League of Nations, can bind either the parties to the Peace Treaties or the Assembly and Council of the League of Nations, as Article 37 purports to bind them. The Assembly's "approval" of the draft Statute and the Council's "adoption" of it may possibly constitute Article 37 as action taken by the League of Nations, but the possibility is not precluded that either body might at a later time set up a "tribunal" or "jurisdiction" other than the Court. As a practical matter this may not be done; the Court's intimate relation to the League may dissuade either body from attempting to set up a different "tribunal." In the case of the *S.S. Wimbledon,* the applicant States relied upon Article 386 of the Treaty of Versailles and Article 37 of the Statute as the foundation of the Court's jurisdiction;

---

[4] See the *Wimbledon Case,* Series A, No. 1, p. 12; §410, *infra.*

[5] Records of First Assembly, Committees, I, p. 382. The phraseology is from the "Brussels draft." *Id.,* p. 488.

[6] *E.g.,* Articles 336, 337, 376, 386 of the Treaty of Versailles; Article 328 of the Treaty of St. Germain; Articles 281, 311 of the Treaty of Trianon; Articles 225, 245 of the Treaty of Neuilly. The texts of these articles are not identical in the references to the jurisdiction instituted by the League of Nations. *Cf.* Article 27 of the Statute.

as Germany did not contest the jurisdiction,[7] the Court found no difficulty in deciding that it had jurisdiction.[8]

The application of Article 37 of the Statute to future treaties or conventions is possibly less important, for it seems unlikely that many such general clauses will be inserted in future treaties. A party to such a future instrument, not also a party to the Protocol of Signature, might insist on the creation of an agency other than the Court, and this would not be beyond the power of the Council or the Assembly.

The conclusion seems to follow that Article 37 is not necessarily to be treated by the Court as a source of jurisdiction in every case to which its terms apply.

§407. General Limits on the Court's Jurisdiction. The jurisdiction of the Court cannot be assimilated to that of a municipal court.[9] There are certain general limits which must be observed as to the consent of the parties, as to the subject-matter of the dispute, and as to other constitutional requirements, for which the experience of many municipal courts furnishes no analogies. Questions as to the observance of these limits may be raised by the Court *proprio motu,* without any objection by a party. No principle can be formulated that in case of doubt the Court should decline to assume jurisdiction; its action must depend on the preponderating force of the arguments militating for or against jurisdiction.[10]

(1) *Consent of the Parties.* The Court has repeatedly declared that its jurisdiction "depends on the will of the parties,"[11] and that jurisdiction exists "only in so far as States have accepted it."[12] However, "the acceptance by a State of the Court's jurisdiction is not, under the Statute, subordinated to the observance of certain forms, such as, for instance, the previous conclusion of a special

---

[7] In correspondence preceding the application, the German Government had suggested the procedure laid down in Article 386 of the Treaty of Versailles. Series C, No. 3 (supplementary volume), p. 38. See also *id.,* p. 33.

[8] Series A, No. 1, p. 20. [9] Series A, No. 15, p. 23.

[10] Series A, No. 9, p. 32. In the first *Mavrommatis Case,* Judge Moore, dissenting, said that no presumption in favor of the jurisdiction of international tribunals may be indulged, and that "their jurisdiction must always affirmatively appear on the face of the record." Series A, No. 2, p. 60.

[11] Series A, No. 15, p. 22. In the case relating to *German Minority Schools in Polish Upper Silesia,* the Court stated that this principle, as established by the first paragraph of Article 36 of the Statute, "only becomes inoperative in those exceptional cases in which the dispute which States might desire to refer to the Court would fall within the exclusive jurisdiction reserved to some other authority." *Id.,* p. 23.

[12] Series A, No. 9, p. 32.

agreement." [13] An express declaration is not necessary, for consent "may be inferred from acts conclusively establishing it." A submission of arguments on the merits without a reservation of the question of jurisdiction is such an act, as is also a request for a decision on the merits without a reservation as to the question of jurisdiction.[14] In the first *Mavrommatis Case,* the Court was willing to exercise jurisdiction on the basis of a protocol ratified after the proceeding had been instituted; [15] and in the *Mavrommatis Jerusalem Concessions Case,* it asserted jurisdiction "in consequence of an agreement between the parties resulting from the written proceedings." [16] It is to be noted that in most of the cases which have arisen there had been an agreement and its effect was merely extended by consent.[17] An interesting question might arise, however, if without any previous agreement whatever State A should file an application against State B and the latter should proceed to defend on the merits, asking judgment in its favor; such action by State B might be regarded by the Court as "an unequivocal indication of the desire of a State to obtain a decision on the merits of the suit." [18] If consent has been given, it cannot be withdrawn during the Court's exercise of the jurisdiction consented to; however, it might be withdrawn "if the applicant had, in the subsequent proceedings, essentially modified the aspect of the case." [19]

(2) *Subject-Matter of the Dispute.* Article 14 of the Covenant envisaged a Court competent "to hear and determine any dispute of an international character"; paragraph 1 of Article 36 of the Statute extends the Court's competence to "all cases" (Fr., *toutes affaires*) referred to it by the parties and to "all matters" (Fr., *tous les cas*) specially provided for in treaties or conventions in force. "Inter-

---

[13] Series A, No. 15, p. 23. See, however, the dissenting opinions of Judge Huber and Judge Nyholm, *id.,* pp. 52, 57.

[14] Series A, No. 15, p. 24. But see the dissenting opinions of Judge Nyholm and Deputy-Judge Negulesco, *id.,* pp. 58, 69.

[15] Series A, No. 2, p. 34.   [16] Series A, No. 5, p. 27.

[17] The Court's judgment No. 4, interpreting judgment No. 3, was based on jurisdiction derived from the request for interpretation by the Greek agent and the submission of a memorandum which did not contest the jurisdiction by the Bulgarian agent; this was said to constitute an "agreement between the parties." Series A, No. 4, p. 6.

[18] Series A, No. 12, p. 24. See, however, the dissent of Judge Huber in Series A, No. 15, pp. 52, 53, insisting that "the absence of a plea to the jurisdiction does not create jurisdiction."

[19] *German Minority Schools in Upper Silesia,* Series A, No. 15, p. 25. In this case it was held that consent given by a counter-case dealing with the merits was not invalidated by an objection contained in a rejoinder.

national character," as the term is used in the Covenant, would seem to involve the necessity of an interstate dispute. If this is all it involves, the expression has no more limiting effect than Article 34 of the Statute, and under Articles 34 and 36, the subject matter of a dispute which may be brought before the Court is not limited if the parties are States which have agreed to the submission.[20] Is there a limitation, however, in that the dispute must be one to which international law applies? In the *Serbian Loans Case,* it was said that "Article 38 of the Statute cannot be regarded as excluding the possibility of the Court's dealing with disputes which do not require the application of international law," [21] though the Court's "true function" was declared to be "to decide disputes between States or Members of the League of Nations on the basis of international law." [22] The Court has also described itself as the "organ" of international law,[23] and as "a tribunal of international law." [24] Yet it is "bound to apply municipal law when circumstances so require," [25] and there would seem to be "no dispute which States entitled to appear before the Court cannot refer to it." [26] In the *Free Zones Case,* however, the Court thought that a settlement of such matters as tariff exemptions "is not a question of law," but depended upon "the interplay of economic interests"; and that "such questions are outside the sphere in which a Court of Justice, concerned with the application of rules of law, can help in the solution of disputes between two States." [27] Article 418 of Part XIII of the Treaty of Versailles, with the corresponding articles in other peace treaties, seems to present a difficult problem in this connection; it would confer on the Court a competence to "indicate the measures, if any, of an economic character which it considers to be appropriate, and which other Governments would be justified in adopting against a defaulting Government." This provision antedates the drafting of the Court's Statute, and Article 26 of the Statute may be taken to incorporate it by reference. Yet express authority for such an indication is not to be found in the Statute; and it would not be surprising if, the case arising, the Court should hesitate to embark upon an exercise of competence under Article 418.

---

[20] See Judge Pessôa dissenting in Series A, No. 20/21, p. 62.
[21] Series A, No. 20/21, p. 20.   [22] *Id.,* p. 19.   [23] Series A, No. 7, p. 19.
[24] Series A, No. 20/21, p. 124.   [25] *Ibid.* See §520, *infra.*
[26] Series A, No. 15, p. 22. See, however, the observations of Judge Kellogg, Series A, No. 24, pp. 37, 41, 43.   [27] Series A/B, No. 46, p. 162.

Questions involved in a dispute may be "abstract" questions; [28] and in some cases at any rate, *e.g.*, where the Court is asked to decide *ex æquo et bono*, they may be "political" questions,[29] though that category is one of changing content.

(3) *Other Constitutional Limits.* Jurisdiction cannot be exercised by the Court, even where the parties consent and where a proper subject matter is presented, except within the *cadre* of its Statute. In other words, the Court cannot act outside its constitutional limits. It could not, even at the request of the parties, give a judgment which was not to be binding, or a decision the force of which was merely advisory. Thus in the *Free Zones Case,* the Court declared "after mature consideration" that "it would be incompatible with the Statute, and with its position as a Court of Justice, to give a judgment which would be dependent for its validity on the subsequent approval of the Parties." [30] The judgment in the *Serbian Loans Case* was not a departure from this principle.[31] Nor can the Court be bound to choose between two incorrect interpretations of a treaty offered by the parties. In the *Free Zones Case,* it refused to communicate to the parties "unofficially" indications as to the results of its deliberations, saying that it could not "on the proposal of the parties, depart from the terms of the Statute." [32] Clearly, States resorting to the Court must take it as they find it and cannot insist upon any departure from

---

[28] Series A, No. 7, p. 18. In the *Statute of Memel Case,* the Court drew attention to the "inconvenience resulting from" the formulation of questions "purely *in abstracto*," though it seems to have admitted the propriety of parties' seeking an interpretation of the Statute of Memel merely "as a guide for the future." Series A/B, No. 49, pp. 311, 337.

[29] It is to be noted, however, that after determining that certain of the Mavrommatis concessions should be readapted, the Court refused to determine the method of such re-adaptation. Series A, No. 5, p. 50.

[30] Series A, No. 46, p. 161. For this reason, the Court refused to give effect to paragraph 2 of Article 2 of the Franco-Swiss special agreement. Its judgment met the condition upon which paragraph 2 was based, for it did "contemplate the import of goods free or at reduced rates through the Federal customs barrier," though no regulations of such importation were made. The Court accepted only a part of the mission entrusted to it, *viz.*, that part covered by paragraph 1 of Article 2, though this part had been said to be "unsuitable to the rôle of a Court of Justice." *Id.*, p. 162. The defense of this course that the "obstacle to fulfilling part of the mission" was due to "the will of the parties," *id.*, p. 163, was most inadequate, as the dissenting judges pointed out. *Id.*, pp. 192, 208.

[31] The special agreement in the *Serbian Loans Case* provided for further negotiations, following the decision of the Court, to constitute "a second possible phase of the proceedings, in which considerations of equity and necessity may come into account." Series A, No. 20/21, p. 20; Series C, No. 16—III, p. 292. The further negotiations resulted in the conclusion of a convention between the Serb-Croat-Slovene Government and the bondholders, on March 31, 1930.

The French-Greek special agreement in the *Lighthouses Case* also provided for a second phase of proceedings before a special arbitral tribunal.

[32] Series A, No. 22, p. 12.

its essential constitutional characteristics. Thus a judgment given by less than the judges required would not be a judgment of the Court.

(4) *Previous Negotiations.* It cannot be laid down as a general condition of the jurisdiction of the Court that the parties must previously have conducted negotiations with a view to the settlement of their differences, and that such negotiations must have failed.[33] In the case of a special agreement, no occasion would arise for applying such a principle; nor can it be formulated for cases which are begun by application. While many treaties provide for the failure of negotiations as a condition precedent to invoking the jurisdiction of the Court, such treaties cannot be said to have established a general law on this point.[34] Article 13 of the Covenant refers to disputes "which cannot be satisfactorily settled by diplomacy," but no similar reference is to be found in the Statute. In the *Mavrommatis Case,* it was said: "The Court realises to the full the importance of the rule laying down that only disputes which cannot be settled by negotiations should be brought before it. It recognises, in fact, that before a dispute can be made the subject of an action at law, its subject matter should have been clearly defined by means of diplomatic negotiations. Nevertheless, in applying this rule, the Court cannot disregard, amongst other considerations, the views of the States concerned, who are in the best position to judge as to the political reasons which may prevent the settlement of a given dispute by diplomatic negotiation."[35] In that case, the Court's jurisdiction under Article 26 of the Palestine mandate was subject to the expressed condition that the dispute could not be settled by negotiation, and the condition was held to have been met. In the case on *German Interests in Polish Upper Silesia,* the Court's jurisdiction related only to "differences of opinion" be-

---

[33] The 1920 Committee of Jurists had proposed a general compulsory jurisdiction of the Court for disputes which it had been found impossible to settle by diplomatic means. Minutes of the 1920 Committee of Jurists, p. 679. In its report, it stated that "it would be inadmissible for a State to bring a direct action against another State before the Court without having previously attempted to settle the case by friendly means." *Id.,* p. 725.

[34] An interesting argument has been made, however, that the Court is bound by the principle of the priority of diplomatic negotiations. Kaasik, *"La Clause de Négociations Diplomatiques,"* 14 *Revue de Droit International et de Législation Comparée* (1933), pp. 62, 69.

[35] Series A, No. 2, p. 15. See the dissenting opinions of Judge Moore and Judge Pessôa, *id.,* pp. 61, 74, 91. Judge Moore wished to prevent the Court's becoming "a mere makeweight in negotiations"; he thought it "a well settled principle of public law that it is inadmissible for courts to assert jurisdiction where, even though there should exist some present ground for complaint, it appears that, for the time being, the power to deal with the subject matter rests with governments."

tween the parties to the Geneva Convention; the Court said that "a difference of opinion does exist as soon as one of the Governments concerned points out that the attitude adopted by the other conflicts with its own views"; it noted that Article 23 of the Geneva Convention did not "stipulate that diplomatic negotiations must first of all be tried," and held that "the absence of diplomatic negotiations" did not "prevent the bringing of an action." [36]

In the application of Article 60 of the Statute, it was held in the *Chorzów Factory Case* that a "dispute as to the meaning or scope of the judgment" does not require manifestation "in a specific manner, as for instance by diplomatic negotiations." [37] The Court added, however: "It would no doubt be desirable that a State should not proceed to take as serious a step as summoning another State to appear before the Court without having previously, within reasonable limits, endeavoured to make it quite clear that a difference of views is in question which has not been capable of being otherwise overcome. But in view of the wording of the article, the Court considers that it cannot require that the dispute should have manifested itself in a formal way." [38]

Where abortive negotiations have preceded an application to the Court, the contentions of the parties are not to be prejudiced by "declarations, admissions or proposals" made in the course of the negotiations.[39]

§408. **Disputes as to the Court's Jurisdiction.** The fourth paragraph of Article 36 confers on the Court power to decide any dispute as to whether it has jurisdiction. This is not expressly limited to disputes arising with reference to other provisions of Article 36,[40] and it seems to apply to the Court's jurisdiction from any source.[41] It constitutes in itself a provision for obligatory jurisdiction, limited to disputes as to jurisdiction.[42] Such a dispute may conceivably have no relation to a case before the Court for a decision on the merits, and might possibly be placed before the Court by special agreement; if it does relate to such a case, however, the dispute may be submitted to

[36] Series A, No. 6, pp. 14, 22. *Cf.*, the observations of Judge Rostworowski, *id.*, p. 36.　　　[37] Series A, No. 13, p. 10.　　　[38] Series A, No. 13, pp. 10–11.
[39] Series A, No. 9, p. 19; No. 17, pp. 51, 62.
[40] A different conclusion may be argued on the history of the drafting of Article 36.
[41] See Judge Anzilotti's observations in the *German Interests in Upper Silesia Case*, Series A, No. 6, pp. 29–30. *Cf.* the explanation by Judge Rostworowski, id., p. 32. *Quære*, as to the application of the fourth paragraph of Article 36 to the cases covered by Article 37 of the Statute.　　　[42] *Cf.*, Series D, No. 2 (add.), p. 91.

the Court either as a preliminary objection under Article 38 of the Rules, or as an objection made in the course of the proceedings on the merits.[43] The existence of a dispute within the meaning of paragraph 4 of Article 36 would seem to require no particular form of manifestation, and possibly previous diplomatic negotiations need not be shown.[44] The Court also has power, *proprio motu*, to raise and to decide questions as to its jurisdiction.[45]

§409. **Objections to the Court's Jurisdiction.** The Statute makes no provision for objections to the Court's jurisdiction *in limine litis*, and the *lacuna* was not filled in the 1922 Rules. In the *Mavrommatis Case*, therefore, the Court felt itself "at liberty to adopt the principle which it considers best calculated to ensure the administration of justice, most suited to procedure before an international tribunal and most in conformity with the fundamental principles of international law." [46] In that case, it refused to "content itself with the provisional conclusion that the dispute falls or not within the terms of the mandate," and it proceeded to "satisfy itself that the suit before it, in the form in which it has been submitted and on the basis of the facts hitherto established, falls to be decided by application of the clauses of the mandate."

In 1926, a new Article 38 of the Rules made provision for the filing of "any preliminary objections" when proceedings are instituted by an application, and such objections have since frequently been made. The State filing the objection is regarded as in the position of instituting a proceeding which is treated as in many respects distinct from the proceeding instituted by the application, and the proceeding based on the objection is given a separate numbering in the Court's general list.[47] Some time-limit may have to be set for the filing of an objection to the jurisdiction. In the case relating to *German Minority Schools in Upper Silesia*, the Polish Government's objection was made in the rejoinder after a counter-case had been filed which dealt with the merits and which contained no reservation; the Court held that "the objection to the jurisdiction made in the rejoinder cannot invalidate the acceptance" of jurisdiction "which ex-

---

[43] See Series A, No. 15, p. 22. See also the observations of Judge Huber, *id.*, p. 50.
[44] See Series A, No. 13, p. 10, for this interpretation of "dispute" as the term is used in Article 60 of the Statute.
[45] Series A /B, No. 52, p. 15.   [46] Series A, No. 2, p. 16.
[47] See, *e.g.*, Series E, No. 8, pp. 184, 187, on the entry of the proceedings as to the *Statute of Memel* in the general list.

isted at the time of the submission of the counter-case."[48] Article 38 of the Rules was construed by the Court to have for its object "to lay down when an objection to the jurisdiction may validly be filed, but only in cases where an objection is submitted as a preliminary question, that is to say, when the respondent asks for a decision upon the objection before any subsequent proceedings on the merits."[49]

The Court may raise questions as to its jurisdiction *proprio motu* —indeed, it ought to do so in any case in which jurisdiction is not clearly conferred upon it by the parties.[50] As Judge Huber said, dissenting in the case relating to *German Minority Schools in Upper Silesia,* "the absence of a plea to the jurisdiction does not create jurisdiction"; and "the Court's jurisdiction is determined by the treaty or special agreement establishing that jurisdiction, and not by the contentions maintained by the parties in the particular case."[51]

In passing upon an objection to its jurisdiction, the Court may sever different parts of an application,[52] and it may have to deal with the merits.[53] When called upon to interpret previous judgments in the *Chorzów Factory Case,* it combined a decision on the objection to its jurisdiction with a decision on the merits.[54] In the *Prince of Pless Case,* a preliminary objection was joined to the merits so that if necessary both should be dealt with by a single judgment.[55]

§410. **Intervention.** Quite apart from the sources of jurisdiction set out in Articles 36 and 37 of the Statute, the Court may acquire contentious jurisdiction as a result of a State's intervention under Article 62 or under Article 63 or possibly under both articles of the Statute.[56] Under Article 62 a State wishing to intervene must establish that "it has an interest of a legal nature which may be affected by the decision in the case" (Fr., *un intérêt d'ordre juridique est pour lui en cause*); otherwise permission to intervene will not be granted.[57]

---

[48] Series A, No. 15, p. 26. But see the dissent by Deputy-Judge Negulesco, *id.,* pp. 68–72.   [49] *Id.,* p. 22.

[50] This was done in the *Prince of Pless Case,* Series A/B, No. 52, p. 16.

[51] Series A, No. 15, pp. 53–54.   [52] Series A, No. 12, p. 29.

[53] In the case relating to *German Interests in Polish Upper Silesia,* the Court noted that the Polish objection had been "submitted at a time when no document of procedure on the merits had been filed," yet some of the Polish arguments related to the merits. Series A, No. 6, p. 15.

[54] Series A, No. 13.   [55] Series A/B, No. 52, p. 16.

[56] On this subject, see Wadie M. Farag, *L'Intervention devant la Cour Permanente de Justice Internationale* (Paris, 1927); Wilhelm Friede, *"Die Intervention im Verfahren vor dem Ständigen Internationalen Gerichtshof,"* 3 *Zeitschrift für ausländisches öffentliches Recht und Völkerrecht* (1932), p. 1.

[57] *Wimbledon Case,* Series A, No. 1, p. 12. *Cf.,* Article 59 of the Statute, and §324, *supra.*

370 PERMANENT COURT OF INTERNATIONAL JUSTICE

Perhaps the request may be denied even though such an interest be shown.[58] Article 62 was drafted when it was proposed to confer on the Court a general obligatory jurisdiction; though that proposal was rejected, no limits were set for the application of Article 62. If two States are before the Court by reason of declarations made under paragraph 2 of Article 36 of the Statute, it seems a derogation from the condition of reciprocity therein laid down to allow a third State which has made no similar declaration to become a party to their case upon its own motion; [59] yet the problem is not essentially different if two States are before the Court under a special agreement and a third State which is not a party to the agreement seeks to intervene.[60] The jurisprudence of the Court has not set additional conditions for the application of Article 62. Under Article 58 of the Rules, the request to be permitted to intervene takes the form of an application, and under Article 59 the Court's decision upon the request takes the form of a judgment upon the application. If the request is granted, the intervenor becomes a party to the case, but apparently a special kind of party, a "third party"; [61] under Article 59 of the Statute, it may be a "party" with reference to which the Court's decision in the case will have "binding force." The difference between Article 62 and Article 63 in this respect, would seem to indicate that the "binding force," so far as the intervenor is concerned, is not limited to the "interest of a legal nature" on which the intervention was based.[62]

Under Article 63 of the Statute, limited intervention is provided for as a matter of right, by any State which is a party to a convention,[63] the construction of which is in question in a case before the Court.[64] Strictly, such a State must have been notified by the Registrar before it may intervene; [65] but the Registrar's duty to

---

[58] See the summary by Deputy-Judge Beichmann, Series D, No. 2, p. 349.

[59] See the discussion in Series D, No. 2, pp. 86–97.

[60] In this case, the intervenor may not be allowed to depart from the terms of the special agreement relating to procedure.

[61] The French version of Article 62 has no equivalent of the words "as a third party," which are in the English version. See the observations of the British agent in the *Wimbledon Case*, Series C, No. 3, vol. 1, p. 107.

[62] *Cf.*, Series D, No. 2, p. 349.

[63] The term *convention* seems to be used in the Statute to imply the existence of more than two parties to the instrument. It is not a term of art in this sense, however. Ordinarily, a party must have ratified and not have denounced the instrument.

[64] The "convention in question," within the terms of Article 63 of the Statute, is "the convention the construction of which is, *prima facie,* decisive for the settlement of the case." Series E, No. 9, p. 176.

[65] In the *Free Zones Case,* "parties to the Treaty of Versailles were not specially

notify is absolute, if he is satisfied that the conditions exist. A State which exercises this right to intervene will be bound by the construction of the convention given by the judgment.[66]

An intervenor may make an independent claim, or it may side with one of the previous parties.[67] The precise character of the "interest of a legal nature" which the intervenor must assert under Article 62 is somewhat uncertain; though the discussions in the Court in 1922 showed some tendency to include under that phrase a State's general interest in the development of international law,[68] a special interest would seem to be required. An application to intervene under Article 62 should be filed before oral proceedings are begun, though it may be considered if filed later. No limit is placed on the time within which intervention under Article 63 must be effected, but doubtless the Court would be reluctant to permit intervention at a late stage of the proceedings in a case. The procedure is governed by Articles 59 and 60 of the Rules.

Intervention has occurred in only one case. On May 22, 1923, Poland requested to be permitted to intervene under Article 62 of the Statute, in the *Wimbledon Case;* [69] the request stated that Poland was a party to the Treaty of Versailles, that its rights and material interests under Article 380 of that Treaty had been violated by the German Government's action which was the subject of the suit, and that Poland desired to intervene "on the side of" the applicant States. When the request came before the Court on June 25, 1923, the British agent contended that the intervention should be under Article 63 of the Statute. The Polish representative made a declaration [70] that the Polish Government wished to avail itself of its right to intervene under Article 63; that it did not insist upon a consideration of its reasons for intervention under Article 62; and that it did not wish to designate a judge *ad hoc*.[71] The Polish request was not withdrawn, however,

---

notified under Article 63 of the Statute, which was considered as inapplicable in this case." Series A/B, No. 46, p. 100. The reason for this is not clear. However, the attention of such States "was drawn to the right which they no doubt possessed to inform the Court, should they wish to intervene in accordance with the said Article [63], in which case it would rest with the Court to decide." *Ibid.* See also Series C, No. 17—I, (vol. 4), p. 2400. This action of the Registrar was contested by the Polish Government, however, *id.*, p. 2423. For the Registrar's reply, see *id.*, p. 2429. See also Series E, No. 7, pp. 299–300.

[66] Series A, No. 1, p. 12. *Quære*, whether as a "party" under Article 59 of the Statute it is otherwise bound by the decision contained in the judgment.

[67] See Minutes of the 1920 Committee of Jurists, p. 745.

[68] Series D, No. 2, pp. 86–90, 349. See §324, *supra*.

[69] Series C, No. 3, Vol. 1, p. 102.   [70] *Id.*, p. 116.   [71] See §385, *supra*.

and the parties left the matter to the Court's appreciation.[72] On June 28, 1923, the Court gave a judgment, in which after "recording" Poland's intention to intervene under Article 63, it "accepted" the intervention.[73]

In 1931, the Government of Iceland notified the Court that it had an interest of a legal nature which might be affected by the decision in the *Eastern Greenland Case,* but apparently it did not ask to be permitted to intervene.[74]

There can be no question of intervention, in the strict sense of the term in an advisory proceeding, in which there are no parties; in such proceedings there seems to be no need for resorting to Articles 62 and 63, as the Court may receive information from any State which is willing to furnish it.[75] In 1923, the Court refused to allow intervention by Rumania under Article 62 of the Statute, in the case concerning the *Acquisition of Polish Nationality.*[76] Under Article 73 of the Rules as amended in 1926, however, notices of requests for advisory opinions are sent by special and direct communications to States or organizations considered to be "likely to be able to furnish information on the question" before the Court, and any State or Member of the League of Nations which fails to receive such a communication may express a desire to submit a written statement or to be heard, it being for the Court to decide. In determining the States which should receive this special and direct communication, Article 63, paragraph 1, of the Statute may be applied by analogy.[77]

It would seem to be impossible for the parties to a special agreement to exclude the possibility of intervention under Articles 62 and 63 of the Statute.[78] On the other hand, a State cannot be forced to intervene.[79]

§411. Types of Jurisdiction. The jurisdiction of the Court is either contentious or advisory. Its contentious jurisdiction must be

---

[72] Series C, No. 3, Vol. 1, p. 9.
[73] Series A, No. 1, p. 11. *Quære,* whether a judgment would be necessary if the request is based on Article 63. The giving of a judgment in this case may be rested on the actual facts.　　　　　　　　　　　[74] Series C, No. 67.
[75] However, the dissenting opinion by five judges, concerning the question of admitting judges *ad hoc* in the case of the *Austro-German Customs Régime,* refers to the "intervention" by Germany under Article 73 of the Rules. Series A/B, No. 41, p. 91.
[76] Series C, No. 3, Vol. 3, pp. 1089, 1090.
[77] Series E, No. 7, pp. 302, 304; Series E, No. 8, p. 274.
[78] Some doubt may be felt on this point if the special agreement asks for a decision *ex æquo et bono.*
[79] See, however, the suggestion in Series D, No. 2, p. 262.

derived either from a special agreement relating to one or more particular questions or disputes which have become the subject of difference between the parties to the agreement; or from the more general provisions of a "treaty or convention in force"; or from declarations under the second paragraph of Article 36. Its advisory jurisdiction is derived from Article 14 of the Covenant as incorporated in Article 1 of the Statute. While it is conceivable that both advisory and contentious jurisdiction might be exercised in a single proceeding, the Court would probably be reluctant to find itself called upon to give an advisory opinion and a judgment at the same time.[80] In the case relating to the *Interpretation of the Caphandaris-Molloff Agreement,* the Court refused to ignore a condition in the request for an advisory opinion, though the agents and counsel of the two Governments represented before the Court desired it to do so; on the facts, it was found unnecessary to say "whether it is possible for an understanding between the representatives of the interested Governments, reached in the course of the [advisory] proceedings, to serve as a kind of 'special agreement,' initiating a contentious proceeding before the Court." [81] Conversely, the Court would doubtless refuse to give an advisory opinion in the course of a contentious proceeding.

The Court's jurisdiction is always original; *i.e.,* the Court is not a part of any international system which includes inferior courts. Yet a dispute between two States may relate to the propriety of a decision taken by some other tribunal, and in exercising jurisdiction over such a dispute, the Court may be empowered to revise such a decision.[82]

§412. **Proposed Appellate Jurisdiction.** The 1929 Committee of Jurists had before it a proposal by M. Rundstein (Poland) that the Court should be given jurisdiction on appeal from special arbitral tribunals, where one party to the arbitration contends that the tribunal has violated a rule of international law or exceeded its competence.[83] Without expressing any opinion on the proposal, the

---

[80] In its opinion on *German Settlers in Poland,* the Court referred to the possibility that under Article 12 of the Polish Minorities treaty the same question might be brought before the Court by the Council for advisory opinion under paragraph 2, and by a single State represented on the Council for judgment under paragraph 3. Series B, No. 6, pp. 22–23.   [81] Series A/B, No. 45, p. 87.
[82] See, for example, Article 34 of the treaty between Denmark and Latvia, of November 3, 1924. 33 League of Nations Treaty Series, p. 393.
[83] Minutes of the 1929 Committee of Jurists, pp. 75, 105. The question had previously been referred to in the Ninth Assembly by the Minister of Foreign Affairs of Finland. Records of Ninth Assembly, Plenary, p. 76. In 1919, Lord Cecil had envisaged extensive appellate jurisdiction for a court. Miller, Drafting of the Covenant, I, p. 63. The question of *excès de pouvoir* had been raised in the optants dispute between Hungary

Committee of Jurists drew it to the attention of the Council,[84] and the latter directed the Secretary-General to examine the proposal.[85] In the Tenth Assembly of the League of Nations, the representative of Finland made a somewhat similar proposal and asked that a special study be made of it.[86] On September 25, 1929, the Tenth Assembly requested that the Council submit to examination the question: "What would be the most appropriate procedure to be followed by States desiring to enable the Permanent Court of International Justice to assume in a general manner, as between them, the functions of a tribunal of appeal from international arbitral tribunals in all cases where it is contended that the arbitral tribunal was without jurisdiction or exceeded its jurisdiction." [87] A special committee set up by the Council was not called upon to express an opinion on the merits of the proposal, and it merely outlined three alternative procedures which might be followed by the Assembly for this purpose: [88] (1) a recommendation that provisions for the Court's appellate jurisdiction be inserted in arbitration treaties; (2) an invitation to States to sign a protocol giving the Court jurisdiction to annul arbitral awards which are vitiated because the tribunal lacked or exceeded its jurisdiction or followed an improper procedure; (3) a resolution declaring that States contesting an award should propose the submission of the question to the Court. The Assembly was reluctant to act on this report, and both in 1930 and in 1931 action was postponed. In 1931, a subcommittee of the First Committee of the Twelfth Assembly drafted an interesting protocol on the subject, as a basis for discussion; [89] but the Assembly concluded that the question "presents many aspects on which sufficient light has not yet been thrown."

and Rumania before the Council of the League of Nations; the Hungarian Government had proposed that it be referred by a *compromis* to the Court, and it was also proposed that the Court be asked for an advisory opinion. League of Nations Official Journal, 1927, pp. 1384ff.   [84] Minutes of the 1929 Committee of Jurists, p. 135.
[85] League of Nations Official Journal, 1929, p. 997.
[86] Records of Tenth Assembly, First Committee, p. 82. The Finnish proposal refers especially to Article 83 of the Hague Convention for Pacific Settlement of 1907, and to Article 5 of the unratified Arbitration treaty between the United States and Great Britain, of January 11, 1897. 28 Martens, N.R.G. (2d ser.), p. 90.
[87] Records of Tenth Assembly, Plenary, p. 174; First Committee, pp. 12–19, 47–50.
[88] League of Nations Official Journal, 1930, pp. 1359–1365. See also, Erich, "Le Projet de conférer à la Cour Permanente de Justice Internationale des fonctions d'une instance de recours," 12 Revue de Droit International et de Législation Comparée (1931), p. 268; Raestad, "Le Recours à la Cour . . . contre les sentences des tribunaux d'arbitrage . . .," 13 id., (1932), p. 302; Rundstein, "La Cour Permanente . . . comme instance de recours," 43 Reçueil des Cours, Académie de Droit International (1933), pp. 1–113.   [89] Records of Twelfth Assembly, First Committee, p. 142.

No unanimity was reached as to the effect of the various declarations under paragraph 2 of Article 36 of the Statute, with reference to "contests of the validity of arbitral awards."

The consideration of the Finnish proposal may have contributed to one result, however; in an agreement signed at Paris on April 28, 1930,[90] Czechoslovakia, Hungary, Rumania and Yugoslavia recognized a right of "appeal" to the Court, without special agreement, "from all judgments on questions of jurisdiction or merits" thereafter given by the Mixed Arbitral Tribunals in proceedings other than those relating to agrarian reforms.[91] An application based upon this agreement is clearly not an appeal in the strict sense of the term; the parties will be different, and the procedure before the Court will be instituted *de novo*.[92] In the case relating to the *Royal Hungarian Peter Pázmány University,* in which the "appeal" was based on this agreement, the Court looked upon the provision in the Paris Agreement as "a special agreement of submission," and found it unnecessary to deal with the nature of the jurisdiction conferred; "the fact that a judgment was given in a litigation to which one of the parties is a private individual does not prevent this judgment from forming the subject of a dispute between two States capable of being submitted to the Court." [93]

§413. **Extra-Judicial Activities.** The constitutional instruments relating to the Court clearly confine its activities to the discharge of judicial functions only. It is therefore subject at all times to the limits within which judicial action is to be effected. In numerous instances, however, provisions have been included in international instruments that the Court or its President may be requested to assume such extra-judicial offices as the appointment of umpires or arbitrators or of members of conciliation commissions.[94] On several occasions, the Court has complied with such requests: [95] in 1925, the Court prepared and submitted to the Turkish Government a list of European legal counsellors who might be selected by Turkey as judicial advisers under the Declaration of July 24, 1923; [96] in 1931, the Court appointed members of the Hungarian-Czechoslovak, Hun-

---

[90] 121 League of Nations Treaty Series, p. 81.

[91] Two "appeals" under this agreement were brought to the Court by Czechoslovakia in 1932, but were later withdrawn. Series A/B, No. 56.

[92] See Series C, No. 68, pp. 209–226.   [93] Series A/B, No. 61, p. 221.

[94] See the texts of such instruments in Series D, No. 6 (4th ed.), pp. 634–679.

[95] Similar requests have also been made by individuals and non-official organizations.   [96] Series E, No. 1, pp. 151ff.

garian-Rumanian and Hungarian-Yugoslav Mixed Arbitral Tribunals, in accordance with an agreement signed at Paris on April 28, 1930; [97] and it later filled a vacancy in the Hungarian-Yugoslav tribunal.[98] On several occasions, also, the President of the Court has made appointments of a similar nature. Such action by the Court or its President is justified by the general interest which it serves; it is in no way a departure from the limits imposed by the Court's judicial character,[99] and it is not in any sense an exercise of jurisdiction.

[97] Series E, No. 7, p. 188.   [98] Series E, No. 8, p. 153.
[99] In the *Free Zones Case,* the Court recognized as binding a Swiss declaration which envisaged the possible appointment of experts by the President of the Court. Series A/B, No. 46, p. 170. *Cf.* Series C, No. 58, p. 706.

CHAPTER 19

JURISDICTION UNDER SPECIAL AGREEMENTS AND UNDER TREATIES IN FORCE

§414. **Formalities of the Special Agreement.** A reference of a case to the Court under the first paragraph of Article 36 of the Statute does not seem to require a definite form. Though Article 40 of the Statute requires that "the subject of the dispute and the contesting parties must be indicated," no writing is necessary. An agreement may be consummated in the course of the proceedings before the Court,[1] and in this case no special form is required. In practice, however, the reference is usually effected under a special agreement or *compromis d'arbitrage*, and Article 35 of the Rules seems to assume that such a form will be given to the reference. Though a special agreement clearly constitutes an international engagement, most of the special agreements have not been registered with the Secretariat of the League of Nations under Article 18 of the Covenant.[2]

§415. **Notification of the Special Agreement.** Where a special agreement is concluded, no application to the Court is made, but jurisdiction will not be exercised until there has been a "notification of the special agreement." The notification may be effected by transmitting a copy of the text of the special agreement, but not by a mere statement that the special agreement has been entered into. All the parties to the special agreement should make such notification,[3] unless it contains provision for notification by less than all the parties.[4] Article 35 of the Rules requires that either the special agreement or the docu-

---

[1] See *e.g.*, Series A, No. 4, p. 6. See also, §407 (1), *supra*.
[2] It seems that only the Brazilian-French agreement of August 27, 1927, and the agreement relating to the Oder Commission of October 30, 1928, have been registered. 75 League of Nations Treaty Series, p. 91; 87 *id.*, p. 103. It may be noted, however, that the agreement between France, Great Britain, Italy and Rumania, of September 18, 1926, for asking the Council to request an advisory opinion on the *Jurisdiction of the European Commission of the Danube*, was registered. 59 *id.*, p. 237.
[3] Series E, No. 9, p. 65.
[4] If the required ratification of the special agreement is notified to the Court by one party, and if the other party informed of the fact fails to raise any objection, it will be assumed to acquiesce in the notification. Series E, No. 1, p. 268. See also, Series D, No. 2 (add.), p. 69.

ment by which it is notified to the Court shall mention the names of the agents of the parties and the addresses at The Hague to which notices are to be sent; this seems to assume that the notification will be effected by all the parties. The notification has the effect of placing the parties before the Court on the same basis; neither is applicant nor respondent, and if the agreement does not otherwise provide, under Article 39 of the Rules the steps in the written procedure will be filed simultaneously by the several parties. The agreement, rather than the submissions of the parties, will determine the points which the Court is to decide.[5] After it has been notified to the Court, under Article 40 of the Statute the Registrar notifies the Members of the League of Nations of the special agreement, and under Article 36 of the Rules copies are transmitted to all Members of the League and to all States entitled to appear before the Court.

§416. **Content of Special Agreements.** In the course of the first twelve years, the following special agreements were made for referring specific disputes to the Court: (1) Greece-Bulgaria, *Interpretation of the Treaty of Neuilly*, March 18, 1924;[6] (2) France-Switzerland, *Free Zones Case*, October 30, 1924;[7] (3) France-Turkey, *Lotus Case*, October 12, 1926;[8] (4) Brazil-France, *Brazilian Loans Case*, August 27, 1927;[9] (5) France—Serb-Croat-Slovene State, *Serbian Loans Case*, April 19, 1928;[10] (6) Czechoslovakia, Denmark, France, Germany, Great Britain, and Sweden–Poland, *Jurisdiction of the Oder Commission*, October 30, 1928;[11] (7) Italy-Turkey, *Territorial Waters Case*, May 30, 1929;[12] (8) France-Greece, *Lighthouses Case*, July 15, 1931.[13] Their terms are not uniform, and the agreements are too few for standards to have developed as to their contents. In most cases the agreement has been subject to ratification. Definite questions are formulated upon which the Court is asked to give its decision. Notification of the agreement to the Court is provided for in most cases, and several of the agreements provide that it may be made by one party; in some of these cases, however, representatives of both parties

---

[5] *Lotus Case*, Series A, No. 10, p. 12.   [6] For the text see Series C, No. 6, p. 9.
[7] For the text see Series C, No. 17—I (vol. 2), p. 490.
[8] For the text see Series C, No. 13—II, p. 25.
[9] For the text see Series C, No. 16—IV, p. 145.
[10] For the text see Series C, No. 16—III, p. 292.
[11] For the text see Series C, No. 17—II, p. 244.
[12] For the text see Series C, No. 61, p. 10. This case was later withdrawn. Series A/B, No. 51. For the text of the final agreement between Italy and Turkey, of January 4, 1932, see 138 League of Nations Treaty Series, p. 243.
[13] Not yet published by the Court.

have made the notification. Several of the agreements set the time-limits for the filing of cases and counter-cases, to be proposed to the Court; in the Franco-Swiss agreement, the parties assumed to fix the time-limits as to cases, counter-cases and replies. Some of the agreements provide that from one month after the expiration of the time limits, the parties will hold themselves at the disposition of the Court; in the Italian-Turkish agreement, the Turkish Government undertook to make the declaration provided for in paragraph 2 of Article 35 of the Rules. French has been agreed upon as the language of the proceedings and judgment in several instances.

Some of the agreements specially envisage the application of the provisions of the Statute in regard to points not covered by their terms; the Italian-Turkish agreement restricts this to questions concerning procedure. The Brazilian-French agreement provided that the Court should not be bound by national jurisprudence in its appreciation of the applicable national law of either party.

In the *Free Zones Case* between France and Switzerland, the Court felt called upon to declare that special agreements should be "formulated with due regard to the forms in which the Court is to express its opinion according to the precise terms of the constitutional provisions governing its activity."[14] In this case, also, the rule was formulated that "every special agreement, like every clause conferring jurisdiction upon the Court, must be interpreted strictly."[15] Yet that interpretation of an agreement will be preferred which will enable the Court to accomplish the task conferred upon it.[16]

§417. **Termination of Proceedings under a Special Agreement.** After the notification of a special agreement to the Court, the parties to the agreement become subject to the Court's jurisdiction, and a single party cannot withdraw. However, it remains within the power of all the parties to say whether the proceedings shall be discontinued. On being notified that the parties wish to discontinue, the Court's recording of the fact will terminate the proceedings, under Article 61 of the Rules. The Italian and Turkish Governments gave such notice with reference to proceedings under the agreement of May 30, 1929, and by order of January 26, 1933, the Court recorded their mutual agreement, declared the proceedings terminated, and removed the case from the Court's list.[17]

---

[14] Series A, No. 22, p. 13.
[15] Series A/B, No. 46, pp. 138–139.
[16] Series A, No. 22, p. 13; No. 24, p. 14.
[17] Series A/B, No. 51.

§418. "Matters Specially Provided for in Treaties and Conventions in Force." The provision in Article 36, paragraph 1, that the Court's jurisdiction comprises "all matters specially provided for in treaties and conventions in force," has given encouragement to States to confer jurisdiction on the Court, and such action has resulted in a wide extension of its jurisdiction. The expression "treaties and conventions" is general in its scope, and it applies to any form of international instrument in force when the Statute took effect or brought into force subsequently. Perhaps the Court would be justified in saying that an international instrument to which two Members of the League of Nations are parties is not brought into force within the meaning of Article 36, however, if it is not registered with the Secretariat of the League of Nations under Article 18 of the Covenant. In the *Mavrommatis Case*, the institution of the proceeding was partly based on a protocol signed at Lausanne on July 24, 1923; when the Greek application was filed on May 13, 1924, this protocol was not yet in force, though it was brought into force on August 6, 1924. The British Government contested the basing of jurisdiction on this protocol, but in its judgment of August 30, 1924, the Court held that even "if the application were premature" on this ground, "this circumstance would now be covered by the subsequent deposit of the necessary ratifications." [18]

The number of treaties and conventions which make special provision for matters to come within the Court's jurisdiction is very large.[19] The provisions vary widely, though some of them tend to follow certain standards. Without attempting to analyze the contents of each of the numerous instruments, certain classes of them may be profitably considered; certain general multipartite instruments relating to pacific settlement stand out as most important, and reference is repeatedly made in this treatise to the Geneva Protocol of October 2, 1924, which has not been brought into force, and to the Geneva General Act of September 26, 1928. In the history of the Court, special importance must also be given to certain bipartite in-

---

[18] Series A, No. 2, p. 34. Judge Moore dissented on this ground. *Id.*, p. 57. It is to be noted that the protocol was not registered at Geneva until September 5, 1924. 28 League of Nations Treaty Series, p. 203.

[19] The texts or excerpts from the texts of 358 instruments relating to the Court's jurisdiction, collected by the Registry down to January 31, 1932, are published in Series D, No. 6 (4th ed.). Two addenda to this volume have been published in Series E, No. 8, pp. 437–488; and Series E, No. 9, pp. 287–345. The total number of listed instruments is now 443; not all of these instruments have been brought into force, however.

struments, such as the Upper Silesia Convention between Germany and Poland of May 15, 1922, which have served as the basis of numerous applications to the Court.

(1) *Protection of Minorities.*[20] The treaties for the protection of minorities made by the Allied and Associated Powers with Poland, Czechoslovakia, Yugoslavia, Rumania and Greece, the Austrian, Bulgarian, Hungarian and Turkish peace treaties, and declarations made by Albania, Lithuania, Latvia, and Iraq, all contain provisions for the Court's exercise of jurisdiction.[21] Article 12 of the Polish Treaty of June 28, 1919, served as a model of such provisions; by Article 12, Poland agreed that any difference of law or fact arising out of certain articles, between Poland and a Member of the League of Nations represented on the Council, should be regarded as a dispute of an international character which might be referred to the Court.[22]

(2) *Mandates.*[23] The various mandates [24] approved by the Council of the League of Nations contain a standard article, modelled on Article 7 of the mandate for German Southwest Africa, under which the mandatory agrees that "if any dispute whatever should arise between the Mandatory and another Member of the League of Nations relating to the interpretation or the application of the provisions of the mandate, such dispute, if it cannot be settled by negotiation, shall be submitted to" the Court. It was on such a provision in the Palestine Mandate (Article 26) that the Greek Government based its applica-

[20] See Nathan Feinberg, *La Juridiction de la Cour Permanente de Justice Internationale dans le système de la Protection Internationale des Minorités* (1931).
[21] See 1 Hudson, International Legislation, pp. 283, 298, 312, 426, 733; 2 *id.*, p. 868; Series D, No. 6 (4th ed.), pp. 538, 539, 542, 543, 545, 549, 550, 554, 558; Series E, No. 9, p. 341; League of Nations Document, C. L. 110. 1927. I. annexe.
[22] This provision is also embodied in the Geneva Convention between Germany and Poland, May 15, 1922, and it was relied upon by Germany in the applications in the case relating to *German Minority Schools in Upper Silesia* in 1928 and in the *Prince of Pless Case* in 1932. The German application in the case relating to *Polish Agrarian Reform and the German Minority* in 1933, was also based on Article 12 of the Polish Minorities Treaty. In all of these cases, Germany acted in its capacity as a Member of the Council. The provision for resort to the Court directly, in Article 12 of the Polish Minorities Treaty, does not render it impossible for the Council acting under another paragraph of the same article to request an advisory opinion. Series B, No. 6, p. 23.
On September 21, 1922, the Third Assembly of the League of Nations recommended "that the Members of the Council appeal without unnecessary delay to the Permanent Court of International Justice for a decision in accordance with the Minorities Treaties," when differences arise. Records of Third Assembly, Plenary, I, p. 186.
[23] See Nathan Feinberg, *La Juridiction de la Cour Permanente de Justice Internationale dans le Système des Mandats* (1930).
[24] For the texts of the mandates, see 1 Hudson, International Legislation, pp. 44–126. Excerpts are given in Series D, No. 6 (4th ed.).

tion of May 13, 1924, in the *Mavrommatis Case*,[25] and that the Court assumed jurisdiction over some of the Greek claims.[26]

(3) *Labor.* Articles 415, 417, and 418 of Part XIII of the Treaty of Versailles and the corresponding articles in other treaties of peace, which serve as the constitution of the International Labor Organization, provide for the jurisdiction of the Court with respect to a complaint by a Member of the International Labor Organization that another Member is not observing a labor convention which both have ratified. Article 416 provides that if a Member fails to take the action required by Article 405, any other Member may refer the matter to the Court; Article 418 provides that the Court may "affirm, vary or reverse" the findings of a Commission of Enquiry and indicate appropriate measures of an economic character to be taken against a defaulting Government; Article 423 provides that any question or dispute relating to the interpretation of Part XIII or of a convention concluded under it shall be referred to the Court for decision. As more than thirty international labor conventions have been brought into force, the effect of these articles is extensive; no application based on them has been addressed to the Court, however.[27]

(4) *Transit and Communications.* The Statute on Freedom of Transit (Article 13) and the Statute on Navigable Waterways (Article 22), annexed to Conventions signed at Barcelona in 1921, provide a jurisdiction of the Court over disputes as to their interpretation or application.[28] Article 38 of the Convention relating to the Statute of the Danube, of July 23, 1921, provides for a "special jurisdiction" to be set up by the League of Nations,[29] which may be the Court.

(5) *Bipartite Arbitration Treaties.* Numerous treaties of conciliation, arbitration, and judicial settlement, concluded since the establishment of the Court, have provided for its jurisdiction in certain types of cases and on certain conditions.[30] Some tendency toward a standardization of these provisions may be noticed. The provisions of the

---

[25] Series C, No. 5—I, p. 88.   [26] Series A, No. 2.

[27] The Court gave an advisory opinion in 1932, relating to the interpretation of the 1919 convention concerning the employment of women during the night. Series A/B, No. 50. See also Article 26, first paragraph, of the Statute.

[28] 1 Hudson, International Legislation, pp. 636, 658. See also Article 35 of the Statute on the International Régime of Railways, and Article 21 of the Statute on the International Régime of Maritime Ports, annexed to the Conventions of December 9, 1923. 2 *id.*, pp. 1151, 1169. See, generally, Jean Hostie, *"Examen de Quelques Règles du Droit International dans le domaine des Communications et du Transit,"* 40 *Recueil des Cours, Académie de Droit International*, pp. 397–524.

[29] 1 Hudson, *op. cit.*, p. 697.   [30] See Series D, No. 6 (4th ed.), pp. 82–482.

bipartite treaties range themselves into various categories.[31] Most of
them provide for the exhaustion of other attempts at settlement before
resort is to be had to the Court, and such resort is usually contemplated only as a result of the action of both parties. Some of them
following the Italian–Swiss treaty of September 20, 1924 (Article
16),[32] provide that on certain conditions disputes may be brought before the Court on the application of one party; but this step is to be
taken only after efforts to arrive at a *compromis* have failed.

(6) *Standard Articles in Multipartite Instruments.* Recent multipartite instruments commonly contain provision for the jurisdiction of
the Court over differences or disputes relating to their interpretation
or application.[33] In many instances, chiefly at the request of States
not parties to the Protocol of Signature of 1920, alternatives to resort
to the Court are provided; but such provisions have undergone an evo-
lution to approach more nearly to conferring obligatory jurisdiction
on the Court. Article 25 of the Convention on the Manufacture of
Narcotic Drugs, of July 13, 1931,[34] represents the most extensive
of these provisions, and may well serve as a model in future international legislation.

§419. **Invocation of the Court's Jurisdiction under a Treaty
in Force.** The Court will not exercise jurisdiction over any matter
specially provided for in a treaty in force, until a case is brought before it. This may be done by all the parties to the treaty, or if the
treaty so provides, by a single party. If all the parties act together,
they may either conclude a special agreement (*compromis*) or file a
written application addressed to the Registrar; if a single party acts,
it must file a written application.

§420. **Applications Made under Treaties in Force.** The Court
has exercised jurisdiction over matters specially provided for in treaties in force in a number of instances, in each of which the case was
brought before it by the application of the party or parties on only one
side of the case. In the *Wimbledon Case,* the application by Great
Britain, France, Italy and Japan on January 16, 1923,[35] instituting
proceedings against Germany, was based on Article 386 of the Treaty
of Versailles; in the *Mavrommatis Case,* the application by Greece on

[31] See Series D, No. 6 (4th ed.), pp. 481–482, 682–683; Habicht, Post-War Treaties
for the Pacific Settlement of International Disputes (1931), pp. 1061–1069.
[32] 33 League of Nations Treaty Series, p. 91.
[33] Series D, No. 6 (4th ed.), pp. 484–532.
[34] Series D, No. 6 (4th ed.), p. 532; U. S. Treaty Series, No. 863.
[35] For the text, see Series A, No. 1, p. 6.

May 13, 1924,[36] instituting proceedings against Great Britain, was based on Article 26 of the Mandate for Palestine; the several German applications of May 15, 1925, and August 25, 1925,[37] instituting proceedings against Poland in the cases relating to *German Interests in Upper Silesia,* were based on Article 23 of the Geneva Convention of May 15, 1922, as was also the German application of February 8, 1927,[38] instituting proceedings against Poland in the case concerning the *Factory at Chorzów;* the Greek application of May 28, 1927,[39] instituting proceedings against Great Britain for the re-adaptation of the *Mavrommatis Jerusalem Concessions,* was based on Article 26 of the Mandate for Palestine; the German application of January 2, 1928,[40] instituting proceedings against Poland concerning the rights of *Minorities in Upper Silesia,* was based upon Article 72 of the Geneva Convention of May 15, 1922; Great Britain, France, Italy, and Japan based their application of April 11, 1932,[41] instituting proceedings against Lithuania concerning the interpretation of the *Statute of Memel,* on Article 17 of the Convention of May 8, 1924, concerning Memel; the German application of May 18, 1932,[42] instituting proceedings against Poland concerning the *Administration of the Prince of Pless,* was based on Article 72 of the Geneva Convention of May 15, 1922; the Czechoslovak applications of July 11 and July 20, 1932, and May 9, 1933,[43] instituting proceedings against Hungary on appeal from the Mixed Arbitral Tribunal, were based on Article 10 of the Agreement (No. II) signed at Paris, April 28, 1930; the German application of July 3, 1933, instituting proceedings against Poland with reference to the *Polish Agrarian Reform and the German Minority,* was based on Article 12 of the Polish Minorities Treaty of June 28, 1919.

§421. **Content of Applications under Treaties in Force.** The applications made to date under treaties in force have tended to follow more or less the same lines. First referring to the provisions of treaties in force which are relied upon and to Article 40 of the Statute of the Court, they then set forth a statement of the dispute; the statements of the dispute are sometimes very long. The application sometimes ends with a prayer for judgment whether the respond-

---

[36] For the text, see Series C, No. 5—I, p. 88.
[37] For the texts, see Series C, No. 9—I, p. 24; No. 11 (vol. 1), p. 340.
[38] For the text, see Series C, No. 13—I, p. 107.
[39] For the text, see Series C, No. 13—III, p. 102.
[40] For the text, see Series C, No. 14—II, p. 87.   [41] Series C, No. 59, p. 12.
[42] Not yet published by the Court.   [43] Series C, No. 68, pp. 9, 103.

ent be "present or absent," and the prayer for judgment may be in the alternative. The Court is usually requested to fix the dates for the filing of cases and other documents of the written procedure. The claims stated in the application are subject to later revision when submissions are formulated.[44]

[44] See §482, infra.

CHAPTER 20

OBLIGATORY JURISDICTION UNDER ARTICLE 36

§422. **Optional Recognition of Obligatory Jurisdiction.** The provision for possible obligatory [1] jurisdiction in the second paragraph of Article 36 of the Court's Statute represented a compromise adopted by the First Assembly between the draft-scheme of the 1920 Committee of Jurists and the amendments proposed by the Council. It was designed to enable those States which were willing to confer on the Court obligatory jurisdiction over their disputes to effect that result in relation to other States similarly situated, and at the same time to set certain limits on the jurisdiction conferred. Such States are to "declare that they recognize as compulsory *ipso facto* and without special agreement" (Fr., *déclarer reconnaître dès à présent comme obligatoire, de plein droit et sans convention spéciale*) a limited jurisdiction of the Court.[2] The declaration may be made either at the time of signature or at the time of ratification of the Protocol of Signature, "or at a later moment" (Fr., *soit ultérieurement*). It is to operate, according to the second paragraph, not *vis-à-vis* all other States, but *vis-à-vis* other States "accepting the same obligation"; the third paragraph of the article adds, however, that it "may be made unconditionally" (Fr., *purement et simplement*), *i.e.*, with the reciprocity described in paragraph 2, or "on condition of reciprocity on the part of several or certain" States. And it may be limited to "a certain time" (Fr., *un délai déterminé*).

§423. **Requirements as to the Declarations.** The Statute prescribes no particular form for the declarations made under Article 36, nor does it in any way refer to the so-called "optional clause" which serves the purpose of suggesting a possible form which the declara-

---

[1] The English version of Article 36 employs the term *compulsory* (Fr., *obligatoire*). Perhaps the term *obligatory* is more exact, for it indicates that the jurisdiction is to be exercised, not as a result of external compulsion, but as a result of the assumption of an obligation by the States concerned.
[2] The English version has no equivalent for *dès à présent* in the French version.

tion may take. The history of the "optional clause" is somewhat obscure. Its text was not referred to in the deliberations of the plenary Assembly in 1920, nor in those of its Third Committee, nor in those of the latter's subcommittee. The text appeared for the first time appended to the draft of the Protocol of Signature which was prepared by the Secretariat of the League of Nations and submitted to and approved by the Council on December 14, 1920. The resolution adopted by the Assembly on December 13, 1920, had entrusted to the Council the duty of submitting the Statute to the Members of the League of Nations "in the form of a Protocol"; and since the Council adopted a draft of this Protocol for such submission with the "optional clause" annexed,[3] the latter may be taken to constitute an authorized part of or addition to the Protocol of Signature.[4] Signature of this "optional clause" serves as a declaration or constitutes a mode of making a declaration as provided in paragraph 2 of Article 36; but such a declaration may be made in another form, without any reference to the "optional clause." Despite this fact, however, the "optional clause" has served as a useful handle, and it has probably facilitated insistence on States' making the declarations provided for in Article 36; it is one of the important innovations of 1920.

§424. **Forms Adopted by States.** In practice, various forms have been adopted by States for their declarations under Article 36.[5] Most States have made their declarations either by signing the "optional clause," or by apposing their declarations to the "optional clause." Several states—Brazil, Estonia and Paraguay—have embodied their declarations in their ratifications of the Protocol of Signature; the first declaration by the Netherlands was contained in a *procès-verbal* of the deposit of its ratification of the Protocol of Signature; the declaration by Panama and Estonia's renewal of its declaration were contained in letters addressed to the Secretary-General of the League of Nations. China's declaration of May 13, 1922, was apposed to the "optional clause," reference being made to it in the ratification of the Protocol of Signature deposited on the same day.[6]

[3] The name given to this form of declaration by which obligatory jurisdiction is recognized, is somewhat paradoxical. On the drafting of the optional clause, see §§110, 157, *supra*. The published records may not be complete on this history. For the texts of declarations under Article 36, see the appendix, p. 610, *infra*.

[4] An Assembly resolution of October 2, 1924, referred to the "optional clause" as "the special Protocol opened for signature in virtue of Article 36, paragraph 2." Records of Fifth Assembly, Plenary, p. 225.

[5] See Series D, No. 6 (4th ed.), pp. 33ff. [6] Series C, No. 16—I, p. 291.

El Salvador's ratification of the Protocol of Signature contained certain reservations to a declaration which had previously been made by a signature of the optional clause. Each of these forms of declaration clearly satisfies the requirements of Article 36.[7]

§425. **Text of the Optional Clause.** The actual text of the "optional clause" does not furnish a very satisfactory model for declarations under Article 36, and it may be for this reason that few States have been content to couch their declarations simply in this form. The language does not follow *verbatim* that of the second paragraph of Article 36. In the English version, the word "accept" is used instead of the word "recognize"; the expression "from this date" (Fr., *dès à présent*) follows the French but not the English version of the Statute, and it fails to take account of a possible necessity for ratification which would postpone the date from which a declaration becomes effective. The expression "under the following conditions" (Fr., *dans les termes suivants*) is not applicable for States desiring to set no conditions, and the French version seems to necessitate a complete additional declaration. In some cases the "optional clause" therefore serves merely as a peg upon which a declaration is hung.

Clearly, the "optional clause" does not stand on any independent basis; it is only a suggested form of the declaration which Article 36 permits to be made at the time of signing or ratifying the Protocol of Signature or at a later moment. It is entirely subsidiary to the Protocol of Signature; a State cannot become a party to the optional clause unless it has become or becomes a party also to the Protocol of Signature, and a State which is not effectively a party to the latter does not make a binding declaration by merely signing the "optional clause" even without conditions.[8] It would seem that a much more satisfactory form might have been found for the "optional clause," which might have saved some of the confusion in references to the effect of signing it.

[7] By the 1930 conventions between Iceland and Denmark, Iceland and Norway, and Iceland and Sweden, disputes covered by paragraph 2 of Article 36 are to be referred to the Court; but these conventions do not constitute declarations under Article 36. For the texts see 118 League of Nations Treaty Series, p. 121; 126 *id.*, p. 417; 127 *id.*, p. 67.

[8] Under the Council resolution of May 17, 1922, a State not a member of the League of Nations and not mentioned in the Annex to the Covenant may make a "general declaration" accepting "the jurisdiction of the Court as compulsory, *ipso facto,* and without special convention, in conformity with Article 36 of the Statute." Such a "general declaration" is not a declaration as envisaged in paragraph 2 of Article 36, and hence States which have made the latter declaration are not thereby bound *vis-à-vis* States which have made such "general declarations." This is expressly recognized in the resolution of May 17, 1922. See §397, *supra*.

§426. **Ratification of Declarations.** A State may make its declaration to be effective forthwith,[9] or subject to later ratification. Many of the declarations have been expressly subject to ratification.[10] The date from which a declaration becomes effective will then depend on its terms and the terms of the ratification; the effect of the words *dès à présent* in the French version of Article 36, of which no equivalent appears in the English version, may easily be overcome with respect to any declaration made under the article. The only question arises where a State makes a declaration, independently of or by a signature of the "optional clause," without mention of ratification. If such State has previously signed and ratified the Protocol of Signature, there is no reason why the declaration cannot become effective immediately if it is so intended; if, on the other hand, such State has not signed and ratified the Protocol of Signature, the declaration would become effective from the date of a later ratification of the Protocol of Signature,[11] or possibly from the deposit of a later ratification. Where ratification is expressly required, it may be effected by a statement in a later ratification of the Protocol of Signature; if no such statement is included, however, it would seem that a later ratification of the Protocol of Signature would not constitute a ratification of the declaration under Article 36.[12]

§427. **Interpretations by the Assembly.** On various occasions the Assembly of the League of Nations has sought to encourage Members of the League of Nations to make the declaration provided for in Article 36, and to this end it has given liberal interpretations to the terms of that Article. On October 2, 1924, after a special report by its First Committee, the Fifth Assembly adopted a resolution which recited that the terms of Article 36 are "sufficiently wide to permit States to adhere to the special Protocol opened for signature in virtue of Article 36, paragraph 2, with the reservations which they regard as indispensable."[13] This interpretation would seem to be too liberal, for Article 36 sets some limits to the action to be taken under it. The Third Committee of the same Assembly was more precise; in its

[9] See the declarations of Norway of September 22, 1926; and of Greece, September 12, 1929. Series D, No. 6 (4th ed.), pp. 41, 44.
[10] In some cases, declarations not expressly subject to ratification have been ratified.
[11] This distinction seems to have been ignored in the first footnote in Series D, No. 6 (4th ed.), p. 33.
[12] Persia, after having made a declaration subject to ratification, ratified the Protocol of Signature only, and later ratified the declaration.
[13] Records of Fifth Assembly, Plenary, p. 225.

report on the Protocol for the Pacific Settlement of International Disputes, which was opened for signature on October 2, 1924, the Third Committee enumerated various possible "reservations" which might be made,[14] and Article 3 of the Protocol itself would have required the parties to "accede" to the "optional clause," subject to "reservations compatible with the said clause."[15] Again at the Ninth Assembly, in connection with the General Act for the Pacific Settlement of International Disputes, Article 36 was studied in some detail, and the Assembly found it "expedient to diminish the obstacles which prevent States from committing themselves." It therefore drew attention in a resolution of September 26, 1928, to the possibility that States might sign the "optional clause" "subject to appropriate reservations limiting the extent of their commitments, both as regards duration and as regards scope"; and it was noted that "reservations conceivable may relate, either generally to certain aspects of any kind of dispute, or specifically to certain classes or lists of disputes, and that these different kinds of reservation can be legitimately combined."[16] This resolution has exercised an important influence on the content of the subsequent declarations.

§428. Scope of Jurisdiction under Article 36. The jurisdiction of the Court recognized under Article 36 must apply to "all or any of the classes of legal disputes concerning" (Fr., *ayant pour objet*), *i.e.,* falling into, four general classes (Fr., *catégories*). The statement of these classes is taken from Article 13 of the Covenant; however, the Covenant fails to describe as "legal" the disputes to which it refers.[17] Does the inclusion of this word in the Statute introduce any limitation on the Court's jurisdiction, in addition to the limitations contained in other terms of Article 36? Must a dispute which falls under one or more of the expressions (a), (b), (c) or (d) also be tested to see if it is a "legal" dispute before the Court will have jurisdiction?[18] An answer

---

[14] Records of Fifth Assembly, Third Committee, pp. 198–200.

[15] Records of Fifth Assembly, Plenary, p. 499. The Protocol of October 2, 1924, was not brought into force.

[16] Records of Ninth Assembly, Plenary, pp. 172, 183.

[17] The language in the Covenant seems to have been based on Articles 16 (1899), 38 (1907) of the Hague Conventions for Pacific Settlement, which applied to cases *d'ordre juridique.* The Netherlands' proposal to use a similar term in the Covenant was not accepted. See 2 Miller, Drafting of the Covenant, p. 613. In some of the later drafts of the Covenant before the Commission on the League of Nations in 1919, these categories of disputes were omitted. *Id.,* pp. 585, 652, 661. Their restoration was proposed by the British delegation on April 1, 1919. *Id.,* p. 670. An early British draft of March 20, 1918, had formulated them. 3 Baker, Woodrow Wilson and World Settlement, pp. 70, 75.

[18] A declaration accepting the Court's jurisdiction may be expressly limited to

to these questions must be preceded by a review of the history of the terms used in the Statute.

The suggestion that the language of Article 13 of the Covenant be adopted in the statement of the Court's jurisdiction was made in Article 21 of the draft formulated by the Conference at The Hague in February, 1920; but that draft did not employ the word "legal." In the 1920 Committee of Jurists, Article 13 of the Covenant was taken to define legal disputes,[19] and various proposals were made for the incorporation of its classification into the Statute.[20] The reference to "legal" disputes was considered, but not at length; [21] the word "legal" was borrowed from Articles 16 (1899), 38 (1907) of the Hague Conventions for Pacific Settlement,[22] as a description of the enumerations in Article 13 of the Covenant. Hence, the text before the Committee for some time read: "disputes concerning cases of a legal nature, that is to say, those dealing with" the four classes.[23] Though the records do not show that the fact was appreciated by members of the Committee of Jurists, the deletion of the "that is to say" phrase [24] gave a wholly different meaning to the text finally adopted by the Committee of Jurists, which read: "to hear and determine cases of a legal nature, concerning" the five categories; the Court was also to be given jurisdiction over "a dispute as to whether a certain case comes within any of the categories above mentioned." Under the text proposed by the Committee of Jurists, then, it is clear that a dispute had to be "legal," in addition to falling within one of the categories. When the Third Committee of the First Assembly decided to seek an optional substitute for compulsory jurisdiction, its subcommittee adopted as a text, "the jurisdiction of the Court in all disputes of a legal nature, concerning" the named categories; [25] a different text was reported by the subcommittee,[26] however, and it was adopted by the Third Committee with some changes, subject to final drafting by a drafting committee.[27] The details of the final phrasing are not explained in the records of the Assembly.

What then is the precise effect of the text as adopted? Two views may be argued.

"legal" disputes. See the Rumanian declaration of October 8, 1930. Series D, No. 6 (4th ed.), p. 53.

[19] Minutes of the 1920 Committee of Jurists, pp. 244, 255, 272.

[20] Id., pp. 252, 253, 272. [21] Id., pp. 260–265. [22] Id., pp. 264, 283.

[23] Id., pp. 272, 277. See also, pp. 547, 566. [24] Id., p. 582.

[25] Records of First Assembly, Committees, I, pp. 408, 611.

[26] Id., p. 566. [27] Id., pp. 312–313.

(1) That the jurisdiction of the Court is confined to disputes which are properly "legal" and which must also concern (have *pour objet*) one or more of the four categories enumerated; *i.e.*, the changes made by the First Assembly did not modify the substance of this phrase as proposed by the Committee of Jurists. This would make the text of the Statute equivalent to the following: "the jurisdiction of the Court in legal disputes in all or any of the following classes: (*a*) disputes concerning," etc. The term "legal" is used as the opposite of *non-legal*, or possibly in contrast to the term "political." A dispute is "legal" if it relates to a claim of right under law; in this connection, possibly a claim of right under international law, or under public international law.[28] A "legal" dispute, therefore, is one which is "susceptible of decision by the application of the principles of law," or in this connection, of international law. Clearly some disputes which are embraced by one or more of the four categories might not be "legal" in this sense. Category (*c*), for instance, covers disputes as to "the existence of any fact which, if established, would constitute a breach of an international obligation"; if the parties to a dispute were agreed upon the legal consequences, and differed only as to the existence of such a fact, would this be a "legal" dispute? The Court's dictum in the *Serbian Loans Case*,[29] based upon a paraphrase of paragraph 2 of Article 36,[30] refers to such a situation and seems to say that the Court would have jurisdiction even though it would be a dispute concerning a "pure matter of fact."

(2) That the jurisdiction of the Court is confined to disputes which fall within one or more of the four classes enumerated, these classes of disputes being merely described as "classes of legal disputes" (Fr., *catégories de différends d'ordre juridique*); *i.e.*, the changes made by the First Assembly modified the substance of the phrase proposed by the Committee of Jurists by restoring the meaning of the language which had been considered and modified by that Committee. This would make the text of the Statute equivalent to the following: "the

[28] An analogy may be drawn to the language used in certain recent arbitration treaties, which apply to all differences relating to international matters in which the parties are "concerned by virtue of a claim of right made by one against the other under treaty or otherwise." See U. S.-France, Treaty of February 6, 1928, U. S. Treaty Series, No. 785. This formula seems to have been first employed in the unratified treaties of the United States with France and Great Britain of August 3, 1911. 5 American Journal of International Law (Supp., 1911), pp. 249, 253.

[29] Series A, Nos. 20/21, p. 19.

[30] The Court refers to Article 36 as providing for jurisdiction "in legal disputes concerning" (Fr., *sur les différends d'ordre juridique ayant pour objet*) the categories. *Ibid.*

jurisdiction of the Court in all or any of the following classes of legal disputes: (a) disputes concerning," etc.[31] It would be very near to the language considered by the Committee of Jurists: "disputes concerning cases of a legal nature, that is to say, those dealing with," etc. On this view, any dispute in one of the four categories would be within the Court's jurisdiction; it would then be improper to inquire whether the dispute meets the additional requirements which may be laid down for "legal" disputes. For the purposes of the Statute, "legal" would be merely a descriptive word, employed to describe disputes which satisfy the requirements of one of the four categories.[32]

Which of these two interpretations of the Statute is to be preferred? A general rule of interpretation, followed by the Court, that where the wording of a treaty provision is not clear "the one which involves a minimum of obligations for the parties should be adopted," [33] would seem to point to the first interpretation.[34] It may also be said that the first interpretation has the advantage of emphasizing the legal, i.e., juridical, character of the problems with which the Court deals. Yet the Court's dictum in the Serbian Loans Case [35] reaches the result of the second interpretation. The directives of Article 13 of the Covenant would seem to point toward the second interpretation; otherwise the jurisdiction of the Court under Article 36 of the Statute would not be so extensive as the indication in Article 13 of the Covenant, as to the disputes which "are generally suitable for submission to arbitration or judicial settlement." The second interpretation is also desirable because it would close the door to discussion whether a dispute within one of the four categories is "legal"; this is a field where definiteness is to be sought, and the second interpretation would avoid controversy about a vague and uncertain term.[36]

[31] Cf., the Italian declaration of September 9, 1929, which refers to les catégories suivantes de différends d'ordre juridique . . . ayant pour objet, etc. Series D, No. 6 (4th ed.), p. 43.

[32] It may be noted that the General Treaty of Inter-American Arbitration, signed at Washington, January 5, 1929, provides (Article 1) that the four classes of disputes enumerated in Article 36 of the Court's Statute "shall be considered as included among the questions of juridical character" for which arbitration is to be required. For the text, see 4 Hudson, International Legislation, p. 2625.   [33] Series B, No. 12, p. 25.

[34] Perhaps Article 17 of the Geneva General Act of September 26, 1928, also points toward the first interpretation; it provides that "all disputes with regard to which the parties are in conflict as to their respective rights" shall be submitted to the Court, and adds that such disputes "include in particular those mentioned in Article 36 of the Statute." 4 Hudson, International Legislation, p. 2534.

[35] Series A, No. 20/21, p. 19.

[36] For an excellent discussion of this question, see H. Lauterpacht, "The British Reservations to the Optional Clause," Economica (June 1930), pp. 160–162; there the view is expressed that the word "legal" is "merely descriptive." "The question whether a

§429. **The Classes of Disputes.** While the classification of disputes in paragraph 2 of Article 36 of the Statute is taken almost *verbatim* from Article 13 of the Covenant,[37] it serves wholly different purposes in the two instruments. As embodied in the Covenant, it is a description of disputes which on principle are to be regarded as "among those which are generally suitable for submission to arbitration or judicial settlement"; [38] in the Statute, on the other hand, it is a description of disputes with reference to some or all of which States desiring to do so may undertake a definite obligation. This difference of purpose may call for a different interpretation of the same language in the two instruments. Clearly, the classification in the Statute may be restricted more narrowly than would be proper for that in the Covenant. The four classes in the Statute are not intended to be mutually exclusive. A State might wish to accept jurisdiction in disputes as to "(*a*) the interpretation of a treaty" without accepting it in disputes as to "(*b*) any question of international law"; if it accepted jurisdiction in disputes covered by (*b*), it would quite clearly have accepted jurisdiction in disputes covered by (*a*).[39] Nor are the four classes stated as embracing every conceivable legal dispute, though few if any such disputes would not be covered by one or more of them.[40]

(*a*) "*The interpretation of a treaty.*" The word "treaty" seems

dispute is 'legal' . . . will be answered in one way by a believer in the law of nature and the principles of natural justice as forming part of international law; in another by the rigid positivist, for whom nothing short of a rule of international conduct expressly accepted by States possesses the authority of a rule of international law; and in still another by the follower of a middle course who, now powerfully supported by Article 38 of the Statute of the Permanent Court, recognizes the practice of States as the principal source of law, but is prepared to extend the sphere of applicable international law by the approved scientific methods of analogy with, and deduction from, general principles of law." Lauterpacht, Function of Law in the International Community (1933), p. 57. See also, Williams, Current International Law and the League of Nations (1929), pp. 37–39; Verzijl, "*La Classification des Différends Internationaux et la Nature du Litige Anglo-Turc relatif au Vilayet de Mossoul*," 6 *Révue de Droit International et de Législation Comparée* (1925), p. 732.

[37] The 1920 Committee of Jurists was reluctant to vary the terminology of the Covenant. Minutes, pp. 284–285.

[38] The words "or judicial settlement" were added by the amendment to the Covenant which came into force on September 26, 1924.

Iceland's conventions of 1930 with Denmark, Norway and Sweden, draw a distinction between legal disputes under paragraph 2 of Article 36 of the Statute, and other disputes, the latter being referable to arbitration while the former are referable to the Court. See 118 League of Nations Treaty Series, p. 121; 126 *id.*, p. 417; 127 *id.*, p. 67.

[39] See, however, the observations of M. Ehrlich, judge *ad hoc*, in Series A, No. 9, p. 37.

[40] "It is believed that every conceivable dispute falls within one of the four categories except when the plaintiff State affirms openly that its claim is contrary to the existing law." H. Lauterpacht, in Economica (June, 1930), p. 154 note.

here to be used in a generic sense to refer to all international agreements. Most questions of treaty interpretation will doubtless be covered also by (b), though perhaps problems of interpretation may arise which will not involve questions of international law. In its opinion on the *Exchange of Greek and Turkish Populations*, however, the Court said that "the difference of opinion which has arisen regarding the meaning and scope of the word 'established,' is a dispute regarding the interpretation of a treaty and as such involves a question of international law."[41] Interpretation does not necessarily include application,[42] and it may be only under one of the following classes (b), (c) or (d) that problems as to the application of treaty provisions are necessarily covered.

(b) *"Any question of international law."* This category is very comprehensive and it serves as a catch-all with reference to legal disputes. This category would also seem to cover disputes under (a) and (d), if not also disputes under (c). A dispute might conceivably involve but not concern (not have *pour objet*) a question of international law. If it concerns a question of private international law, it might fall under (b).

(c) *"The existence of any fact which, if established, would constitute a breach of an international obligation."* The Court's jurisdiction under Article 36 to deal with disputes on questions of fact is stated narrowly. The French version follows that of the Covenant in using *engagement international*, instead of a more exact equivalent of the English "international obligation," in both (c) and (d).[43] The French version is clearly narrower, and the rule of restrictive interpretation might possibly be advanced for emphasizing the French in preference to the English version.[44] It is clear that the Court is not here given power analogous to that of a commission of inquiry set up under the Hague Conventions for Pacific Settlement. The parties to the dispute may agree that the fact if established would constitute a breach of an international obligation;[45] in this case, jurisdiction might not exist if it is to be limited to "legal" disputes. The parties may agree that the fact if established would not constitute a breach of an

---

[41] Series B, No. 10, p. 17.
[42] See Series A, No. 7, p. 18; and §532, *infra*. Articles 16 (1899), 38 (1907) of the Hague Conventions for Pacific Settlement refer to both interpretation and application. *Cf.*, Minutes of the 1920 Committee of Jurists, p. 283.
[43] See Minutes of the 1920 Committee of Jurists, p. 285.
[44] But see the Italian declaration of September 9, 1929. Series D, No. 6 (4th ed.), p. 43.   [45] *Cf.*, the dictum in the *Serbian Loans Case*, Series A, Nos. 20/21, p. 19.

international obligation; in this case, the Court would not have jurisdiction under (c). The parties may disagree as to whether the fact if established would constitute a breach of an international obligation; in this case the Court might exercise jurisdiction under (b) and it might proceed to deal with the dispute as to the facts under (c). The parties may have formulated no attitudes on the question whether the fact if established would constitute a breach of an international obligation; in this case the Court might have the duty *proprio motu* of a preliminary determination that such was the case, and if it determined the question in the negative it would have no jurisdiction under (c) over a dispute as to the existence of a fact. In the *Serbian Loans Case,* the Court stated that "the facts the existence of which the Court has to establish" under (c) "may be of any kind." [46]

(d) *"The nature or extent of the reparation to be made for the breach of an international obligation."* What reparation and how much is owed for a violation of an international obligation, would seem to be a question of international law under (b); in this view, (d) is superfluous for States which also accept jurisdiction under (b).[47] In the *Chorzów Factory Case,* the Court declared that "the decision whether there has been a breach of an engagement involves no doubt a more important jurisdiction than a decision as to the nature or extent of reparation due for a breach of an international engagement the existence of which is already established." [48]

§430. **Disputes as to Jurisdiction Conferred.** The fourth paragraph of Article 36 confers competence on the Court to decide a dispute as to whether it has jurisdiction. This applies to the first paragraph as well as to the second and third paragraphs of Article 36. Therefore, the Court may in the exercise of such competence decide a dispute as to its jurisdiction under (1) an agreement between the parties relating to a particular case, or (2) a treaty or a convention in force, or (3) a declaration made under paragraph 2 of Article 36. The force of the fourth paragraph is therefore not dependent on a declaration made; it may operate independently. It is binding on each party to the Protocol of Signature of 1920, whether or not that party has

[46] Series A, Nos. 20/21, p. 19. See generally, Salvioli, *"La Compétence de la Cour Permanente de Justice Internationale dans les Controverses de Fait,"* 13 *Revue de Droit International et de Législation Comparée* (1932), p. 70.
[47] See *infra,* §445.　　　　　　　　　[48] Series A, No. 9, p. 23.

made a declaration under paragraph 2. No State has made a reservation as to the fourth paragraph, when ratifying the Protocol of Signature; [49] nor has any State included in its declaration under paragraph 2 a reference to paragraph 4. A declaration under paragraph 2 applies only to the matters dealt with in paragraph 2 and paragraph 3; it has and can have no application to any other provision of the Statute.[50] If it is open to a State to make a reservation as to paragraph 4 of Article 36 in connection with its signature or ratification of the Protocol of Signature of 1920, it is not open to a State to make such a reservation in its declaration under paragraph 2 of Article 36. Certainly a mere exclusion of disputes concerning matters which by international law fall within the declarant's domestic jurisdiction, does not have the effect of depriving the Court of competence under paragraph 4 to say what matters are in that category.[51]

§431. **Reciprocity.** The recognition of the Court's jurisdiction by a declaration made under paragraph 2 of Article 36 applies only "in relation to any other Member or State accepting the same obligation." Under paragraph 3 the declaration may be made "on condition of reciprocity on the part of several or certain Members or States." In any event, the declaration recognizing the Court's jurisdiction applies only to disputes between the declaring Member or State and those other Members or States, whether all or some of them, which have accepted the "same obligation." In this sense, all declarations, therefore, are subject to reciprocity, and it adds nothing to a declaration to state this as a "condition" generally, though it is commonly so stated.[52] The declarations of two States do not need to be identical for them to be bound *inter se;* but they must have recognized the Court's jurisdiction with reference to the same dispute. As the declarations made under Article 36 vary widely, this limitation may be the subject of controversy; under paragraph 4, however, it is for the Court to

---

[49] The ratification of the Protocol of Signature by El Salvador contained reservations applying to the Statute as a whole, and cutting down the effect of a previous declaration under Article 36. Series D, No. 6 (4th ed.), p. 52. No other State has made such reservations. It seems clear that El Salvador's reservations do not apply to the fourth paragraph of Article 36, though it might be contended that their effect as to claims of a pecuniary nature is to reserve to El Salvador the power to say what claims are of that character.

[50] *E.g.*, a declaration under paragraph 2 could not exclude the Court's competence to indicate interim measures under Article 41 of the Statute.

[51] But see Lauterpacht, in Economica (June 1930), pp. 152–155, and Lauterpacht, Function of Law in the International Community, p. 188.

[52] See Enriques, *"L'acceptation sans réciprocité de la juridiction obligatoire de la Cour . . . ,"* 13 *Revue de Droit International et de Législation Comparée* (1932), p. 834.

appreciate the identity of the obligations accepted by two or more parties to a dispute.

Most of the declarations made apply *vis-à-vis* all States or Members accepting the same obligation; [53] in a few cases, however, the declarations exclude disputes with certain other States or Members. Each of the members of the British Commonwealth of Nations except the Irish Free State excluded "disputes with the government of any other Member of the League which is a Member of the British Commonwealth of Nations, all of which disputes shall be settled in such manner as the parties may have agreed or shall agree." [54] Rumania and Yugoslavia accepted the Court's jurisdiction *vis-à-vis* other States whose governments may have been recognized by them; [55] and Poland's declaration excluded disputes with States which refuse to establish or maintain normal diplomatic relations with Poland.[56] Brazil's declaration did not include a "condition of reciprocity," but it included a true condition which made the declaration's coming into force dependent on the recognition of compulsory jurisdiction by at least two of the States permanently represented on the Council of the League of Nations.[57] The meaning of the reservation by El Salvador that the obligation extends to "States which accept arbitration in this form," is not clear.[58]

§432. **Exclusions in the Declarations.** Article 36 provides for the recognition of the Court's jurisdiction in "all or any" of the four enumerated "classes of legal disputes." [59] No State has made a declaration covering less than "all" of these classes; [60] but numerous declarations exclude certain kinds of disputes, described in terms other

[53] For the texts of the declarations, see Series D, No. 6 (4th ed.), pp. 32–54; Series E, No. 9, p. 290. See also the appendix, *infra*, p. 610.

[54] Series D, No. 6 (4th ed.), p. 45. With this exclusion, it may be contended that the Irish Free State and the United Kingdom of Great Britain and Northern Ireland did not "accept the same obligation," and that neither is therefore bound to the other. The explicit provision in the declarations other than that of the Irish Free State may possibly be thought to refute the statement by Sir Cecil Hurst to the 1929 Committee of Jurists that disputes between members of the British Commonwealth of Nations *inter se* are not "disputes of an international character" under Article 14 of the Covenant. Minutes of the 1929 Committee of Jurists, p. 72. The United Kingdom has taken the position that neither the Covenant of the League of Nations "nor any conventions concluded under the auspices of the League, are intended to govern the relations *inter se* of the various parts of the British Commonwealth." 27 League of Nations Treaty Series, p. 449.

[55] Series D, No. 6 (4th ed.), pp. 51, 53.   [57] *Id.*, p. 37.   [58] *Id.*, p. 52.
[56] *Id.*, p. 54.

[59] An analogy may be drawn to Article 17 of the Geneva General Act of September 26, 1928. For the text, see 4 Hudson, International Legislation, p. 2534.

[60] The Persian declaration of October 2, 1930, applies, however, only to situations or facts having to do directly or indirectly with the application of a treaty to which Persia is a party. Series D, No. 6 (4th ed.), p. 53.

than those used in the Statute to describe the classes.[61] Strictly such exclusions constitute limitations on the jurisdiction recognized; or they may be described as exceptions. Some of the limitations contained in the declarations of States are frequently referred to as reservations, however, and the Assembly's resolutions sanction the usage of this term though Article 36 makes no mention of reservations. Declarations recognizing jurisdiction in all four of the enumerated classes but excluding "certain aspects of any kind of dispute" or "certain classes or lists of disputes" are said to be made with reservations. A declaration by a State accepting jurisdiction only as to the interpretation of treaties would not be made with a reservation, and it might be more accurate to avoid the term *reservation* in referring to other exclusions.

Several types of exclusions occur repeatedly in the declarations by different States,[62] some of which deserve detailed consideration. Their phraseology, in spite of its variance, suggests that some States have tended to imitate the declarations previously made by other States. It is to be noted that while most of the earlier declarations simply accepted the jurisdiction provided for in Article 36, many of those given since 1928 have contained exclusions; the Assembly resolution of September 26, 1928, may have influenced this development, as did also the Geneva General Act of 1928.

(1) *Past Disputes.* Beginning with the Netherlands declaration of August 6, 1921, many States [63] have limited the jurisdiction either to disputes arising in the future, *i.e.*, subsequently to the declaration or its ratification, or to disputes arising with reference to future events.[64] The Belgian declaration of September 25, 1925, limiting it to

---

[61] In other words, paragraph 2 of Article 36 has been applied in practice as if it provided: "jurisdiction of the Court in all or any classes of the legal disputes which relate to" (*a*), (*b*), (*c*) or (*d*). Thus interpreted, the enumerations do not correspond with "classes," and a declarant is free to choose any class it pleases, so long as it is a class of legal disputes and so long as the disputes covered by the class relate to one or more of the enumerated matters. The difficulty with this interpretation is that it would not permit a declarant to exclude the Court's jurisdiction in all disputes relating to (*a*) or to (*b*) or to (*c*) or to (*d*). Cf., Guatemala's declaration of December 17, 1926. Series D, No. 6 (4th ed.), p. 41.

[62] For convenient reference, the texts of the various declarations, or translations thereof, are reproduced in the appendix, *infra*, p. 610.

[63] Including the Netherlands (Aug. 6, 1921, Sept. 2, 1926); Estonia (May 2, 1923, June 25, 1928); Belgium (Sept. 25, 1925); Spain (Sept. 21, 1928); Italy (Sept. 9, 1929); Latvia (Sept. 10, 1929); France (Sept. 19, 1929); Great Britain (Sept. 19, 1929); South Africa (Sept. 19, 1929); New Zealand (Sept. 19, 1929); India (Sept. 19, 1929); Australia (Sept. 20, 1929); Canada (Sept. 20, 1929); Peru (Sept. 19, 1929); El Salvador (Aug. 29, 1930); Luxemburg (Sept. 15, 1930); Albania (Sept. 17, 1930); Persia (Oct. 2, 1930); Rumania (Oct. 8, 1930); Poland (Jan. 24, 1931).

[64] The British representative referred to this limitation in 1932 when the Council was considering a claim made by Finland. League of Nations Official Journal, 1932, p. 507.

disputes arising after ratification of the declaration with reference to situations or facts subsequent (Fr., *postérieurs*) to the ratification, has been widely copied, though the expression is one of uncertain application.[65] In the first *Mavrommatis Case,* the Court stated that "the reservation made in many arbitration treaties regarding disputes arising out of events previous to the conclusion of the treaty seems to prove the necessity for an explicit limitation of the jurisdiction. . . . The fact of a dispute having arisen at a given moment between two States is a sufficient basis for determining whether, as regards tests of time, jurisdiction exists, whereas any definition of the events leading up to a dispute is in many cases inextricably bound up with the actual merits of the dispute." [66]

(2) *Disputes for Which Treaties in Force Provide Other Means of Settlement.* Beginning also with the Netherlands declaration of August 6, 1921, many States [67] have excluded disputes as to which the parties have agreed upon another method of peaceful settlement. In the Netherlands declaration of September 2, 1926, this was limited to agreements made after the coming into force of the Statute. The Italian declaration of September 9, 1929, adds that the dispute should not have been settled by the diplomatic channel, and the French declaration of September 19, 1929, that it should not have been settled by conciliation; the French declaration also refers to agreements relating to other methods of "arbitral settlement." [68] States which have made these exclusions can of course relieve themselves of the obligation with respect to the Court's compulsory jurisdiction, in some measure, by providing in their future treaties for some other method of settlement. An interesting example of a provision designed to serve this purpose is to be found in draft conventions on foreign judgments, being considered by the British with other Governments in 1932,

---

[65] *Cf.,* Article 1 of the French-German arbitration convention, done at Locarno, October 16, 1925, excluding "disputes arising out of events prior to the present convention and belonging to the past." 54 League of Nations Treaty Series, p. 315.

[66] Series A, No. 2, p. 35.

[67] Including the Netherlands (Aug. 6, 1921; Sept. 2, 1926); Estonia (May 2, 1923; June 25, 1928); Belgium (Sept. 25, 1925); Ethiopia (July 12, 1926); Germany (Sept. 23, 1927); Italy (Sept. 9, 1929); Latvia (Sept. 10, 1929); France (Sept. 19, 1929); Great Britain (Sept. 19, 1929); South Africa (Sept. 19, 1929); New Zealand (Sept. 19, 1929); India (Sept. 19, 1929); Australia (Sept. 20, 1929); Canada (Sept. 20, 1929); Peru (Sept. 19, 1929); Siam (Sept. 20, 1929); Yugoslavia (May 16, 1930); Albania (Sept. 17, 1930); Persia (Oct. 2, 1930); Rumania (Oct. 8, 1930); Poland (Jan. 24, 1931).

[68] Many of the States which have made declarations have concluded among themselves bipartite conventions subject to the provisions of which their declarations may operate.

which state: "Any difficulties which may arise in connection with the interpretation of this convention shall be settled through the diplomatic channel." [69] It may be doubted, however, whether a provision for a method of settlement always open to the parties even if nothing is said, is such a provision as is covered by the exclusion. The typical case for applying the exclusion is that for which a special tribunal is created by a treaty.[70]

(3) *Recourse to the Council.* The abortive French declaration of October 2, 1924, reserved a possibility of bringing a dispute before the Council under Article 15, paragraph 3, of the Covenant; in the French declaration of September 19, 1929, the reference is to paragraph 6 of Article 15 of the Covenant, so that the Court would lack jurisdiction over a dispute as to which the Council had adopted a report unanimously agreed to by its members other than the representatives of the parties. Several States have merely reserved a faculty of submitting the dispute to the Council before there is any recourse to the Court.[71] The declarations by all members of the British Commonwealth except the Irish Free State provide for a suspension of the Court's jurisdiction if a dispute is under consideration by the Council, but notice of the suspension must be given within ten days after an application to the Court and the suspension is limited to "a period of twelve months or such longer period as may be agreed by the Parties to the dispute or determined by a decision of all the Members of the Council other than the Parties to the dispute." [72] The Persian declaration of October 2, 1930, placed no such time limit on the suspension; it would seem, however, that the suspension would cease as soon as the Council has completed its examination of the question.

(4) *Domestic Questions.* The members of the British Commonwealth, except the Irish Free State, in their declarations of September 19 and 20, 1929, excluded disputes concerning questions which

---

[69] British Parliamentary Papers, Cmd. 4213 (1932), p. 41. The draft is said to exclude recourse to an international court under general engagements such as the optional clause. *Id.*, p. 67.

[70] *Id.*, Cmd. 3452 (1929), p. 6.

[71] Including Czechoslovakia (Sept. 19, 1929); Peru (Sept. 19, 1929); Rumania (Oct. 8, 1930).

[72] The British reservations on this point are stated to have been intended to "cover disputes which are really political in character though juridical in appearance." British Parliamentary Papers, 1929, Cmd. 3452 (Misc. No. 12), pp. 6–7. There has been some criticism that this exclusion should have been more complete. See Sir John Fischer Williams, "The Optional Clause," British Year Book of International Law (1930), pp. 63, 79.

by international law fall exclusively within their jurisdiction,[73] and this has since been a popular exclusion.[74] It is obviously traceable to the reservation permitted by Article 39 of the Geneva General Act of 1928, and to the provision in Article 15, paragraph 8, of the Covenant. It is difficult to see how such disputes would fall within any of the four classes enumerated in paragraph 2 of Article 36, and the exclusion seems to be superfluous. The Rumanian declaration of October 8, 1930, does not employ the word "exclusive" in making this exclusion. It would seem quite clear that a State which has excluded disputes concerning questions which by international law fall within its exclusive jurisdiction does not possess a competence to determine finally what questions fall within that description; under paragraph 4 of Article 36, the Court would be competent to decide any dispute on this point.[75] The exclusion does not prevent the Court from having jurisdiction in disputes as to prize law. [76] If a belligerent has failed to set up a prize court, it could not maintain that international law leaves to its domestic jurisdiction the maritime claims of neutrals; if its prize court has decided that a seizure of a neutral vessel was in accordance with international law, it could not maintain that a dispute as to that decision falls exclusively within its domestic jurisdiction.

(5) *Territorial Status.* The reference in Article 39 of the Geneva General Act of 1928 to possible reservations dealing with territorial status, must have led to the exclusion in the Greek declaration of September 12, 1929, of disputes having to do with the territorial status of Greece. This exclusion was copied by several States,[77] two of which also repeat the statement in the Greek declaration that such disputes comprise those relating to sovereignty of their ports and ways of communication. The Rumanian declaration refers to "sovereign

---

[73] Special concern on this point had been voiced by Canada and New Zealand in 1925, in connection with the abortive Protocol of October 2, 1924. See British Parliamentary Papers, 1925, Cmd. 2458.

[74] Such exclusions were also made by Yugoslavia (May 16, 1930); Persia (Oct. 2, 1930); Albania (Sept. 17, 1930); Poland (Jan. 24, 1931). *Cf.,* Article 3 of the French-German Arbitration Convention, done at Locarno, October 16, 1925. 54 League of Nations Treaty Series, p. 315.

[75] On this point, see a discussion by Lauterpacht, in Economica (June, 1930), pp. 151ff.

[76] Some opinion in Great Britain favored an exclusion of such disputes. See British Parliamentary Papers, 1929, Cmd. 3452 (Misc. No. 12), pp. 8–12; Pearce Higgins, British Acceptance of Compulsory Arbitration under the "Optional Clause" and Its Implications (1929). Lauterpacht, in Economica (June 1930), pp. 166–167, favored this view because of the danger to the Court from the exercise of such competence.

[77] Including Albania (Sept. 17, 1930); Persia (Oct. 2, 1930); Rumania (Oct. 8, 1930).

rights including those over its ports and ways of communication." [78]

(6) *Particular Treaties.* The Polish declaration of January 24, 1931, excludes disputes relating to the Treaty of Riga of March 18, 1921.[79] The Greek and Albanian declarations of September 12, 1929, and September 17, 1930,[80] respectively, seem to exclude disputes relating directly or indirectly to the application of treaties or conventions providing for some other means of peaceful settlement to which they are parties.

(7) *Constitutions.* Only El Salvador has excluded disputes concerning questions which under its constitution may not be submitted to arbitration.[81]

(8) *Pecuniary Claims.* El Salvador's reservation of August 29, 1930, also excludes disputes relating to pecuniary claims.[82]

§433. **Effect of Exclusions.** The effect of exclusions raises an interesting question as to who may take advantage of them. Any exclusion must be applied reciprocally, apart from provisions for reciprocity in a declaration.[83] If a dispute arises between States A and B relating to a particular treaty and if A has made a declaration generally and B has excluded disputes relating to that treaty, clearly the Court will not have jurisdiction on the application by A; nor will it have jurisdiction on the application by B, for A is bound only in relation to a State which has accepted the "same obligation." If State A has excluded in its declaration disputes concerning "its ports," and if State B has made a general declaration, clearly the Court would not have jurisdiction over a dispute concerning one of A's ports on the application by either A or B; it would seem, however, that it might not lack jurisdiction over a dispute concerning a port of B on application by A or B.

§434. **Time Limits in the Declarations.** Paragraph 3 of Article 36 provides that the declaration may be made "for a certain time."

---

[78] Series D, No. 6 (4th ed.), p. 53.   [79] *Id.*, p. 54.   [80] *Id.*, pp. 44, 52.

[81] *Id.*, p. 51. See Articles 49, 68 (29) of the El Salvador Constitution of 1886. In a reservation by El Salvador to the General Treaty of Inter-American Arbitration of January 5, 1929, it was stated that "recourse shall be had to international arbitration only in the cases provided in the constitution and laws of El Salvador, that is, in cases of denial of justice or unusual delay in the administration thereof." 4 Hudson, International Legislation, p. 2633.

[82] El Salvador is not a party to the Convention for the Arbitration of Pecuniary Claims, signed at Buenos Aires, August 11, 1910. For the text, see 108 British and Foreign State Papers, p. 829.

[83] This point is better covered in Article 39 of the Geneva General Act of September 26, 1928, which provides, paragraph 3, "if one of the parties to a dispute has made a reservation, the other parties may enforce the same reservation in regard to that party." 4 Hudson, International Legislation, p. 2542.

In some cases, States have not taken advantage of this provision; thus, Panama, Portugal, El Salvador, and Uruguay have made declarations without time limits.[84] Such a recognition of the Court's jurisdiction is therefore permanent, and no power of denunciation is provided for. Most of the declarations have been limited to definite periods of time, however. In the earlier declarations the common period was five years, while many of the later declarations are for longer periods, usually ten years. It is notable that where a period has expired, the declaration is usually renewed for a longer period; thus Austria, Denmark, Netherlands, Norway, Sweden and Switzerland, which originally recognized the jurisdiction for five years, renewed their declarations for ten years when the first period expired. Only China and Ethiopia have failed to renew their declarations upon the expiration of a time limit. In a few instances, where a time limit has been set, it has been provided that after its expiration the declaration shall continue in force until it is denounced; such a provision was made by Albania, all the members of the British Commonwealth except the Irish Free State, India, Luxemburg, and Persia. It would seem that under such a provision a denunciation would not deprive the Court of jurisdiction in any case in which an application is filed before the denunciation is made.

§435. **Extent of Acceptance of Obligatory Jurisdiction.** For several years after 1920, signatories of the Protocol of Signature showed reluctance to make declarations under Article 36 of the Statute. Eight States promptly made such declarations and brought them into force before the end of 1921. This number was increased to eleven by the end of 1922. For several years, thereafter, little progress was made; one of the objects of the abortive Protocol for Pacific Settlement of International Disputes drawn up at Geneva in 1924 was to secure the acceptance of the Court's obligatory jurisdiction. The States whose declarations were in force on January 1, 1928, included none of the States permanently represented on the Council of the League of Nations; Germany, however, took the lead soon thereafter. Some impetus was given by the signing of the Treaty for the Renunciation of War, on August 27, 1928,[85] and by the Assembly resolu-

---

[84] In several other instances of declarations setting no time limit, the declaration has failed to become effective.

[85] The British Government considered its "signature of the Optional Clause as the logical consequence of the acceptance" of the treaty of August 27, 1928. British Parliamentary Papers, Cmd. 3452 (1929), p. 4. For the previous attitude of the British Government, see League of Nations Official Journal, 1928, p. 697.

tion of September 26, 1928; and at the Tenth Assembly in 1929 there was a rush to sign the optional clause. Though a British Imperial Conference in 1926 had pronounced such action to be "premature," all the Members of the League of Nations belonging to the British Commonwealth became signatories in 1929, as did France, Italy and several other States.

At the end of the year 1933, declarations recognizing the obligatory jurisdiction of the Court were in force for forty-one of the forty-nine Members of the League of Nations which had ratified the Protocol of Signature of 1920. The General Act for the Pacific Settlement of International Disputes, opened to adhesion at Geneva on September 26, 1928, is also designed to confer on the Court jurisdiction over the disputes "mentioned in Article 36 of the Statute" (Article 17); but Chapter II of the Act containing this provision has not been adhered to by any Member of the League of Nations which has not also made a declaration under Article 36.

A statement of the situation with reference to the declarations under Article 36 easily leads to a false appreciation of the extent of the Court's obligatory jurisdiction, however, if one does not bear in mind the precise terms of each declaration. Some of the exclusions are so broad that the jurisdiction of the Court is quite limited; this is particularly true of those declarations which have been made since 1929.

§436. Exercise of Obligatory Jurisdiction under Article 36. Four applications have been made to the Court, requesting its exercise of obligatory jurisdiction under Article 36 of the Statute: (1) an application by Belgium against China on November 25, 1926, relating to China's denunciation of a treaty; (2) an application by Denmark against Norway on July 11, 1931, relating to the legal status of certain portions of Eastern Greenland; (3) an application by Norway against Denmark on July 18, 1932, relating to the legal status of certain parts of Southeastern Greenland; and (4) an application by Denmark against Norway on July 18, 1932, relating to the legal status of certain parts of Southeastern Greenland. In none of these instances, has jurisdiction of the Court been contested, and the experience gained furnishes few guides for the future.

(1) *Belgium* v. *China*. The application in this case, communicated to the Registrar on November 25, 1926, prayed for a judgment that the Chinese Government was not entitled unilaterally to denounce

a treaty of November 2, 1865, between Belgium and China, and for an indication of provisional measures of interim protection.[86] In communicating to the Chinese Minister at The Hague copies of the application, on November 26, 1926, the Registrar set out the texts of the declarations made by both States under Article 36. The Chinese Minister did no more than to acknowledge receipt of this and the later communications, stating that they would be transmitted to his Government.[87] The President of the Court proceeded to fix dates for the filing of documents of the written procedure,[88] and on January 8, 1927, he handed down an order indicating measures of interim protection to be taken; [89] thereafter the dates fixed were extended several times at the suggestion of the Belgian agent.[90] On February 15, 1927, the President issued an order declaring that the order indicating measures of interim protection should cease to be effective.[91] The date for the filing of the Chinese counter-case was at one time fixed at February 15, 1928; this date passed without any action by the Chinese Government, and on February 16, 1928, the Registrar reminded the Chinese Minister at The Hague of the fact.[92] Thereafter, at the suggestion of the Belgian agent, the Court agreed to consider the period allowed for filing the Chinese counter-case as expiring on February 25, 1928.[93] A few days later the Belgian agent stated that the Belgian Government was apprised that it would meet the wishes of the Chinese Government to have a further prolongation, and on February 21, 1928, the Court consented to such a prolongation for six months; [94] on August 13, 1928, the date was prolonged for another six months, to expire on February 15, 1929. On November 22, 1928, a preliminary treaty was signed on behalf of Belgium and China; and on February 13, 1929, the Belgian agent asked that the case be terminated; [95] the

---

[86] The Belgian Government had previously proposed to the Chinese Government that a *compromis* should be agreed upon, reference being made to the recognition of the Court's compulsory jurisdiction by both Governments. Series C, No. 16—I, pp. 72, 77. The Chinese Government would have been "prepared to discuss the possibility" of invoking the services of the Court, "if the Belgian Government had indicated a willingness to seek a solution on the broad basis of the universally recognized principle of equality in international intercourse and that of *ex æquo et bono.*" *Id.*, p. 78.

[87] The Chinese Minister seems to have communicated to the Registrar, *à titre purement privé*, certain documents relating to the denunciation of the Sino-Belgian treaty, which had been published by the Chinese Ministry of Foreign Affairs.

[88] Series C, No. 16—I, pp. 302–303.

[89] Series A, No. 8, p. 6. The order referred to Article 36, paragraph 2(d).

[90] Series C, No. 16—I, pp. 334–335, 337.   [91] Series A, No. 8, p. 9.

[92] Series C, No. 16—I, p. 342.   [93] *Id.*, p. 347.   [94] *Id.*, pp. 350–352.

[95] Series C, No. 16—I, p. 355. For the text of the preliminary treaty, see 87 League of Nations Treaty Series, p. 287.

Court was not then in session, and the President decided to await its convening. On May 25, 1929, the Court made an order by which it declared that the proceedings were terminated, and removed the case from the Court's list of cases.[96]

At no time did the Chinese Government enter any appearance in response to the Belgian application; the Chinese Minister and the *chargé d'affaires* at The Hague had some personal correspondence, telephone conversations and interviews with the Registrar, but otherwise confined themselves to formal acknowledgments of communications. No Chinese agent was designated for the case, and it was the Belgian agent who made known to the Court, in connection with the extensions of time limits, the wishes of the Chinese Government as they had appeared in the negotiations between Belgium and China being conducted in China. The Court took no decision as to its jurisdiction, nor can it be said to have exercised jurisdiction by fixing the dates for proceedings. The President's order indicating interim measures was an exercise of jurisdiction, however; but as the order was soon revoked no questions arose under it. The whole incident therefore furnishes an incomplete test of the Court's obligatory jurisdiction. Conditions in China were disturbed by revolutions, and the Belgian Government seems to have found its application a lever for use in connection with the pending negotiations.

The Chinese Government might have contended that it was not bound to recognize the Court's jurisdiction in this case. The Chinese declaration of May 13, 1922, applied to all the disputes covered by Article 36, paragraph 2; the Belgian declaration of September 25, 1925, of which the ratification was deposited on March 10, 1926, applied only to disputes arising subsequently to the ratification of the declaration with reference to situations or facts subsequent (Fr., *postérieurs*) to the ratification. In this case, the Belgian application referred to the Chinese Treaty of 1865, Article 46 of which provided for the manner of its termination, and to the Chinese denunciation on April 26, 1926. The dispute would seem to have related to the question whether under Article 46 the treaty could be denounced unilaterally by China. Under these circumstances, had China and Belgium by their respective declarations "accepted the same obligation"? If so, did the dispute refer to a "situation or fact" subsequent (*postérieur*) to the Belgian ratification of March, 1926? The Chinese declaration

[96] Series A, No. 18/19, p. 7.

had accepted the Court's jurisdiction for a period of five years, which expired on May 13, 1927; as the Belgian application preceded that date, no valid argument could have been made that the exercise of the Court's jurisdiction should not have taken place subsequently.

(2) *Denmark* v. *Norway*. Denmark and Norway having made declarations under paragraph 2 of Article 36, on July 12, 1931 Denmark filed an application asking the Court to give judgment that the promulgation of a Norwegian decree of July 10, 1931, relating to the occupation of certain territories in Eastern Greenland, and any steps taken in this respect by the Norwegian Government, constituted "a violation of the existing legal situation" and were "accordingly illegal and null and void." The application reserved the right to apply for the indication of interim measures and the right to ask for reparation. Both Governments promptly designated agents, and the Court proceeded to fix the time limits. Norway did not at any time contest the Court's jurisdiction, and a judgment was rendered on April 5, 1933.[97]

(3) *Norway* v. *Denmark; Denmark* v. *Norway*. Acting on the view that the whole of the uncolonized part of Greenland was *terra nullius*, on July 12, 1932, the Government of Norway placed the Southeastern territory of Greenland between latitudes 63° 40′ and 60°30′ North under the sovereignty of Norway. On July 18, 1932, Norway filed an application asking the Court to give judgment that this action was "legally valid and that, accordingly, the said territory is subject to the sovereignty of Norway"; and "to decide forthwith to order the Danish Government, as an interim measure of protection, to abstain from any coercive measure directed against Norwegian nationals in the said territory." On July 18, 1932, also, Denmark filed an application asking the Court to give judgment that the promulgation of the Norwegian decree of July 12, 1932, and "any steps taken in this respect by the Norwegian Government constitute an encroachment of the existing legal situation and are accordingly illegal and null and void"; and reserving the right to ask for the indication of interim measures and for reparations. On August 2, 1932, the Court issued an order joining the two "suits," as the applications were found to be "directed to the same object." [98] Taken together the two applications had the effect of creating much the same situation as if the two governments had made a special agreement for submitting a case; as a result of their joinder, the two applicant Governments

[97] Series A/B, No. 53. [98] Series A/B, No. 48, p. 268.

were "held to be simultaneously in the position of Applicant and Respondent." On August 3, 1932, the Court issued an order dismissing the Norwegian request for an indication of interim measures.[99] On April 7, 1933, the Norwegian decree of July 12, 1932, was revoked, and in consequence, on April 18, 1933, both Governments withdrew their applications of July 8, 1932. By an order of May 11, 1933, the Court declared the proceedings to be terminated.[100]

§437. **Necessity of Formal Application.** Even where declarations accepting the Court's obligatory jurisdiction are in force, such jurisdiction will not be exercised by the Court in the absence of a formal application which fulfills the conditions laid down in the Statute and the Rules. In 1933, by an informal application the Peruvian delegate to the League of Nations purported to "submit to the jurisdiction of the Court, under Article 36 of the Statute, the Salomon-Lozano Treaty concluded between the Governments of Peru and Colombia, this Treaty not having been executed in the latter country, as will be established by evidence provided by my Government in due course." Both Peru and Colombia had made declarations accepting the Court's jurisdiction under paragraph 2 of Article 36 of the Statute, but because of the informality of the Peruvian application the case was not entered in the Court's list.[1]

§438. **Conclusion.** The developments which have taken place with respect to the Court's obligatory jurisdiction, suggest that some of the framers of the Statute were too timid. Perhaps the proposal of the 1920 Committee of Jurists was too broad, and it was not well explained; yet it can hardly be said to have been premature. In many ways, 1920 was a more propitious time for abandoning the pre-1914 formulas than the later years. There was little in the early history of the Court itself to lead Governments to reverse their attitudes on this matter. The reversals may be attributed to the educational effect of the continuous efforts made under the Covenant and of the Geneva Protocol of 1924, the Locarno treaties of 1925, the treaty for the renunciation of war of 1928, and the Geneva General Act of 1928; yet the positions taken in 1920 have not been vindicated. Fortunately, the way was left open at that time, and the willingness of so many States to follow it has greatly increased the importance and the usefulness of the Court.

---

[99] *Id.*, p. 277.   [100] Series A/B, No. 55, p. 157.
[1] Series E, No. 9, p. 76 note. Nothing further was done by Peru.

CHAPTER 21

EXERCISE OF CONTENTIOUS JURISDICTION

§439. **Forms Employed.** The Court is not a body which possesses general powers, and it must act strictly within constitutional limitations.[1] Under the Statute, it must employ one of four forms in exercising its jurisdiction: (1) an order, (2) a decision, (3) a judgment, or (4) an advisory opinion.[2] It is not possible to draw from the Statute any clear distinction between a "decision" and a "judgment": the English version uses the terms "decision" (Articles 16, 17, 24, 31, 36, 39, 41, 59, 62), "judgment" (Articles 39, 54, 56, 57, 58, 60, 61, 63), and "sentence" (Article 61); the French version uses the terms *décision* (Articles 55, 59), *jugement* (Articles 24, 39), *arrêt* (Articles 39, 41, 56, 57, 58, 60, 61) and *sentence* (Article 63). Nor is the usage consistent with respect to the equivalence of English and French terms. While Article 24 employs the English term "decision" and the French term *jugement* as equivalents, Article 39 employs "judgment" and "decision" in English as the equivalents of *jugement* and *arrêt* in French; Article 61 employs "judgment" and "sentence" in English as

---

[1] The Court has recognized that "a friendly direct agreement between the parties" to a dispute is "always preferable to the intervention of a third party." Series B, No. 8, p. 56. In the *Free Zones Case* it was said that judicial settlement "is simply an alternative to the direct and friendly settlement" of disputes by the parties, and that "consequently it is for the Court to facilitate, so far as is compatible with its Statute, such direct and friendly settlement." Series A, No. 22, p. 13. In so far as the forms prescribed by the Statute allow such action, the Court may properly assume this function; but it should not go outside these forms. In one instance in 1933, when interim measures had been requested by Germany, the President of the Court sent a telegram to the Polish Minister for Foreign Affairs concerning the possible withholding of action until the Court had passed upon the matter. Series E, No. 9, p. 165 note.

It may be noted in this connection that in 1925 the Danish delegation to the Sixth Assembly of the League of Nations proposed the creation of a "conciliation commission attached to the Court." Records of Sixth Assembly, Committees, I, pp. 10, 51; *id.*, Plenary, p. 103.

[2] On June 16, 1925, the Court adopted a "resolution" containing its decision on a plea to the jurisdiction. Series C, No. 9—I, p. 30. On November 9, 1927, the Court by "resolution" invited the parties to submit statements. Series C, No. 13—V, p. 10. This procedure may now be said to have been exceptional, if not irregular. Of course the Court may adopt resolutions for its own guidance, such as the resolution of January 30, 1931, on the dates of its sessions. Series E, No. 7, p. 285. See also the resolution of February 17, 1928, on dissenting opinions. Series E, No. 4, p. 291.

the equivalent of *arrêt* in French, and Article 63 employs "judgment" in English as the equivalent of *sentence* in French; Article 59 employs "decision" in English and *décision* in French. The process of judging or deciding is also variously described in the Statute.

This confusion necessitated action by the Court to establish a standard use of terms. In 1922, it fixed upon a terminology under which the terms "judgment" in English and *arrêt* in French are to be applied to the Court's final decision.[3] The Rules preserve this usage; but they also employ the term "decision"; Article 31 of the 1926 Rules employs "decision" with reference to the final disposition of a case, as well as with reference to action taken in the course of the proceedings. Both kinds of decisions are usually embodied in either orders or judgments.[4] In one instance, however, the Court has given a decision *eo nomine;* in February 5, 1926, a "decision" (Fr., *décision*) was given joining two suits,[5] though similar action was later taken by an order.[6] The court has never given a "sentence," as such, and that term as used in the Statute must be taken to refer to a judgment. In practice, therefore, judgments, orders and advisory opinions very largely cover the range of the Court's activities, and Article 65 of the 1931 Rules provides for the publication of a collection of "judgments, orders and advisory opinions" without mentioning resolutions, decisions or sentences.[7]

However, the Court takes numerous decisions which may not be cast in any standard form. Some of these decisions relate to administrative matters, such as a decision concerning the Court's composition;[8] others have to do with the conduct of contentious proceedings.[9]

---

[3] Series D, No. 2, p. 79.

[4] The operative part of a judgment is sometimes introduced by "the Court decides." *E.g.,* Series A/B, No. 46, p. 171.

[5] Series A, No. 7, p. 94; Series C, No. 11, p. 42. This decision was later annexed to a judgment. As the Court acted under Article 48 of the Statute, it would seem that the *decision* should have been given as an *order.*

[6] Series A/B, No. 48, p. 268.

[7] Judge Pessôa expressed the view that the Court can render a decision only by a judgment, an opinion or an order. Series A, No. 22, p. 49.

[8] Thus, the decision in 1930 as to the composition of the Court for future phases of the *Free Zones Case.* See Series A/B, No. 46, p. 110.

[9] A decision as to whether a question submitted for advisory opinion relates to a dispute for the purpose of applying the rule as to *ad hoc* judges is taken without formalization in an order. Series A/B, No. 43, p. 131.

Decisions may be taken at private meetings of the Court; thus, "Decision No. 20 of July 9th and No. 1 of July 10, 1923," are referred to in Series E, No. 2, p. 188. See also Series E, No. 8, p. 269. Decisions may be taken by the Court, for instance, under Articles 16, 17, or 24 of the Statute, or under Article 38 (last paragraph) or 46 of the Rules, which will not be formalized in the terms reserved for orders and judgments.

Some questions of interpretation of the Statute may still arise, however. For example, what is the scope of the "decision" (Fr., *décision*) the effect of which is laid down in Article 59? Is the application of that article limited to the judgments of the Court? Does it cover decisions under paragraph 4 of Article 36? The position of Article 59 in the Statute, with the articles preceding and following it referring to "judgment," suggests some special meaning for the term "decision" there used; but the history of its drafting discloses no reason for the use of that term instead of the term "judgment." [10] No clear line of demarcation has been laid down for the Court's choice of the "order" or the "judgment" for giving a decision,[11] but it would seem that in addition to the requirements in the Statute any final pronouncement on submissions by the parties should be made by judgment.

§440. **Orders.** Article 48 of the Statute empowers the Court to "make orders for the conduct of the case" (Fr., *rend des ordonnances pour la direction du procès*). This is the only reference to orders which is to be found in the Statute, and it has been liberally construed. The "order" need not relate to the conduct of the case,[12] for it has been made to serve various other purposes.[13] Indeed, it has become the omnibus form employed by the Court for action preliminary to a final judgment or to an advisory opinion. Thus, orders have been issued fixing time-limits in contentious proceedings and latterly in advisory proceedings; [14] inviting the parties to supply information or to submit arguments or to file submissions; [15] formulating questions to be put to agents; [16] effecting a joinder of two suits; [17] instituting an expert inquiry; [18] excluding documents offered in evidence; [19] disposing of requests for the indication of measures of interim protection; [20] determining upon the designation of *ad hoc* judges; [21] officially recording an agreement to terminate proceedings under Article 61 of the

---

[10] Article 59 originated in the Brussels proposals of the Council. Records of First Assembly, Committees, I, p. 492. See §178, *supra*.

[11] See Series E, No. 8, p. 266 note.   [12] Series E, No. 8, p. 266.

[13] Article 48 is not always invoked in the orders. Series A, No. 7, p. 96; Series A, No. 12, p. 9.

[14] See, *e.g.*, Series A/B, No. 40, p. 6; Series C, No. 52, p. 263; Series A/B, No. 41, p. 40; *id.*, No. 43, p. 130; *id.*, No. 44, p. 71. It has been decided, however, that a decision under Rule 33, paragraph 2, last sentence, need not be given in the form of an order. Series E, No. 4, p. 281.   [15] Series A, No. 7, p. 96; Series A, No. 23, pp. 38, 44.

[16] Series C, No. 18—I, p. 1077.

[17] Series A/B, No. 48, p. 268; but see Series A, No. 7, p. 94.

[18] Series A, No. 17, p. 99.

[19] Series A, No. 23, p. 41. *Cf.*, *id.*, No. 22, pp. 14, 21.

[20] Series A, No. 8, p. 6; No. 12, p. 9; Series A/B, No. 48, p. 277. See also Series E, No. 9, p. 171.   [21] Series A/B, No. 41, p. 55.

Rules.[22] No rules limiting the use of orders can be said to have been established; in general, they are to be given where the action of the Court has not been preceded by contestation or debate. Orders given by the Court are introduced by the statement "after deliberation," or "after due deliberation" (Fr., *après avoir délibéré en Chambre du Conseil*).

In the *Free Zones Case,* the Court was informed of the parties' desire that it should communicate to them indications as to the result of its deliberations on a certain question, and it was asked to accord to the parties, when the deliberation on this question was concluded and before a judgment was rendered, a reasonable time in which to reach an agreement on the new régime to be applied in the districts of the zones. Having decided to comply with this latter request by means of an order, the Court found it possible to give effect to "the common will of the parties" by "indicating in the grounds" (Fr., *exposé des motifs*) of the order the result of its deliberation on the question formulated.[23] This was said to be a "strictly exceptional" procedure, however, and it did not escape castigation by the four judges who expressed disagreement with the grounds of the order in separate opinions. Judge Nyholm thought the order was "rather an interlocutory judgment," [24] and Judge Pessôa thought that the parties were asking for an advisory opinion.[25] In a second stage of the proceeding the conclusions expressed were confirmed and "regarded as established," and it was at least intimated that the Court was not "free to give its judgment on a basis other than that communicated to the parties at the conclusion of its deliberation." [26] This view was expressed also in the third stage of the proceeding.[27]

The President of the Court frequently issues orders in the exercise of his powers under the Rules. He has power under Article 10 of the Rules to "direct the work and administration of the Court," and may therefore issue an order terminating a session. Under Article 33 of the Rules, certain decisions of the Court may be taken by the President when the Court is not sitting; these usually take the form of orders, which may later be varied by action of the Court.[28] Though the Court may vary the terms of an order made by the President, a party

---

[22] Series A, No. 18/19, pp. 5, 11; Series A/B, No. 51.
[23] Series A, No. 22, p. 13.   [24] *Id.,* p. 23.   [25] *Id.,* p. 48.
[26] Series A, No. 24, p. 10.   [27] Series A/B, No. 46, pp. 152–163.
[28] Series E, No. 8, p. 266. The President may also give a *decision.* See Series C, No. 59, p. 638.

has no right of appeal to the Court from such an order.[29] The President has no power to give a judgment.

Orders of the Court have been said to "have no 'binding' force (Article 59 of the Statute) or 'final' effect (Article 60 of the Statute) in deciding the dispute" before the Court.[30] However, they do possess a binding and effective character apart from those articles. If an order relates to the conduct of proceedings, compliance is always a condition which any party desiring to continue the proceedings must respect; if the Court lacks power to compel compliance by a party which does not desire to continue the proceedings, it may still render a judgment under Article 53 of the Statute. If an order indicates provisional measures of interim protection under Article 41 of the Statute, the Court has no power to deal with non-compliance except as it may relate to the proceedings.[31]

Article 58 is sometimes applied by analogy, and orders have frequently been read in open court.[32] The criteria for determining whether this shall be done are not clear; however, apparently orders will usually be read in open court if they have been preceded by an oral argument.[33] The order terminating proceedings in the *Territorial Waters Case* between Italy and Turkey was not read out, but mention of it was made at a later session of the Court.[34] The practice of the Court in this respect has little justification. All orders other than those which merely fix time-limits ought to be read or announced in open court. Of course the orders are promptly communicated to the parties by the Registrar.

§441. **Indication of Interim Protection.**[35] In any contentious proceeding the Court may "if it considers that circumstances so require," exercise a power expressly conferred by Article 41 of the Statute, "to indicate any provisional measures which ought to be taken to reserve [36] the respective rights of either party." It is also provided

---

[29] See Series D, No. 2, p. 67.   [30] Series A, No. 22, p. 13.

[31] In 1922, the Court's committee on procedure expressed the opinion that "the Court could not ensure that its suggestions would be carried out." Series D, No. 2, p. 77.

[32] See Series C, No. 16—II, p. 11. The statement by the Court that orders are "as a general rule read in open Court," Series A, No. 22, p. 13, is hardly borne out by the facts.

[33] The Court's order on the question of judges *ad hoc* in the *Customs Régime Case* was dated July 20, 1931, but it was not read in open court until September 5, 1931. Series C, No. 53, p. 199. See also Series E, No. 9, p. 172.   [34] Series E, No. 9, p. 171.

[35] See E. Dumbauld, Interim Measures of Protection in International Controversies (1932); Paul Guggenheim, in 40 *Recueil des Cours, Académie de Droit International* (1932), p. 645; Niemeyer, *Einstweilige Verfügungen des Weltgerichtshofs, ihr Wesen und ihre Grenzen* (Leipzig, 1932).

[36] The Statute uses the word "reserve" in the English version, though "preserve" was clearly intended. See §162, *supra*.

that "pending the final decision, notice of the measures suggested shall forthwith be given to the parties and the Council." Provision is made in Article 57 of the Rules for applications for "the indication of interim measures of protection" [37] (Fr., *en vue de mesures conserva-toires*), by "one or both of the parties"; it is clear, also, that the Court may make an indication *proprio motu* without awaiting such application, and Article 57 provides for the Court's considering the question even "if no application is made." [38] The indication may be made by an order issued under Article 48 of the Statute, but it is to be noted that the framers of the Statute abstained from attaching any particular effect to an indication. The tenuous character of the term "indicate" [39] is shown by the reference to "measures suggested" (Fr., *ces mesures*) in Article 41 of the Statute. An "indication" seems to be a "suggestion"; it clearly lacks the binding force attributed to a "decision" by Article 59. This view was taken in the Court in 1931.[40] Article 57 of the 1922 Rules provided that "any refusal by the parties to conform to the suggestions [Fr., *indications*] of the Court or of the President, with regard to such measures, shall be placed on record"; this was deleted in 1931, when the Court also rejected a proposal that the members of the Council of the League of Nations should be informed of such a refusal.[41] Possibly the Court could in its judgment take account of a party's refusal to comply with the indication, however.[42] The provision in Article 41 of the Statute that notice of the measures suggested shall be given to the Council seems to be for the purpose of enabling the Council, if it should become necessary, to appreciate the situation created by any refusal.

It would seem that a State which has ratified the Protocol of Signature of December 16, 1920, is bound to carry out measures indicated by the Court; the point is not beyond doubt, however, for no clear undertaking is included in the Statute. Of course, parties may be bound by their own agreement to carry out any measures indicated by the Court; Article 19 of the Locarno treaties of arbitra-

---

[37] A happier expression in the English version of the Rules would have been "provisional measures of interim protection."

[38] See Series A/B, No. 48, pp. 284, 287.

[39] The word "indicate" was borrowed from the Bryan Treaties. Minutes of the 1920 Committee of Jurists, p. 735. Article 5 of the annex to the Treaty to Avoid or Prevent Conflicts between the American States, signed at Santiago, May 3, 1923, gives to a commission of inquiry power "to fix the status in which the parties must remain" pending a report. See 2 Hudson, International Legislation, p. 1014.

[40] Series D, No. 2 (2d add.), pp. 183, 184.

[41] Series D. No. 2 (2d add.), pp. 198, 289.   [42] Series D, No. 2, p. 77.

tion [43] and Article 33 (1) of the Geneva General Act of 1928 contain such agreements.[44]

The Court has power to indicate interim measures only with respect to a case or a dispute which is before it; the use of the word "party" in the English version of paragraph 1 of Article 41 compels this conclusion, though the French version is not precisely equivalent on this point. The Court has declared that "it is in principle arguable" that the power given by Article 41 "exists only in respect of a dispute already submitted to it." [45] This seems to cast doubt where the situation ought to be clear. An indication may be made in the absence of a party, though under Article 57 of the 1931 Rules the parties must be given "an opportunity of presenting their observations on the subject." Nor is it necessary that the Court should determine in advance that it has jurisdiction over the case before it; in other words, jurisdiction to indicate provisional measures is not dependent upon a previous determination of the Court's jurisdiction to deal with the merits.[46] For this reason, it is essential that the limits of the term "indicate" should be strictly observed, and perhaps the Court should hesitate to make an indication in any case in which its jurisdiction has been or is likely to be challenged. If after an indication has been made the Court should later determine that it has no jurisdiction, the Court would have power to order the applicant State to pay the respondent State's costs.

The object of interim measures is to preserve "the respective rights of the parties pending the decision of the Court." The jurisprudence of the Court does not yet enable an adequate judgment to be formed as to the circumstances in which the Court will feel itself justified in giving an indication. If one party is clearly about to take action which would involve an irreparable injury to another party or to nationals of another party, and if the reparation which might be awarded in money damages or in restitution in kind would clearly be inadequate, the indication would be justified. In the *Southeastern Greenland Case*, it was argued that measures might be indicated "for the sole purpose of preventing regrettable events and unfortunate incidents"; but the Court found it unnecessary to pronounce upon the argument.[47] An

[43] 54 League of Nations Treaty Series, pp. 313, 325, 337.

[44] The parties might of course agree upon the nature of interim measures to be indicated. See Series D, No. 2 (2d add.), p. 193.   [45] Series A/B, No. 48, p. 283.

[46] Proceedings relating to a request for interim measures are said to be "distinct from proceedings on the merits." Series E, No. 9, p. 165.

[47] Series A/B, No. 48, p. 284.

omission to act, as well as an act, might lead the Court to make an indication.[48]

The amendment of Article 57 of the Rules of Court in 1931 shows a decided development of the conception of interim protection on the part of the Court. The power was previously conferred on the President, when the Court was not sitting, to indicate interim measures; since 1931 this power may be exercised only by the Court. The change was clearly in line with the envisaging of more frequent sessions of the Court. Yet urgent situations might call for action by the President even before the Court could be convened; in 1933, when the German agent had requested the indication of interim measures in the case of the *Administration of Prince von Pless,* the President met such a situation by telegraphing the Polish Minister for Foreign Affairs a suggestion that it would be desirable to consider the possibility of suspending any contemplated measures of constraint pending the meeting of the Court and pending its decision.[49]

Measures of interim protection have been indicated in only one case. By an order of January 8, 1927,[50] in the *Belgian-Chinese Case,* the President, acting under Article 57 of the 1922 Rules on an application by the Belgian Government, indicated measures provisionally pending a final decision by which the Court might declare itself to have no jurisdiction or give judgment on the merits. It was recited that if there were an infraction of claimed rights, "such infraction could not be made good simply by the payment of an indemnity or by compensation or restitution in some other material form." A new order was made by the President on February 15, 1927, by which the previous order ceased to be operative.[51] By an order of August 3, 1932,[52] the Court dismissed a request of the Norwegian Government for the indication of interim measures of protection in the *Southeastern Greenland Case,* having found that "no Norwegian rights the protection of which might require the indication of such measures" were in issue, and that the circumstances did not require such measures to be taken.

On May 3, 1933, the German agent requested the Court to indicate

---

[48] See the history of Article 41, as given in the German request of October 14, 1927. Series A, No. 12, pp. 6–7. See also, §162, *supra.*
[49] Series E, No. 9, p. 165 note.
[50] Series A, No. 8, p. 6. Previously, on December 20, 1926, the Registrar had communicated to the Belgian agent the view of the President that on the documents then before him he had not been convinced that the circumstances required an indication. Series C, No. 16—I, p. 307.   [51] Series A, No. 8, p. 9.   [52] Series A/B, No. 48, p. 277.

interim measures of protection in the case concerning the *Administration of the Prince of Pless,* asserting that the execution of threatened measures of constraint would irremediably prejudice the rights and interests forming the subject of the dispute. The Court was at once convened in extraordinary session, and a hearing was set for May 11, 1933, to give the agents of the two parties an opportunity to present their "observations." In the interim, however, the Polish Government disavowed the action of certain Polish officials and declared that the threatened measures of constraint would be suspended pending a final disposition of the case before the Court; the German Government having agreed to this course, the German agent requested the Court to take note of the agreement in accordance with Article 61 of the Rules. In consequence, by an order of May 11, 1933, the Court took note of the declarations of the two Governments and declared that the request for the indication of interim measures had ceased to have any object.[53]

On July 3, 1933, the German agent requested the Court to indicate interim measures of protection in the case instituted on the same day with reference to the *Polish Agrarian Reform and the German Minority.* A hearing was set for July 11, 1933, on which date it was adjourned to July 19. Observations were presented orally by the two parties on July 19, 20, and 22, and various documents were submitted by the German agent in the course of the oral proceedings. By an order of July 29, 1933,[54] the Court dismissed the request. It was stated to be "the essential condition" of interim protection that "such measures should have the effect of protecting the rights forming the subject of the dispute submitted to the Court"; whereas the original application by Germany had to do with infractions of the provisions for minority protection in certain individual cases where the Polish agrarian reform law had been applied, and with possible reparation in those cases, the request for interim measures covered all future cases of the application of the Polish law to Polish nationals of German race. Hence the request was regarded as not "solely designed to protect the subject of the dispute and the actual object of the principal claim."

The indication of interim measures must be distinguished from the giving of an interim judgment. On October 14, 1927, the German Government made a request under Article 41 of the Statute, in the

---

[53] Series A/B, No. 54, p. 150.   [54] Series A/B, No. 58, p. 175.

Chorzów Factory Case, that the Court indicate "as a provisional measure" that the Polish Government should pay a sum of money to the German Government, as reparation for an injury sustained, on the ground that liability to that extent was admitted. By an order of November 21, 1927, the Court decided that effect could not be given to the request, which was "designed to obtain an interim judgment." [55] This result was reached without inviting the Polish Government to submit its observations.

§442. Judgments. Under the practice of the Court, *decisions* on the merits are embodied in judgments. This form of action by the Court is not limited to decisions on the merits, however, for it may be employed even at preliminary stages of a proceeding. Thus the Court may by a judgment dispose of a preliminary objection to its jurisdiction,[56] and Article 59 of the 1926 Rules requires that a decision on an application to intervene under Article 62 of the Statute shall be given in the form of a judgment; such a judgment, corresponding to an interlocutory judgment in municipal law, derives its effect from the Court's control of proceedings before it. On the other hand, a judgment on the merits is a "decision" under Article 59 of the Statute, and it therefore has binding force (Fr., *est obligatoire*) "between the parties and in respect of that particular case," as from the time it is read in open court in accordance with the requirements of Article 58.[57] It is imperative under Article 56 of the Statute that "the judgment shall state the reasons on which it is based" (Fr., *l'arrêt est motivé*). Parties are not bound by the "reasons," however.[58] Each of the Court's judgments concludes with an operative part (Fr., *le dispositif*) in which the Court's action or decision is embodied, and the "reasons" serve as

---

[55] Series A, No. 12, pp. 4, 9. See also the dissenting opinion of Judge Anzilotti, in Series A/B, No. 58, p. 181.

[56] In the second *Mavrommatis Case,* Series A, No. 11, p. 23, the objection was upheld by a judgment.

[57] Under Article 64 of the Rules, the judgment is to be "regarded as taking effect on the day on which it is read in open Court." In practice, the greater part of the judgment in the language which is authoritative and only the operative part of the judgment in other language is read out; the non-authoritative version may be read out, however. The President reads out the judgment, but he may be assisted by another member of the Court, or by the Registrar. Series E, No. 9, pp. 162, 175.

[58] Judge Anzilotti has expressed the opinion that "the binding effect attaches only to the operative part of the judgment and not to the statement of reasons." Series A, No. 13, p. 24. With reference to a decision of the League of Nations High Commissioner at Danzig, the Court has said that "the reasons contained in a decision, at least in so far as they go beyond the scope of the operative part, have no binding force as between the parties concerned." Series B, No. 11, pp. 29–30.

The reasons given by the Court may be binding upon it in a later stage of the same proceeding, however. See Series A, No. 24, p. 10; Series A/B, No. 46, pp. 152–163.

aids in the interpretation of what is contained in the operative part. Though this may depend on the submissions of the parties, the operative part of the judgment does not ordinarily contain a command addressed to the parties; [59] it is rather a declaration as to the legal obligations of the parties, a "formulation of what the law is in the case in question." [60] In this sense, it may be said that most of the judgments of the Court are declaratory, even though they are not declaratory judgments in the technical sense of that term.[61] Yet, in some cases, the Court has in its judgment created an obligation which cannot be said to have existed previously. In the *Free Zones Case,* for instance, after formulating the legal obligations of the parties, it appointed a date "by which the withdrawal of the French customs line shall have been effected" (Fr., *doit avoir été effectué*); [62] if France was theretofore under an obligation to withdraw the customs line, there was previously no obligation to effect this action by a particular date.

The terms of the operative part of a judgment are in each instance carefully chosen.[63] In most cases, the Court does not say that the parties shall or shall not do anything; it does not direct them to act. Instead, it declares what they are by law bound to do or to refrain from doing. In the *Wimbledon Case,* the judgment was that the German authorities were wrong in refusing access to the Kiel Canal, that Article 380 of the Treaty of Versailles should have prevented Germany from applying its neutrality order, that "the German Government is bound" (Fr., *est tenu*) to make reparation, that the

---

[59] Perhaps the Court has power to issue an injunction, however. In the *Chorzów Factory Case,* the question was raised but an answer to it was not thought to be necessary. Series A, No. 17, p. 59.

[60] Quoted from Judge Anzilotti's dissent in Series A, No. 13, p. 24. Judgments in municipal law may serve the same purpose. Thus, the 1920 Civil Practice Act of New York, §472, states that "a judgment is the determination of the rights of the parties in an action." See, however, §505. Even in the Anglo-American common law, a judgment is not a command; "it does not advise or recommend, nor on the other hand, does it prescribe any act or course of conduct." 1 Black, Law of Judgments (2 ed.), p. 2. This is not true of a decree of an equity court, however. For an analysis of the French law, see Jèze, *Les Principes Généraux du Droit Administratif* (3d ed.), pp. 5off.

[61] The Court has declared that it has power to give a declaratory judgment in the strict sense of the term. Series A, No. 7, p. 19; No. 13, p. 21. When it was called upon to interpret a previous judgment, the Court said: "The Court's Judgment No. 7 is in the nature of a declaratory judgment, the intention of which is to ensure recognition of a situation at law, once and for all and with binding force as between the parties; so that the legal position thus established cannot again be called in question in so far as the legal effects ensuing therefrom are concerned." Series A, No. 13, p. 20.

[62] Series A/B, No. 46, p. 172. See, also, *id.,* p. 138.

[63] In formulating the operative part of its judgment in the *Serbian Loans Case,* the Court considered itself bound to "keep as closely as possible to the terms used by the parties themselves in the special agreement." Series A, No. 20/21, p. 47.

prejudice was of a certain amount, and finally that the German Government *"sera tenu"* [64] to pay a certain sum to the French Government. The declaratory form has been observed, with more or less consistency, in most of the Court's judgments to date.[65] For the purpose of determining legal obligations, however, the judgment has binding force and finality under Articles 59 and 60 of the Statute,[66] and the Court will not "give a judgment which would be dependent for its validity on the subsequent approval of the parties." [67] Even after a judgment, of course the parties remain "free to dispose of their legal rights," [68] and further negotiations between them may result in an agreement which would render compliance with the judgment unnecessary.

In addition to the offices which have been stated, the judgment also serves an important office with respect to the revision or interpretation of judgments. Under Article 61 of the Statute, a proceeding for revision must be opened by a judgment (Fr., *arrêt*), and Article 66 of the 1926 Rules requires the Court's decision on requests for revision or interpretation to be in the form of a judgment.

All judgments are the judgments of the Court, even though the Court be sitting as a Chamber for Summary Procedure. An early suggestion that judgments be "given in the name of the community of civilised nations" [69] was not adopted. Article 58 of the Statute requires that the judgment be signed by the President and by the Registrar, and a refusal to sign by either of these officials would doubtless prevent a judgment from having legal effect.[70] Yet the signature by these officials is not more than a form of authentication and legalization; it does not indicate that the text of the judgment represents the views of the President.

§443. **Interpretation of Judgments.** In the event of a dispute as to the meaning or scope of a judgment which it has given, the Court has jurisdiction under Article 60 of the Statute to entertain a request

---

[64] This is perhaps improperly rendered in English "shall pay"; the French version is controlling, however. The English translation of Judgment No. 15 is also misleading. Series A, No. 20/21, p. 126. Note also the English rendition of the judgment in the *Free Zones Case.* Series A/B, No. 46, p. 171.

[65] The Court may also give a judgment by consent "in accordance with the spirit of the Statute." Series A, No. 24, p. 14.

[66] Judge Anzilotti has stated that Article 59 "refers to a traditional and generally accepted theory in regard to the material limits of *res judicata.*" Series A, No. 13, p. 27.

[67] Series A/B, No. 46, p. 161.

[68] Series A, No. 24, p. 11; Series A/B, No. 46, p. 153.

[69] Series D, No. 2, p. 266.

[70] In one case a judgment was signed by the Vice-President, and in one case by the judge acting as President.

(Fr., *demande*) by any party for its construction or interpretation. This is in a sense a continuance of the jurisdiction which has previously been exercised; [71] a request for an interpretation is not a continuance of the original suit, however, though it may not be so formal as the ordinary application.[72] The composition of the Court for dealing with the request need not be the same as that when the judgment was given,[73] though Article 66 of the Rules requires the application of Article 13 of the Statute.

No time limit is set for making the request. It may be made by all the parties, under a special agreement between them, or by a single party; Article 66 of the 1926 Rules requires that the request for interpretation be made either by the notification of a special agreement or by an application, and that the Court's decision on the request be given in the form of a judgment. The special agreement or the application must specify the judgment to be interpreted and indicate the precise point or points in dispute. "For the purpose of the interpretation of a judgment," however, the Court "cannot be bound by formulæ chosen by the parties concerned, but must be able to take an unhampered decision." [74] The existence of a "dispute" (Fr., *contestation*) seems to be an essential condition of the jurisdiction to interpret a judgment, but "the manifestation of the existence of the dispute in a specific manner, as for instance by diplomatic negotiations, is not required." [75] The dispute must relate to the "meaning or scope of the judgment," *i.e.*, it must be based upon "a difference of opinion between the parties as to those points in the judgment in question which have been decided with binding force," or as to "whether a particular point has or has not been decided with binding force." [76] The interpretation, once given, "adds nothing to the decision," and "can only have binding force within the limits of what was decided in the judgment construed." [77]

Two requests have been made to the Court for the interpretation of judgments. On November 6, 1924, the Greek Government re-

---

[71] Judge Anzilotti has stated that Article 60 of the Statute establishes "the compulsory jurisdiction of the Court for a certain category of disputes." Series A, No. 13, p. 23.

[72] Series D, No. 2 (add.), pp. 176–177.   [73] Series E, No. 4, p. 295.

[74] *Chorzów Factory Case*, Series A, No. 13, p. 15. The procedure with reference to interpretation resembles summary procedure. Series E, No. 4, p. 295.

[75] *Chorzów Factory Case*, Series A, No. 13, p. 10.

[76] *Id.*, pp. 11, 12. This is to be distinguished from a dispute as to whether the judgment has been complied with. See the British objection in the second *Mavrommatis Case*, Series A, No. 11, p. 12.   [77] Series A, No. 13, p. 21.

quested an interpretation of Judgment No. 3, given by the Court sitting as a Chamber for Summary Procedure on September 12, 1924. This request [78] took the form of a letter which was not a formal application; the letter was communicated to the Bulgarian agent, who submitted a memorandum concerning it without disputing the jurisdiction. The Court found it unnecessary to say whether it had jurisdiction to interpret a judgment in the absence of a dispute between the parties, but assumed jurisdiction in this case on the basis of an agreement between the parties.[79] No oral proceedings were instituted, but the Court sitting as a Chamber for Summary Procedure "declared" that the request could not be granted. On October 18, 1927, the German Government made application for an interpretation of judgments Nos. 7 and 8, of May 25, 1926, and July 26, 1927, respectively.[80] The Polish Government opposed this application, contending that there was no dispute and that the application did not ask for an interpretation of the operative parts of the Court's judgments. Refusing to be bound by the "formulæ chosen by the parties concerned," [81] the Court found it one of the purposes of Article 60 of the Statute "to enable the Court to make quite clear the points which had been settled with binding force in a judgment." [82] In this case, as the grounds given for Judgment No. 7 contained a passage which one of the parties had construed as a reservation restricting the binding force of the judgment, the Court proceeded to give an interpretation by a judgment. It stated, however, that "the interpretation adds nothing to the decision, which has acquired the force of *res judicata,* and can only have binding force within the limits of what was decided in the judgment construed." [83]

The Statute contains no provision for the interpretation of advisory opinions; but the Court might entertain a request for an advisory opinion interpreting a previous advisory opinion, especially if the new Article 68 annexed to the Revision Protocol of September 14, 1929, is incorporated into the Statute.

§444. **Revision of Judgments.** The Court's competence to entertain an application for the revision of a judgment is narrowly restricted by Article 61 of the Statute.[84] A single basis is allowed for an application for revision, the discovery of a fact unknown when the

---

[78] Series C, No. 6 (supplementary volume), p. 13.   [79] Series A, No. 4, p. 6.
[80] Series C, No. 13—V, p. 39.   [81] Series A, No. 13, p. 15.   [82] *Id.,* p. 11.
[83] Series A, No. 13, p. 21.
[84] Revision is to be sharply distinguished from the correction of an error arising from a slip or accidental omission, under Article 75 of the Rules.

judgment was given and "of such a nature as to be a decisive factor." [85]
No application may be entertained after a lapse of ten years, and in
any event it must be made "within six months of the discovery of the
new fact." Article 66 of the 1926 Rules envisages only an application
for revision, though it is recognized that a request for interpretation
may be made either by notification of a special agreement or by
application. The Court may make its "admission of the application
conditional upon previous compliance with the terms of the judgment
impeached." A judgment is required to open a proceeding for revision.
Under Article 66 of the Rules, an application for revision of a judgment given by a Chamber must be dealt with by that Chamber; if the
judgment was given by the full Court, the application for revision must
also be dealt with by the full Court; and Article 13 of the Statute is
to apply in all cases.[86] No application for revision has yet been made.[87]

§445. Reparation and Damages. The competence of the Court
to deal with reparation for an injury suffered by a State or by its
nationals in whose behalf it is proceeding, will depend upon the terms of
the special agreement or upon the extent of the submission of the
parties to the Court's jurisdiction.[88] The parties before the Court
may have expressly excluded its dealing with any question as to reparation or damages; in the absence of an express provision of that
sort, however, an issue may arise as to whether such questions may be
dealt with incidentally to the exercise of jurisdiction. It is important
to note that the classification of disputes contained in Article 13 of
the Covenant of the League of Nations and in paragraph 2 of Article
36 of the Statute makes a special class of disputes as to the nature and
extent of the reparation to be made for a breach of an international

[85] A decision by the Mixed Claims Commission, United States and Germany, rendered
by the Umpire on December 15, 1933, was to the effect that, in spite of a provision in
the agreement creating the Commission that its decisions should be "accepted as final
and binding," the Commission might reopen a proceeding to "correct errors into which
it has been led by fraud and collusion." A petition before the Commission having
averred that the Commission had been "misled by fraud and collusion on the part of
witnesses and suppression of evidence on the part of some of them" when its previous
decision was given, it was stated that "every tribunal has inherent power to reopen and
revise a decision induced by fraud." Manuscript copy of the Decision, p. 19.

[86] Revision and interpretation are thus assimilated. But see Series E, No. 4, p. 295.

[87] The Court has, however, dealt with the question of revision of decisions by other
bodies. See Series B, No. 9, p. 22.

[88] The Court has never been called upon to say what measures an aggrieved State
might take against another State responsible for its injury. Yet it is to be noted that
Article 418 in Part XIII of the Treaty of Versailles states that the Court shall "indicate
the measures, if any, of an economic character which it considers to be appropriate, and
which other Governments would be justified in adopting against a defaulting Government."

obligation. Yet the Court has stated it to be "a principle of international law that the breach of an engagement involves an obligation to make reparation in an adequate form"; [89] if this obligation always exists when a breach has been established, it would seem possible to say that where the Court is competent to determine that a breach of an engagement has taken place, it is also competent, unless this has been expressly excluded by the parties, to deal with the legal consequences of an established breach, *i.e.*, to declare the duty of the defaulting State to make reparation. Moreover, if the Court is competent to pass upon the duty to make reparation, it is also competent, unless this has been expressly excluded by the parties, to determine the form, method and amount of the reparation due.[90] "Jurisdiction as to the reparation due for the violation of an international convention involves jurisdiction as to the forms and methods of reparation." [91]

In the *Wimbledon Case,* in which the jurisdiction depended on Article 386 of the Treaty of Versailles, the Court did not hesitate to declare that Germany was responsible for losses occasioned by the wrongful refusal of passage through the Kiel Canal by the *Wimbledon;* the compensation fixed covered "sums payable for freight during eleven days demurrage and two days deviation and the cost of fuel." Interest was allowed from the date of the judgment, the rate being fixed with reference to "the present financial situation of the world" and the "condition prevailing for public loans." [92]

In the *Chorzów Factory Case,* the Court stated that reparation "is the indispensable complement of a failure to apply a convention" even though this is not stated in the convention itself; hence, its jurisdiction over "differences of opinion, resulting from . . . the application" of certain provisions of the Geneva Convention was held to cover "differences relating to reparations which may be due by reason of failure to apply" those provisions. "The decision whether there has been a breach of an engagement involves no doubt a more important jurisdiction than a decision as to the nature or extent of reparation due for a breach." [93] The estimate of damage in this case was based solely on "the value of property, rights and interests which have been affected." [94] The purpose of reparation is to "wipe out all the con-

---

[89] *Chorzów Factory Case,* Series A, No. 9, p. 21. See also Series A, No. 17, p. 29.
[90] Series A, No. 9, p. 23.　　　　　　　　　[91] Series A, No. 17, p. 61.
[92] Series A, No. 1, pp. 31, 33. Both principal and interest were made payable in French currency, at Paris.
[93] Series A, No. 9, pp. 21, 23.　　　　　　[94] Series A, No. 17, p. 31.

sequences of the illegal act and reëstablish the situation which would, in all probability, have existed if that act had not been committed." Hence, "the amount of compensation due for an act contrary to international law" is to be based on "restitution in kind, or, if this is not possible, payment of a sum corresponding to the value which a restitution in kind would bear," and the award of "damages for loss sustained which would not be covered by restitution in kind or payment in place of it." [95] The compensation awarded consisted of "a lump sum corresponding to the value of the undertaking" at Chorzów; but the Court sought the assistance of an expert inquiry for determining what the sum should be. It observed that "contingent and indeterminate damage" could not be taken into account,[96] but this would not exclude *lucrum cessans*, or unearned profits, covering "future prospects." [97]

§446. **Counter-claims.** The Statute contains no reference to the competence of the Court to deal with counter-claims, but Article 40 of the Rules envisages the inclusion of counter-claims in the conclusions contained in a counter-case, in so far as the counter-claims "come within the jurisdiction of the Court." [98] A distinction is to be made between "direct counter-claims," *i.e.*, those arising out of the facts or transactions upon which the complainant's claim is based, and "indirect counter-claims," *i.e.*, those arising out of facts or transactions extrinsic to those upon which a complainant's claim is based.[99] A "direct counter-claim" must be, to use the Court's expression, "juridically connected with the principal claim." [100] Where a case is before the Court under a special agreement, the questions submitted will usually if not always cover the claims of all the parties; so that the problem of counter-claims will seldom arise.[1] Where a case is

---

[95] Series A, No. 17, p. 47. But see Lord Finlay's dissent, pp. 70–72.

[96] *Id.*, p. 57. The Court gave no decision on the requested prohibition of exports in this case, nor upon its power to issue such an injunction.

[97] *Id.*, pp. 53, 59.

[98] See Anzilotti, *"La riconvenzione nella procedura internazionale,"* 21 *Rivista di Diritto Internazionale* (1929), p. 309.

[99] See 26 American Journal of International Law, Supp. (1932), pp. 490–493, for the adoption of this terminology by the Research in International Law, Harvard Law School.

[100] In the *Chorzów Factory Case*, Series A, No. 17, p. 38. On a set-off as distinguished from a counter-claim, see *id.*, p. 62.

[1] In 1922, Judge Anzilotti "pointed out that in the case of a special agreement, a counter-claim could not be submitted, and that, in the case of an application, a claim of this nature could only be submitted if it came within the conditions subject to which all the parties had accepted the compulsory jurisdiction of the Court." Series D, No. 2, p. 139.

before the Court on an application, the jurisdiction of the Court once established would seem to extend to any direct counter-claim; the Court's power to dispose of the matter covered by the application would include a power to pass upon any submission by either party relating to the facts or transactions upon which the complainant's claim is based. Nor would it be improper for the Court to assume jurisdiction of an indirect counter-claim, if it arises out of facts or transactions which are covered by the same provisions for the Court's jurisdiction as those upon which the application is based. This limitation is important, however, and it seems to have been appreciated in the drafting of Article 40 of the Rules. The mere presence of the parties before the Court does not give it jurisdiction over an indirect counter-claim arising out of facts or transactions other than those which are covered by the text which confers jurisdiction over the application itself. The Court has not yet developed a jurisprudence on this point.[2]

§447. **Award of Costs.** Article 64 of the Statute provides for the possibility of a decision by the Court as to which party shall bear the costs of a proceeding; failing any decision by the Court, each party is to bear its own costs.[3] Article 56 of the 1922 Rules provided that each party may present its bill of costs before the oral proceedings are concluded; in 1926, this was modified to read, "The party in whose favor an order for the payment of costs has been made may present his bill of costs after judgment has been delivered." This goes on the theory that it may be impossible to prepare a complete bill of costs until all the proceedings have been concluded, and that the Court may have decided in the judgment not as to the amount of costs but as to the party by which they should be borne.[4] In no case has it been decided that one party should bear the burden of the other's costs, and no suggestion has been made that an award of costs should be given as a penalty for any action taken; hence there has been no decision as to what expenses are to be included in the costs.[5]

In the *Wimbledon Case,* the Court gave judgment that each party

---

[2] See, however, the *Chorzów Factory Case*, Series A, No. 17, pp. 36–42, 60, 63. See also §483, *infra.*

[3] *Quære,* whether the Court may direct one party to pay the other's costs, except on the request of the other party; and whether the Court may require a deposit in advance for meeting costs.   [4] Series E, No. 3, p. 221.

[5] Costs must be distinguished from the contributions to the Court's expenses, mentioned in Article 35 of the Statute. Such items as the compensation of judges *ad hoc* would not be included in costs.

should pay its own costs; [6] this was wholly unnecessary, for it did not modify the situation which would otherwise have existed. The order of September 13, 1928, instituting an expert enquiry in the *Chorzów Factory Case*, provided that with the exception of fees and expenses of assessors, all fees, costs and expenses of the enquiry should be advanced by the Court and refunded by the parties in the proportion to be fixed by the Court under Article 64 of the Statute, and for this purpose the parties were invited to make a deposit with the Registrar of 25,000 florins each.[7] In the *Eastern Greenland Case,* in 1933, each of the two parties asked the Court to decide that the other party should bear the costs it had incurred, but in the operative part of its judgment the Court declared that there was no need to deviate from the general rule laid down in Article 64 of the Statute that each party should bear its own costs.[8] It seems doubtful whether Article 64 of the Statute should ever be applied in advisory proceedings.[9]

§448. Withdrawal of an Application. Where a proceeding is instituted by an application, it may be terminated by the withdrawal of the application, though this does not seem to be covered by Article 61 of the Rules. If the respondent State has not taken any part in the proceeding, the withdrawal of the application effects a termination; if the respondent has taken part in the proceeding and if the parties have not reached an agreement, a withdrawal may be made by the applicant only on condition that it is formally accepted by the other party. The withdrawal of two suits by the German Government in 1933 and the acquiescence of the Polish Government in this withdrawal were recognized by the Court to have terminated the proceedings instituted by German applications.[10] In the case relating to *German Interests in Polish Upper Silesia,* certain parts of the German application were withdrawn during the course of the oral proceedings; the Court was not clear as to the position of the parties in respect of these parts and called for their explanations, as a result of which it recorded in its judgment that the application was withdrawn *pro tanto.*[11]

On February 13, 1929, the Belgian agent withdrew the Belgian ap-

---

[6] Series A, No. 1, p. 33.

[7] Series A, No. 17, p. 102. These deposits were made, and after the expenses had been met the balance was repaid to the parties. Series C, No. 16—II, pp. 58–60.

[8] Series A/B, No. 53, pp. 74, 75. A similar declaration was made in the case of the *Royal Hungarian Peter Pázmány University of Budapest.* Series A/B, No. 61, p. 249.

[9] In 1923, the expense of certain information furnished in connection with advisory opinions Nos. 6 and 7 was reimbursed by the Court to the German Government. Series E, No. 3, p. 221.

[10] Series A/B, No. 59, p. 195; No. 60, p. 202.   [11] Series A, No. 7, pp. 10–11.

plication of November 25, 1926, and as the respondent, the Chinese Government, had "never taken any proceeding in the suit," the Court held that "there is nothing to prevent the unilateral withdrawal of the suit"; on May 25, 1929, the Court by order declared the proceedings to be terminated.[12] In the case concerning *Southeastern Greenland*, both Denmark and Norway withdrew their applications; the Court had previously joined the two suits, and the Danish Government relied upon Article 61 of the Rules in making its withdrawal; on May 11, 1933, the Court by order declared the proceedings terminated.[13] On April 8, 1933, the agent of the Czechoslovak Government "withdrew the appeals" from certain judgments of the Hungarian-Czechoslovak Mixed Arbitral Tribunal, under the applications of July 7 and 20, 1932, and as this withdrawal was acquiesced in by the Hungarian Government, the Court declared the proceedings terminated.[14]

§449. Sanctions. The Statute contains no provisions relating to sanctions.[15] It confers on the Court no jurisdiction to see that its judgments are carried out. Except for its power to interpret or to revise a judgment, the Court's competence with reference to a dispute is exhausted when its judgment has been rendered. "Between the parties and in respect of that particular case," Article 59 of the Statute provides that the decision of the Court has "binding force."[16] Yet it is no part of the Court's task to oversee the execution of its judgment, to pronounce upon the parties' fulfilment of their obligations under the judgment, or to penalize a defaulting State. The Court has stated that it "neither can nor should contemplate" the contingency that a judgment may not be complied with; therefore, in the *Wimbledon Case*, it refused to "award interim interest at a higher rate in the event of the judgment not being complied with at the expiration of the time fixed for compliance."[17] Only when a State applies for a revision of a judgment may the Court inquire into the parties' "compliance with the

---

[12] Series A, Nos. 18/19, p. 5. [13] Series A/B, No. 55, p. 157.
[14] By order of May 12, 1933. Series A/B, No. 56, p. 162.
[15] The only provision in the Statute operating *in terrorem* is the statement in Article 49 that "formal note shall be taken of any refusal" to produce documents or to supply explanations.
[16] Perhaps the effect of Article 59 is too narrowly stated by the Court in Series A, No. 7, p. 19: "The object of this Article is simply to prevent legal principles accepted by the Court in a particular case from being binding upon other States or in other disputes." This statement was repeated in Series A, No. 13, p. 21. Yet the history of the drafting of Article 59 may justify the view that it establishes only a limitation on the effect of a judgment. The binding force of the judgment may be derived from international law, independently of Article 59.
[17] Series A, No. 1, p. 32. See also *id.*, No. 17, p. 63.

terms of the judgment," and in this case the Court's power of compulsion is limited to its setting a condition to its admitting the proceedings for revision.[18] The question of sanctions does not arise with reference to advisory opinions, since they can never have the effect of placing obligations on States.

Sanctions with which the Court is not immediately or directly concerned may be provided for by agreement. Article 13 of the Covenant, especially since its amendment in 1924, applies quite clearly to "decisions" of the Court; "the Members of the League agree that they will carry out in full good faith any award or decision that may be rendered" when a dispute has been submitted to arbitration or judicial settlement, in accordance with Article 13, and they also agree "that they will not resort to war against a Member of the League which complies therewith." [19] However, it is for the Council of the League of Nations, not for the Court, to "propose what steps should be taken to give effect" to an award or decision "in the event of a failure to carry out" its requirements. In several instances, treaties and conventions in force providing for a possible resort to the Court expressly state that the Court's decision shall have the force and effect of a decision under Article 13 of the Covenant.[20] Article 419 of Part XIII of the Treaty of Versailles and the corresponding articles in other treaties of peace provide specifically for sanctions to be taken by Members of the International Labor Organization.

The judgments of the Court must find their principal sanction in the public opinion which rallies to their support, and the experience of twelve years would seem to justify some confidence that in most cases, at any rate, this sanction will be adequate. If all of the judgments to date have not been executed, in no case has there been a flouting of the Court's authority; and in no instance has there been a flagrant default with respect to a judgment. In most instances the judgments

---

[18] It is a somewhat different question whether the Court has "jurisdiction to decide disputes concerning the non-compliance with the terms of one of its judgments." This question was referred to but not considered in the *Mavrommatis Case*. Series A, No. 11, p. 14.

[19] In the subcommittee of the Third Committee of the First Assembly, in 1920, doubt having been expressed as to the applicability of Article 13 of the Covenant, MM. Hagerup and Fromageot stated "that the sanctions provided in Article 13 must, *a fortiori*, apply to the awards of the Permanent Court, and that in any case Article 16 of the Covenant could be applied, since the non-execution of a judgment of the Court would constitute a violation of the Covenant." Records of First Assembly, Committees, I, p. 377.

[20] This practice originated in Article 12 of the Polish Minorities Treaty of June 28, 1919. 1 Hudson, International Legislation, p. 291.

have not called for the performance of a specific act; some of the judgments have merely established the Court's jurisdiction, some have
merely given authoritative interpretations of international instruments
or directions for the application of the provisions of such instruments.
In the *Wimbledon Case*, Germany was declared bound to pay to France
the sum of 140,749.35 French francs, within three months; within
that period, the German Government sought the permission of the
Guarantee Committee of the Reparation Commission (on which
France was represented) to make the payment, and when such permission was denied the Court was informed of the fact.[21] This cannot
be said to be a case of default, therefore, though the sum has not been
paid. In the *Chorzów Factory Case,* the judgment was that Poland
was under an obligation to pay reparation to Germany, but the
proceeding was discontinued before the amount payable was fixed.
The judgment in the *Lotus Case* put an end to the dispute between
France and Turkey. The judgment in the *Serbian Loans Case* led
to the conclusion of a convention between the Yugoslav Government
and representatives of the bondholders, on March 31, 1930, providing
for payments on the bonds in gold.[22] Following the judgment in the
Brazilian Loans Case, assurance was given by the Brazilian Government that the bonds would be paid in gold.[23] Since the judgment in
the case relating to the *Jurisdiction of the Oder Commission,* the
Commission has exercised the jurisdiction which the Court determined
to exist. The judgment in the *Free Zones Case* gave rise to negotiations between France and Switzerland which led to a settlement.[24] The
difficulties with respect to the *Interpretation of the Statute of the*

---

[21] Series E, No. 1, pp. 167–168.
[22] The text is published in Communication No. 349 (April 18, 1930) of the *Association Nationale des Porteurs Français de Valeurs Mobilières.*
[23] *Id.,* Communication No. 364 (March 31, 1932).
[24] On May 27, 1933, the French Government notified the Swiss Government that
it accepted the procedure envisaged by the Court and referred to in a Swiss declaration
made before the Court. For the text of the Swiss declaration, see Series A/B, No. 46,
p. 169. This procedure called for negotiations to be conducted with the aid and mediation
of experts, who were empowered to lay down, if necessary, the regulations for carrying
out Switzerland's undertaking "to regulate in a manner more appropriate to the economic
conditions of the present day the terms of the exchange of goods between the regions
in question." The direct negotiations between France and Switzerland, conducted at
Montreux-Territet, October 9–12, and November 6–25, 1933, having failed to produce an
agreement on all points, the experts were called upon to draw up the regulations envisaged, and on December 1, 1933, they adopted a *règlement concernant les importations
en Suisse des produits des zones franches* which has obligatory force for the parties as
from January 1, 1934. The text of the *règlement* was published in the French *Journal
Officiel,* December 15, 1933. On January 1, 1934, the French customs line was withdrawn from the Franco-Swiss frontier. See Hudson, in 28 American Journal of International Law (1934), p. 322.

Memel Territory disappeared with the judgment of the Court. The judgment as to the *Legal Status of Eastern Greenland* was followed almost immediately by a cancellation of the Norwegian proclamation which led to the institution of the suit.[25]

On this record as to the compliance with the judgments which have been given, it cannot be said that the Court is rendered ineffective or crippled in any way by the lack of sanctions.

[25] Norsk Lovtidende, 2nen Avdeling, 1933, p. 134.

CHAPTER 22

ADVISORY JURISDICTION

§450. Basis of Advisory Jurisdiction. Article 1 of the Statute of the Court, providing that it is established "in accordance with Article 14 [Fr., *conformément à l'article 14*] of the Covenant of the League of Nations," has the effect of incorporating in the Statute the provision in Article 14 of the Covenant that "the Court may also give [Fr., *elle donnera aussi*] an advisory opinion upon any dispute or question [Fr., *sur tout différend ou tout point*] referred to it by the Council or by the Assembly." [1] The 1920 Committee of Jurists proposed an article on advisory opinions to be included in the Statute, but it was rejected by the First Assembly; the subcommittee of the Third Committee seems to have agreed that since Article 14 of the Covenant "contained a provision in accordance with which the Court could not refuse to give advisory opinions," it "was therefore unnecessary to include a rule to the same effect in the constitution of the Court." [2] It is quite clear that the Court could not refuse altogether to give advisory opinions, and its duty to exercise advisory jurisdiction is recognized in the Rules. The addition to the Statute of the new Articles 65 to 68, annexed to the Revision Protocol of September 14, 1929, will affect only the Court's power over its procedure with respect to advisory opinions, without enlarging its jurisdiction.

§451. Advisory Opinions of National Courts. [3] While it seems doubtful whether the provision in Article 14 of the Covenant was

---

[1] This would seem to be a sounder basis for the Court's jurisdiction than the classification of Article 14 of the Covenant as a provision of a "treaty or convention in force" under Article 36 of the Statute. But see Fachiri, Permanent Court of International Justice (2 ed.), p. 78. In Series A, No. 6, p. 21, the Court noted that Article 14 is "referred to in the Preamble of the Statute."

[2] Records of First Assembly, Committees, I, p. 401. See *supra*, §184; on the work of the First Assembly in this connection, see the memorandum by Judge Moore, in Series D, No. 2, pp. 383–398.

[3] Advisory opinions may also be given by such bodies as the League of Nations Advisory and Technical Committee for Communications and Transit. See Article 13 of the Barcelona Statute on Freedom of Transit of April 20, 1921, 1 Hudson, International Legislation, p. 637; Article 22 of the Barcelona Statute on Navigable Waterways of April 20, 1921, 1 *id.*, p. 658; Article 35 of the Geneva Statute on Railways of

based on national experience, analogies exist in many countries where national courts have advisory jurisdiction. In certain states of the United States, the constitutions provide for advisory opinions to be given by courts or by the judges which compose them.[4] In Canada, the Supreme Court of the Dominion and the Supreme Courts of seven of the provinces exercise such jurisdiction. In Great Britain, advisory opinions are not infrequently given by the Judicial Committee of the Privy Council under the Judicial Committee Act of 1833.[5] Several continental European and Latin-American States have constitutions which provide for some form of advisory jurisdiction to be exercised by their courts.[6] The Austrian Constitution of 1920 (Articles 139, 140),[7] the Colombian Constitution of 1886 (Article 90),[8] the Finnish Constitution of 1919 (Article 18, 19),[9] the Honduran Constitution of 1924 (Article 102),[10] the Nicaraguan Constitution of 1911 (Article 99),[11] the Norwegian Constitution of 1914 (Article 83),[12] the Panama Constitution of 1904 (Article 105),[13] the Salvador Constitution of 1886 (Article 79),[14] and the Swedish Constitution of 1809 (Article 88),[15] contain such provisions. The statutes of some States also provide for the exercise of advisory jurisdiction; thus, the Bulgarian law of 1898 on the organization of courts (Article 47), and the Polish law of 1928 on court organization (Article 41). In view of the extent to which advisory opinions may be

---

December 9, 1923, 2 *id.*, p. 1152; Article 21 of the Geneva Statute on Maritime Ports of December 9, 1923, 2 *id.*, p. 1169; Article 22 of the Convention on the Simplification of Customs Formalities of November 3, 1923, 2 *id.*, p. 1116; and Article 32 of the Opium Convention of February 19, 1925, 3 *id.*, p. 1609.

[4] In Colorado, Florida, Maine, Massachusetts, New Hampshire, Rhode Island, South Dakota; the provision in the Massachusetts constitution dates from 1780. In several states, also, statutory provision is made for advisory opinions. See Hudson, "Advisory Opinions of National and International Courts," 37 Harvard Law Review (1924), p. 970; Frankfurter, "Advisory Opinions," 1 Encyclopedia of the Social Sciences (1930), p. 475. In 1793, the Supreme Court of the United States refused to give an advisory opinion at the request of the President. See Warren, The Supreme Court in United States History, Vol. I, pp. 108ff. Two interesting opinions recently given by state courts, both relating to the procedure for ratifying an amendment to the Constitution of the United States, are to be found in 148 Southern (Alabama, 1933), p. 107; 167 Atlantic (Maine, 1933), p. 176.

[5] The opinion on the *Boundary between Canada and Newfoundland in the Labrador Peninsula* (1927) 43 Times Law Reports 289, applies principles of international law, at least by analogy. See *In re Transferred Civil Servants* [1929] Appeal Cases 242, on the extent to which the Judicial Committee is bound by its previous judgment in giving an opinion.

[6] See Hudson, "The Advisory Opinions of the Permanent Court of International Justice," in International Conciliation (1925), No. 214, p. 321, and in 8 *Recueil des Cours, Académie de Droit International* (1925), p. 345; 15 *Bulletin de l'Institut Inter-médiaire International* (1926), pp. 11–22, 330–332.

[7] 1 Dareste, *Les Constitutions Modernes* (4th ed.), p. 332.

[8] 4 *id.*, p. 120.   [9] 1 *id.*, p. 499.   [10] 4 *id.*, p. 413.   [11] 4 *id.*, p. 425.

[12] 2 *id.*, p. 221.   [13] 4 *id.*, p. 268.   [14] 4 *id.*, p. 439.   [15] 2 *id.*, p. 505.

given by national courts in different parts of the world, it cannot be said that the provision in Article 14 of the Covenant constituted an innovation, therefore.

§452. **Nature of Advisory Jurisdiction.** Does the Court perform a judicial function in exercising its advisory jurisdiction? In 1922, Judge Moore expressed the conclusions that "the giving of advisory opinions, in the sense of opinions having no obligatory character, either on actual disputes or on theoretical questions, is not an appropriate function of a Court of Justice," and that "the exercise of such a function is at variance with the fundamental design of the Permanent Court of International Justice." [16] It is difficult to say what is a judicial function apart from the history of the action of courts and apart from an examination of the procedure actually followed in their determining upon that action. No such uniformity prevails in the action of judicial bodies throughout the world as to enable one to say that the judicial function will always have the same precise attributes. In general, it may be said that the giving of legal advice is not necessarily a discharge of a judicial function. The Court might have developed its procedure and practice with reference to advisory opinions in such a way that the function would have lacked the usual safeguards of judicial action; it has not done so, however. The Rules adopted in 1922 excluded the possibility of its giving opinions which would remain secret, as well as the possibility that the giving of the opinion would be kept secret; they also provided, though not too clearly, for a possible hearing of States or international organizations interested. This procedure has been retained in the revisions of the Rules, and there has been a progressive tendency to assimilate advisory to contentious procedure. The revision of the Statute under the Revision Protocol of September 14, 1929, would incorporate into the Statute the procedural provisions already existing in the Rules, and would provide (Article 68) that "in the exercise of its advisory functions, the Court shall further be guided by the provisions of the Statute which apply in contentious cases to the extent to which it recognizes them to be applicable." Whatever course might have been taken, the actual discharge of its advisory functions by the Court has always been kept within limits which characterize it as a judicial function, and the Court itself has conceived of the function as a judicial one.[17]

---

[16] Series D, No. 2, p. 397.   [17] Series B, No. 13, p. 23.

§453. **Source of Request for Advisory Opinion.** The Court has no competence to offer an advisory opinion *proprio motu;* it can act only when a request is made, and the request must emanate from either the Council or the Assembly of the League of Nations.[18] In practice, the Assembly has made no requests. No other international body is competent to make a request, though such competence was sought in 1920 on behalf of the Governing Body of the International Labor Office and the International Labor Conference.[19] Of course, the Council or the Assembly in making the request may act upon a suggestion by a State or States engaged in a dispute or by another international body; but in each case it is the Council or the Assembly which assumes the responsibility.[20] In practice, the Council has frequently served merely as a channel for requests originating with other bodies. Except as it may proceed through the Council or the Assembly, a State cannot ask for an advisory opinion; [21] nor can two States which are parties to a dispute make the request, or modify in any way a request made by the Council or the Assembly.[22] The Court's jurisdiction as to "matters specially provided for in treaties and conventions in force," under the first paragraph of Article 36 of the Statute, cannot be made to cover a provision in a treaty by which two States might agree to request an advisory opinion.

Neither the Assembly nor the Council is under any duty to request an advisory opinion, even when a legal question is before it.[23] It is

---

[18] Competence to make a request cannot be delegated to a committee set up by the Council or the Assembly. This seems to have been appreciated in the drafting of the Special Assembly's resolution of March 11, 1932, relating to the dispute between China and Japan. See Official Journal, 1932, Special Supplement No. 101, p. 81.

[19] Records of First Assembly, Committees, I, pp. 534, 563.

[20] In several international instruments, provision is made for the Council's requesting advisory opinions. See Article 7 of the agreement between Finland and Sweden, in Minutes of the Thirteenth Session of the Council, p. 53; the Latvian declaration on minorities, League of Nations Official Journal, 1923, p. 933; and the resolution on minorities in Estonia, *id.*, p. 1311.

[21] The Argentine delegation at the First Assembly of the League of Nations proposed that it should be possible for requests to be made "by the Governments of the States composing the League of Nations." Records of First Assembly, Committees, I, p. 519.

[22] *Interpretation of the Caphandaris-Molloff Agreement,* Series A/B, No. 45, p. 87. In this case, the Court found it unnecessary to consider "whether it is possible for an understanding between the representatives of the interested Governments, reached in the course of the proceedings, to serve as a kind of 'special agreement,' initiating a contentious proceeding before the Court." While the Franco-Swiss *compromis* relating to the *Free Zones Case* called for deliberations to be completed prior to a decision, it was not in reality a request for an advisory opinion.

[23] In the Committee set up in 1930 to consider amendments "to bring the Covenant into harmony with the Pact of Paris," there was some disposition to say that the Council should be bound to request an opinion desired by a party to a dispute. Records of Eleventh Assembly, Committees, I, p. 109.

hardly possible to draw a distinction between the competence of the Assembly and that of the Council, with respect to requests for advisory opinions; [24] yet Judge Anzilotti has expressed the opinion that as the admission of Members of the League of Nations falls within the exclusive jurisdiction of the Assembly, only the Assembly could ask the Court for an advisory opinion on a question relating to such admission.[25]

§454. **The Vote in the Council or the Assembly.** The question has been much discussed whether the Council or the Assembly of the League of Nations must be unanimous in voting a request to the Court for an advisory opinion. The two bodies are clearly on the same basis in this respect, and it may be simpler to deal with the question with reference to the Council. It must first be noted that under Article 4 of the Covenant the membership of the Council consists not only of representatives of the Members of the League permanently represented and of the Members selected by the Assembly, but also of representatives of Members whose interests are specially affected by the matter which at the time is under consideration. Under paragraph 1 of Article 5 of the Covenant, "decisions of the Council or of the Assembly" require the agreement of all the Members of the League represented at the meeting, except as otherwise expressly provided in the Covenant or by the terms of the peace treaties.[26] It is "otherwise provided" in paragraph 2 of Article 5 that "all matters of procedure at meetings of the Assembly or of the Council, including the appointment of committees to investigate particular matters" may be decided by a majority vote.[27] The French version (*toutes questions de procédure qui se posent aux réunions de l'Assemblée ou du Conseil*) is perhaps clearer, in that it does not require the "matter of procedure" to relate to procedure merely at meetings of the Assembly or of the Council.

---

[24] The competence of the Council and the Assembly, *vis-à-vis* each other, is not very clearly defined. In 1923, the Lithuanian representative asked the Assembly to request an advisory opinion after the Council had refused to do so. The Sixth Committee of the Fourth Assembly consulted the First Committee on the point, and the latter seems to have replied that the Assembly was not precluded from requesting an opinion under the circumstances. Records of Fourth Assembly, First Committee, p. 57; *id.*, Sixth Committee, pp. 9, 17, 22.   [25] Series B, No. 18, p. 20.

[26] This assumes a single Covenant of the League, and the reference must be taken to be to all the four peace treaties in which the text of the Covenant was embodied. See §89, *supra*.

[27] On the rule of unanimity, see Sir John Fischer Williams, in 19 American Journal of International Law (1925), p. 475; Julius Stone, in British Year Book of International Law, 1933, p. 18; Cromwell A. Riches, The Unanimity Rule and the League of Nations (Baltimore, 1933).

Is the adoption of a resolution to request an advisory opinion a "decision" within the meaning of that term as used in paragraph 1 of Article 5 of the Covenant? Or is it a "matter of procedure" as that term is used in paragraph 2 of Article 5? The unanimity referred to in paragraph 1 of Article 5 is absolute, requiring the "agreement of all the Members of the League represented at the meeting", it is not the limited unanimity referred to in paragraph 6 of Article 15 of the Covenant, which requires agreement by all the members of the Council "other than the representatives of one or more of the parties to the dispute." As it will more probably arise where the proposed request relates to a matter in dispute, the question may be stated, whether all representatives sitting in the Council, including those of the parties to a dispute, must agree before the Council can request an opinion relating to a question involved in that dispute. If it is proposed to request an advisory opinion on a matter which is not the subject of a dispute before the Council, the problem arises in its simpler form. The Court itself has adverted to the question only once, in its reply in the *Eastern Carelia Case,* and it was then unnecessary to give an answer.[28]

The question has arisen or has been discussed in both the Council and the Assembly, and these discussions and the practice of the Council leave the answer in some doubt. On several occasions when it has been proposed that the Council request an advisory opinion and when the proposal has encountered opposition, the Council has refrained from voting a request; as the reasons may have been various, such action by the Council cannot be taken as in any way conclusive with respect to a requirement of unanimity.[29] It may be said, however,

---

[28] Series B, No. 5, p. 27. In the opinion on the Greco-Turkish Agreement of 1926, it was stated that both parties to the agreement had consented to the request for an advisory opinion. Series B, No. 16, p. 12. It may be noted, also, that in the opinion relating to Article 3 of the Treaty of Lausanne, the Court stated that "the rule of unanimity, which is also in accordance with the unvarying tradition of all diplomatic meetings or conferences, is explicitly laid down in Article 5, paragraph 1, of the Covenant," and that "no exceptions to this principle are made other than those provided for in the Covenant itself and in the Peace Treaties of which it constitutes the first part." Series B, No. 12, p. 30. Various treaties confer on the Council power to act by majority vote, however.

[29] In 1923, when a request for an advisory opinion on the Hungarian optants' dispute was proposed, the Hungarian representative thought that the "decision on this question of procedure" could be taken by a majority vote. League of Nations Official Journal, 1923, p. 608. For later discussion of the question in connection with that dispute, see *id.,* 1928, pp. 429, 439. When the *Salamis* dispute was before the Council in 1927, M. Scialoja (Italy) expressed the view that a request for an advisory opinion was a matter of procedure as to which only a majority vote is required; but this view was stoutly contested by M. Titulesco (Rumania). *Id.,* 1927, pp. 1473, 1474.

that the Council has shown some reluctance to adopt a request for an advisory opinion by a majority vote.[30] Though it is not always possible to ascertain from the published minutes the precise character of the vote when the Council has resolved to request an opinion,[31] the following cases are instructive:

(1) On April 21, 1923, the Council unanimously adopted a request for an advisory opinion on instruments relating to the autonomy of Eastern Carelia, though the Soviet Government was not represented and had not been invited to be represented; [32] the questions related to the merits of a dispute between Finland and the Soviet Union.

(2) On July 7, 1923, the decision to make a request for the interpretation of the Polish Minorities Treaty was taken by the Council in spite of the opposition of the Polish representative, who thereupon stated that he would bring the Council's resolution to the notice of his Government; [33] in this case one of the questions related to the competence of the Council itself.[34]

(3) On March 14, 1925, when the Council had before it an appeal by Greece under Article 11 of the Covenant relating to the expulsion of the Œcumenical Patriarch, the Turkish Government had contended that the matter was within its own domestic jurisdiction and had refused to be represented; the Council proceeded to adopt a resolution by unanimous vote, including that of the Greek representative, asking the Court to give an opinion on the question whether the Turkish objections to its competence precluded the Council from dealing with the matter.[35] Thereafter, the Turkish Government, in a letter to the Registrar of the Court, denied the validity of the Council's resolution.[36] As the request was later withdrawn, the case is of doubtful value as a precedent; though a party to the dispute before the Council had expressed its opposition, it was not represented in the Council and the vote was unanimous.

(4) On September 19, 1925, the Council adopted a proposal to

---

[30] See the statement by M. Colban, *rapporteur*, in League of Nations Official Journal, 1932, p. 540; and see *id.*, 1931, p. 232.

[31] The records of the Council are analyzed by M. Hammarskjöld in 9 *Revue de Droit International et de Législation Comparée* (1928), pp. 694–698.

[32] League of Nations Official Journal, 1923, p. 578.

[33] *Id.*, p. 935. The fact that by Article 12 of the Minorities Treaty Poland had agreed to the Court's jurisdiction over disputes under the treaty seems irrelevant to the question as to the nature of the vote in the Council required for requesting the opinion.

[34] Germany was not represented on the Council when the request was adopted, though the matter before the Council related to the protection of German minorities in Poland. [35] League of Nations Official Journal, 1925, p. 488.

[36] Series C, No. 9—II, p. 107.

request the Court to give an opinion on the character of the decision to be taken by the Council in virtue of paragraph 2 of Article 3 of the Treaty of Lausanne and on the character of the vote required in reaching the decision; the Turkish representative who was present saw no necessity for this request, and apparently opposed it, but the record does not state that he voted against it.[37] Thereafter on October 8, 1925, the Turkish Government in a telegram addressed to the Court declared the question to be political and not legal; on November 4, 1925, however, the Turkish *chargé d'affaires* at The Hague replied to certain questions addressed to him by the Court "for the purposes of information," but subject to the reserves previously formulated by his Government.[38] When the Court's opinion came before the Council on December 8, 1925, the Turkish representative stated that "the advisory opinion was not asked for by a unanimous vote" and that the Turkish representative had "voted against it"; [39] he did not object to a consideration of the opinion, however.

On the record of the Council, it may be said that in two cases, those relating to the *Acquisition of Polish Nationality* and to the *Interpretation of the Treaty of Lausanne,* the Council voted to make the request against the opposition of representatives present from States concerned, but in each of these cases, the questions submitted had to do with the powers of the Council. In two other cases, the request was voted in the absence of representatives of one of the States concerned, and in one of these the question submitted related to the merits of the case.

The question arose at the 1926 Conference of Signatories in connection with its consideration of the proposed adhesion of the United States to the Protocol of December 16, 1920. That Conference took the fifth reservation offered by the United States "to rest upon the presumption that the adoption of a request for an advisory opinion by the Council or Assembly requires a unanimous vote"; to this the Conference made the reply in its Final Act that "no such presumption has so far been established," and that "it is therefore impossible to say with certainty whether in some cases, or possibly in all cases, a decision by a majority is not sufficient." [40] In

[37] League of Nations Official Journal, 1925, p. 1382.
[38] Series C, No. 10, p. 287.
[39] League of Nations Official Journal, 1926, p. 122. The President of the Council stated on this occasion that the question of adopting the Court's opinion was a "question of procedure" which did not require unanimity. *Id.,* p. 127. See §464 (12), *infra.*
[40] Minutes of the 1926 Conference of Signatories, p. 79. See also *id.,* pp. 21-45.

1928, the Swiss delegation raised the question at a meeting of the Ninth Assembly of the League of Nations; M. Motta stated that "the view appears already to be fairly generally held that the votes of the States parties to the dispute should not be counted " [41] in a decision to request an advisory opinion, and he thought "the Covenant could easily be interpreted" to require only a majority vote, a result which would be "wise and sound" and would ensure "considerable progress in international jurisprudence." [42] He proposed that the Council be asked to consider "whether it would not be desirable" to submit to the Court for an advisory opinion "the question whether the Council or the Assembly can, by a simple majority, request an advisory opinion." [43] This proposal evoked the expression of a variety of views in the First Committee,[44] some of which indicated a confused understanding of the rôle of advisory opinions. Some delegates in the Assembly thought with M. Fromageot that "the best solution consisted in giving no answer in advance"; some thought with M. Politis that advisory opinions were "in reality no longer" merely advisory. Faced with considerable opposition, the Swiss delegation offered a modified proposal which was adopted by the Assembly; it recited the "necessity for putting an end to the prevailing uncertainty as to the conditions for voting on requests for advisory opinions" and recommended that the Council submit the question to study, "as soon as circumstances permit." This resolution was later noted by the Council, and it was agreed that each member of the Council should study the subject individually in preparation for a later exchange of views.[45]

Under an Assembly resolution of September 24, 1929, a committee was established in 1930 to consider amendments to the Covenant "to bring it into harmony with the Pact of Paris." One of its recommendations was that the following new paragraph 7 *bis* be added to Article 15 of the Covenant:

> At any stage of the examination the Council may, either at the request of one of the parties or on its own initiative, ask the Permanent Court of International Justice for an advisory opinion on points of law

[41] This view had been expressed by Sir Cecil Hurst in 1926. Minutes of the 1926 Conference of Signatories, p. 24. [42] Records of Ninth Assembly, Plenary, p. 64.
[43] *Id.*, p. 73. This course had been suggested by M. Rolin (Belgium) and M. Pilotti (Italy) in 1926. Minutes of the 1926 Conference of Signatories, pp. 23, 25.
[44] Records of Ninth Assembly, First Committee, pp. 40–57.
[45] League of Nations Official Journal, 1929, p. 10. No record has been found of any later exchange of views by members of the Council.

relating to the dispute. Such application shall not require a unanimous vote by the Council.

In its report,[46] this committee stated that "the majority of the Members of the Committee thought that, in order to render the asking of an advisory opinion easier, the Council should be given the possibility of making a request for an advisory opinion by a decision adopted by a simple majority"; it was added, however, that "the Committee has left entirely on one side the question whether, as a general rule, a request for an advisory opinion requires unanimity or may be made by a simple majority." The text of the proposed amendment was not approved by a subcommittee of the First Committee of the Eleventh Assembly,[47] and no amendment along this line has been proposed by the Assembly.

In view of the Ninth Assembly's formulation of doubt, it is impossible to give a definite answer to the question. It is first to be queried whether the adoption of a request for an advisory opinion is a "decision" within the meaning of that term in paragraph 1 of Article 5 of the Covenant; there would seem to be good reason for confining such a "decision" to action which possesses more finality than that of seeking authoritative enlightenment on some matter before the Council. In the second place, it is possible to say that the adoption of a request is a step taken by the Council as "a matter of procedure" within paragraph 2 of Article 5, preparatory to a deliberation which will result in a "decision." Such action is analogous to "the appointment of committees to investigate particular matters" which is said to be included in "matters of procedure," though strictly the Court is not a committee subject to the Council's control.[48] Moreover, when it is dealing with a dispute under Article 15 of the Covenant, the Council is empowered by paragraph 6 of that Article to adopt a report on the agreement of all its members "other than the representatives of one or more of the parties to the dispute," and such a report is given definite consequences;[49] it therefore seems inconsistent to

---

[46] See Records of Eleventh Assembly, First Committee, pp. 104, 109.

[47] Id., pp. 166, 169.

[48] On numerous occasions the Council has set up a special committee of jurists instead of voting a request for an advisory opinion.

[49] The provision in Article 15 was applied when on September 18, 1920, the Council declared itself competent to deal with the Aaland Islands dispute. Minutes of the Council, 9th session, p. 17. The provision was applied also when the special assembly adopted its report on the Sino-Japanese situation, on February 24, 1933. League of Nations Official Journal, Special Supplement No. 112, p. 22.

say that in enlisting the aid of the Court to clarify the legal situation preparatory to making such a report, the Council can vote a request only if all parties to the dispute represented at the meeting agree. It is possible, however, that the nature of the vote required in the Council or the Assembly may be made to depend on the kind of dispute or question to which the advisory opinion would relate; [50] it may be thought that a request for an opinion on a question relating to the Council's competence [51] or procedure can be taken without unanimity, whereas a request for an opinion on a question which constitutes an issue *au fond* would require unanimity. The uncertainty with regard to the whole question has been increased by confusion as to the nature of advisory opinions, and by an improper resort to the analogy of obligatory jurisdiction; [52] as neither the Council nor a party to a dispute is bound by an advisory opinion, it seems wholly unjustified to regard advisory proceedings before the Court as constituting either in substance or in form "litigation between the parties" to a dispute.[53] The continued progress toward a complete assimilation of advisory to contentious jurisdiction may have some effect, however, on the ultimate answer to the question under discussion.

Competence to determine the nature of the vote required for a request for an advisory opinion would seem to reside, in the first instance at any rate, in the Council and Assembly themselves. Possibly a Member of the League which has made a declaration under paragraph 2 of Article 36 of the Statute could institute a proceeding in the Court against other States which have made similar declarations, with a view to procuring the Court's interpretation of Article 5 of the Covenant; a judgment given by the Court in such a proceeding would be binding only on the parties, however. It seems doubtful whether the Court would be competent to give such an interpretation when a

[50] This suggestion is made by Arnold D. McNair, in the British Yearbook of International Law, 1926, p. 9.

[51] When it was proposed to ask for an opinion on the question of the Council's competence in the *Salamis* case, M. Scialoja (Italy) said that "questions of competence belong to the category of the larger questions of procedure." League of Nations Official Journal, 1927, p. 1473.

[52] The fact that a State engaged in a dispute before the Council may have made a declaration under paragraph 2 or Article 36 of the Statute, does not modify its position in the Council with respect to a request for an advisory opinion; by agreeing to become a party before the Court it has not waived any rights in the Council. In 1932, the British representative on the Council seems to have viewed a proposal to request an advisory opinion on the claim of Finland as a "circuitous method" of achieving compulsory arbitration. League of Nations Official Journal, 1932, pp. 508, 509.

[53] See, however, Records of Ninth Assembly, First Committee, pp. 40–57; and McNair, in British Year Book of International Law, 1926, p. 12.

request for an advisory opinion is before it, unless the opinion requested relates to that very matter; and even in this case an opinion by the Court would not be binding. If the Court is seised of a written request signed by the President of the Assembly, by the President of the Council, or by the Secretary-General under instructions from the Assembly or the Council, in accordance with Article 72 of the Rules, it would seem to be no part of the Court's function to inquire how the request was voted; it has no general jurisdiction to interpret the Covenant, and it should not go behind the signature of one of these officials to determine that a request was invalidly adopted.[54] Even if an interested State should oppose the giving of the opinion, it seems doubtful whether the Court should refuse to entertain the request or to give the opinion on the sole ground that the vote to make the request was insufficient.[55]

§455. **Subject-Matter of a Request for an Advisory Opinion.** The provision in Article 14 of the Covenant refers to "an advisory opinion upon any dispute or question" (Fr., *sur tout différend ou tout point*). The Court's Rules envisage in each request for an opinion the formulation of a "question," whether or not it relates to a dispute. The 1920 Committee of Jurists proposed to distinguish between "a question of an international nature which does not refer to any dispute that may have arisen" and "a question which forms the subject of an existing dispute"; but the Third Committee of the First Assembly feared that this distinction was "likely to give rise to practical difficulties." [56] Yet Article 71 of the Rules of Court, as amended in 1927, makes a distinction between "a question relating to an existing dispute" and other questions, providing for the application of Article 31 of the Statute in connection with the Court's consideration of the former. Giving the word "dispute" the broad interpretation of a difference upon which action depends,[57] it may be said that each of the requests for advisory opinions made by the Council has related to a

---

[54] In opposition to this view, it may be said that the Court must interpret the last sentence of Article 14 of the Covenant in the light of other provisions in the Covenant, and that any request for an advisory opinion raises the question as to when the Council or the Assembly has acted.

[55] Under Article 5 of the Protocol for the Accession of the United States, of September 14, 1929, this statement may require some modification with respect to an objection made by the United States. See §238, *supra*.

[56] Records of First Assembly, Committees, I, p. 534. See §184, *supra*.

[57] In another connection, the Court has defined a "dispute" as "a disagreement on a point of law or fact, a conflict of legal views or of interests between two persons." Series A, No. 2, p. 11.

dispute; in every case, the Council acted because it was important that questions as to which varying opinions were held had presented themselves for solution, either to the Council, to some other international body, or to a State or a group of States.[58] In most instances, the difference was actually the subject of a "dispute" between States in the narrower sense to be given to the expression as it is used in Article 71 of the Rules. These facts have a distinct bearing on the judicial character of the advisory function.

The Court has not been requested to give an opinion on any speculative question; it has not been asked to assume the rôle of the Council's schoolmaster. There has been some discussion, however, of the propriety of the Council's making a request for an opinion on an "abstract question." In 1923, following the action taken by the Council in the Corfu dispute between Greece and Italy, certain questions of a general nature were formulated upon which it was proposed that an advisory opinion be requested; the Italian representative expressed some doubt as to the competence of the Court to deal with such questions,[59] and no advisory opinion was requested. A question relating to a dispute existing at the time of the request may later become "abstract" in consequence of the settlement of the dispute; [60] this would not seem to call for the Court's refusing to answer the question. Even though it should refuse to give an answer to the question put, the Court should not refuse to entertain a request for an opinion on an abstract question. In all the cases which have arisen, the question has related to a point of law.[61] May it also involve a point of fact? The Court has said that "under ordinary circumstances, it is certainly expedient that the facts upon which the opinion of the Court is desired should not be in controversy and it should not be left to the Court itself to ascertain what they are." [62] Where the facts had been investigated by the competent body of the League, however, the Court was disposed to accept them without making "new investigations and enquiries." [63]

[58] In each case the Court makes a careful study of the situation which led to the Council's decision to make the request.

[59] League of Nations Official Journal, 1923, p. 1321.

[60] This might be said to have happened with reference to the question concerning the proposed *Austro-German Customs Régime,* in view of the declarations made to the Committee of Enquiry for European Union just before the opinion was handed down. See §464 (20), *infra.*

[61] The Turkish Government contended that the question of the expulsion of the Œcumenical Patriarch, with reference to which a request made was later withdrawn, was a political question. Series C, No. 9—II, p. 107.

[62] Series B, No. 5, p. 28.   [63] Series B, No. 14, p. 46.

§456. **Compliance with Requests for Opinions.** It would seem that the Court is bound to entertain any request for an advisory opinion which is duly communicated to it by the Council or the Assembly. Article 14 of the Covenant merely states that the Court "may give" (Fr., *donnera*) an advisory opinion; under the existing rules, which would be incorporated into the Statute by the additional articles of the Statute annexed to the Revision Protocol of September 14, 1929, the Court could not refuse to take the request into consideration. Even under the original Statute, the Court may not say by rule that it will decline altogether to entertain requests for advisory opinions. Yet the nature of the Court and the process by which its action must be consummated make it impossible to say that the Court must give any particular opinion requested. Many circumstances may arise in which the Court should refuse to give the opinion requested, or should refrain from answering the question put to it. If a majority of the judges are unable to reach any agreement among themselves, no opinion can be given as the opinion of the Court; in the case of the *Austro-German Customs Régime,* the Court found it impossible to answer the whole question put to it. The question may on examination be found to be of such a nature that no answer can be given to it.[64] In 1922, it was proposed that the Rules should contain a provision that "the Court reserves the right to refrain from replying to questions put to it which require an advisory opinion on a theoretical case"; [65] this proposal was not adopted, and no such general rule can be stated. Yet a "theoretical case" might be put in such a way that the Court could give no opinion.[66] If a question of fact were involved, the Court might find that its powers of investigation as conferred by Article 44 of the Statute would not permit any answer to be given. Nor can the Court go outside its constitutional limitations to arrive at an opinion; "being a Court of Justice," it "cannot, even in giving advisory opinions, depart from the essential rules guiding" its "activity as a Court." [67] Hence, if the Council requested the Court to give an opinion on a dispute without hearing States

---

[64] Judge Anzilotti has expressed the view that "it is equally inadmissible for the Court to comply with a request based on a hypothesis which is legally unsound or for the Court to modify the request in order to bring it into harmony with what the Court holds to be the law in force." Series B, No. 18, p. 20.   [65] Series D, No. 2, p. 308.
[66] "It may turn out to be practically impossible to define a principle adequately and safely without previous ascertainment of the exact facts to which it is to be applied." Lord Haldane, in *Attorney-General for British Columbia* v. *Attorney-General for Canada* [1914] A. C. 153, 162.   [67] Series B, No. 5, p. 29.

concerned, the Court would doubtless refuse to answer the questions put. Clearly, therefore, the Court cannot always be bound to give the opinion requested.

This result is confirmed by the "reply" of the Court in 1923 with respect to the request for an advisory opinion on the effect of certain articles in the Treaty of Dorpat and an annexed declaration regarding the autonomy of *Eastern Carelia*. In this case, the Court entertained the request but declined to answer the question.[68] The Soviet Government refused to take any part in the Court's examination of the question. Before hearing the representative of Finland, the Court asked for his "views as to whether it had competence to give effect to the request for an advisory opinion." Examining the documents before it, the Court found that the two Governments were "in acute controversy" with regard to the declaration. Since the question bore "on an actual dispute between Finland and Russia," it concluded that "as Russia is not a Member of the League of Nations, the case is one under Article 17 of the Covenant," and that "the submission of the dispute" "for solution according to the methods provided for in the Covenant, could only take place by virtue of" its consent. Hence the Court found it "impossible to give its opinion on a dispute of this kind." This position is not to be defended. Whatever may be the rule laid down for its own guidance, the Court has no competence to judge the work of the Council, or to say how the Council should deal with a dispute between a Member and a non-member of the League, or to limit the power of the Council to request advisory opinions. The particular dispute had not been "submitted" to the Court "for solution according to the methods provided for in the Covenant"; the Council had asked for an opinion on definite questions which did not relate to the Council's competence, and it was no part of the Court's function to inquire into an application of Article 17 of the Covenant.[69] It was some such view as this which inspired the *caveat* entered by the Council when the Court's reply in this case came before it.[70] "Other cogent reasons" were given by the Court, which were thought to "render it very inexpedient that the

[68] Its "reply" was published in the Court's collection of Advisory Opinions, however, Series B, No. 5; and it has been referred to in Series E, No. 1, p. 200, as an advisory opinion.

[69] It may be noted that in the advisory opinion on *German Settlers in Poland*, the Court upheld the power of the Council to request an opinion in a matter brought before it under Article 12 of the Polish Minorities Treaty. Series B, No. 6, pp. 22–23.

[70] League of Nations Official Journal, 1923, p. 1337. See §464 (5), *infra*.

Court should attempt to deal" with the matter. The question presented was "really one of fact," to answer which an enquiry would have to be made, and in view of the attitude of the Soviet Government the Court found itself "unable to pursue the investigation" which "would require the consent and coöperation of both parties." This, it is submitted, is the sound reason for the Court's refusal to give the opinion, a sounder reason than that which the Court emphasized.

The reply of the Court in the *Eastern Carelia Case* may possibly be taken to have established a limitation on the Court's exercise of advisory jurisdiction with reference to questions relating to existing disputes. On the basis of the "well established" rule of international law that "no State can, without its consent, be compelled to submit its disputes with other States either to mediation or to arbitration or to any other kind of pacific settlement," the Court seems to have been willing to say that where a question relates to the merits of an existing dispute between a Member of the League of Nations and a State not a member of the League of Nations, and where the latter is not a party to any treaty conferring jurisdiction on the Court or the Council and has refused both to participate in the Council's consideration of the dispute and to coöperate in the Court's examination of the question, then the Court is not competent to give an advisory opinion. The 1926 Conference of Signatories expressed its approval of this limitation, by implication, in its Final Act.[71] In the advisory opinion on *German Settlers in Poland*, the Court said that "if, as Poland has claimed, the subject matter of the controversy is not within the competency of the League, the Court would not be justified in rendering an opinion as to the rights of the settlers." [72] This statement seems to be too broad.

§457. **Form of Requests.** Article 14 of the Covenant envisages the reference of a dispute or question to the Court "by the Council or by the Assembly." The Court itself, by Article 72 of the Rules, has provided the manner in which "questions upon which the advisory opinion of the Court is asked shall be laid before the Court"; for this purpose, it prescribes "a written request, signed either by the President of the Assembly or the President of the Council of the League of Nations, or by the Secretary-General of the League under instructions from the Assembly or the Council." This request must "con-

71 Minutes of the 1926 Conferences of Signatories, p. 79.
72 Series B, No. 6, p. 19.

tain an exact statement of the question," and it must "be accompanied by all documents likely to throw light upon the question." The form of the "written request" has undergone some development. It is invariably signed by the Secretary-General and addressed to the Court; it refers to the Council's resolution, of which a certified copy is annexed, and to the authorization thus given to the Secretary-General; the request is that "the Court will, in accordance with Article 14 of the Covenant of the League, give an advisory opinion." The Secretary-General may either present the "request of the Council," or an "application" requesting the Court to give the opinion; in some cases he writes a covering letter to the Registrar. The Secretary-General usually states that he "will be prepared to furnish any assistance which the Court may require in the examination of the matter, and will, if necessary, arrange to be represented before the Court"; [73] in no case to date, however, has the Secretary-General been represented before the Court.[74] In some cases, the Council in its resolution requests that the Court "be so good as to treat the present request for an advisory opinion as a matter of urgency"; it may ask to have the opinion so that it may be dealt with at a particular session of the Council, or it may ask the Court to hold an extraordinary session to deal with the request.[75] The Council sometimes invites interested Governments "to hold themselves at the disposal of the Court for the purpose of supplying any relevant documentation and explanations." A *dossier* of the relevant documents is sent with the request, sometimes by a later despatch, and it usually includes the minutes of the Council at meetings when the question was under consideration.

On several occasions, the Court has found it necessary to interpret the question before it. In connection with its third opinion, it "had to alter the terms of the question put in order to be able to reply thereto." [76] Similarly, in its sixteenth opinion, it found that the question was not exactly stated, and restated it, remarking however that this course might not always be possible.[77] In its request for an

---

[73] In the Council's resolution asking for an opinion on the expulsion of the Œcumenical Patriarch, the Secretary-General was authorized "to explain to the Court the action the Council has taken in the matter." Series C, No. 9—II, p. 14.

[74] But the Court has frequently asked the Secretary-General to supply documents.

[75] Series B, No. 11, p. 9; No. 12, p. 8. In the case relating to the *Exchange of Greek and Turkish Populations*, the Court declared that the question was "by the nature of things, extremely urgent," though the Council's request had not so characterized it. Series B, No. 10, p. 8.　　　　[76] Series B, No. 16, p. 15.　　　　[77] *Id.*, p. 14.

opinion on the *Greco-Bulgarian Communities*, the Council submitted three lists, containing twelve questions, all of which the Court answered. In its resolution concerning a request for an advisory opinion on the dispute relating to the nationality decrees in Tunis and Morocco, adopted on October 4, 1922, the Council decided to "refer" a question to the Court for its opinion; it then requested "the two Governments to bring this matter before the Court." The Secretary-General first transmitted this resolution to the Registrar "for the information of the Court," on October 4, 1922; as this communication was not thought by the Registrar to be a "request" under Article 72 of the Rules, on November 7, 1922 the Secretary-General submitted a formal request.[78] On one occasion, after its request had been communicated to the Court, on the proposal of an interested Government the Council adopted an explanation of the question submitted, and communicated it to the Court; the latter acted upon the explanation in its opinion.[79]

§458. **Procedure on the Request.** In pursuance of the policy of safeguarding the judicial character of its functions, the Court has provided in Article 73 of its Rules that notice of a request shall "forthwith" be given by the Registrar to all Members of the League of Nations and to all States entitled to appear before the Court.[80] In addition, "by means of a special and direct communication," States and international organizations [81] considered "as likely to be able to furnish information on the question" [82] are informed that the Court will be prepared to receive written statements or to hear oral statements relating to the question; a State which has failed to receive such a special communication may nevertheless express a desire to submit a written statement or to be heard, and the Court will decide. In practice, States which are not specially interested are sometimes specially informed that their statements may be received; [83] parties to a multipartite instrument to which the requested opinion relates

---

[78] Series C, No. 2, pp. 248ff.   [79] Series B, No. 6, p. 40.

[80] *Cf.*, Article 36 of the Rules, applying to proceedings instituted by special agreement or application.

[81] Though the last paragraph of Article 26 of the Statute refers only to contentious cases, its principle is applied by analogy in practice. Series E, No. 2, p. 174; No. 8, p. 273. The International Labor Office may be said to be in a special position, therefore.

[82] The Court, or the President if the Court is not sitting, determines which are these States or organizations, and they may be listed in the order fixing time limits. See Series C, No. 15—I, p. 238. The criteria employed in this determination are not clear.

[83] Special interest is not requisite to a State's being admitted to make a statement to the Court. Series E, No. 6, p. 302.

are usually so informed.[84] This practice obviates any need for the application of Articles 62 and 63 of the Statute by analogy; [85] strictly there is no possibility of intervention in advisory proceedings.[86] In the later years, States have usually formulated requests to be heard, and the Court seems to have granted such requests in every instance.

In every case to date save one,[87] Governments have submitted statements in connection with advisory opinions; in every case save one, [88] oral hearings have been held.[89] In several cases, international organizations have submitted statements and their representatives have appeared in oral hearings. Statements have sometimes been presented as "cases" and "counter-cases"; [90] as to such presentations the Court may follow the analogy of contentious proceedings introduced by special agreement. In connection with the request for an opinion relating to the *Greco-Bulgarian Communities,* a curious situation arose; the President of the Greco-Bulgarian Mixed Commission had suggested to each of the two Governments that in the proceedings before the Court, each should submit a written statement concluding with "the submissions which it wishes the Court to confirm"; when the question was before the Court, each Government filed a memorial (case) which contained such "submissions." Without pronouncing on the correctness of this procedure, the Court dealt with the "submissions" as authoritative summaries of the opposing contentions.[91]

Written or oral statements made to the Court in relation to a question before it for advisory opinion are received as "information." [92]

[84] Series E, No. 7, p. 303.

[85] Article 63, paragraph 1, may be applied by analogy in determining the States to which special and direct communications are to be sent. See §410, *supra.*

[86] In 1923, in reply to a request to be allowed to intervene by the Rumanian Government, the President of the Court stated that Articles 62 and 63 of the Statute are not applicable to advisory proceedings, but that under Article 73 of the Rules the Rumanian Government might furnish information. Series C, No. 3 (Vol. 3), pp. 1089, 1090.   [87] This was the thirteenth advisory opinion. Series B, No. 13.

[88] Series B, No. 11, p. 10. In this case no oral hearing was requested.

[89] The Court may express a desire to hear oral statements. Series B, No. 15, p. 7. In connection with the case on the *Jurisdiction of the Danzig Courts,* the Court expressed a desire to hear the parties. Series C, No. 14—I, pp. 9, 548.

[90] This was true in the *Tunis-Morocco Case,* in which also memoranda were directly exchanged between the two Governments interested. Series C, No. 2, p. 265; Series E, No. 1, p. 251. In an order of February 24, 1931, the President clearly refrained from using the term counter-case to apply to a "second written statement" to be filed by an interested State. Series C, No. 52, p. 264.

[91] Series B, No. 17, p. 14. See also Series B, No. 16, p. 13.

[92] This view seems to have been carried too far in 1926 when the President indicated to representatives of international organizations that inasmuch as a question of law had been submitted for an advisory opinion, "it was not for them to indicate the conclusions at which the Court should, in their opinion, arrive." Series C, No. 12, p. 10. In 1923, the German Government was reimbursed certain expenses incurred in supplying information. Series E, No. 3, p. 221.

There are no parties in advisory procedure,[93] even though the opinion requested has to do with a dispute. However, each written statement is communicated to other States or organizations which make statements as to the same question, and comment by the latter is allowed;[94] in this respect the assimilation to contentious procedure tends to become more nearly complete.[95] In several cases, particularly recently, interested States have been represented in advisory proceedings by persons called "agents,"[96] apparently on analogy to Article 42 of the Statute which applies only where there are "parties" in the strict sense of that term.[97]

A State desiring to be heard on a question before the Court must meet the requirements as to time limits which the Court may set.[98] In its earlier years, it seems that the Court did not issue orders in fixing the dates for the conduct of advisory proceedings; more recently, however, such a practice has been followed. In 1923, the Rumanian Government found the interval allowed by a date set by the Court to be too short, and owing to the urgency of the question the period was not extended by the Court.[99]

§459. Assimilation of Advisory to Contentious Procedure. In framing its Rules in 1922, the Court showed a tendency to assimilate the advisory procedure to contentious procedure, without destroying the essentially advisory character of the former. This tendency has become more marked in later years, particularly since the Court's reversal of its former attitude on the admission of judges *ad hoc* in 1927. It has been confirmed also by the proposed addition to the Statute of an Article 68, annexed to the Revision Protocol of September 14, 1929. It was further confirmed by the Court in 1931 when, in revising Article 65 of the Rules, a single collection of judgments, orders and opinions was provided for.[100] The additional Article 68 of the Statute, annexed to the Revision Protocol of Septem-

---

[93] The use of the terms "parties" and "interested parties" in the authoritative English version of Advisory Opinion No. 11, Series B, No. 11, is clearly erroneous.

[94] Permission to file "replies" may be given. Series B, No. 14, p. 10.

[95] See Series E, No. 6, pp. 301–302.

[96] Series A/B, No. 41, p. 41; No. 44, p. 7; No. 45, p. 72. See §469, *infra*.

[97] In 1923, the order of calling on representatives to speak in oral proceedings was put upon the ground that in advisory proceedings the representatives of States do not "appear as representatives of a claimant and respondent." Series C, No. 5—II, p. 10.

[98] On some occasions the Court has invited interested States to make proposals as to time limits. Series E, No. 7, p. 303. Statements may be received also after the expiration of the time limit. Series E, No. 3, p. 213.

[99] Series B, No. 7, p. 9.

[100] Series A and Series B were combined into Series A/B in 1931.

ber 14, 1929, would leave the Court still master in this process of assimilation, for it would merely direct the Court to be "guided by the provisions of the Statute which apply in contentious cases to the extent to which it recognizes them to be applicable." Certain provisions of the Statute would seem to be clearly inapplicable, inasmuch as their application would depend upon the existence of "parties" in a strict sense of the term. Thus, it can hardly be imagined that in advisory proceedings the Court would indicate measures of interim protection under Article 41 of the Statute, or that it would receive an application for revision of an opinion under Article 61; and the application of Articles 62 and 63 as to intervention would seem to serve no purpose in advisory proceedings.[1]

The policy of assimilation is undoubtedly sound; the judicial character of the Court should be safeguarded against any violation in the rendering of advisory opinions, and the opinions themselves will be more authoritative, the prestige of the Court will be better protected, if they are preceded by the thorough explorations which contentious procedure is designed to facilitate. Yet the policy could easily be carried too far. The result of a too complete assimilation might be to encourage a view that an advisory opinion is a species of judgment, that because of the procedure followed before the Court it attains an obligatory character; advisory jurisdiction might then come to be looked upon as an alternative to obligatory jurisdiction, and this might result in diminishing the frequency of requests for advisory opinions.

§460. **Withdrawal of a Request.** The Council or Assembly may withdraw a request for an advisory opinion. The withdrawal may certainly be made at any time prior to the opening of oral hearings, and it would seem that it might be made at any time prior to the actual reading of the opinion in open court.[2] Only one request has been withdrawn. On March 14, 1925, the Council adopted a resolution requesting an opinion on its power to deal with the *Expulsion of the Œcumenical Patriarch;*[3] when as a consequence of an agreement reached by Greece and Turkey the matter was withdrawn from the Council's agenda, the Court was informed on June 8, 1925, that "the Council no longer finds it necessary to ask the Court to give the

---

[1] See Series C, No. 3 (Vol. 3), pp. 1089, 1090. *Cf.* §222, *supra.*
[2] This point might have arisen in connection with the opinion of the *Austro-German Customs Régime.* See §464 (20), *infra.*
[3] See League of Nations Official Journal, 1925, pp. 579, 637.

opinion," and the question was thereafter removed from the list of cases before the Court.[4] The removal, effected without an order by the Court, was viewed as an administrative matter.[5]

§461. **Composition of the Court for Advisory Proceedings.** The 1920 Committee of Jurists proposed that when the Court should give an opinion on a question not related to an existing dispute, a special commission of "from three to five members" should be appointed.[6] No such provision was included in the Statute, and in 1922 the Court took the view that advisory opinions should always be given by the full Court.[7] There has been no disposition to change the provision to this effect in Article 71 of the Rules. Prior to 1927, the Court excluded the participation of judges *ad hoc* appointed by States interested in questions submitted for advisory opinions;[8] in that year, the provision was added in Article 71 of the Rules that "on a question relating to an existing dispute between two or more States or Members of the League of Nations, Article 31 of the Statute shall apply."[9] This can only require that Article 31 of the Statute is to be applied by analogy, for that article deals with "parties" before the Court, and there are no parties before the Court in advisory proceedings. The rule means therefore that on a question relating to an existing dispute, parties to that dispute may claim the benefits of Article 31 of the Statute. In the case relating to the *Austro-German Customs Régime,* the Court thought it was not called upon to pronounce upon the point unless it was officially made cognizant of the question.[10] It must decide in each case whether the opinion requested relates to a dispute[11] and, if so, who are the parties to the dispute. In several instances, judges *ad hoc* have been admitted in advisory proceedings.[12] The decision to exclude judges *ad hoc* in the proceedings relating to the *Austro-German Customs Régime* was based upon the fourth paragraph of Article 31 of the Statute;[13] in this case, five

---

[4] Series C, No. 9—II, pp. 10, 97. The Turkish Government had contested the validity of the Council's resolution of March 14, 1925, and had refused to take any part in the Court's proceedings. *Id.,* p. 107. See §454, *supra.*

[5] Series E, No. 3, p. 184.   [6] Minutes of the 1920 Committee of Jurists, p. 680.

[7] Series D, No. 2, p. 98. This was later explained as an application of Article 25 of the Statute. Series E, No. 4, p. 76.   [8] Series E, No. 3, p. 223.

[9] See Series E, No. 4, pp. 73–78; §337, *supra.*   [10] Series A/B, No. 41, p. 89.

[11] One criterion for this decision is whether the States concerned had been represented or invited to be represented in the Council when it had the matter under consideration. Series E, No. 7, p. 303.

[12] In connection with the advisory opinion on the *Interpretation of the Greco-Turkish Agreement,* the parties to the dispute waived the appointment of judges *ad hoc;* the Court declined to take cognizance of a previous declaration of waiver made before the Council. Series E, No. 5, p. 262.   [13] Series A/B, No. 41, p. 88.

judges were of the opinion that Germany was not a party to the dispute involved in that case.

§462. **Publication of Advisory Opinions.** Article 74 of the 1922 Rules provided that the Court's advisory opinions should be published in a special collection.[14] From the beginning, the opinions have been read in open court,[15] and this has been required by Article 74 of the Rules since 1926. Notice is previously given to the Secretary-General of the League of Nations and to interested States and organizations,[16] and the text is communicated to the Secretary-General, confidentially, in advance.[17] After the opinion is read, signed and sealed copies are deposited in the archives of the Court and of the Secretariat of the League of Nations, and certified copies are transmitted to interested States and organizations. So long as this procedure is maintained—and part of Article 74 of the Rules has been embodied in the new Article 68 of the Statute, annexed to the Revision Protocol of September 14, 1929—no opinion of the Court can remain secret after it is rendered. If any criticism of the Court's practice is to be made, it is that the Court's procedure does not offer a sufficient guarantee of secrecy before the opinion is rendered.[18]

§463. **Legal Force of Advisory Opinions.**[19] An advisory opinion given by the Court is what it purports to be. It is advisory. It is not in any sense a judgment under Article 60 of the Statute, nor is it a decision under Article 59. Hence it is not in any way binding upon any State, even upon a State which is especially interested in the dispute or question to which the opinion relates.[20] Though such a State may have submitted written or oral statements to the Court in the course of the proceedings leading up to the opinion, such statements possessed only the character of information; the State presenting them did not appear before the Court as a party to a suit, and it did not

---

[14] Series B was devoted to the publication of advisory opinions; it was combined with Series A in 1931. Until 1931, the advisory opinions were given serial numbers when published.

[15] It was announced by the President that this would be done, before the first opinion was rendered. Series C, No. 1, p. 5.

[16] Article 58 of the Statute has been applied by analogy. Series C, No. 52, p. 111; No. 53, p. 199.

[17] The text is enclosed in a sealed envelope, and permission to break the seal is given by telegraph. See §340, *supra*.

[18] In connection with the opinion on the proposed *Austro-German Customs Régime*, forecasts of the Court's conclusions were remarkably accurate.

[19] See *Annuaire de l'Institut de Droit International*, 1928, pp. 409–477.

[20] This was insisted upon by Rumania in connection with the agreement that an advisory opinion should be sought with reference to the jurisdiction of the European Commission of the Danube. Series B, No. 14, p. 21.

thereby subject itself to an exercise of jurisdiction by the Court. The Court is therefore without power to impose obligations on any State by the conclusions stated in an advisory opinion,[21] and the conclusions are not binding as formulations of a State's obligations.[22] Nor is the body which had requested the opinion legally bound to accept those conclusions; the Council or the Assembly will not proceed illegally if it opposes the opinion given, or if in a report under paragraph 4 of Article 15 of the Covenant it adopts contrary conclusions on a question of law to which the Court has given an answer. Though the authority of the Court is not to be lightly disregarded, it gives to the Court's opinion only a moral value. The fact that none of the opinions given by the Court has been ignored by the Council, and the fact that many of them have been the basis of decisions taken by the Council, do not serve to give legal force to the opinion itself. Nor is the Court itself bound to adhere to conclusions reached in an advisory opinion; if the question upon which an opinion is given is later submitted to the Court for judgment, the matter is not *res judicata*,[23] and no principle of *stare decisis* compels the Court to abide by the conclusions stated in the opinion. Resort to an analogy to Article 59 of the Statute is not necessary for this result; it flows from the nature of the opinion itself, and that nature is not changed by the Court's policy of assimilating advisory to contentious procedure.

It must be admitted, however, that this view of the nature of advisory opinions has not always been taken. In its reply to the request for an opinion in the *Eastern Carelia Case,* the Court stated that "answering the question would be substantially equivalent to deciding the dispute between the parties." [24] This would depend on what is meant by "substantially equivalent"; certainly the Court could not by its opinion have placed any obligation on either Finland or Soviet Russia. Reference must also be made to views expressed in the Assembly of the League of Nations in connection with the Swiss proposal in 1928; [25] some of the delegates looked upon advisory opinions as

[21] "Nobody would dream of applying to an opinion the rule of Article 13, paragraph 4, of the Covenant, with respect to the execution of an award." M. Erich, in Records of Ninth Assembly, First Committee, p. 54.

[22] In 1927, a committee of the Court, composed of Judges Loder, Moore and Anzilotti, stated that "the view that advisory opinions are not binding is more theoretical than real." Series E, No. 4, p. 76. This must be understood as applying to the problem before the Committee, *i.e.*, a proposed amendment to Article 71 of the Rules.

[23] *Cf.*, de la Grotte, in 10 *Revue de Droit International et de Législation Comparée* (1929), p. 401; Lauterpacht, Function of Law in the International Community (1933), p. 335 note. [24] Series B, No. 5, p. 29.

[25] Records of Ninth Assembly, First Committee, pp. 40–57.

a species of judgment. M. Politis stated that "advisory opinions, being in reality no longer such, were accordingly equivalent in the eyes of the Council, of public opinion and of the interested parties to a judgment." [26] Something of this conception also seems to have been behind the fifth reservation offered by the United States in its proposal to adhere to the Protocol of Signature of 1920. The history of the opinions given by the Court lends no support to the view that the character of advisory opinions has been changed by the reception accorded to them. Of course it is possible that the parties to a dispute may have agreed in advance that an advisory opinion requested by the Council and given by the Court will be binding upon them; [27] in such case, however, the force of the opinion is to be derived from the agreement itself.

§464. **Reception of the Court's Opinions.** Since each of the opinions given by the Court had been requested by the Council, all of them have been communicated to it. In some cases in which the opinion related to its procedure, the Council has taken the opinion for its own guidance; in other cases, it has "adopted" the opinion and used it as a basis for dealing with a dispute or a question before it. In numerous cases, the Council has merely noted the opinion and communicated it to some other body at whose suggestion the request had been made. In some cases the Council has taken no action whatever, the issues before it having dissolved with the rendering of the opinion. Some of the opinions have been formally accepted by interested States; but since such States are "always free to dispose of their rights," [28] their later negotiations may proceed on a basis differing from that of the opinion of the Court.

(1) *Nomination of Netherlands Delegate to the International Labor Conference.* In its opinion of July 31, 1922, the Court answered affirmatively the question whether the Netherlands workers' delegate to the Third International Labor Conference had been nominated in accordance with the provisions of Article 389 of the Treaty of Versailles. The Council merely transmitted this opinion to the Director of the International Labor Office for communication

---

[26] Records of Ninth Assembly, First Committee, p. 47. See also *id.,* p. 61. This view has appeared also in doctrinal writings.

[27] In Article 5 of the abortive Geneva Protocol of October 2, 1924, it was provided that an advisory opinion of the Court on the question whether a matter is by international law solely within the domestic jurisdiction of a State, should be binding on arbitrators. Records of Fifth Assembly, Committees, I, p. 137.

[28] Series A, No. 24, p. 11; Series A/B, No. 46, p. 153.

to the competent authorities of the International Labor Organization which had asked the Council to make the request.[29]

(2) (3) *Competence of the International Labor Organization.* The two opinions given by the Court on August 12, 1922, were similarly transmitted by the Council to the Director of the International Labor Office. The Court's conclusions were accepted in the subsequent International Labor Conference, by a declaration made on behalf of the French Government at whose initiative the Council had made the request.[30]

(4) *Nationality Decrees in Tunis and Morocco.* On February 7, 1923, the Court gave its opinion that this dispute was not by international law solely a matter of domestic jurisdiction. The two parties to the dispute had agreed before the Council made its request that if this answer were given, the whole dispute would be referred to arbitration or judicial settlement under conditions to be agreed upon. The Council seems to have taken no action on the opinion, but on May 24, 1923, the dispute was settled by an exchange of notes, of which the Court took note on June 18, 1923.[31]

(5) *Eastern Carelia Case.* The reply given by the Court on July 23, 1923, by which it refused to answer the questions put concerning provisions for the autonomy of Eastern Carelia, was noted by the Council on September 27, 1923, and the Council adopted a report containing the following *caveat*: "Whilst noting the view of the Court that an advisory opinion concerning this question would have involved an investigation into facts for which certain conditions were lacking, the Council feels sure that the opinion expressed by the Court in connection with the procedure described in Article 17 of the Covenant cannot exclude the possibility of resort by the Council to any action, including a request for an advisory opinion from the Court, on a matter in which a State non-member of the League and unwilling to give information is involved, if the circumstances should make such action necessary to enable the Council to fulfil its functions under the Covenant of the League in the interests of peace." [32]

[29] League of Nations Official Journal, 1922, p. 1173.
[30] Series E, No. 1, p. 193. It may be noted also that the French Government later ratified certain draft conventions adopted by the International Labor Conference, relating to the association and combination of agricultural workers, and to workmen's compensation in agriculture. League of Nations Document, A. 6 (a). 1933. V. annex.
[31] Series C, No. 3, Vol. I, pp. 3, 55.
[32] League of Nations Official Journal, 1923, p. 1336. The *caveat* was formally adopted by the Council, not as part of its resolution but as included in a report. See also the memorandum submitted to the Council by the Government of Finland. *Id.,* p. 1497.

(6) *German Settlers in Poland.* The opinion of September 10, 1923, stated that matters covered by a resolution of the Council involved international obligations of the kind referred to in the Polish Minorities Treaty and therefore came within the competence of the League of Nations, and that the position adopted by the Polish Government "was not in conformity with its international obligations." This opinion was noted by the Council on September 26, 1923, and the Polish Government was invited to inform the Council as to the measures which it proposed to take to settle the question of the German settlers. On December 17, 1923, the Council adopted a resolution stating that the question could be settled only on the basis of the Court's opinion "with which the Council is in agreement." Negotiations ensued under the control of the Council, and on June 17, 1924, the Council took note of a settlement of the question.[33]

(7) *Acquisition of Polish Nationality.* On September 15, 1923, the Court gave an opinion interpreting Article 4 of the Polish Minorities Treaty and stating that consideration of the position of certain persons, arising out of its application, fell within the competence of the League of Nations. Prior to its request for this opinion, the Council had taken advice from a committee of jurists whose interpretation of the treaty the Polish Government had declined to accept. On September 27, 1923, the Council "adopted" the opinion,[34] the Polish representative abstaining from the vote, and offered its good offices for continuing negotiations with reference to the matter.[35] Difficulties having been encountered, on March 14, 1924, the Council suggested the choice of a mediator to preside over negotiations which covered *inter alia* the interpretation and application of Article 4 of the Polish Minorities Treaty. On September 19, 1924, the Council noted the success of these negotiations,[36] which after a fresh arbitral award had led to a convention setting forth the basis for the acquisition of Polish nationality;[37] Article 7 of this convention adopts a rule consistent with the Court's interpretation of Article 4 of the Polish Minorities Treaty, but makes certain exceptions in its application.

(8) *Jaworzina Boundary.* On December 6, 1923, the Court gave the opinion that a question as to the delimitation of the Polish-

[33] League of Nations Official Journal, 1924, p. 927.
[34] The "adoption" of the opinion in this case may have had consequences under Article 12 of the Polish Minorities Treaty; in some cases, however, it is difficult to say what is the effect of the Council's "adoption" of the opinion of the Court.
[35] League of Nations Official Journal, 1923, p. 1334.
[36] *Id.*, 1924, p. 1309. [37] 32 League of Nations Treaty Series, p. 331.

Czechoslovak frontier had been settled by a decision of the Conference of Ambassadors in 1920, and that this definitive decision "must be" (Fr., *doit être*) applied in its entirety. When it came before the Council on December 13, 1923, the opinion was accepted by Poland and Czechoslovakia "in its entirety." The Council "adopted" the opinion,[38] on the basis of which it continued to deal with the dispute, and on March 12, 1924, it adopted a recommendation [39] which led to the fixing of the frontier.[40]

(9) *Monastery of Saint-Naoum.* On September 4, 1924, the Court gave an opinion to the effect that by a decision of the Conference of Ambassadors in 1922 the Principal Allied Powers had exhausted, in regard to the Albanian-Yugoslav frontier, the mission recognized by the interested States and contemplated in a resolution of the Assembly of the League of Nations in 1921. The questions put to the Court by the Council, in substance, had previously been submitted to the Council by the Conference of Ambassadors. On October 3, 1924, the Council resolved that it considered that the Court's opinion "gives the answer" to the questions submitted by the Conference of Ambassadors; the opinion was therefore communicated to the Conference.[41]

(10) *Exchange of Greek and Turkish Populations.* On February 21, 1925, the Court gave an opinion interpreting Article 2 of the Lausanne Convention of January 30, 1923, concerning the exchange of Greek and Turkish populations. The Council's request for the opinion had been in response to a desire expressed by the Greco-Turkish Mixed Commission. On March 11, 1925, the Council took note of the opinion and directed that it be communicated to the President of the Mixed Commission; its *rapporteur's* observation was added to the communication, that "he had no doubt that the Mixed Commission would attribute to this opinion the same high value and authority which the Council always gave to the opinions" of the Court.[42]

---

[38] League of Nations Official Journal, 1924, pp. 356, 364.   [39] *Id.*, p. 520.
[40] See the resolution of the Conference of Ambassadors of March 26, 1924. League of Nations Official Journal, 1924, p. 828.
[41] League of Nations Official Journal, 1924, pp. 1369–1372. By a later rectification of the boundary, confirmed by a final act signed at Paris on July 30, 1926, the monastery of Saint-Naoum was attributed to Yugoslavia. Survey of International Affairs, 1925, Vol. II, p. 287. See also Series E, No. 2, p. 137.
[42] League of Nations Official Journal, 1925, p. 441. A convention of establishment was signed by representatives of Greece and Turkey at Ankara, October 30, 1930. 125 League of Nations Treaty Series, p. 371. Provision for the dissolution of the mixed commission was included in a treaty signed at Ankara, December 9, 1933. League of Nations Official Journal, 1934, p. 389.

(11) *Polish Postal Service in Danzig.* On May 16, 1925, the Court expressed the opinion that points at issue regarding the Polish postal service at Danzig had not been covered by a decision by High Commissioner General Haking; that the Polish postal service within the port of Danzig is entitled to set up letter boxes and collect and deliver postal matter outside its premises in the Heveliusplatz; and that the use of such service may be opened to the public and is not confined to Polish authorities and officials. On June 11, 1925, the opinion was "adopted" by the Council, and it was decided that the boundaries of the port of Danzig should be traced for the purposes of the Polish postal service with due regard to the considerations put forward in the opinion.[43] A final decision on the dispute was taken by the Council on September 19, 1925.[44]

(12) *Article 3, paragraph 2, of the Treaty of Lausanne.* On November 21, 1925, the Court gave its opinion that the "decision to be taken" by the Council under Article 3, paragraph 2, of the Treaty of Lausanne would be binding on the parties and would constitute a definitive determination of the frontier between Turkey and Iraq, and that it should be taken by a unanimous vote, the votes of representatives of the parties not being counted in ascertaining whether there is unanimity. When the opinion came before the Council on December 8, 1925, the Turkish representative stated that as Turkey had voted against the request for the opinion, his Government could not be considered to be bound by the opinion, to which he attributed "only the character of a legal consultation of a theoretical character without any practical bearing." He also drew the Council's attention to an "advisory opinion" by Professor Gilbert Gidel,[45] which he compared with that of the Court. On the question of accepting the Court's opinion, the President of the Council first said that as this was a "question of procedure," the Council might apply the rule in the Covenant relating to a question of procedure; later, the vote was taken on the basis of a stricter rule that unanimity would be required for accepting the opinion, without counting the votes of the parties to the dispute, Great Britain and Turkey. The report "in favor of accepting the advisory opinion . . . was unanimously adopted, the representative of Turkey voting against the report."[46] Thereafter, on December 16, 1925, the Council took a decision under Article 3,

---

[43] League of Nations Official Journal, 1925, p. 882.   [44] *Id.,* 1925, p. 1377.
[45] This opinion had been placed in the hands of members of the Court before the Court's opinion was given. Series C, No. 10, p. 325.
[46] League of Nations Official Journal, 1926, p. 128.

paragraph 2, of the Treaty of Lausanne, in the absence of a Turkish representative, the vote being unanimous; [47] this decision was later made definitive.[48]

(13) *Competence of the International Labor Organization.* On July 23, 1926, the Court gave an opinion that it is within the competence of the International Labor Organization to draw up and to propose labor legislation which, in order to protect certain classes of workers, also regulates incidentally the same work when performed by the employer himself. The Council had been asked by the Governing Body of the International Labor Organization to request this opinion. On June 7, 1926, before the opinion was given, the Council, being informed of the desire of the International Labor Office to have the opinion at the earliest possible date, decided that when it was handed down the opinion should first be communicated to the members of the Council individually and then communicated without further delay to the Director of the International Labor Office.[49]

(14) *Jurisdiction of the European Commission of the Danube.* On December 8, 1927, the Court gave an opinion that under the law at present in force the European Commission of the Danube has the same powers on the maritime sector of the Danube from Galatz to Braila including the port of Braila as on the sector below Galatz, and the opinion defined the extent of these powers. In asking for this opinion, the Council had acted upon a formal request made by the French, British, Italian and Rumanian Governments,[50] transmitted to it by the Chairman of the Advisory and Technical Committee for Communications and Transit. On March 7, 1928, the Council decided to forward the opinion to this Chairman, for transmission to those Governments.[51]

[47] League of Nations Official Journal, 1926, pp. 187–193.
[48] *Id.*, p. 503. The Mosul dispute was finally settled by the Treaty of June 5, 1926, between Great Britain, Iraq and Turkey. For the text, see 64 League of Nations Treaty Series, p. 379.
[49] League of Nations Official Journal, 1926, p. 857.
[50] When the agreement for making this suggestion was concluded on September 18, 1926, the parties also agreed in a protocol that if within six months after the Court's opinion had been given the procedure of conciliation had led to no result, the procedure should be considered as closed. Series B, No. 14, p. 20; Series C, No. 13—IV, p. 812; 59 League of Nations Treaty Series, p. 237.
[51] League of Nations Official Journal, 1928, p. 400. Subsequent negotiations led to the preparation of a draft convention of March 20, 1929, and to the signature of a Declaration of December 5, 1930, by which the parties to the Convention instituting the definitive Statute of the Danube agreed to accept the provisions of the draft convention. For the texts, see *id.*, 1931, pp. 736, 738. Difficulties in completing the draft convention led to the negotiation of a *modus vivendi* and declaration, finally adopted on May 17, 1933, at a meeting of the European Commission of the Danube; Rumania

(15) *Jurisdiction of the Courts of Danzig.* On March 3, 1928, the Court gave an opinion to the effect that a decision given by the League of Nations High Commissioner at Danzig on April 8, 1927, as a result of requests by Danzig, was not legally well founded, in so far as it did not comply with those requests. On March 6, 1928, an agreement was signed on behalf of Danzig and Poland accepting the Court's opinion as an authentic interpretation of their previous agreement of October 2, 1921.[52] On March 9, 1928, the Council took note of the opinion and of the agreement based upon it.[53]

(16) *Interpretation of the Greco-Turkish Agreement of 1926.* In an opinion given on August 28, 1928, the Court interpreted Article 4 of the final protocol annexed to the Greco-Turkish agreement of December 1, 1926. On September 8, 1928, the Council took note of the opinion, and directed that it be communicated to the President of the Mixed Commission for the Exchange of Greek and Turkish Populations, on whose suggestion the Council had requested that the opinion be given.[54]

(17) *The Greco-Bulgarian Communities.* On July 31, 1930, the Court gave an opinion answering three series of questions formulated by the Greco-Bulgarian Mixed Emigration Commission, the Bulgarian Government and the Greek Government. As the opinion was requested at the Mixed Commission's suggestion and for its use, the Council took note of the opinion on September 8, 1930, and directed that it be communicated to the President of the Mixed Commission. This opinion served as the basis of later procedure before the Commission.[55]

(18) *Danzig and the International Labor Organization.* On August 26, 1930, the Court gave an opinion to the effect that the special legal status of Danzig is not such as to enable it to become a Member of the International Labor Organization. As the opinion had been requested at the suggestion of the Governing Body of the International Labor Office and for its use, the Council took note of

agreed to refrain from contesting the jurisdiction of the Commission from the sea to Braila, on the understanding that the Commission was not to exercise a judicial competence between Galatz and Braila, under certain conditions. Series E, No. 9, p. 115. The formal instruments were signed on June 25, 1933. League of Nations Document, C. 98. M. 33. 1934. VIII, p. 41. [52] Series C, No. 14—I, p. 572.
   [53] League of Nations Official Journal, 1928, p. 433. The date of the agreement is there given as March 2, 1928.
   [54] League of Nations Official Journal, 1928, p. 1487.
   [55] Series E, No. 8, p. 213. See S. P. Ladas, The Exchange of Minorities, Bulgaria, Greece and Turkey (1932), *passim.*

the opinion on September 9, 1930, and directed that it be communicated to the Director of the International Labor Office for transmission to the Governing Body.

(19) *Access to German Minority Schools in Upper Silesia.* On May 15, 1931, the Court gave an opinion to the effect that children who had been excluded from German minority schools in Upper Silesia on the basis of the language tests provided for by a Council resolution of 1927 could not then by reason of that circumstance be refused access to those schools. On May 23, 1931, consideration of the matter was postponed by the Council; on September 19, 1931, the Council adopted a report made at its earlier session, deciding that the children in question should be transferred immediately to the minority schools to which their admission had been requested; the Polish representative informed the Council that his Government had complied with the Court's opinion and had informed the children's parents that the admission would be granted.[56]

(20) *Proposed Customs Régime between Germany and Austria.* On September 5, 1931, the Court gave an opinion to the effect that a customs régime established between Germany and Austria in accordance with a Protocol of March 19, 1931, would not be compatible with Protocol No. 1 signed at Geneva on October 4, 1922. Two days before the opinion was handed down, the representatives of Germany and Austria had declared to the Committee of Enquiry for European Union that it was not their intention to proceed with the establishment of the proposed customs régime.[57] On September 7, 1931, the Council took note of the opinion, for which it expressed thanks to the Court. The 1922 protocol was reproduced in a protocol of July 15, 1932.[58]

(21) *Railway Traffic between Lithuania and Poland.* On October 15, 1931, the Court gave an opinion to the effect that the international engagements in force did not oblige Lithuania in the existing circumstances to take the necessary steps to open for traffic or for certain categories of traffic the Landwarów-Kaisiadorys railway sector. On January 28, 1932, the Council took note of this opinion; [59] the Polish representative referred to the matter as a dispute between the

---

[56] League of Nations Official Journal, 1931, pp. 1151, 2263.
[57] *Id.*, pp. 2185–2190. It may be contended that this declaration made the question a moot one, and that the Court should thereupon have refused to give the opinion; but as the declaration had not been communicated to the Court, it could not properly have been taken into account by that body. Of course the Council could have withdrawn the request, however. [58] *Id.*, 1932, p. 1461.
[59] League of Nations Official Journal, 1932, p. 481.

Advisory Committee on Communications and Transit and the Lithuanian Government which had been settled by the Court.

(22) *Polish War Vessels in Danzig.* On December 11, 1931, the Court gave an opinion to the effect that the Treaty of Versailles, the Danzig-Polish Convention of November 9, 1920, and the relevant decisions of the Council and the League of Nations High Commissioner at Danzig, did not confer upon Poland rights or attributions as regards the access to, or anchorage in, the port and waterways of Danzig of Polish war vessels. On January 29, 1932, the Council "adopted" the advisory opinion and directed that it be communicated to the High Commissioner, noting that the legal points of divergence had "been elucidated" by the opinion.[60] A protocol signed by representatives of Poland and Danzig on August 13, 1932, established a series of rules to govern the access of foreign warships to Danzig waters.[61]

(23) *Treatment of Polish Nationals in Danzig.* On February 4, 1932, the Court gave an opinion construing Article 104 (5) of the Treaty of Versailles and Article 33 (1) of the Danzig-Polish Convention of November 9, 1920, as regards the position of Polish nationals and other persons (including Danzig nationals) of Polish origin and speech in Danzig territory. Having requested the opinion for the use of the High Commissioner, on February 6, 1932, the Council directed that it be communicated to him.[62] On November 26, 1932, representatives of Danzig and Poland signed an agreement accepting the conclusions of the Court's opinion.[63]

(24) *Interpretation of the Caphandaris-Molloff Agreement.* On March 8, 1932, the Court gave an opinion to the effect that in the case at issue there was no dispute between Greece and Bulgaria within the meaning of Article 8 of the Caphandaris-Molloff Agreement of December 9, 1927. Previously, on November 11, 1931, Greek and Bulgarian representatives had signed an arrangement concerning the execution of the Caphandaris-Molloff Agreement, but it was not to affect their legal position as it stood when the Council requested the opinion.[64] On May 10, 1932, the Council took note of the Court's opinion and congratulated the two Governments on the conclusion of

---

[60] League of Nations Official Journal, 1932, p. 489.
[61] League of Nations Official Journal, 1933, p. 142; Series E, No. 9, p. 117.
[62] League of Nations Official Journal, 1932, p. 523.
[63] *Id.*, p. 2282; Series E, No. 9, p. 118. See also the agreement initialled on August 5, 1933, and signed on September 18, 1933, implementing the agreement of November 26, 1932. League of Nations Official Journal, 1933, p. 1157.
[64] *Id.*, 1932, p. 270.

the arrangement of November 11, 1931;[65] it appeared, however, that the Greek and Bulgarian representatives were not agreed as to the effect of the Court's opinion.

(25) *Interpretation of the Convention on Employment of Women at Night.* In this opinion given on November 15, 1932, the Court gave an interpretation of the convention concerning employment of women during the night, adopted by the International Labor Conference in 1919. On January 24, 1933, the Council directed that the opinion be transmitted to the Director of the International Labor Office for communication to the Governing Body.[66]

§465. **Purposes Served by Advisory Jurisdiction.** The 1926 Conference of Signatories stated in its Final Act that "great importance is attached by the Members of the League of Nations to the value of the advisory opinions which the Court may give as provided for in the Covenant."[67] This was doubtless because of the purposes which had been served by advisory opinions even in the short period of the Court's experience. On the record to date, it may be said that three distinct advantages have been derived from the Court's exercise of its advisory jurisdiction.

(1) In several instances, advisory opinions have greatly facilitated the Council's handling of international disputes. This is not merely because a request for an advisory opinion may be a means of gaining time or of shifting the theater of discussion in an acute situation; the Court's opinion may clarify difficult questions as to the Council's competence, or it may dispose of legal questions which condition progress in the settlement of political issues. The opinion concerning *German Settlers in Poland,* and that concerning the *Acquisition of Polish Nationality,* both dealt with the competence of the Council; the opinion concerning *Article 3 of the Treaty of Lausanne* gave guidance to the Council as to the nature of the "decision to be taken" and the method by which that decision should be arrived at; the various opinions concerning the relations of Germany and Poland, and of Danzig and Poland, have enabled the Council to push forward settlements of political issues. Indeed, it may be said that the Court's chief contribution to the maintenance of peace has been this assistance given to the Council.

(2) Advisory opinions have also facilitated the efficient functioning of various international institutions other than the Council. Inter-

---

[65] League of Nations Official Journal, 1932, p. 1187.
[66] *Id.,* 1933, p. 184.
[67] Minutes of the 1926 Conference of Signatories, p. 79.

national bodies do not operate automatically, and many legal questions may arise to condition their action. In numerous instances authoritative answers to such questions have been obtained from the Court through the mediation of the Council. Five opinions have dealt with the functioning of the International Labor Organization; the Greco-Turkish Mixed Commission for the Exchange of Greek and Turkish Populations has twice been given such assistance; and opinions have dealt with the attributions of the Greco-Bulgarian Emigration Commission and various international river commissions.

(3) The Court's advisory jurisdiction has also proved to be of value to States engaged in disputes, when they were unable to agree upon the submission of questions to arbitration or adjudication. When Great Britain and France were negotiating concerning the nationality decrees in Tunis and Morocco, no agreement for arbitration could be reached, though such a course was proposed; the two States were able, however, to agree upon asking the Council to request an advisory opinion, and even to agree that if the Court answered a preliminary question by saying that the issue was not "solely a matter of domestic jurisdiction," the "whole dispute" should be "referred to arbitration or to judicial settlement"; and when the Court's opinion was given, a settlement resulted promptly. In the *Jaworzina Boundary Case,* also, Czechoslovakia and Poland seem to have besought the Council to request an opinion because it was the most expeditious way open to them of meeting the demands of public opinion of the two countries, though a "calming effect" had already been produced by the submission of the dispute to the Council.[68] Even though agreements in force may provide for the compulsory jurisdiction of the Court, the States interested in a dispute may prefer to have an advisory opinion which by a clarification of legal questions will aid them in reaching a settlement on broader grounds and which will not have the binding effect of a judgment. In 1931, when the British representative on the Council proposed a request for an advisory opinion relating to the dispute concerning railway traffic between Lithuania and Poland, he stated that under the Memel Convention of 1924 Great Britain and the other parties to the convention had "the opportunity of referring the dispute" to the Court "for final decision"; [69] but a resort to the Court's advisory jurisdiction seemed to be a more efficacious way of handling that dispute.

[68] League of Nations Official Journal, 1923, pp. 1317, 1474.
[69] *Id.,* 1931, p. 214.

PART V

PROCEDURE AND PRACTICE OF THE PERMANENT
COURT OF INTERNATIONAL JUSTICE

CHAPTER 23

REPRESENTATIVES OF STATES BEFORE
THE COURT

§466. Agents in Contentious Proceedings. A party appearing
in a contentious proceeding must be represented by an agent, under
Article 42 of the Statute, and no party can be deprived of this
privilege.[1] If the Court is called upon to exercise obligatory jurisdiction under a declaration made in accordance with paragraph 2 of
Article 36 of the Statute, or under a treaty or convention in force,
the State against which the proceeding is brought may enter no appearance, and in this case it may refrain from appointing an agent;
thus the Chinese Government appointed no agent when Belgium made
application with reference to the *Denunciation of the Belgian-Chinese
Treaty of 1865*. A failure or a refusal by a party to appoint an agent
does not preclude the Court's entertaining the proceeding. Under
Article 35 of the 1926 Rules, the "document notifying the Court" of
a special agreement should mention the names of the agents;[2] in all
other cases, the application should include "the name or names of the
agent or agents,"[3] and the first document sent in reply to the application should mention the "name or names of the agent or agents" of
the State against which the application is made.[4] This can hardly

---

[1] In some cases, the parties have been represented by "representatives." See, *e.g.*,
Series C, No. 9—I, p. 11; No. 11, p. 9.

[2] If the notification is effected by one party, the agent of that party must be
named; Article 35 does not envisage this case. See §473, *infra*.

[3] The requirement that agents be named in the application seems to impose some
inconvenience on States. The application in the case relating to the *Statute of Memel*
failed to give the names of the applicants' agents, but they were given in a covering
letter. Series E, No. 8, p. 256. In several other instances the application has failed to give
the name of the agent of the applicant. The choice of an address at a legation at The
Hague may be taken as a provisional delegation of the powers of an agent to the *chef
de mission*. Series C, No. 59, p. 602.

[4] The name of an agent may be notified to the Court even before an application
is filed. This was done by Germany in the case relating to the *Polish Agrarian Reform
and the German Minority*, but the name of the German agent was also given in the
application.

authorize a State to have more than one agent, for the Court should be able to deal with a single representative of a Government;[5] it seems to envisage the possibility of several parties in the same interest and acting in common, each of which will have an agent. Assistant agents are sometimes appointed. Agents are usually, though not necessarily, nationals of the States which they represent; a party is of course free in the selection of its agent. In many cases, diplomatic representatives at The Hague have been selected,[6] and other persons acting as agents frequently select a legation at The Hague as the address to which communications are to be sent.[7] A person appearing before the Court as an agent must present special powers or credentials, indicating that he is the person who has been named as agent;[8] formal full powers are not required, however, and a notification by a well-known official seems to suffice.[9] An agent may be replaced in the course of the proceedings in a case.[10]

The agent should have an address at The Hague, as he is the representative of his Government to whom notices and communications should be sent. Article 35 of the Rules might be more explicit on this point, as it requires only that a "permanent address at the seat of the Court" be selected by a party.[11]

§467. **Powers and Duties of the Agent.** An agent is the representative of a Government *vis-à-vis* the Court.[12] He is the intermediary between the Court and the State which he represents. He has complete control of the case, so far as the Court is concerned; and he has power to bind his Government by his declarations[13] or con-

---

[5] "Information emanating from the Court should be concentrated in the hands of a single person." Series E, No. 7, p. 294. See also, Series E, No. 4, p. 279. *Cf.*, Minutes of the 1920 Committee of Jurists, p. 340. Belgium seems to have had several agents in the case against China. Series C, No. 16—I, p. 300. In the *Free Zones Case*, Switzerland appointed two agents. Series C, No. 17—I, Vol. 1, p. 10. In the *Statute of Memel Case*, the Italian Government appointed a "second agent." Series C, No. 59, p. 622. In the *Eastern Greenland Case*, the Danish Government appointed two agents and two "agents and counsel." In such situations the Court seems disposed to treat one person as agent.   [6] This practice may raise questions of precedence which ought to be avoided.

[7] Series E, No. 4, p. 279.

[8] For example, see Series C, No. 14—I, p. 525; No. 16—III, p. 767.

[9] See Series C, No. 16—III, p. 771.   [10] Series C, No. 17—II, pp. 9, 648.

[11] The Registrar has explained this rule as being designed to assure "certain and simultaneous communication to all parties," and concentration in a single person's hands of all information emanating from the Court. Series C, No. 18—I, p. 1041.

[12] In some cases in which an agent had been appointed, the Court has dealt with representatives other than the agent. For instance, on August 30, 1924, in the absence of the British agent, the Court took note of an oral request by the British Minister at The Hague. Series C, No. 5—I, p. 17.

[13] In the case concerning *German Interests in Polish Upper Silesia*, the Polish agent made certain declarations to the Court, and the Court was "in no doubt as to

duct.[14] What is said by an agent before the Court engages the responsibility of his Government, but only in connection with the pending case; it may even have the result of conferring jurisdiction on the Court. The agent's position in this respect is quite different from that of counsel or advocates, who are always under the agent's control and who are not in the same sense representative.[15] It is clearly "desirable that agents should have the necessary powers to deal with questions of procedure without reference to their governments."[16] They are subject to having notices served upon them, under Article 44 of the Statute, and even before the hearing begins they may be called upon to produce documents or supply explanations under Article 49. Article 43 of the Statute provides that agents may take part in oral proceedings before the Court, though in many cases this rôle is left to counsel or advocates. Questions put by the Court or the judges are usually addressed to the agents. Under Article 34 of the 1926 Rules, all documents of the written proceedings must be signed by or on behalf of the agent or agents. Under Article 35 of the 1926 Rules, the agent has a duty "whenever possible"[17] to "remain at the seat of the Court pending the trial and determination of the case." The Court would probably be reluctant to conduct hearings in the absence of an agent appointed for the case, unless the circumstances were special, though an agent may for this purpose be represented, by leave of the Court, by a substitute;[18] a judgment may be read in open court in the absence of an agent.[19]

§468. **Counsel and Advocates in Contentious Proceedings.** No distinction is to be made between counsel and advocates before the Court; the term counsel is almost invariably used, and the reference to advocates in Article 42 of the Statute which confers on Governments the privilege of having "the assistance of counsel or advocates,"[20] seems superfluous. The number of counsel is not lim-

the binding character of all these declarations." Series A, No. 7, p. 13. In the *Free Zones Case*, a declaration by the Swiss agent was recorded in the operative part of the judgment. Series A/B, No. 46, p. 172. In the *Mavrommatis Case*, the British agent's statements were used against the position of the British Government. Series A, No. 2, p. 22.

[14] But see Series A, No. 15, p. 53.

[15] The subcommittee of the Third Committee of the First Assembly took the view that "only the agents can represent the parties." Records of First Assembly, Committees, I, p. 535.   [16] Series E, No. 5, p. 250.

[17] The Court has refrained from making this duty absolute. Series D, No. 2 (add.), pp. 73–75.   [18] Series E, No. 8, p. 256.

[19] See, *e.g.*, Series C, No. 6, p. 6; No. 11, p. 38. The agent must have been given "due notice," however, under Article 58 of the Statute.

[20] Advocates were named in the *Austro-German Customs Régime Case*, and in the *Eastern Greenland Case*. Series C, No. 53, pp. 702, 714, 720; No. 67.

ited,[21] apart from any provision to that effect in a special agreement, though the Court may limit the number of speakers on a particular occasion.[22] The position of counsel or advocates is very different from that of agents. It is the agent to whom the Court looks if any issue arises. Counsel and advocates are subject to the agent's authority; they have no power "to take decisions regarding questions of procedure" which will be binding on the Government for which they appear.[23] What is said by counsel before the Court engages only the responsibility of the counsel themselves; [24] in this respect their powers are very different from those of agents. When counsel sought to withdraw certain documents and to suppress passages in the written proceedings in the case of the *Mavrommatis Jerusalem Concessions,* the Court asked that the agents give written notice to this effect.[25] The functions of counsel are not defined in the Statute.[26] Counsel are frequently not nationals of the State for which they appear. Their designation need not be indicated in a notification of a special agreement or in an application; it is usually brought to the Court's notice by a letter addressed to the Registrar,[27] frequently by the agent. *Verbatim* records are taken of speeches by counsel, but correction is allowed within some limits.[28] Though questions may be addressed to counsel, their replies may lack the weight which attaches to replies by agents.[29]

§469. Agents in Advisory Proceedings. In the Court's earlier years, Governments and organizations participating in advisory proceedings usually appointed for this purpose "representatives," named as such and not as agents. Until 1927, this practice was followed in all cases except the case concerning the *Nationality Decrees in Tunis and Morocco,* in which the British and French Governments agreed

[21] Suggestions made to the Court in 1922 would have limited the number of counsel. Series D, No. 2, p. 263. In 1923, the Court held that to avoid repetition the maximum number of oral statements made in the same interest should not as a general rule exceed two, but it was thought that several persons might share the task of stating a case. Series E, No. 3, p. 204.

[22] In the *Southeastern Greenland Case,* in 1932, the Court limited the number of speakers in reply and rejoinder to one on each side. Series E, No. 9, p. 171.

[23] Series E, No. 7, p. 294.

[24] Though this is true of counsel in the ordinary case, the Court might find that in fact counsel has been invested with an agent's powers.

[25] Series C, No. 7—II, pp. 16, 355.

[26] Under Article 62 of the Hague Convention for Pacific Settlement of 1907, the function of counsel and advocates is that of defending rights and interests of a party before an arbitral tribunal.   [27] See, for example, Series C, No. 16—III, p. 790.

[28] Series E, No. 3, p. 208.

[29] On the order in which counsel for different parties will be heard, see §498, *infra.*

upon the appointment of agents.[30] Beginning with the case relating to the *Jurisdiction of the European Commission of the Danube*,[31] however, the representatives participating in advisory proceedings have quite commonly been called agents,[32] and in the more recent cases their designation as agents has become the rule,[33] at least where the questions submitted relate to disputes. This is in line with the Court's tendency to assimilate advisory to contentious procedure. The Court is informed of the designation of agents or other representatives in advisory proceedings by letter.[34]

§470. **Counsel in Advisory Proceedings.** Until recently, the arguments on behalf of States or organizations interested in advisory proceedings were usually presented by "representatives." In the case concerning the *Nationality Decrees in Tunis and Morocco*, however, the British and French Governments agreed that not more than two "counsel" on each side should be appointed.[35] Since 1927, States interested in advisory proceedings have quite commonly appointed counsel to present their arguments, in many cases designating them as such. Such appointments are notified to the Court by letter.

§471. **The Bar of the Court.** Though counsel or advocates are to be chosen by the parties themselves, it would seem to be within the power of the Court to set some limitations on the parties' choice, and to establish the qualifications which counsel or advocates must possess. In other words, the Court would seem to have power to prescribe for the organization of its own bar, and to establish standards with which the members of its bar must comply. At no time has any action been taken in this direction,[36] though some unofficial suggestions have been made,[37] and it seems extremely doubtful whether

---

[30] Series C, No. 2, p. 266. The case of the *Nationality Decrees in Tunis and Morocco* was conducted, in many respects, as if it had been an arbitration between the two Governments, and it has not been regarded as establishing procedural precedents.

[31] Series C, No. 13—IV, Vol. 1, p. 10.

[32] Series C, No. 15—I, p. 11; No. 18—I, p. 12; No. 52, p. 107. Danzig has frequently been represented by non-nationals as agents. See, *e.g.*, Series C, No. 14—I, p. 525.

[33] Series C, No. 53, p. 188; No. 54, p. 304; No. 55, p. 209; No. 56, p. 227; No. 57, p. 265.

[34] Information will be received by the Court from international organizations, in advisory proceedings, though they may not be entitled to representation by agents in any strict sense of the term.   [35] Series C, No. 2, p. 266.

[36] A draft of the rules before the Court in 1922 would have set qualifications for advocates before the Court by requiring that they be either persons admitted to practice as advocates before the highest court of their own country, or university professors of international law, or members of the great international academies of international law. Series D, No. 2, p. 263. On February 21, 1922, it was decided to include in the rules no restriction on appearances before the Court. *Id.*, p. 78.

[37] See 17 Transactions of the Grotius Society (1932), pp. 90, 97; Caloyanni, *"L'Or-*

the establishment of any excluding standards would meet with general approval.[38] In practice, the fact that English and French are the official languages of the Court tends to limit the choice of counsel and advocates by parties and interested States. This probably explains the frequency with which States have been represented by counsel who were non-nationals, as well as the frequency with which the same persons have been chosen to act in different cases by the same Governments and even by different Governments; this practice has given the Court the assistance of experienced counsel in many of its cases.[39]

ganisation de la Cour Permanente de Justice et son avenir," 38 Recueil des Cours, Académie de Droit International (1931), pp. 768–776.

[38] It may be noted that such standards were formulated in the Prize Court Convention of 1907, however. Article 26 of that convention provided that a private person might be represented before the Prize Court by an attorney who should be either an advocate qualified to plead before a court of appeal or a high court in one of the contracting States, or a lawyer practising before a similar court, or a professor of law at a higher teaching center in one of those States. Yet Article 25 of the Convention did not place similar limitations on representatives of States before the Prize Court.

[39] One judge of the Court has stated, though after a short period of service on the Court, that cases are frequently argued by professors and that "professors do not make good advocates." Sir Cecil Hurst, in 75 Solicitors' Journal (1931), p. 564.

CHAPTER 24

WRITTEN PROCEEDINGS

§472. The Court's Law of Procedure. Under the Statute the Court is bound by few procedural limitations. It has the responsibility of building a law of procedure which will meet the needs of inter-state litigation, and to some extent this law must be developed *de novo*. Since its early years the Court has sought to follow the course "which it considers best calculated to ensure the administration of justice, most suited to procedure before an international tribunal and most in conformity with the fundamental principles of international law."[1] Clearly the Court would not be justified in giving to procedural requirements the importance which they have in the municipal law of many countries;[2] in particular, it is not bound by "the various codes of procedure and the various legal terminologies" in use in different countries.[3] To some extent the procedure is governed by Chapter III of the Statute, which is headed "Procedure"; but the Court's law of procedure is largely contained in the Rules "framed" under Article 30 of the Statute "for regulating its procedure." Chapter II of the Rules, subdivided into three headings, deals with contentious procedure, advisory procedure, and errors. Articles 33–70 of the Rules, dealing with contentious procedure, are subject to the provision in Article 32 that they "shall in no way preclude the adoption by the Court of such other rules as may be jointly proposed by the parties concerned, due regard being paid to the particular circumstances of each case." This means that parties before the Court have some control

[1] Series A, No. 2, p. 16.
[2] In the *Free Zones Case*, the Court said that "the decision of an international dispute of the present order should not mainly depend on a point of procedure." Series A/B, No. 46, p. 155.
[3] Series A, No. 6, p. 19. This principle was not applied in the case relating to *German Minority Schools in Upper Silesia*, when the Court stated that "the word *débouter* (dismiss) in the Polish Government's main submission must be taken as possessing the meaning ordinarily attaching to it in French law." Series A, No. 15, p. 20. It seems difficult to justify this statement.

of the procedure, subject to the limitation that the Court cannot depart from the provisions in the Statute; [4] but it is for the Court to make the final decision on the parties' proposals.[5] This is particularly important in shaping the attitude of the Court toward provisions in special agreements; and even in advisory procedure the principle of assimilation may lead the Court to pay regard to the wishes of the States concerned through the application of Article 32 by way of analogy.

§473. **Institution of a Proceeding.**[6] Under Article 40 of the Statute, a contentious proceeding may be instituted in one of the following ways: (1) by the notification of a special agreement; (2) by a written application addressed to the Registrar.[7] In a sense, also, a preliminary objection under Article 38 of the Rules is the institution of a contentious proceeding; and this may be said also of an application to intervene under Article 62 of the Statute. An application for the indication of interim measures of protection, on the other hand, relates to a proceeding already instituted.[8] A proceeding for the revision of a judgment is instituted by application; a proceeding for the interpretation of a judgment, either by the notification of a special agreement concluded by all the parties or by an application by one of the parties. The proceeding for interpretation is largely assimilated to the ordinary contentious proceeding, and the procedure resembles summary procedure.[9] No special method is laid down for instituting, as distinguished from opening, summary proceedings,[10] and under Article 67 of the Rules the ordinary methods for instituting contentious proceedings would seem to apply.

An advisory proceeding is instituted by the filing of a written request of the Assembly or Council of the League of Nations, signed either by the President of the Assembly or the President of the Coun-

---

[4] See the order of August 19, 1929, in the *Free Zones Case*, where it is stated that "the Court cannot, on the proposal of the parties, depart from the terms of the Statute." Series A, No. 22, p. 12. See §416, *supra*.   [5] Series D, No. 2 (add.), pp. 67–68.

[6] There is some confusion in the use of the terms *proceeding* and *proceedings* in the Statute and in the Rules. Article 40 of the Statute deals with bringing cases before the Court, while Articles 35 and 39 of the Rules deal with the institution of proceedings; in this sense a proceeding is a case. However, Article 43 of the Statute deals with written proceedings (Fr., *procédure écrite*) and oral proceedings (Fr., *procédure orale*) and these terms are used in the Rules.

[7] In numerous cases, the application has been addressed to the President and Judges of the Court; in the case concerning the *Statute of Memel*, attention was drawn to the irregularity of thus addressing the covering letter. Series C, No. 59, p. 604.

[8] Two or more applications may be joined for a single proceeding. See Series A, No. 7, p. 94.   [9] See Series E, No. 4, p. 293ff; No. 5, p. 260.

[10] Article 69 of the Rules applies to opening, not to instituting, summary proceedings.

cil, or by the Secretary-General under instructions from the Assembly or the Council.

§474. **Necessity of Written Proceedings.** Article 43 of the Statute seems to envisage a procedure of both written and oral parts in every case.[11] In contentious cases there will normally be written proceedings, and in every case which has come before the Court for judgment written proceedings have been conducted. Yet it would seem that the parties might agree to dispense with written proceedings, and to content themselves with a bare statement of their contentions in the special agreement; in such a case, the Court might call for documents or explanations under Article 49 of the Statute, however. With respect to requests for advisory opinions, there might be no State or international organization considered by the Court "as likely to be able to furnish information on the question" under Article 73 of the Rules,[12] and no State or organization might ask to be permitted to submit a written statement; in such a case, the Court might find the documentation submitted by the Assembly or the Council sufficient to enable it to give the opinion requested, or it might decline to give the opinion for want of information. No advisory opinion has yet been given without the aid of statements filed by interested States or by interested organizations.

§475. **Nature of Written Proceedings.** Article 43 of the Statute provides that "the written proceedings shall consist of the communication to the judges and to the parties of cases, counter-cases, and if necessary, replies; also all papers and documents in support." The Rules distinguish quite sharply between written proceedings in various types of cases.

(a) If a proceeding is instituted by the notification of a special agreement, the nature and order of the documents (Fr., *pièces de procédure*) to be presented is subject to the agreement of the parties; failing an agreement to the contrary,[13] Article 39 of the Rules provides for the simultaneous submission by the parties of cases (Fr., *mémoires*), counter-cases (Fr., *contre-mémoires*), and replies (Fr.,

---

[11] The 1899 Hague Convention for Pacific Settlement provides (Article 39) that "as a general rule the arbitral procedure comprises two distinct phases: pleadings and oral discussions" (Fr., *l'instruction et les débats*). Baron Descamps' report to the 1899 Conference stated that "the first is always indispensable." *Conférence Internationale de la Paix* (1899), p. 134.

[12] Or under the new Article 66 of the Statute, as annexed to the Revision Protocol of September 14, 1929.

[13] Such an agreement was made in the *Brazilian Loans Case*. See Series C, No. 16—IV, p. 318.

répliques).[14] In such a proceeding, there is no applicant and no respondent, and the simultaneous presentation of documents is for the purpose of giving the parties "an equal opportunity reciprocally to discuss their respective contentions." [15] Strictly, the notification of the special agreement, and the agreement itself, do not constitute a part of the written proceedings.

(*b*) If a proceeding is instituted by an application, the respondent is promptly notified of the application; such notification settles the question whether the instrument filed is an application within Article 40 of the Statute, though it does not determine the admissibility of the application.[16] In the absence of an agreement to the contrary between the parties, the documents (Fr., *pièces de procédure*) to be presented are the following, in this order: [17] (1) the applicant's case; (2) the respondent's counter-case; (3) the applicant's reply; (4) the respondent's rejoinder (Fr., *duplique*). After the applicant's case is in, the State against which the proceeding is directed may file a preliminary objection, and the document submitting this objection corresponds in effect to both an application and a case; the "party against whom the plea is directed," *i.e.*, the applicant, submits "a written statement of its observations and conclusions." Thereafter, if the objection is not upheld, a counter-case, a reply and a rejoinder may be filed in dealing with the merits.[18]

(*c*) An application for permission to intervene under Article 62 of the Statute may be followed by "observations" by the parties, and both the would-be intervenor and the original parties may comment on these observations "in Court." [19] Apparently, intervention under Article 63 of the Statute does not require an application; the intervenor is entitled, under Article 60 of the Rules, to submit "observations" on the "documents in the case, in so far as they relate to the interpretation

---

[14] If the special agreement contains no proposal as to replies, the parties may be held to have waived the privilege of presenting them. Series E, No. 4, p. 281.

[15] Series A, No. 23, p. 45.   [16] Series E, No. 9, p. 164.

[17] In the *Statute of Memel Case*, the applicants renounced the right of presenting a written reply, in their application. Series A/B, No. 49, p. 297.

[18] In the case relating to *Appeals from Judgments of the Czechoslovak-Hungarian Mixed Arbitral Tribunal*, the Court called for the views of the parties as to the scope of a treaty provision, time limits being fixed, though this was explained to be not "a step in the proceedings contemplated by the Statute"; the oral proceedings on the preliminary objection were to include the hearing of observations on this treaty provision. Series E, No. 9, pp. 156 note, 172.

[19] The equivalent of "in Court" does not appear in the French version of Article 59 of the Rules, though it is to be implied.

of the convention in question," and other parties may "comment" on these observations, though the intervenor may reply to their comment only with the Court's permission.

(*d*) In a proceeding relating to the revision of a judgment, the application is subject to "observations" by the other party or parties; the Court may invite further written or oral explanations, also.

(*e*) In a proceeding relating to the interpretation of a judgment, an agreement between the parties in the original case may be the sole document presented; if the proceeding is instituted by application by one party, the other party or parties may present "observations" on the application, or may present a preliminary objection. In any case, however, the Court may invite further explanations, written or oral.[20]

(*f*) When the indication of interim measures is requested, the parties must be given an opportunity to present their "observations" (Fr., *observations*), which may be written or oral.[21] In the *Southeastern Greenland Case*, the Court gave opportunity for the parties to submit their observations orally, "such observations to be briefly summarized in a document handed in at the hearing." [22]

(*g*) In the Chamber for Summary Procedure, the written proceedings consist either of a case and a counter-case, or of cases submitted simultaneously which may on the Court's invitation be followed by counter-cases also submitted simultaneously. No replies or rejoinders are provided for, though they may be allowed by the Court.[23]

(*h*) In an advisory proceeding,[24] statements analogous to cases and sometimes called cases, may be presented by interested States and with the permission of the Court, counter-statements analogous to counter-cases are sometimes allowed to be presented; [25] but the purpose of such statements or counter-statements is merely to supply "information" to the Court.

Where a State which is not a Member of the League of Nations and which is not mentioned in the Annex to the Covenant is a party before the Court, it must file with the Registry the declaration required by

[20] Series A, No. 13, p. 6.
[21] In the *Chorzów Case*, in 1927, it was held that the German request for interim measures was not covered by the Statute and Rules, and the decision to give no effect to the request was taken without any invitation to the Polish Government to present its observations. Series A, No. 12, p. 10.
[22] Series A/B, No. 48, p. 280.   [23] Series E, No. 1, p. 267.
[24] "Originally, no written proceedings had been contemplated in the case of advisory opinions." Series E, No. 7, p. 286.
[25] Series E, No. 7, p. 303.

the resolution of the Council of the League of Nations of May 17, 1922,[26] not later than the time fixed for the filing of the first document of the written procedure.[27]

Acts of the written procedure or passages in them may be withdrawn after they are filed, with leave of Court.[28] Corrections or amendments may also be allowed.[29]

§476. **Filing of Acts of Procedure.** Under Article 34 of the Rules, the original of each act of procedure (Fr., *pièce de procédure*) must be dated, and it must be signed by one or more agents. Ten certified[30] copies, and if no other arrangement is made with the Registrar, forty printed copies must be filed, and the President may order additional copies to be supplied.[31] Article 34 is applied by analogy in advisory proceedings.[32] The Registrar has frequently arranged with agents for the printing of acts of procedure to be done under his direction, the expense of drawing off the extra copies being borne by the agent.[33] In such case, it is the filing of the original text which must be effected within the time limit set. The acts of procedure must be in English or French, or if the parties have agreed on the use of one of these languages, in that one of them; if the use of a third language has been authorized, a translation into English or French must be attached to the original.[34]

§477. **Inspection and Publicity of Acts of Procedure.** As soon as each act of procedure is filed, the Registrar forwards a copy or copies to each member of the Court and to each of the other parties.[35] In advisory proceedings, the statements submitted are communicated to interested Governments.[36] Article 42 of the Rules also empowers the Court, or the President if the Court is not sitting, after hearing

---

[26] See §397, *supra.* [27] Series E, No. 7, p. 303.
[28] Series E, No. 3, p. 205; No. 6, p. 290. A proceeding instituted by an application may not be suspended, however. Series E, No. 3, p. 185. [29] Series E, No. 6, p. 290.
[30] The certification should be by the agent or by a person authorized by the agent. *Cf.,* Series E, No. 8, p. 259.
[31] This was done in the case of the *Austro-German Customs Régime.* Series C, No. 53, p. 713.
[32] Series E, No. 4, pp. 279, 297. A failure to comply with Article 34 may be excused by the Court. Series E, No. 4, p. 283.
[33] Series E, No. 6, p. 291; No. 7, p. 294; No. 8, p. 260; No. 9, p. 168.
[34] Series E, No. 3, p. 200. A party is not entitled to a translation from one official language into the other. Series E, No. 4, p. 277. The Registry will usually communicate its own translation to the parties, however.
[35] In the *Eastern Greenland Case,* the Court acquiesced in a proposal for a direct exchange of additional copies by the parties. Series E, No. 9, p. 169. In the case of the *Nationality Decrees in Tunis and Morocco,* there seems to have been a direct exchange between the British and French Governments, and this procedure was noted by the President "as a derogation from the rule laid down in Article 43, paragraph 4, of the Court's Statute." Series C, No. 2, pp. 265, 267. [36] Series E, No. 1, p. 251.

the parties, to hold cases and counter-cases at the disposal of the Government of any State entitled to appear before the Court; [37] this may be very important to a State which is studying the desirability of an application to intervene under Article 62 or of an intervention under Article 63 of the Statute. Since 1931, the acts of procedure may with the consent of the parties be made accessible to the public before a proceeding is terminated.[38] To prevent a partial disclosure, the immediate publication by a party or interested State of its acts of procedure has been discouraged,[39] but such publication has been agreed upon by the parties at the conclusion of the phase of the case in which the acts of procedure were before the Court.[40]

The publication of the acts of procedure *in extenso*, in Series C, is a protection to the Court against any partial reproduction which might be misleading. Article 42 of the Rules is applied by analogy in advisory proceedings.[41]

§478. Preliminary Objections. No mention of preliminary objections [42] is made in the Statute, but Article 38 of the 1926 Rules provides for the filing of "any preliminary objection" (Fr., *toute exception préliminaire*) when a proceeding is begun by means of an application, after the filing of the applicant's case and within the time fixed for the filing of the counter-case. The objection is sometimes called a "plea" or "a plea to the jurisdiction." The Rules refrain from speaking of the State on whose behalf the objection is made as a respondent and in many ways its position is that of an applicant; [43] hence an objection to the jurisdiction is looked upon as instituting a different proceeding from that relating to the merits.[44] No limit is placed on the grounds upon which an objection may be based; in practice, preliminary objections are usually directed against the Court's assumption of jurisdiction on the application, or against its entertaining the application. Article 38 of the Rules has

---

[37] Series E, No. 8, p. 262; No. 9, p. 169. In one case a general authorization was given. Series E, No. 5, p. 253. The action of the Court is not dependent on the agreement of the parties, though it is customary to seek their consent. Series E, No. 9, p. 169. [38] See Series E, No. 7, pp. 282–283; No. 9, p. 170.
[39] Series E, No. 6, p. 284. In the *Serbian Loans Case,* the Registrar objected to a premature publication of extracts from the cases submitted by the parties. Series C, No. 16—III, pp. 776, 781, 789. [40] Series E, No. 7, pp. 280–281.
[41] Series E, No. 8, p. 262; Series C, No. 53, pp. 712, 717, 718, 722.
[42] The usage of this term by the Court is not altogether uniform. See Series A, No. 17, pp. 30, 34, 39. [43] Series E, No. 3, p. 207.
[44] Series E, No. 3, p. 184. The comprehensive general list established in 1931 has separate entries relating to merits and jurisdiction in the same case. See Series E, No. 7, p. 199ff.

been construed by the Court as having for its object "to lay down when an objection to the jurisdiction may validly be filed, but only in cases where the objection is submitted as a preliminary question, that is to say, when the respondent asks for a decision upon the objection before any subsequent proceedings on the merits"; [45] yet it was purposely made to apply to all preliminary objections, not merely to those relating to jurisdiction.[46] A plea of *res judicata* might be offered as a preliminary objection,[47] or possibly a plea of *lis pendens*.[48] The State filing the objection usually has the advantage of knowing the *case* of the applicant before the objection is filed.[49] The proceedings on the objection may be joined to proceedings on the merits.[50] Even before the rule of 1926 was adopted, the Court refused to say that it might not look into the merits in passing on a preliminary objection "which could not be dealt with without recourse to arguments taken from the merits." [51]

(1) On June 16, 1924, the British agent filed a preliminary objection to the jurisdiction in the *Mavrommatis Case*, presenting at the same time a preliminary counter-case; [52] the Greek agent filed a *réponse* to the preliminary counter-case.[53] By the Court's judgment of August 30, 1924,[54] the objection was upheld in part and dismissed in part.

(2) On June 26, 1925, the Polish Government filed a *réponse exceptionnelle* to the German application of May 15, 1924,[55] concerning *German Interests in Polish Upper Silesia*, asking that the Court declare itself incompetent, and alternatively that it declare that the application could not be entertained. The German Government filed

---

[45] Series A, No. 15, p. 22.   [46] Series D, No. 2 (add.), pp. 89–91.

[47] *Cf.*, the Polish objection in the *Chorzów Factory Case*, Series A, No. 17, pp. 32–33.

[48] In the case relating to *German Interests in Polish Upper Silesia*, the Polish Government filed an objection to the jurisdiction and alternatively an objection that the German application could not be entertained until a judgment had been given by the German-Polish Mixed Arbitral Tribunal. Series A, No. 6, pp. 18–21. In the *Free Zones Case*, the term "preliminary objection" was applied to an objection to the admission of evidence. Series A, No. 22, p. 14. See also the use of the term in the judgment in the *Chorzów Factory Case*, Series A, No. 17, p. 30.

[49] The Court noted that this was not true in the case concerning *German Interests in Polish Upper Silesia*. Series A, No. 6, p. 15.

[50] Where the same considerations of fact and of law were adduced, and the conclusions were the same, the objections in two cases relating to appeals from judgments of the Czechoslovak-Hungarian Mixed Arbitral Tribunal were joined. See Series E, No. 9, p. 164.   [51] Series A, No. 6, p. 15.

[52] Series C, No. 5—I, p. 439. The Court was previously informed that the objection would be made, and a date was fixed by the Court for the filing. At this time, the Rules contained no provision for preliminary objections.   [55] Series C, No. 9—I, p. 119.

[53] *Id.*, p. 456.   [54] Series A, No. 2.

"observations" on this *réponse*.[56] The Court's judgment of August 25, 1925,[57] dismissed the plea of the Polish Government. As to the alternative request by Poland, there was no basis for applying the doctrine of *lis pendens,* nor could the Court admit the plea of *fin de non recevoir.*

(3) On April 8, 1927, the Polish agent filed an *exception préliminaire* and preliminary counter-case in the *Chorzów Factory Case,* asking the Court to declare itself incompetent.[58] The German Government filed a *réponse*.[59] On July 26, 1927, the Polish plea was dismissed.[60]

(4) On August 9, 1927, the British agent filed a preliminary objection asking the Court to declare that it had no jurisdiction to entertain a proceeding instituted by the Greek Government in the *Mavrommatis Jerusalem Concessions Case.*[61] To this the Greek agent filed a *réponse*.[62] The objection was upheld by the Court.[63]

(5) In the *Statute of Memel Case,* the Lithuanian Government filed a counter-case and at the same time an objection to the Court's jurisdiction as to certain points in the application before it;[64] this was held to fulfill the requirements of Article 38 of the Rules. The applicants filed observations on the objection, which was "overruled" by the Court on June 24, 1932. Later, however, when the case was heard on the merits, the Lithuanian agent contended that these same points in the application were "inadmissible"; this was deemed to be "in effect a plea to the jurisdiction," and as such it was overruled.[65]

(6) On October 8, 1932, the Polish Government filed a preliminary objection asking that the German Government's application in the case of the *Administration of the Prince of Pless* be declared "inadmissible." The German Government filed a statement in reply, and after oral arguments, on February 4, 1933, the Court gave an order joining the preliminary objection to the merits of the suit "in order to pass upon the objection and, if the latter is overruled, upon the merits, by a single judgment."[66] The grounds of the Polish objection were that no difference of opinion existed under Article 72 (3) of the Geneva Convention, and that Prince von Pless had not exhausted his local remedies; in dealing with these grounds, the Court

---

[56] *Id.,* p. 156. The Court referred to these observations as a counter-case.
[57] Series A, No. 6. [58] Series C, No. 13—I, p. 147. [59] *Id.,* p. 172.
[60] Series A, No. 9. [61] Series C, No. 13—III, p. 451. [62] *Id.,* p. 469.
[63] Series A, No. 11. [64] Series A/B, No. 47, p. 246.
[65] Series A/B, No. 49, pp. 327–328. [66] Series A/B, No. 52, p. 16.

raised *proprio motu* the question whether it had jurisdiction on the basis of Article 72 (3) of the Geneva Convention, to entertain a claim of indemnity put forward by a State in its capacity as a Member of the Council of the League of Nations on behalf of a national of the respondent State.[67]

(7) On October 24, 1932, the agent of the Hungarian Government filed preliminary objections asking the Court to declare that two applications by the Czechoslovak Government, appealing from judgments of a Mixed Arbitral Tribunal, had been submitted too late and could not be entertained.[68]

On this record, it can hardly be said that the Court has shown a marked tendency to aggrandize jurisdiction.

§479. **Procedure on Preliminary Objections.** Proceedings in regard to preliminary objections are "in the nature of summary proceedings," and possess a character of "relative urgency."[69] The procedure with reference to them differs somewhat from that with reference to special agreements or applications, for Article 38 of the Rules seems to envisage a written procedure consisting of two documents: (1) "the document submitting the objection" containing a statement of facts and law, a statement of conclusions, a list of attached documents, and a mention of the evidence to be produced; and (2) "a written statement" of the original applicant's observations and conclusions, with documents attached and with a mention of evidence to be produced. However, the Court may decide upon further written proceedings.[70] In the oral proceedings the Court may call upon the parties under Article 69 of the Rules to supply oral explanations, or may sanction the production of any evidence by witnesses or experts mentioned in the documents.

The tendency seems to be to assimilate the procedure on applications to intervene to that on preliminary objections.[71]

§480. **The Case.** Article 40 of the Rules requires the *case* to have definite contents, whether a proceeding is begun by special agreement or by application. It must contain (1) a statement of the facts on which the claim is based; (2) a statement of law; (3) a statement of

---

[67] As the case was discontinued, this point was not decided. Series A/B, No. 59, p. 194.

[68] The objections were joined by the Court, but the applications were later withdrawn. Series A/B, No. 56.   [69] Series C, No. 13—I, p. 8.

[70] It seemed reluctant to do so in the *Mavrommatis Concessions Case,* saying that "under Article 38 of the Rules, the remainder of the proceedings must be oral." Series A, No. 11, p. 7.   [71] Series E, No. 3, p. 220.

conclusions; and (4) a list of the documents in support, which documents should be attached. The most important part of the case is the statement of conclusions, which must in a general way fall within the terms of the questions submitted by a special agreement or within the indication of the claim in an application. Where a proceeding is under a special agreement, cases are to be filed by all the parties; if it is begun by application, a case is filed only by the applicant.

§481. The Counter-case. Article 40 of the Rules also requires definite contents for a counter-case: (1) an affirmation or contestation of the facts stated in the case; (2) a statement of additional facts, if any; (3) a statement of law; (4) conclusions based on the facts, which may include counter-claims (Fr., *demandes reconventionnelles*) within the Court's jurisdiction; and (5) a list of the documents in support, which documents should be attached.

§482. Conclusions of the Parties.[72] Article 40 of the Statute requires the subject of a dispute to be indicated when a case is brought before the Court, and under Article 48 the Court is to decide as to the form in which a party shall conclude its arguments.[73] The Rules (Article 40) require that cases and counter-cases shall state the conclusions of the parties; Article 38 requires that a document submitting a preliminary objection shall contain a statement of conclusions, and gives the other party the privilege of submitting a statement of observations and conclusions. The Court frequently refers to the parties' conclusions (Fr., *conclusions*) by the English term "submissions," though this latter term is not to be found in the Statute or in the Rules. Conclusions may be stated in an application,[74] though Article 35 of the Rules requires only "an indication of the claim." A special agreement may also deal with the conclusions; thus the Franco-Swiss agreement in the *Free Zones Case,* providing for cases, counter-cases and replies, stated that the reply of each party should contain "its final conclusions."[75] The special agreement in the *Serbian*

---

[72] See A. H. Feller, "Conclusions of the Parties in the Procedure of the Permanent Court of International Justice," 25 American Journal of International Law (1931), p. 490.

[73] Conclusion in the sense of Article 48 may be distinguished from the conclusions contained in a case or counter-case. Series A, No. 17, p. 7.

[74] *Cf.,* Series C, No. 59, p. 602. In the *Statute of Memel Case,* by the covering letters sent when the application was filed, the applicants reserved the right to append their submissions to the case. Series A/B, No. 49, p. 296. Without such a reservation, a party may formulate submissions in its case.

[75] Series A/B, No. 46, p. 99. The French agent filed no statement of conclusions in the second stage of the case. Series A, No. 24, p. 6.

Loans Case provided for additional submissions in the counter-cases,[76] and that in the *Brazilian Loans Case* provided that submissions should be formulated in the cases.[77] Alternative conclusions may be submitted. While the Court will construe conclusions or submissions, it will not formulate them "simply on the basis of arguments and facts advanced." [78] It may call for conclusions to be submitted.[79]

As a general rule, the conclusions will constitute the basis of the Court's action, and only the issues with which they deal will be decided.[80] Yet for the purpose of affording a chart to the Court, some limits may be set on the conclusions themselves. If a case arises under a special agreement, "it is rather to the terms of this agreement than to the submissions of the parties that the Court must have recourse in establishing the precise points which it has to decide"; [81] questions stated in a special agreement "cannot be changed or amplified by one of the parties." [82] If the Court is seised of an application, it seems that the claim put forward in the application cannot be enlarged by conclusions in a later act of procedure.[83] In its order of February 4, 1933, in the case relating to the *Administration of the Prince of Pless*, the Court said: "Under Article 40 of the Statute, it is the Application which sets out the subject of the dispute, and the Case, though it may elucidate the terms of the Application, must not go beyond the limits of the claim as set out therein." [84] In the strict sense of the term, there are no submissions in a request for interpretation of a judgment; the German submissions in connection with a request for the *Interpretation of Judgments Nos. 7 and 8* were therefore regarded as constituting an indication of the points in dispute.[85]

A difficult question may arise as to the extent to which conclusions which have been submitted may later be amended or modified. In the case relating to *German Interests in Polish Upper Silesia*, the submissions in the German applications were modified in the course of the

---

[76] Series A, No. 20/21, p. 9.   [77] *Id.*, p. 95.   [78] Series A, No. 7, p. 35.
[79] See the order of August 15, 1929, inviting the Polish Government to file "any alternative submissions" as to a question placed before the Court by the special agreement in the *Oder Commission Case*. Series A, No. 23, p. 44.
[80] See Series A, No. 17, p. 17. *Cf.*, Series A, No. 2, p. 30.
[81] Series A, No. 10, p. 12. See also Series A, No. 22, p. 40.
[82] Series A, No. 23, p. 18.
[83] See, however, the views of Judge Anzilotti in Series A/B, No. 49, p. 351.
[84] Series A/B, No. 52, p. 14.
[85] Series A, No. 13, p. 16. Judge Anzilotti, dissenting in this case, thought that in such proceedings "the Court has to give judgment upon the submissions of the parties just as in any other contentious proceedings." *Id.*, p. 23.

written and oral proceedings, and in the judgment on the merits the Court stated them as modified.[86] This practice was subsequently followed, though the Court later reserved the power to indicate "at what moment and in what form" the parties must present their final submissions.[87] In the case relating to the *Denunciation of the Belgian-Chinese Treaty,* the applicant was allowed to modify its original submissions before the time had expired for the respondent's presentation of a counter-case.[88] In the *Chorzów Factory Case,* submissions were presented in the applicant's case, to supersede the submissions included in the application; the Court said that no exception could be taken to this, as "this amendment has been effected in the first document of the written proceedings," at a time when "the respondent still retains a completely free hand to file preliminary objections"; but it was noted that in its preliminary pleas, the respondent had referred to the applicant's submissions as stated in its case, and that both sets of submissions were based on the same treaty provision.[89] In that case, also, the parties were allowed "to amend their original submissions, not only in the case and counter-case (Article 40 of the Rules), but also both in the subsequent documents of the written proceedings and in declarations made by them in the course of the hearings (Article 55 of the Rules), subject only to the condition that the other party must always have an opportunity of commenting on the amended submissions"; [90] the Court also allowed the respondent to abandon certain submissions,[91] and the submissions of both parties were reformulated by the Court. During the progress of the *Free Zones Case,* "fresh observations" were submitted by the parties from time to time, containing new submissions, and the presentation of submissions at the conclusion of oral statements was permitted.[92] It may be said, therefore, that no special limit exists as to the stage of proceedings within which the amendment or withdrawal of submissions, or the presentation of new submissions, may be effected; but the principle is to prevail that a party must always have opportunity to comment on the final submissions of another party, and this may set a limit on possible amendment.[93] Possibly this is subject to the provision in Article 48 of the Statute that the Court may always de-

---

[86] Series A, No. 7, p. 12.   [87] Series E, No. 5, p. 258. *Cf.,* Series E, No. 6, p. 294.
[88] Series A, No. 8, p. 10.   [89] Series A, No. 9, pp. 18, 19.
[90] Series A, No. 17, p. 7. It was noted that formal objection had not been made, however. *Id.,* p. 13.
[91] *Id.,* p. 14.   [92] Series A/B, No. 46, p. 114.
[93] Series E, No. 9, p. 173. The same rule holds for the production of new evidence.

cide upon "the form and time in which each party must conclude its arguments."

A submission must of course be supported before the Court.[94] In the case relating to *German Interests in Polish Upper Silesia,* a claim was dismissed "for lack of sufficiently substantiated statements." [95] Alternative and subsidiary submissions are frequently made; and they may even be interrogative in form.[96]

In an advisory proceeding, as there are no parties in the strict sense of the term, conclusions or submissions play a less important rôle. States or organizations appear before the Court in an advisory proceeding to furnish "information," not to present claims.[97] In a few cases, however, formal submissions have been presented. In the case of the *Greco-Bulgarian Communities,* the Court treated submissions as "authoritative summaries of the opposing contentions." [98] In the case relating to the *Caphandaris-Molloff Agreement,* the Court requested the Greek agent to formulate the point of view of his Government in the form of conclusions,[99] thus applying Article 49 of the Statute by analogy.

In a proceeding for the interpretation of a judgment, Article 66 of the Rules provides for an application containing "an indication of the precise point or points in dispute"; this does not seem to envisage submissions. In connection with the *Interpretation of Judgments Nos. 7 and 8,* the Court interpreted "submissions" in the German application "as simply constituting an indication" under Article 66.[100]

§483. Counter-claims. Article 40 of the Rules states that the conclusions set forth in counter-cases "may include counter-claims," in so far as they come within the Court's jurisdiction. It is difficult to see how any counter-claim can be advanced in a proceeding under a special agreement, and perhaps this is not envisaged in the Rules.[1]

---

[94] A submission may have to be construed "in the light of the observations contained in the case" and other documents of the written proceedings. Series A, No. 17, p. 60.   [95] Series A, No. 7, p. 65.

[96] Series A, No. 6, p. 22. An interrogative submission must be supported by a claim, however. Series A, No. 7, p. 34. Judge Anzilotti attached great importance to this point in the *Statute of Memel Case.* Series A/B, No. 49, p. 350.

[97] An extreme application was made of this principle when the representatives of organizations appearing before the Court in a case relating to the *Competence of the International Labor Organization,* were told that they should not indicate the conclusions at which the Court should arrive on a question of law. Series C, No. 12, p. 10.

[98] Series B, No. 17, p. 14. See also Series B, No. 16, p. 13.

[99] Series C, No. 57, p. 433.   [100] Series A, No. 13, p. 16.

[1] Yet Article 40 refers to counter-cases in general, and it may therefore apply to counter-cases in proceedings under special agreements. On the Court's jurisdiction with respect to counter-claims, see §446, *supra.*

If the proceeding has been instituted by an application, however, a counter-claim may be advanced in a counter-case, and the Court may have jurisdiction to consider it either by reason of the applicant's submission to its jurisdiction, or under a declaration made by the applicant in accordance with paragraph 2 of Article 36 of the Statute, or under the provisions of a treaty or convention in force; it would seem that the basis of the Court's jurisdiction over a counter-claim must be the same as the basis of its jurisdiction over the original case, unless the parties agree to a different basis of jurisdiction.[2] In the *Chorzów Factory Case,* in which the German Government sought the payment of an indemnity, the Polish counter-case submitted that "the German Government should in the first place, hand over to the Polish Government the whole of the shares of the *Oberschlesische Company* of the nominal value of 110,000,000 marks, which are in its hands under the contract of December 24, 1919"; the parties were agreed in placing this question before the Court for decision, and the Court observed that the counter-claim was "juridically connected with the principal claim." However, "although in form a counter-claim," the submission was designed only to reduce the indemnity which might be found to be due to Germany;[3] the Court dealt with this submission, but rejected it.[4] In the same case, a submission by the German Government was designed to prevent the set-off of any counter-claim against an indemnity which might be found to be due, or in the alternative to confine any set-off allowed to defined circumstances; as the Polish Government had raised no plea of set-off, it was found unnecessary to pass on this submission.[5]

§484. **Documents.** The term "document" is employed in the Statute (Articles 43, 49) in the sense of "papers and documents in support" of cases, counter-cases and replies.[6] In the Rules, it is employed in three senses: (1) in Articles 34, 35, 37, 38, 39, 69, in the sense of acts of procedure or "documents constituting the written procedure" (Fr., *actes de procédure, pièces de procédure*); (2) in Articles 37, 38, 40, 59, in the sense of "documents in support" of acts of procedure; and (3) in Articles 42, 60, in the sense of both (1) and (2). The term is considered in this section only in the second of these senses.

Article 43 of the Statute requires that "a certified copy of every document produced by one party shall be communicated to the other

---

[2] See §407 (1), *supra.*   [3] Series A, No. 17, pp. 36–39.   [4] *Id.,* pp. 41–42.
[5] *Id.,* pp. 60–63.
[6] The usage in the French version of the Statute is somewhat different.

party," and, though a direct interchange may be allowed, the duty
of communicating them falls upon the Registry. Under Article 37
of the Rules, with the sanction of the Court, a document submitted
may be a translation of the whole or a part of another document.[7]
Cases and counter-cases are required to contain lists of documents
in support, and the Court has decided that these requirements are
applicable by analogy in advisory proceedings;[8] the documents cited
in the list should be annexed,[9] but the Court may permit them to be
presented later if ample opportunity can be given for comment by
other parties or interested States.[10] Documents which are not mentioned in the list, but which are referred to in argument, may be called
for by the Court; [11] in some cases they have been presented after the
termination of the oral hearings.[12] The Court may call for the production of documents, even before the hearing begins.[13] On a few occasions, documents presented have been withdrawn.[14] The Court is not
bound to receive documents from individuals not representing parties
or interested States.[15] A party cannot place on the Court the responsibility of procuring documents from another tribunal.[16] All documents
presented are usually published by the Court; [17] it is not for the
parties themselves to make public the documents in proceedings before
the Court.

[7] In the *Peter Pázmány University Case,* the Czechoslovak agent asked the Court to
call upon the Hungarian agent to produce the original of a document which the Czechoslovak agent desired to present; as this request was based upon a "mistaken idea" that
the Czechoslovak agent was bound to present a certified true copy of the original, it
was denied. Series A/B, No. 61, p. 215.   [8] Series E, No. 8, p. 261.
[9] See Series C, No. 59, pp. 615ff., 621. Objection was made by the Registry when
only copies of the documents were supplied, and this was said to be contrary to Article 34
of the Rules which requires originals, signed and dated, and ten copies. Series E, No. 9,
p. 167. Where necessary, all documents annexed should be translated into one of the
Court's official languages. *Id.,* p. 169. The Registry is not bound to translate documents
filed in one of the Court's official languages, for the use of the parties. *Id.,* p. 162.
[10] Series E, No. 4, p. 285; No. 6, p. 290. In the case relating to the *Royal Hungarian
Peter Pázmány University,* objection to the presentation of documents during the oral
proceedings was overruled, but the Court set a ban on the presentation of further
documents. See Series A/B, No. 61, p. 214.
[11] Series E, No. 6, p. 292. This may be done by the Court *proprio motu* or at the
suggestion of a party. Series E, No. 8, p. 268.
[12] Series E, No. 6, p. 297. See also Series C, No. 16—III, pp. 821–824.
[13] Series C, No. 55, p. 438. The invitation may take the form of an order. In the
case relating to the *Convention on Employment of Women during the Night,* the
Court "had before it certain documents collected on its own behalf." Series A/B, No. 50,
p. 369. These were not listed in the annex to the opinion; this practice must be attributed to the nature of the question with which the Court was called upon to deal.
[14] See, *e.g.,* Series E, No. 3, p. 205; No. 6, p. 291.
[15] By a curious procedure, hardly defensible, petitions and requests from private
individuals and organizations were received in the *Free Zones Case,* and communicated to
the parties during the hearings. Series E, No. 8, p. 264.   [16] Series C, No. 68, p. 247.
[17] Series E, No. 3, p. 209. See, however, Series E, No. 6, p. 296; No. 9, p. 168.

§485. **Time Limits.** Acting under Article 48 of the Statute, the Court has provided in Article 33 of the Rules for the fixing of the time limits "for the completion of the various acts of procedure." [18] In a contentious proceeding, the limits are fixed by the Court, or by the President if the Court is not sitting; [19] since 1928, such action has been taken by order, whether by the Court [20] or by the President.[21] In a contentious proceeding, the fixing of the limits is effected after the filing of the document instituting the proceeding; in an advisory proceeding, after the receipt of the Council's or Assembly's request. The order fixing time limits is communicated to the parties or to the interested States; in advisory proceedings the communication may be made as a part of the "special and direct" communication to interested States provided for in Article 73 (1) of the Rules,[22] or at a later time.[23] Where a proceeding is instituted by an application, the Court may in the first instance fix time limits for only the case and the counter-case, reserving the fixing of time limits for the reply and the rejoinder. The time limits are fixed with regard "as far as possible" to any agreement between the parties; such an agreement may form a part of a special agreement under which proceedings are instituted,[24] or it may be made later.[25] The Court is not bound by the terms of such an agreement, however; [26] for instance, the urgency of the case may have to be taken into account. Parties or interested States are frequently consulted in fixing the time limits, where they have not reached an agreement.[27] Time limits may be fixed, also, with reference to the previous history of a dispute,[28] or with reference to "the exi-

---

[18] For a discussion of this expression, see Series D, No. 2 (2d add.), pp. 170–171.

[19] The President may act for this purpose even in cases in which the Vice-President is to preside over the deliberations. Series E, No. 8, p. 247.

[20] In its earlier years, the Court's decisions fixing time limits were not in the form of orders. Series C, No. 3—II, p. 221.

[21] Series E, No. 4, p. 287. Some of the President's earlier decisions were not in the form of an order. See, *e.g.*, Series C, No. 15—II, p. 526.

[22] Series C, No. 53, pp. 694, 756.   [23] Series C, No. 54, pp. 433, 436, 466.

[24] As in the *Brazilian Loans Case*. Series C, No. 16—IV, p. 318.

[25] Series E, No. 5, p. 255. The time limits may also be fixed subject to variation as a result of a later agreement of the parties.

[26] See Series D, No. 2 (2d add.), pp. 165–171, 176; Series E, No, 7, p. 295.

[27] Series E, No. 7, p. 303; No. 8, p. 257. Following the decision of the Council on May 19, 1931, to request an advisory opinion concerning the *Austro-German Customs Régime*, the Registrar held an interview with members of seven delegations at Geneva on May 21, 1931, for the purpose of obtaining their views as to the time limits to be fixed. Series C, No. 53, p. 687. The President's order of August 6, 1931, fixing time limits in the *Free Zones Case*, seems to have been issued after a hearing of the agents of the parties. Series A/B, No. 46, p. 109.

[28] Series A/B, No. 44, p. 7. Time limits for observations on a request for interpretation of a judgment were fixed on the basis of time limits for a counter-case. Series A, No. 13, p. 5.

gencies of the Court's work as a whole." [29] The fixing of time limits does not prejudge the question whether an application is admissible, or the question whether the Court has jurisdiction.[30]

Time limits which have been fixed may be extended, and requests for extensions are usually granted if they would not unduly affect the readiness of a case for hearing at the opening of a session, or the possibility of dealing with it at a session which is in progress, and if an urgent case would not be delayed.[31] An extension may be granted even if a party objects, or it may be subject to the consent of interested States; [32] and it may be granted even though the time limits have been fixed on the basis of agreed proposals. It may also be granted for the purpose of enabling the parties to continue negotiations.[33] If a preliminary objection is made, the extension of time limits for later proceedings in the case becomes necessary, and it is made *sine die*.[34] An extension is now made by order of the Court, or of the President if the Court is not sitting.

Some elasticity is provided for in that it may be decided in special circumstances that "any proceeding taken after the expiration of a time limit shall be considered as valid." On several occasions the Court has taken decisions in this sense; [35] and such decisions may be made even after a refusal to extend the time limit.[36] Such a decision need not be in the form of an order.[37]

§486. **Computation of Time.** While various systems of national law have developed definite rules for the computation of time, no such rules have been laid down in international law.[38] Yet the need for some such rules is obvious, and a draft was considered by the Court at its preliminary session.[39] Under Article 33 of the Rules, time limits are fixed by the Court or by the President as definite days. When a

---

[29] Series A/B, No. 46, p. 215.
[30] See the Court's order of July 18, 1932, in Series C, No. 58, p. 287.
[31] Series E, No. 4, p. 281. See also Series E, No. 3, pp. 205ff.; No. 9, p. 166.
[32] Series E, No. 8, p. 258.   [33] Series A, No. 14, p. 6.
[34] Series E, No. 2, p. 187. See also Series A, No. 6, p. 31.
[35] Series C, No. 16—IV, p. 288; Series E, No. 3, p. 213.
[36] Series C, No. 13—III, p. 508; Series C, No. 54, p. 451; Series E, No. 8, p. 259.
[37] Series E, No. 4, p. 281.
[38] See Francis Deák, "Computation of Time in International Law," 20 American Journal of International Law (1926), p. 502. The Tripartite Claims Commission (United States, Austria and Hungary) adopted a rule on computation of time in 1926. See Final Report of the Commissioner (1929), p. 181.
[39] Series D, No. 2, p. 462. This draft provided that time limits calculated in days should be reckoned in working days excluding holidays; that a week should be seven days including Sunday; that a month or a year should be reckoned from a given date to the corresponding date, and if there should be no corresponding date to the last day of the month.

document is to be filed by a certain day, a filing on the day fixed is to be deemed a compliance. In the *Free Zones Case,* the parties were given a period expiring on a certain day in which to attempt to reach an agreement.[40] Few indications have yet been given as to the Court's method of measuring periods of time. Where the parties requested that a period of time be fixed in months, the months were reckoned as consisting of twenty-eight days.[41] Holidays observed at the seat of the Court may be taken into account in fixing time limits.[42]

§487. **Closure of Written Proceedings.** Article 41 of the 1931 Rules provides for the fixing of the date for commencing oral proceedings when the written proceedings are terminated, *i.e.,* when all the required acts of the written procedure have been filed. The closure of the written proceedings is not definitely and formally declared, however; documents are frequently, and acts of procedure less frequently, filed after the apparent termination of the written proceedings.[43]

[40] Series A, No. 22, p. 21; No. 24, p. 18.
[41] Series E, No. 4, p. 284.
[42] Series D, No. 2, p. 69.
[43] The written proceedings seem to have been reopened in the *Free Zones Case* to enable the Court to take into account any "new facts." See the order of August 6, 1931, Series A/B, No. 46, p. 213.

CHAPTER 25

ORAL PROCEEDINGS

§488. **Lists of Cases.** A list (Fr., *rôle*) of cases for each session of the Court is envisaged in Article 23 of the Statute. Article 28 of the 1922 Rules provided for a list of cases, and made special mention of "the list for each session," to contain all questions submitted to the Court for advisory opinion [1] and all cases in regard to which the written proceedings are concluded, "in the order in which the documents submitting each question or case have been received by the Registrar"; a separate "list of cases for revision" was also provided for. In 1931, these provisions were recast and a sharp distinction made between "the general list" and "the session list," the revision list being abolished. On the general list are entered all "cases submitted to the Court for decision or for advisory opinion," which are "numbered successively according to the date of the receipt of the document submitting the case to the Court." This list contains notations under twenty headings,[2] and it has been compiled retrospectively since 1922.[3] The session list indicates "the contentious cases and the cases for advisory opinion which are ready for hearing," whether submitted to the full Court or to one of the Chambers. The order of cases on the session list follows the order on the general list. Where a case becomes ready for hearing in the course of a session, it is entered in the session list, unless the Court decides to the contrary.[4] When an advisory proceeding is terminated after its entry on the session list, its removal from the list is an administrative matter to be dealt with by the President.[5] Once a case or request is on the session list, however, the

[1] Originally no written proceedings had been contemplated in the case of advisory opinions. Series E, No. 5, p. 248. See §294, *supra.*
[2] See Series E, No. 7, pp. 198, 286. The entry is marked "approved" in each case.
[3] Series E, No. 7, p. 199ff.; Series D, No. 2 (2d add.), p. 164. See also the Registrar's note published with Series A/B, No. 40.
[4] The 1922 Rules required a positive decision of the Court for such entry. See, *e.g.,* the *Mavrommatis Case,* Series E, No. 1, p. 260.
[5] Series E, No. 3, p. 184; Series C, No. 9—II, pp. 111–112.

Court regards it as incompatible with Article 23 of the Statute to remove it merely for the purpose of postponing the hearing; [6] yet the Court does not feel itself bound to take cases in the order in which they appear on the session list.[7] The session list has lost some of its importance owing to the changes in the Rules as to sessions, made in 1931.[8]

§489. **Priority and Urgency.** The Court does not regard itself as bound to take up cases in the order in which they appear on the general list or on the session list.[9] For various reasons priority may be given to certain proceedings, though under Article 28 of the 1931 Rules, priority is to be given only "in exceptional circumstances." Article 57 of the 1931 Rules gives "priority over all other cases" to applications for the indication of interim measures of protection, and requires the decision thereon to be "treated as a matter of urgency." [10] Priority may be given to a request for an advisory opinion because the Council in making the request has declared the matter to be urgent.[11] Proceedings with regard to preliminary objections are regarded as urgent,[12] but they are not entitled to priority in every case; [13] in connection with the request for an interpretation of Judgments Nos. 7 and 8, in 1927, it was said that the Court viewed a proceeding for interpretation as special and urgent.[14] Urgency may also result from the nature of the issues involved; [15] this result was said to follow where the applicants waived the privilege of filing a written reply and where the application stated that previous negotiations had proved fruitless. The Court may be specially convened to deal with an urgent matter, and less liberality in the application of the Rules may be shown in urgent cases.

The Chamber for Summary Procedure having been established

---

[6] Series E, No. 6, p. 301. [7] Series E, No. 4, p. 272.

[8] Under the present practice, a general agenda is prepared for each session: Section A consists of cases in the list for the session; Section B of other cases pending before the Court; and Section C of administrative questions.

[9] See Series E, No. 4, p. 272.

[10] The degree of urgency must be determined with reference to the facts of a case. In 1933, the Court was twice convened in extraordinary session to deal with requests for the indication of measures of interim protection; the interval between the date of the filing of the request and the date set for the hearing was in each case eight days; in the second case, however, the hearing was adjourned for eight days, at the request of one of the parties.

[11] Series A/B, No. 43, p. 131; Series C, No. 55, p. 422; Series E, No. 8, p. 250.

[12] Series C, No. 13—I, p. 8; Series E, No. 4, pp. 272, 276.

[13] Series E, No. 9, p. 164.   [14] Series C, No. 13—V, p. 78.

[15] Series E, No. 4, p. 284. The case relating to the *German Minority Schools in Upper Silesia* was regarded as urgent. Series A, No. 15, p. 6. There has been some disposition to say that all cases are urgent. Series D, No. 2 (2d add.), p. 77.

"with a view to the speedy despatch of business," all summary proceedings would seem to possess an urgent character.[16] However, after an extension of time limits at the request of the parties or of one party, it would seem that such a proceeding need not be dealt with urgently.[17]

§490. **Necessity of Oral Proceedings.**[18] Though Article 43 of the Statute provides that "the procedure shall consist of two parts: written and oral," it is not necessary that oral proceedings should be conducted in every case.[19] In a contentious case, the Court's decision to dispense with oral proceedings would doubtless require the acquiescence of the parties. In cases before the Chamber for Summary Procedure, Article 69 of the Rules provides that oral proceedings are to be instituted, in the absence of an agreement to the contrary between the parties, only if the Chamber finds that the documents do not furnish adequate information; in the case relating to the *Interpretation of the Treaty of Neuilly* before the Chamber for Summary Procedure, and later when an interpretation of the judgment in that case was requested, the Court found it unnecessary to institute oral proceedings.[20] In proceedings relating to the interpretation of a judgment, the Court has a free hand in determining whether oral hearings will be held.[21] No oral proceedings were held before the Court issued its order of November 21, 1927, refusing to give effect to the German request for the indication of an interim measure of protection, in the *Chorzów Factory Case.*[22] With respect to the request for interim measures of protection in the case of the *Administration of the Prince of Pless*, the Polish agent "waived the right to a hearing afforded him by Article 57" of the Rules,[23] though that article requires merely that parties be given an opportunity to present observations. In advisory cases, oral proceedings may be dispensed with if no request for them is made by the interested States, though this has occurred in only one case;[24] with respect to the request for an advisory opinion on the *Polish Postal Service in Danzig*, no hearings were held, though the Court had inquired whether Poland and Danzig wished "to furnish

[16] Series E, No. 3, p. 191.
[17] Series E, No. 1, p. 266 (*Interpretation of Treaty of Neuilly*).
[18] See generally Guynat, "*La Procédure Orale devant la Cour Permanente de Justice Internationale,* 37 *Revue Générale de Droit International Public* (1930), p. 312.
[19] This seems to have been recognized by the Court in 1922. Series D, No. 2, p. 140.
[20] Series A, No. 3, p. 5; No. 4, p. 5.   [23] Series A/B, No. 54, p. 152.
[21] Series E, No. 5, p. 260.   [24] Series E, No. 3, p. 224; No. 6, p. 301.
[22] Series A, No. 12, p. 10.

information . . . verbally." On the other hand, the Court may express a desire to have oral hearings; this was done in the case relating to the *Jurisdiction of the Danzig Courts*.[25]

§491. **Nature of Oral Proceedings.** Article 43 of the Statute provides that the oral proceedings shall consist of the hearing by the Court of witnesses, experts, agents, counsel and advocates. Hearings are invariably conducted in public sittings, though Article 46 of the Statute empowers the Court or the parties to decide otherwise. The minutes (Fr., *procès-verbaux*) of such sittings are published under Article 55 of the 1926 Rules; [26] they may vary slightly from the verbatim record (Fr., *compte rendu sténographique*), however. The hearings are under the control of the President or his substitute. Since 1931, the date for the hearings is fixed by the Court, or by the President if the Court is not sitting, when the written proceedings have been terminated. If the Court is unable to fix a definite date, it may require the parties to be at its disposal as from a certain date.[27] Under Article 28 of the 1931 Rules, adjournment of hearings may be granted "in case of need." On several occasions the Court has shown itself reluctant to postpone the date which has been fixed, at any rate for reasons of personal convenience.[28] It is not for the parties to fix the date for hearings in a special agreement.[29] The hearings are conducted in one of the Court's two official languages, an interpretation into the other language being made immediately after each statement.[30] If the use of a third language is authorized for the hearing of agents or counsel, the arrangements for an English or French translation must be made by the party or States concerned, under Article 44 of the Rules.[31]

§492. **Evidence.** In the usage of the Court, the term "evidence" has no very exact meaning. Article 48 of the Statute provides that the Court shall "make all arrangements connected with the taking of evidence" (Fr., *prend toutes les mesures que comporte l'administration des preuves*); and Article 52 refers to the receipt by the Court of

---

[25] Series C, No. 14—I, pp. 9, 548.   [26] In Series C.
[27] Series E, No. 8, p. 264.   [28] Series E, No. 6, p. 301; No. 8, p. 263.
[29] Series E, No. 7, p. 295.
[30] See Series D, No. 2 (add.), p. 108. On the advantages of the interpretation, see Series E, No. 9, p. 163. The interpretation has been dispensed with, as an exceptional measure. Series E, No. 6, p. 289. On March 29, 1933, the Court adopted a resolution to the effect that it would decide in sufficient time before the opening of the oral proceedings in each case whether it is desirable to dispense with oral translations at the public hearings. Series E, No. 9, p. 163.
[31] In such case, it is the translation which is authoritative. Series E, No. 3, p. 201.

"the proofs and evidence" (Fr., *les preuves et témoignages*), and "oral or written evidence" (Fr., *dépositions ou documents*). Various articles of the Rules use the term in different senses and with different French equivalents (Articles 45, 47, 48, 50, 54, 55, 69). It is used to refer both to documents introduced and to testimony taken; and the French equivalents are variously *preuves, témoignage, déposition, documents,* and *moyens de preuve.* The parties are entitled to produce documentary evidence and the oral testimony of witnesses; the conditions set by Article 47 of the Rules are not strictly enforced, and the parties seldom communicate to the Court in advance a list of the documents which they intend to introduce.

The Court has developed no law of evidence comparable to the law of evidence in the Anglo-American system. It is seldom called upon to pronounce on issues of fact; in the case relating to the *Jurisdiction of the European Commission of the Danube,* it accepted the findings of fact by a special committee set up by the League of Nations.[32] In only rare cases has any reference been made to burden of proof.[33] The parties must make statements of the facts in their cases, and additional facts may be stated in counter-cases; indeed, parties are free to present statements concerning the facts at any stage of the written proceedings, and even during the oral proceedings. New evidence may be submitted only so long as the opposite party may offer observations concerning it; Article 52 of the Statute enables the Court to refuse to receive further evidence after the expiration of a time limit or after the closing of the written proceedings.[34] The Rules attempt to guard against any party's being surprised by evidence offered by the other party; thus Article 47 requires that "in sufficient time before the opening of the oral proceedings," each party shall inform the other parties of all evidence it intends to produce, giving the names, addresses and descriptions of the intended witnesses and a general indication of the points to be covered. In summary procedure, under Article 69, the cases and counter-cases must mention the evidence which it is desired to produce, including the names of the witnesses. The Court has power to call upon the parties to produce evidence under Article 48 of the Rules.[35] Challenges of statements of

[32] Series B, No. 14, p. 46.
[33] See Judge Anzilotti's dissent in the *Statute of Memel Case,* Series A/B, No. 49, p. 355; and the *Eastern Greenland Case,* Series A/B, No. 53, p. 49.
[34] Series A/B, No. 61, p. 215; Series E, No. 9, p. 173.
[35] Information must not be requested which would raise a question of law not before the Court. Series E, No. 3, p. 212.

fact are not usual, though under Article 45 of the Rules the parties have the right to comment on the evidence given. Questions have arisen on several occasions, however, as to the Court's reception of particular documents as evidence,[36] and on one occasion the Court has rejected the testimony of a witness because it was not approved by him personally.[37] Affidavits have been received by the Court.[38]

In the *Mavrommatis Case*, counsel for the Greek Government cited a volume of Hansard's Parliamentary Debates; though the British counsel objected that the quotation was not admissible, the Court admitted it, reserving appreciation of the importance to be attached to it.[39] In connection with the advisory opinion on the *Jurisdiction of the European Commission of the Danube*, the Rumanian Government invoked the history of the relevant articles of the Treaty of Versailles; the Court declined to consider this history, "the record of the work preparatory to the adoption of these articles being confidential and not having been placed before the Court by, or with the consent of, the competent authority." [40] In the case concerning the *Jurisdiction of the Oder Commission*, the Polish memorial contained references to *travaux préparatoires* relating to the drafting of the Treaty of Versailles; because of objections contained in the British counter-case, the Court found it necessary to give a decision on the "admissibility as evidence" of the minutes and other documents in question. By an order of August 15, 1929, the parties were invited to submit "their observations and final submissions on this question"; and by an order of August 20, 1929,[41] it was "ruled" that "the Minutes of the Commission on Ports, Waterways and Railways of the Conference which prepared the Treaty of Versailles shall be excluded as evidence from the proceedings in the present case." This was put on the ground that certain of the parties had not been represented at that Conference. In the first phase of the *Free Zones Case*, the Court exercised its discretion under Article 52 of the Statute, and by the order of August 19, 1929, it excluded "as evidence at the present stage of the

---

[36] On the responsibility for the production of secret documents, see Series D, No. 2 (add.), pp. 124–126.

[37] Series C, No. 11, vol. I, p. 36; Series E, No. 3, p. 211.

[38] In the *Mavrommatis Case*, Series C, No. 13—III, pp. 488, 490.

[39] Series C, No. 7—II, pp. 10, 30–33, 95.

[40] Series B, No. 14, p. 32. In this case, the Registrar addressed a letter to the French Minister of Foreign Affairs requesting that the citations be verified and asking for his views on the production of these records. The reply, received after the opinion was given, expressed appreciation of the attitude taken by the Court. Series E, No. 4, p. 288.

[41] Series A, No. 23, p. 41.

case" a volume which had been offered by the Swiss agent in the course of his argument.[42]

In any case, however, the Court remains entirely free to estimate the value of evidence received.[43] Thus, the Court has refused to take account of statements made in direct negotiations between parties which had led to no agreement between them,[44] though these statements had been admitted. On the one occasion when the Court has heard witnesses orally, it gave the parties wide latitude in putting questions, reserving its appreciation of the importance to be attached to the questions put and the replies given.[45] During the oral proceedings the Court may set a time limit for the production of further evidence.

In the *Peter Pázmány University Case,* the Court gave the following indication as to its interpretation of Article 52 of the Statute, as to the presentation of "further oral or written evidence" after the expiration of a "time specified for the purpose": [46]

> According to the Court's previous practice, if there is no special decision fixing the time-limit contemplated by Article 52 of the Statute for the production of new documents, this time-limit has been regarded as expiring upon the termination of the written proceedings; if, after a case is ready for hearing, new documents are produced by one Party, the consent referred to in that Article has been presumed unless the other Party, after receiving copies of such documents, lodges an objection; but in the absence of that Party's consent, the Statute allows the Court to refuse to accept the documents in question but does not oblige it to do so.
>
> In these circumstances, it is desirable that, at the opening of the oral proceedings, the Court should know the views of the two Parties with regard to the intended production of new documents by one of them. For this reason, such an intention should, if possible, be expressed early enough to enable the other Party to intimate, before the hearings, whether it gives or withholds its consent.

§493. **Witnesses.** Article 43 of the Statute envisages the Court's hearing of witnesses as a part of the oral proceedings; Article 51 provides that any relevant questions may be put to witnesses under conditions prescribed in the Rules. These conditions are laid down in Articles 47–55 of the Rules, which have undergone but slight modifica-

---

[42] Series A, No. 22, pp. 14, 21. The volume was submitted at too late a stage of the proceedings. See also Series E, No. 6, p. 297. The same volume was resubmitted in a later phase of the case as an annex to a memorial. Series E, No. 7, p. 294.

[43] Series A, No. 23, p. 42. [45] Series C, No. 11 (vol. 1), pp. 25–37.

[44] Series A, No. 9, p. 19. [46] Series A/B, No. 61, p. 215.

tion since 1922. Before the opening of the oral proceedings, each party
to a contentious proceeding is required to inform the Court and the
other party or parties of evidence which it intends to produce, and of
the names, Christian names, description and residence of the witnesses whom it desires to be heard. Article 52 of the Rules deals with
witnesses "who appear at the instance of the Court" (Fr., *qui se
présentent sur l'invitation de la Cour*). The Court may take the initiative by inviting the parties to call witnesses, possibly to call
particular persons as witnesses; but it has been given no power to
summon witnesses, except as this may be done at the request of a
party, and a summons emanating from the Court must derive its force
from the Government of the State upon whose territory it is to be
served.[47] The consent of the Court is not necessary to a party's
producing a witness.[48]

The examination of witnesses may be conducted before the Court,
or under Article 49 of the Rules, "out of Court"; it is subject to the
limitation set by Article 44 of the Statute, however, if any notices are
to be served. The examination and cross-examination are conducted
by the representatives of the parties under the control of the President,
and questions may be put by the President and afterwards by the
judges. Under Article 45 of the Rules, it is for the Court to say whether
witnesses will be heard before or after the arguments by counsel. When
the examination is concluded, a *verbatim* record of the testimony of
each witness must be read to him, and he is given an opportunity subject to the Court's control to correct mistakes; [49] when approved, the
record is signed by the witness. If the testimony is not in English or
French, a party has the duty of providing the Court with a transla-

[47] In the Mixed Arbitral Tribunals created by the Peace Treaties of 1919 and 1920,
"the problem of obtaining evidence and securing the attendance of witnesses was one of
great difficulty." 12 British Year Book of International Law (1931), p. 138. Few
States seem to have legislation which would enable them to produce witnesses to
testify before the Court, and perhaps an international convention concerning the subpœna of witnesses before international tribunals generally would serve a useful purpose. Instruments creating such tribunals have but rarely dealt with the production of
witnesses; the Boundary Waters Treaty between the United States and Great Britain of
January 11, 1909, contains (Art. 12) such a provision, which has been implemented by
legislation in the United States and Canada. See Chandler P. Anderson, "Production of
Evidence by Subpœna before International Tribunals," 27 American Journal of International Law (1933), p. 498. Recent legislation of the United States is designed to
facilitate the summoning of witnesses in international cases to which the United States is
a party. Law of July 3, 1930, 46 Stat. 1005, as amended by the Law of June 7, 1933,
Session Laws, 1933, p. 117. See Philip C. Jessup, "National Sanctions for International
Tribunals," 20 American Bar Association Journal (1934), p. 55.

[48] See Series D, No. 2, pp. 142–143.

[49] "Only slips may be corrected." Series E, No. 3, p. 208.

tion into one of those languages of the record of the testimony of its witness; where a witness appears at the instance of the Court, the arrangements for translation are made by the Registrar.

The indemnities of witnesses will ordinarily be paid by the party which produces them; if they appear at the instance of the Court, however, the indemnities are to be paid out of the funds of the Court.[50]

§494. **Declarations by Witnesses.** The Statute includes no provision that the witness must take an oath; but Article 50 of the Rules requires a "solemn declaration" (Fr., *engagement solennel*) upon the "honor and conscience" of the witness that he will "speak the truth, the whole truth and nothing but the truth." When this article was adopted, it was agreed that a witness is not obliged by his declaration to violate professional secrecy.[51] This declaration may be made by a witness in a language other than English or French.[52] No declaration is required of interpreters who render the testimony of a witness into English or French. The Court has no power to punish for perjury before it, though such perjury may be punishable under some national law; yet the declaration may serve a useful purpose.

§495. **Practice as to Witnesses.** The Court has been asked to hear witnesses on only one occasion. After arguments had been presented in the case concerning *German Interests in Polish Upper Silesia,* the Court by an order of March 22, 1926, invited the parties to furnish information on certain points "at a public hearing, by whatever means they may think fit." Article 47 of the Rules was applied by analogy, and the parties were later invited to inform the Registrar of the evidence they intended to introduce. The German Government replied that it would call four witnesses, whose names were given; the Polish Government replied that it would call one "expert witness." These witnesses were examined before the Court on April 13–15, 1926.[53] All of the witnesses made solemn declarations on April 13. The German witnesses were first produced, and were examined and cross-examined by the German and Polish agents. When objection was made by the German agent to certain questions put by the Polish agent, the Court reserved "its opinion as to the importance to be attached to the questions put and replies given," but it did not exclude the questions.

---

[50] An item to cover such expense appears in the budget of the Court since 1926. Series E, No. 3, p. 211.   [51] Series D, No. 2, p. 211; Series E, No. 1, p. 264.
[52] Series C, No. 11, vol. 1, p. 28.   [53] *Id.,* pp. 25–37.

On one occasion, however, the President reminded the witnesses that their "evidence given at the present hearing must be entirely confined to matters of fact without entering into questions of the construction of the German-Polish Convention." [54] The President and judges also put questions to the witnesses. When all the witnesses had been heard, the agents were given opportunity to comment on the testimony given. The witnesses were permitted to present documents to the Court. The record of the testimony in French [55] was later communicated to the agents for transmission to the witnesses, and on April 16, 1926, a sitting of the Court was devoted to a reading of this record; each witness was given an opportunity to make observations when his testimony was read, and he then signed the record in the presence of the Court.[56] One witness who was unable to be present had empowered the agent who produced him to approve the record of his testimony, and this was allowed, with a reservation as to the Court's appreciation of the value to be attached to the testimony; subsequently on April 21, 1926, the testimony of this witness was "set aside" because it had been approved only by proxy.[57]

§496. **Experts.** The Statute envisages several distinct uses which may be made of experts by the Court. Its most important provision is that in Article 50, which provides that the Court may entrust any individual or organization "with the task of carrying out an enquiry or giving an expert opinion"; under this, experts might be asked to conduct an enquiry, or they might be asked merely to give an opinion.[58] Under Article 43 of the Statute, the agents of the parties may produce experts to be heard as such and not as witnesses,[59] but in no case to date has this been done; [60] possibly the Court might direct that it be done under Article 49 of the Statute. Article 51 of the Statute envisages the examination of experts, but in the Rules the Court has not laid down any conditions for this examination. The Rules (Article 53) deal only with the report or record (Fr., *procès-verbal*) of an enquiry

---

[54] Series C, No. 11, Vol. 1, p. 31.

[55] The French translation was considered as the authoritative record, though the witnesses spoke in German or in Polish. Series E, No. 3, p. 201.

[56] For the form of signature, see Series C, No. 11, Vol. 1, p. 317.

[57] Series E, No. 3, p. 211. The documents published in Series C do not indicate that this action was notified to the parties; nor is the action referred to in the judgment.

[58] In several cases the parties have presented to the Court opinions of lawyers as experts. *E.g.*, Series C, No. 3 (vol. 2), pp. 121, 134ff.; No. 3 (vol. 3), pp. 442ff.; 644; No. 7—I, p. 226; No. 13—II, p. 350; No. 14—I, pp. 166, 272, 287. *Cf.*, Series E, No. 2, p. 168. In one case the opinion was not signed.   [59] Series E, No. 3, p. 213.

[60] In the case relating to *German Interests in Polish Upper Silesia*, the Polish agent produced an "expert witness."

under Article 50 of the Statute, and with reports furnished by experts in accordance with the same article. Article 43 of the Statute may be applied by analogy in advisory proceedings; in one such proceeding the Court expressed a willingness to hear experts.[61]

§497. **Expert Enquiries.** The Court has instituted but one enquiry under Article 50 of the Statute. On September 13, 1928, it decided by order "that an expert enquiry shall be held with a view to enabling the Court to fix, with a full knowledge of the facts," the amount of the indemnity to be paid by the Polish Government to the German Government in accordance with a judgment in the *Chorzów Factory Case.* This enquiry was entrusted to a committee of three experts, each of the parties being given the right to appoint an assessor to take part in the work "in an advisory capacity." The order required of the experts and assessors a solemn declaration to discharge their duties "honorably and faithfully, impartially and conscientiously" and to abstain from divulging or turning to their own use any secrets of an economic or technical nature disclosed to them in the course of the enquiry. The report of the committee was to "contain the reasoned opinion in regard to each question put of each member of the committee"; it was to come before the Court at a public sitting which the experts were to be summoned to attend, to enable the agents of the parties to discuss the report and to enable the Court and the agents to ask the experts for explanations. The expenses were to be borne by the Court and to be refunded by the parties, who were to pay the assessors directly; the parties were invited to make deposits with the Registrar for this purpose, and such deposits were made.[62] The experts were appointed by the President, by order, on October 16, 1928.[63] On November 10, 1928, the experts and assessors met with the President and were installed in their functions after making the required declarations. After hearing the views of the experts, the President by order fixed a date for the filing of their report.[64] The Committee of Experts held five meetings, November 10–12, 1928; [65] it formulated questions for the assessors,[66] and decided upon a visit to certain factories, for which authorization was to be sought from the Governments concerned. On December 15, 1928, in consequence of the settlement of

---

[61] Series C, No. 12, pp. 12, 287–288.   [62] Part of each deposit was later refunded.
[63] Series A, No. 17, p. 99; Series C, No. 16—II, p. 12.
[64] Series C, No. 16—II, p. 14.
[65] For the *procès-verbaux*, see Series C, No. 16—II, pp. 17–24.
[66] The questions appear in German in Series C, No. 16—II, p. 21.

the dispute, the President by order [67] terminated the enquiry and dissolved the Committee of Experts.

Both the French Government and the Swiss Government requested that an expert enquiry be undertaken in the *Free Zones Case,* but the Court did not give effect to the request.[68]

§498. **Hearing of Agents, Counsel and Advocates.** The most important part of the oral proceedings is usually the hearing of agents or counsel, or both agents and counsel. Under Article 45 of the Rules, it is for the Court to determine whether arguments will be heard before or after the presentation of evidence. Under Article 46 of the Rules, the order in which arguments are to be presented is determined, failing any agreement between the parties, by the Court. If a case is before the Court under a special agreement, and if no contrary arrangement is made by the parties, the Court will call upon agents or counsel in the alphabetical order [69] of the names of the States which are parties; [70] but the alphabetical order may be varied if it would result in the presentation of argument on behalf of several parties in the same interest both before and after the presentation of argument on behalf of a party in opposing interest.[71] If a case arises on application, the agent or counsel for the applicant precedes the agent or counsel for the respondent in presenting oral arguments. If the Court is considering a preliminary objection, argument for the State offering the objection will be heard before argument for the applicant.[72] Representatives of a State applying for an indication of interim measures will be heard first, unless the parties agree upon a different order; [73] this is true also of a State which seeks the seating of a judge *ad hoc.*

Oral replies and rejoinders may also be made by agents or counsel. While agents or counsel have a very free rein in presenting arguments, the Court has frequently said that they should come before it "fully prepared to argue the case." The statement that "the reading of

---

[67] Series A, No. 18/19, p. 14. On the fees paid to the experts, see Series C, No. 16—II, p. 57.

[68] Series A/B, No. 46, p. 162. Article 4 of the special agreement in this case provided that either party might request the Court "to delegate one or three of its members for the purposes of conducting investigations on the spot and of hearing the evidence of any interested persons." *Id.,* p. 99. This could hardly have imposed any limitation on the Court, however, and the Court refused to interpret the provision to mean "that it would be bound in any event to comply with such a request." *Id.,* p. 163.

[69] This may be the French or the English alphabetical order, depending on the language in which the proceedings are conducted.

[70] Series C, No. 13—II, p. 10; No. 17—I, p. 10.

[71] Series C, No. 17—II, p. 10. *Cf.,* Series E, No. 8, p. 266.

[72] Series C, No. 13—I, p. 11; No. 13—III, p. 10. On the order, with reference to a preliminary question, see Series E, No. 8, p. 265.   [73] Series E, No. 9, p. 171.

prepared written statements is contrary to the principle underlying oral proceedings," [74] does not seem to be a proper limitation, in view of the fact that agents or counsel may have to speak in a language which is not too familiar to them. Some reluctance has been shown in granting requests for time for the preparation of arguments, after the hearings have been begun. Agents or counsel may be permitted to correct errors in the record of their arguments.[75]

In advisory proceedings, where there is no applicant and no respondent, Article 46 of the Rules is applied by analogy.[76] The States appearing may agree upon the order of their presentations in the oral proceedings.[77] Failing an agreement, the Court applies the alphabetical order; [78] while this has been said to be an "inviolable rule," [79] the alphabetical order may be varied if there is no objection.[80] States which are directly concerned may be heard before other States, also.[81] As to international organizations, no clear rule is discernible as to the order of their presentations.[82]

§499. **Languages in Oral Proceedings.** Under Article 39 of the Statute, agents and counsel are free to employ either English or French in their "pleadings," *i.e.*, in their statements or arguments before the Court, in the absence of an agreement between the parties that one of these languages is to be employed; special agreements frequently contain stipulations on this point. At the request of the parties,[83] also, the Court may authorize a language other than English or French to be employed; in this case, however, under Article 44 of the Rules, the party concerned must make the necessary arrangements for a translation into one of the Court's official languages.

§500. **Questions to Agents and Counsel.** In the course of oral proceedings, the President or judges of the Court may put questions to agents or counsel, but the Court has shown a surprising reluctance in this regard, and in its earlier years its discouragement of questions must have added to the dullness of the hearings. For some reason not easily comprehensible, concern seems to have been felt lest ques-

---

[74] Series E, No. 6, p. 296.
[75] Series E, No. 6, p. 293. See also Series E, No. 7, p. 294.
[76] Series C, No. 14—I, p. 10; No. 15—I, p. 10; No. 52, p. 106; No. 53, p. 188.
[77] Series C, No. 56, p. 227; Series E, No. 9, p. 171.
[78] Series C, No. 7—I, p. 9.   [79] Series C, No. 13—IV, p. 10.
[80] Series C, No. 53, p. 193. The Court has refused to vary this order, even where "weighty reasons" existed for a variance. Series E, No. 8, p. 266.
[81] Series E, No. 3, p. 207.   [82] See Series E, No. 3, p. 207; No. 8, p. 265.
[83] The new text of Article 39 of the Statute, annexed to the Revision Protocol of September 14, 1929, reads "at the request of any party." See §213, *supra*.

tions might lead to some embarrassment.[84] Latterly, more latitude has been allowed in this respect. It was agreed in an advisory proceeding at the Court's 18th session, in 1930, (1) that the questions addressed to agents should be put in the name of the Court; (2) that they should be communicated beforehand to agents of interested States and representatives of interested organizations; (3) that they should be embodied in an order.[85] Beginning with the 20th session, however, more liberality has been shown. It seems to have been agreed, in 1931, that the questions need not be put in the name of the Court, that the judges putting the questions and the President should agree upon a precise formulation, and that questions should be unofficially communicated to the agents in advance.[86] When certain matters of practice were formulated in 1931, it was stated that after giving notice to the President, the judges might put questions to a pleader "in the course of the hearings and before or after each translation"; that the President might give his assent or ask that the question be postponed; that questions ought to refer exclusively to the actual content of the argument; [87] and that the pleader should be given opportunity to postpone his reply if he considered it necessary. Questions on which the judges are in general agreement are still put in the name of the Court.[88] In recent cases, questions have been addressed to agents with some freedom,[89] and occasionally questions have been addressed to counsel.[90] In 1931, the President gave permission to certain judges to put questions to agents in an advisory proceeding; but the agents were reminded that they need not reply immediately,[91] and notice of the questions was given in advance. For the purpose of allowing questions even after the termination of the hearing of counsel, the closure of the oral proceedings is not pronounced immediately.

§501. **Closure of Oral Proceedings.** Under Article 54 of the Statute, the President must declare the hearing closed when agents, counsel and advocates have completed their presentation of the case. "In order to reserve the Court's right to put questions to the parties should it desire to do so," [92] however, the President frequently refrains

[84] Series E, No. 8, pp. 262–263.
[85] Series E, No. 7, p. 301. For the text of such an order, see Series C, No. 18—I, p. 1077.
[86] Series E, No. 8, p. 263.
[87] Series D, No. 2 (2d add.), p. 300.
[88] Series E, No. 8, p. 262.
[89] Series C, No. 52, p. 107; No. 53, pp. 196; No. 54, p. 305; No. 58, p. 335.
[90] Series C, No. 53, p. 481; No. 55, pp. 304, 377.
[91] Series E, No. 7, p. 296.
[92] This does not mean that the parties may produce further evidence as of right, and the Court may require the consent of all parties. Series E, No. 3, p. 213.

from declaring the closure of the oral proceedings, even when the hearings are concluded;[93] since 1925, this has become the common practice. In such a case, the declaration of closure is made when the Court's deliberations have progressed sufficiently to indicate that no further information is needed.[94] The President does not embody the declaration in an order; the parties are informed of the closure by letter of the Registrar.[95] After the declaration of closure, the Court may reopen the oral proceedings;[96] it has on occasion refused to do so, however.[97]

[93] *E.g.*, Series C, No. 11, p. 23. [94] Series E, No. 4, p. 290.
[95] See, *e.g.*, Series C, No. 60, p. 271. [96] Series E, No. 7, p. 301.
[97] Series C, No. 5—II, p. 381; Series E, No. 3, p. 214.

CHAPTER 26

PRACTICE OF THE COURT

§502. **Meaning of the Term "Practice."** The term "practice" is here used to denote the methods followed within the Court itself for determining on the action which is taken by the Court as a body. The internal procedure of the Court is to be distinguished from the procedure followed before the Court, and it is for the most part not covered either by the Statute or the Rules. In 1922, a proposal that the Court should draw up separate *rules of court* as distinguished from *rules of procedure* was not adopted; [1] in 1931, however, a distinction was clearly drawn between the Rules and the practice of the Court. [2]

§503. **Preliminary Examination of Acts of Procedure.** Before any hearing is held, it is incumbent on the members of the Court to make a study of the acts of procedure and any documents filed. [3] A "preliminary exchange of views" may take place before the hearing. [4] This seems to be envisaged in Article 49 of the Statute, for only after such an exchange could the Court call for explanations. On February 20, 1931, the Court formulated the practice as follows: [5] "After the closure of the written procedure, and before the opening of the oral debates, the judges shall meet in council chamber [Fr., *Chambre du Conseil*] to exchange their views on the elements of the written procedure and to note the points concerning which, the case arising, it would be desirable to call for complementary verbal explanations." The preliminary discussion of a case does not constitute a part of the Court's deliberation properly so called. [6]

§504. **Deliberations Subsequent to the Hearings.** Article 54 of the Statute refers to the deliberations of the Court following the presentation by agents and counsel, [7] and provides that they "shall

---

[1] Series D, No. 2, pp. 103, 105.
[2] Series D, No. 2 (2d add.), pp. 218ff.
[3] Series D, No. 2 (2d add.), p. 216.
[4] Series E, No. 8, p. 263.
[5] Series D, No. 2 (2d add.), p. 300.
[6] Series E, No. 6, p. 298.

[7] On one occasion, the deliberations on a case were postponed until after the hearings in another case. Series E, No. 6, p. 298.

take place in private and remain secret." [8] Besides the members of the Court, only the Registrar or Deputy-Registrar [9] is admitted to be present during the deliberations, unless by a special decision taken in exceptional circumstances the Court decides otherwise.[10] Under Article 31 of the Rules, "every member of the Court who is present at the deliberation shall state his opinion together with the reasons on which it is based." The method of conducting these deliberations has been and continues to be in an experimental stage, and the judges have hesitated to commit themselves to any definite lines of procedure. The matter was considered in drafting the 1922 Rules, and it was then decided to include no provision for the appointment of a *rapporteur;* it was agreed that "the utmost possible freedom should be retained by the Court." [11] In the earlier years, no stages were prescribed for the deliberations. At the Court's first session, a *rapporteur* was designated after the oral discussion; under the later practice, a drafting committee of three members, two being elected by secret ballot, has usually been set up. It was the desire of members of the Court to have records of their statements in the oral discussions which led to a system of preparing and circulating notes.

The practice became quite regular [12] that, following the conclusion of the hearings, the members of the Court would meet for a preliminary exchange of views; then each member would prepare a written note setting forth his provisional opinion, and these notes would be simultaneously distributed; a schedule (*schéma*) of the questions raised in these notes was then made by the President, and it became the basis of the further discussions, being taken up point by point; following the discussions, a drafting committee would be elected, consisting of the President and two members elected by secret ballot; [13] suggestions on and amendments to the report of this drafting committee were then prepared by each member of the Court, which with the report were considered in plenary session point by point; a

---

[8] The Court deliberates *en Chambre du Conseil.* On the method of deliberation in the earlier years, see Å. Hammarskjöld, "Sidelights on the Permanent Court of International Justice," 25 Michigan Law Review (1927), pp. 327, 331. The results of the deliberations, as distinguished from the deliberations themselves, are made public. Series E, No. 6, p. 295.

[9] In practice, both the Registrar and the Deputy-Registrar may be present.

[10] A decision has been taken to admit interpreters. Series E, No. 3, p. 25.

[11] Series D, No. 2, p. 305. [12] Series E, No. 4, p. 290.

[13] In 1932, the Court held that a judge of the nationality of one of the parties should not be a member of the drafting committee. Series E, No. 8, p. 269. The Registrar takes part in the work of the drafting committee. Instructions for Registry (Article 3).

final draft of the judgment or opinion was then prepared by the drafting committee and offered for the Court's approval; a rendition of this draft into the other of the Court's official languages was also offered for approval by the Court.[14] While it has been agreed that members are not committed by preliminary votes or expressions, the psychological effect of formulating a position leads to a danger that once ideas have been expressed they will become fixed and difficult to change.[15]

In the *Chorzów Factory Case*, it was agreed at the preliminary discussion that the President should prepare a list of preliminary questions to be considered, to guide the members in drafting their notes; two series of notes, one on questions of principle and one on questions of application, were then presented and a second preliminary discussion was held.[16] In 1928, in connection with the advisory opinion on the *Greco-Turkish Agreement,* no preliminary discussion was held.[17] In 1929, it was held that as the preliminary discussion "did not constitute a part of the Court's deliberation properly so-called," it might be conducted in the temporary absence of a judge; [18] the presence of judges *ad hoc* at the deliberations is necessary, however. On one occasion in 1932, notes expressing provisional opinions were dispensed with.[19]

§505. **Formulation of the Court's Practice in 1931.** In 1931, the practice of the Court was carefully studied,[20] and on February 20, 1931, the Court decided "to complete provisionally its existing practice by the following": [21]

(1) After the closure of the written procedure, and before the opening of the oral debates, the judges shall meet in council chamber (Fr., *en Chambre du Conseil*) to exchange their views on the elements of the written procedure and to note the points concerning which, the case arising, it would be desirable to call for complementary verbal explanations.

(2) In the course of the hearings and before or after each translation, questions may be put to the pleader by the judges individually after notice has been given to the President.

---

[14] More recently, the non-authoritative versions are not verified by the full Court. Series E, No. 6, p. 289.

[15] Series D, No. 2 (2d add.), p. 218.

[16] The usual summary by the President was not made in this case. Series E, No. 5, p. 259.

[17] *Ibid.*   [18] Series E, No. 6, p. 298.   [19] Series E, No. 8, p. 269.

[20] Series D, No. 2 (2d add.), pp. 218–226, 231–251, 267–268.

[21] *Id.*, pp. 300–301. The translation is by the writer.

The questions ought to refer exclusively to the actual content of the argument.

The President may either give his assent or he may ask the judge interested to postpone his question.

It shall be pointed out to counsel that he has the freedom of delaying his response if he should deem it necessary.

(3) After the hearings, a period appropriate to the nature of the case shall be given to the judges for a study of the oral presentations of the parties.

(4) At the expiration of this period, a deliberation shall take place, conducted by the President, with a view to a common examination of the matter as it has been presented to the Court, and for the purpose of selecting the questions to be resolved and of discussing them. The President shall make sure that all the questions raised either by himself or by the judges have been discussed, and that each judge has made known his view with regard to them.

(5) Following this deliberation and within an appropriate period, each judge shall give his personal point of view in writing in the form of a note, without stating his definitive opinion.

(6) Having regard to the notes of the respective judges, the President shall elaborate and submit to the appreciation of the Court a plan of discussion, determining provisionally the order and position of questions on which the Court ought to pronounce.

The adoption of this plan shall not affect the right of judges in any stage of the proceedings to ask the Court to pronounce itself on any question, and in any form that they may deem desirable, nor the freedom of the Court itself to determine at a later time the modifications which it may deem desirable in the order of the discussion and the position of the questions.

(7) In the subsequent and final deliberation, each question is discussed, put to vote by the President, and resolved.

(8) On the basis of the votes cast by a majority of the judges at the time of the final deliberation, the preparation of a draft of the decision is to be confided to a committee composed of the President and two judges, chosen by the Court by secret ballot and by absolute majority.

(9) The editing of the draft decision shall be examined by the Court and decided upon.

It was later decided that this formulation should not be published in the annual report, further consideration and experience being needed.[22] Nor has the Court since followed the formulation strictly, though complete information on this point has not been published.

[22] Series E, No. 7, p. 297.

§506. **Voting.** Article 55 of the Statute provides that "all questions shall be decided by a majority of the judges present at the hearing" (the French version omits "at the hearing"); in practice this rule is applied at all sittings of the Court. Article 31 of the Rules states that a decision "shall be based upon the conclusions adopted after final discussion by a majority of the members." The order of voting is inverse to the order of precedence. On the request of any member of the Court the question to be voted on must be drawn up in precise terms, in both English and French, and distributed in advance. It has been held by the Court that judges are obliged to take part in all the votes on questions for judgment or advisory opinion,[23] and this applies both to the operative part and to the grounds thereof; [24] for a final decision on a case, nine judges must be present and voting.[25] The final vote covers the whole of the judgment or opinion; [26] it applies both to the reasons and to the operative part. Under Article 62 of the Rules, each judgment or opinion must mention the number of the judges constituting the majority; this is not true of orders, however.[27] "In the event of an equality of votes," the President has a "casting vote"; in practice this means an additional and decisive vote.[28] This power of the President has been exercised in the final adoption of a judgment only in the *Lotus Case;* but it has frequently been exercised as to points in the discussion, both in open and in secret ballots.[29] The President has usually, though not invariably,[30] given his casting vote in the same sense as his original vote.[31]

§507. **Order of Giving Opinions.** In deliberations of the Court, as well as in the reading of individual opinions at a public session, members of the Court deliver their opinions in the inverse order of precedence,[32] the order of precedence being that provided for in Article 2 of the Rules.

§508. **Separate and Dissenting Opinions.** Judgments and opinions are given in the name of the Court; they are sealed, and are signed

---

[23] Series E, No. 3, p. 188. See also Minutes of the 1929 Committee of Jurists, p. 65.
[24] Series E, No. 9, p. 174.   [25] See §375, *supra.*
[26] A Polish law of October 27, 1932, on the Supreme Administrative Court, provides (Article 82) that a judge whose opinion on a given point has been rejected by a previous vote is bound to take part in the deliberations and votes on other points, subordinating his opinion to the decisions previously taken. *Dziennik Ustaw, 1932, Poz.* 806.

[27] While the nature of the majority is not indicated in the introduction to the operative part of the order, in some cases a paragraph is inserted after the order indicating the names of judges who dissent. Series E, No. 6, p. 295.

[28] For a discussion of this point, see §377, *supra.*

[29] However, in 1931 a provision for a casting vote by the President in the election of the Registrar was deleted from Article 17 of the Rules, as "incompatible with a secret ballot." Series E, No. 7, p. 281.   [30] Series E, No. 3, p. 216; No. 6, p. 299.

[31] Series E, No. 7, p. 298; No. 9, p. 174.   [32] Series E, No. 3, p. 215.

by the President or acting President [33] and by the Registrar or his deputy. Article 57 of the Statute provides that if a judgment "does not represent in whole or in part the unanimous opinion of the judges, dissenting judges are entitled to deliver a separate opinion" (Fr., *opinion individuelle*). Article 62 of the 1922 Rules provided that the opinions of dissenting judges should be attached to the judgment, if such judges expressed a desire to that effect; in 1926, this was changed to a provision that "dissenting judges may, if they so desire, attach to the judgment either an exposition of their individual opinion or the statement of their dissent." [34] Article 71 of the Rules, as amended in 1926, contains a similar provision for dissenting opinions to be attached to advisory opinions. In the *Free Zones Case* dissenting opinions were allowed to be attached to an order for the first time; and in the case of the *Austro-German Customs Régime,* they were attached to an order concerning the admission of judges *ad hoc*.[35] In the earlier years, dissenting opinions were allowed to be attached to the minutes of private sittings of the Court, without being published; [36] this is now precluded by the last paragraph of Article 31 of the 1926 Rules which requires any judge who desires to set forth his individual opinion, to do so in accordance with Article 57 of the Statute. Nothing in the Rules requires a disclosure of the name of a dissenting judge; [37] though four judges voted against the adoption of the Court's opinion on *Danzig and the International Labor Organization,* the names of only three dissenting judges were stated.[38] In some cases, several judges have combined in a joint dissenting opinion, a practice which has been criticized and which is hardly in accord with the English version of Article 57 of the Statute. Separate or dissenting opinions may be read or summarized in open court; but this is optional with the judge concerned.[39] Separate opinions are sometimes published as "observations," or "declarations."

It has been said that dissenting opinions are "not intended to be a reasoned criticism of the judgment or opinion," and that they "are

---

[33] In one case by both. Series E, No. 8, p. 270.

[34] The President shares this privilege with the other judges, and his signature of a judgment or opinion does not indicate that he agrees with the majority. The President has rarely dissented, however.

[35] Series A/B, No. 41, p. 91. This was regarded as exceptional, however.

[36] Series E, No. 3, p. 217.

[37] The number of the votes for the adoption of a judgment or opinion must be stated, however.

[38] Series B, No. 18, pp. 16–17. For a criticism of this practice, see Series D, No. 2 (2d add.), p. 294.   [39] Series E, No. 4, p. 292.

designed solely to set forth the reasons for which judges do not feel able to accept the opinion of the Court"; [40] but it would be difficult to say that this limitation has been respected in practice. It is clearly desirable that the majority should be acquainted with the views expressed in dissenting opinions before the final text of a judgment or opinion is adopted; hence, on February 17, 1928, the Court formally decided that, failing a contrary decision "in exceptional circumstances, the time for the submission of dissenting opinions shall be fixed after the first reading of the draft judgment or opinion so as to cause the presentation of dissenting opinions to coincide with the presentation of the draft judgment or opinion as prepared for second reading." [41] All judges are thus informed of the contents of dissenting opinions before the final vote is taken.

§509. **Minutes of Private Sittings.** Under Article 31 of the 1926 Rules, the confidential minutes of private meetings for deliberation upon judgments or advisory opinions are not detailed, but record the subject of the debates, the votes of each of the judges, and "statements expressly made for insertion in the minutes." [42] The Court has experimented with a system of skeleton minutes, supplemented by an unofficial schedule of votes and decisions which would be destroyed at the end of the session; but this system was short-lived.[43] Minutes of deliberations on administrative matters do not necessarily have to be kept secret, and the Court has published its minutes relating to the drafting of the Rules.[44] Each member of the Court is allowed to correct the minutes before their approval.[45]

§510. **Texts of Judgments and Opinions.** Under Article 39 of the Statute, if the parties have agreed to conduct a case in one of the Court's two official languages, the Court's judgment must be delivered in that language; [46] failing any such agreement, the judgment must be given in English and French. The judgments in the *Lotus Case* and the *Brazilian Loans Case* were drawn up in French, and English

---

[40] *Id.,* p. 291. Judge Anzilotti has expressed the view that "a dissenting opinion should not be a criticism of that which the Court has seen fit to say, but rather an exposition of the views of the writer." Series B, No. 18, p. 18.

[41] Series E, No. 4, p. 291.   [42] But see Series E, No. 8, p. 269.

[43] *Id.,* pp. 269–270.

[44] Series D, No. 2; No. 2 (add.); No. 2 (2d add.); Series E, No. 4, pp. 73–78. A verbatim record of the deliberations in connection with the preparation of the Rules in 1922 was also prepared and filed, but not published. Series E, No. 3, p. 215.

[45] Series E, No. 7, p. 298.

[46] The special agreement in the *Brazilian Loans Case* provided that both the procedure and the judgment should be in French. Series C, No. 16—IV, p. 146. The special agreement in the *Lotus Case* contained a similar provision.

translations were attached; but the translations were not officially approved by the Court.[47] Where the judgment is in two languages, the Court must say which of the two is authoritative; this determination will depend both on the language used before the Court and on the history of the drafting of the judgment.[48] In practice, equality of the two languages does not exist.[49] Of twenty judgments delivered, two have been in French, with English translations; eighteen have been in English and French, in only two of which was the English version made authoritative.[50] Each judgment is "done" in a number of originals, of which one is placed at the disposal of each of the parties.

In advisory proceedings, it seems that a decision to apply Article 39 of the Statute by analogy has been avoided, and in view of the bilingual practice of the Council of the League of Nations effort has been made to give effect to the equality of the two languages. Of twenty-five advisory opinions rendered to date, all have been in English and French, the English version being authoritative in twelve and the French version in thirteen cases. In the advisory opinion on the *Jurisdiction of the European Commission of the Danube,* the English version was made authoritative, though most of the proceedings had been conducted in French.[51]

Judgments, orders and opinions of the Courts are signed by the President and the Registrar, for the purpose of giving to them legal force.

§511. Publication of Judgments, Orders and Opinions. Every precaution is taken by the Court to guard the secrecy of judgments and opinions until they are read in open Court.[52] It is the general practice to send sealed copies of judgments and opinions to the Secretary-General of the League of Nations in advance, so that they will be in his hands on the day of the reading in open Court; as to advisory

[47] Series A, No. 10, p. 32; No. 20/21, p. 126. See also Series E, No. 4, p. 278; No. 6, p. 289. This was not true in the *Lighthouses Case* in 1934, however.

[48] In general, where a judgment or opinion is drawn up in one language the version in that language will be made authoritative.

[49] In the oral hearings, translations from one of the official languages into the other have been provided. On March 29, 1933, however, the Court adopted a resolution to the effect that it would decide in sufficient time before the opening of the oral proceedings in each case whether it is desirable to dispense with oral translations at the public hearings. See §491, *supra.*

[50] See Lord Finlay's letter in Series C, No. 16—III, p. 797.

[51] Series E, No. 4, p. 277.

[52] Forecasts of the division in the Court in the case of the *Austro-German Customs Régime* were remarkably accurate, however.

opinions this is required by Article 74 of the 1926 Rules, the object being to avoid giving publicity to an opinion before it is available to the Council or Assembly which requested it.[53] With reference to certain judgments concerning financial interests, the general practice was not followed, however.[54] The publication of judgments and opinions follows their being read in open Court, the 1931 Rules providing for publication in a single series.[55] Certain orders are published in the same series, but orders which are merely interlocutory, such as orders fixing time-limits, are commonly published only in Series C. All the orders have not been promptly published.[56]

§512. **Termination of Proceedings.** Proceedings before the Court may be terminated as a consequence of the agreement of the parties to that effect, as provided in Article 61 of the Rules. Thus the parties may cancel the effect of a special agreement, or an application may be withdrawn. In consequence of events, also, an application may cease to have any object, and the action of the Court may be confined to a declaration to this effect. Termination is formally effected by an order issued by the Court, and the parties may or may not be heard in connection with this order.[57] The order also directs the removal of the case from the Court's general list.

[53] The envelope containing the text is opened only on receipt by the Secretary-General of telegraphic notice of the publication at The Hague.

[54] Series E, No. 6, p. 299. See also, Series C, No. 16—III, p. 831.

[55] Series A and Series B were combined into Series A/B in 1931. Until that time, the judgments and opinions bore serial numbers.

[56] The Court's order of July 20, 1931, relating to the admission of judges *ad hoc* in the case of the *Austro-German Customs Régime* was not published until September 5, 1931, though the conclusion was made public without delay.

[57] Series E, No. 9, p. 175. When the Council's request for an advisory opinion on the *Expulsion of the Œcumenical Patriarch* was withdrawn, no order was issued.

PART VI

THE APPLICATION OF LAW BY THE PERMANENT COURT OF INTERNATIONAL JUSTICE

CHAPTER 27

THE LAW APPLICABLE BY THE COURT

§513. **Application of International Law.** The Court is directed by Article 38 of the Statute to "apply" four categories of legal materials. The text is clumsily drafted, and the direction is not altogether clear. The four sub-paragraphs seem to list sources of the law to be applied, rather than statements of the law itself,[1] and the list of sources cannot be taken to be exhaustive.[2] The 1920 Committee of Jurists explained that this article was based on Article 7 of the International Prize Court Convention of October 18, 1907, which provided that in the absence of treaty provisions the International Prize Court "should apply the rules of international law," and that "if no generally recognized rule exists" judgment should be given "in accordance with the general principles of justice and equity." Yet the Committee of Jurists purposely refrained from going so far, refusing to give "such an unrestricted field to the decisions of the Court"; [3] this attitude was partly due to the proposal to confer on the Court a general obligatory jurisdiction.[4] The result is that Article 38 does not expressly state

---

[1] This seems to have been recognized by the Court in the opinion on the *Jurisdiction of the European Commission of the Danube,* where it referred to a convention as "the first source" of law to be applied. Series B, No. 14, p. 22.

[2] On the sources of international law, see the dissenting opinion of Judge Weiss, in the *Lotus Case,* Series A, No. 10, pp. 43–44.

The list of sources in Article 38 of the Statute has had a wide influence on international jurisprudence. It was adopted with some additions by the German-American Mixed Claims Commission, in its Administrative Decision No. 2, in 1923. See Hudson, Cases on International Law, p. 1280. It was followed by the German-Portuguese special tribunal in 1928 (*The Maziua and Naulilaa Cases*). 8 *Recueil des Décisions des Tribunaux Arbitraux Mixtes,* 409, 412; Annual Digest, 1927–1928, Case No. 317. The list has also been incorporated into numerous arbitration treaties of recent years. See, *e.g.,* Article 19 of the Polish-Czechoslovak treaty of April 23, 1925, 48 League of Nations Treaty Series, p. 383; Article 2 of the Danish-German treaty of June 2, 1926, 61 *id.,* p. 325; Article 5 of the German-Estonian treaty of August 10, 1925, 63 *id.,* p. 111; Article 1 of the General Treaty of Inter-American Arbitration of January 5, 1929, 4 Hudson, International Legislation, p. 2627.

[3] Minutes of the 1920 Committee of Jurists, p. 729.

[4] *Id.,* pp. 294, 308ff.

that the Court shall apply international law, and the omission of such a provision is the more surprising because of the reference in Article 36 to "any question of international law." Yet it must be clear that the Court is to apply international law. This may be rested on the direction to the Court to apply "the general principles of law recognized by civilized nations"; but independently of any explicit provision in the Statute, the very nature of the Court compels it to apply international law. Article 14 of the Covenant of the League of Nations envisaged a court competent to "hear and determine any dispute of an international character," and as States are the parties before the Court it must necessarily apply international law as the law by which their relations are governed.

On numerous occasions the Court has sought a rule or principle of international law to be applied,[5] and it has consistently conceived itself to be bound to apply international law. In the judgment on *German Interests in Polish Upper Silesia*, it spoke of itself as the "organ" of international law, and in the *Brazilian Loans Case*, as "a tribunal of international law."[6] In the judgment in the *Serbian Loans Case*, it was said that "from a general point of view, it must be admitted that the true function of the Court is to decide disputes between States or Members of the League of Nations on the basis of international law: Article 38 of the Statute contains a clear indication to this effect."[7] Almost all the cases before the Court have required the interpretation of a treaty, and the Court has held that this "involves a question of international law."[8]

The international law which the Court is to apply would seem to be that law which is "in force between all independent nations."[9] The nature of this law was stated in the *Lotus Case* too restrictively: "International law governs relations between independent States. The rules of law binding upon States therefore emanate from their own free will as expressed in conventions or by usages generally accepted as expressing principles of law and established in order to regulate

---

[5] Series A, No. 2, p. 28; No. 7, p. 42; No. 9, p. 21; No. 17, p. 28; Series B, No. 4, pp. 24, 28; No. 5, p. 27; No. 15, p. 24; Series A/B, No. 44, pp. 24, 25.

[6] Series A, No. 7, p. 19; Nos. 20/21, p. 124. *Cf.*, Series A/B, No. 46, p. 138.

[7] Series A, No. 20/21, p. 19. See also *id.*, p. 79. *Cf.*, Articles 15 (1899), 37 (1907) of the Hague Conventions for Pacific Settlement, stating that international arbitration has for its object the settlement of disputes "on the basis of respect for law."

[8] Series B, No. 10, p. 17.

[9] *Lotus Case*, Series A, No. 10, p. 17. In a dissenting opinion in the *Mavrommatis Concessions Case*, Judge Altamira insisted that "law is not an abstract or merely speculative science," but "a practical force which reacts on human life, and generally with a view to the achievement of practical aims." Series A, No. 11, p. 45.

the relations between these co-existing independent communities or with a view to the achievement of common aims." [10] Yet the Court has shown some disposition to appreciate that international law is not a static body of inspired doctrine, and that its content may change from century to century or from generation to generation; [11] as it was put by Judge Nyholm in the *Lotus Case*, "international law is liable to continual variations." [12]

§514. **International Conventions.** The Court is directed to "apply," *i.e.*, to take as a source of international law, "international conventions, whether general or particular, establishing rules expressly recognized by the contesting States." The term "conventions" is used in Article 38, as in Article 63 of the Statute,[13] in an inclusive sense, and it would seem to apply to any treaty, convention, protocol, act or agreement, regardless of its title or form.[14] A "general" convention may be a multipartite instrument to which the contesting States are parties with other States; or it may be a multipartite or bipartite instrument to which only the contesting States are parties but which is of general application to their relations. A "particular" (Fr., *spécial*) convention may be one to which only the contesting States are parties, or it may be a multipartite or bipartite convention concerning a specific subject-matter. In a sense, a special agreement between the parties upon which the Court's jurisdiction is based in a particular case, would seem to be a "particular" international convention as that term is used in Article 38, and the parties may by their special agreement determine, perhaps within some limits, the rules of law which the Court should apply; [15] yet it would seem that Article 38 was not drafted with special agreements in view, and it may be thought that they are outside the scope of this direction to the Court.

As the reference in Article 38 (1) is limited to conventions which establish "rules [Fr., *règles*] expressly recognized by the contesting States," it may not include all conventions. The Declaration of Paris of 1856, the American-British Treaty of Washington of 1871, the Protocol of London of 1871, and the London Naval Treaty of 1930

---

[10] Series A, No. 10, p. 18.
[11] *Cf.*, the *Eastern Greenland Case*, Series A/B, No. 53, p. 46.
[12] Series A, No. 10, p. 63.
[13] The usage in the Statute is not uniform. Article 36 employs "treaty," and "treaties and conventions"; Article 37, "treaty or convention."
[14] "Engagements may be taken in the form of treaties, conventions, declarations, agreements, protocols, or exchanges of notes." Series A/B, No. 41, p. 47. In the *Eastern Greenland Case*, the Court even recognized an oral statement as a binding undertaking. Series A/B, No. 53, p. 73.
[15] *Cf.*, the *Brazilian Loans Case*, Series A, Nos. 20/21, p. 123. See §416, *supra*.

(Article 22), are clear examples of conventions "establishing rules expressly recognized" by the parties. It may be argued, however, that the ordinary treaty does not fall within that category, that it creates obligations without stating recognized rules, and that the assumption of an obligation is not the recognition of a rule. Such a treaty must of course be applied by the Court; if it is not a source of law under Article 38, the obligations it creates will be performable under the general international law which the Court must apply. Though the word "rules" may be given a broad meaning, the Statute should have included a definite provision that the Court should apply conventions by which the parties have assumed obligations. On this analysis, the provision in Article 38 (1) adds little to the situation which would exist if it were omitted. One object of the provision may have been to enable the Court to apply conventions to which contesting States may not be parties but which have been recognized by them.

§515. **International Custom.** The Court is directed to "apply," *i.e.,* to take as a source of international law, "international custom, as evidence of a general practice accepted as law" (Fr., *la coutume internationale comme preuve d'une pratique générale acceptée comme étant la droit*). This provision in Article 38 (2) is an awkward reference to the well-understood customary international law. A practice itself is not accepted as law, though it may be due to a conception of law. The meaning of this sub-paragraph would seem to be that the Court is to find international law by reference to a general practice based upon a conception of law,[16] which is to be regarded as evidence of customary international law. It is difficult to ascertain the content of customary international law by such evidence, and perhaps this content is not so extensive as is generally supposed. The immunity of ambassadors from local process is quite clearly a rule of customary law; the practice of States in observing this rule and their frequent insistence that other States observe it furnish clear evidence of the custom upon which it is based as a part of customary law. Yet it is not a simple matter to say when a general practice is proved to exist; [17] the laws of a number of states may be evidence tending to prove

---

[16] In the *Lotus Case,* the Court stated that the action of States in abstaining from instituting criminal proceedings would show an international custom "only if such abstention were based on their being conscious of having a duty to abstain." Series A, No. 10, p. 28. See also *id.,* pp. 23, 60.

[17] On what constitutes a *general* practice, see M. Negulesco's remarks in the case on the *Jurisdiction of the European Commission of the Danube,* Series B, No. 14, pp. 105, 114; and Judge Altamira's statement in the *Lotus Case* is of interest in this connection,

a general practice, but only if it can be shown that such laws were enacted in conformity with international law.[18]

§516. **General Principles.** The Court is also directed to "apply," *i.e.*, to take as a source of international law, "the general principles of law recognized by civilized nations." [19] Though differing views of the meaning of this expression were expressed in the 1920 Committee of Jurists which framed it,[20] it seems to have been intended to prevent "the possibility of a *non-liquet*," *i.e.*, to prevent the Court's having to refuse to decide a case because of its inability to find any applicable law.[21] It may be questioned whether it is necessary for this purpose. First, it must be borne in mind that most courts are not confined to the application of a clearly preëxisting law; the judicial function is not so barren. In the second place, courts act on claims presented to them, and judge whether these claims are or are not substantiated by the law to be applied; a judgment dismissing a claim is based on the applicable law, quite as much as a judgment by which a claim is upheld. The danger of a *non-liquet* does not seem to call for the listing of this special source of law, therefore; [22] but the provision serves a most useful purpose in that it indicates quite clearly the creative nature of the Court's functions. Its terms are sufficiently

that often in the process of the development of a customary rule "there are moments of time in which the rule, implicitly discernible, has not as yet taken shape in the eyes of the world, but is so forcibly suggested by precedents that it would be rendering good service to the cause of justice and law to assist its appearance in a form in which it will have all the force rightly belonging to rules of positive law appertaining to that category." Series A, No. 10, pp. 106–107.

[18] In a dissenting opinion in the *Lotus Case,* Judge Nyholm said: "the foundation of a custom must be the united *will* of several and even of many States constituting a *union of wills,* or a general *consensus of opinion* among the countries which have adopted the European system of civilization, or a manifestation of *international legal ethics* which takes place through the continual recurrence of events with an *innate consciousness of their being necessary.*" Series A, No. 10, p. 60.

[19] See the reports on *"Les principes généraux de droit comme source du droit des gens,"* in the *Annuaire de l'Institut de Droit International,* 1932, pp. 283–328; Balladore Pallieri, *"I 'Principi Generali del Diritto Riconosciuti dalle Nazioni Civili' "* (Turin, 1931).

[20] This expression was the subject of some confusion in the 1920 Committee of Jurists. Lord Phillimore thought that it referred to principles "accepted by all nations *in foro domestico,*" and to the "maxims of law." Minutes, p. 335. M. Loder thought the expression "was necessary to meet the possibility of a *non-liquet.*" *Id.,* p. 336.

[21] Minutes of the 1920 Committee of Jurists, pp. 296, 336. The President of the Committee of Jurists referred to "the blind alley of *non-liquet.*" *Id.,* p. 322.

[22] But see Judge Huber's reference to *non liquet* in Series A, No. 15, p. 54.

Some national codes contain provisions for meeting the problem of *non liquet.* In some States, courts are required to decide cases before them and cannot evade this responsibility because of the non-existence of applicable law. The French Civil Code (Article 4) forbids a judge to refuse to decide under pretext of the silence, obscurity, or insufficiency of the law. The Swiss Civil Code of 1907 (Article 1) requires a judge, in default of applicable code provisions, to apply the rules which he would establish if he were acting as a legislator.

elastic to give the Court great freedom, and no purpose would be served by an attempt to restrict their meaning to a fixed and definite content. It has been widely hailed as a refutation of the extreme positivist conception of international law.

The "general principles of law recognized by civilized nations" may be principles of international law, or principles common both to international law and to various systems of national law. Though it may be unnecessary for this purpose, this provision may be taken to confer on the Court a mandate to apply general principles of international law.[23] Some of these principles may also be common to various systems of national law; *res judicata* is the stock example,[24] and the Court has not hesitated to apply it.[25] Principles which various nations—the word "civilized" can do no more than exclude primitive systems of law—have embodied in their national law can also be drawn upon to enrich the content of international law; yet some caution is to be exercised in the process. To say with Holland that "the law of nations is but private law 'writ large,'" [26] is to ignore essential differences between States and individuals; the aphorism would conceal the psychology which underlies the action of States, and it may easily lead to a false appreciation of the ends to be served by a law of nations. It would be indeed a dangerous practice for judges of an international court to conceive of themselves as permitted to introduce into international law principles of the particular system of national law with which they happen to be familiar; progress in international legislation has frequently been defeated when this attitude was taken by State representatives in international conferences. The borrowing of national law principles must be subordinated to the Court's resort to other sources, and this may explain the slight extent to which the Court has attempted to apply general principles of national law.[27]

---

[23] See, however, C. de Visscher, "*Contribution à l'étude des sources du droit international*," 14 *Revue de Droit International et de Législation Comparée* (1933), p. 395.

[24] In the 1920 Committee of Jurists, Lord Phillimore referred to *res judicata* as one of the general principles included. Minutes of the 1920 Committee of Jurists, p. 335. And Judge Anzilotti has expressed the view that this reference was "not without reason." Series A, No. 13, p. 27.

[25] *Chorzów Factory Case*, Series A, No. 17, p. 29. In the first *Mavrommatis Case*, the Court spoke of "the general principle of subrogation" as a "general principle of international law." Series A, No. 2, p. 28. In the case on *German Interests in Polish Upper Silesia*, the "principle of respect for vested rights" was said to form a part of "generally accepted international law." Series A, No. 7, p. 42.

[26] Holland, Studies in International Law, p. 152. See also Lauterpacht, Private Law Sources and Analogies in International Law (1927).

[27] The "principle known in Anglo-Saxon law as estoppel" was held to be inapplicable in the *Serbian Loans Case*. Series A, Nos. 20/21, pp. 38–39.

§517. **Judicial Decisions and the Teachings of Publicists.** The Court is also directed to apply, *i.e.*, to take as a source of international law, "judicial decisions and the teachings of the most highly qualified publicists of the various nations." [28] In this case, however, the "application" is limited; such decisions and teachings are to be regarded only "as subsidiary means [Fr., *moyen auxiliaire*] for the determination of rules of law." What is meant by "subsidiary" is not clear; it would seem to mean that these sources are to be subordinated to the other sources mentioned in this article, *i.e.*, to international conventions, international custom, and general principles. Moreover, the direction to the Court in Article 38 (4) is "subject to the provisions of Article 59" of the Statute; this indicates that even the judicial decisions of the Court itself are covered by the provision. The Court's own decisions have "no binding force except between the parties and in respect of that particular case," as provided in Article 59, but they are to be regarded "as subsidiary means for the determination of rules of law." The term "judicial decisions" applies also to the decisions of other international tribunals, and to the decisions of national tribunals; Judge Moore has stated it to be a "well-settled rule" that international tribunals "are not to treat the judgments of the courts of one State on questions of international law as binding on other States," and should "follow them only so far as they may be found to be in harmony with international law, the law common to all countries." [29]

In the *Lotus Case*, the Court referred to the question of the value of the teachings of publicists (Fr., *la doctrine*) "from the point of view of establishing the existence of a rule of customary law," without attempting to answer it; and it gave a survey of writers' opinions without citations. [30] No rules can be laid down as to the relative authority of publicists, [31] but the following *caveat* formulated by Judge de Bustamante deserves to be borne in mind: "Writers of legal treatises just as much as anyone else, without wanting to and without knowing it, come under the irresistible influence of their surroundings, and the

[28] The French version has no equivalent for "of the various nations," but corresponding words would be added by the amendment annexed to the Revision Protocol of September 14, 1929.

[29] *Lotus Case*, Series A, No. 10, p. 74.

[30] *Id.*, p. 26.

[31] Members of the Court have not hesitated to cite the works of living authors in their individual opinions; even the published works of members of the Court have been cited against their positions. See Series A, No. 22, p. 44.

requirements of the national situation are reflected in their thoughts and have a great influence on their teachings." [32] Time is also a factor to be borne in mind in appraising the teachings of publicists.

§518. **Decisions ex æquo et bono.** The concluding paragraph of Article 38 states that "this provision" (Fr., *la présente disposition*), *i.e.*, the direction contained in the first paragraph, "shall not prejudice the power of the Court to decide a case *ex æquo et bono*, if the parties agree thereto." [33] In contrast with the direction as to the sources of law to be applied by the Court, this seems to mean that if the parties so request or agree, the Court may base its decision or judgment on considerations of fairness and good conscience. In this connection the term *ex æquo et bono* can hardly be called a term of art,[34] but its usage has been sufficiently frequent to give it significance.[35] It is not to be confused with the term "equity," for the Court's power to take equitable considerations into account in finding the law is not limited by the necessity of an agreement of the parties. The provision in the Statute enables the Court under the condition set to go outside the realm of law to reach a solution of a problem presented; it relieves the Court altogether from the necessity of deciding according to law; [36] it removes the limitations both of the existing law and of a law which might be made for future cases; it makes possible a solution based either on law or solely on considerations of fair dealing and

[32] *Brazilian Loans Case*, Series A, Nos. 20/21, p. 133. Judge Weiss has also pointed out, in his dissenting opinion in the *Lotus Case*, that the source of international law is not "a sum total of judgments, even if they agree with each other." Series A, No. 10, p. 43.

[33] On the interpretation of this provision, see Schindler, *"Les Progrès de l'arbitrage obligatoire,"* 25 *Recueil des Cours, Académie du Droit International* (1928), pp. 334ff.

[34] The expression *ex æquo et bono* has its roots in the Roman law. See Dig. 1.1.1. pr. See also Heumann-Seckel, *Handlexicon, s.v. bonus* (1).

[35] The Chilean-American arbitration under the agreement of November 10, 1858, was conducted *ex æquo et bono*. 2 Moore, International Arbitrations, p. 1463; 5 *id.*, p. 4689. Provisions for decisions *ex æquo et bono* are to be found in a number of recent arbitration treaties. See Series D, No. 6 (4th ed.), p. 482, note 2. The Italian-Swiss treaty of September 20, 1924, provides (Art. 15) for the Court's deciding *ex æquo et bono* in cases not of a judicial nature. 33 League of Nations Treaty Series, p. 93. This provision has been widely copied, especially in treaties to which Italy is a party. The Belgian-Swedish treaty of April 30, 1926, provides that arbitral tribunals shall decide *ex æquo et bono* disputes other than those relating to the rights of the parties. 67 *id.*, p. 91. Similar provisions are to be found in the Rumanian-Swiss treaty of February 3, 1926, 55 *id.*, p. 91; the Spanish-Swiss treaty of April 20, 1926, 60 *id.*, p. 23; the Austro-Swedish treaty of May 28, 1926, 61 *id.*, p. 193; and the Danish-Belgian treaty of March 3, 1927, 67 *id.*, p. 117. The General Convention of Inter-American Conciliation, signed at Washington, January 5, 1929, also envisages (Article 13) the possibility of decisions *ex æquo et bono*. See 4 Hudson, International Legislation, p. 2640.

[36] This is recognized in numerous treaty provisions which provide for decision by the Court *ex æquo et bono* if the question in dispute is not a legal question and if no rule of international law can be applied. *E.g.*, in Article 26 of the treaty between Bulgaria and Turkey of March 6, 1929, and in Article 21 of the treaty between Greece and Turkey of October 30, 1930. See Series D, No. 6 (4th ed.), pp. 345, 461.

good faith, which may be independent of and even contrary to law.[37] Acting *ex æquo et bono,* the Court might call upon a party to give up legal rights.[38] This does not mean, however, that the Court has a complete freedom of action when it is deciding *ex æquo et bono,* or that it has the same freedom which the parties themselves would enjoy in reaching a solution. Capricious and purely arbitrary action is excluded. Objective considerations of fair and honest dealing must be found, and the action taken must be kept within their limitations. The application of such considerations may depend in large measure on the judges' personal appreciation; yet the Court would not be justified in reaching a result which could not be explained on rational grounds.

A decision *ex æquo et bono* becomes binding on the parties, and it may therefore be said that in giving it the Court is laying down, *making,* the law governing their relations *pro tanto.* Yet the law so made applies only to the particular case before the Court, and it may be made without any inquiry as to the desirability of a similar disposition of other analogous cases. It may be doubted whether Article 38 (4) of the Statute applies to decisions *ex æquo et bono.*

Arbitral tribunals have frequently been invested with power to make awards based on international law and equity,[39] or on justice and equity; by such a mandate, they are not relieved of the necessity of finding a juridical basis for their awards, and they cannot act *ex æquo et bono* in the sense in which that term is used in Article 38.[40] Nor is a recommendation by an arbitral tribunal that certain action be

[37] Article 28 of the Geneva General Act of September 26, 1928, provides: "If nothing is laid down in the special agreement or no special agreement has been made, the Tribunal shall apply the rules in regard to the substance of the dispute enumerated in Article 38 of the Statute of the Permanent Court of International Justice. In so far as there exists no such rule applicable to the dispute, the Tribunal shall decide *ex æquo et bono.*" 4 Hudson, International Legislation, p. 2537. This applies to disputes other than those "with regard to which the parties are in conflict as to their respective rights." It is a curious and a confused variation of the provision in the Statute. If the limitation in Article 28 is ever to be applied, it may seriously detract from the usefulness of a decision *ex æquo et bono.* See the criticism of Article 28 by Professor J. L. Brierly, in British Year Book of International Law, 1930, pp. 125–133.
[38] In the final phase of the *Free Zones Case,* Judge *ad hoc* Dreyfus, dissenting, explained the Court's power to decide *ex æquo et bono* as a power "to play the part of an arbitrator in order to reach the solution which, in the light of present conditions, appeared to be the best, even if that solution required the abolition of the Zones." Series A/B, No. 46, p. 212.
[39] See, *e.g.,* the award in the United States-Norway arbitration of 1922. Scott, Hague Court Reports (2d ser.), pp. 63–65.
[40] See the opinion of the Anglo-American tribunal in the case of *The Cayuga Indians* (1926), Hudson's Cases on International Law, p. 1283; Ralston, Law and Procedure of International Tribunals (1926), §§61–67.

taken *ex gratia* [41] equivalent to a judgment *ex æquo et bono;* the Court is not competent to make such a recommendation.

No case has yet arisen in which the Court has decided *ex æquo et bono.* The special agreement in the *Serbian Loans Case* provided for a later phase of negotiations, not to be conducted before the Court, in which considerations of equity were to be taken into account.[42] In the second phase of the *Free Zones Case,* the Court observed that an agreement that it might decide *ex æquo et bono* should be "clear and explicit"; Judge Kellogg expressed the opinion that the last paragraph of Article 38 "merely empowers" the Court "to apply the principles of equity and justice in the broader signification of this latter word," and that it was not "intended to give the Court jurisdiction of political and economic questions which the Court might settle without regard to treaty rights or principles of law and equity." [43] This seems to be an undue narrowing of the provision.[44]

As there are no parties before the Court when it is considering a request for an advisory opinion, the last paragraph of Article 38 clearly has no reference to advisory opinions, which must be formulated according to law, and not *ex æquo et bono.*

§519. **Private International Law.** In the discharge of its duty to apply the international law which governs the relations of States *inter se,* the Court may be called upon to apply the principles which

---

[41] Such a recommendation was made, for example, by the Anglo-American tribunal in the *Home Missionary Society Case* (1920). Hudson's Cases on International Law, p. 1172.

The French-Mexican Claims Convention of September 25, 1924, and the British-Mexican Claims Convention of November 19, 1926, are of interest in this connection. For the texts, see 79 League of Nations Treaty Series, p. 417; 85 *id.,* p. 51. Article 2 of the latter convention required the tribunal to judge "with impartiality, in accordance with the principles of justice and equity, all claims presented, since it is the desire of Mexico *ex gratia* fully to compensate the injured parties, and not that her responsibility should be established in conformity with the general principles of international law; and it is sufficient therefore that it be established that the alleged damage actually took place, and was due to any of the causes enumerated in Article 3 of this Convention, for Mexico to feel moved *ex gratia* to afford such compensation." For the application of a similar provision in the French-Mexican convention, see the *Georges Pinson Case,* Annual Digest, 1927-28, p. 467.

[42] Series C, No. 16—III, p. 294.

[43] Series A, No. 24, pp. 10, 40. Judge Kellogg relied on the records of the drafting of the Statute. When this paragraph of Article 38 was adopted by the Assembly subcommittee in 1920, M. Fromageot had proposed the addition to No. 3 of "the general principles of law and justice," explaining that this would "enable the Court to state as the sole reason for its judgment that the award had seemed to it to be just," but that "this did not imply that the Court might disregard existing rules." Records of First Assembly, Committees, I, pp. 385-386. After M. Fromageot's phrasing was adopted, it was later modified, and the sense was radically changed by the modification. *Id.,* p. 403.

[44] See Roden, *"La Compétence de la Cour Permanente, Les Observations Kellogg,"* 12 *Révue de Droit International et de Législation Comparée* (1931), p. 727.

govern the choice of the national law which is to regulate the creation
or exercise of the rights or duties of individuals. It is not precluded
from doing so by Article 38 of the Statute; [45] indeed, there may be said
to be certain principles of private international law which are "general
principles of law recognized by civilized nations." The Court may
have before it "a dispute involving the question as to the law which
governs the contractual obligations at issue," as in the *Serbian Loans
Case*.[46] It may be called upon to deal with such a question under
private international law as codified in an international convention; [47]
in this case, the Court has declared that the rules of private international law "may possess the character of true international law governing the relations between States," whereas in other cases they are
to be considered as a "part of municipal law." [48]

§520. **Municipal Law.** Ordinarily, in its application of international law, the Court will not have to deal with questions of municipal
law, and if municipal laws must be taken into account they will be
regarded as "merely facts which express the will and constitute the
activities of States, in the same manner as do legal decisions or administrative measures." [49] A typical case of this is one in which it is
contended that a municipal law of a State violates its obligations under
international law, or in which a State relies upon a law of another
State.[50] However, in the discharge of its duty to apply the international law which governs the relations of States *inter se,* it was recognized in the *Brazilian Loans Case* that the Court may be called
upon "to apply municipal law when circumstances so require." [51]
"Once the Court has arrived at the conclusion that it is necessary to
apply the municipal law of a particular country, there seems no doubt
that it must seek to apply it as it would be applied in that country." [52]
Hence, the Court will be guided by the decisions of the courts of that

---

[45] But see the views of M. Novacovitch, judge *ad hoc,* in Series A, No. 20/21, p. 79.
[46] *Id.,* p. 41.
[47] A protocol was opened to signature at The Hague on March 27, 1931, for conferring on the Court jurisdiction to deal with differences arising with reference to the
interpretation of the various international conventions on private international law.
Series D, No. 6, p. 529.
[48] Series A, No. 20/21, p. 41.   [49] Series A, No. 7, p. 19.
[50] "According to generally accepted principles, a State cannot rely, as against another
State, on the provisions of the latter's constitution." *Treatment of Polish Nationals in
Danzig,* Series A/B, No. 44, p. 24.
[51] Series A, No. 20/21, p. 124. See also Series B, No. 6, p. 29. Sir Cecil Hurst has
stated that "the Court cannot apply or enforce the municipal law of an individual State,"
and that "in no case would the Court be qualified to interpret the meaning of a national
enactment." 75 Solicitors' Journal (1931), p. 535.
[52] Series A, No. 20/21, p. 124.

State. "For the Court itself to undertake its own construction of municipal law, leaving on one side existing judicial decisions, with the ensuing danger of contradicting the construction which has been placed on such law by the highest national tribunal and which, in its results, seems to the Court reasonable, would not be in conformity with the task for which the Court has been established and would not be compatible with the principles governing the selection of its members. It would be a most delicate matter to do so." [53] In the *Brazilian Loans Case,* the special agreement expressly provided that "in estimating the weight to be attached to any municipal law of either country which may be applicable," the Court should "not be bound by the decisions of the respective courts." This was not interpreted as requiring the Court to disregard the decisions of the national courts; indeed, "to compel the Court to disregard that jurisprudence would not be in conformity with its [the Court's] function when applying municipal law." [54] It must apply municipal law "as it would be applied in that country," and must therefore "pay the utmost regard to the decisions of the municipal courts of a country." [55] If the jurisprudence of a State's municipal courts "is uncertain or divided, it will rest with the Court to select the interpretation which it considers most in conformity with the law." [56] The extent to which special proof of municipal law may be required, has not been indicated.

§521. **Resort to Sources.** The Court has described itself as "a tribunal of international law" which "in this capacity, is deemed itself to know what this law is." [57] As no ready-made and complete body of international law is at hand for it to know and to apply, this merely means that the Court is free to *find* the international law which must be applied. The process of finding the law is of course to be conducted within some general limitations. The Court is not free to cut out of whole cloth. It must make use of the jural materials at hand, embarking into new realms only as those materials guide the way. Little is to be gained by the oft-repeated statement that the Court cannot legislate; within very indefinite limits it must make new law where preëxisting rules do not suffice for reaching results, and there is no need for alarm if this process is described as legislation.

[53] *Serbian Loans Case,* Series A, No. 20/21, p. 46.
[54] See, however, the view of Judge de Bustamante, *id.,* p. 135.
[55] *Id.,* p. 124.
[56] *Ibid.*
[57] *Brazilian Loans Case,* Series A, No. 20/21, p. 124.

Where a development or extension of the law would demand an elaborate legislative framework, the Court may very well hesitate; other agencies may be better equipped to deal with such a situation. In many cases, however, this will not be true, and if the Court is to serve the needs of a society of States, it must *find, i.e., create,* law.

This process of *finding* the law is not subject to any special limitations, either in the Statute or in the Court's own practice. Of course the Court is not limited by the presentations placed before it by the parties or the interested States; its explorations will naturally be guided by such presentations, but may well go beyond them. Thus, in the *Lotus Case,* the Court observed "that in the fulfilment of its task of itself ascertaining what the international law is, it has not confined itself to a consideration of the arguments put forward, but has included in its researches all precedents, teachings and facts to which it had access and which might possibly have revealed the existence of one of the principles of international law contemplated in the agreement." [58] Nor does Article 38 of the Statute set any special limitations. No order is prescribed in which the four sources there enumerated must be resorted to. The 1920 Committee of Jurists had proposed that the order of the enumerations should be the order of a successive application, which was thought to be the "logical" and the "natural" order; [59] but fortunately that proposal was not adopted.[60] When it finds a conventional law which is applicable, the Court is not forbidden to take account also of customary law and of general principles; this might be unnecessary in some cases, but in others the conventional law may need to be supplemented by resort to other sources. Few conventions are susceptible of automatic application; the very existence of a conventional rule may be determinable only in application of customary rules or general principles; [61] or a course of judicial decisions may exist to impel a particular application. Article 38 seems to offer one special limitation in that judicial decisions and the teachings of publicists are to be applied only "as subsidiary means for the determination of rules of law"; yet it seems doubtful whether in practice this is a limitation of much consequence. If there were a clear course of judicial decision, or even a generally

---

[58] Series A, No. 10, p. 31. This applies also to the Court's ascertainment of municipal law. Series A, No. 20/21, p. 124.
[59] Minutes of the 1920 Committee of Jurists, pp. 333, 337.
[60] Records of First Assembly, Committees, I, p. 535.
[61] See particularly, Series A, No. 23, p. 26.

accepted view of publicists, with reference to a conventional rule, the Court could not fail to be influenced by it. Only as its appreciation is left free, only as it is unfettered in its *ascertaining* or *finding* the law, is the Court likely to produce the results which are expected of it, or to contribute to the development of international law.

§522. **Stare decisis.** Article 59 of the Statute, providing that "the decision of the Court has no binding force except between the parties and in respect of that particular case," clearly precludes the Court from adopting any doctrine similar to the Anglo-American doctrine of *stare decisis*. It seems to be recognized in Article 62 of the Statute that "an interest of a legal nature" of a State not a party to a case before the Court may be "affected by the decision in the case," *i.e.*, may be *en cause;* but intervention on this ground is never compulsory, and the provision in Article 62 does not weaken the effect of Article 59. If a question has arisen in a dispute between States A and B and has been decided by the Court, this decision may not be treated as determinative of the decision of the same question when it arises before the Court in a dispute between States A and C, or in a dispute between States C and D, or even in another dispute between States A and B. This means that the Court cannot treat its former decisions as binding upon it for the future; freedom must be maintained to vary in any later case the law or the rule of law applied in an earlier case. The Statute does not require the Court to ignore its previous decisions, however, nor does it prevent great weight from being given to them; on the contrary, Article 38 (4) indicates that they are to be treated as a subsidiary source of law. On numerous occasions the Court has referred to its formulations in earlier judgments or opinions; [62] if it has not built up a *body* of precedents, as such, it has maintained its positions with general consistency, and a coherent case-law is developing in its jurisprudence.

In its negative sense, possibly Article 59 may be applied by analogy to advisory opinions. A pronouncement by the Court in an opinion is not to be regarded as binding upon the Court in connection with a later request for an advisory opinion, nor are the interested States which appear with reference to the later request in any way foreclosed in their contentions by what the Court may have said in an earlier opinion. Similarly, if a question upon which the Court has given an advisory opinion later comes up for judgment, the conclu-

---

[62] See Series E, No. 3, p. 218; and §524 (1), *infra*.

sions of the opinion may be departed from.[63] Yet the Court may give weight to its earlier opinions as part of the materials available for its use in finding the law to be applied in a judgment or in an advisory opinion.

§523. **Res judicata.** The elimination of the possibility of the Court's developing a doctrine of *stare decisis* does not preclude it from applying the general principle of *res judicata*. Indeed, the application of that principle seems to be required by Article 59 of the Statute, for otherwise a decision of the Court would not be binding on the parties.[64] Once a final decision has been given in a case, the Court cannot be called upon to give a second decision in that same case, except as it may construe or revise the earlier judgment in accordance with Articles 60 and 61 of the Statute. When it was asked to give an interpretation of its Judgment No. 7, in which it was "decided that the attitude of the Polish Government in regard to the Oberschlesische was not in conformity with the provisions of the Geneva Convention," the Court stated that this conclusion had "indisputably acquired the force of *res judicata*." [65] Moreover, a decision taken at some intermediate stage of the proceedings must be regarded as binding in the later stages of the proceedings in the same case; progress toward a final disposition would be thwarted without such a rule. Hence, where a judgment has been given on a preliminary objection to the Court's jurisdiction and where the objection is not upheld, the same objection cannot be raised when the merits are being dealt with.[66]

The Court has even gone further. When an indemnity was claimed in the *Chorzów Case* (merits), the Court viewed the claim as a demand for reparation for an injury to rights previously determined by the judgment relating to *German Interests in Polish Upper Silesia;* "having been of opinion that the Oberschlesische's right to the Chorzów factory justified the conclusion that the Polish Govern-

---

[63] If a dispute on which the Court has given a judgment should later come before it for advisory opinion, the Court would doubtless be reluctant to depart from the conclusions which led to the judgment. Such a situation has not actually arisen, however; the advisory opinion concerning access to the German minority schools in Upper Silesia (Series A/B, No. 40) related to questions which were not before the Court when it gave an earlier judgment on the treaty provisions relating to the German minority schools (Series A, No. 15).

[64] Judge Anzilotti has expressed the view that Article 59 "determines the material limits of *res judicata*." Series A, No. 13, pp. 23, 27. See also Limburg, *"L'autorité de Chose Jugée des décisions des juridictions internationales,"* 30 *Recueil des Cours, Académie de Droit International* (1929), p. 523.　　　　　[65] Series A, No. 13, p. 20.

[66] *Cf.,* the *Mavrommatis Jerusalem Concessions Case*, Series A, No. 11, p. 14; but see the Lithuanian contention in the *Statute of Memel Case*, Series A/B, No. 49, p. 327.

ment's attitude in respect of that Company was not in conformity with Article 6 and the following articles of the Geneva Convention," the Court felt that it "must necessarily maintain that opinion when the same situation at law has to be considered for the purpose of giving judgment in regard to the reparation claimed as a result of the act which has been declared by the Court not to be in conformity with the Convention." [67]

§524. **Citations Made by the Court.** The citations made by the Court give a very incomplete indication of the sources to which it has resorted in finding the law to be applied.[68] An international court has possibly less freedom in citations than a national court applying private law; previous decisions are less frequently in point, and at times a delicacy may be felt in relying on them. It is first to be noted that the Court has formulated no rules as to what it may cite.[69] Though its citations cover a variety of materials, the paucity of citations in most of the judgments and opinions is quite striking; a much greater freedom is evident in the individual opinions of the judges than in the judgments and opinions of the Court. At various times, the following have been cited and relied upon or distinguished by the Court: (1) the Court's previous judgments and opinions; (2) decisions and awards of other international tribunals; (3) decisions of the Council of the League of Nations and other political bodies; (4) conventions concluded by States other than the parties; (5) decisions by national courts; (6) national legislation; (7) and diplomatic correspondence of States other than the parties. It is to be noted that treatises do not figure in this list, though they have often been cited in the individual opinions of judges.[70]

(1) *The Court's Judgments and Opinions.* Numerous references have been made by the Court to its previous formulations of rules or principles. The advisory opinion on the *Competence of the International Labor Organization* to deal with conditions of labor in agriculture [71] has been cited in later opinions concerning the International

---

[67] Series A, No. 17, p. 32. See also Series A/B, No. 46, p. 151.

[68] The documents submitted to the Court by the parties or interested States form a part of the record in a case, and references to them are not citations in the sense in which the term is used here.

[69] It has excluded certain documents offered by the parties as evidence, however. Series B, No. 14, p. 32; Series A, No. 22, p. 21; Series A, No. 23, p. 42.

[70] English and French dictionaries have been cited by the Court in one instance. Series B, No. 2, pp. 33, 35. The works of living authors, and even of judges of the Court, have been cited in the individual opinions. *E.g.*, Series A, No. 2, p. 59.

[71] Series B, No. 2.

Labor Organization,[72] and the series of these opinions follows a consistent view of the functions of the Organization. The statement in the *Wimbledon Case* that the Court cannot contemplate the failure of a State to comply with its judgment,[73] has been repeated with a reference to the earlier judgment; [74] and the *Wimbledon Case* has also been cited on the power of States to enter into treaties.[75] The principle formulated in the *Mavrommatis Case* [76] that in espousing a claim by its national a State asserts its own rights, has been followed with citation in a later case,[77] and the line of decisions on this point is consistent. In the case concerning the *Readaptation of the Mavrommatis Concessions,* the Court thought its earlier decisions "must undoubtedly be taken into account," though it was held that the suit was not a continuation of the earlier proceedings.[78] In the case relating to *German Interests in Polish Upper Silesia,* a previous opinion was relied upon, as nothing had been advanced "to alter the Court's opinion" on the point.[79] The principle of informal submission to the jurisdiction, enunciated in the *Mavrommatis Jerusalem Concessions Case,*[80] was followed with citation in a later case.[81] The interpretation of the term "minorities" given in the opinion on *Acquisition of Polish Nationality* [82] was cited and relied upon in the opinion concerning *Polish Nationals in Danzig.*[83] In its opinion on the *Interpretation of the Greco-Turkish Agreement,*[84] the Court followed "the precedent afforded by its advisory opinion No. 3," in restating a question submitted by the Council.[85] The construction of a convention given in the judgment relating to *German Minority Schools in Upper Silesia* was followed when the Court was later asked for an advisory opinion on the execution of a decision of the Council based on the same convention.[86] In the advisory opinion on the *St. Naoum Monastery,*[87] the Court referred to its earlier holding, in the advisory opinion on the *Jaworzina Boundary,* on the "general legal considerations determining the nature and effects of a decision" taken by the Conference of Ambassadors.[88] On the use of *travaux préparatoires,* frequent reference

---

[72] Series B, No. 3, p. 55; No. 13, p. 20; Series A/B, No. 50, p. 275.
[73] Series A, No. 1, p. 32.   [74] Series A, No. 17, p. 63.
[75] Series B, No. 10, p. 21. See also Series B, No. 14, p. 36.
[76] Series A, No. 2, p. 12.   [77] Series A, No. 20/21, p. 17. See also *id.,* p. 96.
[78] Series A, No. 11, p. 14.   [84] Series B, No. 16, p. 15.
[79] Series A, No. 7, p. 31.   [85] Series B, No. 3, p. 59.
[80] Series A, No. 5, p. 28.   [86] Series A/B, No. 40, pp. 13, 19.
[81] Series A, No. 15, pp. 23–24.   [87] Series B, No. 9, p. 15.
[82] Series B, No. 7, pp. 14–15.   [88] Series B, No. 8, p. 28.
[83] Series A/B, No. 44, p. 39.

has been made to what the Court has said on previous occasions.[89] The judgment in the case on *German Interests in Polish Upper Silesia* was cited and relied on in the advisory opinion on *Polish Nationals in Danzig*, as were also several of the earlier advisory opinions.[90]

Since most of the cases which have come before the Court have related to the interpretation or application of treaty provisions, and since the treaties involved have been varied and numerous, this possibly incomplete list of the Court's citations of its own judgments and opinions is impressive. It indicates quite clearly an effort by the Court to build a cumulating body of case-law, and this effort has not been thwarted by Article 59 of the Statute.

(2) *Decisions of Other International Tribunals.* On a few occasions the Court has cited decisions of other international tribunals. In the judgment relating to the *Interpretation of the Treaty of Neuilly*, reference was made to the interpretations placed on certain texts by the Mixed Arbitral Tribunals, but they were said to be "of no importance in connection with the dispute before the Court." [91] In the *Lotus Case*, the decision of a British-Netherlands tribunal in the case of the *Costa Rica Packet* [92] was cited and distinguished.[93] In the *Chorzów Factory Case*, a conclusion was said to be "in accordance with the jurisprudence of arbitral tribunals," but no cases were cited.[94] In the advisory opinion on *Polish Postal Service in Danzig*, the Court cited approvingly the award of a tribunal of the Permanent Court of Arbitration in the *Pious Fund Case;* [95] in the judgment on *Eastern Greenland*, the award of a similar tribunal in the *Palmas Island Case* was cited.[96] On the other hand, there have been some questions before the Court on which international jurisprudence might have been and was not cited.

(3) *Decisions of the Council of the League of Nations and Other Political Bodies.* In the advisory opinion on the *Nationality Decrees in Tunis and Morocco*, the Court cited the view taken by the Council

---

[89] Series A, No. 10, p. 16; Series B, No. 14, p. 28; Series A/B, No. 47, p. 249.
[90] Series A/B, No. 44, pp. 24, 25, 28, 31.
[91] Series A, No. 3, p. 7.
[92] 5 Moore, International Arbitrations, p. 4948.
[93] Series A, No. 10, p. 27. The case had been referred to in the argument. Series C, No. 13—II, p. 33.
[94] Series A, No. 17, p. 57.
[95] Series B, No. 11, p. 30.
[96] Series A/B, No. 53, p. 45. In the opinion on the *Jaworzina Boundary,* also, the Court cited the award of September 13, 1902, in the *Meerauge Case* between Austria and Hungary, 3 Martens, *Nouveau Recueil Général* (3 Ser.), p. 71.

of the League of Nations as to the proper interpretation of paragraph 8 of Article 15 of the Covenant.[97] In the opinion concerning *Polish Nationals in Danzig*, the Court cited "the practice of the Council," in connection with a reference to its own previous opinion on the meaning of the term "minority."[98] In the judgment on the *Interpretation of the Treaty of Neuilly*, the Court found confirmation of its views in a decision of the Reparation Commission.[99] In the judgment on the *Statute of Memel*, reference was made to reports submitted to the Conference of Ambassadors and to the Council.[100]

(4) *Conventions Concluded by States Other than the Parties.* Numerous references have been made to the course of international legislation by States not parties before the Court, either for distinguishing it or for drawing some general conclusions. In the *Wimbledon Case*, the conventions relating to the Panama and Suez Canals were cited and their provisions and their execution were examined in some detail; the Court found them to be "illustrations of the general opinion" which tended to "invalidate in advance" certain contentions of the German agent.[1] In the first *Mavrommatis Case*, a general conclusion was based on the "reservation made in many arbitration treaties," but no citations were given.[2] In the judgment on the *Interpretation of the Treaty of Neuilly*, the Court refused to take into account provisions in the Treaty of Versailles.[3] In the *Lotus Case*, a general reference was made to "conventions expressly reserving jurisdiction exclusively to the State whose flag is flown," but the Court refused to make any deduction from them.[4] In the opinion on the *Interpretation of the Treaty of Lausanne*, the Court cited the 1907 Hague Convention for the Pacific Settlement of International Disputes, repeating the statement there made as to the object of arbitration.[5]

(5) *Decisions of National Courts.* Even though it was applying international law, the Court has on several occasions examined the effect of decisions of municipal courts. In the *Lotus Case*, reference was made to applications of criminal law by "the courts of many countries" without citations;[6] later several decisions of national courts were cited, though the Court did not pause "to consider the value to be attributed to the judgments of municipal courts in connection with

[97] Series B, No. 4, p. 25.
[98] Series A/B, No. 44, p. 39.
[99] Series A, No. 3, p. 9.
[100] Series A/B, No. 47, p. 253.
[1] Series A, No. 1, pp. 25–28.

[2] Series A, No. 2, p. 35.
[3] Series A, No. 3, p. 9.
[4] Series A, No. 10, p. 27.
[5] Series B, No. 12, p. 26.
[6] Series A, No. 10, p. 23.

the establishment of the existence of a rule of international law," and the conclusion was reached that "municipal jurisprudence is thus divided" in its results.[7] In its advisory opinion on the *Competence of the International Labor Organization* to regulate the personal work of the employer, an interesting reference was made to municipal jurisprudence on the constitutionality of legislation, but no cases were cited.[8] When the Court is applying municipal law, it must of course determine how the law is applied in the country in question;[9] in the *Serbian Loans Case*, it referred to "the doctrine of French courts" without citation,[10] and in the *Brazilian Loans Case* reference was made to the "jurisprudence of the French courts" without citation.[11]

(6) *National Legislation.* In its finding of municipal law to be applied, of course reference is made by the Court to national legislation;[12] it may also be referred to in the finding of international law. In the *Wimbledon Case*, reference was made to executive orders and proclamations of the United States relating to the Panama Canal, and the absence of protests by other States was taken to indicate a view as to what may be compatible with neutrality.[13] In the judgment on the *Statute of Memel*, the Court refused "to consider the extent to which the constitutions of other countries can be used as a guide [in] interpreting the Statute of Memel."[14]

(7) *Diplomatic Correspondence of States Other than the Parties.* Little reliance has been placed by the Court on legal positions taken by States not parties, in their diplomatic correspondence.[15] In the *Lotus Case*, reference was made to the British Government's failure to honor a request for extradition by the United States,[16] "to show that the principle of the exclusive jurisdiction of the country whose flag the vessel flies is not universally accepted."[17]

[7] Series A, No. 10, pp. 28, 29, 30.
[8] Series B, No. 13, p. 20.
[9] Series A, No. 20/21, p. 124.
[10] *Id.*, p. 47.
[11] *Id.*, p. 125.
[12] *Id.*, pp. 44–47.
[13] Series A, No. 1, pp. 25–28.
[14] Series A/B, No. 49, p. 320. In the Lithuanian counter-case, the American, German, and Swiss Constitutions had been cited. Series C, No. 59, p. 51.
[15] The danger of such reliance is admirably pointed out by Professor Viktor Bruns in *Fontes Juris Gentium*, Series A, No. 1, I, p. xxiv.
[16] *Anderson's Case*, in 1 Moore's Digest of International Law, pp. 932–935.
[17] Series A, No. 10, p. 27.

CHAPTER 28

INTERNATIONAL ENGAGEMENTS AND THEIR INTERPRETATION BY THE COURT

§525. International Engagements in the Court's Jurisprudence. In almost every case which has come before it, either for judgment or for advisory opinion, the Court has been confronted with the necessity of dealing with an international engagement,[1] and the issues drawn have called for the Court's determining whether an engagement existed or what interpretation was to be placed upon the text of an engagement admitted to exist. The law of treaties and of the interpretation of treaties is by far the largest subject in the Court's jurisprudence. Indeed, the value of this jurisprudence for general purposes is limited by the fact that the Court is usually dealing with a specific text, and the texts are seldom the same in two different cases. Yet the Court has appreciated the necessity of its maintaining a consistent attitude in dealing with the texts which have come before it, and the result has been both a clarification of the legal situations to which the texts have related and a significant contribution to the approach to be made in international law to the interpretation and application of conventional arrangements.

§526. The Form of Engagements. For the present purpose, the term "international engagement" is borrowed from Article 18 of the Covenant of the League of Nations as a general term applicable to the assumption of an international obligation. It is broader than the term "treaty," also employed in Article 18 of the Covenant, or the term "treaties and conventions" employed in Article 36 of the Statute of the Court; it is also broader than the term "agreement" if that term is taken to involve action by more than one State. The Court has shown a decided preference for this term in its fre-

---

[1] In the *Serbian* and *Brazilian Loans Cases,* before the Court under special agreements, no treaty engagements other than the special agreements were involved. Series A, Nos. 20/21. In the *Lotus Case,* on the other hand, the question submitted referred to Article 15 of the Convention of Lausanne of July 24, 1923. Series A, No. 10.

quent references to the obligations resulting from "engagements." In the opinion on the *Austro-German Customs Régime,* the Court said of a provision in the Geneva Protocol of 1922 that "though it took the form of a declaration,[2] Austria did thereby assume certain undertakings in the economic sphere"; adding that "from the standpoint of the obligatory character of international engagements, it is well known that such engagements may be taken in the form of treaties, conventions, declarations, agreements, protocols, or exchanges of notes." [3]

The Court has not been compelled to lay down rules governing capacity to enter into international engagements, though it has declared that "the right of entering into international engagements is an attribute of state sovereignty." [4] It has not adverted to the question whether the international capacity of States is subject to their own constitutional limitations, though in the *Eastern Greenland Case* Judge Anzilotti expressed the view that "the question whether Norwegian constitutional law authorized the [Norwegian] Minister for Foreign Affairs to make the [Ihlen] declaration . . . does not concern the Danish Government." [5] Nor have any rules been laid down by the Court as to the conditions of validity of engagements,[6] or as to the formalities necessary for entering into an engagement; it has not even adverted to the effect of non-compliance with the formality of registration required by Article 18 of the Covenant.[7] In the *Eastern Green-*

---

[2] The multipartite instrument in question, denominated "Protocol No. 1," contained bilateral "declarations." For the text, see 12 League of Nations Treaty Series, p. 385; 2 Hudson, International Legislation, p. 882.

[3] Series A/B, No. 41, p. 47. The list given by the Court cannot have been intended to be exhaustive; the terms "arrangement," "act," "statute," and *"modus vivendi"* are common, and other names of instruments are sometimes employed. The choice of a name for an instrument is frequently determined by political considerations, and the name selected generally has little juridical significance. The Court has not clearly defined the nature of a mandate issued under Article 22 of the Covenant; in the *Mavrommatis Case,* Judge Moore regarded the Palestine mandate as "in a sense a legislative act of the Council." Series A, No. 2, p. 69.

[4] Series A, No. 1, p. 25; Series B, No. 10, p. 21.

[5] Series A/B, No. 53, pp. 91–92. See, however, the dissenting opinion in the *Free Zones Case* by Judge ad hoc Dreyfus, Series A/B, No. 46, pp. 209–210.

[6] Dissenting judges have addressed themselves to conditions of validity, however. See Judge Schücking in Series A, No. 1, p. 47; Judge Negulesco in Series B, No. 14, p. 126; Judge Anzilotti in Series A/B, No. 53, p. 92.

[7] It may be doubted whether the Court should give any effect to an unregistered treaty or engagement concluded by two Members of the League of Nations since January 10, 1920, and the practice ought to be adopted of citing the League of Nations Treaty Series when reference is made to registered treaties or engagements. Perhaps an exception must be made in the application of Article 18 of the Covenant, of special agreements for the reference of disputes to the Court; certainly most of the special agreements to date have not been registered with the Secretariat of the League of Nations. It may be noted, however, that the Court has not refused to give effect to an unregistered treaty. In the judgment in the *Mavrommatis Case,* given on August 30, 1924, the Concessions

land Case, an oral reply "given by the Minister for Foreign Affairs on behalf of his Government in response to a request by the diplomatic representative of a foreign Power, in regard to a question falling within his province" was held to constitute an "undertaking" which was "binding upon the country to which the Minister belongs." [8] In the advisory opinion as to the *Jurisdiction of the European Commission of the Danube,* the Court refused to consider an interpretative protocol signed by delegates to the European Commission attending the Danube Conference in an advisory capacity, as "an international agreement between the parties to the Definitive Statute" of the Danube.[9] In its reply to the request for an advisory opinion concerning *Eastern Carelia,* the Court gave no answer to the question whether a declaration inserted in a *procès-verbal* at the time of the signature of the Treaty of Dorpat constituted an engagement; the question was said to be, "in the very nature of things, a question of fact." [10] In the judgment in the *Free Zones Case,* the Court treated a manifesto of the Royal Sardinian Court of Accounts, issued on royal orders following a favorable reception by the King of Sardinia of a request of the Canton of Valais based on Article 3 of the Treaty of Turin, as a "concord of wills" which conferred on the delimitation of the zone of Saint Gingolph "the character of a treaty stipulation." [11] In the opinion on *German Minority Schools in Upper Silesia,* an arrangement adopted by the Council of the League of Nations and accepted by Germany and Poland was said to be "valid and binding for both countries." [12]

It has been recognized in several cases that an engagement may

Protocol of Lausanne was held to be applicable between Great Britain and Greece, Series A, No. 2, p. 33, though it was not registered until September 5, 1924 (28 League of Nations Treaty Series, p. 203); one of the parties to the Protocol, Turkey, was not at the time a member of the League of Nations. The Danzig-Polish agreement of October 24, 1921, was interpreted and relied upon in the opinion on the *Polish Postal Service in Danzig,* given on May 16, 1925, Series B, No. 11, though it was not registered until May 5, 1931 (116 League of Nations Treaty Series, p. 5); Danzig is not a member of the League of Nations, however, and the agreement had been noted by the Council in 1922.

[8] Series A/B, No. 53, pp. 71, 73. Judge Anzilotti said in this case that "there does not seem to be any rule of international law requiring that agreements of this kind must necessarily be in writing, in order to be valid." *Id.,* p. 91.

Possibly an agreement may be expressed in a map, also. In the *Jaworzina Case,* confirmatory evidence was found in maps, though it was said that independently maps could not be regarded as conclusive proof. Series B, No. 8, p. 33. In the *Monastery of St. Naoum Case,* the map in question was unsigned, and its authentic character was not established. Series B, No. 9, p. 21.

[9] Series B, No. 14, pp. 32–34. Judge Moore referred to this interpretative protocol as a "legally unclassified paper." *Id.,* p. 81.

[10] Series B, No. 5, p. 26. *Sed quære.*

[11] Series A/B, No. 46, p. 145. See also Series A, No. 24, p. 17.

[12] Series A/B, No. 40, p. 16.

be undertaken by a State as a consequence of its agent's declaration before the Court. In the *Mavrommatis Case,* the British agent made a declaration which was incorporated in the Court's judgment with the statement that its binding character was beyond question.[13] In the case relating to *German Interests in Polish Upper Silesia,* the Polish agent made various declarations as to the binding character of which the Court was in no doubt.[14] In the *Free Zones Case,* the Swiss agent made a declaration in the course of the oral proceedings which was incorporated in the judgment of the Court, and in the operative part of the judgment the Court placed it on record.[15]

It may also be noted that the same text may serve several purposes; it may constitute an international engagement and a provision of national law, and its legal consequences may depend upon the aspect in which it is to be considered. Thus the Statute of Memel was regarded by the Court as "a conventional arrangement binding upon Lithuania," because it was an annex to the Convention of May 8, 1924, and referred to in Article 16 of that Convention, though the Statute had also "been enacted as a Lithuanian law."[16]

§527. **Effectiveness of Engagements.** The Court has not been called upon to fix the precise time when an international engagement becomes effective. In the case relating to the *Jurisdiction of the Oder Commission,* reference was made to the "ordinary rules of international law amongst which is the rule that conventions, save in certain exceptional cases, are binding only by virtue of their ratification."[17] In the judgment on *German Interests in Polish Upper Silesia,* it seems to have been admitted that a "principle of good faith" requires a signatory to ratify, but it was found to be unnecessary to "consider the question whether, and if so how far, the signatories of a treaty are under an obligation to abstain from any action likely to interfere with its execution when ratification has taken place."[18] In determining its jurisdiction in the *Mavrommatis Case,* the Court recognized the Lausanne Protocol which came into force after the proceeding was

---

[13] Series A, No. 5, p. 37.   [14] Series A, No. 7, p. 13.

[15] Series A/B, No. 46, pp. 170, 172. In the order in the case relating to *Southeastern Greenland,* it was stated that where intentions have "been officially proclaimed before the Court, the latter must not and cannot presume that the two Governments concerned might act otherwise than in conformity with the intentions thus expressed." Series A/B, No. 48, p. 287.

[16] Series A/B, No. 49, p. 300.

[17] Series A, No. 23, p. 20. If taken out of its context, this statement by the Court would clearly be too broad.

[18] Series A, No. 7, p. 40. See also, *passim,* Series B, No. 6.

instituted as having effects which "extend to legal situations dating from a time previous to its own existence," and therefore relied upon its provisions; [19] on another occasion, however, it refused to "examine the question whether" this protocol might, before its ratification, "have produced certain legal effects as regards the contracting parties." [20] In that case, also, it was recognized that a later may prevail over an earlier instrument.[21]

§528. **Performance of Obligations Undertaken.** The Court has acted upon the principle of *pacta sunt servanda*, though without frequent reference to it, and it has repeatedly declared that international engagements are binding on the parties thereto. Throughout its jurisprudence, the assumption runs that States will in good faith observe and carry out the obligations which they have undertaken. Hence, little hospitality has been shown to reasons advanced by parties for the non-fulfillment of their obligations. In the opinion on *Exchange of Greek and Turkish Populations*, the principle was declared to be "self-evident" that "a State which has contracted valid international obligations is bound to make in its legislation such modifications as may be necessary to ensure the fulfilment of the obligations undertaken." [22] It follows that a State cannot rely upon its own constitution or legislation as an excuse for non-performance of its obligations. In the case concerning the *Polish Nationals in Danzig*, it was said that "a State cannot adduce as against another State its own Constitution with a view to evading obligations incumbent upon it under international law or treaties in force." [23] In the opinion on the *Jurisdiction of Danzig Courts*, it was made clear that Poland could not rely upon its own failure to enact legislation for the purpose of avoiding the obligations undertaken with Danzig.[24] In the opinion on the *Greco-Bulgarian Communities*, it was declared to be "a generally accepted principle of international law that in the relations between Powers who are contracting parties to a treaty, the provisions of municipal law cannot prevail over those of the treaty." [25]

At various times, excuses for non-performance have been advanced,

---

[19] Series A, No. 2, p. 34. In this case, Judge Moore, dissenting, said that "the doctrine that governments are bound to ratify whatever their plenipotentiaries, acting within the limits of their instructions, may sign, and that treaties may therefore be regarded as legally operative and enforceable before they have been ratified, is obsolete, and lingers only as an echo from the past." *Id.*, p. 57.   [20] Series A, No. 5, p. 39.
[21] Series A, No. 2, pp. 30, 31. *Cf.*, Judge Nyholm's dissent in Series A, No. 15, p. 59.
[22] Series B, No. 10, p. 20.   [24] Series B, No. 15, pp. 26–27.
[23] Series A/B, No. 44, p. 24.   [25] Series B, No. 17, p. 32.

usually in the form of limitations on the extent of the obligation undertaken. In the *Wimbledon Case,* two dissenting judges would have excused non-performance of Germany's obligations with respect to the Kiel Canal: "If, as a result of a war, a neutral or belligerent State is faced with the necessity of taking extraordinary measures temporarily affecting the application of such conventions in order to protect its neutrality or for the purpose of national defence, it is entitled to do so even if no express reservations are made in the convention." [26] This view was not shared by the Court, however. In the *Serbian Loans Case,* the impossibility of performance contended for was found not to exist, and in the *Brazilian Loans Case* no basis was found for a defense of impossibility of performance based on *force majeure;* [27] but the judgments intimate that these might in a proper case be excuses for non-performance. In the *Eastern Greenland Case,* Judge Anzilotti was willing to consider the effect of a mistake if it was "of an excusable character," but he concluded that no mistake had been made in that case.[28]

§529. **Rebus Sic Stantibus.** The Court has not been confronted with a necessity of deciding on the so-called *clausula rebus sic stantibus.* In the opinion on *Nationality Decrees in Tunis and Morocco,* the French agent contended that certain treaties had "lapsed by virtue of the principle known as the *clausula rebus sic stantibus";* the Court was of the opinion that any pronouncement on this point would involve "recourse to the principles of international law concerning the duration of the validity of treaties," but it was unnecessary for it to make such a pronouncement at that stage of the case.[29] In the *Free Zones Case,* the principle of the *clausula* was invoked in the earlier stages; [30] and in the final judgment it was considered at some length.[31] The French agent's contention was that the zones were created in 1815 "in view of and because of the existence of a particular state of facts," *viz.,* that the Canton of Geneva was a free trade area which by the zones became an economic unit with other territory; that this state of facts disappeared when "the institution of Swiss Federal Customs in 1849 destroyed this economic unit"; and that in

[26] Series A, No. 1, p. 36. [27] Series A, No. 20/21, pp. 40, 120.
[28] Series A/B, No. 53, p. 92. [29] Series B, No. 4, p. 29.
[30] Series A, No. 22, pp. 29, 36, 41.
[31] Series A/B, No. 46, pp. 156–158. On this and other questions discussed in this chapter, see W. E. Beckett, *"Les questions d'intérêt général au point de vue juridique dans la jurisprudence de la Cour . . . ,"* 39 Recueil des Cours, Académie de Droit International (1932), pp. 131–272.

consequence the Court should declare the stipulations creating the zones to have lapsed. The Court stated that "to establish this position it is necessary, first of all, to prove that it was in consideration of the absence of customs duties at Geneva that the Powers decided, in 1815, in favour of the creation of the zones." As this was not proved to the Court's satisfaction, "the French argument fails on the facts," and it therefore became "unnecessary for the Court to consider any of the questions of principle which arise in connection with the theory of the lapse of treaties by reason of change of circumstances, such as the extent to which the theory can be regarded as constituting a rule of international law, the occasions on which and the method by which effect can be given to the theory if recognized, and the question whether it would apply to treaties establishing rights such as that which Switzerland derived from the treaties of 1815 and 1816." This statement leaves wholly unanswered the question whether the *clausula rebus sic stantibus* has become a principle of international law.[32]

§530. **Effect of Engagements on States Not Parties.** On several occasions the Court has had to deal with the effect of international instruments upon the position of States which are not parties to them. In general, a treaty may create rights for States not parties if this is clearly intended,[33] but it cannot impose obligations on such States.[34] In the case relating to *German Interests in Polish Upper Silesia*, Poland relied upon the Armistice of November 11, 1918, and the Protocol of Spa of December 1, 1918; though Poland was not expressly a party to either instrument at the time of its signature, it was claimed that by virtue of being one of the Allied and Associated Powers Poland was entitled to be considered a party from the time of the later recognition

---

[32] In the first phase of the *Free Zones Case*, Deputy-Judge Negulesco expressed the view that Article 19 of the Covenant of the League of Nations "confirms the validity of the clause *rebus sic stantibus* and at the same time rejects any claim to apply it unilaterally." Series A, No. 22, p. 30.

[33] In the *Wimbledon Case*, Judge *ad hoc* Schücking, dissenting, expressed the view that "a legally binding contractual obligation cannot be undertaken to perform acts which would violate the rights of third parties." Series A, No. 1, p. 47.

[34] On this latter point, agreements forming part of a general continental settlement, such as those concluded at the end of the World War, may be viewed as exceptional. The commission of jurists which dealt with certain questions involved in the Aaland Islands dispute in 1920, emphasized the "European character" of the Convention of March 30, 1856, and the intention thereby to create "European law." League of Nations Council Document 69 (20/4/238), 1920, pp. 25–26. However, in a dissenting opinion on the *Jurisdiction of the European Commission of the Danube*, Judge Negulesco expressed the view that "decisions of the Great Powers, met together as the Concert of Europe, . . . have never been held to be legally binding upon States not represented in the Concert." Series B, No. 14, p. 95. See also Series A, No. 24, p. 27.

accorded to it during the peace negotiations.[35] The Court found "no subsequent tacit adherence or accession on the part of Poland." As the instruments made no provision for adhesion, it was said to be "just as impossible to presume the existence of such a right—at all events in the case of an instrument of the nature of the Armistice Convention—as to presume that the provisions of these instruments can *ipso facto* be extended to apply to third States. A treaty only creates law as between the States which are parties to it; in case of doubt, no rights can be deduced from it in favour of third States." [36] This language was so guarded as to leave open the general question of rights of third States. In the *Free Zones Case,* the Court held that "Article 435 of the Treaty of Versailles is not binding upon Switzerland, who is not a party to that Treaty, except to the extent to which that country accepted it." [37] Switzerland had acceded to the Declaration of the Powers of March 20, 1815, and in consequence it was found to be unnecessary to "consider the legal nature of the Gex zone from the point of view of whether it constitutes a stipulation in favour of a third party." It was added, *obiter:* "It cannot be lightly presumed that stipulations favourable to a third State have been adopted with the object of creating an actual right in its favour. There is, however, nothing to prevent the will of sovereign States from having this object and this effect. The question of the existence of a right acquired under an instrument drawn between other States is therefore one to be decided in each particular case: it must be ascertained whether the States which have stipulated in favour of a third State meant to create for that State an actual right which the latter has accepted as such." [38] Judges Altamira and Hurst, dissenting in this case, made "every reservation in regard to a theory seeking to lay down, as a principle, that rights accorded third parties by international conventions, to which the favoured State is not a party, cannot be amended or abolished, even by the States which accorded them, without the consent of the third State." [39]

§531. **International Engagements and Private Individuals.** In general, it may be said that an international engagement entered

---

[35] Series C, No. 11, vol. II, pp. 616ff.

[36] Series A, No. 7, pp. 28–29. *Cf.,* Lord Finlay's dissent, asserting that on analogy to "contracts on behalf of companies not yet incorporated," the "Allied States made the Armistice on behalf of Poland, which was about to become a State." *Id.,* p. 84.

[37] Series A/B, No. 46, p. 141.

[38] Series A/B, No. 46, pp. 147–148. *Cf.,* Series A, No. 22, pp. 20, 26; and the dissenting opinions of Judge Negulesco and of Judge Dreyfus, *id.,* pp. 36–37, 43–44.

[39] Series A/B, No. 46, p. 185.

into by two States creates rights and obligations for those States only, and it does not of its own force confer rights or impose obligations on individuals, though this may be the consequence of its incorporation into the municipal law of a State which is a party. This was recognized by the Court in its opinion on the *Jurisdiction of Danzig Courts:* "It may be readily admitted that, according to a well established principle of international law, the *Beamtenabkommen,* being an international agreement, cannot, as such, create direct rights and obligations for private individuals." [40] However, the parties may accomplish that result, and in that case an intention was found to adopt "definite rules creating individual rights and obligations and enforceable by the national courts"; the Court therefore held that the *Beamtenabkommen* governed the relations between the Polish Railways Administration and the Danzig officials, and constituted a part of the latter's "contract of service."

§532. **Interpretation and Application.** The Court may be called upon to interpret a provision in a treaty apart from any question of its application.[41] "There seems to be no reason why States should not be able to ask the Court to give an abstract interpretation of a treaty; rather would it appear that this is one of the most important functions which it can fulfil. It has, in fact, already had occasion to do so in Judgment No. 3." [42] However, the Court is usually called upon to interpret the text of an instrument in connection with some problem of its application, and the cases are rare in which an abstract question of interpretation will be presented. Many instruments confer on the Court jurisdiction over disputes or differences as to the "interpretation and application" of their provisions; the word "or" is sometimes employed instead of "and," but "and" may be construed to be both alternative and cumulative.[43] Just as interpretation will usually be connected with application, any difference as to the application of a provision will almost invariably involve some question of its interpretation. In the *Mavrommatis Case,* the term "application" used in

[40] Series B, No. 15, p. 17.

[41] Interpretation is the process of giving a meaning to a text; application is the process of determining its consequences in a given situation. *Cf.,* the explanation by M. Ehrlich, in Series A, No. 9, p. 39.
As the Court stated in the judgment relating to *German Interests in Polish Upper Silesia,* "the interpretation of other international agreements is indisputably within the competence of the Court if such interpretation must be regarded as incidental to a decision on a point in regard to which it has jurisdiction." Series A, No. 6, p. 18.

[42] *German Interests in Polish Upper Silesia,* Series A, No. 7, pp. 18–19. Judgment No. 3 related to the *Interpretation of the Treaty of Neuilly.*

[43] Series A, No. 6, p. 14; No. 7, p. 18. But see the views of Judge Rostworowski, in Series A, No. 6, p. 35.

a contract was thought to be broader than the term "execution," the latter involving "a form of application." [44] In the judgment on *German Interests in Polish Upper Silesia,* differences of opinion as to interpretation and application were said to "include differences of opinion as to the extent of the sphere of application," [45] and they were held to include also differences relating to reparation for non-application. [46]

If it is true that interpretation is usually connected with application, this may very well influence the conception to be entertained as to the nature of the function of interpretation; the consequences of a particular interpretation must be given greater importance in the discharge of that function, if interpretation and application are not dissociated.

§533. **The Function of Interpretation.** The process of interpreting the text of an international instrument [47] is not to be viewed as a search for some preëxisting meaning. It may be true, as was said in the opinion on *German Minority Schools in Polish Upper Silesia,* that "in accordance with a rule of law," an interpretation once arrived at is to be given "retrospective effect," "in the sense that the terms . . . must be held to have always borne the meaning placed upon them by this interpretation"; [48] yet this does not mean that the interpretation merely gives form to a meaning which previously existed. Interpretation involves *giving* a meaning to the text. Few terms of art may be said to exist in international law, and as the terms employed in international instruments seldom have an exact meaning, [49] they can be interpreted only as content is given to them. This is not a matter of a mechanical operation; it is not a process which performs itself automatically; results have to be kept in mind, [50] judgment must be exercised, many factors must be appreciated. [51] Given a text, the

---

[44] Series A, No. 5, p. 48. [45] Series A, No. 6, p. 16. *Cf., id.,* pp. 29–30.
[46] Series A, No. 9, pp. 20–24.

[47] Of course the interpretation of a treaty does not "fall solely within the domestic jurisdiction of a single State." Series B, No. 4, p. 30. In the interpretation of international instruments, an international tribunal should be on its guard against the improper use of analogies based upon the interpretation of private instruments by national courts.

[48] Series A/B, No. 40, p. 19.

[49] The chemical formulas in the Convention on Manufacture of Narcotic Drugs of July 13, 1931, are exceptional. See League of Nations Official Journal, 1931, p. 1795; United States Treaty Series, No. 863.

[50] This was recognized by the Court in its opinion on the *Interpretation of the Treaty of Lausanne,* when it said that "any article designed to fix a frontier should, if possible, be so interpreted that the result of the application of its provisions in their entirety should be the establishment of a precise, complete and definite frontier." Series B, No. 12, p. 20. See also Series A, No. 5, p. 49; No. 22, p. 13.

[51] This process is sometimes hidden under an imputation to the parties of an intention to arrive at "the best possible solution of the difficulty." See, *e.g.,* Series B, No. 14, p. 27. Judge Anzilotti has found it to be "a fundamental rule in the interpretation of

Court may have to "look to its practical effect rather than to the predominant motive that may be conjectured to have inspired it." [52] There may be no danger in saying that it is the function of the Court to "ascertain the precise meaning" of a text,[53] if the nature of this process is kept in mind. Yet it serves little purpose to say that the Court must look for a "true meaning," or that "the question in every case must resolve itself into what the terms of the treaty actually mean." [54] Such expressions sometimes serve merely to hide the operations through which the Court must pass before it can arrive at a determination of the meaning to be given to a text. It is more proper to say that "the duty of the Court is to interpret the text as it stands, taking into consideration all the materials at the Court's disposal." [55]

Of course the Court does not enjoy a complete freedom in the process of interpretation thus conceived.[56] It is always under a duty to respect the text before it; unlike a legislative body, it cannot substitute a new text. Nor can any complete list be made of the "materials at the Court's disposal" for explaining a given text.[57] Canons or technical rules of interpretation can serve but a limited usefulness, and none of them can be of rigid and universal application. Within wide limits the Court must have a free hand; and it must be bound by no hard and fast rules of its own making.[58]

This has been appreciated by the Court. Fortunately, it has formulated but few rules. Most of the rules formulated have been stated in such guarded form as to leave it open to the Court to refuse to apply them; and it would be difficult to say that all of them have been applied by the Court.

§534. **Authentic Interpretation.** The Court must of course follow any interpretation of an instrument which may have been agreed

legal texts" that "when there are two interpretations, one of them attributing a reasonable meaning to each part of the text and the other not fulfilling these conditions, the first must be preferred." Series A/B, No. 41, p. 62.

[52] Series B, No. 13, p. 19.   [53] Series A/B, No. 44, p. 33.

[54] Series B, No. 2, pp. 23, 39.   [55] Series A/B, No. 44, p. 40.

[56] Dealing with national courts' function of interpretation, Austin characterized the process here described by the terrifying epithets of *bastard* and *spurious* interpretation. Austin, Lectures on Jurisprudence (3d ed.), II, pp. 597, 1029.

[57] The following statement in the *Chorzów Factory Case* indicates that this has been appreciated by the Court: "For the interpretation of Article 23 of the Geneva Convention between Germany and Poland, account must be taken not only of the historical development of arbitration treaties, as well as of the terminology of such treaties, and of the grammatical and logical meaning of the words used, but also and more especially of the function which, in the intention of the contracting parties, is to be attributed to this provision." Series A, No. 9, p. 24.

[58] The Court has also refused to be "bound by the views of the interested Governments" in giving an advisory opinion. Series A/B, No. 44, p. 35.

upon by the parties after the instrument had taken final form, though it has been scrupulously attentive to the facts in its willingness to find any such agreement. In the *Jaworzina Case,* it refused to admit the power of the Conference of Ambassadors to give a binding interpretation to its own previous decision after the task entrusted to the Conference had been fulfilled, saying that "it is an established principle that the right of giving an authoritative interpretation of a legal rule belongs solely to the person or body who has power to modify or suppress it." [59] Apart from this principle, it was said also that "the opinion of the authors of a document cannot be endowed with a decisive value when that opinion has been formulated after the drafting of that document and conflicts with the opinion which they expressed at the time." [60] In the case concerning the *Polish Postal Service in Danzig,* it was said that "a so-called authentic interpretation of a judicial decision is in effect a new decision," and the Court denied that the proper meaning of a decision could be altered by an expression of a personal opinion by its author.[61] In the case relating to the *Jurisdiction of the European Danube Commission,* an "interpretative protocol" annexed to the minutes of the Danube Conference was treated as a part of the preparatory work which could not prevail against the text of the Statute drawn up by the Conference.[62]

§535. **Intention of the Parties.** The judgments and opinions of the Court contain numerous references to the "intention of the parties" as a guide for interpretation. It is of first importance that the definitely entertained and expressed intentions of the parties should be effectuated,[63] and in some cases the results reached by the Court may be so explained. Yet it is necessary to be on guard against the use of this criterion merely as a palliating description of a result which has been arrived at by some other method than the ascertainment of intention. In litigation, the simple case is relatively rare in which the parties may be said to have foreseen and endeavored to effect a solution of the precise problem presented.[64] The parties seldom proclaim

---

[59] Series B, No. 8, p. 37.   [60] *Id.,* p. 38.
[61] Series B, No. 11, p. 31.   [62] Series B, No. 14, p. 32.

[63] It has been suggested that the criterion of intention is "hardly applicable" to "treaties imposed by force." Lauterpacht, Function of Law in the International Community (1933), p. 272.

[64] This is true also of contracts before national courts. "Litigation usually reveals the absence of genuine agreement between the parties *ab initio.* If both parties had foreseen the difficulty, provision would have been made for it in the beginning when the contract was drawn up. When courts thus proceed to interpret the terms of the contract they are generally not merely seeking to discover the actual past meanings"; the "legal

their intention in unmistakable terms; and even if an intention is pro-claimed, it must be found to have been expressed in the text.[65] More often, the problem raised before the Court was not foreseen when the instrument in question was being drafted, neither the particular prob-lem nor the general class to which it belongs; or if it was foreseen its solution was not definitely agreed upon. The compromises which are inevitable in framing an international instrument frequently result in the acceptance of a "formula" which is possible only because it does not foreclose the contentions of any party. No great experience in international conferences is required to know that terms are sometimes employed in treaties of which no common understanding is reached in advance.[66] In some situations, a lack of clarity may even be a *desideratum;* the chief desire may be to continue uncertainty.[67] Where a text is not consciously "so framed as to perpetuate the divergence of views which had arisen," however, "a formula" may be chosen which will leave the solution even of the definitely foreseen problem to await future developments.[68]

It is precisely these kinds of situations which are calculated to produce the differences of which the Court will be seised; either (1) a situation was not foreseen, or (2) it was foreseen and no clear and definite provision was made for it. In a case involving an unfore-seen situation, it can only be conjectured what the parties might have thought or said if their attention had been directed to a given pos-sibility; the Court may very properly be asked to deal with this situation, though it cannot do so by a simple reference to the intention of the parties, and any reliance on assumed intention would be

relations are determined by the courts and the jural system and not by the agreed will of the contesting parties." Morris R. Cohen, "The Basis of Contract," 46 Harvard Law Review (1933), p. 577.

[65] Series A/B, No. 43, p. 144.

[66] In 1919, the author served as a member of the Commissions which drafted the articles in the Treaty of Versailles relating to the Kiel Canal and those in the Polish Minorities Treaty, and as a member of the drafting committee which shaped the Inter-national Labor Conventions of 1919. While he shares fully the view expressed by Lord Halsbury in *Hilder* v. *Dexter* [1902] A. C. 474, 477, that "the worst person to construe" a text, "is the person who is responsible for its drafting," a refreshing of recollection from the official records only confirms his impression that the conferences which drafted these texts did not have their attention drawn to the precise problems presented to the Court in the cases which have called for their interpretation and application.

[67] This may have been true of the provision relating to the Danube, of which the Court said that its authors "were not all well acquainted with the situation which existed before the War between Galatz and Braila," but that they had agreed to main-tain "that situation whatever it may have been." Series B, No. 14, pp. 31–32.

[68] In the *Free Zones Case,* Judges Altamira and Hurst insisted that account should be taken "of human psychology and more particularly of Governmental psychology." Series A/B, No. 46, p. 182.

artificial.[69] This was recognized in the advisory opinion on the *Convention on Employment of Women at Night* when the Court said: "The mere fact that, at the time when the convention . . . was concluded, certain facts or situations, which the terms of the convention in their ordinary meaning are wide enough to cover, were not thought of, does not justify interpreting those of its provisions which are general in scope otherwise than in accordance with their terms." [70] Where the "facts or situations" were foreseen and no definite provision was made for them, also, the Court may be called upon to apply a "formula'" and to give it a content based upon considerations other than intention. Important as it may be, therefore, that effect be given to the intentions of the parties, it must be recognized that the problem of interpretation is not so simple that it can be resolved by a mere statement of that principle. In fact, no purpose is served by an assumption that the Court's function is so limited.

It is also possible that a treaty may contain provisions which were envisaged to apply to situations which could not be foreseen, and in such a case the task of interpretation may be still less confined to a mere effectuation of entertained intention.

§536. "Natural" Meaning. Throughout the Court's jurisprudence, a tendency is manifest to seek first the so-called "natural" meaning of the terms to be construed, and once it is found to weigh other considerations with a disposition to say that the "natural" meaning is not to be disturbed.[71] This may be a wise tendency, and no objection is to be made to a term which has a soothing effect and which tends to avoid arousals because of its indefinite content. Yet there may be some danger in allowing the "natural" meaning to overcome the results of other investigations. Numerous substitutions have been made for the term "natural" from time to time: a meaning may be described as "literal," [72] "grammatical," [73] "ordinary," [74] "normal," [75] "logical," [76] "reasonable." [77] It is often said that the meaning is

---

[69] It has been suggested that it is the duty of the judge "to find what, having regard to the available data, was the intention of the parties or what the intention of the parties must be presumed to have been." Lauterpacht, Function of Law in the International Community (1933), p. 130. This makes a farce of the criterion of intention.

[70] Series A/B, No. 50, p. 377.

[71] See especially Series A/B, No. 50, pp. 373, 378.

[72] Series A, No. 9, p. 24.   [73] *Ibid.;* Series A, No. 23, p. 26.

[74] Series B, No. 11, p. 37.

[75] *Id.,* p. 39; Series A/B, No. 41, p. 61 (dissenting opinion).

[76] Series A, No. 9, p. 24.

[77] Series B, No. 7, p. 20; Series B, No. 11, p. 39.

"clear" [78] or "sufficiently clear," [79] in spite of the fact that the States concerned do not place the same construction on the text, or that some members of the Court do not agree with this conclusion.[80] It would be difficult to say that the various adjectives are always used by the Court synonymously, or that any of them is used as a term of art. "Natural" seems to have reference to ordinary usage.[81] On one occasion, standard dictionaries were consulted to determine usage, though "common use" was made to yield to context.[82] The legal terminology of the States concerned is not necessarily controlling.[83] Ordinary usage must clearly yield to the usage of the time, place and occasion, however, and the Court has therefore admitted that "natural" meaning may be displaced. It has been laid down as "a cardinal principle of interpretation that words must be interpreted in the sense which they would normally have in their context, unless such interpretation would lead to something unreasonable or absurd." [84] In the advisory opinion on the *Convention on Employment of Women at Night,* a willingness was expressed "to find some valid ground for interpreting the provision otherwise than in accordance with the natural sense of the words"; but the grounds on which it had been suggested that the natural meaning could be displaced, did not "appear to the Court to be well-founded." [85]

§537. **Context.** Even in arriving at the natural meaning of terms, the Court insists upon looking at them in their context, and it early announced that "the context is the final test." [86] The context is not simply the particular sentence, or the particular paragraph in which the term to be construed occurs.[87] It may be (1) a particular part of the instrument, or (2) the instrument as a whole, or (3) the versions

[78] Series B, No. 7, p. 20; Series A/B, No. 50, p. 373. [79] Series B, No. 12, p. 22.
[80] In the advisory opinion on the *Convention on Employment of Women at Night,* a majority of the Court found the terms of Article 3 "in themselves clear and free from ambiguity"; while Judge Anzilotti found them, "to say the least . . . ambiguous." Series A/B, No. 50, pp. 373, 388.
[81] In one case, the Court referred to the "etymology" of the word and the "current practice of the language." Series B, No. 10, p. 18.
[82] Series B, No. 2/3, pp. 33, 35.
[83] "If an expression, not in itself of a legal nature, is used in a convention which derives legal consequences from it, it does not in the least follow" that a criterion for interpreting the expression "must be sought in the legislation of the respective contracting States." Series B, No. 10, p. 21.
[84] Series B, No. 11, p. 39. See also Series A/B, No. 41, p. 60. In a dissenting opinion in the *Eastern Greenland Case,* Judge Anzilotti said that "a literal interpretation fails where it would lead to absurd or inconsistent results." Series A/B, No. 53, p. 82.
[85] Series A/B, No. 50, pp. 373, 378.
[86] Series B, No. 2, p. 35. See also Series B, No. 11, p. 39.
[87] A scientific approach to the problem might also insist on the "context of situation."

of the text in different languages, or (4) the texts of several inter-related and interdependent instruments.

(1) *A Particular Part of an Instrument.* The various parts of a single instrument may be quite independent, either because of the history of their drafting or because each deals completely with a distinct subject-matter. Thus, in the judgment in the *Free Zones Case,* though it was said to be "impossible to interpret the second paragraph without regard to the first paragraph" of Article 435 of the Treaty of Versailles, that Article was taken by itself, independently of other articles in the same treaty, to form "a complete whole," both because of its position in the treaty and because of its origin.[88] In determining the competence of the International Labor Organization, the Court has considered Part XIII of the Treaty of Versailles as a whole; [89] and it has referred to "the entire framework of Part XIII." [90] In the *Wimbledon Case,* also, the provisions relating to the Kiel Canal, Section VI of Part XII of the Treaty of Versailles, were held to be "self-contained"; and it was said that "they would lose their *raison d'être*" if they had to be interpreted in connection with other sections of that part of the treaty.[91] On the other hand, one part of an instrument may be dependent on another part, in connection with which it must be construed; thus in the judgment concerning *German Interests in Polish Upper Silesia,* the Court held that a "system of rules relating to large scale industry," forming part of the Geneva Convention, should be construed as a whole.[92]

(2) *An Instrument as a Whole.* In some cases, the Court has insisted that "the treaty must be read as a whole, and that its meaning is not to be determined merely upon particular phrases which, if detached from the context, may be interpreted in more than one sense." [93] Thus in the opinion concerning the *Interpretation of the Treaty of Lausanne,* the Court not only read paragraph 2 of Article 3 in the light of paragraph 3 of the same article, but also inquired whether any other articles of the treaty were "calculated to throw any light

---

[88] Series A/B, No. 46, p. 140. In this case, it was also a matter of some importance to say whether a reference to Article 435 in the special agreement was to be construed as a reference to that article and its annexes. See *id.,* p. 182.

[89] Series B, No. 2, pp. 23, 35.   [90] Series B, No. 13, p. 18.

[91] Series A, No. 1, p. 24.

[92] Series A, No. 7, pp. 33, 48. See also Series A, No. 15, p. 31.

[93] Series B, No. 2, p. 23. See also Series A/B, No. 49, p. 317. "A law cannot set up a rule in one article and, changing its mind, a contrary rule in the next article. Any such interpretation must be ill-founded." Judge Nyholm in Series B, No. 14, p. 76.

upon the scope of Article 3." [94] This is especially so when the treaty sets up a *régime;* in such cases the Court tends to construe the provision before it by reference to its place in a whole system. This may be seen in the Court's construction of provisions relating to Danzig and to Memel. In the advisory opinion concerning the *Polish Postal Service in Danzig* it was said that "the construction which the Court has placed on the various treaty stipulations is not only reasonable but is also supported by reference to the various articles taken by themselves and in their relation one to another." [95] In the case concerning the interpretation of the *Statute of Memel,* there being no clear provision governing the question in dispute, the Court stated that "the Convention of Paris of 1924 and the Statute annexed to it must be considered as a whole in order to understand the *régime* which the Four Powers and Lithuania intended to establish for the Memel Territory"; [96] and it rejected an argument of the applicants on the ground that "such an interpretation would destroy the general scheme of the Convention of Paris of 1924 and the Statute annexed to it." [97] On the other hand, the Court has refused in some cases to allow its construction of a part of a treaty to be influenced by other parts.[98]

(3) *Versions in Different Languages.* The text of an international instrument may be drawn up in two or more languages,[99] without provision as to which is to prevail in case of difference; [100] in such a case, it seems better to speak not of several texts in different languages, but of several versions of a single text.[1] The versions in all languages must be considered together, and a meaning is to be given to the composite of them.[2] Ordinarily, neither version should be subordinated

[94] Series B, No. 12, p. 21. But see *id.,* p. 22.
[95] Series B, No. 11, pp. 39–40.
[96] Series A/B, No. 49, p. 317. See also *id.,* p. 321.
[97] *Cf.,* Series B, No. 6, p. 37.   [98] Series A, No. 17, p. 42.
[99] Where a text is in one language, it must of course be given a meaning in that language. Series B, No. 10, p. 18.
[100] This is true of the Covenant of the League of Nations and the Statute of the Court. Where a text is in two or more languages one of which is to prevail in case of difference, the version in the other language may not improperly be taken into account in interpretation.
[1] The Court has employed the term "version." Series A, No. 2, p. 18. It frequently refers to the English and French "versions" of its judgments and opinions.
[2] The statement in 1 Oppenheim, International Law (2d ed.), p. 586, (3d ed.), p. 704, (4th ed.), p. 765, that in this case "each party is only bound by the text in its own language," seems clearly erroneous; nor can his statement be accepted that "a party cannot claim the benefit of the text in the language of the other party." Oppenheim's statement may have been due to the views expressed by English courts in such cases as *Rex* v. *Brixton Prison* [1912] 3 K. B. 190, 197. *Cf.,* Ehrlich, *"L'Interprétation des Traités,"* 24 Recueil des Cours, *Académie de Droit International* (1928), pp. 95–104.

to the other, though a history of both should be taken into account. This was recognized in the second advisory opinion relating to the *Competence of the International Labor Organization.*[3] The rule was formulated in the *Mavrommatis Case* that "where two versions possessing equal authority exist one of which appears to have a wider bearing than the other," the Court "is bound to adopt the more limited interpretation which can be made to harmonise with both versions and which, as far as it goes, is doubtless in accordance with the common intention of the parties."[4] In that case it was held that "the wider meaning of the English text appears to be the only one which does not nullify the expression *contrôle public* in the French version." "Especial force" was said to be given to the rule "because the question concerns an instrument laying down the obligations of Great Britain in her capacity as Mandatory for Palestine and also because the original draft of this instrument was probably made in English"; the latter ground smacks of a reference to *travaux préparatoires* for taking account of the fact that the text in one language was constructed by the process of translating from another language, and the Court has frequently stated that this should be done only in cases of doubt.

(4) *Related and Interdependent Instruments.* Two or more instruments may be so related, or so interdependent, that the text of one must be construed with reference to that of the other. Hence the Court held that in case of doubt as to the meaning of the provisions of the Polish-Danzig Convention of November 9, 1920, "recourse may be had to the Treaty of Versailles, not for the purpose of discarding the terms of the Convention, but with a view to elucidating their meaning."[5] In its judgment relating to *German Minority Schools in Upper Silesia,* the Court "presumed" that provisions in the Polish Minorities Treaty which had been incorporated into the later Geneva Convention were not thereby given a different meaning: "there is a presumption that the provisions of the Convention are in conformity with the principles underlying the Minorities Treaty."[6] In the case concerning *German Interests in Polish Upper Silesia,* the application of the Geneva Con-

---

[3] Series B, No. 2. If one version is clear and the other is not, the former might be allowed to prevail. *Reparation Commission* v. *German Government,* Annual Digest, 1923–1924, p. 334.

[4] Series A, No. 2, p. 19. See, also, Judge Moore's dissent, *id.,* p. 69.

[5] Series A/B, No. 44, p. 32.

[6] Series A, No. 15, p. 33. It seems difficult to justify the Court's willingness in this case to consider a German argument based upon the attitude taken by Poland in negotiating an agreement with Danzig, even though the Court did not attach "much importance" to the argument. *Id.,* p. 40.

vention was found to be "hardly possible without giving an interpretation of Article 256 of the Treaty of Versailles and the other international stipulations cited by Poland," and it was held that the "interpretation of other international agreements is indisputably within the competence of the Court if such interpretation must be regarded as incidental to a decision on a point in regard to which it has jurisdiction." [7] In the opinion on the *Jurisdiction of the European Commission of the Danube,* the Court spoke of "the whole system of international acts applicable before the War to the Maritime Danube." [8] In his opinion on *Danzig and the International Labor Organization,* Judge Huber thought that the Covenant of the League of Nations and Part XIII of the Treaty of Versailles were "organically connected." [9]

§538. **Nature and Purpose of an Instrument.** A consideration of the setting of an instrument necessarily leads to appreciation of the office it was designed to serve, and the Court has frequently referred to the "nature," [10] "spirit," [11] "scheme," [12] "purpose," [13] "function," [14] "intention," [15] "tenor," [16] "rôle," [17] "object," [18] "aim" [19] or "system" [20] of, or "principles underlying," [21] an instrument.[22] That interpretation is to be favored which will make the instrument effective to serve its purpose. No rules of interpretation, therefore, can be of universal validity, applicable in the same way to all international instruments.[23]

[7] Series A, No. 6, p. 18.　　　　　　　[8] Series B, No. 14, p. 55.
[9] Series B, No. 18, p. 30.　　　　　　[10] Series A/B, No. 50, p. 388.
[11] Series B, No. 16, pp. 19, 24.　　　[12] Series A/B, No. 49, p. 317.
[13] Series A, No. 15, p. 33; Series B, No. 17, p. 19.
[14] Series A, No. 9, p. 24.　　　　　　[15] Series B, No. 6, p. 25.
[16] Series B, No. 14, p. 52.　　　　　[17] Series B, No. 12, p. 23.
[18] Series A/B, No. 44, p. 27; Series B, No. 6, p. 25; Series B, No. 8, p. 40; Series B, No. 13, pp. 19, 28; Series B, No. 17, p. 21.
[19] Series B, No. 13, p. 18; *id.,* No. 17, p. 21; Series A/B, No. 50, p. 383 (Judge Anzilotti dissenting).　　　　　　[20] Series A, No. 5, p. 49; Series B, No. 14, p. 37.
[21] Series A/B, No. 43, pp. 142, 157; Series A, No. 1, p. 23; *id.,* No. 23, p. 26.
[22] Mr. Charles Cheney Hyde states the task of the interpreter to be "to get at the truth concerning the design of the parties as exemplified by their treaty." See his studies in 24 American Journal of International Law (1930), p. 1; 27 *id.* (1933), p. 502.
[23] Thus, the Covenant of the League of Nations may have to be interpreted less strictly than many other international instruments. In a memorandum signed by President Wilson, M. Clemenceau, and Mr. Lloyd George on May 6, 1919, it was said that "the articles of the Covenant are not subject to a narrow or technical construction." Miller, Drafting of the Covenant, I, p. 489. See also Ray, *Commentaire du Pacte de la Société des Nations* (1930), pp. 12ff.
　　Mr. Quincy Wright has suggested that different approaches are to be followed in interpreting multipartite and bipartite treaties: "With respect to interpretation it seems both reasonable and in accord with practice to regard treaties between two or a small number of States as analogous to contracts, while multilateral law-making treaties bear more resemblance to statutes." Wright, "The Interpretation of Multilateral Treaties," 23 American Journal of International Law (1929), pp. 94, 104. Both of these analogies are misleading, and little support in practice is to be found for the general distinction drawn.

Such appreciation has been shown by the Court, particularly in connection with its interpretation of treaties for the protection of minorities. In the opinion on *German Settlers in Poland,* the Court rejected a contention that the competence conferred on the Council of the League of Nations by the Polish Minorities Treaty did not apply to Poland's exercise of rights conferred by the Treaty of Versailles, stating: "The main object of the Minorities Treaty is to assure respect for the rights of minorities and to prevent discrimination against them by any act whatsoever of the Polish State. . . . If the Council ceased to be competent whenever the subject before it involved the interpretation of such an international engagement, the Minorities Treaty would to a great extent be deprived of value. . . . In order that the pledged protection may be certain and effective, it is essential that the Council, when acting under the Minorities Treaty, should be competent, incidentally, to consider and interpret the laws or treaties on which the rights claimed to be infringed are dependent." [24] Later it was said that "an interpretation which would deprive the Minorities Treaty of a great part of its value is inadmissible." [25] The same attitude was shown in the construction of the words "interpretation and application" in Article 23 of the German-Polish Convention of May 18, 1922, when the Court took account "not only of the historical development of arbitration treaties as well as of the terminology of such treaties, and of the grammatical and logical meaning of the words used, but also and more especially of the function which, in the intention of the contracting Parties, is to be attributed to this provision." [26] When called upon to interpret an international labor convention, the Court considered "the fact that the improvement of the lot of the manual worker was the aim of Part XIII" of the Treaty of Versailles. [27] In the case relating to *German Settlers in Poland,* however, the Court refused to give weight to an alleged purpose of de-Germanization where this would involve an extension inconsistent with the provisions of a treaty; [28] and in an opinion on the *Competence of the International Labor Organization,* it was said that "the Court, in determining the nature and scope of a measure, must look to its practical effect rather than to the predominant motive that may be conjectured to have inspired it." [29]

[24] Series B, No. 6, p. 25.   [25] Series B, No. 7, p. 17.
[26] Series A, No. 9, p. 24. See also *id.,* p. 25.
[27] Series A/B, No. 50, p. 374. See also Series B, No. 3, p. 57.
[28] Series B, No. 6, p. 37.   [29] Series B, No. 13, p. 19.

The jurisprudence of the Court does not establish any rigid time-table for the various steps in the process of interpretation. Yet it is to be noted that in the opinion on the *Convention on Employment of Women at Night*, the Court did not take account of the policy to be served by the instrument until after it had arrived at a conclusion as to the "natural" meaning of terms in the convention, and then only for the purpose of determining whether the "natural" meaning could be displaced. This was made the target of a brilliant dissent by Judge Anzilotti, who protested that it is not "possible to say that an article of a convention is clear until the subject and aim of the convention have been ascertained." "The first question which arises," he said, "is what is the subject [Fr., *objet*] and aim of the convention." [30]

§539. **Use of Travaux Préparatoires.** It is doubtless a sound principle that when negotiations have resulted in the text of an instrument which is formalized by signature and possibly by ratification, that text should ordinarily be taken to embody the whole of the agreement reached in the course of the negotiations. Additions to the text are not to be made as a consequence of a study of preliminary drafts which were not incorporated into the instrument which was signed; nor are subtractions to be made by that means. A preliminary question may arise as to what is the text which was agreed upon.[31] Yet after it is disposed of, the construction of the text cannot be arrived at without a consideration of its setting, and the development of the negotiations forms a part of the history which constitutes that setting. Where a dispute revolves about issues connected with the preparation of a text, as did the dispute concerning the *Interpretation of the Treaty of Lausanne*, it would be merely stultifying to say that. *travaux préparatoires* cannot be examined.

While the Court has always been careful to trace the history of the negotiations which have led to the signing of an instrument, it has shown itself somewhat reluctant to make use of preliminary drafts, *travaux préparatoires*.[32] The actual rules formulated on this subject have been stated in such a way as to leave the Court wide latitude; and it is doubtful whether the Court's practice has been in any way circumscribed by such formulations. Even when the use of *travaux*

---

[30] Series A/B, No. 50, p. 383. [31] See Series B, No. 14, p. 34.

[32] This term may also be applied to materials other than preliminary drafts. Using it in this broader sense, the Court may be said to have referred to *travaux préparatoires* in the *Jaworzina Case*, when it expressed a willingness to study instructions given to representatives composing the Conference of Ambassadors in interpreting a decision of that Conference. Series B, No. 8, p. 26.

préparatoires has been said to be excluded, in most cases they have been used to confirm conclusions reached. The rule has frequently been stated that "there is no occasion to have regard to preparatory work if the text of a convention is sufficiently clear in itself." [33] This leaves the door open for saying that *travaux préparatoires* may be resorted to because the text is not "sufficiently clear"; [34] on this point, individual judges have sometimes dissented from the majority's view. On a few occasions the Court has shown a willingness to refer to *travaux préparatoires* without referring to this rule.[35] In the case relating to *Polish Nationals in Danzig,* where a text was found to be not "absolutely clear," the Court thought it "useful, in order to ascertain its precise meaning, to recall here somewhat in detail the various drafts which existed prior to the adoption of the text now in force"; [36] yet one judge in this case found the text to be "so clear that a reference to the *travaux préparatoires* of the convention seems hardly justifiable." [37] Even in cases where the text has been found to be "sufficiently clear," however, usually the Court does not altogether refuse to examine *travaux préparatoires,* and it sometimes uses them to buttress the conclusions which have been reached independently. Thus, in its second advisory opinion, after the Court had reached its conclusion "on the construction of the text itself," it was observed that "there is certainly nothing in the preparatory work to disturb this conclusion." [38] In the *Lotus Case,* after a construction was given to the expression "principles of international law" as used in the Lausanne Convention, it was said that "the records of the preparation of the Convention . . . would not furnish anything calculated to overrule the construction indicated by the actual terms" of the Article, and *travaux préparatoires* were gone into to justify this statement.[39] In the opinion on the *Interpretation of the Treaty of Lausanne,* a text was found to be "sufficiently clear," and yet the Court proceeded to consider it "in the light of the

[33] Series A, No. 10, p. 16; Series B, No. 14, p. 28; Series A, No. 20/21, p. 30; Series A/B, No. 47, p. 249; *id.,* No. 50, p. 378.
 The Supreme Court of the United States has followed a similar rule with reference to national legislation. *Standard Fashion Co.* v. *Magrane-Houston Co.* (1922) 258 U. S. 346, 356; *Ozawa* v. *U. S.* (1922) 260 U. S. 178, 194; *Van Camp & Sons* v. *American Can Co.* (1929) 278 U. S. 245, 253; *U. S.* v. *Missouri Pacific R. R. Co.* (1929) 278 U. S. 269, 278.
[34] The mere fact that the Council has asked for an interpretation of a provision ought not to cast doubt upon its clarity. *Cf.,* Series B, No. 12, p. 25.
[35] See the *Mavrommatis Case,* Series A, No. 2, p. 24; *id.,* No. 5, p. 47; and see Series B, No. 9, pp. 17–18; *id.,* No. 10, p. 16. In individual opinions, the judges refer to *travaux préparatoires* quite frequently. *E.g.,* Series A, No. 22, p. 32.
[36] Series A/B, No. 44, p. 33.　　　　　[38] Series B, No. 2, p. 41.
[37] *Id.,* p. 56.　　　　　[39] Series A, No. 10, p. 17.

negotiations." [40] With reference to the bonds in question in the *Serbian Loans Case,* the Court said that "as the words themselves are not ambiguous, there is no occasion to refer to the preliminary documents. But if these are examined, it will appear that they tend to confirm the agreement for gold payments." [41] In its interpretation of the *Convention on Employment of Women during the Night,* the Court was "so struck with the confident opinions expressed" that it was "led to examine the preparatory work of the Convention," disclaiming an intention "to derogate in any way from the rule" laid down as to *travaux préparatoires;* its conclusion was only confirmed in consequence. [42]

The conclusion to be drawn from the jurisprudence is that while the Court professes a willingness to look into *travaux préparatoires* only for the purpose of resolving a doubt as to the text, it has on many occasions done so to confirm constructions as to which it had no doubt. In spite of the frequency of these occasions, it must be said that the Court has not exercised a complete freedom in the use of *travaux préparatoires;* a resort to them only after a conclusion has been reached is not the same as a resort to them before the conclusion is formulated. [43]

Once the decision is taken that *travaux préparatoires* may be resorted to, the Court has not been very definite in saying to what extent they may be relied upon. It has said, however, that "preparatory work should not be used for the purpose of changing the plain meaning of a text." [44] Judge Anzilotti has formulated a more definite rule, that preparatory work is to be "adduced not to extend or limit the scope of a text clear in itself, but to verify the existence of an intention not necessarily emerging from the text but likewise not excluded by that text." [45] Under the approach made by the Court, it seems improbable that it will have a case in which it admits the "plain meaning" to be clear and in which it will feel compelled by the *travaux préparatoires* to assign a different meaning to the text.

One quite definite ground for refusing to consider *travaux préparatoires* was stated in the advisory opinion relating to the *Jurisdic-*

---

[40] Series B, No. 12, p. 22. See also *id.,* No. 14, pp. 28–31.
[41] Series A, No. 20/21, p. 30.   [42] Series A/B, No. 50, pp. 378–380.
[43] The element of time may be less important than the above indicates. Where *travaux préparatoires* are referred to in documents or argument before the Court, they will doubtless have been studied even before any conclusions are reached; this fact robs the actual formulations by the Court of some of their importance.
[44] Series B, No. 14, p. 31.   [45] Series A/B, No. 50, p. 388.

tion of the European Commission of the Danube. The history of certain articles of the Treaty of Versailles having been invoked, the Court said: "The record of the work preparatory to the adoption of these articles being confidential and not being placed before the Court by, or with the consent of, the competent authority, the Court is not called upon to consider to what extent it might have been possible for it to take this preparatory work into account." [46] Perhaps it is a somewhat different question whether *travaux préparatoires* may be admitted as evidence; usually they are admitted without question, and in consequence they constitute a part of the judges' background of knowledge, whatever rule may be formulated as to their use. In connection with the second advisory opinion, the objection was made that such materials should not be considered by the Court, not that they should not be admitted as evidence.[47] In the case on the *Jurisdiction of the Oder Commission,* however, the Court was asked to rule that no attention should be paid to passages in the Polish case and counter-case which referred to records of the preparatory work of the Treaty of Versailles, *viz.,* the minutes of the Commission on Ports, Waterways and Railways; and by its order of August 20, 1929, the Court ruled that these minutes should "be excluded as evidence from the proceedings in the present case." [48] The chief ground of this order was that "three of the parties concerned in the present case did not take part in the work of the conference which prepared the Treaty of Versailles." [49]

§540. **Legal Background.** Any international instrument must be interpreted in the light of the prevailing international law, by which the parties must be taken to have charted their course.[50] Judges Anzilotti and Huber insisted on this point in the *Wimbledon Case,* stating that "treaty stipulations cannot be interpreted as limiting" a State's right of self-protection, "even though these stipulations do not

---

[46] Series B, No. 14, p. 32. For the correspondence of the Registrar with the President of the Conference of Ambassadors at Paris, see Series C, No. 13—IV, pp. 2172, 2188.

[47] Series B, No. 2, p. 41; Series C, No. 1, pp. 187–189.

[48] Series A, No. 23, pp. 41–43.

[49] This refers to Denmark, Germany and Sweden. As to Germany, the statement is somewhat surprising, though it is true that Germany was not represented in the Commission on Ports, Waterways and Railways of the Preliminary Peace Conference at Paris; Denmark and Sweden were not parties to the Treaty of Versailles.

[50] The following statement by the French-Mexican Claims Commission seems to be apposite: "Every international convention must be deemed tacitly to refer to general principles of international law for all questions which it does not itself resolve in express terms or in a different way." *Georges Pinson Case* (1928), Annual Digest, 1927–1928, Case No. 292.

conflict with such an interpretation."[51] In the judgment relating to *German Interests in Polish Upper Silesia*, the Court took the "generally accepted international law" to constitute, at least in part, "the basis of the Geneva Convention."[52] In the case relating to the *Jurisdiction of the Oder Commission*, the Court found it proper to explore "the principles underlying the matter to which the text refers," and Article 331 of the Treaty of Versailles was "interpreted in the light of these principles," *viz.*, "the principles governing international fluvial law in general";[53] and in interpreting Article 338 of the same treaty, it was said to be "hardly justifiable to deduce from a somewhat ill-chosen expression an intention to derogate from a rule of international law so important as that relating to the ratification of conventions."[54] In the opinion on the *Interpretation of the Treaty of Lausanne*, the Court took the provisions of the Covenant concerning unanimity to be subject to the "well-known rule that no one can be judge in his own suit."[55] To some extent also, the Court might take account of the municipal laws of the parties as a part of the legal background of an instrument, though in the opinion on the *Exchange of Greek and Turkish Populations* it showed itself reluctant to do so.[56] It has also referred to the "precedents supplied by international practice."[57]

§541. **Political and Social Background.** Quite clearly, the Court would not be justified in dealing with an international instrument as if it had been concluded *in vacuo*. It must take account of the general setting in which the parties acted if it would understand their purposes, and its construction of an instrument may very properly be influenced by factors of a political or social significance. International legislation which the Court must apply is frequently designed to deal with such factors. As the Court has phrased it, "the making of laws, whether national or international, is a political act and as such may involve the application of political principles."[58] If international law is to be builded on sound foundations, it is no more possible to ignore the political and social phases of the prevailing international order than it is possible to ignore similar phases of the prevailing national order in the building of municipal law.[59]

---

[51] Series A, No. 1, p. 37.
[52] Series A, No. 7, p. 42. *Cf. id.*, pp. 21, 22.
[53] Series A, No. 23, pp. 26, 29.
[54] *Id.*, p. 20.
[55] Series B, No. 12, p. 32.
[56] Series B, No. 10, pp. 19, 21.
[57] Series B, No. 7, p. 17.
[58] Series B, No. 13, p. 22.
[59] This is shown in the foundations of the public law of the United States as they were laid by Chief Justice John Marshall, and in the decisions of the United States Supreme Court with reference to the 14th amendment to the Constitution of the United States.

This has been appreciated by the Court in a long course of action. In the judgment on *German Interests in Polish Upper Silesia,* the Geneva Convention was interpreted "in the light of war-time legislation," and a city was included in the term "national." [60] In the *Jaworzina Case,* extended reference was made to the general political situation in which decisions had been taken by the Supreme Council and the Conference of Ambassadors for defining the Polish-Czechoslovak frontier.[61] In determining the nature of the vote to be taken by the Council of the League of Nations under Article 3 of the Treaty of Lausanne, the Court had in mind the "political position" of certain States which might require them to "bear the larger share of the responsibilities and consequences." [62] The Definitive Statute of the Danube was viewed by the Court with reference to "the historical facts upon which it rests." [63] The construction placed on the treaties applicable to the proposed Austro-German customs régime was preceded by a reference to "the existing political settlement which has laid down in Europe the consequences of the break-up of the Austro-Hungarian monarchy"; the existence of Austria was thought to be "an essential feature" of that settlement, and the Court's conclusions were based on this background of "circumstances." [64] This was surely a sounder attitude than that taken by a minority of the Court which was not "concerned with political considerations," and which saw the question presented as "purely legal." [65] In the advisory opinion on *Polish War Vessels in Danzig,* the Court "took notice," as of a "matter of history," of the assurances given to Poland of a free and secure access to the sea,[66] but it found no reasons for assuming that these assurances had not been completely fulfilled in the later agreements. In the advisory opinion on the treatment of *Polish Nationals in Danzig,* an interpretation of the treaty provisions was made "in the light of the circumstances which led to the creation of Danzig as a Free City." [67] In the opinion concerning the *Greco-Bulgarian Communities,* the Court insisted on the "traditional conception" of a "community"

---

[60] Series A, No. 7, p. 74.
[61] Series B, No. 8, pp. 20–22.
[62] Series B, No. 12, p. 29.
[63] Series B, No. 14, p. 28.
[64] Series A/B, No. 41, p. 42. Judge Anzilotti also insisted in this case that "account must be taken of the movement . . . the aim of which is to effect the political union" of Austria and Germany. *Id.,* p. 70.
[65] Some of the criticism of the Court's opinion in this case was due to a failure to appreciate the nature of the judicial process which had to be followed in order to reply to the question put. See Edwin M. Borchard, in 25 American Journal of International Law (1931), p. 711.
[66] Series A/B, No. 43, p. 144.
[67] Series A/B, No. 44, p. 27.

in Eastern countries, and held that the Greco-Bulgarian Convention should be taken to embody that conception.[68]

§542. **Analogous Provisions.** An aid to the interpretation of a text may sometimes be found in analogous provisions either in the same instrument, or more rarely in an instrument to which other States are parties. Even if a part of a treaty or convention is taken to be a self-contained whole, analogies may be drawn from other parts; thus, in the *Wimbledon Case,* though the provisions of the Treaty of Versailles relating to the Kiel Canal were said to be self-contained, the wording of Article 380 was "compared with that of the other provisions to be found in Part XII." [69] In the opinion concerning *German Settlers in Poland,* the Court drew upon analogies in Article 75 of the Treaty of Versailles relating to Alsace-Lorraine and in other articles, in its application of Article 256 of the same treaty.[70] In the *Chorzów Factory Case,* the Court refused to draw any conclusion from the terminology in general arbitration agreements, for interpreting a compromissory clause in the Geneva Convention, though it found some analogy in the classification of disputes in Article 13 of the Covenant and Article 36 of the Court's Statute.[71] In interpreting the *Convention on the Employment of Women at Night,* the Court was willing "to attach some importance" to provisions in the eight-hour day convention, also drawn up by the International Labor Conference in 1919, because of its "similarity both in structure and in expression." [72] On the other hand, the Court has declared it to be a general principle of interpretation that "an obligation imposed on one contracting party cannot be based on the fact that it is mentioned in the annex to a section of a treaty dealing with a different subject matter." [73]

§543. **Action by the Parties.** In the process of *giving* a meaning to a text, the Court cannot ignore action which may have been taken by the parties to an instrument, either contemporaneously with its drafting or subsequently,[74] though as the Court said in the *Brazilian Loans Case,* "where reference is had to the conduct of the Parties as an aid to interpretation, it is necessary to consider whether that conduct itself permits of but one inference." [75] Contemporaneous

[68] Series B, No. 17, p. 21.
[69] Series A, No. 1, p. 23.
[70] Series B, No. 6, p. 38. *Cf.,* Series A, No. 7, p. 30.
[71] Series A, No. 9, pp. 22–23.
[72] Series A/B, No. 50, pp. 380–381.
[73] Series A, No. 3, p. 9.
[74] *Cf.,* M. Ehrlich's statement, Series A, No. 9, p. 43.
[75] Series A, No. 20/21, p. 119.

action by the parties, related to the instrument itself, may be taken to indicate the purpose which the instrument was designed to serve.[76] In an advisory opinion on the *Competence of the International Labor Organization,* the Court relied upon the inclusion of an item in the agenda of the first International Labor Conference, "as a contemporaneous practical interpretation made by the High Contracting Parties of the scope of the competence which they had conferred upon the International Labour Organization."[77] Subsequent action taken by the parties may also furnish some indication of the purpose with which an instrument was concluded, though great caution must be exercised in finding such an indication. In its opinion on the *Interpretation of the Treaty of Lausanne,* the Court declared that "the facts subsequent to the conclusion of the Treaty of Lausanne can only concern the Court in so far as they are calculated to throw light on the intention of the parties at the time of the conclusion of the treaty."[78] It seems doubtful whether this limitation has always been observed, however.

In an advisory opinion on the *Competence of the International Labor Organization,* a willingness was expressed "if there were any ambiguity"[79] to "consider the action which has been taken under the Treaty" for the "purpose of arriving at the true meaning"; and though no ambiguity was found to exist, the Court did refer to action taken under the Treaty.[80] In a later opinion on the same general subject, the Court referred to the actual exercise of competence by the International Labor Organization in the convention on the use of white lead in painting.[81] In these two cases, the function of interpretation bore a close resemblance to the function exercised by certain national courts in passing upon the constitutionality of legislation, and in the second case the Court pointed out that "it is not an unusual thing, in countries in which legislative power is limited by a fundamental charter, for the courts, in deciding whether certain legislation is constitutional, or *intra vires,* to resort to practice, national or international, for the determination of the extent of a particular governmental power."[82] Such action by national courts is based upon a

---

[76] In the *Jaworzina Case,* one of the contemporary documents relied upon was not related to the decision to be interpreted. Series B, No. 8, pp. 33, 38. See also Series B, No. 14, p. 58.

[77] Series B, No. 13, p. 19. However, this result might have been rested on reading Part XIII of the Treaty of Versailles as a whole. See also Series B, No. 8, p. 33.

[78] Series B, No. 12, p. 24.   [80] Series B, No. 2, p. 39.

[79] *Cf.,* Series A, No. 20/21, pp. 38, 119.   [81] Series B, No. 13, p. 19.

[82] Series B, No. 13, p. 20. This is particularly true of the Supreme Court of the United States.

reluctance to disturb a course of action under legislation and upon a desire to take into account the results of a particular interpretation given in practice to a constitutional provision. It would seem that the consideration of subsequent action by the Court in these two cases was based upon a similar reluctance and a similar desire; in other words, the Court has not observed the limitation placed upon itself in the opinion relating to the *Interpretation of the Treaty of Lausanne*. With the lapse of time, intentions entertained by the draftsmen of an instrument may lose some of their importance, and a course of action by those who must live with and under the provisions of the instrument may assume a correspondingly greater significance. In the advisory opinion relating to the *Jurisdiction of Danzig Courts*, the fact that the *Beamtenabkommen* had been actually put into force by the parties was taken to indicate their intention that it should govern directly the relations between the Polish Railways Administration and the Danzig officials.[83]

What has been said applies to action which is common to all the parties to an instrument. Action taken by a single party may involve an admission which will militate against some position it may assume,[84] but it is not otherwise to be taken into account in interpretation.

§544. **Liberal or Restrictive Interpretation.** The Court has not attempted to formulate any general principle that instruments must be liberally or strictly construed. A national court may be justified in adopting a policy of the liberal construction of treaties to which the State is a party, for it will seldom be called upon to construe a treaty with other States before it; [85] an international court before which only States may be parties would not be justified in adopting any such principle. The Court has said that "rules as to a strict or liberal construction of treaty stipulations can be applied only in cases where ordinary methods of interpretation have failed." [86] No rules for extensive interpretation have been formulated; [87] and where specific rules for a restrictive interpretation are announced,[88] a *caveat* is usually entered to avoid their automatic application. First, the Court has

---

[83] Series B, No. 15, pp. 18, 20–21.   [84] See Series A, No. 3, p. 8.

[85] The Supreme Court of the United States has frequently stated that "treaties are to be liberally construed." See *Jordan* v. *Tashiro* (1928) 278 U. S. 123; *Nielsen* v. *Johnson* (1929) 279 U. S. 47. *Quaere*, whether even in a national court the principle should be stated so broadly.   [86] Series B, No. 11, p. 39.

[87] However, the Court said in the *Jaworzina Case* that as the object of a clause in a decision was "one of equity, it must not be interpreted in too rigid a manner." Series B, No. 8, p. 40.

[88] In their individual opinions, judges have sometimes referred to rules of restrictive interpretation as "presumptions." *E.g.*, Series A, No. 9, p. 40.

adopted a rule of restrictive interpretation of texts conferring jurisdiction upon itself. "Every special agreement, like every clause conferring jurisdiction on the Court, must be interpreted strictly"; yet it
was added that this rule is not to be so applied that the special agreement would fail to enunciate the question in dispute and prejudge the
answer,[89] or fail to have "appropriate effects." [90] Again, it has been
said that limitations on the exercise of sovereign rights must be strictly
construed; but this is only "in case of doubt," [91] and in applying this
rule in the *Wimbledon Case* the Court felt itself "obliged to stop at the
point where the so-called restrictive interpretation would be contrary
to the plain terms of the article and would destroy what has clearly
been granted." [92] In the *Oder Commission Case,* it was contended that
where a text is doubtful, that construction should be given to it "which
imposes the least restriction on the freedom of States"; the Court
thought that while the argument was "sound in itself," the rule was to
be "employed only with the greatest caution." "Only when in spite of
all pertinent considerations, the intention of the parties remains doubtful," is that interpretation to be given "which is most favourable to
the freedom of States." [93] In the advisory opinion concerning the
Interpretation of the Treaty of Lausanne, it was said to be a sound
principle that "if the wording of a treaty provision is not clear, in
choosing between several admissible interpretations, the one which
involves the minimum of obligations for the parties should be adopted";
but the text there involved was said to be clear.[94]

A clear instance of restrictive interpretation is to be found in the
interpretation of texts which form an exceptional part of a system
or régime into which they must be fitted. Thus, in the case concerning *Nationality Decrees in Tunis and Morocco,* it was said that since
paragraph 8 of Article 15 of the Covenant is "an exception to the
principles affirmed in the preceding paragraph," it "does not therefore lend itself to an extensive interpretation." [95] In the case concerning the *Mavrommatis Concessions,* "a strict interpretation" was given

[89] Series A/B, No. 46, pp. 138–139, 167.
[90] Series A, No. 22, p. 13. See also Series A, No. 24, p. 14.
[91] Series A, No. 1, p. 24; No. 24, p. 12; Series A/B, No. 46, p. 167.
[92] Series A, No. 1, pp. 24–25. In this case, Judge Schücking declared that "all
treaties concerning servitudes must be interpreted strictly." *Id.,* p. 43. Judges Anzilotti
and Huber were reluctant to interpret a treaty so as to limit a State's self-protection,
and this consideration was said to apply "with particular force in the case of perpetual
provisions without reciprocity which affect the interests of third States." *Id.,* p. 37.
[93] Series A, No. 23, p. 26.   [94] Series B, No. 12, p. 25.
[95] Series B, No. 4, p. 25. See also Series A, No. 2, p. 85; Series A, No. 7, pp. 22, 42.

to Article 6 of the Lausanne Protocol as "the only one which is in harmony with the system of the Protocol." [96] In the judgment on *German Interests in Polish Upper Silesia*, it was said that "the liability to expropriation of rural property constitutes, under the Geneva Convention, an exception; in case of doubt as to the scope of this provision, its terms must therefore be strictly construed." [97]

§545. **Special Rules of Interpretation.** On a few occasions the Court has formulated special rules of interpretation, some of which it borrowed from municipal law. Thus, in the *Mavrommatis Case*, it held that as between Article 11 of the Palestine Mandate and the Lausanne Protocol XII, "in cases of doubt, the Protocol, being a special and more recent agreement, should prevail." [98] In the *Serbian Loans Case*, being called upon to interpret provisions in a bond the Court declared that "the special words, according to elementary principles of interpretation, control the general expressions." [99] In the *Brazilian Loans Case*, it was said to be "a familiar rule for the construction of instruments that, where they are found to be ambiguous, they should be taken *contra proferentem";* and it was held that an ambiguity in a prospectus of the loans might be resolved against the Brazilian Government which was responsible for it, that meaning being given which the terms "would naturally carry to those taking the bonds under the prospectus." [100] The Court has also applied the maxim *expressio unius exclusio alterius*.[1]

---

[96] Series A, No. 5, p. 49. [97] Series A, No. 7, p. 76.
[98] Series A, No. 2, p. 31. *Cf.*, Series A, No. 7, p. 29.
[99] Series A, No. 20/21, p. 30. *Cf.*, Series A, No. 7, p. 33.
[100] Series A, No. 20/21, p. 114. [1] Series A/B, No. 42, p. 121.

APPENDICES

I. INSTRUMENTS RELATING TO THE CONSTITUTION OF THE COURT

APPENDIX NO. 1

Resolution of the Assembly of the League of Nations, Geneva, December 13th, 1920

Text from Series D, No. 1, 2d. ed., p. 6.

1. L'Assemblé à l'unanimité déclare approuver, avec les amendements qu'elle y a apportés, le projet de Statut de la Cour permanente de Justice internationale, qui, préparé par le Conseil aux termes de l'article 14 du Pacte,[1] a été soumis à son approbation.

2. Le Statut de la Cour, vu les termes particuliers dudit article 14, sera soumis, dans le plus bref délai, aux Membres de la Société des Nations pour adoption sous forme de Protocole dûment ratifié constatant qu'ils reconnaissent ce Statut. Le soin de procéder à cette présentation est confié au Conseil.

3. Dès que ce Protocole aura été ratifié par la majorité des Membres

1. The Assembly unanimously declares its approval of the draft Statute of the Permanent Court of International Justice—as amended by the Assembly—which was prepared by the Council under Article 14 of the Covenant[1] and submitted to the Assembly for its approval.

2. In view of the special wording of Article 14, the Statute of the Court shall be submitted within the shortest possible time to the Members of the League of Nations for adoption in the form of a Protocol duly ratified and declaring their recognition of this Statute. It shall be the duty of the Council to submit the Statute to the Members.

3. As soon as this Protocol has been ratified by the majority of the

---

[1] *Article 14 du Pacte de la Société des Nations.*
Le Conseil est chargé de préparer un projet de Cour permanente de Justice internationale et de le soumettre aux Membres de la Société. Cette Cour connaîtra de tous différends d'un caractère international que les Parties lui soumettront. Elle donnera aussi des avis consultatifs sur tout différend ou tout point dont la saisira le Conseil ou l'Assemblée.

[1] *Article 14 of the Covenant of the League of Nations.*
The Council shall formulate and submit to the Members of the League for adoption plans for the establishment of a Permanent Court of International Justice. The Court shall be competent to hear and determine any dispute of an international character which the Parties thereto submit to it. The Court may also give an advisory opinion upon any dispute or question referred to it by the Council or by the Assembly.

de la Société, le Statut de la Cour sera en vigueur et la Cour sera appelée à siéger, conformément audit Statut, dans tous les litiges entre les Membres ou États ayant ratifié, ainsi que pour les autres États auxquels la Cour est ouverte aux termes de l'article 35, alinéa 2, dudit Statut.

4. Ledit Protocole restera également ouvert à la signature des États mentionnés à l'annexe au Pacte.

Members of the League, the Statute of the Court shall come into force and the Court shall be called upon to sit in conformity with the said Statute in all disputes between the Members or States which have ratified, as well as between the other States to which the Court is open under Article 35, paragraph 2, of the said Statute.

4. The said Protocol shall likewise remain open for signature by the States mentioned in the Annex to the Covenant.

APPENDIX NO. 2

Protocol of Signature of the Statute of the Permanent Court of International Justice, Geneva, December 16, 1920

Text from Series D, No. 1, 2d. ed., p. 7.

Les Membres de la Société des Nations, représentés par les soussignés dûment autorisés, déclarent reconnaître le Statut ci-joint de la Cour permanente de Justice internationale de la Société des Nations, approuvé par le vote unanime de l'Assemblée de la Société, en date, à Genève, du 13 décembre 1920.

En conséquence, ils déclarent accepter la juridiction de la Cour dans les termes et conditions prévus dans le Statut ci-dessus visé.

Le présent Protocole, dressé conformément à la décision de l'Assemblée de la Société des Nations du 13 décembre 1920, sera ratifié. Chaque Puissance adressera sa ratification au Secrétariat général de la Société des Nations, par les soins duquel il en sera donné avis à toutes les autres

The Members of the League of Nations, through the undersigned, duly authorized, declare their acceptance of the adjoined Statute of the Permanent Court of International Justice, which was approved by a unanimous vote of the Assembly of the League on the 13th December, 1920, at Geneva.

Consequently, they hereby declare that they accept the jurisdiction of the Court in accordance with the terms and subject to the conditions of the above-mentioned Statute.

The present Protocol, which has been drawn up in accordance with the decision taken by the Assembly of the League of Nations on the 13th December, 1920, is subject to ratification. Each Power shall send its ratification to the Secretary-General of the League of Nations; the

Puissances signataires. Les ratifications resteront déposées dans les archives du Secrétariat de la Société des Nations.

Le présent Protocole restera ouvert à la signature des États visés à l'annexe du Pacte de la Société.

Le Statut de la Cour entrera en vigueur ainsi qu'il est prévu par ladite décision.

Fait à Genève, en un seul exemplaire, dont les textes français et anglais feront foi.

Le 16 décembre 1920.

latter shall take the necessary steps to notify such ratification to the other signatory Powers. The ratification shall be deposited in the archives of the Secretariat of the League of Nations.

The said Protocol shall remain open for signature by the Members of the League of Nations and by the States mentioned in the Annex to the Covenant of the League.

The Statute of the Court shall come into force as provided in the above-mentioned decision.

Executed at Geneva, in a single copy, the French and English texts of which shall both be authentic.

December 16th, 1920.

[Signatures omitted.]

SIGNATURE AND RATIFICATION OF THE PROTOCOL OF SIGNATURE OF DECEMBER 16, 1920

(As of June 1, 1934)

States [1]	Date of Signature [2]	Date of Deposit of Ratification [2]
Albania	June 18, 1921	July 13, 1921
Argentine Republic		
Australia	June 16, 1921	Aug. 4, 1921
Austria	June 18, 1921	July 23, 1921
Belgium	May 9, 1921	Aug. 29, 1921
Bolivia	June 20, 1921	
Brazil	Before Feb. 25, 1921	Nov. 1, 1921
Bulgaria	April 10, 1921	Aug. 12, 1921
Canada	March 30, 1921	Aug. 4, 1921
Chile	Sept. 7, 1921	July 20, 1928
China	Before Feb. 25, 1921	May 13, 1922
Colombia	Before Feb. 25, 1921	Jan. 6, 1932
Costa Rica	Before Jan. 28, 1921	
Cuba	Before Feb. 25, 1921	Jan. 12, 1922
Czechoslovakia	May 19, 1921	Sept. 2, 1921
Denmark	Before Jan. 28, 1921	June 13, 1921
Dominican Republic	Sept. 30, 1924	Feb. 4, 1933
Ecuador		

[1] The States to which the Protocol of Signature was opened for signature are listed. They include all of the Members of the League of Nations since 1920, and the three additional States mentioned in the Annex to the Covenant of the League of Nations.

[2] The dates have been compiled from various official documents, more especially League of Nations Document A. 6(a). 1933. V. Annex.

States	Date of Signature	Date of Deposit of Ratification
Estonia	Oct. 18, 1921	May 2, 1923
Ethiopia	July 12, 1926	July 16, 1926
Finland	June 28, 1921	Apr. 6, 1922
France	Before Feb. 25, 1921	Aug. 7, 1921
Germany	Dec. 10, 1926	Mar. 11, 1927
Great Britain	Before Feb. 25, 1921	Aug. 4, 1921
Greece	Before Feb. 25, 1921	Oct. 3, 1921
Guatemala	Dec. 17, 1926	
Haiti	Before Sept. 5, 1921	Sept. 7, 1921
Hedjaz [3]		
Honduras		
Hungary	August 1, 1923	Nov. 20, 1925
India	Before Feb. 25, 1921	Aug. 4, 1921
Iraq		
Irish Free State		[4] From Aug. 21, 1926
Italy	Before Feb. 25, 1921	June 20, 1921
Japan	Before Feb. 25, 1921	Nov. 16, 1921
Latvia	Sept. 11, 1923	Feb. 12, 1924
Liberia	Before Sept. 1, 1921	
Lithuania	Oct. 5, 1921	May 16, 1922
Luxemburg	Before Feb. 25, 1921	Sept. 15, 1930
Mexico		
Netherlands	Before Feb. 25, 1921	Aug. 6, 1921
New Zealand	Before Feb. 25, 1921	Aug. 4, 1921
Nicaragua	Sept. 14, 1929	
Norway	Before Feb. 25, 1921	Aug. 20, 1921
Panama	Before Feb. 25, 1921	June 14, 1929
Paraguay	Before Feb. 25, 1921	May 11, 1933
Persia	April 4, 1921	Apr. 25, 1931
Peru	Sept. 14, 1929	Mar. 29, 1932
Poland	Before Feb. 25, 1921	Aug. 26, 1921
Portugal	Before Jan. 28, 1921	Oct. 8, 1921
Rumania	April 15, 1921	Aug. 8, 1921
El Salvador	Before Jan. 28, 1921	Aug. 29, 1930
Siam	Before Feb. 25, 1921	Feb. 27, 1922
South Africa	Before Feb. 25, 1921	Aug. 4, 1921
Spain	April 6, 1929	Aug. 30, 1921
Sweden	Before Dec. 31, 1920	Feb. 21, 1921
Switzerland	Before Jan. 28, 1921	July 25, 1921
Turkey		
United States of America	Dec. 9, 1929	
Uruguay	Before Jan. 28, 1921	Sept. 27, 1921
Venezuela	Before Feb. 25, 1921	Dec. 2, 1921
Yugoslavia	May 30, 1921	Aug. 12, 1921

Total number of signatory States . . . 55
Total number of ratifying States . . . 49

[3] Now united with the Nejd in Saudi Arabia.
[4] The signing by Great Britain on behalf of the British Empire, before February 25, 1921, applied to what later became the Irish Free State. A letter dated August 21, 1926, informed the Secretary-General of the League of Nations that the Irish Free State should be listed as having ratified the Protocol of Signature.

APPENDIX NO. 3

Statute of the Permanent Court of International Justice, Annexed to the Protocol of Signature of December 16, 1920 [1]

Text from Series D, No. 1, 2d. ed., pp. 8–22.

Article premier. Indépendamment de la Cour d'Arbitrage, organisée par les Conventions de La Haye de 1899 et 1907, et des Tribunaux spéciaux d'Arbitres, auxquels les États demeurent toujours libres de confier la solution de leurs différends, il est institué, conformément à l'article 14 du Pacte de la Société des Nations, une Cour permanente de Justice internationale.

Article 1. A Permanent Court of International Justice is hereby established, in accordance with Article 14 of the Covenant of the League of Nations. This Court shall be in addition to the Court of Arbitration organized by the Conventions of The Hague of 1899 and 1907, and to the special Tribunals of Arbitration to which States are always at liberty to submit their disputes for settlement.

Chapter I. Organization of the Court

Article 2. La Cour permanente de Justice internationale est un corps de magistrats indépendants, élus, sans égard à leur nationalité, parmi les personnes jouissant de la plus haute considération morale, et qui réunissent les conditions requises pour l'exercice, dans leurs pays respectifs, des plus hautes fonctions judiciaires, ou qui sont des jurisconsultes possédant une compétence notoire en matière de droit international.

Article 2. The Permanent Court of International Justice shall be composed of a body of independent judges elected regardless of their nationality from amongst persons of high moral character, who possess the qualifications required in their respective countries for appointment to the highest judicial offices, or are jurisconsults of recognized competence in international law.

Article 3. La Cour se compose de quinze membres: onze juges titulaires et quatre juges suppléants. Le nombre des juges titulaires et des juges suppléants peut être éventuellement augmenté par l'Assemblée, sur la pro-

Article 3. The Court shall consist of fifteen members: eleven judges and four deptuy-judges. The number of judges and deputy-judges may hereafter be increased by the Assembly, upon the proposal

[1] For the reader's convenience, the amendments provided for by the Revision Protocol of September 14, 1929, which has not yet been brought into force (June 1, 1934), are reproduced in connection with the text of the articles to which they relate.

position du Conseil da la Société des Nations, à concurrence de quinze juges titulaires et de six juges suppléants.

of the Council of the League of Nations, to a total of fifteen judges and six deputy-judges.

[New text, 1929 Revision Protocol.]

La Cour se compose de quinze membres.

The Court shall consist of fifteen members.

Article 4. Les membres de la Cour sont élus par l'Assemblée et par le Conseil sur une liste de personnes présentées par les groupes nationaux de la Cour d'Arbitrage, conformément aux dispositions suivantes.

En ce qui concerne les Membres de la Société qui ne sont pas représentés à la Cour permanente d'Arbitrage, les listes de candidats seront présentées par des groupes nationaux, désignés à cet effet par leurs Gouvernements, dans les mêmes conditions que celles stipulées pour les membres de la Cour d'Arbitrage par l'article 44 de la Convention de La Haye de 1907 sur le règlement pacifique des conflits internationaux.

Article 4. The members of the Court shall be elected by the Assembly and by the Council from a list of persons nominated by the national groups in the Court of Arbitration, in accordance with the following provisions.

In the case of Members of the League of Nations not represented in the Permanent Court of Arbitration, the lists of candidates shall be drawn up by national groups appointed for this purpose by their Governments under the same conditions as those prescribed for members of the Permanent Court of Arbitration by Article 44 of the Convention of The Hague of 1907 for the pacific settlement of international disputes.

[Additional paragraph, 1929 Revision Protocol.]

En l'absence d'accord spécial, l'Assemblée, sur la proposition du Conseil, réglera les conditions auxquelles peut participer à l'élection des membres de la Cour un Etat qui, tout en ayant accepté le Statut de la Cour, n'est pas Membre de la Société des Nations.

The conditions under which a State which has accepted the Statute of the Court but is not a member of the League of Nations, may participate in electing the members of the Court shall, in the absence of a special agreement, be laid down by the Assembly on the proposal of the Council.

Article 5. Trois mois au moins avant la date de l'élection, le Secrétaire général de la Société des Nations

Article 5. At least three months before the date of the election, the Secretary-General of the League of

invite par écrit les membres de la Cour d'Arbitrage appartenant aux États mentionnés à l'annexe au Pacte ou entrés ultérieurement dans la Société des Nations, ainsi que les personnes désignées conformément à l'alinéa 2 de l'article 4, à procéder dans un délai déterminé, par groupes nationaux, à la présentation de personnes en situation de remplir les fonctions de membre de la Cour.

Chaque groupe ne peut, en aucun cas, présenter plus de quatre personnes, dont deux au plus de sa nationalité. En aucun cas il ne peut être présenté un nombre de candidats plus élevé que le double des places à remplir.

Article 6. Avant de procéder à cette désignation, il est recommandé à chaque groupe national de consulter la plus haute cour de justice, les facultés et écoles de droit, les académies nationales et les sections nationales d'académies internationales vouées à l'étude du droit.

Article 7. Le Secrétaire général de la Société des Nations dresse, par ordre alphabétique, une liste de toutes les personnes ainsi désignées; seules ces personnes sont éligibles, sauf le cas prévu à l'article 12, paragraphe 2.

Le Secrétaire général communique cette liste à l'Assemblée et au Conseil.

Article 8. L'Assemblée et le Conseil procèdent, indépendamment l'une de l'autre, à l'élection, d'abord des juges titulaires, ensuite des juges suppléants.

Nations shall address a written request to the members of the Court of Arbitration belonging to the States mentioned in the Annex to the Covenant or to the States which join the League subsequently, and to the persons appointed under paragraph 2 of Article 4, inviting them to undertake, within a given time, by national groups, the nomination of persons in a position to accept the duties of a member of the Court.

No group may nominate more than four persons, not more than two of whom shall be of their own nationality. In no case must the number of candidates nominated be more than double the number of seats to be filled.

Article 6. Before making these nominations, each national group is recommended to consult its Highest Court of Justice, its Legal Faculties and Schools of Law, and its National Academies and national sections of International Academies devoted to the study of Law.

Article 7. The Secretary-General of the League of Nations shall prepare a list in alphabetical order of all the persons thus nominated. Save as provided in Article 12, paragraph 2, these shall be the only persons eligible for appointment.

The Secretary-General shall submit this list to the Assembly and to the Council.

Article 8. The Assembly and the Council shall proceed independently of one another to elect, firstly the judges, then the deputy-judges.

[New text, 1929 Revision Protocol.]

L'Assemblée et le Conseil procèdent indépendamment l'un de l'autre à l'élection des membres de la Cour.

The Assembly and the Council shall proceed independently of one another to elect the members of the Court.

Article 9. Dans toute élection, les électeurs auront en vue que les personnes appelées à faire partie de la Cour, non seulement réunissent individuellement les conditions requises, mais assurent dans l'ensemble la représentation des grandes formes de civilisation et des principaux systèmes juridiques du monde.

Article 9. At every election, the electors shall bear in mind that not only should all the persons appointed as members of the Court possess the qualifications required, but the whole body also should represent the main forms of civilization and the principal legal systems of the world.

Article 10. Sont élus ceux qui ont réuni la majorité absolue des voix dans l'Assemblée et dans le Conseil.

Article 10. Those candidates who obtain an absolute majority of votes in the Assembly and in the Council shall be considered as elected.

Au cas où le double scrutin de l'Assemblée et du Conseil se porterait sur plus d'un ressortissant du même Membre de la Société des Nations, le plus âgé est seul élu.

In the event of more than one national of the same Member of the League being elected by the votes of both the Assembly and the Council, the eldest of these only shall be considered as elected.

Article 11. Si, après la première séance d'élection, il reste encore des sièges à pourvoir, il est procédé, de la même manière, à une seconde et, s'il est nécessaire, à une troisième.

Article 11. If, after the first meeting held for the purpose of the election, one or more seats remain to be filled, a second and, if necessary, a third meeting shall take place.

Article 12. Si, après la troisième séance d'élection, il reste encore des sièges à pourvoir, il peut être à tout moment formé, sur la demande soit de l'Assemblée, soit du Conseil, une Commission médiatrice de six membres, nommés trois par l'Assemblée, trois par le Conseil, en vue de choisir pour chaque siège non pourvu un nom à présenter à l'adoption séparée de l'Assemblée et du Conseil.

Article 12. If, after the third meeting, one or more seats still remain unfilled, a joint conference consisting of six members, three appointed by the Assembly and three by the Council, may be formed, at any time, at the request of either the Assembly or the Council, for the purpose of choosing one name for each seat still vacant, to submit to the Assembly and the Council for their respective acceptance.

Peuvent être portées sur cette liste, à l'unanimité, toutes personnes satisfaisant aux conditions requises, alors même qu'elles n'auraient pas figuré sur la liste de présentation visée aux articles 4 et 5.

If the Conference is unanimously agreed upon any person who fulfils the required conditions, he may be included in its list, even though he was not included in the list of nominations referred to in Articles 4 and 5.

Si la Commission médiatrice constate qu'elle ne peut réussir à assurer l'élection, les membres de la Cour déjà nommés pourvoient aux sièges vacants, dans un délai à fixer par le Conseil, en choisissant parmi les personnes qui ont obtenu des suffrages soit dans l'Assemblée, soit dans le Conseil.

If the joint conference is satisfied that it will not be successful in procuring an election, those members of the Court who have already been appointed shall, within a period to be fixed by the Council, proceed to fill the vacant seats by selection from amongst those candidates who have obtained votes either in the Assembly or in the Council.

Si parmi les juges il y a partage égal des voix, la voix du juge le plus âgé l'emporte.

In the event of an equality of votes amongst the judges, the eldest judge shall have a casting vote.

Article 13. Les membres de la Cour sont élus pour neuf ans.

Ils sont rééligibles.

Ils restent en fonction jusqu'à leur remplacement. Après ce remplacement, ils continuent de connaître des affaires dont ils sont déjà saisis.

Article 13. The members of the Court shall be elected for nine years.

They may be reëlected.

They shall continue to discharge their duties until their places have been filled. Though replaced, they shall finish any cases which they may have begun.

[Additional paragraphs, 1929 Revision Protocol.]

En cas de démission d'un membre de la Cour, la démission sera adressée au Président de la Cour, pour être transmise au Secrétaire général de la Société des Nations.

In the case of the resignation of a member of the Court, the resignation will be addressed to the President of the Court for transmission to the Secretary-General of the League of Nations.

Cette dernière notification emporte vacance de siège.

This last notification makes the place vacant.

Article 14. Il est pourvu aux sièges devenus vacants selon la méthode suivie pour la première élection. Le

Article 14. Vacancies which may occur shall be filled by the same method as that laid down for the

membre de la Cour élu en remplacement d'un membre dont le mandat n'est pas expiré achève le terme du mandat de son prédécesseur.

first election. A member of the Court elected to replace a member whose period of appointment had not expired will hold the appointment for the remainder of his predecessor's term.

[New text, 1929 Revision Protocol.]

Il est pourvu aux sièges devenus vacants selon la méthode suivie pour la première élection, sous réserve de la disposition ci-après: dans le mois qui suivra la vacance, le Secrétaire général de la Société des Nations procédera à l'invitation prescrite par l'article 5, et la date d'élection sera fixée par le Conseil dans sa première session.

Vacancies which may occur shall be filled by the same method as that laid down for the first election, subject to the following provision: the Secretary-General of the League of Nations shall, within one month of the occurrence of the vacancy, proceed to issue the invitations provided for in Article 5, and the date of the election shall be fixed by the Council at its next session.

Article 15. Les juges suppléants sont appelés dans l'ordre du tableau.

Le tableau est dressé par la Cour, en tenant compte d'abord de la priorité d'élection et ensuite d' l'ancienneté d'âge.

Article 15. Deputy-judges shall be called upon to sit in the order laid down in a list.

This list shall be prepared by the Court and shall have regard firstly to priority of election and secondly to age.

[New text, 1929 Revision Protocol.]

Le membre de la Cour élu en remplacement d'un membre dont le mandat n'est pas expiré achève le terme du mandat de son prédécesseur.

A member of the Court elected to replace a member whose period of appointment has not expired, will hold the appointment for the remainder of his predecessor's term.

Article 16. Les membres de la Cour ne peuvent exercer aucune fonction politique ou administrative. Cette disposition ne s'applique pas aux juges suppléants en dehors de l'exercice de leurs fonctions près de la Cour.

Article 16. The ordinary members of the Court may not exercise any political or administrative function. This provision does not apply to the deputy-judges except when performing their duties on the Court.

[New first paragraph, 1929 Revision Protocol.]

Les membres de la Cour ne peuvent exercer aucune fonction politique ou administrative, ni se livrer à aucune autre occupation de caractère professionnel.

The members of the Court may not exercise any political or administrative function, nor engage in any other occupation of a professional nature.

En cas de doute, la Cour décide.

Any doubt on this point is settled by the decision of the Court.

Article 17. Les membres de la Cour ne peuvent exercer les fonctions d'agent, de conseil ou d'avocat dans aucune affaire d'ordre international. Cette disposition ne s'applique aux juges suppléants que relativement aux affaires pour lesquelles ils sont appelés à exercer leurs fonctions près de la Cour.

Article 17. No member of the Court can act as agent, counsel or advocate in any case of an international nature. This provision only applies to the deputy-judges as regards cases in which they are called upon to exercise their functions on the Court.

[New first paragraph, 1929 Revision Protocol.]

Les membres de la Cour ne peuvent exercer les fonctions d'agent, de conseil ou d'avocat dans aucune affaire.

No member of the Court may act as agent, counsel or advocate in any case.

Ils ne peuvent participer au règlement d'aucune affaire dans laquelle ils sont antérieurement intervenus comme agents, conseils ou avocats de l'une des parties, membres d'un tribunal national ou international, d'une commission d'enquête, ou à tout autre titre.

No member may participate in the decision of any case in which he has previously taken an active part, as agent, counsel or advocate for one of the contesting parties, or as a member of a national or international Court, or of a commission of enquiry, or in any other capacity.

En cas de doute, la Cour décide.

Any doubt on this point is settled by the decision of the Court.

Article 18. Les membres de la Cour ne peuvent être relevés de leurs fonctions que si, au jugement unanime des autres membres, ils ont cessé de répondre aux conditions requises.

Article 18. A member of the Court cannot be dismissed unless, in the unanimous opinion of the other members, he has ceased to fulfil the required conditions.

Le Secrétaire général de la Société

Formal notification thereof shall

des Nations en est officiellement informé par le Greffier.

Cette communication emporte vacance de siège.

Article 19. Les membres de la Cour jouissent dans l'exercice de leurs fonctions des privilèges et immunités diplomatiques.

Article 20. Tout membre de la Cour doit, avant d'entrer en fonctions, en séance publique, prendre engagement solennel d'exercer ses attributions en pleine impartialité et en toute conscience.

Article 21. La Cour élit, pour trois ans, son Président et son Vice-Président; ils sont rééligibles.

Elle nomme son Greffier.

La fonction de Greffier de la Cour n'est pas incompatible avec celle de Secrétaire général de la Cour permanente d'Arbitrage.

Article 22. Le siège de la Cour est fixé à La Haye.

Le Président et le Greffier résident au siège de la Cour.

Article 23. La Cour tient une session chaque année.

Sauf disposition contraire du Règlement de la Cour, cette session commence le 15 juin et continue tant que le rôle n'est pas épuisé.

Le Président convoque la Cour en session extraordinaire quand les circonstances l'exigent.

be made to the Secretary-General of the League of Nations, by the Registrar.

This notification makes the place vacant.

Article 19. The members of the Court, when engaged on the business of the Court, shall enjoy diplomatic privileges and immunities.

Article 20. Every member of the Court shall, before taking up his duties, make a solemn declaration in open Court that he will exercise his powers impartially and conscientiously.

Article 21. The Court shall elect its President and Vice-President for three years; they may be re-elected.

It shall appoint its Registrar.

The duties of Registrar of the Court shall not be deemed incompatible with those of Secretary-General of the Permanent Court of Arbitration.

Article 22. The seat of the Court shall be established at The Hague.

The President and Registrar shall reside at the seat of the Court.

Article 23. A session of the Court shall be held every year.

Unless otherwise provided by Rules of Court, this session shall begin on the 15th of June, and shall continue for so long as may be deemed necessary to finish the cases on the list.

The President may summon an extraordinary session of the Court whenever necessary.

[New text, 1929 Revision Protocol.]

La Cour reste toujours en fonction, excepté pendant les

The Court shall remain permanently in session except during

vacances judiciaires, dont les périodes et la durée sont fixées par la Cour.

Les membres de la Cour dont les foyers se trouvent à plus de cinq jours de voyage normal de La Haye auront droit, indépendamment des vacances judiciaires, à un congé de six mois, non compris la durée des voyages, tous les trois ans.

Les membres de la Cour sont tenus, à moins de congé régulier, d'empêchement pour cause de maladie ou autre motif grave dûment justifié auprès du Président, d'être à tout moment à la disposition de la Cour.

Article 24. Si, pour une raison spéciale, l'un des membres de la Cour estime devoir ne pas participer au jugement d'une affaire déterminée, il en fait part au Président.

Si le Président estime qu'un des membres de la Cour ne doit pas, pour une raison spéciale, siéger dans une affaire déterminée, il en avertit celui-ci.

Si, en pareils cas, le membre de la Cour et le Président sont en désaccord, la Cour décide.

Article 25. Sauf exception expressément prévue, la Cour exerce ses attributions en séance plénière.

Si la présence de onze juges titulaires n'est pas assurée, ce nombre est parfait par l'entrée en fonctions des juges suppléants.

Toutefois, si onze juges ne sont pas disponibles, le quorum de neuf est suffisant pour constituer la Cour.

the judicial vacations, the dates and duration of which shall be fixed by the Court.

Members of the Court whose homes are situated at more than five days' normal journey from The Hague shall be entitled, apart from the judicial vacations, to six months' leave every three years, not including the time spent in travelling.

Members of the Court shall be bound, unless they are on regular leave or prevented from attending by illness or other serious reason duly explained to the President, to hold themselves permanently at the disposal of the Court.

Article 24. If, for some special reason, a member of the Court considers that he should not take part in the decision of a particular case, he shall so inform the President.

If the President considers that for some special reason one of the members of the Court should not sit on a particular case, he shall give him notice accordingly.

If in any such case the member of the Court and the President disagree, the matter shall be settled by the decision of the Court.

Article 25. The full Court shall sit except when it is expressly provided otherwise.

If eleven judges cannot be present, the number shall be made up by calling on deputy-judges to sit.

If, however, eleven judges are not available, a quorum of nine judges shall suffice to constitute the Court.

[New second and third paragraphs, 1929 Revision Protocol.]

Sous la condition que le nombre des juges disponibles pour constituer la Cour ne soit pas réduit à moins de onze, le Règlement de la Cour pourra prévoir que, selon les circonstances et à tour de rôle, un ou plusieurs juges pourront être dispensés de siéger.

Toutefois, le quorum de neuf est suffisant pour constituer la Cour.

Subject to the condition that the number of judges available to constitute the Court is not thereby reduced below eleven, the Rules of Court may provide for allowing one or more judges, according to circumstances and in rotation, to be dispensed from sitting.

Provided always that a quorum of nine judges shall suffice to constitute the Court.

Article 26. Pour les affaires concernant le travail, et spécialement pour les affaires visées dans la Partie XIII (Travail) du Traité de Versailles et les parties correspondantes des autres traités de paix, la Cour statuera dans les conditions ci-après:

La Cour constituera pour chaque période de trois années une chambre spéciale composée de cinq juges désignés en tenant compte, autant que possible, des prescriptions de l'article 9. Deux juges seront, en outre, désignés pour remplacer celui des juges qui se trouverait dans l'impossibilité de siéger. Sur la demande des parties, cette chambre statuera. A défaut de cette demande, la Cour siégera avec le nombre de juges prévu à l'article 25. Dans tous les cas, les juges sont assistés de quatre assesseurs techniques siégeant à leurs côtés avec voix consultative et assurant une juste représentation des intérêts en cause.

Si l'une seulement des parties a un de ses ressortissants siégeant

Article 26. Labour cases, particularly cases referred to in Part XIII (Labour) of the Treaty of Versailles and the corresponding portions of the other Treaties of Peace, shall be heard and determined by the Court under the following conditions:

The Court will appoint every three years a special chamber of five judges, selected so far as possible with due regard to the provisions of Article 9. In addition, two judges shall be selected for the purpose of replacing a judge who finds it impossible to sit. If the parties so demand, cases will be heard and determined by this Chamber. In the absence of any such demand, the Court will sit with the number of judges provided for in Article 25. On all occasions the judges will be assisted by four technical assessors sitting with them, but without the right to vote, and chosen with a view to ensuring a just representation of the competing interests.

If there is a national of one only of the parties sitting as a judge in the

comme juge dans la chambre prévue à l'alinéa précédent, le Président priera un autre juge de céder sa place à un juge choisi par l'autre partie, en conformité de l'article 31.

Les assesseurs techniques sont choisis dans chaque cas spécial d'après les règles de procédure visées à l'article 30, sur une liste d' "Assesseurs pour litiges de travail," composée de noms présentés à raison de deux par chaque Membre de la Société des Nations et d'un nombre égal présenté par le Conseil d'administration du Bureau international du Travail. Le Conseil désignera par moitié des représentants des travailleurs et par moitié des représentants des patrons pris sur la liste prévue à l'article 412 du Traité de Versailles et les articles correspondants des autres traités de paix.

Chamber referred to in the preceding paragraph, the President will invite one of the other judges to retire in favour of a judge chosen by the other party in accordance with Article 31.

The technical assessors shall be chosen for each particular case in accordance with rules of procedure under Article 30 from a list of "Assessors for Labour cases" composed of two persons nominated by each Member of the League of Nations and an equivalent number nominated by the Governing Body of the Labour Office. The Governing Body will nominate, as to one-half, representatives of the workers, and as to one-half, representatives of employers from the list referred to in Article 412 of the Treaty of Versailles and the corresponding articles of the other Treaties of Peace.

[New second, third and fourth paragraphs, 1929 Revision Protocol.]

La Cour constituera pour chaque période de trois années une chambre spéciale composée de cinq juges désignés en tenant compte, autant que possible, des prescriptions de l'article 9. Deux juges seront, en outre, désignés pour remplacer celui des juges qui se trouverait dans l'impossibilité de siéger. Sur la demande des parties, cette chambre statuera. A défaut de cette demande, la Cour siégera en séance plénière. Dans les deux cas, les juges sont assistés de quatre assesseurs techniques siégeant à leurs côtés avec voix consultative et

The Court will appoint every three years a special Chamber of five judges, selected so far as possible with due regard to the provisions of Article 9. In addition, two judges shall be selected for the purpose of replacing a judge who finds it impossible to sit. If the parties so demand, cases will be heard and determined by this Chamber. In the absence of any such demand, the full Court will sit. In both cases, the judges will be assisted by four technical assessors sitting with them, but without the right

assurant une juste représentation des intérêts en cause.

Les assesseurs techniques sont choisis dans chaque cas spécial d'après les règles de procédure visées à l'article 30, sur une liste d' "Assesseurs pour litiges de travail," composée de noms présentés à raison de deux par chaque Membre de la Société des Nations et d'un nombre égal présenté par le Conseil d'administration du Bureau international du Travail. Le Conseil désignera par moitié des représentants des travailleurs et par moitié des représentants des patrons pris sur la liste prévue à l'article 412 du Traité de Versailles et les articles correspondants des autres traités de paix.

Le recours à la procédure sommaire visée à l'article 29 reste toujours ouvert dans les affaires visées à l'alinéa premier du présent article, si les parties le demandent.

Dans les affaires concernant le travail, le Bureau international aura la faculté de fournir à la Cour tous les renseignements nécessaires et, à cet effet, le Directeur de ce Bureau recevra communication de toutes les pièces de procédure présentées par écrit.

Article 27. Pour les affaires concernant le transit et les communications, et spécialement pour les affaires visées dans la Partie XII (Ports, Voies d'eau, Voies ferrées) du Traité de Versailles et les parties correspondantes des autres traités de

to vote, and chosen with a view to ensuring a just representation of the competing interests.

The technical assessors shall be chosen for each particular case in accordance with rules of procedure under Article 30 from a list of "Assessors for Labour Cases" composed of two persons nominated by each Member of the League of Nations and an equivalent number nominated by the Governing Body of the Labour Office. The Governing Body will nominate, as to one-half, representatives of the workers, and, as to one-half, representatives of employers from the list referred to in Article 412 of the Treaty of Versailles and the corresponding Articles of the other Treaties of Peace.

Recourse may always be had to the summary procedure provided for in Article 29, in the cases referred to in the first paragraph of the present Article, if the parties so request.

In Labour cases the International Labour Office shall be at liberty to furnish the Court with all relevant information, and for this purpose the Director of that Office shall receive copies of all the written proceedings.

Article 27. Cases relating to transit and communications, particularly cases referred to in Part XII (Ports, Waterways and Railways) of the Treaty of Versailles and the corresponding portions of the other Treaties of Peace shall be heard and

paix, la Cour statuera dans les conditions ci-après:

La Cour constituera, pour chaque période de trois années, une chambre spéciale composée de cinq juges désignés en tenant compte autant que possible des prescriptions de l'article 9. Deux juges seront, en outre, désignés pour remplacer celui des juges qui se trouverait dans l'impossibilité de siéger. Sur la demande des parties, cette chambre statuera. A défaut de cette demande, la Cour siégera avec le nombre de juges prévu à l'article 25. Si les parties le désirent, ou si la Cour le décide, les juges seront assistés de quatre assesseurs techniques siégeant à leurs côtés avec voix consultative.

Si l'une seulement des parties a un de ses ressortissants siégeant comme juge dans la chambre prévue à l'alinéa précédent, le Président priera un autre juge de céder sa place à un juge choisi par l'autre partie, en conformité de l'article 31.

Les assesseurs techniques seront choisis dans chaque cas spécial d'après les règles de procédure visées à l'article 30, sur une liste d' "Assesseurs pour litiges de transit et de communications," composée de noms présentés à raison de deux par chaque Membre de la Société des Nations.

determined by the Court under the following conditions:

The Court will appoint every three years a special chamber of five judges, selected so far as possible with due regard to the provisions of Article 9. In addition, two judges shall be selected for the purpose of replacing a judge who finds it impossible to sit. If the parties so demand, cases will be heard and determined by this chamber. In the absence of any such demand, the Court will sit with the number of judges provided for in Article 25. When desired by the parties or decided by the Court, the judges will be assisted by four technical assessors sitting with them, but without the right to vote.

If there is a national of one only of the parties sitting as a judge in the chamber referred to in the preceding paragraph, the President will invite one of the other judges to retire in favour of a judge chosen by the other party in accordance with Article 31.

The technical assessors shall be chosen for each particular case in accordance with rules of procedure under Article 30 from a list of "Assessors for Transit and Communications cases" composed of two persons nominated by each Member of the League of Nations.

[New second, third and fourth paragraphs, 1929 Revision Protocol.]

La Cour constituera, pour chaque période de trois années, une chambre spéciale composée de cinq juges désignés en tenant compte autant que possible des prescriptions de l'article 9. Deux juges

The Court will appoint every three years a special Chamber of five judges, selected so far as possible with due regard to the provisions of Article 9. In addition, two judges shall be selected for the

seront, en outre, désignés pour remplacer celui des juges qui se trouverait dans l'impossibilité de siéger. Sur la demande des parties, cette chambre statuera. A défaut de cette demande, la Cour siégera en séance plénière. Si les parties le désirent, ou si la Cour le décide, les juges seront assistés de quatre assesseurs techniques siégeant à leurs côtés avec voix consultative.

Les assesseurs techniques seront choisis dans chaque cas spécial d'après les règles de procédure visées à l'article 30, sur une liste d' "Assesseurs pour litiges de transit et de communications," composée de noms présentés à raison de deux par chaque Membre de la Société des Nations.

Le recours à la procédure sommaire visée à l'article 29 reste toujours ouvert dans les affaires visées à l'alinéa premier du présent article, si les parties le demandent.

Article 28. Les chambres spéciales prévues aux articles 26 et 27 peuvent, avec le consentement des parties en cause, siéger ailleurs qu'à La Haye.

Article 29. En vue de la prompte expédition des affaires, la Cour compose annuellement une chambre de trois juges, appelée à statuer en procédure sommaire lorsque les parties le demandent.

purpose of replacing a judge who finds it impossible to sit. If the parties so demand, cases will be heard and determined by this Chamber. In the absence of any such demand, the full Court will sit. When desired by the parties or decided by the Court, the judges will be assisted by four technical assessors sitting with them, but without the right to vote.

The technical assessors shall be chosen for each particular case in accordance with rules of procedure under Article 30 from a list of "Assessors for Transit and Communications Cases" composed of two persons nominated by each Member of the League of Nations.

Recourse may always be had to the summary procedure provided for in Article 29, in the cases referred to in the first paragraph of the present Article, if the parties so request.

Article 28. The special chambers provided for in Articles 26 and 27 may, with the consent of the parties to the dispute, sit elsewhere than at The Hague.

Article 29. With a view to the speedy despatch of business, the Court shall form annually a chamber composed of three judges who, at the request of the contesting parties, may hear and determine cases by summary procedure.

[New text, 1929 Revision Protocol.]

En vue de la prompte expédition des affaires, la Cour compose

With a view to the speedy despatch of business, the Court shall

annuellement une Chambre de cinq juges, appelés à statuer en procédure sommaire lorsque les parties le demandent. Deux juges seront, en outre, désignés, pour remplacer celui des juges qui se trouverait dans l'impossibilité de siéger.

form annually a Chamber composed of five judges who, at the request of the contesting parties, may hear and determine cases by summary procedure. In addition, two judges shall be selected for the purpose of replacing a judge who finds it impossible to sit.

Article 30. La Cour détermine par un règlement le mode suivant lequel elle exerce ses attributions. Elle règle notamment la procédure sommaire.

Article 31. Les juges de la nationalité de chacune des parties en cause conservent le droit de siéger dans l'affaire dont la Cour est saisie.

Si la Cour compte sur le siège un juge de la nationalité d'une seule des parties, l'autre partie peut désigner pour siéger un juge suppléant s'il s'en trouve un de sa nationalité. S'il n'en existe pas, elle peut choisir un juge, pris de préférence parmi les personnes qui ont été l'objet d'une présentation en conformité des articles 4 et 5.

Si la Cour ne compte sur le siège aucun juge de la nationalité des parties, chacune de ces parties peut procéder à la désignation ou au choix d'un juge de la même manière qu'au paragraphe précédent.

Lorsque plusieurs parties font cause commune, elles ne comptent, pour l'application des dispositions qui précèdent, que pour une seule. En cas de doute, la Cour décide.

Les juges désignés ou choisis, comme il est dit aux paragraphes 2

Article 30. The Court shall frame rules for regulating its procedure. In particular, it shall lay down rules for summary procedure.

Article 31. Judges of the nationality of each contesting party shall retain their right to sit in the case before the Court.

If the Court includes upon the Bench a judge of the nationality of one of the parties only, the other party may select from among the deputy-judges a judge of its nationality, if there be one. If there should not be one, the party may choose a judge, preferably from among those persons who have been nominated as candidates as provided in Articles 4 and 5.

If the Court includes upon the Bench no judge of the nationality of the contesting parties, each of these may proceed to select or choose a judge as provided in the preceding paragraph.

Should there be several parties in the same interest, they shall, for the purpose of the preceding provisions, be reckoned as one party only. Any doubt upon this point is settled by the decision of the Court.

Judges selected or chosen as laid down in paragraphs 2 and 3 of this

et 3 du présent article, doivent satisfaire aux prescriptions des articles 2, 16, 17, 20, 24 du présent acte. Ils statuent sur un pied d'égalité avec leurs collègues.

article shall fulfil the conditions required by Articles 2, 16, 17, 20, 24 of this Statute. They shall take part in the decision on an equal footing with their colleagues.

[New text, 1929 Revision Protocol.]

Les juges de la nationalité de chacune des parties en cause conservent le droit de siéger dans l'affaire dont la Cour est saisie.

Si la Cour compte sur le siège un juge de la nationalité d'une des parties, l'autre partie peut désigner une personne de son choix pour siéger en qualité de juge. Celle-ci devra être prise de préférence parmi les personnes qui ont été l'objet d'une présentation en conformité des articles 4 et 5.

Si la Cour ne compte sur le siége aucun juge de la nationalité des parties, chacune de ces parties peut procéder à la désignation d'un juge de la même manière qu'au paragraphe précédent.

La présente disposition s'applique dans le cas des articles 26, 27 et 29. En pareils cas, le Président priera un, ou, s'il y a lieu, deux des membres de la Cour composant la Chambre, de céder leur place aux membres de la Cour de la nationalité des parties intéressés et, à défaut ou en cas d'empêchement, aux juges spécialement désignés par les parties.

Lorsque plusieurs parties font cause commune, elles ne comptent, pour l'application des dispositions qui précèdent, que pour une seule.

Judges of the nationality of each of the contesting parties shall retain their right to sit in the case before the Court.

If the Court includes upon the Bench a judge of the nationality of one of the parties, the other party may choose a person to sit as judge. Such person shall be chosen preferably from among those persons who have been nominated as candidates as provided in Articles 4 and 5.

If the Court includes upon the Bench no judge of the nationality of the contesting parties, each of these parties may proceed to select a judge as provided in the preceding paragraph.

The present provision shall apply to the case of Articles 26, 27 and 29. In such cases, the President shall request one or, if necessary, two of the members of the Court forming the Chamber to give place to the members of the Court of the nationality of the parties concerned, and, failing such or if they are unable to be present, to the judges specially appointed by the parties.

Should there be several parties in the same interest, they shall, for the purpose of the preceding provisions, be reckoned as

En cas de doute, la Cour décide.

Les juges désignés, comme il est dit aux paragraphes 2, 3 et 4 du présent article, doivent satisfaire aux prescriptions des articles 2; 17, alinéa 2; 20 et 24 du présent Statut. Ils participent à la décision dans des conditions de complète égalité avec leurs collègues.

one party only. Any doubt upon this point is settled by the decision of the Court.

Judges selected as laid down in paragraphs 2, 3 and 4 of this Article shall fulfil the conditions required by Articles 2, 17 (paragraph 2), 20 and 24 of this Statute. They shall take part in the decision on terms of complete equality with their colleagues.

Article 32. Les juges titulaires reçoivent une indemnité annuelle à fixer par l'Assemblée de la Société des Nations sur la proposition du Conseil. Cette indemnité ne peut être diminuée pendant la durée des fonctions du juge.

Le Président reçoit une indemnité spéciale déterminée de la même manière pour la durée des ses fonctions.

Le Vice-Président, les juges et les juges suppléants reçoivent dans l'exercice de leurs fonctions une indemnité à fixer de la même manière.

Les juges titulaires et suppléants qui ne résident pas au siège de la Cour reçoivent le remboursement des frais de voyage nécessités par l'accomplissement de leurs fonctions.

Les indemnités dues aux juges désignés ou choisis conformément à l'article 31 sont réglées de la même manière.

Le traitement du Greffier est fixé par le Conseil sur la proposition de la Cour.

L'Assemblée de la Société des Nations, sur la proposition du Conseil, adoptera un règlement spécial fixant

Article 32. The judges shall receive an annual indemnity to be determined by the Assembly of the League of Nations upon the proposal of the Council. This indemnity must not be decreased during the period of a judge's appointment.

The President shall receive a special grant for his period of office, to be fixed in the same way.

The Vice-President, judges and deputy-judges, shall receive a grant for the actual performance of their duties, to be fixed in the same way.

Travelling expenses incurred in the performance of their duties shall be refunded to judges and deputy-judges who do not reside at the seat of the Court.

Grants due to judges selected or chosen as provided in Article 31 shall be determined in the same way.

The salary of the Registrar shall be decided by the Council upon the proposal of the Court.

The Assembly of the League of Nations shall lay down, on the proposal of the Council, a special regu-

les conditions sous lesquelles des pensions seront allouées au personnel de la Cour.

lation fixing the conditions under which retiring pensions may be given to the personnel of the Court.

[New text, 1929 Revision Protocol.]

Les membres de la Cour reçoivent un traitement annuel.

Le président reçoit une allocation annuelle spéciale.

Le vice-président reçoit une allocation spéciale pour chaque jour où il remplit les fonctions de président.

Les juges désignés par application de l'article 31, autres que les membres de la Cour, reçoivent une indemnité pour chaque jour où ils exercent leurs fonctions.

Ces traitements, allocations et indemnités sont fixés par l'Assemblée de la Société des Nations sur la proposition du Conseil. Ils ne peuvent être diminués pendant la durée des fonctions.

Le traitement du Greffier est fixé par l'Assemblée sur la proposition de la Cour.

Un règlement adopté par l'Assemblée fixe les conditions dans lesquelles les pensions sont allouées aux membres de la Cour et au Greffier, ainsi que les conditions dans lesquelles les membres de la Cour et le Greffier reçoivent le remboursement de leurs frais de voyage.

Les traitements, indemnités et allocations sont exempts de tout impôt.

The members of the Court shall receive an annual salary.

The President shall receive a special annual allowance.

The Vice-President shall receive a special allowance for every day on which he acts as President.

The judges appointed under Article 31, other than members of the Court, shall receive an indemnity for each day on which they sit.

These salaries, allowances and indemnities shall be fixed by the Assembly of the League of Nations on the proposal of the Council. They may not be decreased during the term of office.

The salary of the Registrar shall be fixed by the Assembly on the proposal of the Court.

Regulations made by the Assembly shall fix the conditions under which retiring pensions may be given to members of the Court and to the Registrar, and the conditions under which members of the Court and the Registrar shall have their travelling expenses refunded.

The above salaries, indemnities and allowances shall be free of all taxation.

Article 33. Les frais de la Cour sont supportés par la Société des Na-

Article 33. The expenses of the Court shall be borne by the League

tions de la manière que l'Assemblée décide sur la proposition du Conseil.

of Nations, in such a manner as shall be decided by the Assembly upon the proposal of the Council.

Chapter II. Competence of the Court

Article 34. Seuls les États ou les Membres de la Société des Nations ont qualité pour se présenter devant la Cour.

Article 35. La Cour est ouverte aux Membres de la Société des Nations, ainsi qu'aux États mentionnés à l'annexe au Pacte.

Les conditions auxquelles elle est ouverte aux autres États sont, sous réserve des dispositions particulières des traités en vigueur, réglées par le Conseil, et dans tous les cas, sans qu'il puisse en résulter pour les parties aucune inégalité devant la Cour.

Lorsqu'un État, qui n'est pas Membre de la Société des Nations, est partie en cause, la Cour fixera la contribution aux frais de la Cour que cette partie devra supporter.

Article 34. Only States or Members of the League of Nations can be parties in cases before the Court.

Article 35. The Court shall be open to the Members of the League and also to States mentioned in the Annex to the Covenant.

The conditions under which the Court shall be open to other States shall, subject to the special provisions contained in treaties in force, be laid down by the Council, but in no case shall such provisions place the parties in a position of inequality before the Court.

When a State which is not a Member of the League of Nations is a party to a dispute, the Court will fix the amount which that party is to contribute towards the expenses of the Court.

[New text of third paragraph, 1929 Revision Protocol.]

Lorsqu'un État, qui n'est pas Membre de la Société des Nations, est partie en cause, la Cour fixera la contribution aux frais de la Cour que cette partie devra supporter. Toutefois cette disposition ne s'appliquera pas, si cet État participe aux dépenses de la Cour.

When a State which is not a Member of the League of Nations is a party to a dispute, the Court will fix the amount which that party is to contribute towards the expenses of the Court. This provision shall not apply if such State is bearing a share of the expenses of the Court.

Article 36. La compétence de la Cour s'étend à toutes affaires que les parties lui soumettront, ainsi qu'à

Article 36. The jurisdiction of the Court comprises all cases which the parties refer to it and all mat-

tous les cas spécialement prévus dans les traités et conventions en vigueur.

Les Membres de la Société et États mentionnés à l'annexe au Pacte pourront, soit lors de la signature ou de la ratification du Protocole, auquel le présent acte est joint, soit ultérieurement, déclarer reconnaître dès à présent comme obligatoire, de plein droit et sans convention spéciale, vis-à-vis de tout autre Membre ou État acceptant la même obligation, la juridiction de la Cour sur toutes ou quelques-unes des catégories de différends d'ordre juridique ayant pour objet:

(a) l'interprétation d'un traité;
(b) tout point de droit international;
(c) la réalité de tout fait qui, s'il était établi, constituerait la violation d'un engagement international;
(d) la nature ou l'étendue de la réparation due pour la rupture d'un engagement international.

La déclaration ci-dessus visée pourra être faite purement et simplement ou sous condition de réciprocité de la part de plusieurs ou de certains Membres ou États, ou pour un délai déterminé.

En cas de contestation sur le point de savoir si la Cour est compétente, la Cour décide.

Article 37. Lorsqu'un traité ou convention en vigueur vise le renvoi à une juridiction à établir par la Société des Nations, la Cour constituera cette juridiction.

ters specially provided for in Treaties and Conventions in force.

The Members of the League of Nations and the States mentioned in the Annex to the Covenant may, either when signing or ratifying the Protocol to which the present Statute is adjoined, or at a later moment, declare that they recognize as compulsory *ipso facto* and without special agreement, in relation to any other Member or State accepting the same obligation, the jurisdiction of the Court in all or any of the classes of legal disputes concerning:

(a) the interpretation of a treaty;
(b) any question of international law;
(c) the existence of any fact which, if established, would constitute a breach of an international obligation;
(d) the nature or extent of the reparation to be made for the breach of an international obligation.

The declaration referred to above may be made unconditionally or on condition of reciprocity on the part of several or certain Members or States, or for a certain time.

In the event of a dispute as to whether the Court has jurisdiction, the matter shall be settled by the decision of the Court.

Article 37. When a treaty or convention in force provides for the reference of a matter to a tribunal to be instituted by the League of Nations, the Court will be such tribunal.

Article 38. La Cour applique:

1. Les conventions internationales, soit générales, soit spéciales, établissant des règles expressément reconnues par les États en litige;

2. La coutume internationale comme preuve d'une pratique générale acceptée comme étant le droit;

3. Les principes généraux de droit reconnus par les nations civilisées;

4. Sous réserve de la disposition de l'article 59, les décisions judiciaires et la doctrine des publicistes les plus qualifiés, comme moyen auxiliaire de détermination des règles de droit.

Article 38. The Court shall apply:

1. International conventions, whether general or particular, establishing rules expressly recognized by the contesting States;

2. International custom, as evidence of a general practice accepted as law;

3. The general principles of law recognized by civilized nations;

4. Subject to the provisions of Article 59, judicial decisions and the teachings of the most highly qualified publicists of the various nations, as subsidiary means for the determination of rules of law.

[New sub-paragraph 4, French version, 1929 Revision Protocol.]

4. Sous réserve de la disposition de l'article 59, les décisions judiciaires et la doctrine des publicistes les plus qualifiés des différentes nations, comme moyen auxiliaire de détermination des règles de droit.

La présente disposition ne porte pas atteinte à la faculté pour la Cour, si les parties sont d'accord, de statuer *ex æquo et bono*.

This provision shall not prejudice the power of the Court to decide a case *ex æquo et bono*, if the parties agree thereto.

Chapter III. Procedure

Article 39. Les langues officielles de la Cour sont le français et l'anglais. Si les parties sont d'accord pour que toute la procédure ait lieu en français, le jugement sera prononcé en cette langue. Si les parties sont d'accord pour que toute la procédure ait lieu en anglais, le jugement sera prononcé en cette langue.

Article 39. The official languages of the Court shall be French and English. If the parties agree that the case shall be conducted in French, the judgment will be delivered in French. If the parties agree that the case shall be conducted in English, the judgment will be delivered in English.

A défaut d'un accord fixant la langue dont il sera fait usage, les parties pourront employer pour les plaidoiries celle des deux langues qu'elles préféreront, et l'arrêt de la Cour sera rendu en français et en anglais. En ce cas, la Cour désignera en même temps celui des deux textes qui fera foi.

La Cour pourra, à la requête des parties, autoriser l'emploi d'une langue autre que le français ou l'anglais.

In the absence of an agreement as to which language shall be employed, each party may, in the pleadings, use the language which it prefers; the decision of the Court will be given in French and English. In this case the Court will at the same time determine which of the two texts shall be considered as authoritative.

The Court may, at the request of the parties, authorize a language other than French or English to be used.

[New third paragraph, 1929 Revision Protocol.]

La Cour pourra, à la demande de toute partie, autoriser l'emploi d'une langue autre que le français ou l'anglais.

The Court may, at the request of any party, authorise a language other than French or English to be used.

Article 40. Les affaires sont portées devant la Cour, selon le cas, soit par notification du compromis, soit par une requête, addressées au Greffe; dans les deux cas, l'objet du différend et les parties en cause doivent être indiqués.

Le Greffe donne immédiatement communication de la requête à tous intéressés.

Il en informe également les Membres de la Société des Nations par l'entremise du Secrétaire général.

Article 40. Cases are brought before the Court, as the case may be, either by the notification of the special agreement, or by a written application addressed to the Registrar. In either case the subject of the dispute and the contesting parties must be indicated.

The Registrar shall forthwith communicate the application to all concerned.

He shall also notify the Members of the League of Nations through the Secretary-General.

[New third paragraph, 1929 Revision Protocol.]

Il en informe également les Membres de la Société des Nations par l'entremise du Secrétaire général, ainsi que les Etats admis à ester en justice devant la Cour.

He shall also notify the Members of the League of Nations through the Secretary-General, and also any States entitled to appear before the Court.

Article 41. La Cour a le pouvoir d'indiquer, si elle estime que les circonstances l'exigent, quelles mesures conservatoires du droit de chacun doivent être prises à titre provisoire.

En attendant l'arrêt définitif, l'indication de ces mesures est immédiatement notifiée aux parties et au Conseil.

Article 42. Les parties sont représentées par des agents.

Elles peuvent se faire assister devant la Cour par des conseils ou des avocats.

Article 43. La procédure a deux phases: l'une écrite, l'autre orale.

La procédure écrite comprend la communication à juge et à partie des mémoires, des contre-mémoires et, éventuellement, des répliques, ainsi que de toute pièce et document à l'appui.

La communication se fait par l'entremise du Greffe dans l'ordre et les délais déterminés par la Cour.

Toute pièce produite par l'une des parties doit être communiquée à l'autre en copie certifiée conforme.

La procédure orale consiste dans l'audition par la Cour des témoins, experts, agents, conseils et avocats.

Article 44. Pour toute notification à faire à d'autres personnes que les agents, conseils et avocats, la Cour s'adresse directement au gouvernement de l'État sur le territoire duquel la notification doit produire effet.

Il en est de même s'il s'agit de

Article 41. The Court shall have the power to indicate, if it considers that circumstances so require, any provisional measures which ought to be taken to reserve the respective rights of either party.

Pending the final decision, notice of the measures suggested shall forthwith be given to the parties and the Council.

Article 42. The parties shall be represented by agents.

They may have the assistance of counsel or advocates before the Court.

Article 43. The procedure shall consist of two parts: written and oral.

The written proceedings shall consist of the communication to the judges and to the parties of Cases, Counter-Cases and, if necessary, Replies; also all papers and documents in support.

These communications shall be made through the Registrar, in the order and within the time fixed by the Court.

A certified copy of every document produced by one party shall be communicated to the other party.

The oral proceedings shall consist of the hearing by the Court of witnesses, experts, agents, counsel and advocates.

Article 44. For the service of all notices upon persons other than the agents, counsel and advocates, the Court shall apply direct to the government of the State upon whose territory the notice has to be served.

The same provision shall apply

faire procéder sur place à l'établissement de tous moyens de preuve.

Article 45. Les débats sont dirigés par le Président et à défaut de celui-ci par le Vice-Président; en cas d'empêchement, par le plus ancien des juges présents.

whenever steps are to be taken to procure evidence on the spot.

Article 45. The hearing shall be under the control of the President or, in his absence, of the Vice-President; if both are absent, the senior judge shall preside.

[New text, English version, 1929 Revision Protocol.]

The hearing shall be under the control of the President or, if he is unable to preside, of the Vice-President; if neither is able to preside, the senior judge present shall preside.

Article 46. L'audience est publique, à moins qu'il n'en soit autrement décidé par la Cour ou que les deux parties ne demandent que le public ne soit pas admis.

Article 47. Il est tenu de chaque audience un procès-verbal signé par le Greffier et le Président.

Ce procès-verbal a seul caractère authentique.

Article 48. La Cour rend des ordonnances pour la direction du procès, la détermination des formes et délais dans lesquels chaque partie doit finalement conclure; elle prend toutes les mesures que comporte l'administration des preuves.

Article 49. La Cour peut, même avant tout débat, demander aux agents de produire tout document et de fournir toutes explications. En cas de refus, elle en prend acte.

Article 50. A tout moment, la Cour peut confier une enquête ou une expertise à toute personne, corps,

Article 46. The hearing in Court shall be public, unless the Court shall decide otherwise, or unless the parties demand that the public be not admitted.

Article 47. Minutes shall be made at each hearing, and signed by the Registrar and the President.

These minutes shall be the only authentic record.

Article 48. The Court shall make orders for the conduct of the case, shall decide the form and time in which each party must conclude its arguments, and make all arrangements connected with the taking of evidence.

Article 49. The Court may, even before the hearing begins, call upon the agents to produce any document, or to supply any explanations. Formal note shall be taken of any refusal.

Article 50. The Court may, at any time, entrust any individual, body, bureau, commission or other

bureau, commission ou organe de son choix.

Article 51. Au cours des débats, toutes questions utiles sont posées aux témoins et experts dans les conditions que fixera la Cour dans le règlement visé à l'article 30.

Article 52. Après avoir reçu les preuves et témoignages dans les délais déterminés par elle, la Cour peut écarter toutes dépositions ou documents nouveaux qu'une des parties voudrait lui présenter sans l'assentiment de l'autre.

Article 53. Lorsqu'une des parties ne se présente pas, ou s'abstient de faire valoir ses moyens, l'autre partie peut demander à la Cour de lui adjuger ses conclusions.

La Cour, avant d'y faire droit, doit s'assurer non seulement qu'elle a compétence aux termes des articles 36 et 37, mais que les conclusions sont fondées en fait et en droit.

Article 54. Quand les agents, avocats et conseils ont fait valoir, sous le contrôle de la Cour, tous les moyens qu'ils jugent utiles, le Président prononce la clôture des débats.

La Cour se retire en Chambre du Conseil pour délibérer.

Les délibérations de la Cour sont et restent secrètes.

Article 55. Les décisions de la Cour sont prises à la majorité des juges présents.

En cas de partage de voix, la voix

organization that it may select, with the task of carrying out an enquiry or giving an expert opinion.

Article 51. During the hearing, any relevant questions are to be put to the witnesses and experts under the conditions laid down by the Court in the rules of procedure referred to in Article 30.

Article 52. After the Court has received the proofs and evidence within the time specified for the purpose, it may refuse to accept any further oral or written evidence that one party may desire to present unless the other side consents.

Article 53. Whenever one of the parties shall not appear before the Court, or shall fail to defend his case, the other party may call upon the Court to decide in favour of his claim.

The Court must, before doing so, satisfy itself, not only that it has jurisdiction in accordance with Articles 36 and 37, but also that the claim is well founded in fact and law.

Article 54. When, subject to the control of the Court, the agents, advocates and counsel have completed their presentation of the case, the President shall declare the hearing closed.

The Court shall withdraw to consider the judgment.

The deliberations of the Court shall take place in private and remain secret.

Article 55. All questions shall be decided by a majority of the judges present at the hearing.

In the event of an equality of votes,

du Président ou de celui qui le remplace est prépondérante.

Article 56. L'arrêt est motivé.

Il mentionne les noms des juges qui y ont pris part.

Article 57. Si l'arrêt n'exprime pas en tout ou en partie l'opinion unanime des juges, les dissidents ont le droit d'y joindre l'exposé de leur opinion individuelle.

Article 58. L'arrêt est signé par le Président et par le Greffier. Il est lu en séance publique, les agents dûment prévenus.

Article 59. La décision de la Cour n'est obligatoire que pour les parties en litige et dans le cas qui a été décidé.

Article 60. L'arrêt est définitif et sans recours. En cas de contestation sur le sens et la portée de l'arrêt, il appartient à la Cour de l'interpréter, à la demande de toute partie.

Article 61. La revision de l'arrêt ne peut être éventuellement demandée à la Cour qu'à raison de la découverte d'un fait de nature à exercer une influence décisive et qui, avant le prononcé de l'arrêt, était inconnu de la Cour et de la partie qui demande la revision, sans qu'il y ait, de sa part, faute à l'ignorer.

La procédure de revision s'ouvre par un arrêt de la Cour constatant expressément l'existence du fait nouveau, lui reconnaissant les caractères qui donnent ouverture à la

the President or his deputy shall have a casting vote.

Article 56. The judgment shall state the reasons on which it is based.

It shall contain the names of the judges who have taken part in the decision.

Article 57. If the judgment does not represent in whole or in part the unanimous opinion of the judges, dissenting judges are entitled to deliver a separate opinion.

Article 58. The judgment shall be signed by the President and by the Registrar. It shall be read in open Court, due notice having been given to the agents.

Article 59. The decision of the Court has no binding force except between the parties and in respect of that particular case.

Article 60. The judgment is final and without appeal. In the event of dispute as to the meaning or scope of the judgment, the Court shall construe it upon the request of any party.

Article 61. An application for revision of a judgment can be made only when it is based upon the discovery of some fact of such a nature as to be a decisive factor, which fact was, when the judgment was given, unknown to the Court and also to the party claiming revision, always provided that such ignorance was not due to negligence.

The proceedings for revision will be opened by a judgment of the Court expressly recording the existence of the new fact, recognizing that it has such a character as to lay the case

revision, et déclarant de ce chef la demande recevable.

La Cour peut subordonner l'ouverture de la procédure en revision à l'exécution préalable de l'arrêt.

La demande en revision devra être formée au plus tard dans le délai de six mois après la découverte du fait nouveau.

Aucune demande de revision ne pourra être formée après l'expiration d'un délai de dix ans à dater de l'arrêt.

Article 62. Lorsqu'un État estime que dans un différend un intérêt d'ordre juridique est pour lui en cause, il peut adresser à la Cour une requête, à fin d'intervention.

La Cour décide.

Article 63. Lorsqu'il s'agit de l'interprétation d'une convention à laquelle ont participé d'autres États que les parties en litige, le Greffe les avertit sans délai.

Chacun d'eux a le droit d'intervenir au procès, et s'il exerce cette faculté, l'interprétation contenue dans la sentence est également obligatoire à son égard.

Article 64. S'il n'en est autrement décidé par la Cour, chaque partie supporte ses frais de procédure.

open to revision, and declaring the application admissible on this ground.

The Court may require previous compliance with the terms of the judgment before it admits proceedings in revision.

The application for revision must be made at latest within six months of the discovery of the new fact.

No application for revision may be made after the lapse of ten years from the date of the sentence.

Article 62. Should a State consider that it has an interest of a legal nature which may be affected by the decision in the case, it may submit a request to the Court to be permitted to intervene as a third party.

It will be for the Court to decide upon this request.

Article 63. Whenever the construction of a convention to which States other than those concerned in the case are parties is in question, the Registrar shall notify all such States forthwith.

Every State so notified has the right to intervene in the proceedings: but if it uses this right, the construction given by the judgment will be equally binding upon it.

Article 64. Unless otherwise decided by the Court, each party shall bear its own costs.

[Additional chapter, 1929 Revision Protocol.]

Chapter IV. Advisory Opinions

Nouvel article 65.

Les questions sur lesquelles l'avis consultatif de la Cour est demandé

New Article 65.

Questions upon which the advisory opinion of the Court is

sont exposées à la Cour par une requête écrite, signée soit par le président de l'Assemblée ou par le président du Conseil de la Société des Nations, soit par le Secrétaire général de la Société agissant en vertu d'instructions de l'Assemblée ou du Conseil.

La requête formule, en termes précis, la question sur laquelle l'avis de la Cour est demandé. Il y est joint tout document pouvant servir à élucider la question.

Nouvel article 66.

1. Le Greffier notifie immédiatement la requête demandant l'avis consultatif aux Membres de la Société des Nations par l'entremise du Secrétaire général de la Société, ainsi qu'aux Etats admis à ester en justice devant la Cour.

En outre, à tout Membre de la Société, à tout Etat admis à ester devant la Cour et à toute organisation internationale jugés, par la Cour ou par le Président si elle ne siège pas, susceptibles de fournir des renseignements sur la question, le Greffier fait connaître, par communication spéciale et directe, que la Cour est disposée à recevoir des exposés écrits dans un délai à fixer par le Président, ou à entendre des exposés oraux au cours d'une audience publique tenue à cet effet.

Si un des Membres de la Société ou des États mentionnés au premier alinéa du présent paragraphe,

asked shall be laid before the Court by means of a written request, signed either by the President of the Assembly or the President of the Council of the League of Nations, or by the Secretary-General of the League under instructions from the Assembly or the Council.

The request shall contain an exact statement of the question upon which an opinion is required, and shall be accompanied by all documents likely to throw light upon the question.

New Article 66.

1. The Registrar shall forthwith give notice of the request for an advisory opinion to the Members of the League of Nations, through the Secretary-General of the League, and to any States entitled to appear before the Court.

The Registrar shall also, by means of a special and direct communication, notify any Member of the League or State admitted to appear before the Court or international organisation considered by the Court (or, should it not be sitting, by the President) as likely to be able to furnish information on the question, that the Court will be prepared to receive, within a time-limit to be fixed by the President, written statements, or to hear, at a public sitting to be held for the purpose, oral statements relating to the question.

Should any Member or State referred to in the first paragraph have failed to receive the com-

n'ayant pas été l'objet de la communication spéciale ci-dessus visée, exprime le désir de soumettre un exposé écrit ou d'être entendu, la Cour statue.

2. Les Membres, États ou organisations qui ont présenté des exposés écrits ou oraux sont admis à discuter les exposés faits par d'autres Membres, États et organisations dans les formes, mesures et délais fixés, dans chaque cas d'espèce, par la Cour, ou, si elle ne siège pas, par le Président. A cet effet, le Greffier communique en temps voulu les exposés écrits aux Membres, États ou organisations qui en ont eux-mêmes présentés.

munication specified above, such Member or State may express a desire to submit a written statement, or to be heard; and the Court will decide.

2. Members, States, and organisations having presented written or oral statements or both shall be admitted to comment on the statements made by other Members, States, or organisations in the form, to the extent and within the time-limits which the Court, or, should it not be sitting, the President, shall decide in each particular case. Accordingly, the Registrar shall in due time comunicate any such written statements to Members, States, and organisations having submitted similar statements.

Nouvel article 67.

La Cour prononcera ses avis consultatifs en audience publique, le Secrétaire générale de la Société des Nations et les représentants des Membres de la Société, des États et des organisations internationales directement intéressés étant prévenus.

New Article 67.

The Court shall deliver its advisory opinions in open Court, notice having been given to the Secretary-General of the League of Nations and to the representatives of Members of the League, of States and of international organisations immediately concerned.

Nouvel article 68.

Dans l'exercice de ses attributions consultatives, la Cour s'inspirera en outre des dispositions du Statut qui s'appliquent en matiére contentieuse, dans la mesure où elle les reconnaîtra applicables.

New Article 68.

In the exercise of its advisory functions, the Court shall further be guided by the provisions of the Statute which apply in contentious cases to the extent to which it recognises them to be applicable.

APPENDIX NO. 4

The "Optional Clause" and Declarations Accepting the Court's Obligatory Jurisdiction

(As of June 1, 1934)

Les soussignés, dûment autorisés, déclarent en outre, au nom de leur Gouvernement, reconnaître dès à présent comme obligatoire, de plein droit et sans convention spéciale, la juridiction de la Cour conformément à l'article 36, paragraphe 2, du Statut de la Cour et dans les termes suivants:

The undersigned, being duly authorized thereto, further declare, on behalf of their Government, that, from this date, they accept as compulsory *ipso facto* and without special convention, the jurisdiction of the Court in conformity with Article 36, paragraph 2, of the Statute of the Court, under the following conditions:

Albania.—On behalf of the Kingdom of Albania and subject to ratification, I recognize as compulsory *ipso facto* and without special agreement in relation to any other Member of the League of Nations or State accepting the same obligation, that is to say, on condition of reciprocity, the Optional Clause provided for by Article 36 of the Statute of the Permanent Court of International Justice, for a period of five years from the date of the deposit of the instrument of ratification, in any of the disputes enumerated in the said article arising after the ratification of the present declaration with regard to situations or facts subsequent to this ratification, other than

(*a*) disputes relating to the territorial status of Albania;

(*b*) disputes with regard to questions which, by international law, fall exclusively within the jurisdiction of the Kingdom of Albania;

(*c*) disputes relating directly or indirectly to the application of treaties or conventions accepted by the Kingdom of Albania and providing for another method of pacific settlement.

Geneva, September 17, 1930.[1]

(Signed)   MEHDI FRASHERI.

Australia.—On behalf of His Majesty's Government in the Commonwealth of Australia and subject to ratification, I accept as compulsory *ipso facto* and without special convention on condition of reciprocity the juris-

[1] Translation. Ratification deposited September 17, 1930.

diction of the Court in conformity with Article 36, paragraph 2, of the Statute of the Court, for a period of ten years and thereafter until such time as notice may be given to terminate the acceptance, over all disputes arising after the ratification of the present declaration with regard to situations or facts subsequent to the said ratification;

> other than disputes in regard to which the parties to the dispute have agreed or shall agree to have recourse to some other method of peaceful settlement; and

> disputes with the Government of any other Member of the League which is a member of the British Commonwealth of Nations, all of which disputes shall be settled in such manner as the parties have agreed or shall agree; and

> disputes with regard to questions which by international law fall exclusively within the jurisdiction of the Commonwealth of Australia;

and subject to the condition that His Majesty's Government in the Commonwealth of Australia reserve the right to require that proceedings in the Court shall be suspended in respect of any dispute which has been submitted to and is under consideration by the Council of the League of Nations, provided that notice to suspend is given after the dispute has been submitted to the Council and is given within ten days of the notification of the initiation of the proceedings in the Court, and provided also that such suspension shall be limited to a period of twelve months or such longer period as may be agreed by the parties to the dispute or determined by a decision of all the Members of the Council other than the parties to the dispute.

Geneva, September 20, 1929.[2]

(Signed)   GRANVILLE RYRIE.

Austria.—On behalf of the Austrian Republic, I declare that the latter recognizes in relation to any other Member or State which accepts the same obligation, that is to say, on the condition of reciprocity, the jurisdiction of the Permanent Court as compulsory, *ipso facto* and without any special convention, for a period of five years.

March 14, 1922.[3]

(Signed)   EMERICH PFLÜGL.

(Renewal).—On behalf of the Austrian Republic and subject to ratification, the undersigned recognizes in relation to any other Member of the League of Nations or State accepting the same obligation, that is to say, on condition of reciprocity, the jurisdiction of the Court as compulsory *ipso facto*

---

[2] Ratification deposited August 18, 1930.
[3] Translation. Not subject to ratification.

and without special convention, for a further period of ten years from the date of deposit of the instrument of ratification.

Geneva, January 12, 1927.[4]

(Signed) EMERICH PFLÜGL.

Belgium.—On behalf of the Belgian Government, I recognize as compulsory, *ipso facto* and without special agreement, in relation to any other Member or State accepting the same obligation, the jurisdiction of the Court in conformity with Article 36, paragraph 2, of the Statute of the Court, for a period of fifteen years, in any disputes arising after the ratification of the present declaration with regard to situations or facts subsequent to this ratification, except in cases where the parties have agreed or shall agree to have recourse to another method of pacific settlement.

Geneva, September 25, 1925.[5]

(Signed) P. HYMANS.

Brazil.—[The instrument of ratification of the Protocol deposited November 1, 1921, with the Secretariat of the League of Nations by the Brazilian Government contains the following passage:] ". . . we declare to recognize as compulsory, in accordance with the said resolution of the National Legislature, the jurisdiction of the said Court for the period of five years, on condition of reciprocity and as soon as it has likewise been recognized as such by two at least of the Powers permanently represented on the Council of the League of Nations."[6]

Bulgaria.—On behalf of the Government of the Kingdom of Bulgaria, I recognize, in relation to any other Member or State which accepts the same obligation, the jurisdiction of the Court as compulsory, *ipso facto* and without any special convention, unconditionally.

July 29, 1921.[7]

(Signed) S. POMENOV.

Canada.—On behalf of His Majesty's Government in Canada and subject to ratification, I accept as compulsory *ipso facto* and without special convention, on condition of reciprocity, the jurisdiction of the Court in conformity with Article 36, paragraph 2, of the Statute, for a period of ten years and thereafter until such time as notice may be given to terminate the acceptance, in all disputes arising after ratification of the present declaration with regard to situations or facts subsequent to said ratification:

[4] Translation. Ratification deposited March 13, 1927.
[5] Translation. Ratification deposited March 10, 1926.
[6] Translation. The condition was met on February 5, 1930.
[7] Translation. This declaration became effective August 12, 1921. No ratification was required.

other than disputes in regard to which the parties to the dispute have agreed or shall agree to have recourse to some other method of peaceful settlement; and

disputes with the Government of any other Member of the League which is a member of the British Commonwealth of Nations, all of which disputes shall be settled in such manner as the parties have agreed or shall agree; and

disputes with regard to questions which by international law fall exclusively within the jurisdiction of the Dominion of Canada;

and subject to the condition that His Majesty's Government in Canada reserve the right to require that proceedings in the Court shall be suspended in respect of any dispute which has been submitted to and is under consideration by the Council of the League of Nations, provided that notice to suspend is given after the dispute has been submitted to the Council and is given within ten days of the notification of the initiation of the proceedings in the Court, and provided also that such suspension shall be limited to a period of twelve months or such longer period as may be agreed by the parties to the dispute or determined by a decision of all the Members of the Council other than the parties to the dispute.

Geneva, September 20, 1929.[8]

(Signed)   R. DANDURAND.

China.—The Chinese Government recognizes as compulsory *ipso facto* and without special convention, in relation to any Member or State which accepts the same obligation, that is to say, on the sole condition of reciprocity, the jurisdiction of the Court in conformity with Article 36, paragraph 2, of the Statute of the Court, for a period of five years.

May 13, 1922.[9]

(Signed)   Ts. F. TANG.

Colombia.—The Republic of Colombia recognizes as compulsory *ipso facto* and without special agreement, on condition of reciprocity, in relation to any other State accepting the same obligation, the jurisdiction of the Permanent Court of International Justice, in accordance with Article 36 of the Statute.

Geneva, January 6, 1932.[10]

(Signed)   A. J. RESTREPO.

[8] Ratification deposited July 28, 1930.
[9] Translation. The period of five years expired in 1927, and the declaration was not renewed.
[10] Translation. Ratification not required.

[Costa Rica.—On condition of reciprocity.

(Signed) MANUEL M. DE PERALTA.] [11]

Czechoslovakia.—On behalf of the Czechoslovak Republic and subject to ratification, I recognize as compulsory *ipso facto* and without special agreement in relation to any other Member of the League of Nations or State accepting the same obligation, that is to say, on condition of reciprocity, the jurisdiction of the Court, in conformity with Article 36, paragraph 2, of its Statute, for a period of ten years from the date of the deposit of the instrument of ratification, in any dispute arising after the ratification of the present declaration with regard to situations or facts subsequent to this ratification, except in cases where the parties have agreed or shall agree to have recourse to another method of pacific settlement, and subject to the right, for either of the parties to the dispute, to submit the dispute, before any recourse to the Court, to the Council of the League of Nations.

Geneva, September 19, 1929.[12]

(Signed) DR. EDUARD BENĚS.

Denmark.—On behalf of the Danish Government and subject to ratification, I recognize, in relation to any Member or State accepting the same obligation, that is to say, on the sole condition of reciprocity, the jurisdiction of the Court as compulsory, *ipso facto* and without special convention, for a period of five years.[13]

[Before January 28, 1921.]

(Signed) HERLUF ZAHLE.

(Renewal).—On behalf of the Government of Denmark and subject to ratification I recognize, in relation to any other Member or State accepting the same obligation, that is to say, on the sole condition of reciprocity, the jurisdiction of the Court as compulsory, *ipso facto* and without special convention, for a further period of ten years.

Geneva, December 11, 1925.[14]

(Signed) ANDREAS OLDENBURG.

Dominican Republic.—On behalf of the Government of the Dominican Republic and subject to ratification, I recognize, in relation to any other Member or State accepting the same obligation, that is to say, on the sole

[11] Translation. The Costa Rican declaration was signed before January 28, 1921. Costa Rica has not deposited a ratification of the Protocol of Signature of December 16, 1920, and the declaration has not come into force.

[12] Translation. No ratification has been deposited.

[13] Translation. Ratification deposited June 13, 1921.

[14] Translation. Ratification deposited on March 28, 1926, counted as dating from June 13, 1926, on which date the previous acceptance expired by limitation.

condition of reciprocity, the jurisdiction of the Court as compulsory *ipso facto* and without special convention.

September 30, 1924.[15]

(Signed)   JACINTO R. DE CASTRO.

Estonia.—[The instrument of ratification [16] of the Protocol of Signature contains the following:] "The Estonian Republic declares that it recognizes as compulsory *ipso facto* and without special agreement, in relation to any other Member or State accepting the same obligation, that is to say, on condition of reciprocity, the jurisdiction of the Court, in conformity with Article 36, paragraph 2, of the Statute of the Court, for a period of five years, in any future dispute in respect of which the parties have not agreed to have recourse to another method of pacific settlement." [17]

Ethiopia.—On behalf of the Imperial Ethiopian Government the undersigned recognizes as compulsory, *ipso facto* and without special agreement, in relation to any other Member or State accepting the same obligation, that is to say, on the sole condition of reciprocity, the jurisdiction of the Court in conformity with Article 36, paragraph 2, of the Statute, for a period of five years, excepting future disputes in respect of which the parties have agreed to have recourse to another method of pacific settlement.

July 12, 1926.[18]

(Signed)   LAGARDE, DUC D'ENTOTTO.

(Renewal).—On behalf of the Imperial Ethiopian Government the undersigned recognizes as compulsory, *ipso facto* and without special agreement, in relation to any other Member or State accepting the same obligation, that is to say, on condition of reciprocity, the jurisdiction of the Court in conformity with Article 36, paragraph 2 of the Statute, for a period of two years taking effect as from July 16, 1931, excepting future disputes in respect of which the parties have agreed to have recourse to another method of pacific settlement.

Geneva, April 15, 1932.[19]

(Signed)   LAGARDE, DUC D'ENTOTTO.

Finland.—On behalf of the Republic of Finland, and subject to ratification, I recognize, in relation to any other Member or State which accepts the same obligation, that is to say, on the sole condition of reciprocity, the

---

[15] Translation. Ratification deposited February 4, 1933.
[16] Deposited May 2, 1923. The original is in French.
[17] Renewed for 10 years from May 2, 1928, by letter of June 25, 1928. See Series D, No. 6 (4th ed.), p. 42.
[18] Translation. Ratification deposited July 16, 1926.
[19] Translation. Not subject to ratification.

jurisdiction of the Court as compulsory, *ipso facto* and without any special convention, for a period of five years.[20]

[June 28, 1921.]

(Signed)   ENCKELL.

(Renewal.)—On behalf of the Government of the Republic of Finland, and as from April 6, 1927, I recognize in relation to any other Member or State accepting the same obligation, that is to say, on the sole condition of reciprocity, the jurisdiction of the Court as compulsory, *ipso facto* and without any special convention, for a period of ten years.

Geneva, March 3, 1927.[21]

(Signed)   R. ERICH.

France.—On behalf of the Government of the French Republic and subject to ratification, I recognize as compulsory *ipso facto* and without special agreement, in relation to any other Member or State accepting the same obligation, the jurisdiction of the Court, in conformity with Article 36, paragraph 2, of the Statute of the Court, for a period of five years, in any disputes arising after the ratification of the present declaration with regard to situations or facts subsequent to this ratification, and which could not have been settled by a procedure of conciliation or by the Council, according to the terms of Article 15, paragraph 6, of the Covenant, with reservation as to the case where the parties have agreed or shall agree to have recourse to another method of settlement by arbitration. This declaration replaces the declaration of October 2, 1924, which has now lapsed.[22]

Geneva, September 19, 1929.[23]

(Signed)   LOUCHEUR.

Germany.—On behalf of the German Government, I recognize as compulsory, *ipso facto* and without special agreement, in relation to any other Member or State accepting the same obligation, the jurisdiction of the Court in conformity with Article 36, paragraph 2, of the Statute of the Court, for a period of five years, in any disputes arising after the ratification of the present declaration with regard to situations or facts subsequent to this ratification, except in cases where the parties have agreed or shall agree to have recourse to another method of pacific settlement.

Geneva, September 23, 1927.[24]

(Signed)   G. STRESEMANN.

[20] Translation. Ratification deposited April 6, 1922.
[21] Translation. Not subject to ratification.
[22] The declaration of October 2, 1924, which was not ratified, did not come into force. For the text, see Series D, No. 6 (4th ed.), p. 45.
[23] Translation. Ratification deposited April 25, 1931.
[24] Translation. Ratification deposited February 29, 1928.

(Renewal.)—On behalf of the German Government, I recognize as compulsory *ipso facto* and without special agreement, in relation to any Member or State accepting the same obligation, the jurisdiction of the Court in conformity with Article 36, paragraph 2, of the Statute of the Court, for a period of five years, from March 1, 1933. The present declaration applies to any disputes which might have arisen after February 29, 1928, date of the ratification of the declaration made on this subject at Geneva on September 23, 1927, or to disputes arising in future with regard to situations or facts subsequent to the said ratification. Cases where the parties have agreed or shall agree to have recourse to another method of pacific settlement are excepted. The present declaration shall enter into force on the date of its ratification.

Geneva, February 9, 1933.[25]

(Signed)   VON KELLER.

Great Britain.—On behalf of His Majesty's Government in the United Kingdom and subject to ratification, I accept as compulsory *ipso facto* and without special convention on condition of reciprocity the jurisdiction of the Court in conformity with Article 36, paragraph 2, of the Statute of the Court, for a period of ten years and thereafter until such time as notice may be given to terminate the acceptance, over all disputes arising after the ratification of the present declaration with regard to situations or facts subsequent to the said ratification:

other than disputes in regard to which the parties to the dispute have agreed or shall agree to have recourse to some other method of peaceful settlement; and

disputes with the Government of any other Member of the League which is a member of the British Commonwealth of Nations, all of which disputes shall be settled in such manner as the parties have agreed or shall agree; and

disputes with regard to questions which by international law fall exclusively within the jurisdiction of the United Kingdom;

and subject to the condition that His Majesty's Government reserve the right to require that proceedings in the Court shall be suspended in respect of any dispute which has been submitted to and is under consideration by the Council of the League of Nations, provided that notice to suspend is given after the dispute has been submitted to the Council and is given within ten days of the notification of the initiation of the proceedings in the Court, and provided also that such suspension shall be limited to a period of twelve months or such longer period as may be agreed by the parties to the dispute

[25] Translation. Ratification deposited July 5, 1933.

or determined by a decision of all the Members of the Council other than the parties to the dispute.

Geneva, September 19, 1929.[26]

(Signed)   ARTHUR HENDERSON.

Greece.—Duly authorized by the Hellenic Government, acting in virtue of special approval by the legislative power, I declare that I accept on behalf of Greece the Optional Clause provided in Article 36 of the Statute of the Permanent Court of International Justice, for a period of five years and on condition of reciprocity for all the classes of disputes mentioned in the said Article 36, with the exception of:

(*a*) disputes relating to the territorial status of Greece, including disputes relating to its rights of sovereignty over its ports and lines of communication;

(*b*) disputes relating directly or indirectly to the application of treaties or conventions accepted by Greece and providing for another procedure.

This acceptance is effective as from the date of signature of the present declaration.

Geneva, September 12, 1929.[27]

(Signed)   A. MICHALAKOPOULOS.

Guatemala.—On behalf of the Republic of Guatemala, I accept, subject to ratification and on the sole condition of reciprocity, the jurisdiction of the Court in all classes of legal disputes concerning:

(*a*) the interpretation of a treaty;

(*b*) any question of international law;

(*c*) the existence of any fact which, if established, would constitute a breach of an international obligation;

(*d*) the nature or extent of the reparation to be made for the breach of an international obligation.

Geneva, December 17, 1926.[28]

(Signed)   F. A. FIGUEROA.

Haiti.—On behalf of the Republic of Haiti, I recognize the jurisdiction of the Permanent Court of International Justice as compulsory.[29]

[1921.]

(Signed)   F. ADDOR.

[26] Ratification deposited February 5, 1930.
[27] Translation. Not subject to ratification.
[28] Translation. No ratification has been deposited.
[29] Translation. Not subject to ratification.

Hungary.—On behalf of the Royal Hungarian Government, and subject to ratification, I recognize, in relation to any other Member or State accepting the same obligation, that is to say, on the sole condition of reciprocity, the jurisdiction of the Court as compulsory *ipso facto* and without special convention, in conformity with Article 36, paragraph 2, of the Statute, for a period of five years to be reckoned as from the deposit of the instrument of the ratification.

Geneva, September 14, 1928.[30]

(Signed) Louis Walko.

(Renewal).—On behalf of the Royal Hungarian Government and subject to ratification, I recognise, in relation to any other Member or State accepting the same obligation, that is to say, on condition of reciprocity, the jurisdiction of the Court as compulsory *ipso facto* and without special convention, in conformity with Article 36, Paragraph 2 of the Statute of the Court, for a further period of five years as from August 13th, 1934.

Geneva, May 30, 1934.[31]

(Signed) Ladislas de Tahy.

India.—On behalf of the Government of India and subject to ratification, I accept as compulsory *ipso facto* and without special convention on condition of reciprocity the jurisdiction of the Court in conformity with Article 36, paragraph 2, of the Statute of the Court, for a period of ten years and thereafter until such time as notice may be given to terminate the acceptance, over all disputes arising after the ratification of the present declaration with regard to situations or facts subsequent to the said ratification:

other than disputes in regard to which the parties to the dispute have agreed or shall agree to have recourse to some other method of peaceful settlement; and

disputes with the Government of any other Member of the League which is a member of the British Commonwealth of Nations, all of which disputes shall be settled in such manner as the parties have agreed or shall agree; and

disputes with regard to questions which by international law fall exclusively within the jurisdiction of India;

and subject to the condition that the Government of India reserve the right to require that proceedings in the Court shall be suspended in respect to any dispute which has been submitted to and is under consideration by the Council of the League of Nations, provided that notice to suspend is given after the dispute has been submitted to the Council and is given within ten days of the notification of the initiation of the proceedings in the

[30] Translation. **Ratification deposited August 13, 1929.**
[31] Translation.

Court, and provided also that such suspension shall be limited to a period of twelve months or such longer period as may be agreed by the parties to the dispute or determined by a decision of all the Members of the Council other than the parties to the dispute.

Geneva, September 19, 1929.[32]

(Signed)   MD. HABIBULLAH.

Irish Free State.—On behalf of the Irish Free State, I declare that I accept as compulsory *ipso facto* and without special convention the jurisdiction of the Court in conformity with Article 36 of the Statute of the Permanent Court of International Justice for a period of twenty years and on the sole condition of reciprocity. This declaration is subject to ratification.

Geneva, September 14, 1929.[33]

(Signed)   P. McGILLIGAN.

Italy.—The Italian Government declares to recognize as compulsory *ipso facto*, in relation to any other Member or State accepting the same obligation, and for a period of five years, subject to any other method of settlement provided by a special convention, and in any case where a solution through the diplomatic channel or further by the action of the Council of the League of Nations could not be reached, the jurisdiction of the Court on the following classes of legal disputes arising after the ratification of the present declaration, and concerning:

(*a*) the interpretation of a treaty;

(*b*) any question of international law;

(*c*) the existence of any fact which, if established, would constitute a breach of an international obligation;

(*d*) the nature or extent of the reparation to be made for the breach of an international obligation.

Geneva, September 9, 1929.[34]

(Signed)   VITTORIO SCIALOJA.

Latvia.—On behalf of the Latvian Government and subject to ratification by the Saeima, I recognize as compulsory, *ipso facto* and without special agreement in relation to any other Member or State accepting the same obligation, that is to say, on condition of reciprocity, the jurisdiction of the Court in conformity with Article 36, paragraph 2, of the Statute of the Court, for a period of five years, in any disputes arising after the ratification of the present declaration with regard to situations or facts subsequent to this ratification, except in cases where the parties have agreed or shall agree

---

[32] Ratification deposited February 5, 1930.
[33] Ratification deposited July 11, 1930.
[34] Translation. Ratification deposited September 7, 1931.

to have recourse to another method of pacific settlement. This declaration replaces the declaration made on September 11, 1923.

Geneva, September 10, 1929.[35]

(Signed)   A. BALODIS.

Liberia.—On behalf of the Government of the Republic of Liberia, and subject to ratification by the Liberian Senate, I recognize, in relation to any other Member or State which accepts the same obligation, that is to say, on the sole condition of reciprocity, the jurisdiction of the Court as compulsory, *ipso facto* and without any special convention.[36]

[Before September 1, 1921.]

(Signed)   B. LEHMANN.

Lithuania.—For a period of five years.

October 5, 1921.[37]

(Signed)   GALVANAUSKAS.

(Renewal).—For a period of five years with effect as from January 14, 1930.

January 14, 1930.[38]

(Signed)   ZAUNIUS.

Luxemburg.—The Government of the Grand-Duchy of Luxemburg recognizes as compulsory, *ipso facto* and without special agreement, in relation to any other State accepting the same obligation, that is to say, on condition of reciprocity, the jurisdiction of the Court in conformity with Article 36, paragraph 2, of the Statute, in any disputes arising after the signature of the present declaration with regard to situations or facts subsequent to this signature, except in cases where the parties have agreed or shall agree to have recourse to another procedure or to another method of pacific settlement. The present declaration is made for a period of five years. Unless it is denounced six months before the expiration of that period, it shall be considered as renewed for a further period of five years and similarly thereafter.

Geneva, September 15, 1930.[39]

(Signed)   BECH.

---

[35] Translation. Ratification deposited February 26, 1930. The declaration of September 11, 1923, was not ratified, and never came into force. For the text, see Series D, No. 6, (4th ed.), p. 44.   [36] Translation. No ratification has been deposited.
[37] Translation. Ratification deposited May 16, 1922.
[38] Translation. Not subject to ratification.
[39] Translation. Not subject to ratification. A previous declaration made by Luxemburg in 1921 was not ratified. For the text, see Series D, No. 6 (4th ed.), p. 52.

Netherlands.—On behalf of the Government of the Netherlands, I recognize, in relation to any other Member or State which accepts the same obligation, that is to say, on the condition of reciprocity, the jurisdiction of the Court as compulsory, *ipso facto* and without any special convention, in conformity with Article 36, paragraph 2, of the Statute of the Court, for a period of five years, in respect of any future dispute in regard to which the parties have not agreed to have recourse to some other means of friendly settlement.

August 6, 1921.[40]

(Signed)   MOSSELMANS.

(Renewal).—On behalf of the Netherlands Government, I recognize as compulsory, *ipso facto* and without special agreement, in relation to any other Member or State accepting the same obligation, that is to say, on condition of reciprocity, the jurisdiction of the Court, in conformity with Article 36, paragraph 2, of the Statute of the Court, for a period of ten years as from August 6, 1926, for any future disputes excepting those in regard to which the parties have agreed, since the coming into force of the Statute of the Permanent Court of International Justice, to have recourse to another method of pacific settlement.

Geneva, September 2, 1926.[41]

(Signed)   W. DOUDE VAN TROOSTWYK.

New Zealand.—On behalf of His Majesty's Government in the Dominion of New Zealand and subject to ratification, I accept as compulsory *ipso facto* and without special convention on condition of reciprocity the jurisdiction of the Court in conformity with Article 36, paragraph 2, of the Statute of the Court, for a period of ten years and thereafter until such time as notice may be given to terminate the acceptance, over all disputes arising after the ratification of the present declaration with regard to situations or facts subsequent to the said ratification:

other than disputes in regard to which the parties to the dispute have agreed or shall agree to have recourse to some other method of peaceful settlement; and

disputes with the Government of any other Member of the League which is a member of the British Commonwealth of Nations, all of which disputes shall be settled in such manner as the parties have agreed or shall agree; and

disputes with regard to questions which by international law fall exclusively within the jurisdiction of the Dominion of New Zealand;

[40] Translation. Not subject to ratification.
[41] Translation. Not subject to ratification.

and subject to the condition that His Majesty's Government in New Zealand reserve the right to require that proceedings in the Court shall be suspended in respect of any dispute which has been submitted to and is under consideration by the Council of the League of Nations, provided that notice to suspend is given after the dispute has been submitted to the Council and is given within ten days of the notification of the initiation of the proceedings in the Court, and provided also that such suspension shall be limited to a period of twelve months or such longer period as may be agreed by the parties to the dispute or determined by a decision of all the Members of the Council other than the parties to the dispute.

Geneva, September 19, 1929.[42]

(Signed)   C. J. PARR.

Nicaragua.—On behalf of the Republic of Nicaragua I recognize as compulsory unconditionally the jurisdiction of the Permanent Court of International Justice.

Geneva, September 24, 1929.[43]

(Signed)   T. F. MEDINA.

Norway.—On behalf of the Government of His Majesty the King of Norway, and subject to ratification, I recognize, in relation to any other Member or State which accepts the same obligation, that is to say, on the sole condition of reciprocity, the jurisdiction of the Court as compulsory, *ipso facto* and without any special convention, for a period of five years.

September 6, 1921.[44]

(Signed)   FRIDTJOF NANSEN.

(Renewal).—On behalf of the Norwegian Government, and without any reserve of ratification, I recognize, in relation to any other Member or State accepting the same obligation, that is to say, on condition of reciprocity, the jurisdiction of the Court as compulsory, *ipso facto* and without special agreement, for a period of ten years as from October 3, 1926.

Geneva, September 22, 1926.[45]

(Signed)   FRIDTJOF NANSEN.

Panama.—On behalf of the Government of Panama, I recognize, in relation to any other Member or State which accepts the same obligation,

---

[42] Ratification deposited March 29, 1930.
[43] Translation. As Nicaragua has not ratified the Protocol of Signature, this declaration has not become effective.
[44] Translation. Ratification deposited October 3, 1921.
[45] Translation. Not subject to ratification.

that is to say, on the sole condition of reciprocity, the jurisdiction of the Court as compulsory, *ipso facto* and without any special convention.

October 25, 1921.[46]

(Signed)   R. A. AMADOR.

Paraguay.—Paraguay accepts, purely and simply, as compulsory, *ipso facto* and without special convention, the jurisdiction of the Permanent Court of International Justice, as set out in Article 36, paragraph 2, of the Statute.

May 11, 1933.[47]

Persia.—The Imperial Government of Persia recognizes as compulsory *ipso facto* and without special agreement in relation to any other State accepting the same obligation, that is to say, on condition of reciprocity, the jurisdiction of the Permanent Court of International Justice, in accordance with Article 36, paragraph 2, of the Statute of the Court, in any disputes arising after the ratification of the present declaration with regard to situations or facts relating directly or indirectly to the application of treaties or conventions accepted by Persia and subsequent to the ratification of this declaration, with the exception of:

(*a*) disputes relating to the territorial status of Persia, including those concerning the rights of sovereignty of Persia over its islands and ports;

(*b*) disputes in regard to which the parties have agreed or shall agree to have recourse to some other method of peaceful settlement;

(*c*) disputes with regard to questions which, by international law, fall exclusively within the jurisdiction of Persia.

However, the Imperial Government of Persia reserves the right to require that proceedings in the Court shall be suspended in respect of any dispute which has been submitted to the Council of the League of Nations.

The present declaration is made for a period of six years. At the expiration of that period, it shall continue to bear its full effects until notification is given of its abrogation.

Geneva, October 2, 1930.[48]

(Signed)   HUSSEIN ALA.

Peru.—On behalf of the Republic of Peru and subject to ratification, I recognize as compulsory *ipso facto* without special agreement in relation to any other Member of the League of Nations or to any State accepting the same obligation, the jurisdiction of the Court, in conformity with Article

[46] Translation. Ratification deposited June 14, 1929.
[47] Translation. Declaration on deposit of ratification of Protocol of Signature.
[48] Translation. Ratification deposited September 19, 1932.

36, paragraph 2, of its Statute, for a period of ten years from the date of deposit of the instrument of ratification, in any dispute arising with regard to situations and facts subsequent to that ratification, except in cases where the parties have agreed either to have recourse to another method of settlement by arbitration, or to submit the dispute previously to the Council of the League of Nations.

Geneva, September 19, 1929.[49]

(Signed)   M. H. CORNEJO.

Poland.—On behalf of the Republic of Poland, subject to ratification, the undersigned recognizes as compulsory *ipso facto* and without special agreement, in relation to any other Member of the League of Nations or State accepting the same obligation, the jurisdiction of the Permanent Court of International Justice in conformity with Article 36, paragraph 2, of the Statute of the Court, for a period of five years, in any future dispute arising after the ratification of the present declaration with regard to situations or facts subsequent to such ratification, except in cases where the parties have agreed or shall agree to have recourse to another method of peaceful settlement.

The present declaration does not apply to disputes:

(1) with regard to matters which by international law are solely within the domestic jurisdiction of States, or

(2) arising between Poland and States which refuse to establish or maintain normal diplomatic relations with Poland, or

(3) connected directly or indirectly with the World War or with the Polish-Soviet war, or

(4) resulting directly or indirectly from the provisions of the treaty of peace signed at Riga, on March 18, 1921,[50] or

(5) relating to provisions of internal law connected with points (3) and (4).

Geneva, January 24, 1931.[51]

(Signed)   AUGUSTE ZALESKI.

Portugal.—On behalf of Portugal, I recognize, in relation to any Member or State accepting the same obligation, the jurisdiction of the Court as compulsory, *ipso facto* and without special convention.[52]

(Signed)   AFFONSO COSTA.

[49] Translation. Ratification deposited March 29, 1932.
[50] 6 *League of Nations Treaty Series*, p. 52.—Ed.
[51] Translation. No ratification has been deposited.
[52] Translation. The signature and declaration were affixed prior to January 28, 1921. Ratification deposited October 8, 1921.

Rumania.—The Rumanian Government declares that it accedes to the Optional Clause of Article 36 of the Statute of the Permanent Court of International Justice for a period of five years in respect of the Governments recognized by Rumania and on condition of reciprocity in regard to legal disputes arising out of situations or facts subsequent to the ratification by the Rumanian Parliament of this accession and with the exception of matters for which a special procedure has been or may be established and subject to the right of Rumania to submit the dispute to the Council of the League of Nations before having recourse to the Court.

The following are, however, excepted:

(*a*) any question of substance or of procedure which might directly or indirectly cause the existing territorial integrity of Rumania and her sovereign rights, including her rights over her ports and communications, to be brought into question.

(*b*) disputes relating to questions which, according to international law, fall under the domestic jurisdiction of Rumania.

Geneva, October 8, 1930.[53]

(Signed)   C. ANTONIADE.

El Salvador.—On condition of reciprocity.[54]

(Signed)   J. GUSTAVO GUERRERO.
ARTURO R. AVILA.

Siam.—On behalf of the Siamese Government, I recognize, subject to ratification, in relation to any other Member or State which accepts the same obligation, that is to say, on the condition of reciprocity, the jurisdiction of the Court as compulsory *ipso facto* and without any special convention, in conformity with Article 36, paragraph 2, of the Statute of the Court for a period of ten years, in all disputes as to which no other means of pacific settlement is agreed upon between the parties.

Geneva, September 20, 1929.[55]

(Signed)   VARNVAIDYA.

---

[53] Translation. Ratification deposited June 9, 1931.

[54] Translation. The signature and declaration were affixed prior to January 28, 1921. The ratification of the Protocol of Signature of 1920 was subject to reservations expressed in the decision of the Executive Power of El Salvador of May 26, 1930, and translated from the instrument of ratification, which was deposited on August 29, 1930, in the following terms:

"The provisions of this Statute do not apply to any disputes or differences concerning points or questions which cannot be submitted to arbitration in accordance with the political Constitution of this Republic.

"The provisions of this Statute also do not apply to disputes which arose before that date or to pecuniary claims made against the nation, it being further understood that Article 36 binds El Salvador only in regard to States which accept the arbitration in that form."—Ed.

[55] Ratification deposited May 7, 1930.

South Africa.—On behalf of His Majesty's Government in the Union of South Africa and subject to ratification, I accept as compulsory *ipso facto* and without special convention on condition of reciprocity the jurisdiction of the Court in conformity with Article 36, paragraph 2, of the Statute of the Court, for a period of ten years and thereafter until such time as notice may be given to terminate the acceptance, over all disputes arising after the ratification of the present declaration with regard to situations or facts subsequent to the said ratification:

other than disputes in regard to which the parties to the dispute have agreed or shall agree to have recourse to some other method of peaceful settlement; and

disputes with the Government of any other Member of the League which is a member of the British Commonwealth of Nations, all of which disputes shall be settled in such manner as the parties have agreed or shall agree; and

disputes with regard to questions which by international law fall exclusively within the jurisdiction of the Union of South Africa;

and subject to the condition that His Majesty's Government in the Union of South Africa reserve the right to require that proceedings in the Court shall be suspended in respect of any dispute which has been submitted to and is under consideration by the Council of the League of Nations, provided that notice to suspend is given after the dispute has been submitted to the Council and is given within ten days of the notification of the initiation of the proceedings in the Court, and provided also that such suspension shall be limited to a period of twelve months or such longer period as may be agreed by the parties to the dispute or determined by a decision of all the Members of the Council other than the parties to the dispute.

Geneva, September 19, 1929.[56]

(Signed)   ERIC H. LOUW.

Spain.—On behalf of the Government of His Majesty the King of Spain, I recognize as compulsory *ipso facto* and without special agreement in relation to any other Member or State accepting the same obligation, that is to say, on condition of reciprocity, the jurisdiction of the Court for a period of ten years, in any dispute arising after the signature of the present declaration with regard to situations or facts subsequent to this signature, except in cases where the parties have agreed or shall agree to have recourse to another method of pacific settlement.

Geneva, September 21, 1928.[57]

(Signed)   J. QUIÑONES DE LEÓN.

---

[56] Ratification deposited April 7, 1930.   [57] Translation. Not subject to ratification.

Sweden.—On behalf of the Government of His Majesty the King of Sweden, I recognize, in relation to any other Member or State which accepts the same obligation, that is to say, on the condition of reciprocity, the jurisdiction of the Court as compulsory, *ipso facto* and without any special convention, for a period of five years.

Geneva, August 16, 1921.[58]

(Signed)   P. DE ADLERCREUTZ.

(Renewal).—On behalf of the Royal Swedish Government, I recognize, in relation to any other Member or State accepting the same obligation, that is to say, on the sole condition of reciprocity, the jurisdiction of the Court as compulsory, *ipso facto* and without special convention, for a period of ten years to be reckoned from the date on which the Swedish Declaration of August 16, 1921, ceases to be in force.

Geneva, March 18, 1926.[58]

(Signed)   EINAR HENNINGS.

Switzerland.—On behalf of the Swiss Government and subject to ratification by the Federal Assembly, I recognize, in relation to any Member or State accepting the same obligation, that is to say, on the sole condition of reciprocity, the jurisdiction of the Court as compulsory, *ipso facto* and without special convention, for a period of five years.[59]

[Before January 28, 1921.]

(Signed)   MOTTA.

(Renewal).—On behalf of the Swiss Confederation and subject to ratification, the undersigned recognizes, in relation to any other Member of the League of Nations or State accepting the same obligation, that is to say, on the sole condition of reciprocity, the jurisdiction of the Court as compulsory, *ipso facto* and without special convention, for a period of ten years to be reckoned as from the deposit of the instrument of ratification.

Geneva, March 1, 1926.[60]

(Signed)   MOTTA.

Uruguay.—On behalf of the Government of Uruguay, I recognize, in relation to any Member or State accepting the same obligation, that is to say, on the sole condition of reciprocity, the jurisdiction of the Court as compulsory, *ipso facto* and without special convention.[61]

(Signed)   B. FERNANDEZ Y MEDINA.

[58] Translation. Not subject to ratification.
[59] Translation. Ratification deposited July 25, 1921.
[60] Translation. Ratification deposited July 24, 1926.
[61] Translation. The declaration was made prior to January 28, 1921. Ratification deposited September 27, 1921.

Yugoslavia.—On behalf of the Kingdom of Yugoslavia and subject to ratification, I recognize, as compulsory *ipso facto* and without special agreement, in relation to any other Member of the League of Nations, or State the Government of which is recognized by the Kingdom of Yugoslavia, and accepting the same obligation, that is to say, on condition of reciprocity, the jurisdiction of the Permanent Court of International Justice, in conformity with Article 36 of its Statute, for a period of five years from the date of the deposit of the instrument of ratification, in any disputes arising after the ratification of the present declaration, except disputes with regard to questions which, by international law, fall exclusively within the jurisdiction of the Kingdom of Yugoslavia, and except in cases where the parties have agreed or shall agree to have recourse to some other method of peaceful settlement.

May 16, 1930.[62]

(Signed)   DR. V. MARINKOVICH.

SIGNATURE AND RATIFICATION OF THE "OPTIONAL CLAUSE" AND DECLARATIONS ACCEPTING OBLIGATORY JURISDICTION

(Asterisks (*) indicate States bound on June 1, 1934)

States	Date of Signature	Date of Deposit of Ratification	Effective Until
*Albania	Sept. 17, 1930	Sept. 17, 1930	Sept. 17, 1935
*Australia	Sept. 20, 1929	Aug. 18, 1930	Aug. 18, 1940
*Austria	{ Mar. 14, 1922 { Jan. 12, 1927	{ Not required { Mar. 13, 1927	{ Mar. 14, 1927 { Mar. 13, 1937
*Belgium	Sept. 25, 1925	Mar. 10, 1926	Mar. 10, 1941
*Brazil	Nov. 1, 1921	[Nov. 1, 1921 [1]]	Feb. 5, 1935 [2]
*Bulgaria	July 29, 1921	[Aug. 12, 1921 [1]]	Indefinite
*Canada	Sept. 20, 1929	July 28, 1930	July 28, 1940
China	May 13, 1922	[May 13, 1922 [1]]	May 13, 1927
*Colombia	Jan. 6, 1932	Jan. 6, 1932	Indefinite
Costa Rica	Before Jan. 28, 1921		
Czechoslovakia	Sept. 19, 1929		
*Denmark	{ Before Jan. 28, 1921 { Dec. 11, 1925	{ June 13, 1921 { Mar. 28, 1926	{ June 13, 1926 { June 13, 1936
*Dominican Republic	Sept. 30, 1924	Feb. 4, 1933	Indefinite
*Estonia	{ May 2, 1923 { June 25, 1928	{ [May 2, 1923 [1]] { Not required	{ May 2, 1928 { May 2, 1938
Ethiopia	{ July 12, 1926 { Apr. 15, 1932	{ July 16, 1926 { Not required	{ July 16, 1931 { July 16, 1933
*Finland	{ June 28, 1921 { Mar. 3, 1927	{ Apr. 6, 1922 { Not required	{ Apr. 6, 1927 { Apr. 6, 1937
*France	Sept. 19, 1929	Apr. 25, 1931	Apr. 25, 1936
*Germany	{ Sept. 23, 1927 { Feb. 9, 1933	{ Feb. 29, 1928 { July 5, 1933	{ Feb. 28, 1933 { Feb. 28, 1938
*Great Britain	Sept. 19, 1929	Feb. 5, 1930	Feb. 5, 1940

[1] Ratification was not a condition of the declaration. The date given is that of the ratification of the Protocol of Signature.

[2] The Brazilian acceptance was subject to a condition that it was to become effective when the Court's jurisdiction was recognized "by two at least of the Powers permanently represented on the Council of the League of Nations." That condition was met on February 5, 1930.

[62] Translation. Ratification deposited November 24, 1930.

States	Date of Signature	Date of Deposit of Ratification	Effective Until
*Greece	Sept. 12, 1929	Not required	Sept. 12, 1934
Guatemala	Dec. 17, 1926		
*Haiti	Before Sept. 1, 1921	[Sept. 7, 1921 [3]]	Indefinite
*Hungary	{ Sept. 14, 1928 { May 30, 1934	Aug. 13, 1929	Aug. 13, 1934
*India	Sept. 19, 1929	Feb. 5, 1930	Feb. 5, 1940
*Irish Free State	Sept. 14, 1929	July 11, 1930	July 11, 1950
*Italy	Sept. 9, 1929	Sept. 7, 1931	Sept. 7, 1936
*Latvia	Sept. 10, 1929	Feb. 26, 1930	Feb. 26, 1935
Liberia	Before Sept. 1, 1921		
*Lithuania	{ Oct. 5, 1921 { Jan. 14, 1930	{ May 16, 1922 { Not required	{ May 16, 1927 { Jan. 14, 1935
*Luxemburg	Sept. 15, 1930	Sept. 15, 1930	Sept. 15, 1935
*Netherlands	{ Aug. 6, 1921 { Sept. 2, 1926	{ Not required { Not required	{ Aug. 6, 1926 { Aug. 6, 1936
*New Zealand	Sept. 19, 1929	Mar. 29, 1930	Mar. 29, 1940
Nicaragua	Sept. 24, 1929		
*Norway	{ Sept. 6, 1921 { Sept. 22, 1926	{ Oct. 3, 1921 { Not required	{ Oct. 3, 1926 { Oct. 3, 1936
*Panama	Oct. 25, 1921	June 14, 1929	Indefinite
*Paraguay	May 11, 1933	May 11, 1933	Indefinite
*Persia	Oct. 2, 1930	Sept. 19, 1932	Sept. 19, 1938
*Peru	Sept. 19, 1929	Mar. 29, 1932	Mar. 29, 1942
Poland	Jan. 24, 1931		
*Portugal	Before Jan. 28, 1921	[Oct. 8, 1921 [3]]	Indefinite
*Rumania	Oct. 8, 1930	June 9, 1931	June 9, 1936
*Salvador	Before Jan. 28, 1921	Aug. 29, 1930	Indefinite
*Siam	Sept. 20, 1929	May 7, 1930	May 7, 1940
*South Africa	Sept. 19, 1929	Apr. 7, 1930	Apr. 7, 1940
*Spain	Sept. 21, 1928	Not required	Sept. 21, 1938
*Sweden	{ Aug. 16, 1921 { Mar. 18, 1926	{ Not required { Not required	{ Aug. 16, 1926 { Aug. 16, 1936
*Switzerland	{ Before Jan. 28, 1921 { Mar. 1, 1926	{ July 25, 1921 { July 24, 1926	{ July 25, 1926 { July 25, 1936
*Uruguay	Before Jan. 28, 1921	Sept. 27, 1921	Indefinite
*Yugoslavia	May 16, 1930	Nov. 24, 1930	Nov. 24, 1935

Number of signatory States 49
Number of States bound 41

[3] Ratification was not a condition of the declaration. The date given is that of the ratification of the Protocol of Signature.

II. INSTRUMENTS NOT IN FORCE RELATING TO THE CONSTITUTION OF THE COURT

APPENDIX NO. 5

Protocol for the Revision of the Statute of the Permanent Court of International Justice, Geneva, September 14, 1929

(Not in force, June 1, 1934)

Text from *League of Nations Official Journal*, 1929, p. 1842.

1. Les soussignés, dûment autorisés, conviennent, au nom des gouvernements qu'ils représentent, d'apporter au Statut de la Cour permanente de Justice internationale les amendements qui sont indiqués dans l'annexe au présent Protocole et qui font l'objet de la résolution de l'Assemblée de la Société des Nations du 14 septembre 1929.

2. Le présent Protocole, dont les textes français et anglais feront également foi, sera soumis à la signature de tous les signataires du Protocole du 16 décembre 1920, auquel est annexé le Statut de la Cour permanente de Justice internationale, ainsi qu'à celle des Etats-Unis d'Amérique.

3. Le présent Protocole sera ratifié. Les instruments de ratification seront déposés, si possible avant le 1er septembre 1930, entre les mains du Secrétaire général de la Société des Nations, qui en informera les Membres de la Société et les Etats mentionnés dans l'annexe au Pacte.

1. The undersigned, duly authorised, agree, on behalf of the Governments which they represent, to make in the Statute of the Permanent Court of International Justice the amendments which are set out in the Annex to the present Protocol and which form the subject of the resolution of the Assembly of the League of Nations of September 14th, 1929.

2. The present Protocol, of which the French and English texts are both authentic, shall be presented for signature to all the signatories of the Protocol of December 16th, 1920, to which the Statute of the Permanent Court of International Justice is annexed, and to the United States of America.

3. The present Protocol shall be ratified. The instruments of ratification shall be deposited, if possible before September 1st, 1930, with the Secretary-General of the League of Nations, who shall inform the Members of the League of Nations and the States mentioned in the Annex to the Covenant.

4. Le présent Protocole entrera en vigueur le 1er septembre 1930, à condition que le Conseil de la Société des Nations se soit assuré que les Membres de la Société des Nations et les Etats mentionnés dans l'annexe au Pacte, qui auront ratifié le Protocole du 16 décembre 1920, mais dont la ratification sur le présent Protocole n'aurait pas encore été reçue à cette date, ne font pas d'objection à l'entrée en vigueur des amendements au Statut de la Cour qui sont indiqués dans l'annexe au présent Protocole.

5. Dés l'entrée en vigueur du présent Protocole, les nouvelles dispositions feront partie du Statut adopté en 1920 et les dispositions des articles primitifs objet de la revision seront abrogées. Il est entendu que, jusqu'au 1er janvier 1931, la Cour continuera à exercer ses fonctions conformément au Statut de 1920.

6. Dés l'entrée en vigueur du présent Protocole, toute acceptation du Statut de la Cour signifiera acceptation du Statut revisé.

7. Aux fins du présent Protocole, les Etats-Unis d'Amérique seront dans la même position qu'un Etat ayant ratifié le Protocole du 16 décembre 1920.

Fait à Genève, le quatorzième jour de septembre mil neuf cent vingt-neuf, en un seul exemplaire qui sera déposé dans les archives du Secrétariat de la Société des Nations. Le Secrétaire général adressera des copies

4. The present Protocol shall enter into force on September 1st, 1930, provided that the Council of the League of Nations has satisfied itself that those Members of the League of Nations and States mentioned in the Annex to the Covenant which have ratified the Protocol of December 16th, 1920, and whose ratification of the present Protocol has not been received by that date, have no objection to the coming into force of the amendments to the Statute of the Court which are annexed to the present Protocol.

5. After the entry into force of the present Protocol, the new provisions shall form part of the Statute adopted in 1920 and the provisions of the original articles which have been made the subject of amendment shall be abrogated. It is understood that, until January 1st, 1931, the Court shall continue to perform its functions in accordance with the Statute of 1920.

6. After the entry into force of the present Protocol, any acceptance of the Statute of the Court shall constitute an acceptance of the Statute as amended.

7. For the purposes of the present Protocol, the United States of America shall be in the same position as a State which has ratified the Protocol of December 16th, 1920.

Done at Geneva, the fourteenth day of September nineteen hundred and twenty-nine, in a single copy which shall be deposited in the archives of the Secretariat of the League of Nations. The Secretary-

certifiées conformes aux Membres de la Société des Nations et aux Etats mentionnés dans l'annexe au Pacte.

General shall deliver authenticated copies to the Members of the League of Nations and to the States mentioned in the Annex to the Covenant.

[Signatures omitted.]

ANNEX TO THE PROTOCOL OF SEPTEMBER 14, 1929

AMENDMENTS TO THE STATUTE OF THE PERMANENT COURT OF INTERNATIONAL JUSTICE

Les articles 3, 4, 8, 13, 14, 15, 16, 17, 23, 25, 26, 27, 29, 31, 32 et 35 sont remplacés par les dispositions suivantes:

Articles 3, 4, 8, 13, 14, 15, 16, 17, 23, 25, 26, 27, 29, 31, 32 and 35 are replaced by the following provisions:

Nouvelle rédaction de l'article 3.

New text of Article 3.

La Cour se compose de quinze membres.

The Court shall consist of fifteen members.

Nouvel article 4.

New text of Article 4.

Les membres de la Cour sont élus par l'Assemblée et par le Conseil sur une liste de personnes présentées par les groupes nationaux de la Cour d'Arbitrage, conformément aux dispositions suivantes.

The members of the Court shall be elected by the Assembly and by the Council from a list of persons nominated by the national groups in the Court of Arbitration, in accordance with the following provisions.

En ce qui concerne les Membres de la Société qui ne sont pas représentés à la Cour permanente d'Arbitrage, les listes de candidats seront présentées par des groupes nationaux, désignés à cet effet par leurs Gouvernements, dans les mêmes conditions que celles stipulées pour les membres de la Cour d'Arbitrage par l'article 44 de la Convention de La Haye de 1907 sur le règlement pacifique des conflits internationaux.

In the case of Members of the League of Nations not represented in the Permanent Court of Arbitration, the lists of candidates shall be drawn up by national groups appointed for this purpose by their Governments under the same conditions as those prescribed for members of the Permanent Court of Arbitration by Article 44 of the Convention of The Hague of 1907 for the pacific settlement of international disputes.

En l'absence d'accord spécial, l'Assemblée, sur la proposition du Conseil, réglera les conditions auxquelles peut participer à l'élection

The conditions under which a State which has accepted the Statute of the Court but is not a member of the League of Nations, may par-

des membres de la Cour un Etat qui, tout en ayant accepté le Statut de la Cour, n'est pas Membre de la Société des Nations.

Nouvelle rédaction de l'article 8.

L'Assemblée et le Conseil procèdent indépendamment l'un de l'autre à l'élection des membres de la Cour.

Nouvelle rédaction de l'article 13.

Les membres de la Cour sont élus pour neuf ans.

Ils sont rééligibles.

Ils restent en fonction jusqu'à leur remplacement. Après ce remplacement, ils continuent de connaître des affaires dont ils sont déjà saisis.

En cas de démission d'un membre de la Cour, la démission sera adressée au Président de la Cour, pour être transmise au Secrétaire général de la Société des Nations.

Cette dernière notification emporte vacance de siège.

Nouvelle rédaction de l'article 14.

Il est pourvu aux sièges devenus vacants selon la méthode suivie pour la première élection, sous réserve de la disposition ci-après: dans le mois qui suivra la vacance, le Secrétaire général de la Société des Nations procédera à l'invitation prescrite par l'article 5, et la date d'élection sera fixée par le Conseil dans sa première session.

ticipate in electing the members of the Court shall, in the absence of a special agreement, be laid down by the Assembly on the proposal of the Council.

New text of Article 8.

The Assembly and the Council shall proceed independently of one another to elect the members of the Court.

New text of Article 13.

The members of the Court shall be elected for nine years.

They may be rëelected.

They shall continue to discharge their duties until their places have been filled. Though replaced, they shall finish any cases which they may have begun.

In the case of the resignation of a member of the Court, the resignation will be addressed to the President of the Court for transmission to the Secretary-General of the League of Nations.

This last notification makes the place vacant.

New text of Article 14.

Vacancies which may occur shall be filled by the same method as that laid down for the first election, subject to the following provision: the Secretary-General of the League of Nations shall, within one month of the occurrence of the vacancy, proceed to issue the invitations provided for in Article 5, and the date of the election shall be fixed by the Council at its next session.

Nouvelle rédaction de l'article 15.

Le membre de la Cour élu en remplacement d'un membre dont le mandat n'est pas expiré achève le terme du mandat de son prédécesseur.

Nouvelle rédaction de l'article 16.

Les membres de la Cour ne peuvent exercer aucune fonction politique ou administrative, ni se livrer à aucune autre occupation de caractère professionnel.

En cas de doute, la Cour décide.

Nouvelle rédaction de l'article 17.

Les membres de la Cour ne peuvent exercer les fonctions d'agent, de conseil ou d'avocat dans aucune affaire.

Ils ne peuvent participer au règlement d'aucune affaire dans laquelle ils sont antérieurement intervenus comme agents, conseils ou avocats de l'une des parties, membres d'un tribunal national ou international, d'une commission d'enquête, ou à tout autre titre.

En cas de doute, la Cour décide.

Nouvelle rédaction de l'article 23.

La Cour reste toujours en fonction, excepté pendant les vacances judiciares, dont les périodes et la durée sont fixées par la Cour.

Les membres de la Cour dont les foyers se trouvent à plus de cinq jours de voyage normal de La Haye auront droit, indépendamment des vacances judiciaires, à un congé de

New text of Article 15.

A member of the Court elected to replace a member whose period of appointment has not expired, will hold the appointment for the remainder of his predecessor's term.

New text of Article 16.

The members of the Court may not exercise any political or administrative function, nor engage in any other occupation of a professional nature.

Any doubt on this point is settled by the decision of the Court.

New text of Article 17.

No member of the Court may act as agent, counsel or advocate in any case.

No member may participate in the decision of any case in which he has previously taken an active part as agent, counsel or advocate for one of the contesting parties, or as a member of a national or international Court, or of a commission of enquiry, or in any other capacity.

Any doubt on this point is settled by the decision of the Court.

New text of Article 23.

The Court shall remain permanently in session, except during the judicial vacations, the dates and duration of which shall be fixed by the Court.

Members of the Court whose homes are situated at more than five days' normal journey from The Hague shall be entitled, apart from the judicial vacations, to six months'

six mois, non compris la durée des voyages, tous les trois ans.

Les membres de la Cour sont tenus, à moins de congé régulier, d'empêchement pour cause de maladie ou autre motif grave dûment justifié auprès du Président, d'être à tout moment à la disposition de la Cour.

Nouvelle rédaction de l'article 25.

Sauf exception expressément prévue, la Cour exerce ses attributions en séance plénière.

Sous la condition que le nombre des juges disponibles pour constituer la Cour ne soit pas réduit à moins de onze, le Règlement de la Cour pourra prévoir que, selon les circonstances et à tour de rôle, un ou plusieurs juges pourront être dispensés de siéger.

Toutefois, le quorum de neuf est suffisant pour constituer la Cour.

Nouvelle rédaction de l'article 26.

Pour les affaires concernant le travail, et spécialement pour les affaires visées dans la partie XIII (Travail) du Traité de Versailles et les parties correspondantes des autres traités de paix, la Cour statuera dans les conditions ci-après:

La Cour constituera pour chaque période de trois années une chambre spéciale composée de cinq juges désignés en tenant compte, autant que possible, des prescriptions de l'article 9. Deux juges seront, en outre, désignés pour remplacer celui des juges qui se trouverait dans l'impossibilité de siéger. Sur la demande

leave every three years, not including the time spent in travelling.

Members of the Court shall be bound, unless they are on regular leave or prevented from attending by illness or other serious reason duly explained to the President, to hold themselves permanently at the disposal of the Court.

New text of Article 25.

The full Court shall sit except when it is expressly provided otherwise.

Subject to the condition that the number of judges available to constitute the Court is not thereby reduced below eleven, the Rules of Court may provide for allowing one or more judges, according to circumstances and in rotation, to be dispensed from sitting.

Provided always that a quorum of nine judges shall suffice to constitute the Court.

New text of Article 26.

Labour cases, particularly cases referred to in Part XIII (Labour) of the Treaty of Versailles and the corresponding portions of the other Treaties of Peace, shall be heard and determined by the Court under the following conditions:

The Court will appoint every three years a special Chamber of five judges, selected so far as possible with due regard to the provisions of Article 9. In addition, two judges shall be selected for the purpose of replacing a judge who finds it impossible to sit. If the parties so demand, cases will be heard and

des parties, cette chambre statuera. A défaut de cette demande, la Cour siégera en séance plénière. Dans les deux cas, les juges sont assistés de quatre assesseurs techniques siégeant à leurs côtés avec voix consultative et assurant une juste représentation des intérêts en cause.

Les assesseurs techniques sont choisis dans chaque cas spécial d'après les règles de procédure visées à l'article 30, sur une liste d' "Assesseurs pour litiges de travail," composée de noms présentés à raison de deux par chaque Membre de la Société des Nations et d'un nombre égal présenté par le Conseil d'administration du Bureau international du Travail. Le Conseil désignera par moitié des représentants des travailleurs et par moitié des représentants des patrons pris sur la liste prévue à l'article 412 du Traité de Versailles et les articles correspondants des autres traités de paix.

Le recours à la procédure sommaire visée à l'article 29 reste toujours ouvert dans les affaires visées à l'alinéa premier du présent article, si les parties le demandent.

Dans les affaires concernant le travail, le Bureau international aura la faculté de fournir à la Cour tous les renseignements nécessaires et, à cet effet, le Directeur de ce Bureau recevra communication de toutes les pièces de procédure présentées par écrit.

Nouvelle rédaction de l'article 27.

Pour les affaires concernant le transit et les communications, et

determined by this Chamber. In the absence of any such demand, the full Court will sit. In both cases, the judges will be assisted by four technical assessors sitting with them, but without the right to vote, and chosen with a view to ensuring a just representation of the competing interests.

The technical assessors shall be chosen for each particular case in accordance with rules of procedure under Article 30 from a list of "Assessors for Labour Cases" composed of two persons nominated by each Member of the League of Nations and an equivalent number nominated by the Governing Body of the Labour Office. The Governing Body will nominate, as to one-half, representatives of the workers, and, as to one-half, representatives of employers from the list referred to in Article 412 of the Treaty of Versailles and the corresponding Articles of the other Treaties of Peace.

Recourse may always be had to the summary procedure provided for in Article 29, in the cases referred to in the first paragraph of the present Article, if the parties so request.

In Labour cases, the International Office shall be at liberty to furnish the Court with all relevant information, and for this purpose the Director of that Office shall receive copies of all the written proceedings.

New text of Article 27.

Cases relating to transit and communications, particularly cases re-

spécialement pour les affaires visées dans la partie XII (Ports, Voies d'eau, Voies ferrées) du Traité de Versailles et les parties correspondantes des autres traités de paix, la Cour statuera dans les conditions ci-après:

La Cour constituera, pour chaque période de trois années, une chambre spéciale composée de cinq juges désignés en tenant compte autant que possible des prescriptions de l'article 9. Deux juges seront, en outre, désignés pour remplacer celui des juges qui se trouverait dans l'impossibilité de siéger. Sur la demande des parties, cette chambre statuera. A défaut de cette demande, la Cour siégera en séance plénière. Si les parties le désirent, ou si la Cour le décide, les juges seront assistés de quatre assesseurs techniques siégeant à leurs côtés avec voix consultative.

Les assesseurs techniques seront choisis dans chaque cas spécial d'après les règles de procédure visées à l'article 30, sur une liste d' "Assesseurs pour litiges de transit et de communications," composée de noms présentés à raison de deux par chaque Membre de la Société des Nations.

Le recours à la procédure sommaire visée à l'article 29 reste toujours ouvert dans les affaires visées à l'alinéa premier du présent article, si les parties le demandent.

Nouvelle rédaction de l'article 29.

En vue de la prompte expédition des affaires, la Cour compose annuellement une Chambre de cinq juges, appelés à statuer en procédure som-

ferred to in Part XII (Ports, Waterways and Railways) of the Treaty of Versailles and the corresponding portions of the other Treaties of Peace, shall be heard and determined by the Court under the following conditions:

The Court will appoint every three years a special Chamber of five judges, selected so far as possible with due regard to the provisions of Article 9. In addition, two judges shall be selected for the purpose of replacing a judge who finds it impossible to sit. If the parties so demand, cases will be heard and determined by this Chamber. In the absence of any such demand, the full Court will sit. When desired by the parties or decided by the Court, the judges will be assisted by four technical assessors sitting with them, but without the right to vote.

The technical assessors shall be chosen for each particular case in accordance with rules of procedure under Article 30 from a list of "Assessors for Transit and Communications Cases" composed of two persons nominated by each Member of the League of Nations.

Recourse may always be had to the summary procedure provided for in Article 29, in the cases referred to in the first paragraph of the present Article, if the parties so request.

New text of Article 29.

With a view to the speedy despatch of business, the Court shall form annually a Chamber composed of five judges who, at the request of the con-

maire lorsque les parties le demandent. Deux juges seront, en outre, désignés, pour remplacer celui des juges qui se trouverait dans l'impossibilité de siéger.

Nouvelle rédaction de l'article 31.

Les juges de la nationalité de chacune des parties en cause conservent le droit de siéger dans l'affaire dont la Cour est saisie.

Si la Cour compte sur le siège un juge de la nationalité d'une des parties, l'autre partie peut désigner une personne de son choix pour siéger en qualité de juge. Celle-ci devra être prise de préférence parmi les personnes qui ont été l'objet d'une présentation en conformité des articles 4 et 5.

Si la Cour ne compte sur le siège aucun juge de la nationalité des parties, chacune de ces parties peut procéder à la désignation d'un juge de la même manière qu'au paragraphe précédent.

La présente disposition s'applique dans le cas des articles 26, 27 et 29. En pareils cas, le Président priera un, ou, s'il y a lieu, deux des membres de la Cour composant la Chambre, de céder leur place aux membres de la Cour de la nationalité des parties intéressées et, à défaut ou en cas d'empêchement, aux juges spécialement désignés par les parties.

Lorsque plusieurs parties font cause commune, elles ne comptent, pour l'application des dispositions qui précèdent, que pour une seule. En cas de doute, la Cour décide.

testing parties, may hear and determine cases by summary procedure. In addition, two judges shall be selected for the purpose of replacing a judge who finds it impossible to sit.

New text of Article 31.

Judges of the nationality of each of the contesting parties shall retain their right to sit in the case before the Court.

If the Court includes upon the Bench a judge of the nationality of one of the parties, the other party may choose a person to sit as judge. Such person shall be chosen preferably from among those persons who have been nominated as candidates as provided in Articles 4 and 5.

If the Court includes upon the Bench no judge of the nationality of the contesting parties, each of these parties may proceed to select a judge as provided in the preceding paragraph.

The present provision shall apply to the case of Articles 26, 27 and 29. In such cases, the President shall request one or, if necessary, two of the members of the Court forming the Chamber to give place to the members of the Court of the nationality of the parties concerned, and, failing such or if they are unable to be present, to the judges specially appointed by the parties.

Should there be several parties in the same interest, they shall, for the purpose of the preceding provisions, be reckoned as one party only. Any doubt upon this point is settled by the decision of the Court.

Les juges désignés, comme il est dit aux paragraphes 2, 3 et 4 du présent article, doivent satisfaire aux prescriptions des articles 2; 17, alinéa 2; 20 et 24 du présent Statut. Ils participent à la décision dans des conditions de complète égalité avec leurs collègues.

Nouvelle rédaction de l'article 32.

Les membres de la Cour reçoivent un traitement annuel.

Le président reçoit une allocation annuelle spéciale.

Le vice-président reçoit une allocation spéciale pour chaque jour où il remplit les fonctions de président.

Les juges désignés par application de l'article 31, autres que les membres de la Cour, reçoivent une indemnité pour chaque jour où ils exercent leurs fonctions.

Ces traitements, allocations et indemnités sont fixés par l'Assemblée de la Société des Nations sur la proposition du Conseil. Ils ne peuvent être diminués pendant la durée des fonctions.

Le traitement du Greffier est fixé par l'Assemblée sur la proposition de la Cour.

Un règlement adopté par l'Assemblée fixe les conditions dans lesquelles les pensions sont allouées aux membres de la Cour et au Greffier, ainsi que les conditions dans lesquelles les membres de la Cour et le Greffier reçoivent le remboursement de leurs frais de voyage.

Les traitements, indemnités et allocations sont exempts de tout impôt.

Judges selected as laid down in paragraphs 2, 3 and 4 of this Article shall fulfil the conditions required by Articles 2, 17 (paragraph 2), 20 and 24 of this Statute. They shall take part in the decision on terms of complete equality with their colleagues.

New text of Article 32.

The members of the Court shall receive an annual salary.

The President shall receive a special annual allowance.

The Vice-President shall receive a special allowance for every day on which he acts as President.

The judges appointed under Article 31, other than members of the Court, shall receive an indemnity for each day on which they sit.

These salaries, allowances and indemnities shall be fixed by the Assembly of the League of Nations on the proposal of the Council. They may not be decreased during the term of office.

The salary of the Registrar shall be fixed by the Assembly on the proposal of the Court.

Regulations made by the Assembly shall fix the conditions under which retiring pensions may be given to members of the Court and to the Registrar, and the conditions under which members of the Court and the Registrar shall have their travelling expenses refunded.

The above salaries, indemnities and allowances shall be free of all taxation.

Nouvelle rédaction de l'article 35.

La Cour est ouverte aux Membres de la Société des Nations, ainsi qu'aux Etats mentionnés à l'annexe au Pacte.

Les conditions auxquelles elle est ouverte aux autres Etats sont, sous réserve des dispositions particulières des traités en vigueur, réglées par le Conseil, et dans tous les cas, sans qu'il puisse en résulter pour les parties aucune inégalité devant la Cour.

Lorsqu'un Etat, qui n'est pas Membre de la Société des Nations, est partie en cause, la Cour fixera la contribution aux frais de la Cour que cette partie devra supporter. Toutefois cette disposition ne s'appliquera pas, si cet Etat participe aux dépenses de la Cour.

Le texte français de l'article 38, n° 4, est remplacé par la disposition suivante:

4. Sous réserve de la disposition de l'article 59, les décisions judiciaires et la doctrine des publicistes les plus qualifiés des différentes nations, comme moyen auxiliare de détermination des règles de droit.

[*Il n'y a pas de changement dans le texte anglais.*]

Les articles 39 et 40 sont remplacés par les dispositions ci-après:

Nouvelle rédaction de l'article 39.

Les langues officielles de la Cour sont le français et l'anglais. Si les parties sont d'accord pour que toute

New text of Article 35.

The Court shall be open to the Members of the League and also to States mentioned in the Annex to the Covenant.

The conditions under which the Court shall be open to other States shall, subject to the special provisions contained in treaties in force, be laid down by the Council, but in no case shall such provisions place the parties in a position of inequality before the Court.

When a State which is not a Member of the League of Nations is a party to a dispute, the Court will fix the amount which that party is to contribute towards the expenses of the Court. This provision shall not apply if such State is bearing a share of the expenses of the Court.

The French text of Article 38, No. 4, is replaced by the following provision:

4. Sous réserve de la disposition de l'article 59, les décisions judiciaires et la doctrine des publicistes les plus qualifiés des différentes nations, comme moyen auxiliare de détermination des règles de droit.

[*There is no change in the English text.*]

Articles 39 and 40 are replaced by the following provisions:

New text of Article 39.

The official languages of the Court shall be French and English. If the parties agree that the case shall be

la procédure ait lieu en français, le jugement sera prononcé en cette langue. Si les parties sont d'accord pour que toute la procédure ait lieu en anglais, le jugement sera prononcé en cette langue.

A défaut d'un accord fixant la langue dont il sera fait usage, les parties pourront employer pour les plaidoiries celle des deux langues qu'elles préféreront, et l'arrêt de la Cour sera rendu en français et en anglais. En ce cas, la Cour désignera en même temps celui des deux textes qui fera foi.

La Cour pourra, à la demande de toute partie, autoriser l'emploi d'une langue autre que le français ou l'anglais.

Nouvelle rédaction de l'article 40.

Les affaires sont portées devant la Cour, selon le cas, soit par notification du compromis, soit par une requête, adressées au Greffe; dans les deux cas, l'objet du différend et les parties en cause doivent être indiqués.

Le Greffe donne immédiatement communication de la requête à tous intéressés.

Il en informe également les Membres de la Société des Nations par l'entremise du Secrétaire général, ainsi que les Etats admis à ester en justice devant la Cour.

Le texte anglais de l'article 45 est remplacé par la disposition suivante:

The hearing shall be under the control of the President, or if he is

conducted in French, the judgment will be delivered in French. If the parties agree that the case shall be conducted in English, the judgment will be delivered in English.

In the absence of an agreement as to which language shall be employed, each party may, in the pleadings, use the language which it prefers; the decision of the Court will be given in French and English. In this case the Court will at the same time determine which of the two texts shall be considered as authoritative.

The Court may, at the request of any party, authorise a language other than French or English to be used.

New text of Article 40.

Cases are brought before the Court, as the case may be, either by the notification of the special agreement or by a written application addressed to the Registrar. In either case the subject of the dispute and the contesting parties must be indicated.

The Registrar shall forthwith communicate the application to all concerned.

He shall also notify the Members of the League of Nations through the Secretary-General, and also any States entitled to appear before the Court.

The English text of Article 45 is replaced by the following provision:

The hearing shall be under the control of the President or, if he is

unable to preside, of the Vice-President; if neither is able to preside, the senior judge present shall preside.

[*Il n'y a pas de changement dans le texte français.*]

Le nouveau chapitre suivant est ajouté au Statut de la Cour:

CHAPITRE IV.—AVIS CONSULTATIFS

Nouvel article 65.

Les questions sur lesquelles l'avis consultatif de la Cour est demandé sont exposées à la Cour par une requête écrite, signée soit par le président de l'Assemblée ou par le président du Conseil de la Société des Nations, soit par le Secrétaire général de la Société agissant en vertu d'instructions de l'Assemblée ou du Conseil.

La requête formule, en termes précis, la question sur laquelle l'avis de la Cour est demandé. Il y est joint tout document pouvant servir à élucider la question.

Nouvel article 66.

1. Le Greffier notifie immédiatement la requête demandant l'avis consultatif aux Membres de la Société des Nations par l'entremise du Secrétaire général de la Société, ainsi qu'aux Etats admis à ester en justice devant la Cour.

En outre, à tout Membre de la Société, à tout Etat admis à ester devant la Cour et à toute organisation internationale jugés, par la Cour ou par le Président si elle ne siège pas, susceptibles de fournir des renseignements sur la question, le Greffier fait connaître, par communi-

unable to preside, of the Vice-President; if neither is able to preside, the senior judge present shall preside.

[*There is no change in the French text.*]

The following new chapter is added to the Statute of the Court:

CHAPTER IV.—ADVISORY OPINIONS

New Article 65.

Questions upon which the advisory opinion of the Court is asked shall be laid before the Court by means of a written request, signed either by the President of the Assembly or the President of the Council of the League of Nations, or by the Secretary-General of the League under instructions from the Assembly or the Council.

The request shall contain an exact statement of the question upon which an opinion is required, and shall be accompanied by all documents likely to throw light upon the question.

New Article 66.

1. The Registrar shall forthwith give notice of the request for an advisory opinion to the Members of the League of Nations, through the Secretary-General of the League, and to any States entitled to appear before the Court.

The Registrar shall also, by means of a special and direct communication, notify any Member of the League or State admitted to appear before the Court or international organisation considered by the Court (or, should it not be sitting, by the President) as likely to be able to

cation spéciale et directe, que la Cour est disposée à recevoir des exposés écrits dans un délai à fixer par le Président, ou à entendre des exposés oraux au cours d'une audience publique tenue à cet effet.

Si un des Membres de la Société ou des Etats mentionnés au premier alinéa du présent paragraphe, n'ayant pas été l'objet de la communication spéciale ci-dessus visée, exprime le désir de soumettre un exposé écrit ou d'être entendu, la Cour statue.

2. Les Membres, Etats ou organisations qui ont présenté des exposés écrits ou oraux sont admis à discuter les exposés faits par d'autres Membres, Etats et organisations dans les formes, mesures et délais fixés, dans chaque cas d'espèce, par la Cour, ou, si elle ne siège pas, par le Président. A cet effet, le Greffier communique en temps voulu les exposés écrits aux Membres, Etats ou organisations qui en ont eux-mêmes présentés.

Nouvel article 67.

La Cour prononcera ses avis consultatifs en audience publique, le Secrétaire général de la Société des Nations et les représentants des membres de la Société, des Etats et des organisations internationales directement intéressés étant prévenus.

Nouvel article 68.

Dans l'exercice de ses attributions consultatives, la Cour s'inspirera en

furnish information on the question, that the Court will be prepared to receive, within a time-limit to be fixed by the President, written statements, or to hear, at a public sitting to be held for the purpose, oral statements relating to the question.

Should any Member or State referred to in the first paragraph have failed to receive the communication specified above, such Member or State may express a desire to submit a written statement, or to be heard; and the Court will decide.

2. Members, States, and organisations having presented written or oral statements or both shall be admitted to comment on the statements made by other Members, States, or organisations in the form, to the extent and within the time-limits which the Court, or, should it not be sitting the President, shall decide in each particular case. Accordingly, the Registrar shall in due time communicate any such written statements to Members, States, and organisations having submitted similar statements.

New Article 67.

The Court shall deliver its advisory opinions in open Court, notice having been given to the Secretary-General of the League of Nations and to the representatives of Members of the League, of States and of international organisations immediately concerned.

New Article 68.

In the exercise of its advisory functions, the Court shall further be

outre des djspositions du Statut qui s'appliquent en matière contentieuse, dans la mesure où elle les reconnaîtra applicables.

guided by the provisions of the Statute which apply in contentious cases to the extent to which it recognises them to be applicable.

SIGNATURE AND RATIFICATION OF THE PROTOCOL FOR THE REVISION OF THE STATUTE, SEPTEMBER 14, 1929

(As of June 1, 1934)

States	Date of Signature	Date of Deposit of Ratification
Albania	Jan. 21, 1930	Sept. 12, 1930
Australia	Sept. 16, 1929	Aug. 28, 1930
Austria	Sept. 16, 1929	Feb. 26, 1930
Belgium	Sept. 16, 1929	Nov. 18, 1929
Bolivia	Sept. 16, 1929	
Brazil	Sept. 16, 1929	
Bulgaria	Sept. 16, 1929	Apr. 27, 1931
Canada	Sept. 16, 1929	Aug. 28, 1930
Chile	Sept. 20, 1929	Nov. 20, 1933
China	Sept. 16, 1929	Oct. 14, 1930
Colombia	Sept. 16, 1929	Jan. 6, 1932
Cuba	Jan. 5, 1931	[1] Jan. 5, 1931
Czechoslovakia	Sept. 16, 1929	Oct. 30, 1930
Denmark	Sept. 16, 1929	Mar. 11, 1930
Dominican Republic	Sept. 20, 1929	Feb. 4, 1933
Estonia	Before Nov. 10, 1929	Sept. 8, 1930
Ethiopia	Apr. 15, 1932	
Finland	Sept. 16, 1929	Aug. 28, 1930
France	Sept. 16, 1929	May 8, 1931
Germany	Sept. 16, 1929	Aug. 13, 1930
Great Britain	Sept. 19, 1929	Feb. 12, 1930
Greece	Sept. 16, 1929	Aug. 29, 1930
Guatemala	Sept. 20, 1929	
Haiti	Sept. 21, 1929	Sept. 30, 1930
Hungary	Sept. 24, 1929	Aug. 13, 1930
India	Sept. 19, 1929	Feb. 26, 1930
Irish Free State	Sept. 16, 1929	Aug. 2, 1930
Italy	Sept. 16, 1929	Apr. 2, 1931
Japan	Nov. 6, 1929	Nov. 14, 1930
Latvia	Sept. 17, 1929	Aug. 29, 1930
Liberia	Sept. 17, 1929	Aug. 29, 1930
Lithuania	Jan. 14, 1930	Jan. 23, 1933
Luxemburg	Sept. 17, 1929	Sept. 15, 1930
Netherlands	Sept. 16, 1929	Aug. 8, 1930
New Zealand	Sept. 19, 1929	June 4, 1930
Nicaragua	Sept. 16, 1929	
Norway	Sept. 16, 1929	Apr. 10, 1930
Panama	Sept. 19, 1929	
Paraguay	Sept. 23, 1929	May 11, 1933
Persia	Before Nov. 10, 1929	Apr. 25, 1931
Peru	Sept. 16, 1929	
Poland	Sept. 16, 1929	May 13, 1930
Portugal	Sept. 16, 1929	June 12, 1930
Rumania	Sept. 24, 1929	Aug. 4, 1930
El Salvador	Sept. 23, 1929	Aug. 29, 1930

[1] The reservations originally made by Cuba were withdrawn, after various States had refused to agree to them.

States	Date of Signature	Date of Deposit of Ratification
Siam	Sept. 16, 1929	June 2, 1930
South Africa	Sept. 23, 1929	Feb. 17, 1930
Spain	Sept. 16, 1929	July 15, 1930
Sweden	Sept. 16, 1929	Mar. 20, 1930
Switzerland	Sept. 16, 1929	July 5, 1930
United States of America	Dec. 9, 1929	
Uruguay	Sept. 16, 1929	Sept. 19, 1933
Venezuela	Sept. 16, 1929	Aug. 4, 1933
Yugoslavia	Sept. 20, 1929	Aug. 27, 1930

Total number of signatory States . . . 54 [2]
Total number of ratifying States . . . 46 [3]

APPENDIX NO. 6

Protocol for the Accession of the United States of America to the Protocol of Signature, Geneva, September 14, 1929

(Not in force, June 1, 1934)

Text from *League of Nations Official Journal, 1929, p. 1856.*

Les Etats signataires du Protocole de signature du Statut de la Cour permanente de Justice internationale du 16 décembre 1920, et les Etats-Unis d'Amérique, représentés par les soussignés dûment autorisés, sont convenus des dispositions suivantes, relativement à l'adhésion des Etats-Unis d'Amérique audit Protocole sous condition des cinq réserves formulées par les Etats-Unis dans la résolution adoptée par le Sénat le 27 janvier 1926.

Article premier. Les Etats signa-

The States signatories of the Protocol of Signature of the Statute of the Permanent Court of International Justice, dated December 16th, 1920, and the United States of America, through the undersigned duly authorised representatives, have mutually agreed upon the following provisions regarding the adherence of the United States of America to the said Protocol subject to the five reservations formulated by the United States in the resolution adopted by the Senate on January 27th, 1926.

Article 1. The States signatories

[2] Five of the signatories of the Protocol for the Revision of the Statute—Bolivia, Guatemala, Liberia, Nicaragua and the United States of America—have not ratified the Protocol of Signature of December 16, 1920.

[3] The Protocol for the Revision of the Statute can be brought into force only by the deposit of ratifications by all the States which have ratified the Protocol of Signature of December 16, 1920. On June 1, 1934, deposits of ratifications necessary to bring the Protocol into force were lacking by Brazil, Ethiopia, Panama and Peru. Liberia has deposited a ratification of the Revision Protocol, without having deposited a ratification of the Protocol of Signature.

taires dudit Protocole acceptent, aux termes des conditions spécifiées dans les articles ci-après, les conditions spéciales mises par les Etats-Unis à leur adhésion audit Protocole et énoncées dans les cinq réserves précitées.

Article 2. Les Etats-Unis sont admis à participer, par le moyen de délégués qu'ils désigneront à cet effet et sur un pied d'égalité avec les Etats signataires, Membres de la Société des Nations, représentés, soit au Conseil, soit à l'Assemblée, à toutes délibérations du Conseil ou de l'Assemblée ayant pour objet les élections de juges ou de juges suppléants de la Cour permanente de Justice internationale visées au Statut de la Cour. Leur voix sera comptée dans le calcul de la majorité absolue requise dans le Statut.

Article 3. Aucune modification du Statut de la Cour ne pourra avoir lieu sans l'acceptation de tous les Etats contractants.

Article 4. La Cour prononcera ses avis consultatifs en séance publique, après avoir procédé aux notifications nécessaires et avoir donné aux intéressés l'occasion d'être entendus, conformément aux dispositions essentielles des articles 73 et 74 actuels du Règlement de la Cour.

Article 5. En vue d'assurer que la Cour ne donne pas suite, sans le consentement des Etats-Unis, à une demande d'avis consultatif concernant une question ou un différend auquel les Etats-Unis sont ou dé-

of the said Protocol accept the special conditions attached by the United States in the five reservations mentioned above to its adherence to the said Protocol upon the terms and conditions set out in the following Articles.

Article 2. The United States shall be admitted to participate, through representatives designated for the purpose and upon an equality with the signatory States Members of the League of Nations represented in the Council or in the Assembly, in any and all proceedings of either the Council or the Assembly for the election of judges or deputy-judges of the Permanent Court of International Justice, provided for in the Statute of the Court. The vote of the United States shall be counted in determining the absolute majority of votes required by the Statute.

Article 3. No amendment of the Statute of the Court may be made without the consent of all the contracting States.

Article 4. The Court shall render advisory opinions in public session after notice and opportunity for hearing substantially as provided in the now existing Articles 73 and 74 of the Rules of Court.

Article 5. With a view to ensuring that the Court shall not, without the consent of the United States, entertain any request for an advisory opinion touching any dispute or question in which the United States

clarent être intéressés, le Secrétaire général avisera les Etats-Unis, par la voie indiquée par eux à cet effet, de toute proposition soumise au Conseil ou à l'Assemblée de la Société des Nations et tendant à obtenir de la Cour un avis consultatif et, ensuite, si cela est jugé désirable, il sera procédé, avec toute la rapidité possible, à un échange de vues entre le Conseil ou l'Assemblée de la Société des Nations et les Etats-Unis sur la question de savoir si les intérêts des Etats-Unis sont affectés.

Lorsqu'une demande d'avis consultatif parviendra à la Cour, le Greffier en avisera les Etats-Unis en même temps que les autres Etats mentionnés à l'article 73 actuel du Règlement de la Cour en indiquant un délai raisonnable fixé par le Président pour la transmission d'un exposé écrit des Etats-Unis, concernant la demande. Si, pour une raison quelconque, l'échange de vues au sujet de ladite demande n'a pu avoir lieu dans des conditions satisfaisantes, et si les Etats-Unis avisent la Cour que la question au sujet de laquelle l'avis de la Cour est demandé est une question qui affecte les intérêts des Etats-Unis, la procédure sera suspendue pendant une période suffisante pour permettre ledit échange de vues entre le Conseil ou l'Assemblée et les Etats-Unis.

Lorsqu'il s'agira de demander à la Cour un avis consultatif dans un cas tombant sous le coup des paragraphes précédent, il sera at-

has or claims an interest, the Secretary-General of the League of Nations shall, through any channel designated for that purpose by the United States, inform the United States of any proposal before the Council or the Assembly of the League for obtaining an advisory opinion from the Court, and thereupon, if desired, an exchange of views as to whether an interest of the United States is affected shall proceed with all convenient speed between the Council or Assembly of the League and the United States.

Whenever a request for an advisory opinion comes to the Court, the Registrar shall notify the United States thereof, among other States mentioned in the now existing Article 73 of the Rules of Court, stating a reasonable time-limit fixed by the President within which a written statement by the United States concerning the request will be received. If for any reason no sufficient opportunity for an exchange of views upon such request should have been afforded and the United States advises the Court that the question upon which the opinion of the Court is asked is one that affects the interests of the United States, proceedings shall be stayed for a period sufficient to enable such an exchange of views between the Council or the Assembly and the United States to take place.

With regard to requesting an advisory opinion of the Court in any case covered by the preceding paragraphs, there shall be attributed to

taché à l'opposition des Etats-Unis la même valeur que celle qui s'attache à un vote émis par un Membre de la Société des Nations au sein du Conseil ou de l'Assemblée pour s'opposer à la demande d'avis consultatif.

Si, après l'échange de vues prévu aux paragraphes 1 et 2 du présent article, il apparaît qu'on ne peut aboutir à aucun accord et que les Etats-Unis ne sont pas disposés à renoncer à leur opposition, la faculté de retrait prévue à l'article 8 s'exercera normalement, sans que cet acte puisse être interprété comme un acte inamical, ou comme un refus de coopérer à la paix et à la bonne entente générales.

Article 6. Sous réserve de ce qui sera dit à l'article 8 ci-après, les dispositions du présent Protocole auront la même force et valeur que les dispositions du Statut de la Cour et toute signature ultérieure du Protocole du 16 décembre 1920 sera réputée impliquer une acceptation des dispositions du présent Protocole.

Article 7. Le présent Protocole sera ratifié. Chaque Etat adressera l'instrument de sa ratification au Secrétaire général de la Société des Nations, par les soins duquel il en sera donné avis à tous les autres Etats signataires. Les instruments de ratification seront déposés dans les archives du Secrétariat de la Société des Nations.

Le présent Protocole entrera en vigueur dès que tous les Etats ayant ratifié le Protocole du 16 décembre

an objection of the United States the same force and effect as attaches to a vote against asking for the opinion given by a Member of the League of Nations in the Council or in the Assembly.

If, after the exchange of views provided for in paragraphs 1 and 2 of this Article, it shall appear that no agreement can be reached and the United States is not prepared to forgo its objection, the exercise of the powers of withdrawal provided for in Article 8 hereof will follow naturally without any imputation of unfriendliness or unwillingness to coöperate generally for peace and goodwill.

Article 6. Subject to the provisions of Article 8 below, the provisions of the present Protocol shall have the same force and effect as the provisions of the Statute of the Court and any future signature of the Protocol of December 16th, 1920, shall be deemed to be an acceptance of the provisions of the present Protocol.

Article 7. The present Protocol shall be ratified. Each State shall forward the instrument of ratification to the Secretary-General of the League of Nations, who shall inform all the other signatory States. The instruments of ratification shall be deposited in the archives of the Secretariat of the League of Nations.

The present Protocol shall come into force as soon as all States which have ratified the Protocol of De-

1920, ainsi que les Etats-Unis, auront déposé leur ratification.

Article 8. Les Etats-Unis pourront, en tout temps, notifier au Secrétaire général de la Société des Nations qu'ils retirent leur adhésion au Protocole du 16 décembre 1920. Le Secrétaire général donnera immédiatement communication de cette notification à tous les autres Etats signataires du Protocole.

En pareil cas, le présent Protocole sera considéré comme ayant cessé d'être en vigueur dès réception par le Secrétaire général de la notification des Etats-Unis.

De leur côté, chacun des autres Etats contractants pourra, en tout temps notifier au Secrétaire général de la Société des Nations qu'il désire retirer son acceptation des conditions spéciales mises par les Etats-Unis à leur adhésion au Protocole du 16 décembre 1920. Le Secrétaire général donnera immédiatement communication de cette notification à tous les Etats signataires du présent Protocole. Le présent Protocole sera considéré comme ayant cessé d'être en vigueur dès que, dans un délai ne dépassant pas une année à compter de la date de la réception de la notification susdite, au moins deux tiers des Etats contractants, autres que les Etats-Unis, auront notifié au Secrétaire général de la Société des Nations qu'ils désirent retirer l'acceptation susvisée.

Fait à Genève, le quatorzième jour de septembre mil neuf cent vingt-

cember 16th, 1920, and also the United States, have deposited their ratifications.

Article 8. The United States may at any time notify the Secretary-General of the League of Nations that it withdraws its adherence to the Protocol of December 16th, 1920. The Secretary-General shall immediately communicate this notification to all the other States signatories of the Protocol.

In such case, the present Protocol shall cease to be in force as from the receipt by the Secretary-General of the notification by the United States.

On their part, each of the other contracting States may at any time notify the Secretary-General of the League of Nations that it desires to withdraw its acceptance of the special conditions attached by the United States to its adherence to the Protocol of December 16th, 1920. The Secretary-General shall immediately give communication of this notification to each of the States signatories of the present Protocol. The present Protocol shall be considered as ceasing to be in force if and when, within one year from the date of receipt of the said notification, not less than two-thirds of the contracting States other than the United States shall have notified the Secretary-General of the League of Nations that they desire to withdraw the above-mentioned acceptance.

Done at Geneva, the fourteenth day of September, nineteen hundred

neuf, en un seul exemplaire, dont les	and twenty-nine, in a single copy,
textes français et anglais feront	of which the French and English
également foi.	texts shall both be authoritative.

[Signatures omitted.]

SIGNATURE AND RATIFICATION OF PROTOCOL FOR THE ACCESSION OF THE UNITED STATES, SEPTEMBER 14, 1929

(As of June 1, 1934)

States	Date of Signature	Date of Deposit of Ratification
Albania	Jan. 21, 1930	Sept. 12, 1930
Australia	Sept. 16, 1929	Aug. 28, 1930
Austria	Sept. 16, 1929	Feb. 26, 1930
Belgium	Sept. 16, 1929	Oct. 5, 1931
Bolivia	Sept. 16, 1929	
Brazil	Sept. 16, 1929	
Bulgaria	Sept. 16, 1929	Apr. 27, 1931
Canada	Sept. 16, 1929	Aug. 28, 1930
Chile	Sept. 20, 1929	
China	Sept. 16, 1929	Oct. 14, 1930
Colombia	Sept. 16, 1929	Jan. 6, 1932
Cuba	Sept. 20, 1929	Nov. 26, 1930
Czechoslovakia	Sept. 16, 1929	Oct. 30, 1930
Denmark	Sept. 16, 1929	Mar. 11, 1930
Dominican Republic	Sept. 20, 1929	Feb. 4, 1933
Estonia	Before Nov. 10, 1929	Sept. 8, 1930
Ethiopia	Apr. 15, 1932	
Finland	Sept. 16, 1929	Aug. 28, 1930
France	Sept. 16, 1929	May 8, 1931
Germany	Sept. 16, 1929	Aug. 13, 1930
Great Britain	Sept. 19, 1929	Feb. 12, 1930
Greece	Sept. 16, 1929	Aug. 29, 1930
Guatemala	Sept. 16, 1929	
Haiti	Sept. 21, 1929	
Hungary	Sept. 24, 1929	Aug. 13, 1930
India	Sept. 19, 1929	Feb. 26, 1930
Irish Free State	Sept. 16, 1929	Aug. 2, 1930
Italy	Sept. 16, 1929	Apr. 2, 1931
Japan	Sept. 21, 1929	Nov. 14, 1930
Latvia	Sept. 17, 1929	Aug. 29, 1930
Liberia	Sept. 17, 1929	
Lithuania	Jan. 14, 1930	Jan. 23, 1933
Luxemburg	Sept. 17, 1929	Sept. 15, 1930
Netherlands	Sept. 16, 1929	Aug. 8, 1930
New Zealand	Sept. 19, 1929	June 4, 1930
Nicaragua	Sept. 16, 1929	
Norway	Sept. 16, 1929	Apr. 10, 1930
Panama	Sept. 19, 1929	
Paraguay	Sept. 23, 1929	
Persia	Before Nov. 10, 1929	Apr. 25, 1931
Peru	Sept. 16, 1929	
Poland	Sept. 16, 1929	May 13, 1930
Portugal	Sept. 16, 1929	June 12, 1930
Rumania	Sept. 24, 1929	Aug. 4, 1930
El Salvador	Sept. 23, 1929	
Siam	Sept. 16, 1929	June 2, 1930
South Africa	Sept. 23, 1929	Feb. 17, 1930

States	Date of Signature	Date of Deposit of Ratification
Spain	Sept. 16, 1929	July 15, 1930
Sweden	Sept. 16, 1929	Mar. 20, 1930
Switzerland	Sept. 16, 1929	July 5, 1930
United States of America	Dec. 9, 1929	
Uruguay	Sept. 16, 1929	Sept. 19, 1933
Venezuela	Sept. 16, 1929	Sept. 14, 1932
Yugoslavia	Sept. 20, 1929	Aug. 27, 1930

Total number of signatory States . . . 54 [1]
Total number of ratifying States . . . 41 [2]

[1] Five of the signatories of the Protocol for the Accession of the United States— Bolivia, Guatemala, Liberia, Nicaragua and the United States of America—have not ratified the Protocol of Signature of December 16, 1920.

[2] The Protocol for the Accession of the United States can be brought into force only by the deposit of ratifications by all the States which have ratified the Protocol of Signature of December 16, 1920, and by the United States. On June 1, 1934, deposits of ratifications were lacking by Brazil, Chile, Ethiopia, Haiti, Panama, Paraguay, Peru, El Salvador, and the United States of America.

III. INSTRUMENTS GOVERNING THE COURT'S PROCEDURE AND ADMINISTRATION

APPENDIX NO. 7

Revised Rules Adopted by the Court, February 21, 1931

Text from Series D, No. 1, 2d ed., pp. 23–49.

Preamble

The Court,

By virtue of Article 30 of its Statute,

Adopts the present Rules:

CHAPTER I. THE COURT

Heading 1. Constitution of the Court

SECTION A. JUDGES AND ASSESSORS

Article 1. Subject to the provisions of Article 14 of the Statute, the term of office of judges and deputy-judges shall commence on January 1st of the year following their election.

*†**Article 2.**[1] Judges and deputy-judges elected at an earlier session of the Assembly and of the Council of the League of Nations shall take precedence respectively over judges and deputy-judges elected at a subsequent session. Judges and deputy-judges elected during the same session shall take precedence according to age. Judges shall take precedence over deputy-judges.

National judges chosen from outside the Court, under the terms of Article 31 of the Statute, shall take precedence after deputy-judges in order of age.

The list of deputy-judges shall be prepared in accordance with these principles.

The Vice-President shall take his seat on the right of the President.

---

[1] The articles revised in 1926 are marked with an asterisk; those amended in 1931 are marked with a dagger. For convenience, the earlier texts are also reproduced here.

The other members of the Court shall take their seats on the left and right of the President in the order laid down above.

[1922 and 1926 text of the fourth paragraph:]

The Vice-President shall take his seat on the right of the President. The other members of the Court shall take their seats to the right and left of the President in the order laid down above.

[The 1926 Rules also contained as a final paragraph:]

Nevertheless the retiring President, whatever may be his seniority according to the preceding provisions, shall take his seat on the right of the President, the Vice-President taking in such case his seat on the left. This rule, however, shall not affect the other privileges or the powers conferred by the Statute or Rules of Court upon the Vice-President or the eldest judge.

*†**Article 3.** Deputy-judges whose presence is necessary shall be summoned in the order laid down in the list referred to in the preceding article, that is to say, each of them will be summoned in rotation throughout the list.

Should a deputy-judge be so far from the seat of the Court that, in the opinion of the President, a summons would not reach him in sufficient time, the deputy-judge next on the list shall be summoned; nevertheless, the judge to whom the summons should have been addressed shall be called upon, if possible, on the next occasion that the presence of a deputy-judge is required.

Should a deputy-judge be summoned to take his seat in a particular case as a national judge, under the terms of Article 31 of the Statute or of Article 71 of the Rules, such summons shall not be regarded as coming within the terms of the present article.

[1922 text of a third paragraph:]

A deputy-judge who has begun a case shall be summoned again, if necessary out of his turn, in order to continue to sit in the case until it is finished.

[1922 and 1926 text of the final paragraph:]

Should a deputy-judge be summoned to take his seat in a particular case as a national judge, under the terms of Article 31 of the Statute, such summons shall not be regarded as coming within the terms of the present article.

***Article 4.** In case in which one or more parties are entitled to choose a judge *ad hoc* of their nationality, the full Court may sit with a number of judges exceeding the number of regular judges fixed by the Statute.

When the Court has satisfied itself, in accordance with Article 31 of the Statute, that there are several parties in the same interest and that none of them has a judge of its nationality upon the bench, the Court shall invite them, within a period to be fixed by the Court, to select by common agreement a deputy-judge of the nationality of one of the parties, should there be one; or, should there not be one, a judge chosen in accordance with the the principles of the above-mentioned article.

Should the parties have failed to notify the Court of their selection or choice when the time limit expires, they shall be regarded as having renounced the right conferred upon them by Article 31.

[1922 text of the first paragraph:]

In cases in which one or more parties are entitled to choose a judge ad hoc of their nationality, the full Court may sit with a number of judges exceeding eleven.

Article 5. Before entering upon his duties, each member of the Court or judge summoned to complete the Court, under the terms of Article 31 of the Statute, shall make the following solemn declaration in accordance with Article 20 of the Statute:

"I solemnly declare that I will exercise all my powers and duties as a judge honorably and faithfully, impartially and conscientiously."

A special public sitting of the Court may, if necessary, be convened for this purpose.

At the public inaugural sitting held after a new election of the whole Court the required declaration shall be made first by the President, secondly by the Vice-President, and then by the remaining judges in the order laid down in Article 2.

Article 6. For the purpose of applying Article 18 of the Statute, the President, or if necessary the Vice-President, shall convene the judges and deputy-judges. The member affected shall be allowed to furnish explanations. When he has done so the question shall be discussed and a vote shall be taken, the member in question not being present. If the members present are unanimously agreed, the Registrar shall issue the notification prescribed in the above-mentioned article.

Article 7. The President shall take steps to obtain all information which might be helpful to the Court in selecting technical assessors in each case. With regard to the questions referred to in Article 26 of the Statute, he shall, in particular, consult the Governing Body of the International Labour Office.

The assessors shall be appointed by an absolute majority of votes, either by the Court or by the special Chamber which has to deal with the case in question.

Article 8. Assessors shall make the following solemn declaration at the first sitting of the Court at which they are present:

"I solemnly declare that I will exercise my duties and powers as an assessor honorably and faithfully, impartially and conscientiously, and that I will scrupulously observe all the provisions of the Statute and of the Rules of Court."

SECTION B. THE PRESIDENCY

†**Article 9.** The election of the President and the Vice-President shall take place in the last quarter of the last year of office of the retiring President and Vice-President.

After a new election of the whole Court, the election of the President and of the Vice-President shall take place at the commencement of the following session. The President and Vice-President elected in these circumstances shall take up their duties on the day of their election. They shall remain in office until the end of the second year after the year of their election.

Should the President or the Vice-President cease to belong to the Court before the expiration of their normal term of office, an election shall be held for the purpose of appointing a substitute for the unexpired portion of their term of office.

The elections referred to in the present article shall take place by secret ballot. The candidate obtaining an absolute majority of votes shall be declared elected.

[1922 and 1926 text of the first and third paragraphs:]

The election of the President and Vice-President shall take place at the end of the ordinary session immediately before the normal termination of the period of office of the retiring President and Vice-President.

Should the President or the Vice-President cease to belong to the Court before the expiration of their normal term of office, an election shall be held for the purpose of appointing a substitute for the unexpired portion of their term of office. If necessary, an extraordinary session of the Court may be convened for this purpose.

Article 10. The President shall direct the work and administration of the Court; he shall preside at the meetings of the full Court.

†**Article 11.** The Vice-President shall take the place of the President, should the latter be unable to fulfill his duties, or, should he cease to hold office, until the new President has been appointed by the Court.

[1922 and 1926 text:]

The Vice-President shall take the place of the President, should the latter be unable to be present, or, should he cease to hold office, until the new President has been appointed by the Court.

†**Article 12.** The discharge of the duties of the President shall always be assured at the seat of the Court, either by the President himself or by the Vice-President.

If at the same time both the President and the Vice-President are unable to fulfill their duties, or if both appointments are vacant at the same time, the duties of President are discharged by the oldest among the judges who have been longest on the bench.

After a new election of the whole Court, and until the election of the President and the Vice-President, the duties of President are discharged by the oldest judge.

[1922 and 1926 text:]

The President shall reside within a radius of ten kilometres from the Peace Palace at The Hague.

The main annual vacation of the President shall not exceed three months.

*†**Article 13.** If the President is a national of one of the Parties to the case, the functions of President pass in respect of that case to the Vice-President, or if he is similarly prevented from presiding, to the oldest among the judges who have been longest on the bench and who is not for the same reason prevented from presiding.

[1922 text:]

After a new election of the whole Court and until such time as the President and Vice-President have been elected, the judge who takes precedence according to the order laid down in Article 2, shall perform the duties of President.

The same principle shall be applied should both the President and the Vice-President be unable to be present, or should both appointments be vacant at the same time.

[The 1926 text added to the second paragraph of the 1922 text:]

Whenever, according to the rules in force, the functions of President should be exercised by a national of one of the parties to the suit, they shall pass, for the purposes of the case in question, in the order of seniority established by the Rules of Court, to the first judge not similarly situated.

SECTION C. THE CHAMBERS

†**Article 14.** The members of the Chambers constituted by virtue of Articles 26, 27 and 29 of the Statute shall be appointed at a meeting of the full Court by an absolute majority of votes, regard being had for the purposes of this selection to any preference expressed by the judges, so far as the provisions of Article 9 of the Statute permit.

The substitutes mentioned in Articles 26 and 27 of the Statute shall be appointed in the same manner. Two judges shall also be chosen to replace any member of the Chamber for summary procedure who may be unable to sit.

The election shall take place in the last quarter of the year, and the period of appointment of the members elected shall commence on January 1st of the following year.

Nevertheless, after a new election of the whole Court, the election shall take place at the beginning of the following session. The period of appointment shall commence on the date of election and shall terminate, in the case of the Chamber referred to in Article 29 of the Statute, at the end of the same year and, in the case of the Chambers referred to in Articles 26 and 27 of the Statute, at the end of the second year after the year of election.

The Presidents of the Chambers shall be appointed at a sitting of the full Court. Nevertheless, the President of the Court shall, *ex officio,* preside over any Chamber of which he may be elected a member; similarly, the Vice-President of the Court shall, *ex officio,* preside over any Chamber of which he may be elected a member, provided that the President is not also a member.

[1922 and 1926 text of the third paragraph:]

The election shall take place at the end of the ordinary session of the Court, and the period of appointment of the members elected shall commence on January 1st of the following year.

Article 15. The special Chambers for labor cases and for communications and transit cases may not sit with a greater number than five judges.

Except as provided in the second paragraph of the preceding article, the composition of the Chamber for summary procedure may not be altered.

Article 16. Deputy-judges shall not be summoned to complete the special Chambers or the Chamber for summary procedure, unless sufficient judges are not available to complete the number required.

SECTION D. THE REGISTRY

*†**Article 17.** The Court shall select its Registrar from amongst candidates proposed by members of the Court. The latter shall receive adequate notice of the date on which the list of candidates will be closed so as to enable nominations and information concerning the nationals of distant countries to be received in sufficient time.

Nominations must give the necessary particulars regarding age, nationality, university degrees and linguistic attainments of candidates, as also regarding

their judicial and diplomatic qualifications, their experience in connection with the work of the League of Nations and their present profession.

The election shall be by secret ballot and by an absolute majority of votes.

The Registrar shall be elected for a term of seven years commencing on January 1st of the year following that in which the election takes place. He may be reëlected.

Should the Registrar cease to hold his office before the expiration of the term above mentioned, an election shall be held for the purpose of appointing a successor. Such election shall be for a full term of seven years.

The Court shall appoint a Deputy-Registrar to assist the Registrar, to act as Registrar in his absence, and, in the event of his ceasing to hold the office, to perform its duties until a new Registrar shall have been appointed. The Deputy-Registrar shall be appointed under the same conditions and in the same way as the Registrar.

[1922 text:]

The Court shall select its Registrar from amongst candidates proposed by members of the Court.

The election shall be by secret ballot and by a majority of votes. In the event of an equality of votes, the President shall have a casting vote.

The Registrar shall be elected for a term of seven years commencing on January 1st of the year following that in which the election takes place. He may be reëlected.

Should the Registrar cease to hold his office before the expiration of the term above mentioned, an election shall be held for the purpose of appointing a successor.

[1926 text of the fourth, and a fifth, paragraph:]

Should the Registrar cease to hold his office before the expiration of the term above mentioned, an election shall be held for the purpose of appointing a successor. Each election shall be for a full term of seven years.

The Court shall appoint a Deputy-Registrar to assist the Registrar, to act as Registrar in his absence, and, in the event of his ceasing to hold the office, to perform its duties until a new Registrar shall have been appointed. The Deputy-Registrar shall be appointed in the same way as the Registrar.

*Article 18. Before taking up his duties, the Registrar shall make the following declaration at a meeting of the full Court:

"I solemnly declare that I will perform the duties conferred upon me as **Registrar of the Permanent Court of International Justice** in all loyalty, discretion and good conscience."

The Deputy-Registrar shall make a similar declaration in the same conditions.

[1922 text of the second paragraph:]

The other members of the Registry shall make a similar declaration before the President, the Registrar being present.

*†Article 19. The Registrar is entitled to two months holiday in each year.

[1922 text:]

The Registrar shall reside within a radius of ten kilometres from the Peace Palace at The Hague.

The main annual vacation of the Registrar shall not exceed two months.

[1926 text of the first paragraph:]

The Registrar and the Deputy-Registrar shall reside within a radius of ten kilometres from the Peace Palace at The Hague.

*Article 20. The officials of the Registry, other than the Deputy-Registrar, shall be appointed by the Court on proposals submitted by the Registrar.

On taking up their duties, such officials shall make the following declaration before the President, the Registrar being present:

"I solemnly declare that I will perform the duties conferred upon me as official of the Permanent Court of International Justice in all loyalty, discretion and good conscience."

[1922 text:]

The staff of the Registry shall be appointed by the Court on proposals submitted by the Registrar.

†Article 21. The Court shall determine or modify the organization of the Registry upon proposals submitted by the Registrar.

The Regulations for the staff of the Registry shall be drawn up having regard to the organization decided upon by the Court and to the provisions of the Regulations for the staff of the Secretariat of the League of Nations, to which they shall as far as possible, conform. They shall be adopted by the President, on the proposal of the Registrar, subject to subsequent approval by the Court.

[1922 and 1926 text:]

The Regulations for the Staff of the Registry shall be adopted by the President on the proposal of the Registrar, subject to subsequent approval by the Court.

*†**Article 22.** On the proposal of the Registrar or Deputy-Registrar, as the case may be, the Court, or, if it is not sitting, the President, shall appoint the official of the Registry who is to act as substitute for the Registrar, should both the Registrar and Deputy-Registrar be unable to be present, or, should both appointments be vacant at the same time, until a successor to the Registrar has been appointed.

[1922 text:]

The Court shall determine or modify the organization of the Registry upon proposals submitted by the Registrar. On the proposal of the Registrar, the President shall appoint the member of the Registry who is to act for the Registrar in his absence or, in the event of his ceasing to hold his office, until a successor has been appointed.

[1926 text:]

The Court shall determine or modify the organization of the Registry upon proposals submitted by the Registrar. On the proposal of the Registrar or Deputy-Registrar, as the case may be, the Court, or, if it is not in session, the President, shall appoint the official of the Registry who is to act as substitute for the Registrar, should both the Registrar and Deputy-Registrar be unable to be present, or, should both appointments be vacant at the same time, until a successor to the Registrar has been appointed.

Article 23. The registers kept in the archives shall be so arranged as to give particulars with regard to the following points amongst others:

(1) For each case or question, all documents pertaining to it and all action taken with regard to it in chronological order; all such documents shall bear the same file number and shall be numbered consecutively within the file;

(2) All decisions of the Court in chronological order, with references to the respective files;

(3) All advisory opinions given by the Court in chronological order, with references to the respective files;

(4) All notifications and similar communications sent out by the Court, with references to the respective files.

Indexes kept in the archives shall comprise:

(1) A card index of names with necessary references;

(2) A card index of subject matter with like references.

***Article 24.** The Registrar shall be the channel for all communications to and from the Court.

The Registrar shall reply to any enquiries concerning its activities, in-

cluding enquiries from the Press, subject, however, to the provisions of Article 42 of the present Rules and to the observance of professional secrecy.

[1922 text:]

During hours to be fixed by the President, the Registrar shall receive any documents and reply to any enquiries, subject to the provisions of Article 38 of the present Rules and to the observance of professional secrecy.

* Article 25. The Registrar shall ensure that the date of despatch and receipt of all communications and notifications may readily be verified. Communications and notifications sent by post shall be registered. Communications addressed to the official representatives or to the agents of the parties shall be considered as having been addressed to the parties themselves. The date of receipt shall be noted on all documents received by the Registrar, and a receipt bearing this date and the number under which the document has been registered shall be given to the sender, if a request to that effect be made.

[The 1922 text contained as a first paragraph:]

The Registrar shall be the channel for all communications to and from the Court.

*Article 26. The Registrar shall be responsible for the archives, the accounts and all administrative work. He shall have the custody of the seals and stamps of the Court. He, or the Deputy-Registrar, shall be present at all meetings of the full Court and either he, or the Deputy-Registrar, or an official appointed by the Registrar, with the approval of the Court, to represent him, shall be present at all sittings of the various Chambers; the Registrar shall be responsible for drawing up the minutes of the meetings.

He shall further undertake all duties which may be laid upon him by the present Rules.

The duties of the Registry shall be set forth in detail in a list of instructions to be submitted by the Registrar to the President for his approval.

[1922 text of the first paragraph:]

The Registrar shall be responsible for the archives, the accounts and all administrative work. He shall have the custody of the seals and stamps of the Court. He shall himself be present at all meetings of the full Court and either he, or a person appointed to represent him with the approval of the Court, shall be present at all sittings of the various Chambers; he shall be responsible for drawing up the minutes of the meetings.

Heading 2. Working of the Court

†**Article 27.** 1. The ordinary session of the Court opens on February 1st in each year.

2. The session continues until the session list referred to in Article 28 is finished. The President declares the session closed when the agenda is exhausted.

3. The President may summon an extraordinary session of the Court whenever he thinks it desirable, as, for instance, when a case submitted to the Court is ready for hearing or to deal with urgent administrative matters.

4. Judges are bound to be present at the ordinary session of the Court and at all sessions to which they are summoned by the President, unless they are on leave or are prevented by illness or other serious reasons duly explained to the President and communicated by him to the Court.

Deputy-judges are bound to be present at all sessions to which they are summoned by the President unless they are prevented by some reason duly explained to the President and communicated by him to the Court.

5. Judges whose homes are situated at more than five days' normal journey from The Hague and who by reason of the fulfilment of their duties in the Court are obliged to live away from their own country are entitled in the course of each period of three years of duty to leave for six months in addition to the time spent on travelling.

The order in which these leaves are to be taken shall be laid down in a list drawn up by the Court according to the seniority in age of the persons entitled. This order can only be departed from for serious reasons duly admitted by the Court.

The number of judges on leave at any one time must not exceed two.

The President and the Vice-President must not take their leave at the same time.

6. If the day fixed for the opening of a session is regarded as a holiday at the place where the Court is sitting, the session shall be opened on the working day following.

[1922 and 1926 text:]

In the year following a new election of the whole Court the ordinary annual session shall commence on the fifteenth of January.

If the day fixed for the opening of a session is regarded as a holiday at the place where the Court is sitting, the session shall be opened on the working day following.

†**Article 28.** The general list of cases submitted to the Court for decision or for advisory opinion shall be prepared and kept up to date by the Registrar on the instructions and subject to the authority of the President.

Cases shall be entered in the list and numbered successively according to the date of the receipt of the document submitting the case to the Court.

For each session of the Court a session list shall be prepared in the same way, indicating the contentious cases and the cases for advisory opinion which are ready for hearing, whether submitted to the full Court or to the Special Chambers or the Chamber for Summary Procedure. Cases shall be entered in the order which they occupy in the general list, but subject to the priority resulting from Article 57 or accorded by the Court to a particular case in exceptional circumstances.

When the list includes no cases other than those submitted to the Special Chambers or the Chamber for Summary Procedure, the session shall only continue as a session of the Special Chamber or of the Chamber for Summary Procedure, as the case may be.

If in the course of the session a case submitted to the Court, either for decision or for an advisory opinion, becomes ready for hearing, it shall be entered in the session list, unless the Court decides to the contrary.

Adjournments which are applied for in cases which are submitted to the Court for decision or for advisory opinion and are ready for hearing may be granted by the Court in case of need. If the Court is not sitting, adjournments may in such cases be granted by the President.

[1922 and 1926 text:]

The list of cases shall be prepared and kept up to date by the Registrar under the responsibility of the President. The list for each session shall contain all questions submitted to the Court for an advisory opinion and all cases in regard to which the written proceedings are concluded, in the order in which the documents submitting each question or case have been received by the Registrar. If in the course of a session, a question is submitted to the Court or the written proceedings in regard to any case are concluded, the Court shall decide whether such question or case shall be added to the list for that session.

The Registrar shall prepare and keep up to date extracts from the above list showing the cases to be dealt with by the respective Chambers.

The Registrar shall also prepare and keep a list of cases for revision.

Article 29. During the sessions the dates and hours of sittings shall be fixed by the President.

*Article 30. If at any sitting of the full Court it is impossible to obtain the prescribed quorum, the Court shall adjourn until the quorum is obtained. Judges *ad hoc* shall not be taken into account for the calculation of the quorum.[2]

---

[2] The second sentence of this article was added in 1926.

*Article 31. The Court shall sit in private to deliberate upon the decision of any case or upon any advisory opinion; also, when dealing with any administrative matter.

During the deliberation referred to in the preceding paragraph, only persons authorized to take part in the deliberation and the Registrar or, in his absence, the Deputy-Registrar, shall be present. No other person shall be admitted except by virtue of a special decision taken by the Court, having regard to exceptional circumstances.

Every member of the Court who is present at the deliberation shall state his opinion together with the reasons on which it is based.

The decision of the Court shall be based upon the conclusions adopted after final discussion by a majority of the members voting in an order inverse to the order of precedence established by Article 2.

Any member of the Court may request that a question which is to be voted upon shall be drawn up in precise terms in both the official languages and distributed to the Court. A request to this effect shall be complied with.

No detailed minutes shall be prepared of the Court's private meetings for deliberation upon judgments or advisory opinions; such minutes, which are to be considered as confidential, shall record only the subject of the debates, votes taken, with the names of those voting for and against a motion, and statements expressly made for insertion in the minutes.

Subject to a contrary decision by the Court, the same procedure shall apply to private meetings for deliberation upon administrative matters.

After the final vote taken on a judgment or advisory opinion, any judge who desires to set forth his individual opinion must do so in accordance with Article 57 of the Statute.

[1922 text:]

The Court shall sit in private to deliberate upon the decision of any case or on the reply to any question submitted to it.

During the deliberation referred to in the preceding paragraph, only persons authorized to take part in the deliberation and the Registrar shall be present. No other person shall be admitted except by virtue of a special decision taken by the Court, having regard to exceptional circumstances.

Every member of the Court who is present at the deliberation shall state his opinion together with the reasons on which it is based.

The decision of the Court shall be based upon the conclusions adopted after final discussion by a majority of the members.

Any member of the Court may request that a question which is to be voted upon shall be drawn up in precise terms in both the official languages and distributed to the Court. A request to this effect shall be complied with.

CHAPTER II. PROCEDURE

Heading 1. Contentious Procedure

SECTION A. GENERAL PROVISIONS

Article 32. The rules contained under this heading shall in no way preclude the adoption by the Court of such other rules as may be jointly proposed by the parties concerned, due regard being paid to the particular circumstances of each case.

Article 33. The Court shall fix time limits in each case by assigning a definite date for the completion of the various acts of procedure, having regard as far as possible to any agreement between the parties.

The Court may extend time limits which it has fixed. It may likewise decide in certain circumstances that any proceeding taken after the expiration of a time limit shall be considered as valid.

If the Court is not sitting, the powers conferred upon it by this article shall be exercised by the President, subject to any subsequent decision of the Court.

*Article 34. The originals of all documents of the written proceedings submitted to the Court shall be signed by the agent or agents duly appointed; they shall be dated.

The original shall be accompanied by ten copies certified as correct. Subject to any contrary arrangement between the Registrar and the agent or agents, it shall likewise be accompanied by a further forty printed copies.

The President may order additional printed copies to be supplied.

[1922 text:]

All documents of the written proceedings submitted to the Court shall be accompanied by not less than thirty printed copies certified correct. The President may order additional copies to be supplied.

SECTION B.—PROCEDURE BEFORE THE COURT AND BEFORE THE SPECIAL CHAMBERS (ARTICLES 26 AND 27 OF THE STATUTE)

I. Institution of Proceedings

*Article 35. (1) When a case is brought before the Court by means of a special agreement, the latter, or the document notifying the Court of the agreement, shall mention:

> (a) the names of the agents appointed by the respective parties for the purposes of the case;

(*b*) the permanent addresses at the seat of the Court to which notices and communications intended for the respective parties are to be sent.

In all other cases in which the Court has jurisdiction, the application, in addition to the specification of the subject of the dispute and the names of the parties concerned, a succinct statement of facts, and an indication of the claim, shall include:

(*a*) the name or names of the agent or agents appointed for the purposes of the case;

(*b*) the permanent addresses at the seat of the Court to which subsequent notices and communications in regard to the case are to be sent.

Should proceedings be instituted by means of an application, the first document sent in reply thereto shall likewise mention the name or names of the agent or agents and the addresses at the seat of the Court.

Whenever possible, the agents should remain at the seat of the Court pending the trial and determination of the case.

(2) The declaration provided for in the Resolution of the Council of the League of Nations of May 17th, 1922 (Annex [3]), shall, when it is required under Article 35 of the Statute, be filed with the Registry not later than the time fixed for the deposit of the first document of the written procedure.

[3] ANNEX TO ARTICLE 35. *Resolution adopted by the Council on May 17, 1922.*
The Council of the League of Nations, in virtue of the powers conferred upon it by Article 35, paragraph 2, of the Statute of the Permanent Court of International Justice, and subject to the provisions of that article,

RESOLVES:

1. The Permanent Court of International Justice shall be open to a State which is not a Member of the League of Nations or mentioned in the Annex to the Covenant of the League, upon the following condition, namely: that such State shall previously have deposited with the Registrar of the Court a declaration by which it accepts the jurisdiction of the Court, in accordance with the Covenant of the League of Nations and with the terms and subject to the conditions of the Statute and Rules of the Court, and undertakes to carry out in full good faith the decision or decisions of the Court and not to resort to war against a State complying therewith.

2. Such declaration may be either particular or general.
A particular declaration is one accepting the jurisdiction of the Court in respect only of a particular dispute or disputes which have already arisen.
A general declaration is one accepting the jurisdiction generally in respect of all disputes or of a particular class or classes of disputes which have already arisen or which may arise in the future.
A State in making such a general declaration may accept the jurisdiction of the Court as compulsory, *ipso facto,* and without special convention, in conformity with Article 36 of the Statute of the Court; but such acceptance may not, without special convention, be relied upon *vis-à-vis* Members of the League or States mentioned in the Annex to the Covenant which have signed or may hereafter sign the "optional clause" provided for by the additional Protocol of December 16th, 1920.

3. The original declarations made under the terms of this Resolution shall be kept in the custody of the Registrar of the Court, in accordance with the practice of the Court. Certified true copies thereof shall be transmitted, in accordance with the practice

(3) Should the notice of a special agreement, or the application, contain a request that the case be referred to one of the special Chambers mentioned in Articles 26 and 27 of the Statute, such request shall be complied with, provided that the parties are in agreement.

Similarly, a request to the effect that technical assessors be attached to the Court, in accordance with Article 27 of the Statute, or that the case be referred to the Chamber for Summary Procedure, shall also be granted; compliance with the latter request is, however, subject to the condition that the case does not relate to the matters dealt with in Articles 26 and 27 of the Statute.

[1922 text:]

When a case is brought before the Court by means of a special agreement, the latter, or the document notifying the Court of the agreement, shall mention the addresses selected at the seat of the Court to which notices and communications intended for the respective parties are to be sent.

In all other cases in which the Court has jurisdiction, the application shall include, in addition to an indication of the subject of the dispute and the names of the parties concerned, a succinct statement of facts, an indication of the claim and the address selected at the seat of the Court to which notices and communications are to be sent.

Should proceedings be instituted by means of an application, the first document sent in reply thereto shall mention the address selected at the seat of the Court to which subsequent notices and communications in regard to the case are to be sent.

Should the notice of a special agreement, or the application, contain a request that the case be referred to one of the special Chambers mentioned in Articles 26 and 27 of the Statute, such request shall be complied with, provided that the parties are in agreement.

Similarly, a request to the effect that technical assessors be attached to the Court, in accordance with Article 27 of the Statute, or that the case be referred to the Chamber for summary procedure, shall also be granted; compliance with the latter request is, however, subject to the condition that the case does not refer to any of the questions indicated in Articles 26 and 27 of the Statute.

of the Court, to all Members of the League of Nations, and States mentioned in the Annex to the Covenant, and to such other States as the Court may determine, and to the Secretary-General of the League of Nations.

4. The Council of the League of Nations reserves the right to rescind or amend this Resolution by a Resolution which shall be communicated to the Court; and on the receipt of such communication and to the extent determined by the new Resolution, existing declarations shall cease to be effective except in regard to disputes which are already before the Court.

5. All questions as to the validity or the effect of a declaration made under the terms of this Resolution shall be decided by the Court.

*Article 36. The Registrar shall forthwith communicate to all members of the Court special agreements or applications which have been notified to him.

He shall also transmit them through the channels provided for in the Statute or by special arrangement, as the case may be, to all Members of the League of Nations and to all states not Members of the League entitled to appear before the Court.[4]

II. Written Proceedings

Article 37. Should the parties agree that the proceedings shall be conducted in French or in English, the documents constituting the written procedure shall be submitted only in the language adopted by the parties.

In the absence of an agreement with regard to the language to be employed, documents shall be submitted in French or in English.

Should the use of a language other than French or English be authorized, a translation into French or into English shall be attached to the original of each document submitted.

The Registrar shall not be bound to make translations of documents submitted in accordance with the above rules.

In the case of voluminous documents the Court, or the President if the Court is not sitting, may, at the request of the party concerned, sanction the submission of translations of portions of documents only.

*Article 38. When proceedings are begun by means of an application, any preliminary objection shall be filed after the filing of the case by the applicant and within the time fixed for the filing of the counter-case.

The document submitting the objection shall contain a statement of facts and of law on which the plea is based, a statement of conclusions and a list of the documents in support; these documents shall be attached; it shall mention the evidence which the party may desire to produce.

Upon receipt by the Registrar of the document submitting the objection, the Court, or the President if the Court is not sitting, shall fix the time within which the party against whom the plea is directed may submit a written statement of its observations and conclusions; documents in support shall be attached and evidence which it is proposed to produce shall be mentioned.

Unless otherwise decided by the Court, the further proceedings shall be oral. The provisions of paragraphs 4 and 5 of Article 69 of the Rules shall apply.

[1922 text:]

The Court, or the President, if the Court is not sitting, may, after hearing the parties, order the Registrar to hold the Cases and Counter-Cases of each

---

[4] The second paragraph of this article was added in 1926.

suit at the disposal of the government of any State which is entitled to appear before the Court.

Article 39. In cases in which proceedings have been instituted by means of a special agreement, the following documents may be presented in the order stated below, provided that no agreement to the contrary has been concluded between the parties:

a case, submitted by each party within the same limit of time;

a counter-case, submitted by each party within the same limit of time;

a reply, submitted by each party within the same limit of time.

When proceedings are instituted by means of an application, failing any agreement to the contrary between the parties, the documents shall be presented in the order stated below:

the case by the applicant;

the counter-case by the respondent;

the reply by the applicant;

the rejoinder by the respondent.

Article 40. Cases shall contain:

(1) a statement of the facts on which the claim is based;

(2) a statement of law;

(3) a statement of conclusions;

(4) a list of the documents in support; these documents shall be attached to the case.

Counter-cases shall contain:

(1) the affirmation or contestation of the facts stated in the case;

(2) a statement of additional facts, if any;

(3) a statement of law;

(4) conclusions based on the facts stated; these conclusions may include counter-claims, in so far as the latter come within the jurisdiction of the Court;

(5) a list of the documents in support; these documents shall be attached to the counter-case.

†**Article 41.** Upon the termination of the written proceedings the Court, or the President, if the Court is not sitting, shall fix a date for the commencement of the oral proceedings.

[1922 and 1926 text:]

Upon the termination of the written proceedings the President shall fix a date for the commencement of the oral proceedings.

*†**Article 42.** The Registrar shall forward to each of the members of the Court, and to the parties, a copy or copies of all documents in the case as he receives them.

The Court, or the President, if the Court is not sitting, may, after hearing the parties, order the Registrar to hold the cases and counter-cases of each suit at the disposal of the government of any State which is entitled to appear before the Court.

In the same way, the Court or the President may, with the consent of the parties, authorize the documents of the written proceedings in regard to a particular case to be made accessible to the public before the termination of the case.[5]

[1922 text:]

The Registrar shall forward to each of the members of the Court, a copy of all documents in the case as he receives them.

III. Oral Proceedings

Article 43. In the case of a public sitting, the Registrar shall publish in the Press all necessary information as to the date and hour fixed.

Article 44. The Registrar shall arrange for the interpretation from French into English and from English into French of all statements, questions and answers which the Court may direct to be so interpreted.

Whenever a language other than French or English is employed, either under the terms of the third paragraph of Article 39 of the Statute or in a particular instance, the necessary arrangements for translation into one of the two official languages shall be made by the party concerned. In the case of witnesses or experts who appear at the instance of the Court, these arrangements shall be made by the Registrar.

Article 45. The Court shall determine in each case whether the representatives of the parties shall address the Court before or after the production of the evidence; the parties shall, however, retain the right to comment on the evidence given.

Article 46. The order in which the agents, advocates or counsel shall be called upon to speak shall be determined by the Court, failing an agreement between the parties on the subject.

Article 47. In sufficient time before the opening of the oral proceedings, each party shall inform the Court and the other parties of all evidence which it intends to produce, together with the names, Christian names, description and residence of witnesses whom it desires to be heard.

It shall further give a general indication of the point or points to which the evidence is to refer.

Article 48. The Court may, subject to the provisions of Article 44 of the Statute, invite the parties to call witnesses, or may call for the production of any other evidence on points of fact in regard to which the parties are not in agreement.

---

[5] The third paragraph of this article was added in 1931.

Article 49. The Court, or the President should the Court not be sitting, shall, at the request of one of the parties or on its own initiative, take the necessary steps for the examination of witnesses out of Court.

Article 50. Each witness shall make the following solemn declaration before giving his evidence in Court:

"I solemnly declare upon my honor and conscience that I will speak the truth, the whole truth and nothing but the truth."

Article 51. Witnesses shall be examined by the representatives of the parties under the control of the President. Questions may be put to them by the President and afterwards by the judges.

Article 52. The indemnities of witnesses who appear at the instance of the Court shall be paid out of the funds of the Court.

Article 53. Any report or record of an enquiry carried out at the request of the Court, under the terms of Article 50 of the Statute, and reports furnished to the Court by experts, in accordance with the same article, shall be forthwith communicated to the parties.

*Article 54. A verbatim record shall be made of the oral proceedings, including the evidence taken, under the supervision of the Registrar.

The report of the evidence of each witness shall be read to him in order that, subject to the direction of the Court, any mistakes may be corrected.

The report of statements made by agents, advocates or counsel, shall be communicated to them for their correction or revision, subject to the direction of the Court.

[1922 text:]

A record shall be made of the evidence taken. The portion containing the evidence of each witness shall be read over to him and approved by him.

As regards the remainder of the oral proceedings, the Court shall decide in each case whether verbatim records of all or certain portions of them shall be prepared for its own use.

*Article 55. The minutes mentioned in Article 47 of the Statute shall in particular include:

(1) the names of the judges;
(2) the names of the agents, advocates and counsel;
(3) the names, Christian names, description and residence of witnesses heard;
(4) a specification of other evidence produced;
(5) any declarations made by the parties;
(6) all decisions taken by the Court during the hearing.

The minutes of public sittings shall be printed and published.[6]

[6] This paragraph was added in 1926.

*Article 56. The party in whose favor an order for the payment of costs has been made may present his bill of costs after judgment has been delivered.

[1922 text:]

Before the oral proceedings are concluded, each party may present his bill of costs.

IV. Interim Protection

†Article 57. An application made to the Court by one or both of the parties, for the indication of interim measures of protection, shall have priority over all other cases. The decision thereon shall be treated as a matter of urgency, and if the Court is not sitting it shall be convened without delay by the President for the purpose.

If no application is made, and if the Court is not sitting, the President may convene the Court to submit to it the question whether such measures are expedient.

In all cases, the Court shall only indicate measures of protection after giving the parties an opportunity of presenting their observations on the subject.

[1922 and 1926 text:]

When the Court is not sitting, any measures for the preservation in the meantime of the respective rights of the parties shall be indicated by the President.

Any refusal by the parties to conform to the suggestions of the Court or of the President, with regard to such measures, shall be placed on record.

V. Intervention

Article 58. An application for permission to intervene, under the terms of Article 62 of the Statute, must be communicated to the Registrar at latest before the commencement of the oral proceedings.

Nevertheless the Court may, in exceptional circumstances, consider an application submitted at a later stage.

*Article 59. The application referred to in the preceding article shall contain:

(1) a specification of the case in which the applicant desires to intervene;

(2) a statement of law and of fact justifying intervention;

(3) a list of the documents in support of the application; these documents shall be attached.

Such application shall be immediately communicated to the parties, who

shall send to the Registrar any observations which they may desire to make within a period to be fixed by the Court, or by the President, should the Court not be sitting.

Such observations shall be communicated to the State desiring to intervene and to all parties. The intervener and the original parties may comment thereon in Court; for this purpose the matter shall be placed on the agenda for a hearing the date and hour of which shall be notified to all concerned. The Court will give its decision on the application in the form of a judgment.[7]

If the application is not contested, the President, if the Court is not sitting, may, subject to any subsequent decision of the Court as regards the admissibility of the application, fix, at the request of the State by which the application is made, time limits within which such State is authorized to file a case on the merits and within which the other parties may file their counter-cases. These time limits, however, may not extend beyond the beginning of the session in the course of which the case shall be heard.[7]

*Article 60. The notification provided for in Article 63 of the Statute shall be sent to every State or Member of the League of Nations which is a party to the convention relied upon in the special agreement or in the application as governing the case submitted to the Court.

The Court, or the President if the Court is not sitting, shall fix the times within which States desiring to intervene are to file any cases.

The Registrar shall take the necessary steps to enable the intervening State to inspect the documents in the case, in so far as they relate to the interpretation of the convention in question, and to submit its observations thereon to the Court. Such observations shall be communicated to the parties, who may comment thereon in Court. The Court may authorize the intervening State to reply.

[1922 text:]

Any State desiring to intervene, under the terms of Article 63 of the Statute, shall inform the Registrar in writing at latest before the commencement of the oral proceedings.

The Court, or the President if the Court is not sitting, shall take the necessary steps to enable the intervening State to inspect the documents in the case, in so far as they relate to the interpretation of the convention in question, and to submit its observations thereon to the Court.

VI. Agreement

Article 61. If the parties conclude an agreement regarding the settlement of the dispute and give written notice of such agreement to the Court before the close of the proceedings, the Court shall officially record the conclusion of the agreement.

[7] This paragraph was added in 1926.

Should the parties by mutual agreement notify the Court in writing that they intend to break off proceedings, the Court shall officially record the fact and proceedings shall be terminated.

VII. Judgment

*Article 62. The judgment shall contain:
  (1) the date on which it is pronounced;
  (2) the names of the judges participating;
  (3) the names and style of the parties;
  (4) the names of the agents of the parties;
  (5) the conclusions of the parties;
  (6) the matters of fact;
  (7) the reasons in point of law;
  (8) the operative provisions of the judgment;
  (9) the decision, if any, referred to in Article 64 of the Statute;
  (10) the number of the judges constituting the majority contemplated in Article 55 of the Statute.[8]

Dissenting judges may, if they so desire, attach to the judgment either an exposition of their individual opinion or the statement of their dissent.

[1922 text of the second paragraph:]

The opinions of judges who dissent from the judgment, shall be attached thereto should they express a desire to that effect.

*Article 63. When the judgment has been read in public, duly signed and sealed copies thereof shall be forwarded to the parties.

This text shall forthwith be communicated by the Registrar, through the channels agreed upon, to Members of the League of Nations and to States entitled to appear before the Court.

[1922 text:]

After having been read in open Court the text of the judgment shall forthwith be communicated to all parties concerned and to the Secretary-General of the League of Nations.

Article 64. The judgment shall be regarded as taking effect on the day on which it is read in open Court, in accordance with Article 58 of the Statute.

†Article 65. A collection of the judgments, orders and advisory opinions

---

[8] This sub-paragraph was added in 1926.

of the Court shall be printed and published under the responsibility of the Registrar.

[1922 and 1926 text:]

A collection of the judgments of the Court shall be printed and published under the responsibility of the Registrar.

VIII. Revision and Interpretation

*Article 66. 1. Application for revision shall be made in the same form as the application mentioned in Article 40 of the Statute.

It shall contain:

(*a*) a specification of the judgment impeached;

(*b*) the facts upon which the application is based;

(*c*) a list of the supporting documents; these documents shall be attached to the application.

It shall be the duty of the Registrar to give immediate notice of an application for revision to the other parties concerned. The latter may submit observations within a time limit to be fixed by the Court, or by the President should the Court not be sitting.

If the Court, under the third paragraph of Article 61 of the Statute, by a special judgment makes the admission of the application conditional upon previous compliance with the terms of the judgment impeached, this condition shall be immediately communicated to the applicant by the Registrar, and proceedings in revision shall be stayed pending receipt by the Registrar of proof of previous compliance with the original judgment and until such proof shall have been accepted by the Court.

2. A request to the Court to construe a judgment which it has given may be made either by the notification of a special agreement between all the parties or by an application by one or more of the parties.

The agreement or application shall contain:

(*a*) a specification of the judgment the interpretation of which is requested;

(*b*) an indication of the precise point or points in dispute.

If the request for interpretation is made by means of an application, it shall be the duty of the Registrar to give immediate notice of such application to the other parties, and the latter may submit observations within a time limit to be fixed by the Court or by the President, as the case may be.

The Court may, whether the request be made by agreement or by application, invite the parties to furnish further written or oral explanations.

3. If the judgment impeached or to be construed was pronounced by the full Court, the application for revision or the request for interpretation shall also be dealt with by the full Court. If the judgment was pronounced by

one of the Chambers mentioned in Article 26, 27 or 29 of the Statute, the application for revision or the request for interpretation shall be dealt with by the same Chamber. The provisions of Article 13 of the Statute shall apply in all cases.

4. Objections to the Court's jurisdiction to revise or to construe a judgment, or other similar preliminary objections, shall be dealt with according to the procedure laid down in Article 38 of the present Rules.

5. The Court's decision on requests for revision or interpretation shall be given in the form of a judgment.

[1922 text:]

Application for revision shall be made in the same form as the application mentioned in Article 40 of the Statute.

It shall contain:

(1) the reference to the judgment impeached;

(2) the fact on which the application is based;

(3) a list of the documents in support; these documents shall be attached.

It shall be the duty of the Registrar to give immediate notice of an application for revision to the other parties concerned. The latter may submit observations within a time limit to be fixed by the Court, or by the President should the Court not be sitting.

If the judgment impeached was pronounced by the full Court, the application for revision shall also be dealt with by the full Court. If the judgment impeached was pronounced by one of the Chambers mentioned in Articles 26, 27 or 29 of the Statute, the application for revision shall be dealt with by the same Chamber. The provisions of Article 13 of the Statute shall apply in all cases.

If the Court, under the third paragraph of Article 61 of the Statute, makes a special order rendering the admission of the application conditional upon previous compliance with the terms of the judgment impeached, this condition shall be immediately communicated to the applicant by the Registrar, and proceedings in revision shall be stayed pending receipt by the Registrar of proof of previous compliance with the original judgment and until such proof shall have been accepted by the Court.

Section C. Summary Procedure

Article 67. Except as provided under the present section, the rules for procedure before the full Court shall apply to summary procedure.

*Article 68. Upon receipt by the Registrar of the document instituting proceedings in a case which, by virtue of an agreement between the parties, is to be dealt with by summary procedure, the President of the Court shall,

as soon as possible, notify the members of the Chamber referred to in Article 29 of the Statute. The Chamber or, if it is not in session, its President, shall fix the time within which the first document of the written procedure, provided for in the following article, shall be filed.

The President shall convene the Chamber at the earliest date that may be required by the circumstances of the case.

[1922 text:]

Upon receipt by the Registrar of the document instituting proceedings in a case which, by virtue of an agreement between the parties, is to be dealt with by summary procedure, the President shall convene as soon as possible the Chamber referred to in Article 29 of the Statute.

*Article 69. Summary proceedings are opened by the presentation of cases according to the provisions of Article 39, paragraph 1, of the present Rules. If a case is presented by one party only, the other party or parties shall present a counter-case. In the event of the simultaneous presentation of cases by the parties, the Chamber may invite the presentation, under the same conditions, of counter-cases.

The cases and counter-cases, which shall be communicated by the Registrar to the members of the Chamber and to opposing parties, shall mention all evidence which the parties may desire to produce.

Should the Chamber consider that the documents do not furnish adequate information, it may, in the absence of an agreement to the contrary between the parties, institute oral proceedings. It shall fix a date for the commencement of the oral proceedings.

At the hearing, the Chamber shall call upon the parties to supply oral explanations. It may sanction the production of any evidence mentioned in the documents.

If it is desired that witnesses or experts whose names are mentioned in the documents should be heard, such witnesses or experts must be available to appear before the Chamber when required.

[1922 text:]

The proceedings are opened by the presentation of a Case by each party. These Cases shall be communicated by the Registrar to the members of the Chamber and to the opposing party.

The Cases shall contain reference to all evidence which the parties may desire to produce.

Should the Chamber consider that the Cases do not furnish adequate information, it may, in the absence of an agreement to the contrary between the parties, institute oral proceedings. It shall fix a date for the commencement of the oral proceedings.

At the hearing, the Chamber shall call upon the parties to supply oral explanations. It may sanction the production of any evidence mentioned in the Cases.

If it is desired that witnesses or experts whose names are mentioned in the Case should be heard, such witnesses or experts must be available to appear before the Chamber when required.

Article 70. The judgment is the judgment of the Court rendered in the Chamber for Summary Procedure. It shall be read at a public sitting of the Chamber.

Heading 2. Advisory Procedure

*Article 71. Advisory opinions shall be given after deliberation by the full Court. They shall mention the number of the judges constituting the majority.

On a question relating to an existing dispute between two or more States or Members of the League of Nations, Article 31 of the Statute shall apply. In case of doubt the Court shall decide.[9]

Dissenting judges may, if they so desire, attach to the opinion of the Court either an exposition of their individual opinion or the statement of their dissent.

[1922 text:]

Advisory opinions shall be given after deliberation by the full Court.

The opinions of dissenting judges may, at their request, be attached to the opinion of the Court.

Article 72. Questions upon which the advisory opinion of the Court is asked shall be laid before the Court by means of a written request, signed either by the President of the Assembly or the President of the Council of the League of Nations, or by the Secretary-General of the League under instructions from the Assembly or the Council.

The request shall contain an exact statement of the question upon which an opinion is required, and shall be accompanied by all documents likely to throw light upon the question.

*Article 73. 1. The Registrar shall forthwith give notice of the request for an advisory opinion to the members of the Court, to the Members of the League of Nations, through the Secretary-General of the League, and to any States entitled to appear before the Court.

The Registrar shall also, by means of a special and direct communication, notify any Member of the League or States admitted to appear before the

---

[9] This paragraph was added by amendment on September 7, 1927.

Court or international organizations considered by the Court (or, should it not be sitting, by the President) as likely to be able to furnish information on the question, that the Court will be prepared to receive, within a time limit to be fixed by the President, written statements, or to hear, at a public sitting to be held for the purpose, oral statements relating to the question.

Should any State or Member referred to in the first paragraph have failed to receive the communication specified above, such State or Member may express a desire to submit a written statement, or to be heard; and the Court will decide.

2. States, Members and organizations having presented written or oral statements or both shall be admitted to comment on the statements made by other States, Members or organizations, in the form, to the extent and within the time limits which the Court or, should it not be sitting, the President shall decide in each particular case. Accordingly, the Registrar shall in due time communicate any such written statements to States, Members and organizations having submitted similar statements.

[1922 text:]

The Registrar shall forthwith give notice of the request for an advisory opinion to the members of the Court, and to the Members of the League of Nations, through the Secretary-General of the League, and to the States mentioned in the Annex to the Covenant.

Notice of such request shall also be given to any international organizations which are likely to be able to furnish information on the question.

*†Article 74. Advisory opinions shall be read in open Court, notice having been given to the Secretary-General of the League of Nations and to the representatives of States, of Members of the League and of international organizations immediately concerned. The Registrar shall take the necessary steps in order to ensure that the text of the advisory opinion is in the hands of the Secretary-General at the seat of the League at the date and hour fixed for the meeting held for the reading of the opinion.

Signed and sealed original copies of advisory opinions shall be placed in the archives of the Court and of the Secretariat of the League. Certified copies thereof shall be transmitted by the Registrar to States, to Members of the League, and to international organizations immediately concerned.

[1922 text:]

Any advisory opinion which may be given by the Court and the request in response to which it was given, shall be printed and published in a special collection for which the Registrar shall be responsible.

[The 1926 text included as a third paragraph:]

Any advisory opinion which may be given by the Court and the request in response to which it is given, shall be printed and published in a special collection for which the Registrar shall be responsible.

Heading 3. Errors

Article 75. The Court, or the President if the Court is not sitting, shall be entitled to correct an error in any order, judgment or opinion, arising from a slip or accidental omission.

APPENDIX NO. 8

Staff Regulations for the Registry of the Court, Approved February 20, 1931 [1]

Preamble

The present statute for the staff has been drawn up in accordance with Article 21 of the Rules of Court and with the relevant decisions of the Assembly of the League of Nations; it applies to all officials of the Registry.

Article 1. The staff of the Registry comprises established, temporary and auxiliary officials.

Article 2. The appointment of established officials is subject to the provisions of the present regulations.

Temporary or auxiliary appointments are made, subject to the provisions of Article 5 below, on conditions to be fixed in each particular case, having regard to the provisions above mentioned.

Article 3. Appointments shall be made in all cases by means of a letter addressed by the Registrar to the person concerned and replied to by the latter. This letter, which shall contain an express reference to the present regulations, shall indicate the position offered, the category in which it is placed, the commencing salary and the special conditions, if any, applicable to the case.

The letter above mentioned, together with the reply thereto, shall constitute the official's title to his appointment.

Any question arising in connection with the rights and duties resulting from this appointment which is not expressly dealt with in the present Regulations shall be settled by the Registrar, who will supply any deficiencies, having regard to the rules in force in the staff regulations of the Secretariat of the League of Nations and the International Labour Office.

---

[1] These regulations were adopted by the President of the Court, February 6, 1931, and approved by the Court, February 20, 1931. Series E, No. 7, p. 75. Later annual reports give the modifications of the regulations due to financial decisions.

Differences between the Registrar and officials of the Registry which may arise in connection with the application of the provisions of the present regulations and of those referred to in the preceding paragraph shall, failing agreement with the Registrar and without prejudice to the application of the provisions of the regulations concerning a pensions scheme for the staff of the League of Nations, be submitted, either by the Registrar or by the official concerned, to the Court or to any person or persons selected by it from amongst its members and to whom the necessary powers are delegated.

Article 4. (1) Established officials are appointed for periods of seven years. Save in the case of the post of Deputy-Registrar (Rules of Court, Article 17), the appointment, at the expiration of each period of seven years and failing notice to the contrary, shall be automatically renewed for a further period of seven years, until the age-limit is reached. In the event of the non-renewal of the appointment, six months' notice shall be given.

(2) Even during a period of seven years and without prejudice to the terms of Article 13 (below), the Registrar, subject to the notice laid down above, may terminate the appointment of an official in the case of incompetency, not calling for disciplinary measures, as also in the event of the suppression of the post as a result of reorganization.

In these circumstances, the official concerned shall receive an equitable indemnity, fixed in accordance with the principles indicated in Article 3, paragraph 3, above.

(3) At any time during the period of their appointment, officials may terminate it by giving six months' notice, which may, in any particular case, be reduced by agreement between the Registrar and the person concerned.

(4) The age-limit referred to in No. 1 above shall be sixty years, though the Registrar shall have the right to retain the services of an official for a further period, which, normally, will not exceed five years.

Article 5. (1) Temporary appointments shall be made for uninterrupted periods of a duration of less than seven years and more than six months.

(2) Auxiliary appointments shall be made for isolated or consecutive periods not in principle exceeding the duration of a session of the Court.

Article 6. (1) The officials of the Registry are appointed in the following categories, classified according to the minimum salaries attaching thereto; these salaries are:

Category (a)	14,000 florins
Category (b)	6,000 florins
Category (c)	5,625 florins
Category (d)	5,000 florins
Category (e)	4,250 florins
Category (f)	3,750 florins
Category (g)	3,250 florins

Category (h)	.	.	.	.	.	.	.	2,250 florins
Category (i)	.	.	.	.	.	.	.	2,000 florins
Category (k)	.	.	.	.	.	.	.	1,500 florins

(2) The commencing salary of an official in his category shall be fixed by the Registrar. The salary thus fixed may be increased in the proportion and up to the maximum indicated below:

Category (a)	. . . . .florins. . . . .[2]
Category (b)	400 florins per annum up to 14,000 florins
	then, in the event of
	promotion by selection,
	. . . . . . florins per annum
	up to. . . .
Category (c)	250 florins per annum up to	8,125 florins
Category (d)[3]	150 florins per annum up to	7,200 florins
Category (e)	125 florins per annum up to	5,625 florins
Category (f)	100 florins per annum up to	4,750 florins
Category (g)	90 florins per annum up to	4,000 florins
Category (h)[4]	75 florins per annum up to	3,500 florins
Category (i)	65 florins per annum up to	3,000 florins
Category (k)	50 florins per annum up to	2,000 florins

The provisions of this paragraph shall not affect rights acquired under contracts in force on January 1st, 1931.

(3) The salaries of all officials entitled to a pension under the regulations of the Pensions Fund of the League of Nations shall be payable subject to deduction of the contributions prescribed by those regulations.

The salaries of all officials who, after the coming into force of the regulations of the Pensions Fund, remain members of the Staff Provident Fund, shall be payable subject to deduction of the prescribed contribution to that fund.

Article 7. The daily rates of subsistence allowance shall be as follows:

for category (a) of Article 6: 30 florins;

for categories (b), (c) and (d) of Article 6: 20 florins;

for categories (e), (f), (g), (h), (i) and (k) of Article 6: 15 florins.

Travelling expenses incurred on official business will be refunded on presentation of a detailed statement approved by the Registrar.

---

[2] The schedules were changed by the 12th Assembly of the League of Nations, in 1931, without adhering to the categories of the Regulations. For the minimum, maximum and annual increment of the current salary groups see *League of Nations Official Journal*, 1931, p. 1980; 1932, p. 1672.—Ed.

[3] In the case of a lady secretary, the increase will be 200 florins.

[4] In the case of the chief messenger, the increase will be 100 florins.

Article 8. Salaries shall be fixed in Dutch florins and payable in the same currency. The same rule shall apply as regards any allowances and travelling expenses.

Article 9. The hours of work shall be 42 per week. The Registrar may, however, in so far as the pressure of work permits, reduce this number to 38 by deciding that the office shall be closed on Saturday afternoon.

The office hours shall, in general, be from 9.30 A.M. to 6 P.M. The luncheon interval is one hour and a half.

These hours may be modified by the Registrar as the work of the office may require.

Officials whose annual salary does not exceed 5,000 florins shall be entitled to overtime pay for each hour of work done during the week over and above the regulation 42 hours. The rate of overtime pay shall be fixed by the Registrar.

In the case of officials whose salary is between 5,000 and 5,625 florins, corresponding additional leave shall be granted in place of overtime pay.

In all circumstances, the staff whose salary is between 3,000 and 5,000 florins, and who do not form part of shifts which relieve each other, shall be entitled to receive overtime pay for work done either after 8 P.M. or on Sundays or holidays.

Article 10. (1) Without prejudice to the Registrar's right to grant leave in special circumstances, officials belonging to one of categories (*a*) to (*g*) of Article 6 above shall be entitled annually to 36 working days' holidays; those belonging to categories (*h*), (*i*) or (*k*), to from 15 to 21 working days. The holidays of staff engaged locally or on a temporary or auxiliary basis shall be fixed by the Registrar in each particular case; the Registrar shall prepare a roster of holidays.

(2) The public holidays observed in the Netherlands shall not be regarded as working days.

(3) The members of the staff engaged on an international basis shall be entitled to have refunded the cost of one return journey each year for the purpose of proceeding to their recognized homes. Similarly, they shall be entitled, once every three years, to have refunded the travelling expenses incurred by their wives and children under age in proceeding to their recognized homes. In order to take advantage of this right, each member of the staff must have informed the Registrar, as soon as possible after his appointment, of the name of the place which is to be regarded as his or her recognized home.

Article 11. Sick leave is granted in accordance with conditions to be determined after paying due regard to each particular case.

In principle, such leave shall be granted without reduction of salary. Should the leave be of long duration, a reduction may be considered. Any

decision as to a reduction of salary shall be taken by the Registrar, subject to the approval of the President.

In the event of absence from duty on the ground of illness extending over more than three consecutive days, the official concerned must furnish a medical certificate.

Article 12. (1) The officials of the Registry shall have the benefit of the pensions scheme instituted for the staff of the League of Nations, under the conditions and with the rights and obligations resulting from the regulations establishing this scheme.

(2) Officials of the Registry who, *ipso facto,* are entitled to benefit by this scheme and those who desire to do so, shall undergo medical examination by a duly qualified doctor selected by the Registrar, in order to verify that they suffer from no infirmity or illness likely to prevent them from satisfactorily fulfilling their duties.

(3) The Court undertakes to refund 50 per cent of the premiums payable on sickness insurance policies taken out by officials of the Registry and duly approved for the purpose by the Registrar.

Article 13. The Registrar may, with the approval of the President, adopt disciplinary measures in regard to any official of the Registry involving:

(*a*) a reprimand, addressed to the official in writing and entered in the personal file relating to the official;

(*b*) a reduction of salary;

(*c*) suspension, with or without total or partial deprivation of salary; except in special cases, suspensions shall have no effect upon the seniority of the official concerned from the point of view of his right to pension;

(*d*) dismissal, with or without notice.

In all the cases enumerated under (*a*) to (*d*) above, the official concerned shall have the right of appeal to the full Court.

Article 14. The present Statute of the staff may be modified by the Registrar with the approval of the President. The Registrar shall take into consideration any proposal made to this effect by at least three members of the staff.

APPENDIX NO. 9

Instructions for the Registry, 1929 [1]

Text from Series E, No. 5, pp. 58–76.

Preamble

The present instructions are drawn up in accordance with Article 26, paragraph 3, of the Rules of Court.

[1] Some modifications of these instructions have been made since 1931.

PART I. The Registrar

Article 1. The Registrar is responsible for all departments of the Registry. The Staff is under his control and he alone is authorized to direct the work of the Registry of which he is the Head.

Article 2. The Deputy-Registrar will replace the Registrar, amongst other things in his capacity as Head of the Registry, as laid down in Article 17 of the Rules of Court.

Should both the Registrar and the Deputy-Registrar be unable to perform their duties, a substitute as provided in Article 22 of the Rules will be appointed. His powers will be those of the Registrar in his capacity as the Head of the Registry.

The letter from the Registrar or Deputy-Registrar proposing the name of the substitute, bearing duly noted upon it the latter's appointment by the President, will, should the appointment take place when the Court is not sitting, constitute the substitute's authority; otherwise the minute of the Court's decision will constitute such authority.

The officials of the Registry will have the same duties towards the Deputy-Registrar and towards the substitute referred to in the preceding paragraphs, when replacing the Registrar, as towards the Registrar himself.

The provisions of the present article do not preclude the exercise by the Registrar of the right to appoint a deputy in the circumstances contemplated in Article 26 of the Rules of Court.

PART II. Duties of the Registrar

a. GENERAL

Article 3. 1. The Registrar is responsible for the preparation of cases for consideration by the Court. He assists the Drafting Committee appointed by the Court for the preparation of the text of judgments or opinions.

2. The official correspondence of the Court is prepared under the responsibility of the Registrar in conformity with Article 25 of the Rules. Letters not reserved for the President's signature are signed by the Registrar, or by the Deputy-Registrar or Heads of Services, in so far as he may delegate this duty to them.

Notes drawn up in the third person are prepared in the Registrar's name.

The following are to be considered as reserved for the President's signature:

(*a*) answers to letters addressed to the President otherwise than under Article 25 of the Rules of Court;

(*b*) letters prepared by the President not expressly reserved by him for the Registrar's signature.

Article 4. The Registrar will make the necessary arrangements for the temporary engagement of the additional staff required during sessions, in particular under the terms of Article 44 of the Rules of Court. Such staff is not included in the expression "Officials of the Registry."

Article 5. The Registrar will inform the members of the Court of the date fixed for the commencement of each session.

Article 6. The Registrar will prepare the agenda setting out the administrative questions to be dealt with during a session and will append explanatory notes relating to them.

The list of cases and the agenda with explanatory notes will, after receiving the approval of the President, be distributed to the members of the Court.

Administrative questions not included on the agenda thus distributed may be added before or during the session with the permission of the President.

Article 7. The Registrar will place on the administrative agenda for ordinary sessions of the Court the appointment of a representative to be present at meetings of the Supervisory Commission and of the Assembly and its Financial Commission when those bodies discuss questions concerning the Court.

He will, if necessary, also place on the administrative agenda of ordinary sessions the question of granting the President all powers for the approval of the budget estimates for the next year but one and on the agenda of extraordinary sessions meeting in a given year before the month of April, the approval of the budget estimates for the next year.

Similarly he will place on the agenda of ordinary sessions the election of members of the Chamber for Summary Procedure for the following year and, every third year commencing with the ordinary session of 1924, the election of the President and Vice-President and of members of the Chambers mentioned in Articles 26 and 27 of the Statute.

Article 8. Whenever, on the list for any session, a case appears which has already been considered, the Registrar will notify any judge who has already had cognizance of the case, even if he is not called upon to attend the whole of the session in question.

Article 9. The Registrar will collect for submission to the President all information with regard to technical assessors likely to be of use for the purpose of the application of Article 7 of the Rules of Court.

Article 10. Should a session be held in a place other than that in which the seat of the Court is established, the Registrar will cause the necessary preparations to be made.

Article 11. The Registrar will issue the notifications and communications referred to in Article 40 of the Statute and Articles 36 and 73 of the Rules of Court; he will also inform States which are parties to a convention the interpretation of which constitutes the subject of a dispute brought before the Court.

Article 12. The relevant information referred to in paragraph 5 of Article 26 of the Statute will be supplied through the intermediary of the Registrar.

Article 13. For each case the Registrar will prepare for the use of members of the Court and the Parties a statement of the rules of procedure applicable in the particular case, in conformity with Article 32 of the Rules of Court.

Article 14. The Registrar will inform all concerned of the dates and hours of sittings. He will communicate to the judges the agenda, which must include all questions to be dealt with during the sitting, including elections (if any).

He will cause the dates and times of all public sittings to be published; in the case of a public sitting for the reading of a judgment or advisory opinion, he will send a special notification to all agents whose appointment and address at the seat of the Court have been duly brought to his knowledge.

Article 15. For every document of procedure filed with the Registry, a receipt upon a special form, prepared in accordance with the terms of Article 25 of the Rules, will be given.

Article 16. Should an application—whether instituting proceedings, or for permission to intervene, or for revision—or a request for an advisory opinion, or a case, counter-case, reply or rejoinder addressed to the Court, not be prepared in accordance with the forms prescribed by the Rules of Court, the Registrar will inform the Party which has deposited the document in question; if the document is not amended within the time fixed for its presentation, he will inform the Court.

Article 17. In the case of a request of the nature contemplated in Article 72 of the Rules of Court, the Registrar may ask the Secretary-General of the League of Nations for any additional information.

Article 18. The Registrar will obtain from witnesses or experts called at the instance of the Court a statement of their expenses and of the subsistence allowance claimed by them. He will cause the amount of the expenses and allowances to be paid to the persons concerned.

The Registrar will take the necessary steps to recover from the Parties to a suit concerning a question of transit or communications the amount of any expenses and allowances which he may have paid to technical assessors sitting at their request.

Article 19. The Registrar must ascertain the language used by witnesses called at the instance of the Court, in order if necessary to be able to arrange for interpretation.

Article 20. The Registrar will obtain the Court's approval in respect of any interpreter called upon to translate at a sitting who is not an official of the Registry.

Article 21. The Registrar will be responsible for the preparation of the record of the evidence given by witnesses and for the drawing up of the minutes referred to in Article 47 of the Statute.

Article 22. The Registrar will place the necessary staff at the disposal of any individual or body entrusted with an enquiry or with the preparation of an expert opinion, under the terms of Article 50 of the Statute.

Article 23. The communication of the text of judgments, in accordance with Article 63 of the Rules, and of the text of advisory opinions, in accordance with Article 74 of the Rules, shall be undertaken by the Registrar. Opinions will, like judgments, be communicated to any States entitled to appear before the Court.

Article 24. The Registrar will communicate to the Press information concerning the activities of the Court in accordance with Article 24 of the Rules.

Before the 25th of each month he will supply to the Secretariat at Geneva all information concerning the Court's activities, the publication of which in the *Monthly Bulletin* of the Secretariat of the League of Nations appears desirable.

Article 25. The Registrar will arrange for the printing of separate collections of the judgments, advisory opinions and minutes of public sittings, and of any other documents relating to cases, the publication of which is not prohibited by decision of the Court. Similarly, he will be responsible for the publication of the Court's annual reports, and for such other volumes as the Court may from time to time decide to issue. For this purpose he will conclude the necessary printing contracts.

Of each publication the Registrar will reserve not less than 750 copies for gratuitous distribution by the Court. This distribution will be as follows:

(1) Members of the Court.   } (Through the
(2) Members of the League of Nations.   } Secretariat at
(3) Organizations of the League of Nations.   } Geneva.)

(4) National associations for the League of Nations.
(5) States not Members of the League of Nations which are entitled to appear before the Court.
(6) Persons or institutions making special application, in accordance with a decision taken by the Registrar in each particular case in agreement with the Court's publisher.

Article 26. The Registrar will bring to the knowledge of the Court, or of the President if the Court is not sitting, any clerical error which may be found in an order, judgment or opinion, in order that it may be corrected in accordance with Article 75 of the Rules.

Article 27. The Registrar will inform the Secretary-General of any vacancy which may occur amongst the members of the Court and of any sentence of dismissal pronounced in accordance with Article 18 of the Statute.

b. FINANCIAL ADMINISTRATION

Article 28. The Registrar is responsible for estimating the financial requirements of the Court and for submitting such estimates first to the Court or the President, as the case may be, and then to the Supervisory Commission. He will be responsible for the expenditure of all funds voted and for the appropriation of such expenditure to the proper items of the budget.

Article 29. Budget estimates for each year will be divided into two sections, one including ordinary expenditure and the other capital expenditure.

The sections will be sub-divided into chapters corresponding to the various categories of expenditure.

Article 30. The budget estimates will consist of:

(*a*) a summary of chapters;

(*b*) a full statement of items indicating in each case, in addition to the sum asked for, the sum voted for the current year and the sum voted for and the amount actually expended in the preceding year;

(*c*) whenever possible, detailed schedules and explanatory statements.

Important differences in the amounts estimated for the same items in successive years will be fully explained by means of notes.

Article 31. Receipts other than funds obtained from the League of Nations (such as interest or contributions from States not Members of the League) will, if possible, be estimated in advance and be deducted, as appropriations in aid, from the budget estimates.

Article 32. Budget estimates will be submitted for approval to the Court or, if the Court is not sitting, to the President, in the last week of March.

Article 33. Budget estimates duly approved will be communicated by the Registrar to the Secretary-General of the League of Nations, for transmission to the Supervisory Commission, upon a date between April 1st and May 1st to be agreed upon between the Registrar and the Secretary-General.

Article 34. When the Supervisory Commission considers the Court's

budget, the latter will be represented before the Commission by the Registrar or such other official as the Court may appoint for the purpose.

Article 35. In order to prevent any excess of expenditure over the amount voted for each item of the budget, the Registrar will cause a record to be prepared of all appropriations made and of liabilities incurred, showing at any time the balance available under each item.

Article 36. If necessary, the Registrar may ask the Court to authorize by a special resolution transfers from one item to another of the same chapter of the budget. He will immediately communicate such resolutions to the Secretary-General of the League of Nations, in order to enable the latter to take the measures necessary under Article 29 of the League's Financial Regulations.

The Registrar may himself authorize any transfers, which circumstances may render necessary, as between sub-heads of the same item of the budget. Such transfers need not be communicated to the Secretary-General.

Article 37. Between March 1st and 15th of each year the Registrar will submit to the Court, or to the President if the Court is not sitting, the accounts of the previous year, with annexes.

Between March 15th and April 1st he will forward the documents in question to the Supervisory Commission.

Article 38. The Registrar alone is entitled to incur liabilities in the name of the Court. It is for him to judge in what cases he should obtain previous authorization from the Court or the President.

Article 39. The Registrar will cause an accurate record to be kept of all capital acquisitions and of all supplies purchased and used during each year. He will submit to the Auditor of the League of Nations between 15th and 30th January a statement showing the stores in hand on December 31st, distinguishing the stores purchased from capital and the stores purchased from revenue.

The Registrar will cause to be submitted annually to the Auditor, before January 15th, a statement of unpaid debts incurred during the preceding year; should the accounts not be received in sufficient time, the orders or deliveries will be entered in the statement for an approximate amount.

Article 40. The Registrar will hold at the disposal of the Auditor, should he make a request to that effect, any document which may be of use to him in his examination of the accounts or other duties.

The Registrar will send to the Auditor, on or about the 10th of each month, a statement of receipts and expenditure for the preceding month.

Article 41. The funds of the Court will be placed by the Registrar on deposit at interest with the Amsterdamsche Bank (Hague branch). The interest obtained will be taken to account in accordance with Article 32.

PART III. The Officials of the Registry

Article 42. Appointments in the Registry which are provided for in the Staff Regulations, shall be filled, in the case of the appointment as Deputy-Registrar, in accordance with the procedure laid down in Article 17 of the Rules of Court, and in the case of any other appointment, in accordance with Article 20 of those Rules.

The Registrar may, if desirable, make announcements in the publications of the Court or of the League of Nations in order to obtain applications calculated to facilitate the preparation of the lists of candidates; due regard shall also be had to the Court's waiting lists.

Article 43. Before entering upon his duties, every official of the Registry will make the following declaration before the President, the Registrar being present:

"I solemnly declare that I will perform the duties conferred upon me as an official of the Permanent Court of International Justice in all loyalty, discretion and good conscience."

A record of this declaration will be made by the Registrar, signed by the President and the Registrar and deposited in the archives of the Court.

Article 44. The Registrar will take all steps necessary to preserve the diplomatic character conferred upon officials of the Registry under Article 7 of the Covenant of the League of Nations.

Article 45. The Deputy-Registrar shares the duties of the Registrar, both as regards his functions in connection with the exercise of the judicial and advisory powers of the Court (Rules of Court, Articles 26 and 31) and as concerns his functions as Head of the Registry (Part II above).

The manner in which the work is divided between the Registrar and the Deputy-Registrar during periods when both are present will be settled from time to time by the Registrar.

The arrangement of the work shall be such that both the Registrar and the Deputy-Registrar shall at all times be fully acquainted with all branches of the work of the Court and of the Registry.

Article 46. The officials of the Registry are intended to serve as a framework for the absorption of the staff temporarily engaged for the duration of a session or in similar circumstances.

In this respect, in addition to one of the editing secretaries being entrusted with the duties of Secretary to the Presidency, another will be responsible for interpretation and editing and a third for translation.

Similarly, one of the shorthand-secretaries will be in charge of typing and roneography; another will be detached for duty to the Drafting Committee; finally, yet another will have the qualifications of a verbatim reporter.

PART IV. The Duties of the Officials of the Registry

A. THE EDITING SECRETARIES

Article 47. The Editing Secretary entrusted with the duties of Secretary to the Presidency will in the first place perform tasks entrusted to him by the President or the Registrar, as the case may be. He is in charge of the editing, under the Registrar's control, of the Court's Confidential Bulletin.

The Editing Secretary, who is amongst other things in charge of editing, is responsible for the editing of the manuscript of all documents which have to be printed, unless another official has also been made responsible for the printing of a document the preparation of which has been entrusted to him.

The Editing Secretary in charge of translations will, as far as possible, prepare them himself with the assistance of another editing secretary whose native language is the official language of the Court which is not the native language of the editing secretary responsible for translation.

B. THE ARCHIVIST

Article 48. The Court's Archivist is responsible to the Registrar for keeping the archives and the library in accordance with the following provisions.

She is assisted by an Assistant or Assistants appointed for this purpose.

The Archivist is likewise responsible for the handling and distribution of documents in accordance with the system provided for under Article 57 below.

Article 49. No file or original of any document registered in the archives may be taken out of the offices of the Registry without express permission from the Registrar.

Article 50. The archives will contain amongst other things files duly kept up to date containing information as to the following:

(1) The States Members of the League of Nations or mentioned in the Annex to the Covenant which have accepted the compulsory jurisdiction of the Court, together with the text of the declarations of acceptance, also the list of States outside the League of Nations which have made the general declaration, in accordance with the Council Resolution of May 12th, 1922, to accept the jurisdiction of the Court, together with a statement whether this acceptance does or does not include compulsory jurisdiction.

(2) The articles of treaties, conventions or international agreements, including mandates, in which provision is made for recourse to the Court, together with the text of the articles, a list of the States affected and the conditions governing the competence of the Court in each case.

(3) The channel to be used for direct communications between the Court and each Government.

Subject to the above provisions and to Article 23 of the Rules of Court, the distribution of subject matter in the various files will be decided by the Registrar.

Article 51. In addition to the registers mentioned in Article 23 of the Rules, the archives shall contain:

(1) A list of judges.

(2) A list of deputy-judges.

(These two lists shall mention: (*a*) the age of each judge; (*b*) whether they have or have not made the solemn declaration provided for in Article 20 of the Statute of the Court, and (*c*) their successive addresses.)

(3) The list in chronological order of substitutes or deputy-judges who have been summoned to complete the Chambers and the Court respectively.

A reference to the file of each case dealt with by him shall be entered against the name of each judge.

(4) The lists of technical assessors for labour cases in the alphabetical order of the Members of the League of Nations by whom they have been nominated, and in alphabetical order of names within each list.

(5) The lists of technical assessors for transit and communications cases in the alphabetical order of the Members of the League of Nations by whom they have been nominated, and in alphabetical order of names within each list.

(6) The lists of nominations referred to in Articles 4 and 5 of the Court's Statute.

Article 52. Every incoming document will be handed to the Archivist, who will open official letters. Every document will be immediately registered and submitted to the Registrar, together with previous correspondence (if any).

Every outgoing document bearing the signature or initials of the Registrar, in token of its official character, will be handed, together with the necessary number of copies, any enclosures and the requisite envelope, to the Archivist for registration and despatch.

Article 53. Incoming documents will be registered by writing in the register entitled "In Register" the particulars indicated by the various columns of this register, and by writing upon the document itself the date of receipt, the consecutive number in the register, the reference to the file concerned and the reference number within this file.

Outgoing documents will be registered by entering similar particulars in the register entitled "Out Register" and by writing on the document itself the consecutive number in the "Out Register" and the reference number

of the document, if any, to which the outgoing document is a reply. On the copies kept in the archives will also be written the consecutive number in the "In Register" of the document, if any, which has given rise to the preparation of the outgoing document. The entry of the reference numbers and of the "in" numbers will be made by the typist in accordance with the instructions of the person drafting the document.

To each of the files to which the various documents are allotted will be attached a list of the documents contained therein (file register).

In the case of outgoing letters a second copy will be inserted in the chronological file.

The card indexes provided for in Article 23 of the Rules of Court, as also the file registers, will be brought up to date as each document is registered. Nevertheless, in order to prevent delay in the despatch of outgoing documents, the necessary entries concerning them, except those which must appear on the documents themselves, may be made as soon as possible from the copies.

Article 54. The Archivist will keep a diary in which will be entered at the required date a note to the effect that a given document is to be handed to the official who has given instructions for the note to be made.

Article 55. The Archivist is responsible for the despatch of any document inscribed in the "Out Register." She will ascertain that the required annexes are attached thereto; she will also satisfy herself that every letter, note or telegram is duly signed or initialled.

A confirmation of every telegram, upon a special form, will be immediately sent by post to the person to whom the telegram is addressed.

Within the town, any packet which is not sent by post will be delivered in return for a receipt, to be made out according to the detailed provisions in the Annex.

Article 56. Every book belonging to the Court Library will be stamped with the stamp of the Court and entered in an "In Register"; it will be furnished with a consecutive number. Card indexes will be prepared by names of authors and by subjects. These card indexes will contain, in addition to a reference to the register, particulars enabling each book to be readily found (shelf and consecutive number).

C. CORRESPONDENCE AND DISTRIBUTION OF DOCUMENTS

Article 57. [Article 57 regulates the preparation, translation and distribution of documents; it is not reproduced here.]

Article 58. [Article 58 and its annex set out the rules to be observed for the preparation of letters, including modes of address, etc.; it is not reproduced here.]

D. LIAISON WITH THE PRESS

Article 59. Communications intended for the public and concerning the Court's activities may be issued by the Registrar in accordance with the agreement entered into between him and the Director of the Geneva Information Section and approved by the President. Whenever held to be necessary, the Registrar shall submit such communications to the President for approval.

E. ACCOUNTANT–ESTABLISHMENT OFFICER

Article 60. The Accountant-Establishment Officer is responsible to the Registrar for the following:

(1) accounts,

(2) payments,

(3) purchases,

(4) equipment and supplies.

Article 61. The following ledgers will be kept:

(1) budget ledger,

(2) bank book,

(3) current account ledger,

(4) cash book.

In the budget ledger will be inscribed under the headings corresponding to the chapters and items of the budget: (*a*) the credit originally voted; (*b*) this credit with modifications resulting from possible transfers; and twice weekly (*c*) actual expenditure chargeable to the various chapters and items.

For the purpose of keeping this ledger, every cheque issued by the Court shall be regarded as expended, whether or not it has been presented to the Bank for payment.

In the bank book will be inscribed all operations affecting the Court's banking account, in particular the issue of cheques and their presentation for payment according to the notification forms sent by the Bank.

In the current account ledger will be inscribed, on receipt of notification from the Bank, cheques issued by the Court which have been presented for payment.

In the cash book will be noted all payments in cash as they are made.

Article 62. The budget ledger will be kept so as to show at any time payments made as regards each member of the Court and each official. Each person concerned has the right to inspect his personal account.

Article 63. The cash shall be checked at the commencement of each working day. It will be controlled by the Registrar at intervals to be fixed by him. He will approve the accounts by means of his signature in the cash book.

Article 64. The Accountant-Establishment Officer will prepare in the first week of each month a summary of the accounts of the preceding month upon a special form.

Article 65. All payments shall be made in return for receipts, which in the case of transactions falling under the jurisdiction of the Courts of the Netherlands will be stamped in accordance with local legislation. Other receipts will be prepared on a special form.

Payment of subsistence allowance and travelling expenses to the judges will only be made on presentation of a claim for repayment upon a special form duly signed by the person concerned, countersigned by the Registrar and approved by the President.

Payment of salaries of members of the permanent and temporary staff will be made in accordance with lists duly signed by the Registrar.

Payments to the staff of subsistence allowance and refunds of travelling expenses (including journeys authorized to an official's native country) shall be made upon receipt of a detailed application drawn up on a special form signed by the person concerned and by the Registrar, in token of his approval. In the case of journeys on duty, the application, to be valid, must be accompanied by a signed letter from the Registrar instructing the person concerned to undertake the journey in question.

Except with the approval of the Registrar, accounts for supplies will only be paid if the account is accompanied by the order form signed by him.

Salaries of less than 6,000 florins per annum will be paid half monthly; other salaries will be paid monthly in arrears.

Except with the written permission of the Registrar, payment of advances is forbidden; should an advance be made, interest from the date of payment until the day the sum advanced falls due will be deducted.

Article 66. All purchases will be made by means of an order form signed by the Registrar.

Whenever necessary, the Accountant-Establishment Officer will obtain at least three tenders for submission to the Registrar for his decision.

Article 67. Every Monday the Chief messenger will receive a sum to cover postage and telegrams and other minor expenses. He will enter postal and telegraph charges in a book which will be verified every morning by the Archivist.

Every Monday the account will be balanced.

Every Monday the Hall porter will receive a sum for minor expenses. He will render an account on a special form.

Article 68. The Registrar will ensure that no expenditure is incurred which is not provided for in the Budget, that no payment is made except where an obligation actually exists and that the strictest economy is observed in incurring liabilities.

Article 69. The Accountant-Establishment Officer will prepare and keep up to date separate inventories (*a*) for the supplies of stationery and the like, and (*b*) for furniture and equipment.

The inventory of supplies will be brought up to date each week and submitted to the Registrar.

The inventory of furniture, etc., will be kept up to date as purchases are made or losses occur.

Article 70. Every Monday the Accountant-Establishment Officer will place at the disposal of the staff in the various offices supplies of stationery sufficient to meet the consumption estimated for the week.

Every person who uses the stationery thus made available will immediately enter on the control-sheet attached to the particular species the quantity taken, and will sign his name.

The Accountant-Establishment Officer will verify the entries when bringing the inventory up to date.

Article 71. Officials are forbidden to use stationery belonging to the Court for private purposes.

Members of the Court may apply to the Registrar for the use of the Court's services and stationery for work which is not strictly speaking within the domain of the Court. As regards the Court's services, the Registrar will comply in so far as it is compatible with the requirements of the work of the Court; as regards stationery, he will comply subject to repayment by the member concerned of the cost price. The amount will be deducted from the next monthly payment of salary to the member.

Article 72. The Accountant-Establishment Officer is responsible that a sufficient stock of all necessary material is available both for the normal work of the Registry and for sessions of the Court.

F. PRINTING DEPARTMENT

Article 73. The duties of the Head of the Printing Department include:

(1) preparation and examination of all estimates, "dummies," etc., relating to the Court's publications;

(2) correction of proofs and supervision of time devoted to the author's corrections;

(3) preparation of the manuscript of the alphabetical and analytical indexes inserted at the end of volumes and of general indexes to be published by the Court;

(4) verification of costs of printing.

Generally speaking, the Head of the Printing Department shall act as intermediary in all dealings between the Registry and the printers of the Court's publications.

Furthermore, the Head of the Printing Department will keep in close and permanent contact with the Publisher, with a view to the elaboration and carrying out of all measures calculated to ensure a wider circulation of the publications of the Court.

In this respect he is in particular entrusted with the preparation and bringing up to date of the catalogues of these publications.

Article 74. The order to print may only be given when the Registrar's approval, after inspection of definitive, paginated proofs, has been obtained.

Article 75. With regard to the correction of proofs and the verification of charges, the Head of the Printing Department shall ensure that the conditions of the printing contract and the *Typographical Rules for the Publications of the Court* are strictly complied with. He is also responsible for concordance between the French and English texts of each publication.

Article 76. As regards the printing of documents urgently required (judgments, advisory opinions, preliminary volumes, etc.), the Head of the Printing Department shall take all measures necessary to ensure that the work is carried out as promptly as possible.

As the Court's publications are printed at Leyden, he may proceed to that town whenever he may consider it necessary to do so to ensure satisfactory performance of the work. He must on each occasion inform the Registrar beforehand.

PART V. Amendments

Article 77. The present instructions may be modified by means of amendments to be approved by the President.

IV. INFORMATION CONCERNING THE COURT

APPENDIX NO. 10

Members and Registrar of the Court

(1) Judges and Deputy-Judges Elected for the First Period, 1922–30 [1]

Judge	Nationality
Rafael ALTAMIRA y Crevea	Spanish
Dionisio ANZILOTTI (*President*, 1928–30) . . .	Italian
Ruy BARBOSA [2]	Brazilian
Antonio Sánchez DE BUSTAMANTE y Sirven . . .	Cuban
Viscount FINLAY [3]	British

[1] For biographical data, see Publications of the Court, Series E, No. 1, pp. 14–26; No. 5, pp. 25, 33; No. 6, p. 20.   [2] Deceased March 1, 1923.
[3] Deceased March 9, 1929.

Judge	Nationality
Henri FROMAGEOT [4]	French
Hans Max HUBER (*President*, 1925–27)	Swiss
Charles Evans HUGHES [5]	American
Cecil James Barrington HURST [6]	British
Frank Billings KELLOGG [7]	American
Bernard Cornelis Johannes LODER (*President*, 1922–24)	Dutch
John Bassett MOORE [8]	American
Didrik Galtrup Gjedde NYHOLM	Danish
Yorozu ODA	Japanese
Epitacio da Silva PESSÔA [9]	Brazilian
Charles André WEISS [10]	French

Deputy-Judge	Nationality
Frederik Waldemar Nikolai BEICHMANN	Norwegian
Demètre NEGULESCO	Rumanian
WANG Ch'ung-hui	Chinese
Mikhailo YOVANOVITCH	Serb-Croat-Slovene

(2) JUDGES AND DEPUTY-JUDGES ELECTED FOR THE SECOND PERIOD, 1931–39 (TO JUNE 1, 1934) [11]

Judge	Nationality
Minéitcirô ADATCI (*President*, 1931–33)	Japanese
Rafael ALTAMIRA y Crevea	Spanish
Dionisio ANZILOTTI	Italian
Antonio Sánchez DE BUSTAMANTE y Sirven	Cuban
Willem Jan Marie VAN EYSINGA	Dutch
Henri FROMAGEOT	French
J. Gustavo GUERRERO	Salvadorean
Cecil James Barrington HURST (*President*, 1934–36)	British
Frank Billings KELLOGG	American
Demètre NEGULESCO	Rumanian
Edouard ROLIN-JAEQUEMYNS	Belgian
Michel ROSTWOROWSKI	Polish
Walther SCHÜCKING	German
Francisco José URRUTIA	Colombian
WANG Ch'ung-hui	Chinese

Deputy-Judge	Nationality
Rafael Waldemar ERICH	Finnish
José Caeiro DA MATTA	Portuguese
Mileta NOVAKOVICH	Yugoslav
Josef REDLICH	Austrian

[4] Elected September 19, 1929, to succeed Charles André Weiss.
[5] Elected September 8, 1928, to succeed John Bassett Moore; resigned on February 15, 1930. [6] Elected September 19, 1929, to succeed Viscount Finlay.
[7] Elected September 25, 1930, to succeed Charles Evans Hughes.
[8] Resigned by letter dated April 11, 1928.
[9] Elected September 10, 1923, to succeed Ruy Barbosa.
[10] Deceased August 30, 1928.
[11] For biographical data, see Publications of the Court, Series E, No. 7, pp. 21–41.

(3) REGISTRAR OF THE COURT SINCE 1922

Åke HAMMARSKJÖLD . . . . Swedish

APPENDIX NO. 11

Sessions of the Court, 1922–1933

Preliminary	January 30 to March 24, 1922
First (ordinary)	June 15 to August 12, 1922
Second (extraordinary)	January 8 to February 7, 1923
Third (ordinary)	June 15 to September 15, 1923
Fourth (extraordinary)	November 12 to December 6, 1923
Fifth (ordinary)	June 16 to September 4, 1924
Sixth (extraordinary)	January 12 to March 26, 1925
Seventh (extraordinary)	April 14 to May 16, 1925
Eighth (ordinary)	June 15 to June 19 July 15 to August 25, 1925
Ninth (extraordinary)	October 22 to November 21, 1925
Tenth (extraordinary)	February 2 to May 25, 1926
Eleventh (ordinary)	June 15 to July 31, 1926
Twelfth (ordinary)	June 15 to December 16, 1927
Thirteenth (extraordinary)	February 6 to April 26, 1928
Fourteenth (ordinary)	June 15 to September 13, 1928
Fifteenth (extraordinary)	November 12 to November 21, 1928
Sixteenth (extraordinary)	May 13 to July 12, 1929
Seventeenth (ordinary)	June 17 to September 10, 1929
Eighteenth (ordinary)	June 16 to August 26, 1930
Nineteenth (extraordinary)	October 23 to December 6, 1930
Twentieth (ordinary)	January 15 to February 21, 1931
Twenty-first (extraordinary)	April 20 to May 15, 1931
Twenty-second (extraordinary)	July 16 to October 15, 1931
Twenty-third (extraordinary)	November 5, 1931, to February 4, 1932
Twenty-fourth (ordinary)	February 1 to March 8, 1932
Twenty-fifth (extraordinary)	April 18 to August 11, 1932
Twenty-sixth (extraordinary)	October 14, 1932, to April 5, 1933

Twenty-seventh (ordinary)   February 1 to April 19, 1933
Twenty-eighth (extraordinary)   May 10 to May 16, 1933
Twenty-ninth (extraordinary)   July 10 to July 29, 1933
Thirtieth (extraordinary)   October 20 to December 15, 1933

APPENDIX NO. 12

Publications of the Court Relating to Judgments, Orders and Advisory Opinions [1]

Series A

No. 1. *The S.S. Wimbledon.* [Great Britain, France, Italy, Japan, Poland (Intervenor) *v.* Germany.] Judgment No. 1, August 17, 1923.
See also Series C, No. 3, Vols. I, II and additional volume.

No. 2. *The Mavrommatis Palestine Concessions.* [Greece *v.* Great Britain.] Judgment No. 2, August 30, 1924.
See also Series C, No. 5—I.

No. 3. *Treaty of Neuilly, Article 179, Annex, Paragraph 4 (Interpretation).* [Bulgaria-Greece] Judgment No. 3, September 12, 1924.
See also Series C, No. 6.

No. 4. *Interpretation of Judgment No. 3.* [Bulgaria-Greece.] Judgment No. 4, March 26, 1925.
See also Series C, No. 6, additional volume.

No. 5. *The Mavrommatis Jerusalem Concessions.* [Greece *v.* Great Britain.] Judgment No. 5, March 26, 1925.
See also Series C, No. 7—II.

No. 6. *Case Concerning Certain German Interests in Polish Upper Silesia.* [Germany *v.* Poland.] Judgment No. 6, August 25, 1925.
See also Series C, No. 9—I.

No. 7. *Case Concerning Certain German Interests in Polish Upper Silesia (Merits).* [Germany *v.* Poland.] Judgment No. 7, May 25, 1926.
See also Series C, No. 11, Vols. I, II, III.

No. 8. *Denunciation of the Treaty of November 2nd, 1865, between China and Belgium.* [Belgium *v.* China.] Orders of January 8th, February 15th and June 18th, 1927.
See also Series C, No. 16—I.

---

[1] This list does not include a reference to Series C, No. 9—II, containing Acts and Documents relating to the Expulsion of the Œcumenical Patriarch. For the new numbering given retrospectively to Series A and Series B, and to Series C prior to No. 52, see Series E, No. 8, pp. 310, 314.

No. 9. *Case Concerning the Factory at Chorzów (Claim for Indemnity) (Jurisdiction.)* [Germany v. Poland.] Judgment No. 8, July 26, 1927.
See also Series C, No. 13—I.

No. 10. *The Case of the S.S. "Lotus."* [France-Turkey.] Judgment No. 9, September 7, 1927.
See also Series C, No. 13—II.

No. 11. *Case of the Readaptation of the Mavrommatis Jerusalem Concessions (Jurisdiction).* [Greece v. Great Britain.] Judgment No. 10, October 10, 1927.
See also Series C, No. 13—III.

No. 12. *Case Concerning the Factory at Chorzów (Indemnities).* [Germany v. Poland.] Order of November 21st, 1927.

No. 13. *Interpretation of Judgments Nos. 7 and 8 (The Chorzów Factory).* [Germany v. Poland.] Judgment No. 11, December 16, 1927.
See also Series C, No. 13—V.

No. 14. *Denunciation of the Treaty of November 2nd, 1865, between China and Belgium.* [Belgium v. China.] Order of February 21st, 1928.
See also Series C, No. 16—I.

No. 15. *Rights of Minorities in Upper Silesia (Minority Schools).* [Germany v. Poland.] Judgment No. 12, April 26, 1928.
See also Series C, No. 14—II.

No. 16. *Denunciation of the Treaty of November 2nd, 1865, between China and Belgium.* [Belgium v. China.] Order of August 13th, 1928.
See also Series C, No. 16—I.

No. 17. *Case Concerning the Factory at Chorzów (Claim for Indemnity) (Merits).* [Germany v. Poland.] Judgment No. 13, September 13, 1928.
See also Series C, No. 15—II.

Nos. 18/19. *Denunciation of the Treaty of November 2nd, 1865, between China and Belgium.* [Belgium v. China.] Order of May 25th, 1929.
See also Series C, No. 16—I.

Case Concerning the Factory at Chorzów (Indemnities). [Germany v. Poland.] Order of May 25th, 1929.
See also Series C, No. 16—II.

Nos. 20/21. *Case Concerning the Payment of Various Serbian Loans Issued in France.* [France–Serb-Croat-Slovene State.] Judgment No. 14, July 12, 1929.
See also Series C, No. 16—III.

Case Concerning the Payment in Gold of the Brazilian Federal Loans Issued in France. [France-Brazil.] Judgment No. 15, July 12, 1929.
See also Series C, No. 16—IV.

No. 22. *Case of the Free Zones of Upper Savoy and the District of Gex.* [France-Switzerland.] Order of August 19th, 1929.
See also Series C, No. 17—I, Vols. I, II, III, IV.

No. 23. *Case Relating to the Territorial Jurisdiction of the International Commission of the River Oder.* [Great Britain, Czechoslovakia, Denmark, France, Germany, Sweden and Poland.] Judgment No. 16, September 10, 1929.
See also Series C, No. 17—II.

No. 24. *Case of the Free Zones of Upper Savoy and the District of Gex (Second Phase).* [France-Switzerland.] Order of December 6th, 1930.
See also Series C, No. 19—I, Vols. I, II, III, IV, V.

Series B

No. 1. *Nomination of Netherlands Delegate at the Third Session of the International Labor Conference.* [Great Britain, Netherlands, International Federation of Trades Unions, International Federation of Christian Trades Unions, International Labor Office.] Advisory Opinion No. 1, July 31, 1922.
See also Series C, No. 1.

Nos. 2 & 3. *Competence of the International Labor Organization as to Agricultural Labor.* [Great Britain, France, Hungary, Portugal, International Agricultural Commission, International Labor Office, International Federation of Trades Unions.] Advisory Opinion No. 2, August 12, 1922.
See also Series C, No. 1.

Competence of the International Labor Organization as to Methods of Agricultural Production. [France, International Labor Office.] Advisory Opinion No. 3, August 12, 1922.
See also Series C, No. 1.

No. 4. *Nature of Dispute as to Application of Nationality Decrees in Tunis and Morocco (French Zone).* [France and Great Britain.] Advisory Opinion No. 4, February 7, 1923.
See also Series C, No. 2, and No. 2, additional volume.

No. 5. *Dispute over the Autonomy of Eastern Carelia.* [Finland.] Reply of the Court, July 23, 1923.
See also Series C, No. 3, Vols. I and II.

No. 6. *Protection of German Settlers in Poland.* [Germany and Poland.]
Advisory Opinion No. 6, September 10, 1923.
See also Series C, No. 3, Vols. I and III.

No. 7. *Acquisition of Polish Nationality.* [Germany and Poland.] Advisory
Opinion No. 7, September 15, 1923.
See also Series C, No. 3, Vols. I and III.

No. 8. *Question of Jaworzina (Polish-Czechoslovakian Frontier).* [Czecho-
slovakia and Poland.] Advisory Opinion No. 8, December 6, 1923.
See also Series C, No. 4.

No. 9. *Question of the Monastery of Saint-Naoum (Albanian Frontier).*
[Albania, Greece and Serb-Croat-Slovene State.] Advisory
Opinion No. 9, September 4, 1924.
See also Series C, No. 5—II.

No. 10. *Exchange of Greek and Turkish Populations (Lausanne Conven-
tion VI, January 30th, 1923, Article 2).* [Greece and Turkey.]
Advisory Opinion No. 10, February 21, 1925.
See also Series C, No. 7—I.

No. 11. *Polish Postal Service in Danzig.* [Danzig and Poland.] Advisory
Opinion No. 11, May 16, 1925.
See also Series C, No. 8.

No. 12. *Article 3, Paragraph 2, of the Treaty of Lausanne (Frontier between
Turkey and Iraq).* [Great Britain and Turkey.] Advisory
Opinion No. 12, November 21, 1925.
See also Series C, No. 10.

No. 13. *Competence of the International Labor Organization to Regulate,
Incidentally, the Personal Work of the Employer.* [International
Labor Organization, International Organization of Industrial
Employers, International Federation of Trades Unions, Interna-
tional Confederation of Christian Trades Unions.] Advisory
Opinion No. 13, July 23, 1926.
See also Series C, No. 12.

No. 14. *Jurisdiction of the European Commission of the Danube between
Galatz and Braila.* [France, Great Britain, Italy and Rumania.]
Advisory Opinion No. 14, December 8, 1927.
See also Series C, No. 13—IV, Vols. I, II, III, IV.

No. 15. *Jurisdiction of the Courts of Danzig (Pecuniary Claims of Danzig
Railway Officials Who Have Passed into the Polish Service,
against the Polish Railways Administration).* [Danzig and
Poland.] Advisory Opinion No. 15, March 3, 1928.
See also Series C, No. 14—I.

No. 16. *Interpretation of the Greco-Turkish Agreement of December 1st, 1926 (Final Protocol, Article IV).* [Greece and Turkey.] Advisory Opinion No. 16, August 28, 1928.
See also Series C, No. 15—I.

No. 17. *The Greco-Bulgarian "Communities."* [Bulgaria and Greece.] Advisory Opinion No. 18, July 31, 1930.
See also Series C, No. 18—I.

No. 18. *Free City of Danzig and International Labor Organization.* [Danzig, Poland, International Labor Organization.] Advisory Opinion No. 18, August 26, 1930.
See also Series C, No. 18—II.

Series A/B

No. 40. *Access to German Minority Schools in Upper Silesia.* [Germany and Poland.] Advisory Opinion, May 15, 1931.
See also Series C, No. 52.

No. 41. *Customs Régime between Germany and Austria (Protocol of March 19th, 1931).* [Austria, Czechoslovakia, France, Germany and Italy.] Advisory Opinion, September 5, 1931; Order of July 20, 1931.
See also Series C, No. 53.

No. 42. *Railway Traffic between Lithuania and Poland (Railway Sector Landwarów-Kaisiadorys).* [Lithuania, Poland, Advisory and Technical Committee for Communications and Transit.] Advisory Opinion, October 15, 1931.
See also Series C, No. 54.

No. 43. *Access to, or Anchorage in, the Port of Danzig, of Polish War Vessels.* [Danzig and Poland.] Advisory Opinion, December 11, 1931.
See also Series C, No. 55.

No. 44. *Treatment of Polish Nationals and Other Persons of Polish Origin or Speech in the Danzig Territory.* [Danzig and Poland.] Advisory Opinion, February 4, 1932.
See also Series C, No. 56.

No. 45. *Interpretation of the Greco-Bulgarian Agreement of December 9th, 1927.* [Bulgaria and Greece.] Advisory Opinion, March 8, 1932.
See also Series C, No. 57.

No. 46. *Case of the Free Zones of Upper Savoy and the District of Gex.* [France-Switzerland.] Judgment, June 7, 1932.
See also Series C, No. 58.

No. 47. *Interpretation of the Statute of the Memel Territory (Preliminary Objection).* [France, Great Britain, Italy, Japan v. Lithuania.] Judgment, June 24, 1932.
See also Series C, No. 59.

No. 48. *Legal Status of the South-eastern Territory of Greenland.* [Norway *v.* Denmark: Denmark *v.* Norway.] Orders of August 2nd and 3rd, 1932.

> See also Series C, No. 69.

No. 49. *Interpretation of the Statute of the Memel Territory.* [Great Britain, France, Italy, Japan *v.* Lithuania.] Judgment, August 11, 1932.

> See also Series C, No. 59.

No. 50 *Interpretation of the Convention of 1919 Concerning Employment of Women during the Night.* [Germany, Great Britain, International Labor Organization, International Federation of Trades Unions, International Confederation of Christian Trades Unions.] Advisory Opinion, November 15, 1932.

> See also Series C, No. 60.

No. 51. *Case Concerning the Delimitation of the Territorial Waters between the Island of Castellorizo and the Coasts of Anatolia.* [Italy-Turkey.] Order of January 26, 1933.

> See also Series C, No. 61.

No. 52. *Case Concerning the Administration of the Prince von Pless (Preliminary Objection).* [Germany *v.* Poland.] Order of February 4, 1933.

No. 53. *Legal Status of Eastern Greenland.* [Denmark *v.* Norway.] Judgment, April 5, 1933.

> See also Series C, Nos. 62–67 and annex (maps).

No. 54. *Case Concerning the Administration of the Prince von Pless (Interim Measures of Protection).* [Germany v. Poland.] Order of May 11, 1933.

No. 55. *Legal Status of the South-eastern Territory of Greenland.* [Norway *v.* Denmark: Denmark *v.* Norway.] Order of May 11, 1933.

> See also Series C, No. 69.

No. 56. *Appeals from Certain Judgments of the Hungaro-Czechoslovak Mixed Arbitral Tribunal.* [Czechoslovakia *v.* Hungary.] Order of May 12, 1933.

> See also Series C, No. 68.

No. 57. *Case Concerning the Administration of the Prince von Pless (Prorogation).* [Germany *v.* Poland.] Order of July 4th, 1933.

No. 58. *Case Concerning the Polish Agrarian Reform and the German Minority (Interim Measures of Protection).* [Germany v. Poland.] Order of July 29, 1933.

No. 59. *Case Concerning the Administration of the Prince von Pless.* [Germany v. Poland.]　Order of December 2, 1933.

No. 60. *Case Concerning the Polish Agrarian Reform and the German Minority.* [Germany v. Poland.]　Order of December 2, 1933.

No. 61. *Appeal from Judgment of the Hungaro-Czechoslovak Mixed Arbitral Tribunal* (The Peter Pázmány University v. The State of Czechoslovakia).　[Czechoslovakia v. Hungary.]　Judgment, December 15, 1933.

APPENDIX NO. 13

Other Publications of the Court

Series D.—Acts and Documents Concerning the Organization of the Court.

No. 1.　Statute of the Court: Rules of Court (as amended on July 31, 1926).

Addendum to No. 1:

Rules of Court, Article 71 as amended on September 7, 1927.

No. 1. (Second edition). Statute and Rules of Court and other constitutional documents, rules or regulations (with the modifications effected therein up to February 15th, 1931).

No. 2. Preparation of the Rules of Court.—Minutes of meetings during the preliminary session of the Court, with annexes.

Addendum to No. 2:

Revision of the Rules of Court, 1926 (Minutes of meetings of the Court; report by the President; notes, observations and suggestions by members of the Court; report by the Registrar).

Second Addendum to No. 2:

Modification of the Rules, 1931 (Minutes of meetings of the Court; resolutions of the 11th Assembly of the League of Nations, 1930, etc.; proposals of members of the Court and of the Registrar).

No. 3. Collection of Texts governing the jurisdiction of the Court.

No. 4. Collection of Texts governing the jurisdiction of the Court. Second edition (June 1st, 1924).

Addendum to No. 4:

Agreements signed at London, August 30, 1924.

Second Addendum to No. 4:

Resolutions relating to the Pacific Settlement of International Disputes, adopted by the Fifth Assembly of the League of Nations, Geneva, October, 1924.

No. 5. Collection of Texts governing the jurisdiction of the Court. Third edition (brought up to date, October 1st, 1926).

No. 6. Collection of Texts governing the jurisdiction of the Court. Fourth edition (January 31st, 1932).

Series E.—Annual Reports.

No. 1. Annual Report (January 1st, 1922–June 15th (1925).

No. 2. Second Annual Report (June 15th, 1925–June 15th, 1926).

No. 3. Third Annual Report (June 15th, 1926–June 15th, 1927).

No. 4. Fourth Annual Report (June 15th, 1927–June 15th, 1928).

No. 5. Fifth Annual Report (June 15th, 1928–June 15th, 1929).

No. 6. Sixth Annual Report (June 15th, 1929–June 15th, 1930).

No. 7. Seventh Annual Report (June 15th, 1930–June 15, 1931).

No. 8. Eighth Annual Report (June 15th, 1931–June 15th, 1932).

No. 9. Ninth Annual Report (June 15th, 1932–June 15th, 1933).

Series F.—General Indexes.

No. 1. First General Index to the Publications of the Court (Series A, B and C).—First–Eleventh Sessions (1922–1926). (English and French in one volume.)

No. 2. Second General Index to the Publications of the Court (Series A, B and C)—Twelfth–Nineteenth Sessions (1927–1930). (English and French in one volume.)

No. 7 — Seventh Annual Report (June 15th, 1930-June 15th, 1931).

LIST OF REFERENCES TO AUTHORS

LIST OF REFERENCES TO CASES

Aaland Islands Dispute, 180 n, 442 n, 549 n.
Adela, The, 68 n.
American-British Claims Arbitration under Agreement of 1910, 12.
Anderson's Case, 542 n.
Appeals from Judgments of the Czecho-slovak-Hungarian Mixed Arbitral Tribunal, 429, 480 n, 484 n, 486.
Attorney-General for British Columbia *v.* Attorney-General for Canada, 446 n.
Austro-German Customs Régime, 335, 335 n, 372 n, 414 n, 445 n, 446, 453 n, 454, 455 n, 464, 473 n, 482 n, 493 n, 516, 518 n, 519 n, 544, 568.

Belgian-Chinese Treaty of 1865, Denunciation of, 405, 417, 429, 471, 489.
Bermúdez y Nuñez *v.* Costa Rica, 51.
Brazilian Loans Case, 298 n, 378, 431, 479 n, 488, 493 n, 517, 524, 525 n, 530 n, 533, 534, 542, 543 n, 548, 569, 573.
Brooks-Scanlon Corp. *v.* U. S., 25 n.

Camouna Inquiry, 32.
Canevaro Case, 20.
Caphandaris-Molloff Agreement, Interpretation of, 373, 436 n, 465, 490.
Carthage and *Manouba* Cases, 21, 22, 32.
Casablanca Case, 16.
Cayuga Indians Case, 531 n.
Cerda, Salvador, *v.* Costa Rica, 46, 48.
Chevreau Claim Arbitration, 11 n, 26, 29 n.
Chorzów Factory Case, 307, 344, 356 n, 357, 357 n, 367, 369, 384, 396, 419, 420 n, 422 n, 425, 425 n, 426 n, 427 n, 428, 431, 481 n, 484 n, 485, 488, 489, 490, 491, 497, 498, 506, 513, 528 n, 537, 540, 553 n, 569.
Colombian-Peruvian Dispute (Leticia), 409.
Costa Rica *v.* Nicaragua, 52.
Costa Rica Packet, 540.

Danzig and the International Labor Organization. *See* International Labor Organization.
Danzig Courts, Jurisdiction of, 338, 463, 499, 547, 551, 571.
Dashing Wave, The, 68 n.
Diaz *v.* Guatemala, 47.
Dogger Bank Affair, 30, 31, 33.
Dreyfus Case, 24.

Eastern Carelia Case, 438, 439, 447, 448, 456, 458, 545.

Eastern Greenland Case, 334, 372, 408, 428, 432, 472 n, 473 n, 482 n, 500 n, 525 n, 540, 544, 548, 557 n.
Employment of Women at Night, Interpretation of Convention on, 466, 492 n, 556, 557, 563, 565, 569.
European Commission of the Danube, 286, 377 n, 462, 475, 500, 501, 518, 523 n, 526 n, 545, 549 n, 554, 561, 566.
Exchange of Greek and Turkish Populations, 395, 449 n, 460, 547, 567.

Flores, González, Election of as President in Costa Rica, 51.
Free Zones Case, 326, 327 n, 330, 331 n, 339, 364, 365, 370 n, 376, 378, 379, 410 n, 411 n, 413, 420, 431, 436 n, 472 n, 473 n, 477 n, 478 n, 487, 489, 492 n, 495, 495 n, 501, 507, 516, 531 n, 532, 544 n, 545, 546, 548, 549 n, 550, 555 n, 558.

Gaulois Inquiry, 32.
Georgia, The, 68 n.
German Interests in Polish Upper Silesia, 275, 279, 298 n, 330, 349, 350, 354 n, 366, 367 n, 369 n, 384, 428, 472 n, 484, 484 n, 488, 490, 504, 505 n, 524, 528 n, 537, 539, 540, 546, 549, 551 n, 552, 558, 560, 567, 568, 573.
German Minority Schools in Polish Upper Silesia, 340, 362 n, 363 n, 368, 369, 381 n, 464, 477 n, 497 n, 539, 545, 552, 560.
German Settlers in Poland, 373 n, 447 n, 448, 459, 466, 562, 569.
Greco-Bulgarian Communities, 338, 450, 451, 463, 490, 547, 568.
Greco-Turkish Agreement of 1926, Interpretation of, 454 n, 463, 513, 539.
Guatemala-Honduras Boundary Arbitration (1933), 65 n.

Hiawatha, The, 68 n.
Hilder *v.* Dexter, 223, 555 n.
Home Missionary Society Case, 532 n.
Honduras and Nicaragua *v.* Guatemala and El Salvador, 46.
Hungarian-Rumanian Optants, 374 n.

International Labor Organization, Competence of, 458, 462, 490 n, 538, 542, 558, 560, 562, 570.
International Labor Organization, Membership of Danzig in, 463, 516, 561.
Isabella Thompson, The, 68 n.

INDEX OF SUBJECTS

(The references are to page numbers. *See also* the List of references to Authors, the List of references to Persons, and the List of references to Cases)

INDEX

721

reform of, 62.
revival of, effort for, 62.
rules of court, 43.
seat, 41.
sessions, 41.
successor to, 63.
Challenge of judges, 44, 49, 149, 149 n.
Chambers, 150, 151, 152, 153, 267, 328, 329, 421.
See also Communications and transit cases, Labor cases, Summary procedure.
Chambre du Conseil, 328 n, 511, 512 n.
China
  declaration under Article 36, 407.
  denunciation of treaty of 1865, 406, 407.
  membership in League, 95 n.
Citations
  conventions, 541.
  Court's freedom in, 538.
  Court's judgments and opinions, 538, 539, 540.
  decisions of Council, 540, 541; of other courts, 540, 541.
  dictionaries, 538 n, 557.
  diplomatic correspondence, 542.
  living authors, 529 n.
  national legislation, 542.
Cleveland award (1888), 52, 59.
Commissions of inquiry. *See* Inquiry.
Committee of Jurists (1920)
  agenda of, 109.
  attitude toward Hague Conferences, 109.
  conception of Court, 104.
  draft scheme, 109, 110; attitude of Council, 110; attitude of Assembly, 111.
  organization, 106; members, 106, 107; secretariat, 108; expenses, 108; minutes, 109; procedure, 109; mandate, 109.
  rôle in drafting Statute, 109, 122.
Committee of Jurists (1929)
  creation of, 185, 186.
  meetings, 186.
  membership, 185, 186.
  report on U.S. reservations, 216, 217.
Communications and Transit Cases
  chamber for, 152, 153, 328; abolition proposed, 195, 328; no cases in, 328.
  summary procedure in, 195.
Communications with Governments
  channels for, 355, 356.
  languages used, 355 n.
Compromis. *See* Special agreements.
Compulsory jurisdiction. *See* Jurisdiction.
Conclusions
  amendment of, 385, 488, 489.
  Court will not formulate, 488.
  in advisory proceedings, 490.
  limits on, 488.
  must be supported, 490.
  not prejudiced by abortive negotiations, 367.

referred to as submissions, 487.
statement of, 486, 487.
Confederacy of Six Nations of Grand River, 355.
Conference of Signatories (1926)
  calling, 213.
  final act, 214.
  nature, 214.
  recommendations, 216.
Conference of Signatories (1929)
  adopts draft of U.S. Protocol, 218.
  independence, 186 n.
  States represented, 187.
"Conscience of civilized nations," 165.
Convention, use of term in Statute, 370, 371 n.
Costs, 179, 280, 427, 428.
Council of the League of Nations
  adoption of advisory opinions, 461.
  assisted by advisory opinions, 466.
  attitude towards obligatory jurisdiction, 110, 111, 161, 162, 163.
  Brussels session (1920), 110, 122.
  creation of 1920 Committee of Jurists, 106.
  decisions as to individuals, 239.
  decisions cited, 540, 541.
  mandate under Article 14 of Covenant, 97, 98.
  "plans" for Court, 111, 113, 115.
  power as to salaries, 156, 308, 309.
  requests for advisory opinions, 436, 437, 438, 439, 440, 441.
  resolution of 1922 on access to Court, 274, 348, 349, 350, 351, 352, 353, 354, 388 n, 482.
  rôle in creating Court, 97; in drafting Statute, 122.
  San Sebastian session (1920), 110, 122.
  unanimity, 437, 438, 439, 440, 441, 442.
  voting in elections, 135, 238, 239, 241.
  See also League of Nations.
Counsel
  agent's control of, 474.
  correction of errors, 279.
  designation of, 474.
  hearing of, 277, 278, 507.
  in advisory proceedings, 475.
  nationality, 476.
  not distinguished from advocates, 473.
  number, 473.
  powers, 474.
  provision in Statute, 169.
  qualifications, 475, 476.
  questions to, 173, 474, 508, 509, 514.
  service of notices on, 170.
Counter-cases
  contents of, 486.
  in advisory proceedings, 451.
  provisions in Statute, 170.
Counter-claims
  jurisdiction of Court, 426, 427.
  provision in Rules, 426.
  time for presentation, 490, 491.